HIGHER EDUCATION:
Handbook of Theory and Research

Volume X

Associate Editors

HIGHER EDUCATION:
Handbook of Theory and Research

Volume X

Edited by

John C. Smart

Memphis State University

Published under the sponsorship of
The Association for Institutional Research (AIR)
and
The Association for the Study of Higher Education (ASHE)

AGATHON PRESS

New York

5648 Riverdale Avenue
Bronx, NY 10471-2106

ISBN: 0-87586-111-3
ISSN: 0882-4126

Library of Congress Catalog Card Number: 86-642109

Printed in the United States

Contents

The Contributors

SHEILA M. ARREDONDO is a Ph.D. candidate in the Higher Education Program at the University of Denver. She is also a policy analyst at the Education Commission of the States. She has coordinated several national conferences on mathematics and science education reform, and also provides technical assistance to policymakers and educators who are trying to redesign their education systems. Her scholarly interests focus on academic ethics, governance and policy formulation, minority access, and persistence, as well as reform of the undergraduate curriculum. She is currently coediting the *State Postsecondary Education Structures Handbook: State Coordinating and Governing Boards,* to be published by the Education Commission of the States. She is also a former nationally ranked weightlifter and a competitive swimmer.

ALBERTO F. CABRERA is an assistant professor in educational administration and policy analysis at SUNY-Albany. On the basis of his work for the Wisconsin Center for the Study of Higher Education and Finance, he has published several papers evaluating the equity and effectiveness of student aid programs. His research interests also embrace the development of persistence models addressing the role of finances, testing and merging of economic and noneconomic student persistence models, and exploring determinants of persistence among minority students and the role of perceptions of prejudice in the academic and social integration of students in college.

DANA DUNN is an Assistant Professor of Sociology at the University of Texas at Arlington. Her primary research and teaching interests are in the areas of stratification, gender, sociology of work, and sociology of education. She has published articles and book chapters on women and work, comparable worth, women and politics, and macrostructural theories of gender stratification.

RICHARD J. ELLIOTT is Professor of Educational Foundations at the University of New Orleans. Dr. Elliott's research has focused on issues related to philosophy and social science in education. He is a fellow of the Philosophy of Education Society and 1995 President Elect for the Philosophy and History of Education Society. He has served on various editorial and review boards and is currently on the editorial board of the *International Review of History and Political Science Journal.*

JOHN FRYE is Professor of History at Triton College in River Grove, Illinois where he has held several administrative positions as well. He is author of *Vision of the Public Junior College, 1900–1940: Professional Goals and Popular Aspirations* and several articles on the history of the two-year college.

ROBIN B. GLASER is a Ph.D. candidate in the Higher Education Program at the University of Denver. A registered nurse for 15 years, he has a special perspective in seeking healthy lifestyles within the academic community. His interests include not only integrating wellness into the curriculum but also understanding junior faculty burnout, particularly at the United States Air Force Academy, where he is a captain and assistant professor of

Spanish, French, and German. His most recent publication is ''The Significance of Ethnic and Gender Identity in Childhood" in *Educating Young Children in a Diverse Society* (Allyn and Bacon, 1994).

LESTER F. GOODCHILD is an associate professor of education and coordinator of the Higher Education Program at the University of Denver. His research centers on foundational studies related to higher education, including history, academic ethics, and policy studies. Recent efforts resulted in two coedited works: *Administration as a Profession* (Jossey-Bass, 1991) and *The ASHE Reader on the History of Higher Education* (Ginn Press, 1989).

KENNETH A. KIEWRA is an Associate Professor of Educational Psychology and Director of the Academic Success Center at the University of Nebraska-Lincoln. He received his Ph.D. in Educational Psychology and Instructional Design from Florida State University in 1982. He served as an Assistant Professor of Educational Psychology from 1982–1986 at Kansas State University and as Associate Professor of Psychology from 1986–1988 at Utah State University. Kiewra's research investigates note taking and text representations. He is the Immediate Past President of the Midwestern Educational Research Association, the former Chair of the Special Interest Group on Academic Studying, and a member of four editorial boards.

LEE E. KREHBIEL is a doctoral student in higher education and public policy and a research assistant with the Indiana Education Policy Center at Indiana University-Bloomington. Formerly Director of Student Activities at Berea College, his research interests include the historical relationship of philanthropy to special purpose postsecondary institutions, student involvement, and the collection and use of student activity fees.

GEORGE D. KUH is a professor of higher education at Indiana University-Bloomington where he is affiliated with the Center for Postsecondary Research and Planning. His research over the past two decades has focused on student development, assessment strategies for student learning and postsecondary environments, and the use of cultural perspectives in research and college and university administration.

GARY R. PIKE is the senior research analyst, Center for Educational Assessment, and adjunct assistant professor, department of Counseling and Educational Psychology, at the University of Missouri-Columbia. He also serves as founding editor of the ''Assessment Measures'' column in *Assessment Update*. Pike's research interests include college effects on students, psychometric theory, and statistics.

LINDA P. ROUSE is an Associate Professor of Sociology at the University of Texas at Arlington. Her primary research and teaching interests are in the areas of social psychology, sociology of education, family, and statistics. Her published articles and book chapters address issues in higher education, domestic violence, racial/ethnic stereotyping, and gender.

EDWARD P. ST. JOHN is a Professor of Educational Leadership at the University of New Orleans. His research focuses on organizational and financial issues in higher education.

He has published numerous studies examining the effects of student aid. Dr. St. John was awarded the Robert P. Huff Golden Quill Award by the National Association for Financial Aid Administrators in 1993 for his contributions to the literature on student aid. He is a Contributing Editor for *Research in Higher Education.*

MONICA A. SEFF is an Assistant Professor of Sociology at Bowling Green State University. Her primary research and teaching interests are in the areas of family, research methods and social psychology, particularly socialization and self concept. Her publications include articles on adolescents, social class and self-esteem, work-family linkages, and welfare dependence.

FRANS A. VAN VUGHT is professor of public administration at the University of Twente in the Netherlands. He also is director of the Center for Higher Education Policy Studies (CHEPS), a policy-oriented international research center, based at the same university. Frans van Vught has published fifteen books and a large number of articles and book chapters on policy-analysis, futures studies, and higher education. Two recent books, both written together with Guy Neave, are *Prometheus Bound: The Changing Relationship Between Government and Higher Education in Western Europe* (1991) and *Government and Higher Education Relationships Across Three Continents* (1993) (both Pergamon Press). Van Vught regularly acts as a consultant for international organisations like the European Communities, the Organisation for Economic Cooperation and Development, UNESCO, and the World Bank. He is executive secretary of the *Consortium of Higher Education Researchers* (CHER) and participates in the boards of several journals in the field of higher education studies.

NICK VESPER is a policy analyst for the Indiana Education Policy Center at Indiana University-Bloomington. He has had extensive experience in institutional research and information systems. His current research and writing concentrates on college choice, college student learning, and policy issues of financing education. He is a Ph.D. candidate in higher education and public policy at Indiana University.

Student Learning at Metropolitan Universities

George D. Kuh, Nick Vesper,

and

Lee E. Krehbiel
School of Education, Indiana University—Bloomington

The great universities of Europe—Paris, Salerno, Bologna, Prague—were established in cities where the safety of students and faculty was easier to insure and lodging, food, and drink were readily available (Bender, 1989; McGrane, 1963; Spaights, 1980). In contrast, the American practice was to put colleges in small towns and rural areas. Jefferson chose rural Charlottesville for his "academical village," a place of solitude removed from the evils and distractions of the city; by charter, the University of North Carolina had to be at least five miles from the nearest government office or law court (Klotsche, 1966); the University of Georgia trustees selected a forested hilltop for their institution because it was "far away from civilization . . ." (Rudolph, 1962, p. 92). Some institutions commonly associated today with urban areas (Harvard and Boston, Columbia University—originally King's College—and New York City) were located originally some distance from the nearest settlement only to be surrounded subsequently by urban sprawl (Rudolph, 1962; Waetjen and Muffo, 1983). There were, of course, notable exceptions to seeking a rural setting: Brown in Providence, Temple and the College of Philadelphia (now University of Pennsylvania) in Philadelphia, Northeastern in Boston, Wayne State in Detroit, and the University of Cincinnati (Klotsche, 1966; Skardon, 1983).

The preference for locating the university in an isolated setting was a product primarily of two factors: the influence of the English residential college and the rural, agrarian character of the country (Hofstadter and Smith, 1961). Until about 1875, the majority of the country's work force was engaged in jobs related to agriculture (Williams and Cowley, 1991). By 1920, however, the majority of citizens were living in urban areas (Berube, 1978). Today, about 85 percent of the population in the contiguous 48 states live in cities (Grobman, 1988), with only 10 percent of working adults engaged in agricultural jobs. Moreover, the majority of undergraduate students attend a public institution located near a metropolitan area (Berube, 1978; Levine, 1986). In fact, in the past 30 years, most of the enrollment growth in American higher education has been realized by institutions in or near major metropolitan areas (Grobman, 1988).

Whether state-assisted (Portland State University, Wright State University) as the vast majority are, or privately controlled (Roosevelt University, University of Detroit), metropolitan universities are magnets for ''new majority students'' (Ehrlich, 1991), the fastest growing segment of undergraduates (Cedar, 1970; Grobman, 1988; Levine, 1989). New majority students are people of color or are over the age of 23, attend college part time, live off campus, have families, and work more than 20 hours a week (Kuh, 1992; The Landscape, 1993). For reasons discussed later, most of these students have no alternative for obtaining a baccalaureate degree other than the nearby metropolitan institution.

The bulk of the studies on student learning in college is based on experiences of predominantly white, traditional-age students at residential institutions (Pascarella and Terenzini, 1991). It is not known whether the processes that influence student learning and personal development at residential institutions are similar for metropolitan institutions, given their urban location and substantially more diverse students (Baird, 1991). Therefore, ''specifying the effects of college with the vast numbers of [new majority] students who now populate American post-secondary education may be the single most important area of research on college impacts in the next decade'' (Pascarella and Terenzini, 1991, p. 632). Another reason for examining the student experience in metropolitan universities is the desire to increase learning productivity (Johnstone, 1993). State legislators, taxpayers, governing board members, and students are seeking ways to produce more learning for the same cost or equal learning for less cost (Wingspread Group on Higher Education, 1993).

The purposes of this chapter are twofold. First, the metropolitan university is described as an emerging institutional form in American higher education. We review its historical roots, character, and function in order to identify institutional characteristics likely to be associated with, or that have the potential to affect, student learning. Second, approaches developed for assessing student learning of traditional-age students at residential colleges are examined to determine if they are appropriate for students who attend metropolitan universities. Findings are summarized from a series of exploratory studies on student learning at metropolitan universities and an alternative model of student learning is described. Suggestions for additional research on student learning at metropolitan universities are offered and implications for institutional policy and practice are discussed.

THE EVOLUTION OF THE METROPOLITAN UNIVERSITY

The metropolitan institution differs from other types of four-year colleges and universities because of its mission, which is to address the educational, economic, and social needs of people who live in the surrounding service region (Grobman, 1988; Kuh et al., 1991; Riesman, 1975). Thus, the functions and character of the metropolitan university are shaped both by traditions of academe and the needs and aspirations of their local environment and people. Almost a half century ago, Samuel P. Capen, then chancellor of the University of Buffalo, articulated the goals of the metropolitan university:

> to respond to the immediate educational needs of the community in which it is set; that is, without compromising the standards appropriate to university instruction and investigation, [the metropolitan university] plans its offerings with direct reference to these needs, and that within the limits of its resources it is hospitable to all local requests for those intellectual services which the university may legitimately render. (in Crooks, 1982, p. 38)

Thus, the metropolitan university is not merely a university located *in* a city; it is also *of* the city, with an obligation to serve the needs of the city's diverse citizenry (Klotsche, 1966; Grobman and Sanders, 1984; Hathaway, Mulhollan and White, 1990). This means that not all institutions in urban areas are metropolitan universities. Consider Northeastern and Harvard in Boston, Cleveland State and Case Western Reserve in Cleveland, and California State University-Los Angeles and the University of Southern California in Los Angeles. The first institution in each of these pairs has a metropolitan mission, meaning they draw their students almost exclusively from within commuting distance and they offer programs and services that meet local area needs. The second institution in these pairs may focus on urban problems, but not because of a mission-driven set of priorities (Waetjen and Muffo, 1983); equally important, they attract large numbers of students who live well beyond commuting distance. In Britain, the analog to the U.S. metropolitan university is the polytechnic where:

> teaching is emphasized over research, access is valued, the ability to succeed is more important to admission than meeting specific entry requirements, underprivileged and underrepresented groups are assured access, links are fostered with local and regional communities through industry commerce and public service, greater effort is made to link academic programs with the world of work, part-time students form a significant proportion of enrollment. (Lewis, 1992, p. 25)

The metropolitan university has five historical roots: (a) the municipal university, (b) Roman Catholic colleges located in urban areas, (c) some other private institutions located in cities; (d) YMCA colleges; and (e) state-assisted institutions established in urban areas (Skardon, 1983). Of these, the municipal university, the YMCA colleges, and the state-assisted universities had the most influence on the mission and educational programs of the contemporary metropolitan university. Adapting Crooks (1982) approach, our examination of the evolution of the metropolitan university is divided into three phases.

Phase I: The Early Colleges in Cities (1800 to 1950)

The first institution with a declared mission to focus on the needs of the city was the municipal college or university, an institution supported by local taxes and administered by a local governing board (Carlson, 1962; Klotsche, 1966). The early municipals were created primarily out of convenience. Most were private institutions which came under municipal control to keep the institution open when its future was in doubt (Grobman, 1988; Levine, 1986). For example, The College of Charleston (now a state-assisted institution) was founded in 1790 as a private institution but became a municipal in 1837 (Carlson, 1962; Easterby, 1935; McGrane, 1963) to offer ''to all classes of our citizens an opportunity for their children to receive a classical education, and yet to be under parental control'' (Diekhoff, 1950, p. 28). The University of Louisville, originally chartered in 1798 as Jefferson Seminary, was the second municipal institution (1846), but the first with university status (Skardon, 1983). The third was the College of the City of New York (1849), which was the first tuition-free institution (Rudy, 1949). Other examples of municipals that began as private institutions include The Toledo University of Arts and Trades (established as a private institution in 1872, becoming a municipal in 1883), Wichita State University (founded in 1895 as Fairmount College, becoming a municipal in 1926), and the University of Nebraska at Omaha (founded in 1908 as the University of Omaha, becoming a municipal in 1931).

Between 1880 and 1900, the number of municipal institutions increased markedly (Skardon, 1983). In part, cities created a new institution, or began to support an existing college, in order to produce more technically trained specialists and to better educate its citizens to address the complex industrial, political, and social problems that were becoming clearly visible (Eckelberry, 1932).

During the same period, Roman Catholic colleges and universities, particularly those sponsored by the Jesuits, recognized that the majority of Catholics were living in urban areas. They established colleges nearby to serve their constituents. These institutions included the Loyola Universities of New Orleans, Chicago, and Los Angeles, and many others named after the city in which they were located (e.g., University of Dallas, University of Dayton, University of Detroit, University of Niagara, University of Portland, St. Louis University, Seattle University) (Skardon, 1983). Other private institutions also were established in cities, depending in part on community contributions for support (e.g., Temple University, University of Hartford, University of Houston, New York University) (Skardon, 1983).

By the turn of the century, these institutions—particularly the municipals—had introduced several noteworthy educational innovations including cooperative learning arrangements (pioneered at the University of Cincinnati) and community service (the University of Toledo at one point required students to work for either a state or city agency) (Kolbe, 1928; McGrane, 1963). They modified their curriculum to respond to such urban challenges as industrialization, the growing size and complexity of public school systems, and increased numbers of high school graduates desiring postsecondary education. Sociology and psychology were featured and programs of study in education, business, and engineering were established. As Kolbe (1928, p. 225) noted, ''the very essence of the urban trend in higher education'' was a curriculum emphasizing professional and vocational training. At the same time, he counseled against emphasizing vocational training over general education, the latter being critical to an educated populace.

The growth of municipal universities and of other urban institutions led to the establishment of the Association of Urban Universities (AUU) in 1914, due in large part to the efforts of Charles William Dabney, then president of the University of Cincinnati. Realizing the importance of providing postsecondary educational opportunities to place-bound students (Crooks, 1982), Dabney organized the first AUU meeting of 16 city colleges and universities during the National Association of State Universities conference. Crooks (1982) likened the role of the AUU to the development of postsecondary education in urban areas to John Dewey's influence on the reform of primary and secondary education.

In addition to the municipal university, the other pre-World War II institution that directly addressed the needs of the city and its residents was the YMCA college (Hopkins, 1950; Skardon, 1983). A primary mission of the Young Men's Christian Association was to provide educational opportunities for young men residing in the cities. In response to the business boom of the 1920s and the aforementioned need for technical education and arts and sciences preparation, the YMCA began to offer classes, often at night though not always at collegiate level. As the demand for lawyers increased, several YMCAs initiated law schools. As these institutions matured, their governance structures became more complex, creating an inevitable friction between YMCA officials and college administrators and faculty. During the 1930s and 1940s, these tensions were exacerbated by accreditation agencies insisting that institutions of higher education be incorporated and administered independent of other organizations, such as a YMCA. Accreditation was becoming increasingly important, particularly for students wishing to transfer or to pursue graduate studies. As a result, some YMCA colleges closed, and others ''pulled-away'' (Bouseman, 1970) from YMCA sponsorship in order to obtain accreditation. Most of the former YMCA colleges in existence today are independently controlled, such as Roosevelt University in Chicago, Northeastern University in Boston, Southeastern University in Washington, D.C., and Golden Gate University in San Francisco. Two notable exceptions are Cleveland State University (founded as Fenn College) and Youngstown State University.

By 1950, then, four of the five roots of the metropolitan institution had appeared, with the municipal and YMCA colleges being the most influential in terms of the subsequent development of the contemporary metropolitan university.

Phase II: The Urban University and the Crisis of the City (1950 to 1980)
The second phase in the evolution of the metropolitan university was dominated by four themes: (a) the response of the urban university to the crisis in the cities, (b) the creation of urban universities by state systems of higher education (the fifth root of the metropolitan university), (c) tenuous relations between the urban institution and its neighbors, and (d) confusion over the appropriate mission for the urban university.

The enrollment surges immediately following World War II prompted by the GI Bill, and in the 1960s by the post-war baby boom, put tremendous pressure on institutions of higher education (Bonner, 1986), particularly those in urban areas. Urbanization continued at a rapid pace, fueled by immigration, emigration of Blacks from the rural south to an industrialized north, and the dominance of large industrial concerns. This confluence of factors created crises in many cities. At the 1958 AUU conference, Paul Ylvisaker of the Ford Foundation sounded a prescient warning:

> To flee the city denies the purpose and potential of the urban university. . . . Put broadly and simply, the neglected job of the urban university in these changing times is to commit itself to the life of the City, and to help educate its students and neighboring community to the potential for urban learning. (Crooks, 1982, p. 36)

Initially, the higher education community appeared eager to take on the challenge articulated by Ylvisaker. Its track record in meeting economic, social, and technological challenges was good: the land grant institutions helped diversify an agriculture-based economy and the emerging research universities developed advanced forms of technology in the wake of Sputnik. Surely the urban universities could solve the crises of the cities!

The Higher Education Act of 1965 (Community Services Program of Title I) provided resources for addressing such problems unique to urban areas as unemployment, health delivery, and urban planning (Crooks, 1982; Grobman and Sanders, 1984). At the same time, college enrollments expanded at unprecedented rates. In some states, new institutions were created in urban areas to respond to the demand for access (Northeastern in Chicago, University of Maryland-Baltimore County). In other states, the shift to more centralized coordination of public institutions (Layzell and Lyddon, 1990) resulted in the integration of existing municipal institutions into state systems of higher education (e.g., Wayne State joined the Michigan state university system, the University of Kansas City joined the Missouri state university system, becoming the University of Missouri-Kansas City). According to the American Council on Education, there were 17 municipal universities and colleges in 1961 (McGrane, 1963); by 1964, only 10 remained: Brooklyn, City, Hunter, and Queens Colleges of the City University of New York, University of Cincinnati, Municipal University of

Omaha, University of Toledo, University of Akron, University of Louisville, and Washburn University of Topeka (Klotsche, 1966). In 1967, the state of Ohio accepted responsibility for Akron, Toledo, and Cincinnati (Gappert, 1986). Youngstown University, founded as a YMCA college, also was incorporated into the Ohio state university system at this time. Today, the only remaining municipal university is Washburn, located in Topeka; Washburn has tried for years to be admitted into the state university system of Kansas.

During this same period, considerable attention was given to the appropriate role of the university in the city, particularly with regard to the impact of its presence and concomitant responsibilities (Ashworth, 1964; Carothers, 1963; Doxiadis, 1972; Hester, 1966; Knox, 1967; Levi, 1961; Pang, 1993; Parsons, 1963; Wright, 1961). The relationship often was uneasy. Many educationally and economically disadvantaged city dwellers perceived the university to be "a gateway to economic security" while at the same time others who lived nearby feared "being trampled by [its] wealth . . ." (Berube, 1978, p. 49). In part, this fear was exacerbated by what seemed to be an insatiable appetite for acquiring land, a process that often resulted in the demolition of low-income housing and other changes in the character of the neighborhood (Folger, 1963; Pierce, 1981; Seyffert, 1975).

In some cities, the metropolitan university was an influential source of influence and revenue, its policies and practices affecting people well beyond the campus through training and retraining such local service providers as police and social workers (Adamany, 1992; Berube, 1978). On occasion, though, universities offended their neighbors (Seyffert, 1975). Irresponsible behavior by students (e.g., late night noisy social events, activism) irritated local residents. The tax-exempt status of institutions of higher education created (and continue to create) problems when universities own and operate book stores, cafeterias, faculty and student residences, parking facilities, and other services that compete with local business and industry (Adamany, 1992; Knowles, 1970). The American Association of State Colleges and Universities started the *Urban Affairs Newsletter* in 1968 to inform member institutions about the efforts of urban universities to meet the needs of the city and live in harmony with their neighbors.

By the late 1960s, the intractable nature of urban problems became apparent and optimism waned about the urban university's ability to perform all the tasks expected of a traditional institution of higher education as well as address needs peculiar to the urban area. The teaching mission was re-emphasized by most urban institutions, with a promise that a byproduct would be an enhanced quality of life for all. Some observers interpreted this revised urban university mission to be similar enough to that of the traditional university so as to signal a retreat from the emerging metropolitan mission of direct service to the local community. Gardner (1969, p. 5) cajoled:

> Very few [metropolitan universities] have pursued any aspect of the urban crisis with the intellectual rigor it requires. Even fewer have accepted the real world of the city on their doorstep as a laboratory in which they can advance those intellectual pursuits.

But the prospect that a university with a metropolitan mission could successfully address issues particular to urban life remained of interest in some quarters. The Carnegie Commission produced two volumes on the university's role in the city (Carnegie Commission on Higher Education, 1972; Nash, 1973) and the Ford Foundation funded a newsletter (*Connections*) to disseminate information about urban programs between universities as well as a series of *Higher Education in the Cities* reports (Cafferty and Spangenberg, 1983; College Entrance Examination Board, 1981; Ford Foundation, 1981). Even though membership in the Association of Urban Universities (AUU) continued to increase, attendance at its annual meetings declined precipitously in the 1970s. For example, 122 institutions held membership, yet only 42 participated in the 1973 meeting; the 1974 meeting was canceled for lack of a quorum. The AUU disbanded at the end of 1977, in part because other organizations (e.g., American Association of State Colleges and Universities, National Association of State Universities and Land Grant Colleges) developed their own divisions to address the university-city nexus (Crooks, 1982).

Phase III: The Metropolitan University Comes of Age (1980 to the present)

This phase is characterized by a sharpened sense of institutional mission and confidence. To discover the mission of a college or university, both its espoused mission (what a college writes or says about itself) and its living or enacted mission (what a college does and the characteristics of its programs and clients) must be considered (Davies, 1986). The clearest statement of the mission of the contemporary metropolitan university is "The Declaration of Metropolitan Universities" (1990–91) issued by a self-appointed group of leaders and endorsed by more than 100 presidents of metropolitan universities (Appendix A). As this document indicates, the basic functions of the metropolitan university are the same as other universities: teaching, research, and service. These functions, however, are oriented substantially toward serving the needs of the metropolis and its inhabitants, thereby strengthening the community and surrounding metropolitan area (Dillon, 1980; Gappert, 1986; Goldstein, 1979; Grobman, 1988; Sussman, Gollattsheck, MacIntyre and Schilt, 1981).

The metropolitan university has a deep sense of responsibility for improving the quality of life for its many constituencies (Dillon, 1980). One way the metropolitan university pursues this goal is through educational, economic, and social-oriented programs in collaboration with other organizations and institutions in the metropolitan area, particularly cooperative arrangements with schools and agencies (American Association of State Colleges and Universities, 1990).

For example, Wichita State University, through its Hugo Wall Center for Urban Studies, is attempting to establish a neighborhood resource center which would offer tutoring, counseling, and health services for adults and children who live in the predominantly Black neighborhoods near the campus (Sevetson, 1993). Similarly, Indiana University–Purdue University–Indianapolis is working with local Black churches in an effort to increase the college-going rate of students of color (J. H. Blake, personal communication, October 16, 1993).

The metropolitan university has come of age in the past decade for three reasons: (a) enrollment growth (Kinnick and Ricks, 1990) resulting from needs for lifelong learning and work force retraining (American Association of State Colleges and Universities, 1985); (b) demands for access to higher education by members of historically underrepresented ethnic and racial groups; and (c) the inexorable trend of cities toward becoming ''knowledge-dense'' (Blakely, 1991). That is, to attract and support business, commerce, and the arts, a city must host a ''configuration of knowledge institutions such as universities and colleges, and knowledge transfer and information centres'' (Fox-Przeworski, 1991, p. 231). The existence of a metropolitan university contributes to the availability of more knowledge-base workers, resulting in access to more information and an enhanced capacity to address the complicated challenges of economic development and technology transfer (Fox-Przeworski, 1991; Gappert, 1986; Potter and Chickering, 1991).

With a more clearly defined role and sense of confidence, metropolitan universities have become more aggressive in competing for resources, often putting them at odds with the older, and typically non-metropolitan state university flagship campuses (Jaschik, 1988). Effective lobbying by urban college presidents (Hill, 1981; Kerr, 1991) led to the inclusion in 1980 of Title XI in the Amendments to the Higher Education Act, which created the ''urban-grant'' program, modeled in part after the land-grant legislation of 1862 and 1890 (Berube, 1978; Grobman, 1980; Horn, 1977; National Association of State Universities and Land Grant Colleges, 1989; Olson, 1977). The purpose of these grants was to fund projects considered worthy by municipal government officials and community leaders that promised to ameliorate some of the intolerable conditions faced by urban dwellers (Grobman, 1980). However, funds have not to date been appropriated for this program.

The metropolitan university provides a wide range of educational programs, offering at least the baccalaureate degree and professional school programs and, perhaps, opportunities for graduate study in order to address the needs of part-time students and older students through various formats (regular degree, continuing education). As does the community college, the metropolitan university provides an opportunity for anyone, regardless of academic credentials, to pursue personal and vocational goals (Berube, 1978). Thus, it serves both the traditional 18-to-23-year-old cohort as well as older students resuming interrupted educations and those seeking additional professional training. Academic support services are available for those who have been previously disadvantaged but have the potential and motivation to succeed academically. A closer look at the students who attend metropolitan universities is warranted.

Characteristics of Students at Metropolitan Universities

Because of its location and inclusive philosophy, the metropolitan university attracts a student body diverse in terms of race, ethnicity, age, educational preparation, and socioeconomic background. For this reason, perhaps, much of what has been published about metropolitan university students is descriptive in nature, reporting biographical characteristics.

The average age of students at metropolitan universities usually exceeds 25 or 26 (Chandler and Galerstein, 1982); thus, students tend to have considerable life and work experience. Many are the first in their family to go to college. A substantial proportion are members of groups that have been historically underrepresented in American higher education. Although many students at metropolitan universities are underprepared for college level work (Richardson and Bender, 1985; Smartt, 1981), the vast majority expect to complete a degree program (The Landscape, 1993). Many, though not all (Morstain and Smart, 1977), expect their studies to have practical applications to their lives beyond the classroom, particularly to their work (Schlossberg et al., 1989). At the same time, older students often have families and full-time jobs that severely restrict their postsecondary options (Campbell, Wilson and Hanson, 1980). Other students, many of whom are traditional age, lack the resources to go away to college. Indeed, because of inflation and reduced rates of income growth through the 1970s and 1980s, going away to college became financially prohibitive for many students from middle-class families. The metropolitan university also attracts many transfer students, some of whom started college at residential institutions and who, for various reasons (work, family circumstances, changing career or academic preferences), return to the city to continue or resume their education. Other students prefer to attend school in the city because they do not want to give up their job, or because they need to work in order to pay for college.

To depict the diversity of students attending the metropolitan university, Rhatigan (1986) developed a typology based on 13,000 undergraduates at Wichita State University; the typology includes 256 potential categories of students. Students at WSU were about evenly divided between full-time and part-time students; about a third were married. More students owned their own home (30 percent) than lived with their parents or a relative (27 percent); about a third worked 40 or more hours per week. What most of these students have in common with their counterparts at other metropolitan institutions is that they commute to campus. In fact, commuting students now account for over 80 percent of all undergraduates (Jacoby, 1989).

Kasworm (1990) reviewed 345 papers describing the characteristics and experiences of a specific subset of metropolitan university students: those older than 24 years of age. She found that the literature described this group as deficient and marginal with regard to certain qualities that would make them effective learners (e.g., Prusok, 1960; Mueller, 1961; Shaffer, 1959). This observation also characterizes much of the literature on commuter students, part-time students, and students of color attending predominantly white campuses (Saufley, Cowan and Blake, 1983). In short, with few exceptions (e.g., Cross, 1976; Peterson, 1981), new majority students are described as needy and marginalized. It is no surprise, then, that metropolitan universities provide programs and services to meet the needs of new majority students. Certainly such efforts are well intentioned; whether they are viewed as desirable by new majority students, or address the factors in their lives that limit their learning, are separate matters. Perhaps this is why such services at metropolitan institutions are not always used by new majority students. For example, in a study of students at five urban state universities, Davila (1985) found that although 86 percent of the students used campus parking facilities and 91 percent used the library, only about 21 percent used the academic skill and tutoring programs. Similarly, 80 percent were aware of orientation, counseling, and career planning and placement services but less than half took advantage of them.

The Davila study points to what the college outcomes literature suggests is a potential obstacle to student learning and personal development inherent in metropolitan university environments: low levels of interaction between students and socialization agents (e.g., faculty, peers) and infrequent use of institutional resources. Compared with their counterparts at residential colleges, students at metropolitan universities generally do not spend as much time on the campus and, as a result, may not benefit as much from the company of faculty, staff, and other students (Pascarella and Terenzini, 1991).

This snapshot of metropolitan university students suggests that they are ''citizen-students''; that is, for many their educational program is their third or fourth priority after work, family, community service, church, and so forth. They juggle these competing commitments along with transportation issues, multiple life roles, and relationships with parents, siblings, spouses, children, employers, co-workers, and friends (Schlossberg et al., 1989). The citizen-student role common to metropolitan students is evident in their attire; at residential campuses, traditional-age students often wear jeans and sweatshirts with institutional logos. At metropolitan universities, many students wear clothing suitable for the workplace as they move directly from class to their job and vice-versa.

Summary

Universities are defined by their functions. As functions change in response to external influences, institutional missions may change (Berube, 1978; Davies,

1986; Pew Higher Education Roundtable, 1993). The land-grant universities experimented with curricular offerings for several decades before clarifying their appropriate mission. At the present moment, metropolitan universities are doing the same, offering classes and degree programs at both campus and off-campus locations to address such needs and challenges of their service area as human resource development, transportation, health and human services, housing, and planning (Berube, 1978). At the same time, they attempt to maintain relatively open admissions and low tuition rates in order to be accessible to virtually anyone seeking postsecondary education, particularly first generation college students and those from economically and educationally disadvantaged backgrounds. As a result, students attending metropolitan universities are diverse in virtually every way.

RESEARCH ON STUDENT LEARNING AT METROPOLITAN UNIVERSITIES

According to Pascarella and Terenzini (1991), "within-college" differences in student learning are typically greater than "between-college" differences. Between-college effects refer to differences in gains in learning related to the kind of institution attended (e.g., residential liberal arts college, metropolitan university), whereas within-college effects represent changes attributable to differences in the experiences of students on any given campus (Pascarella and Terenzini, 1991). Pascarella and Terenzini (1991) also found that gains in learning and personal development tend to be specific (e.g., intellectual development is influenced by classroom involvement, changes in values are linked to interactions with peers). Indeed, contacts with influential agents of socialization (e.g., faculty, peers supportive of the student's academic goals) are related both directly and indirectly to student learning. Also, students who use institutional resources (e.g., library, laboratories, studios, recreational facilities, theaters, and so on) usually benefit more than their counterparts who do not. This is consistent with the involvement principle, whereby student learning is a function of the amount of physical and psychological energy that a student devotes to the academic experience (Astin, 1984; The Study Group on the Conditions of Excellence in American Higher Education, 1984; Pace, 1987). This would suggest that students attending metropolitan universities will benefit to a degree commensurate with the amount of effort they invest in educationally purposeful activities (Schuh, Andreas and Strange, 1992).

Relatively little research has been published comparing learning and personal development outcomes of students attending metropolitan campuses and their counterparts at other types of institutions. The few studies that analyze differences between residential, full-time, traditional-age students and one or more groups of new majority students present somewhat mixed findings.

Compared with commuters, students who live in a campus residence exhibit greater gains in critical thinking during the first year (Pascarella, Bohr, Nora, Zusman, Inman and Desler, 1993) and are more likely to graduate (Astin, 1975). Chickering (1974, pp. 84–85) also compared the learning and personal development outcomes of commuter students with counterparts who lived on campus. He concluded:

> Students who live at home with their parents fall short of the kinds of learning and personal development typically desired. . . . [I]n comparison with those who live in college dormitories, [they] are less fully involved in academic activities, and extracurricular activities, and in social activities. . . . Their degree aspirations diminish and they become less committed to a variety of long-range goals.

Because most students at metropolitan institutions do not live in a residence hall, they do not benefit to the same degree from peer interactions (Astin, 1977, 1993; Feldman and Newcomb, 1969; Pascarella, 1985b; Pascarella and Terenzini, 1991).

Using the College Student Experience Questionnaire (Pace, 1987), Arnold, Kuh, Vesper and Schuh (1993) attempted to determine the relationships between age, enrollment status, and the learning and personal development of students at four metropolitan universities. Assuming influences on student learning were mutually dependent, age (22 years and younger, 28 years or older) and enrollment status (full-time and part-time) were controlled to determine their effects on outcomes in combination with student effort and perceptions of the institution's environment. The findings were inconclusive; that is, for some gain areas, age and enrollment status had a positive influence; for other gain areas they had a negative influence. For example, older students reported smaller gains in areas related to personal and social development. Part-time students reported greater gains in general education, literature and the arts, and vocational preparation. When the amount of time invested in academic activities was held constant, however, part-time and older students gained more than full-time traditional-age students. Arnold et al. (1993) speculated that because the amount of time new majority students have to spend on campus is limited, they concentrate harder on learning tasks because of the need to balance multiple commitments.

Also using the CSEQ, Pace (1991) attempted to determine whether the location of an institution (i.e., urban, suburban, rural) was related to differences in students' perceptions of the institution's environment, amount of effort expended, and self-reported gains in learning and personal development. He developed a "breadth index" (the number of CSEQ scales on which an institution's mean score is higher than the mean score of institutions of a similar type) to examine the overall level of student effort in taking advantage of opportunities for learning and personal development. The 14 Activity scales represent the quality of effort a student devotes to educationally purposeful behavior, such as talking with faculty or peers about assignments, using the library and union, and so forth. Pace found that city size was more clearly associated with breadth score differences than institutional size or institutional type. The smaller and less urban the location, the greater the breadth scores. Students who put forth highest levels of effort did so mainly in academic areas; students at non-urban institutions reported above average levels of effort in virtually all aspects of the college experience—academic, use of institutional facilities, and informal contacts with peers, faculty and others. Pace suggested that the size of the city be considered in studies of student learning at metropolitan institutions. It should be noted that the versions of the CSEQ used in the Arnold et al. and Pace studies did not include items that take into account the multiple off-campus learning environments (place of employment, community service, family, church) experienced by many students attending metropolitan universities.

That is, a city offers a variety of educational opportunities beyond those typically available on campus: voluntarism (e.g., tutoring disadvantaged students), internships (e.g., working for an accounting firm or a social service agency), and exposure to the arts (e.g., museums, live theater productions) to name a few. Students generally report they learn more through off-campus internships than from the classroom (Kantrowitz, Mitchell, and Davidson, 1983; Starke, 1985). Internships and cooperative work-education experiences provide opportunities for students to apply what they are learning in class to real world problems, helping students develop such interpersonal and practical competencies as getting along with people from different backgrounds and decisionmaking under real-time, stressful conditions (Bowen, 1977; Eyler, 1992; Kuh, 1993). However, attempts to demonstrate gains in factual knowledge associated with such experiences generally have been disappointing (Balutis, 1977; Eyler and Halteman, 1981); that is, students do not always perceive connections between what they learn in their academic program and their experiences in the field (Hursch and Borzak, 1979). But when students are asked to reflect systematically on what they learned in their internship, they are more likely to see the relevance of the curriculum to their work (Eyler, 1992).

Learning and personal development are enhanced when an institution's programs, policies, and practices ''are mutually supporting and relevant to a particular educational outcome'' (Pascarella and Terenzini, 1991, p. 626). In the context of a metropolitan university, this would mean that, among other things, faculty and administrators encourage and reward students to augment what they are learning in the classroom (and vice versa!) by using the resources of the city (e.g., art galleries, employment opportunities). This approach to teaching and learning contradicts the belief dating back to colonial times that anything worth knowing is best obtained in classrooms on campuses isolated from cities replete with distractions.

CREATING A MODEL OF STUDENT LEARNING AT METROPOLITAN UNIVERSITIES

The limited research on student learning at metropolitan universities is based on a residential paradigm—assumptions and measures that reflect the experiences of full-time, traditional-age students attending residential colleges. This paradigm treats aspects of the metropolitan student experience (e.g., competing multiple priorities, commuting to campus, working many hours a week) as—at best—irrelevant to learning or—at worst—deficits to be overcome. As a result, the literature unwittingly has promulgated negative images of new majority students and their experiences, emphasizing difficulties with regard to finances, personal, social and academic adjustment, and self-confidence (Jacoby, 1989; Kasworm, 1990). As Jacoby (1989) and others (Kuh, 1992; Stewart, 1983) have suggested, many of the students attending metropolitan universities differ in important ways from their traditional-age counterparts attending residential institutions.

> What works with full-time, single, well-prepared residential students does not necessarily work with part-time students who have jobs and families, and who have often experienced less academic success in their previous schooling. . . . More creative ways must be found to extend the discourse, build the relationships, and stir a spirit of shared goals. (Commission on the Future, 1988, pp. 7, 30)

Answers to the following questions, however tentative, would extend the discourse: Do the methods, models, and measures designed to assess student learning of traditional-age students at residential colleges adequately account for what happens to students at metropolitan universities? Are the factors that influence learning of traditional-age students enrolled at metropolitan universities similar to, or different from, those at work in residential colleges? Do out-of-class interactions with faculty influence academic gains for new majority students as is the case for traditional-age students at residential institutions? Are students more involved, and learn more, at certain metropolitan universities compared with others? If so, do the environments of these institutions—enacted by administrators, faculty and peers—differ in systematic ways? Finally, what can institutional agents do to enhance the learning productivity of all students at metropolitan universities (Johnstone, 1993)?

With these questions in mind, we conducted three exploratory studies (Kuh and Vesper, 1991, 1992; Vesper and Kuh, 1993) which differed in approaches and methods. One study (Kuh and Vesper, 1991) used path analysis to test a sub-model of Pascarella's (1985a) general causal model of student learning with students at metropolitan universities. The other two studies compared student learning at different types of metropolitan institutions (involving and other), one using path analysis (Kuh and Vesper, 1992), the other discriminant analysis (Vesper and Kuh, 1993). Because all the studies used data collected with the

College Student Experience Questionnaire (Pace, 1987), a brief description of this instrument follows.

College Student Experience Questionnaire (CSEQ)

The CSEQ is a survey instrument that collects information in four areas. Student gains are self reported on 21 Estimate of Gains scales representing areas frequently mentioned in the higher education literature (e.g., general education, analytical thinking, vocational competence) and used in national surveys over the past several decades to assess important outcomes of college (Pace, 1988). Scored on a four-point rating scale (4 = very much,3 = quite a bit, 2 = some, 1 = very little), these scales represent value-added measures. The 14 Quality of Effort scales (scored 4 = very often, 3 = often, 2 = occasionally, 1 = never) measure the frequency with which students engage, and the amount of effort they expend, in such activities as studying, using the library, union, or recreational facilities, and talking with peers and faculty about academic matters or personal concerns.

Eight rating scales (from 7 = strong emphasis to 1 = weak emphasis) measure students' perceptions of various aspects of their institution's environment. Five scales refer to the extent to which the institution emphasizes certain aspects of learning (scholarship, estheticism, critical thinking, vocational competence, practical relevance of courses); the remaining three scales refer to the quality and nature of relationships among students, faculty, and administrators. The fourth section collects biographical information about the student's personal characteristics and academic preparation indicating readiness to handle college-level work. Items from these four sections can be combined and analyzed in many different ways to determine the factors that influence student learning.

Three Exploratory Studies of Student Learning at Metropolitan Universities

The studies have three things in common. First, they examined the relationships between outcomes, student effort, and student perceptions of institutional environments, while controlling for selected student background characteristics. Second, they were intended to be practical (Ewell, 1988); we hoped the findings would point to changes in policy and practice that would enhance learning productivity. Third, the studies were fairly consistent in explaining student learning at metropolitans. Only the major findings of these studies are reported. The methods and results are described in detail in the respective papers which are available from the authors upon request.

1. Does a sub-model derived from the general causal model of student learning based on the experiences of traditional-age students accurately describe the experiences of students attending metropolitan universities?

To answer this question, CSEQs completed by 1,043 students from four metropolitan universities (University of Alabama at Birmingham, University of Louisville, University of North Carolina-Charlotte, Wichita State University) were analyzed (Kuh and Vesper, 1991). Following Pascarella (1985a) and Pascarella and Terenzini (1991), the sub-model (Figure 1) assumes student background characteristics, effort, and environmental influences are mutually reinforcing, and influence gains in learning. However, the sub-model differs in two ways from the general model described by Pascarella (1985a). Institutional characteristics included in the general model (e.g., enrollment) were omitted because the four institutions in this study were the same general type, metropolitan. No claim was made that the institutions were identical, only that the context of learning at each institution was similar (e.g., Kuh et al., 1991). In addition, institutional characteristics are far less important than some other variables (e.g., student effort) in explaining gains (Pascarella and Terenzini, 1991). Second, we assumed that perceptions of the environment have direct effects on student gains. This approach seemed justified because in the general model this category of influences includes interactions with agents of socialization (peers, faculty, administrators) which directly affect learning.

Student background characteristics descriptive of new majority students were included in addition to the sociological variables (grades, sex, race, educational aspirations, parents' education) typically used to explain student outcomes. These include age, marital status, enrollment status (full or part-time), and place of residence (on or off campus). The two criterion variables, gains in intellectual skills and gains in interpersonal skills, were created by combining relevant gains scales (e.g., analytical skills, synthesizing information, quantitative skills, inquiry skills, knowledge of computers; self-awareness, awareness of others, personal values, team skills, personal health). These variables represent a student's ability to "learn to learn" and interact with others in a complex, information-based society, both of which are useful to the individual and the society as a whole.

Three of the five independent variables were indices of student effort devoted to academics, interpersonal relations, and science and technology-related activities. The remaining two reflected the perceived quality of the intellectual environment (i.e., scholarship, estheticism, critical thinking, vocational competence, practical relevance of courses) and the intrapersonal environment (i.e., relations with students, faculty, and administrators). Structural equation models were estimated using LISREL (Joreskog and Sorbom, 1989) for each of the dependent variables (intellectual gains, interpersonal gains).

The most important finding was that student background variables which have direct effects on learning and personal development of traditional-age students at residential colleges, such as grades, sex, race, and educational aspirations (Pascarella, 1985a; Pascarella and Terenzini, 1991), did not have any direct effects on gains of students at metropolitan institutions. The results were mixed as to the influence of enrollment status, marital status, and place of residence on effort and gains. Students living off campus (including those who were married) devoted

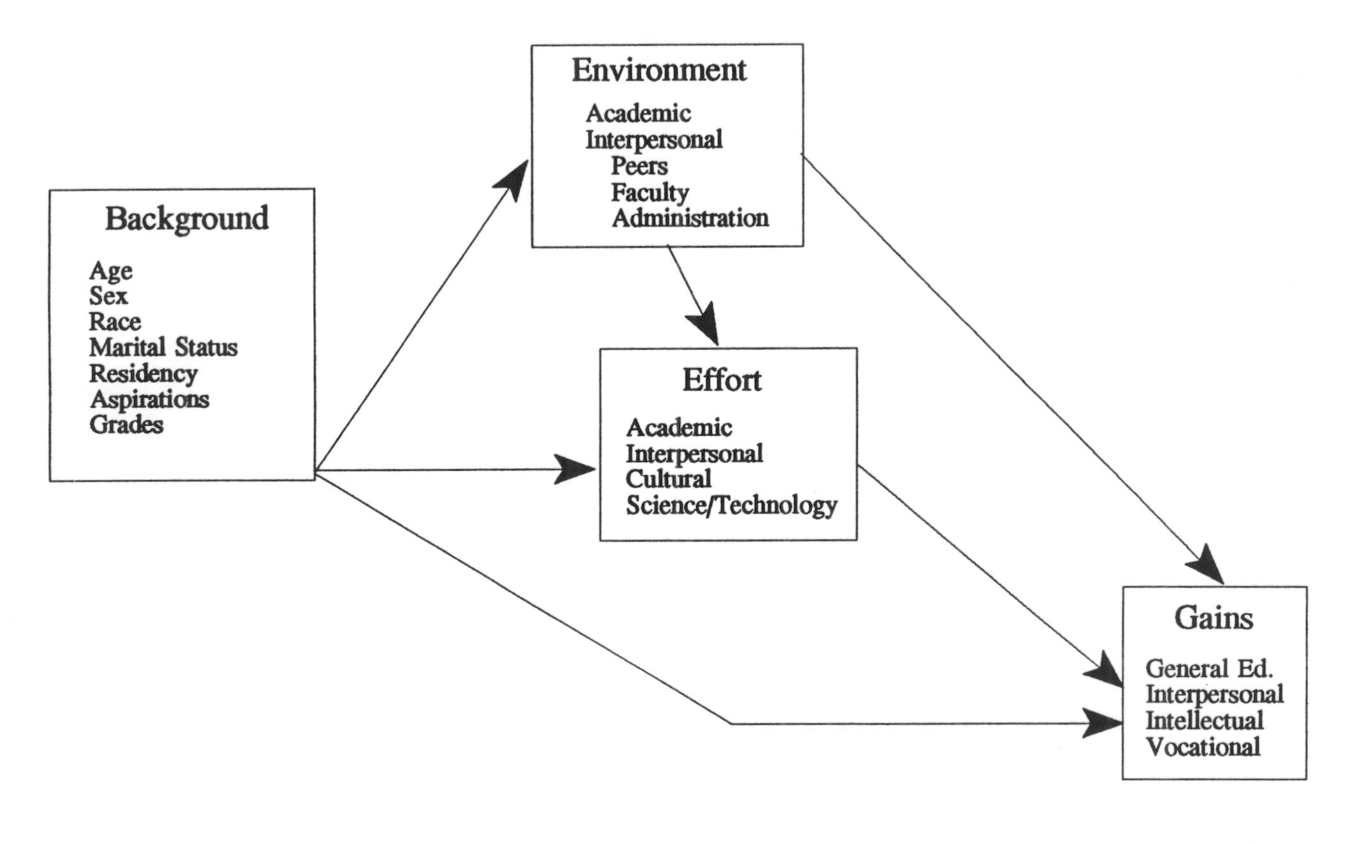

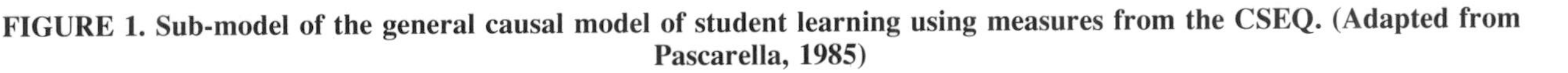

FIGURE 1. Sub-model of the general causal model of student learning using measures from the CSEQ. (Adapted from Pascarella, 1985)

less effort to peer interactions. This is to be expected as most people over the age of 25 have resolved the psycho-social developmental tasks common to late adolescence (Chickering, 1969), their needs for affiliation being met by family members and co-workers. Moreover, devoting less effort to interpersonal activities did not seem to have a negative effect on gains in intellectual skills. In general, gains seemed to be due mostly to student effort and the general intellectual atmosphere of the institution.

These findings suggest that the factors associated with student learning at metropolitan universities, although similar to traditional students in many ways, also may differ in some important ways. With judicious selection of measures and elimination of institutional characteristics, the sub-model explained the environmental effects on learning of students at metropolitan universities about as well as the general model does for traditional-age students.

2. Do the learning and personal development outcomes of students attending various metropolitan universities differ?

To answer this question, the relationships were examined between student background characteristics, perceptions of institutional environments, and gains of students attending three metropolitan universities classified as ''involving'' (n = 579) and three ''other'' metropolitan institutions (n = 579). Involving metros (University of Alabama-Birmingham, University of Louisville, Wichita State University) were those known to provide rich out-of-class learning opportunities for their students (Kuh et al., 1991). CSEQ data from students at the ''other'' three metropolitan universities (Cleveland State University, University of Lowell, University of Toledo) were provided by C. Robert Pace.

Four structural equation models (two for each set of institutions) were estimated using LISREL (Joreskog and Sorbom, 1989) to explain gains in intellectual development, general education, science and technology, personal and social competence, and vocational and practical skills. Environmental influences were composed of three factors: (a) the quality of personal relationships among peers, faculty, and administrators; (b) degree of emphasis on academics (scholarly and intellectual climate); and (c) degree of emphasis on pragmatic concerns (vocational and practical competence). As with the previous study, the models assumed student effort and environmental influences were mutually reinforcing and influenced gains in learning. The models differed, however, in how background characteristics were introduced.

The first set of models assumed that student background variables had no direct effects on any of the environmental variables but did directly affect effort and gains. In other words, both groups of institutions treat all students in the same way (or at least environmental influences are perceived by students to be similar) and that students' experiences and perceptions are independent of such characteristics as age, race, sex, marital status, enrollment status, place of residence, grades, educational aspirations, and parents' education. The second set of models assumed that only four variables (marital status, age, college grades, educational aspirations) influenced environmental perceptions and directly affected effort and gains. These variables were selected because they appeared to distinguish between those students who either have considerable time to devote to their studies and other aspects of campus life and those students whose time on campus is limited because of personal circumstances (e.g., marriage, family).

The assumption that background variables did not directly influence environmental variables proved to be tenable for the involving metros but not for the other institutions. The second assumption, that marital status, age, grades, and educational aspirations directly affected the environment at both types of metropolitan universities, produced two models, neither of which could be rejected. Students at involving metros devoted more or the same amount of effort to academic activities (depending on controls) and reported greater gains in intellectual development, general education, and vocational competence (independent of controls) compared with their counterparts at other metros.

The literature (Astin, 1977; Chickering, 1974; Pascarella and Terenzini, 1991) indicates that students enrolled full-time become more involved in the life of the institution and, as a result, benefit more from their experiences than older, part-time students. This was not the case for students at involving metros, where part-time students exhibited gains comparable to those reported by full-time students (see also Arnold et al., 1993). Moreover, background characteristics had a stronger influence on the effort and gains of students at the other metropolitan universities. This indicates that background characteristics made a difference in student learning at the other institutions, but had little influence on students at involving metros.

Equally important, the influence of the environments of the two groups of institutions on student effort and learning also differed, except for students' perceptions of administrators which were, as a rule, unrelated to student learning at either type of metropolitan institution. At the other metros, students' effort and gains were influenced by the quality of relations among students and faculty. That is, students who perceived the faculty to be supportive devoted more effort than those who viewed the faculty as neutral or disinterested; students who did not perceive the faculty to be supportive expended less effort. Thus, the environments of involving metros had less influence on gains in learning and personal development, but in an interesting and effective way. No matter how the environment was perceived by students at involving metros (more or less emphasis on critical or intellectual qualities, more or less positive relations among students and faculty), the environment was a neutral factor; that is, the environments of involving metros never hindered effort or gains.

In summary, students at involving metropolitan universities reported greater gains than their counterparts at other metropolitan universities, and these gains were independent of their background characteristics and perceptions of the institutional environment. Also noteworthy was that fewer variables accounted for student effort and outcomes at involving metros compared with the other metros. Therefore, factors other than those captured by the CSEQ apparently are operating that influence student learning at the involving metros. Taken together, the results of this study suggest that the two types of metropolitan universities differed in ways that affected learning productivity.

3. What is the relative contribution of the student and institutional agents to student learning and personal development at metropolitan universities? The previous two studies looked at student learning at metropolitan universities from a macro perspective, using measures in the form of factors derived empirically from the CSEQ gains, effort, and environment scales. This study was designed to see if learning and personal development gains could be further explained by examining specific student and faculty behaviors over which students and institutional agents could exert some influence in order to enhance learning productivity. This examination of the relationships between student learning and the local campus and classroom conditions of the involving and other metropolitans was guided by theories of the transmission of social and cultural capital (Coleman, 1988; Persell, Catsambis, and Cookson, 1992). According to these theories, the assets (or educational advantages) a family makes available to a child determines in part the benefits the child derives from formal schooling. Social and cultural capital is represented in part by family expectations, the amount of time and attention parents give to their children, and such status attainment variables as socioeconomic level, ability, and aspirations (Hossler and Vesper, 1993).

Extrapolating from this view to the university setting, faculty, and administrators are agents of socialization (the ''family'') and do things that induce the student (''child'') to behave in desirable ways in the larger world (take advantage of the institution's educational resources). Thus, faculty and administrators influence student learning and personal development through direct interventions, as in classroom interactions, as well as through indirect means by creating environments that establish high expectations for achievement while simultaneously communicating to students that they can succeed (see Persell et al., 1992, for K-12 schools and Pascarella and Terenzini, 1991, for higher education). Learning, then, is not only a function of what the student does, nor can it be the sole responsibility of the student; faculty and institutional environments contribute to student learning in significant ways by encouraging (or discouraging) students to use their capital (i.e, ability and effort) to take advantage of institutional resources.

For this analysis, student capital variables were three clusters of learning skills considered important to academic success: (a) writing and classroom note taking; (b) integrating and reflecting on the content of courses; and (c) library research. Faculty capital included four behaviors: (a) treating students as collaborators in various settings, such as on a research project or submitting a paper for publication; (b) treating students as friends in a social setting, such as having coffee or snacks; (c) providing students feedback and general information about courses, such as discussing a term paper or career plans; and (d) providing students specific feedback about their academic performance, such as offering advice on writing or talking with students about comments on a paper. Finally, the institutional capital variables were the eight environment scales from the CSEQ divided into two categories: (a) students' perceptions of the degree to which the institution emphasized such areas as scholarship, creativity, analysis, vocational competence, and relevance of academic programs; and (b) the quality of relations between students, faculty, and administrators.

A sample of students was drawn from the six institutions described in the previous analysis (Kuh and Vesper, 1992). The sample differed, however, in one important respect: only traditional-age (22 or less), unmarried, full-time students were included. This is the single fastest growing group of students at many metropolitan universities (Mulhollan, 1992). The dependent variable was a form of social stratification represented by the average of scores on the 21 CSEQ gains scales (e.g., career information, vocational training, writing clearly and effectively, awareness of other philosophies, understanding other people, understanding science, thinking analytically). That is, gains represented the degree to which students said they benefited from their college experience and, therefore, differed from one another. Students were assigned to one of three groups: high gain, medium gain, and low gain. Medium gainers were those whose gain scores were one half standard deviation on either side of the overall average gain, and the high and low gainers were outside that range. The independent variables were the clusters of student learning skills (student capital), the four selected faculty behaviors (faculty capital) and the perceptions of the environment (institutional capital). Thus, both between-college and within-college effects (Pascarella and Terenzini, 1991) were examined by comparing gains in student learning at each set of institutions (involving metros, other metros) as well as subsets of students (high gainers, medium gainers, low gainers) within the two types of metropolitan universities (Vesper and Kuh, 1993).

Using discriminant analysis (Stevens, 1986), two comparisons were conducted for each type of institution: The H and M groups which consisted of all the high and medium gainers, and the H and L groups which consisted of the high and low gainers. The high gainers were the standard to which the other groups (for both kinds of institutions) were compared. The results revealed that, consistent with the vast majority of studies on student outcomes, the most important variable linked to learning at metropolitan universities was the student's use of their capital (effort). For example, the more students engaged in such activities as note-taking, reflecting on what they are learning, and using institutional resources (e.g., library), the more they learned. The amount of time students spent with faculty discussing personal problems, having coffee, and so forth was not related to gains in either type of institution. What did matter was when faculty spent time with students in activities related to their academic performance. As has been suggested by others (Pace, 1990; Pascarella and Terenzini, 1991), the substance of what is discussed when students interact with faculty was more important to learning than the frequency of contact.

The institutional environment was quite important, particularly for students at the other institutions. That is, compared with low gainers, the high gainers at the other metros perceived that the institution placed a higher value on critical thinking, vocational skills, and practical concerns and viewed more positively the relations among peers and faculty. Three of these environmental variables differentiated the high from the medium gainers: emphasis on scholarship and vocational skills and the quality of relations between students and faculty. The group affected most negatively by their perceptions of the institution were the low gainers at the other metros; these students did not engage in the kinds of activities that lead to learning, in part because they perceived the environment to be inhospitable. In contrast, the institutional environments of the involving metropolitan universities were perceived in very similar ways by all groups. Only two differences were noted: the high gainers perceived a greater emphasis on scholarship (compared with low gainers) and on critical analysis (compared with medium gainers). Student perceptions of the environment, then, also seem to matter to student learning at metropolitan universities.

Summary

Some results from these exploratory studies corroborate the findings from research on traditional-age students at residential colleges. Other results, however, suggest that the role of faculty and the environments at metropolitan universities differed in ways that affect learning productivity. The results suggest three tentative conclusions. First, student learning at metropolitan institutions is primarily a function of classroom-related activities and student effort. At first blush, this seems to be self-evident. What takes place in classrooms is obviously important to learning. However, students at residential institutions often report that out-of-class experiences on campus—particularly interactions with peers—are at least as important to their learning—and often more important—than what happens in the classroom (Astin, 1993; Kuh, 1993; Light, 1992; Moffatt, 1989; Wilson, 1966). But at metropolitan universities, the classroom, and contacts with faculty related to academic expectations and activities, were the critical points of contact between institution and student, even for traditional-age students, because they spend a limited amount of time on campus.

Second, involving and other metros differ in ways that influence learning productivity. At the other metros, effort and gains were influenced by students' perceptions of their institution's environment, especially those aspects that focused on relations among students and faculty. In general, students at the involving metros tended to see the campus in the same way, meaning that the institutional environments did not alienate or disadvantage any group (e.g., older, married, commuter, students of color) in terms of their learning and personal development. Moreover, student background characteristics had a stronger influence on student effort and gains in learning and personal development of students at other metropolitan universities than at involving metros. Intentionally or not, the involving metros seem to have created a level playing field, whereby unalterable student characteristics (age, sex, race and ethnicity, marital status) were less relevant to how much a student gains from attending college.

Finally, the sub-model derived from the general causal model of student learning (Pascarella, 1985a), as estimated using variables contained in the CSEQ, did not account for some factors that seem to be related to student learning at metropolitan universities. Multiple commitments (e.g., full-time job, childrearing) which limit time on campus may explain some of the contradictory findings, one of which was the absence of influence of social-personal gains on intellectual gains; this empirical relationship is common for traditional-age students at residential colleges (Astin, 1993; Pascarella and Terenzini, 1991). In addition, necessary information about the learner was not represented in the sub-model, such as the amount of knowledge the student brings to the classroom and their sources of motivation. Data from the CSEQ reflect a student's choice of tasks (e.g., using a thesaurus, writing and revising drafts of papers several times, taking detailed notes and listening attentively in class, thinking about practical applications of course learning, explaining material to other students) and the amount of effort devoted to the tasks. The CSEQ does not, however, indicate a student's willingness to persist at various tasks nor does it include items that refer to off-campus activities in which students have opportunities to apply what they are learning in class and through which they might acquire knowledge and skills related to practical and interpersonal competence. These experiences (e.g., work, family relationships, community service obligations) may have direct effects on student learning or indirect effects through the student's commitment of time and energy (i.e., effort).

Although most new majority students say they aspire to earn a baccalaureate degree, they graduate at rates much lower than traditional-age students attending residential colleges (The Landscape, 1993). Learning productivity is, in part, a function of persistence. The reasons new majority students go to college, and why they persist, must be understood, even though the institution may not be able to influence some of these sources of motivation (e.g., family encouragement—or discouragement—to work hard to meet course requirements). It is to these challenges we now turn.

A Heuristic Model of Student Learning at Metropolitan Universities

People are influenced by social and historical forces operating throughout their lives. For traditional-age students, much of their experience reflects learning how to adapt to the expectations of their families and teachers, and to people from other institutions in which they have participated (e.g., church and social organizations). The historical and social forces impinging on many new majority students often are more varied, including years of full-time employment, child-rearing, military service, and other experiences that diverted them from taking the "old majority" route of 16 years of unbroken formal schooling. Therefore, any model of learning appropriate for students at metropolitan universities must take into account the factors that compelled older students to return to college and affect their ability to manage multiple commitments while pursuing their educational, vocational, and personal goals.

Figure 2 represents an approach to assessing student learning at metropolitan universities that incorporates some of the variables contained in Pascarella's general model of learning, although somewhat different labels are used. The model differs from the general causal model in several ways, however. First, institutional characteristics, such as size and selectivity, are not included. Student perceptions of the environment are featured because the exploratory studies showed that the effects of the institutional environment on learning were indirect through student effort; that is, learning was affected by the existence of a climate where student effort was encouraged, or at least not inhibited. Second, this approach emphasizes the relationships between the student's experiences (past and present) with classrooms and other learning environments (e.g., job, community service, home). The background characteristics of ability and socioeconomic status are replaced in the model by personal, social, and historical processes that need to be taken into account to understand and predict motivation to succeed. For example, older students have had, and still have, a life external to the institution, particularly a work history that has given them knowledge that might inhibit or encourage the acquisition of new information and that, in turn, affects their motivation to study hard (or not) and enroll in additional classes.

The model is heavily influenced by Schunk's (1991) overview of learning theory and the conceptual change model of learning presented by Pintrich, Marx, and Boyle (1993). As such, motivation is featured as the central mechanism by which students learn. Introducing motivation as a key variable—however messy and inconvenient it is to define and measure—requires a change in focus from the search for macro or general effects to a micro-level analysis of what occurs in the classroom (as attempted to a limited degree in the Vesper and Kuh study). For example, a positive relationship typically is found between intellectual gains and indicators of academic effort, such as the CSEQ item, use of the card catalog in the library. But the CSEQ does not provide any insight into what the institution, or its agents (faculty, student affairs staff) might do to motivate students to go to

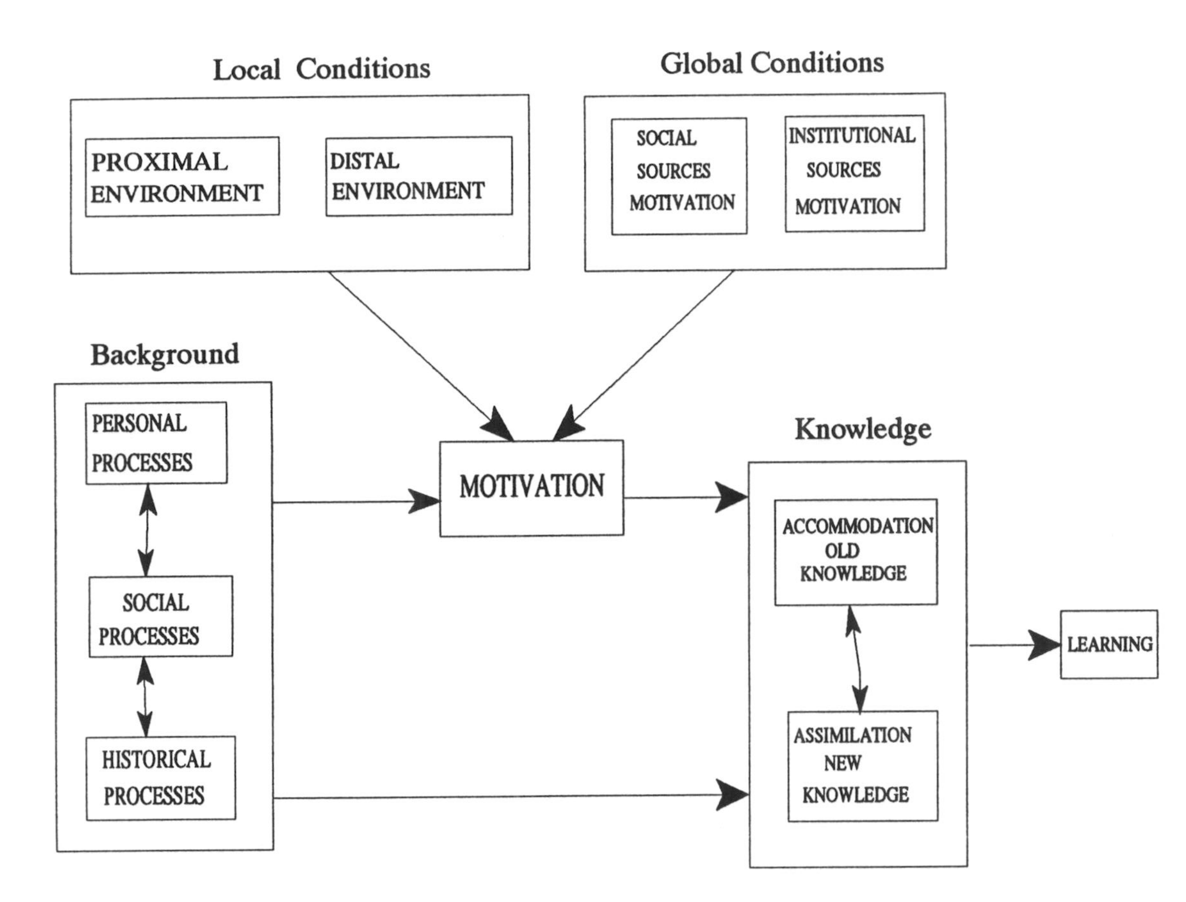

Figure 2. A heuristic model of student learning at metropolitan universities.

the library in the first place and then use the card catalog. Measures are needed of both student effort and institutional effort in the form of faculty behavior that prompts students to use the library. Featuring motivation in the model acknowledges that both the teacher and the student play important roles in enhancing learning productivity (Johnstone, 1993).

The model is proposed as a heuristic framework, not something to be estimated empirically. It is presented to extend the discourse on alternative approaches to understanding student learning at metropolitan universities, to identify constructs that warrant consideration in studies of student learning at metropolitan universities, and to suggest institutional policies and practices that can enhance learning productivity at metropolitan universities.

The components of the model are discussed briefly in the following order: learning, motivation, background processes, proximal and distal learning environments, global sources of motivation, and approaches to knowledge acquisition. These categories are interactive and not mutually exclusive; variables in one category may be found in, and influence variables from, one or more other categories.

Learning. According to Pintrich et al. (1993), learning is "the interaction that takes place between an individual's experiences and his or her conceptions and ideas. These conceptions create a framework for understanding and interpreting information gathered through experience" (p. 170). Prior knowledge plays a paradoxical role in learning by impeding the acquisition of new information when the new knowledge conflicts with a student's strongly held set of beliefs, such as those gained through experience in the work world. At the same time, prior knowledge in an area can facilitate learning in that area by providing a framework for judging the validity and adequacy of new information. Affective variables (personal interests, values, beliefs) and situational factors also determine whether students can identify discrepancies between what they already know and the new knowledge being presented and will cognitively engage in tasks that help them accommodate the discrepancies.

Motivation. Three aspects of a student's behavior indicate motivation: choice of a task, level of engagement or activity in the task, and willingness to persist at the task (Pintrich et al., 1993). By definition, highly motivated students invest more time and energy in learning tasks (i.e., they try harder to learn). Thus, motivation precedes effort. Relying on student effort alone tends to place most, if not all, of the responsibility on the student, and too little on institutional agents. For example, instead of a faculty member telling a student, "You must try harder," the faculty member should ask herself or himself, "What can I do to motivate the student to try harder?"

Background processes. As in the general model, prior experiences are thought to directly influence a student's motivation to learn. These include, but are not limited to, the sociological variables usually included in models based on traditional-age students (e.g., family socioeconomic status, high school grades). A key difference between the heuristic model and the general model is that background variables are not viewed as static or fixed; rather they are considered to be ongoing influences made up of personal, social, and historical processes mediated through motivation and the ways in which students acquire knowledge. Thus, background characteristics interact with the student's experience over time and continue to do so while they are taking classes.

Personal processes include a student's achievement orientation (high achiever, low achiever, "satisfier"), locus of control, preferred learning style (Kolb, 1981), level of cognitive development (Perry, 1970), aptitude (not necessarily reflected by high school grades or test scores), personality characteristics such as perseverance to complete tasks and, perhaps, even age. Social processes include ethnicity and gender, whether the student is responsible for children or others (spouse, parents), level of community involvement, preferred learning conditions (e.g., cooperative or independent settings), and enrollment status (full or part-time). Historical processes include work experience, career aspirations, prior experiences in formal schooling including their influence on expectations for present learning settings, how long they have been out of school, and again, possibly, age.

Local conditions. In class and out of class environments influence learning (Pascarella and Terenzini, 1991). The model acknowledges the possibility that the mix of relative effects of proximal and distal campus learning environments (Pace and Baird, 1966) may differ for new majority and traditional-age students, assuming that environmental factors act through motivation (as do background processes) to influence learning. The proximal environment refers to classrooms and other sub-environments (Baird, 1988) immediate to the core academic experience where contact occurs with faculty or classmates related to course objectives (e.g., library, laboratories, faculty offices). In addition to direct contacts with faculty, other factors to consider include the structure of the class (e.g., is competition or cooperation emphasized?), the ways in which instructors recognize and use student experience and knowledge to foster assimilation and accommodation of new knowledge, and the instructor's expectations that students will apply information and ideas from class to their lives beyond the classroom.

The distal environment refers to settings beyond the immediate classroom and includes interactions with peers and faculty as well as the campus physical arrangements that enhance student effort, such as availability of places on campus to study and meet with classmates after class and access to the library and computing facilities on weekends, evenings, and holidays. These physical features and policies may be especially important if the campus is some distance from a student's home. This category also includes off-campus locations where learning may occur, particularly settings such as internship sites or work where students encounter opportunities to apply or augment what they are learning in the classroom.

Global conditions. Because classmates, faculty members, and other institutional agents motivate students directly or indirectly, two other sources of motivation also must be considered: (a) social sources, and (b) institutional sources. Social sources of motivation include interactions with co-workers, employers, spouses, and family members, the amount of stress these relationships and other commitments create, and the degree to which significant others support the student in completing learning tasks and the program of study. Acknowledging the influence of social sources of motivation is akin to the way the environmental pull and push concept is used in retention studies (Bean and Metzner, 1985). Institutional agents may not be able to do much about whether a student's family encourages or discourages the student to work hard to meet course requirements. Yet, to accurately assess learning productivity for either institutional accountability or improvement purposes (Ewell, 1988), these sources must be taken into account.

Institutional sources of motivation include grading policies (e.g., a student's motivation might increase if the institution's grading system directly involved the student's employer in the assessment), whether the university offers some classes at employment sites (and other forms of distance learning), whether the university cooperates with local business and industry in designing courses, and whether classes are scheduled for the convenience of students (as contrasted with the preferences of faculty). Other institutional sources of motivation include faculty behavior and students' perceptions of the environment including cultural properties difficult to define or measure directly but which make a difference in terms of student learning (Vesper and Kuh, 1993) including whether students feel as though they ''matter'' (Kuh et al., 1991; Schlossberg et al., 1989).

Approaches to knowledge acquisition and use. This factor is the most difficult to account for, particularly if Figure 2 is operationalized as a path model to be estimated. Nevertheless, to increase learning productivity at metropolitan universities, how new knowledge is acquired, adopted, and used by the student is a key process that must not be overlooked. This is another face of the learning paradox mentioned earlier, the interplay between assimilation and accommodation. That is, people ''with relatively little prior conception of content to be learned have few barriers to learning new content'' (Pintrich et al., 1993, p. 171). If a student knows little about the topic being studied (as is the case for many traditional-age students), new information is likely to be combined easily with existing ideas, a process that Posner, Strike, Hewson, and Gertzog (1982) referred to as assimilation.

But for students who have relatively well-developed concepts about the topic under study, as might be the case with many students, or students who work while attending school, new concepts may conflict with, or be contrary to, what they already "know" or believe; thus, they find it difficult to assimilate the information being presented, particularly when it conflicts with, or seems unrelated to, what they have experienced or know to be true in the workplace. Existing ideas often are highly resistant to change, requiring what Posner et al. referred to as accommodation. For this reason, information presented in class might not be learned, or at best be learned only with unnecessary difficulty. Moreover, new knowledge can be a negative source of personal motivation when information seems to conflict with the student's external realities. On the other hand, prior knowledge can be a bridge for acquiring and integrating new knowledge within the student's present knowledge schema. Clearly, engaging new majority students in the process of accommodation is a special challenge, both to students and their teachers.

To promote accommodation, four conditions are necessary (Posner et al., 1982):

> The first condition is that of *dissatisfaction* with current conceptions. This suggests that, the less dissatisfied an individual is with his or her current understandings and ideas, the less likely he or she will be to consider a radical change of view. The second condition is that a new conception be *intelligible*. In order for an individual to consider a new concept as a better means of explaining experience than his or her current conception, he or she must be able to understand it. The third condition is that the new concept be *plausible*. While the learner might be able to understand the new concept, he or she may not see how it can be applied or may deem the new concept too inconsistent with other understandings to merit further consideration. Finally, the new concept must appear *fruitful*; that is, it must have explanatory power and/or suggest new areas for investigation. (Pintrich et al., 1993, p. 172)

These conditions (dissatisfaction, intelligibility, plausibility, fruitfulness) do not necessarily operate in a "cold," rational manner, meaning that people routinely acknowledge the need to have new or different information. Thus, to enhance learning productivity, instructors must create conditions that encourage new majority students to integrate their experiences, currently held knowledge, and new information.

IMPLICATIONS

This section identifies areas where additional research and development work is needed to better understand student learning at metropolitan universities. Also, suggestions are offered for institutional agents responsible for shaping policies and practices to increase learning productivity at these institutions.

Research and Development

The exploratory studies failed to corroborate a relationship between student background characteristics and gains. However, student effort and their perceptions of the institutional environment did affect gains, consistent with the general model (Pascarella, 1985a). Thus, some variables (e.g., effort) directly affect learning and personal development of both traditional-age students at residential colleges and new majority students at metropolitan universities. At the same time, there is much more to discover about the factors associated with learning productivity at metropolitan universities.

The sub-model of Pascarella's (1985a) general causal model must be tested with students at additional institutions to determine whether the findings from the exploratory studies adequately represent the student experience at metropolitan universities and to verify its capacity to explain student learning. Such studies may well result in modifications to the sub-model that increase its predictive power. Assuming the results of the exploratory studies are corroborated, new or revised measurement instruments are needed if the predictive power of the sub-model is to increase. The CSEQ (and many other instruments) do not ask the right questions of metropolitan university students. For example, although the CSEQ is an excellent tool for assessing effort and gains for traditional-age students at residential colleges, it does not take into account the effort metropolitan university students devote to off-campus activities (work, church, community service) nor what students gain from their participation in them.

Discovering the relationships between motivational beliefs, effort, institutional environments, and gains should be a high priority in instrument development. Student capital in the form of motivation and effort and institutional capital must be accounted for, including whether faculty hold high expectations for all students. For example, faculty members seem to be more important than peers at metropolitan universities to fostering student effort and learning; this is not the case at many residential colleges (Astin, 1993). Scales are needed that address specific categories of classroom behavior by both instructors and students, including instructor efforts to motivate students to accommodate new knowledge. Other potential influences that must be taken into account include the distal environments and global sources of motivation (e.g., social sources of support by family, co-workers).

A place to start is to adapt the Community College Student Experience Questionnaire (Freidlander, Pace and Lehman, 1990) for use in four-year metropolitan universities or to substantially revise the current version of the CSEQ with these concerns in mind. Qualitative studies of the experiences of new majority students at metropolitan universities could examine the mutually shaping influences of the components of the heuristic model, particularly the relationships between student background (i.e., personal, social, and historical processes), faculty behavior, and motivation. Whitt (1994) is an example of this kind of work. She found that faculty were important sources of encouragement for older students:

> Faculty believed . . . in the abilities and potential of adult learners, in some cases before the adult learners believed in themselves. This faith motivated the students to take risks

> and get involved: "They force you to do things that you don't feel comfortable doing or you haven't done before. Even at this stage of the game, I tend to sit on my rear end a little bit, and I need an extra nudge and they give me that nudge." (p. 313)

Finally, the theoretical underpinnings of the relationship between involvement and learning of new majority students should be reconsidered in the context of the metropolitan university. Research and theory development on learning productivity at metropolitan universities must explicitly acknowledge that the student's life outside the institution can be as important to their learning as what takes place in class. Taking into account the influence of social sources of motivation emphasizes the blurred boundaries between the institution and other important learning environments where knowledge has been obtained and assimilated, and that have potentially positive and negative influences on the student's ability to accommodate new knowledge. It would be particularly useful to discover more about the role of motivation as a precursor of effort and how a student's background (experiences that have a continuing influence—positively and negatively) affects motivation and other behaviors related to assimilation and accommodation of new knowledge.

Institutional Policy and Practice

The easiest way for an institution to increase learning productivity is to recruit talented, highly motivated students who devote the bulk of their time and effort to academic activities. Metropolitan universities do not have that luxury. To enhance learning productivity, metropolitan universities must concentrate their capital on three activities: (a) motivating students to devote effort to academic activities; (b) creating classroom conditions that help new majority students accommodate new knowledge with what they have learned previously; and (c) auditing the institution's distal and proximal environments to be certain all students experience the institution as affirming. With these ends in mind, three recommendations are offered.

1. Faculty must become proficient with effective instructional approaches and teach students academic survival skills.

For most new majority students the classroom is the primary point of contact with the institution. As a result, faculty capital is the single most important lever that a metropolitan university can pull to increase learning productivity. Students learn more, faster, when teachers accommodate differences in student learning styles, and use such active, collaborative learning strategies (Bruffee, 1984; Goodsell, Maher, Tinto, Smith, and MacGregor, 1992; Smith and MacGregor, 1992) as case studies, as contrasted with the more passive lecture format (Cross, 1988; Cross and Angelo, 1988; Pascarella and Terenzini, 1991). Effective instructional skills that can be learned by faculty include how to teach students to take notes and to teach one another (peer teaching), individualized systems of instruction, audio-tutorial instruction, computer-based instruction, and electronic classrooms (Murray, 1991); the latter is particularly effective in encouraging interaction among classmates and instructors. Cooperative learning can be fostered by designating a portion of class time for group projects. At residential colleges, this kind of activity often occurs after class. Because many new majority students are unable to spend time on campus other than attending class, metropolitan institutions should consider longer class periods to incorporate such activities. For example, instead of meeting one night a week for 2.5 hours, the class length could be increased to 3.5 hours to allow students to spend time together working on group projects; this avoids returning to the campus at another time.

Faculty also should require students to record periodically their thoughts about what is going on in the classroom, including their reactions to the material and the observations of their peers expressed during class discussions (Murray, 1991; Pintrich et al., 1993). As Eyler (1992) noted, students are more likely to see the connections between what they are learning in class and other areas of their lives (e.g., job, family relations) when they reflect systematically on what they are learning. Using assignments and class discussions to require students to reflect on what they are learning on their job, or from relationships with classmates, co-workers and family members, increases active engagement in academic work, fosters intellectual development, and facilitates the processes of assimilation and accommodation of new knowledge.

To increase the chances that students will complete these tasks (e.g., reflecting on what they are learning), faculty must take into account the multiple sources of motivation pushing and pulling (Bean and Metzner, 1988) their students and teach students the behaviors that will produce learning (e.g., taking class notes, using the library and other institutional resources, how much time is needed to complete various the assignments). For example, social sources of motivation include employers and co-workers; as mentioned earlier, directly involving the employer in determining the grade in a course related to the nature of the job would probably increase the student's motivation. Other approaches likely to motivate new majority students are those in which students can exercise some control over what to work on, how to work, and what products to create (Pintrich et al., 1993), and when and how to monitor their own work as they complete assignments during a course, and seek connections between material learned in different courses in a program of study.

2. Clarify the institution's educational purposes and philosophy.

Institutions unclear about what they are trying to do, and how best to accomplish these ends, send mixed messages to faculty and students about their aspirations, expectations, priorities, and values. The metropolitan university mission is distinctive compared with other types of postsecondary institutions in the United States. But every metropolitan university must interpret this mission on a continuing basis in its particular context, periodically clarify its aims (Davies, 1986), and translate these aims into appropriate expectations for student behavior (Kuh et al., 1991). The key questions are: "What are we trying to accomplish?" and "By what means (policies, practices)—given our students—can we best attain our educational purposes?" To answer these questions, faculty and administrators must know a good deal about their students (especially how multiple sources of motivation affect their enrolling and staying in college), and how they perceive various aspects of the institution's environment. For example, many new majority students at metropolitan universities are experiencing a major life transition—from married to divorced, from one job to another, from children in the home to an empty nest, and so on. Faculty and staff at metropolitan institutions must be certain their institutions's policies and practices, and their own behavior, acknowledge this transition-facilitation role.

From their study of 14 involving colleges and universities, Kuh et al. (1991) concluded that faculty at these institutions behaved in ways that communicated a sense of belonging and empowerment to all their students. A key factor, then, in motivating metropolitan university students is establishing an institution-wide ethic of inclusion; that is, treating all students the same regardless of background characteristics (e.g., sex, age, enrollment status, ethnicity). One way to start the dialogue about assumptions is with a series of colloquia or workshops designed to flesh out the characteristics that faculty believe make for the "ideal" student. Unless they subscribe to the principle, that, and behave as if, any student in their class can learn what they have to teach, faculty will send subtle signals to students that some people belong here (and can succeed) while others do not.

3. Monitor institutional environments with student learning in mind. Institutional environments affect student learning (Astin, 1977, 1993; Baird, 1988; Feldman and Newcomb, 1969; Heath, 1968; Kuh, 1993b; Pascarella, 1985a, Pascarella and Terenzini, 1991). In the Vesper and Kuh study, student perceptions of the institution's distal and proximal environments distinguished between high gainers and low gainers at the other metropolitan institutions. Although the classroom is the most important proximal environment for students at metropolitan universities, the climates of academic departments also warrant attention. For example, students for whom affirmation is a source of social motivation appreciate gestures that make them feel welcome, such as a personal mail box in the department office or occasional social events following class.

Activities designed to foster interaction must view family members, friends, and co-workers as sources of social motivation, an approach that differs from residential campuses initiatives where the goal is to get students to substitute new peer acquaintances for family and friends. Kuh and Vesper (1992) found a negative relationship between intellectual gains and perceptions of the quality of relations between faculty and students for married students at the other metropolitan universities. To alter this perception, and possibly motivate married students to spend more time interacting with their classmates on academic tasks, the institution could assist them in fulfilling family obligations (e.g., cooperative learning projects conducted in the evening with child-care available on campus). Also, family members should have an open invitation to participate in institutional events, another source of personal and social motivation. For example, rather than celebrating commencement with a dinner-dance, a picnic or some other event to which children, parents and co-workers are invited—and would feel comfortable—would be more appropriate.

Taken together, the proximal and distal environments of an institution can be thought of as its ethos. The word, ethos, is from the Greek, "habit." The concept as used here refers to a belief system widely shared by faculty, students and administrators (Kuh, 1993). An institution's ethos evokes an emotional commitment to the institution and helps people decide what is appropriate. Although viewed by some as a soft, vague notion, the ethos is a key factor in explaining institutional effectiveness in a variety of areas (Heath, 1981; Kuh and Whitt, 1988). Colleges that have cultivated an ethos of learning expect all students to be successful in their chosen area of study and make status distinctions among students irrelevant to learning (Kuh et al., 1991). This was the case with students at the involving metropolitan universities in the exploratory studies where background characteristics of students did not directly affect gains in learning and personal development.

Finally, although perceptions of administrators were unrelated to student learning, a metropolitan university with an ethos of learning does not just happen. In addition to the desired classroom behavior of faculty described earlier, academic and student life administrators should audit periodically institutional policies and practices to be certain they are consistent with the institution's mission and contribute to the campus-wide ethos of learning and do not inhibit student access to needed resources.

CONCLUSION

The metropolitan university has emerged as a distinctive institutional type in American higher education (Grobman, 1988), in part because it was uniquely situated to capitalize on what is now a defining characteristic of American higher education—student diversity. The character and purposes of the metropolitan university, and the characteristics of its students differ substantially from the traditional residential campus and its students. As a result, increasing learning productivity at metropolitan institutions requires approaches that do not simply mimic best practices from residential institutions. The models and assessment instruments most frequently used, such as the CSEQ, do not address some of the more important variables and contexts that may increase our understanding of what contributes to student learning at metropolitan institutions. Experimentation is needed with assessment instruments that take into account the experiences of new majority students and with institutional policies and instructional practices that encourage students to assimilate and accommodate new knowledge. Instead of tacitly endorsing the assumption that students must be removed from the distractions of the city in order to learn (the assumption that resulted in many American colleges and universities being located in rural areas), researchers must recognize that students are citizen-students, *of* the city as are the metropolitan universities they attend.

To increase learning productivity at metropolitan universities, faculty and staff must concentrate their capital (i.e., time, energy) on activities that motivate students to become cognitively engaged in tasks that foster learning. As the exploratory studies summarized in this chapter indicated, at some metropolitan universities, students devoted more effort to learning tasks and exhibited greater gains, compared with their counterparts at other similar institutions. Apparently, at the former institutions, faculty and institutional environments encourage students to use their social and cultural capital in educationally productive ways. As a result, what students learn is a function of what they do, not of who they are or where they are from.

APPENDIX A

DECLARATION OF METROPOLITAN UNIVERSITIES

MAY 8, 1990

We, the undersigned leaders of metropolitan universities and colleges, embracing the historical values and principles which define all universities and colleges, and which make our institutions major intellectual resources for their metropolitan regions.

- reaffirm that the creation, interpretation, dissemination, and application of knowledge are the fundamental functions of our universities;
- assert and accept a broadened responsibility to bring these functions to bear on the needs of our metropolitan regions;
- commit our institutions to be responsive to the needs of our metropolitan areas by seeking new ways of using our human and physical resources to provide leadership in addressing metropolitan problems, through teaching, research, and professional services.

Our teaching must:

- educate individuals to be informed and effective citizens, as well as capable practitioners of professions and occupations;
- be adapted to the particular needs of metropolitan students, including minorities and other underserved groups, adults of all ages, and the placebound;
- combine research-based knowledge with practical application and experience, using the best current technology and pedagogical techniques.

Our research must:

- seek and exploit opportunities for linking basic investigation and practical application, and for creating synergistic interdisciplinary and multidisciplinary scholarly partnerships for attacking complex metropolitan problems, while meeting the highest scholarly standards of the academic community.

Our professional service must include:

- development of creative partnerships with public and private enterprises that ensure that the intellectual resources of our institutions are fully engaged with such enterprises in mutually beneficial ways;
- close working relationships with the elementary and secondary schools of our metropolitan regions, aimed at maximizing the effectiveness of the entire metropolitan education system, from preschool through postdoctoral levels;
- the fullest possible contributions to the cultural life and general quality of life of our metropolitan regions.

(*Metropolitan University*, 1990–91, pp. 3–5)

REFERENCES

Adamany, D. (1992). The university as urban citizen. *Educational Record* 73(2), 6–9.

American Association of State Colleges and Universities (1985). *Urban State Colleges and Universities*. Washington, DC: American Association of State Colleges and Universities. (HE 022 914)

American Association of State Colleges and Universities (1990). *City Learning Laboratories: Urban State Colleges and Universities*. Washington, DC: American Association of State Colleges and Universities. (ed 332 643)

Arnold, J. A., Kuh, G. D., Vesper, N., and Schuh, J. H. (1993). Student age and enrollment status as determinants of learning and personal development at metropolitan institutions. *Journal of College Student Development* 34: 11–16.

Ashworth, K. H. (1964). Urban renewal and the university: A tool for campus expansion and neighborhood improvement. *Journal of Higher Education* 35: 393–396.

Astin, A. W. (1975). *Preventing Students from Dropping Out*. San Francisco: Jossey-Bass.

Astin, A. W. (1977). *Four Critical Years.* San Francisco: Jossey-Bass.
Astin, A. W. (1984). Student involvement: A developmental theory for higher education. *Journal of College Student Personnel* 25: 297–308.
Astin, A. W. (1985). *Achieving Educational Excellence.* San Francisco: Jossey-Bass.
Astin, A. W. (1993). *What Matters in College: Four Critical Years Revisited.* San Francisco: Jossey-Bass.
Baird, L. L. (1988). The college environment revisited: a review of research and theory. In J. Smart (ed.), *Higher Education: Handbook of Theory and Research,* Vol IV. New York: Agathon.
Baird, L. L. (1991, November). The urban university: student experiences and campus features. Paper presented at the meeting of the Association for the Study of Higher Education, Boston.
Balutis, A. (1977). Participation through politics. *Teaching Political Science* 4: 319–328.
Bean, J. P., and Metzner, B. S. (1985). A conceptual model of nontraditional undergraduate student attrition. *Review of Educational Research* 55: 485–540.
Bender, T. (ed.), (1989). *The University and the City: From Medieval Origins to the Present.* New York: Oxford University Press.
Berube, M. R. (1978). *The Urban University in America.* Westport, Ct: Greenwood.
Blakely, E. (1991). The New Technology City: Infostructure for the Future Community. In J. Brotchie, M. Batty, P. Hall and P. Newton (eds.), *Cities of the 21st Century: New Technologies and Spacial Systems.* New York: Longman Cheshire.
Bonner, T. N. (1986). The unintended revolution in America's colleges since 1940. *Change* 18(5): 44–51.
Bouseman, J. W. (1970). The pulled away college. Unpublished doctoral dissertation, University of Chicago.
Bowen, H. R. (1977). *Investment in Learning.* San Francisco: Jossey-Bass.
Bruffee, K. A. (1984). Collaborative learning and the conversation of mankind. *College English* 46: 635–652.
Cafferty, P. S. J., and Spangenberg, G. (1983). *Backs Against the Wall: Urban Oriented Colleges and the Urban Poor and Disadvantaged.* Series on Higher Education and the Cities, No. 3. New York: Ford Foundation.
Campbell, M. D., Wilson, L. G., and Hanson, G. R. (1980). *The Invisible Minority: A Study of Adult University Students.* Austin: Office of the Dean of Students, University of Texas.
Carlson, W. S. (1962). *The Municipal University.* Washington, DC: The Center for Applied Research in Education.
Carnegie Commission on Higher Education (1972). *The Campus and the City.* New York: McGraw-Gill.
Carothers, N. (1963, May). University circle institutions round out urban site. *College and University Business* 34: 53–57.
Cedar, T. B. (1970). The unique clientele of the urban university. *College and University* 45(2): 138–147.
Chandler, J. M., and Galerstein, C. (1982). Students over 30: need their classes be different? *Alternative Higher Education* 7(1): 44–51.
Chickering, A. W. (1969). *Education and Identity.* San Francisco: Jossey-Bass.
Chickering, A. W. (1974). *Commuting Versus Resident Students.* San Francisco: Jossey-Bass.
Chickering, A. W., and Gamson, Z. F. (1987). Seven principles for good practice in undergraduate education. *AAHE Bulletin* 39(7): 3–7.

Coleman, J. S. (1988). Social capital in the creation of human capital. *American Journal of Sociology* 94(Suppl.): S95–S120
College Entrance Examination Board (1981). *Student Aid and the Urban Poor.* Higher Education and the Cities: No. 1. New York: Ford Foundation.
Commission on the Future of Community Colleges (1988). *Building Communities: A Vision for a New Century.* Washington, DC: American Association of Community and Junior Colleges. (ed 293 578)
Crooks, J. B. (1982). The AUU and the mission of the urban university. *Urbanism Past and Present* 7(2): 34–39.
Cross, K. P. (1976). *Accent on Learning.* San Francisco: Jossey-Bass.
Cross, K. P. (1988). In search of zippers. *AAHE Bulletin* 40(10): 3–7.
Cross, K. P., and Angelo, T. (1988). *Classroom Assessment Techniques: A Handbook for Faculty.* Ann Arbor: University of Michigan, NCRIPTAL.
Davies, G. K. (1986). The importance of being general: philosophy, politics, and institutional mission statements. In J. Smart (ed.), *Higher Education: Handbook of Theory and Research,* Vol. II. New York: Agathon.
Davila, E. M. (1985). *Today's Urban University Students: Part 1. Profile of a New Generation. Final Report on the Urban University Study.* Washington, DC: College Entrance Examination Board.
Declaration of Metropolitan Universities (1990–91). *Metropolitan Universities,* 1 (3): 3–5.
Diekhoff, J. S. (1950). *Democracy's College: Higher Education in the Local Community.* New York: Harper and Row.
Dillon, J. A., Jr. (1980). The evolution of the American urban university. *Urban Education* 15(1): 33–48.
Doxiadis, C. A. (1969). Cities in crisis and the university. *College and University Business* 47(4): 49–56.
Easterby, J. H. (1935). *A History of the College of Charleston.* Charleston, SC: Scribner.
Eckelberry, R. H. (1932). *The History of Municipal University in the United States.* Washington, DC Office of Education Bulletin No. 2.
Ehrlich, T. (1991). *Our University in the State: Educating the New Majority.* Bloomington, IN: Indiana University.
Ewell, P. T. (1988). Outcomes, assessment, and academic improvement: in search of usable knowledge. In J. Smart (ed.), *Higher Education: Handbook of Theory and Research,* Vol. IV. New York: Agathon, 1988.
Eyler, J. (1992, April). Comparing the impact of two internship experiences on student learning. Paper presented at the meeting of the American Educational Research Association, San Francisco.
Eyler, J., and Halteman, B. (1981). The impact of a legislative internship on students' political skill and sophistication. *Teaching Political Science* 9: 27–34.
Feldman, K. A., and Newcomb, T. M. (1969). *The Impact of College on Students.* San Francisco: Jossey-Bass.
Folger, J. K. (1963). Urban sprawl in the academic community: alleviating the university's growing pains. *Journal of Higher Education* 34: 450–457.
Ford Foundation (1981). *A Tale of Three Cities—Boston, Birmingham, Hartford.* Series on Higher Education and the Cities, No. 2. New York: Ford Foundation.
Fox-Przeworski, J. (1991). Concentration of new information technologies: are there spacial policy concerns? In J. Brotchie, M. Batty, P. Hall and P. Newton (eds.), *Cities of the 21st Century: New Technologies and Spacial Systems.* New York: Longman Cheshire.

Friedlander, J., Pace, C. R., and Lehman, P. (1990). *Community College Student Experiences Questionnaire*. Los Angeles: UCLA Center for the Study of Evaluation.

Gappert, G. (1986). The present and future nature of the urban mission in higher education: from 1966 to 2006. In A. S. J. Artibise and W. A. Fraser (eds.), *New Directions for Urban Universities: International Perspectives*. University of Winnipeg: Institute of Urban Studies.

Gardner, J. W. (1969). The university and the city. *Educational Record* 50 (1): 5–8.

Goldstein, M. B. (1979). Toward the urban university: the needs and the obstacles. *The Innovator: Newsletter of the Center for Program Development* 6(4): 2–9.

Goodsell, A., Maher, M., Tinto, V., Smith, B. L., and MacGregor, J. (1992). *Collaborative Learning: A Sourcebook for Higher Education*. University Park, Pa: National Center on Postsecondary Teaching, Learning, and Assessment.

Grobman, A. B. (1980). The missions of urban institutions. *Liberal Education* 66(2): 200–207.

Grobman, A. B. (1988). *Urban State Universities: An Unfinished Agenda*. New York: Praeger.

Grobman, A. B., and Sanders, J. S. (1984). *Interactions Between Public Urban Universities and Their Cities*. A Report of the Division of Urban Affairs of the National Association of State Universities and Land-grant Colleges. St. Louis: University of Missouri.

Hathaway, C. E., Mulhollan, P. E., and White, K. A. (1990). Metropolitan universities: models for the twenty-first century. *Metropolitan Universities* 1(1): 9–20.

Heath, D. H. (1981). A college's ethos: a neglected key to effectiveness and survival. *Liberal Education* 67: 89–111.

Hester, J. M. (1966). Urbanization and higher education. In G. Kerry Smith (ed.), *1966 Current Issues in Higher Education*, the Proceedings of the Twenty-first Annual National Conference on Higher Education. Washington, DC.

Hill, S. R., Jr. (1981). Urban universities: twentieth-century phenomena. *National Forum*, 61 (3): 38–39.

Hofstadter, R., and Smith, W. (1961). *American Higher Education: A Documented History*. Chicago: University of Chicago Press.

Hopkins, C. H. (1950). *The History of the YMCA in North America*. New York: Association Press.

Horn, S. (1977). Opportunities for the public urban university. *Phi Delta Kappan* 59 (1): 14–15.

Hossler, D., and Vesper, N. (1993). Factors associated with parental college savings. *Journal of Higher Education* 16: 140–166.

Hursch, B. A., and Borzak, L. (1979). Toward cognitive development through field studies. *Journal of Higher Education* 50: 63–77.

Jacoby, B. (1989). *The Student as Commuter: Developing a Comprehensive Institutional Response*. ASHE-ERIC Higher Education Report No. 7. Washington, DC: School of Education and Human Development, the George Washington University.

Jaschik, J. (1988, February 10). City campuses balk at secondary roles in state systems. *The Chronicle of Higher Education*, Pp. A1, A24–25.

Johnstone, D. B. (1993). Learning productivity: a new imperative for American higher education. *Studies in Public Higher Education*, No. 3. Albany, NY: Office of the Chancellor, State University of New York.

Jöreskog, K. G., and Sörbom, D. (1989). *Lisrel 7: A Guide to the Program and Applications* (2nd Ed.). Chicago: Jöreskog and Sörbom/spss.

Kantrowitz, R., Mitchell, C., and Davidson, W. S., II (1983). Varying formats of teaching undergraduate courses: an experimental examination. *Teaching of Psychology* 9: 186–188.

Kasworm, C. E. (1990). Adult undergraduates in higher education: a review of past research perspectives. *Review of Educational Research*, 60: 345–372.

Kerr, C. (1991). An urban versus a rural society—the urban-grant university: a model for the future. In C. Kerr (ed.), *the Great Transformation in Higher Education, 1960–1980*. Albany, NY: SUNY Press.

Kinnick, M. K., and Ricks, N. F. (1990). The urban public university in the United States: an analysis of change, 1977–1987. *Research in Higher Education* 31: 15–38.

Klotsche, J. M. (1966). *The Urban University: And the Future of Our Cities*. New York: Harper and Row.

Knowles, A. S. (1970). *Handbook of College and University Administration—general*. New York: McGraw-Hill.

Knox, N. H. (1967). The urban community: a planning guide. *College and University Business* 42: 58–63.

Kolb, D. (1981). Learning styles and disciplinary differences. In A. W. Chickering and Associates (eds.), *The Modern American College*. San Francisco: Jossey-Bass.

Kolbe, P. R. (1928). *Urban Influences on Higher Education in England and the United States*. New York: Macmillan.

Kuh, G. D. (1992). A landmark in scholarly synthesis: what do we do now? Implications for educators of *How College Affects Students*. *The Review of Higher Education* 15: 349–363.

Kuh, G. D. (1993). In their own words: what students learn outside the classroom. *American Educational Research Journal* 30: 277–304.

Kuh, G. D. (1993). Ethos: its influence on student learning. *Liberal Education*, 79(4): 22–31.

Kuh, G. D., Schuh, J. H., Whitt, E. J., Andreas, R. E., Lyons, J. W., Strange, C. C., Krehbiel, L. E., and Mackay, K. A. (1991). *Involving Colleges: Successful Approaches to Fostering Student Learning and Development Outside the Classroom*. San Francisco: Jossey-Bass.

Kuh, G. D., and Vesper, N. (November 1991). *Influences on student learning at metropolitan universities: a structural model*. Presented at the meeting of the Association for the Study of Higher Education, Boston. (ED 339 316)

Kuh, G. D., and Vesper, N. (April 1992). *A comparison of student learning at "involving" and other metropolitan universities*. Presented at the meeting of the American Educational Research Association, San Francisco.

Kuh, G. D., and Whitt, E. J. (1988). *The Invisible Tapestry: Culture in American Colleges and Universities*. AAHE-ERIC/Higher Education Research Report, No. 1. Washington, DC: American Association for Higher Education.

Layzell, D.T., and Lyddon, J.W. (1990). *Budgeting for Higher Education at the State Level: Enigma, Paradox, and Ritual*. AAHE-ERIC/Higher Education Research Report, No. 4. Washington, DC: George Washington University.

Levi, J. H. (1961). The influence of environment on urban institutions. *The Educational Record* 42: 37–141.

Levine, A. and Associates (1989). *Shaping Higher Education's Future: Demographic Realities and Opportunities, 1990–2000*. San Francisco: Jossey-Bass.

Levine, D. O. (1986). *The American College and the Culture of Aspiration, 1915–1940*. Ithaca: Cornell University Press.

Lewis, M. S. (1992). The polytechnics: a peculiarly British phenomenon. *Metropolitan Universities* 2(4): 24–34.

Light, R.J. (1992). *The Harvard Assessment Seminars: Explorations with Students and Faculty about Teaching, Learning, and Student Life* (Second Report). Cambridge, MA: Harvard University Graduate School of Education and Kennedy School of Government.

McGrane, R.C. (1963). *The University of Cincinnati*. New York: Harper and Row.

Moffatt, M. (1988). *Coming of Age in New Jersey: College and American Culture*. New Brunswick, NJ: Rutgers University Press.

Morstain, B. R., and Smart, J. C. (1977). A motivational typology of adult learners. *Journal of Higher Education* 48: 665–679.

Mueller, K. H. (1961). *Student Personnel Work in Higher Education*. Cambridge, Mass: Riverside.

Mulhollan, P. E. (1992, April). Recent developments at metropolitan universities. Paper presented at the annual meeting of the American Association for Higher Education, Chicago.

Murray, H. G. (1991). Effective teaching behaviors in the college classroom. In J. Smart (ed.), *Higher Education: Handbook of Theory and Research*, Vol. VII. New York: Agathon.

Nash, G. (1973). *The University and the City*. New York: McGraw-Hill.

National Association of State Universities and Land-grant Colleges (1989). *America's People: An Imperiled Resource*. Washington, DC: National Association of State Universities and Land-grant Colleges. (ed 310 214)

Olson, J. C. (1977). Proposed for urban universities: a federal urban grant program. *Phi Delta Kappan* 59(1): 21–22.

Pace, C. R. (1987). *CSEQ: Test Manual and Norms: College Student Experiences Questionnaire*. Los Angeles: the Center for the Study of Evaluation, Graduate School of Education, University of California, Los Angeles.

Pace, C. R. (1990). *The Undergraduates: A Report of Their Activities and Progress in College in the 1980s*. Los Angeles: Center for the Study of Evaluation, UCLA Graduate School of Education.

Pace, C. R. (1991, November). Is urbanness a useful variable? Paper presented at the meeting of the Association for the Study of Higher Education, Boston.

Pace, C. R., and Baird, L. L. (1966). Attainment patterns in the environmental press of college subcultures. In T. Newcomb and E. Wilson (eds.), *College Peer Groups*. Chicago: Aldine.

Pang, V. O. (1993). Universities as good neighbors for ethnic communities. *Equity and Excellence in Education* 26(1): 46–51.

Parsons, K. C. (1963). Universities and cities. *Journal of Higher Education* 34: 205–216.

Pascarella, E. T. (1985a). College environmental influences on learning and cognitive development: A critical review and synthesis. In J. Smart (ed.), *Higher Education: Handbook of Theory and Research*, Vol I. New York: Agathon.

Pascarella, E. T. (1985b). The influence of on-campus living versus commuting to college on intellectual and interpersonal self-concept. *Journal of College Student Personnel* 26: 292–299.

Pascarella, E. T., Bohr, L., Nora, A, Zusman, B., Inman, P., and Desler, M. (1993). Cognitive impacts of living on campus versus commuting to college. *Journal of College Student Development* 34: 216–220.

Pascarella, E. T., and Terenzini, P. T. (1991). *How College Affects Students: Findings and Insights from Twenty Years of Research*. San Francisco: Jossey-Bass.

Persell, C., Catsambis, S., and Cookson, P. (1992). Differential asset conversion: Class and gendered pathways to selective colleges. *Sociology of Education* 65: 208–225.

Perry, W. G., Jr. (1970). *Forms of Intellectual and Ethical Development in the College Years: A Scheme*. New York: Holt, Rinehart and Winston.
Peterson, R. E. (1981). Opportunities for adult learners. In A. W. Chickering and Associates (eds.), *The Modern American College*. San Francisco: Jossey-Bass.
Pew Higher Education Roundtable (1993). A transatlantic dialogue. *Policy Perspectives* 5(1): 1A–11A.
Pierce, G. A. (1981). Competition for space: Planning policy for urban universities. *Planning for Higher Education* 9(3): 1–12.
Pintrich, P., Marx, R., and Boyle, R. (1993). Beyond cold conceptual change: The role of motivational beliefs and classroom contextual factors in the process of conceptual change. *Review of Educational Research* 63: 167–199.
Posner, G., Strike, K, Hewson, P., and Gertzog, W. (1982). Accommodation of a scientific conception: Toward a theory of conceptual change. *Science Education* 66: 211–227.
Potter, D., and Chickering, A. (1991). Reshaping the university for the metropolitan area. *Metropolitan Universities* 2(2): 7–20.
Prusok, R. E. (1960). The off-campus student. *Journal of College Student Personnel* 2: 2–9.
Rhatigan, J. J. (1986). Developing a campus profile of commuting students. *NASPA Journal* 24: 4–10.
Richardson, R. C., Jr., and Bender, L. W. (1985). *Students in Urban Settings: Achieving the Baccalaureate Degree*. ASHE-ERIC Higher Education Report No. 6. Washington, DC: Association for the Study of Higher Education.
Riesman, D. (1975). The mission of the urban grant universities. *The Journal of General Education* 27(2): 149–156.
Rudolph, F. (1962). *The American College and University*. New York: Knopf.
Rudy, S. W. (1949). *The College of the City of New York: A History 1847–1947*. New York: The City College Press.
Saufley, R.W., Cowan, K.O., and Blake, J.H. (1983). The struggles of minority students at predominantly white campuses. In J. Cones, J. Noonan, and D. Janha (eds.), *Teaching Minority Students, New Directions for Teaching and Learning*, No. 16. San Francisco: Jossey-Bass.
Schlossberg, N. K., Lynch, A. Q., and Chickering, A. W. (1989). *Improving Higher Education Environments for Adults*. San Francisco: Jossey-Bass.
Schuh, J. H., Andreas, R. E., and Strange, C. C. (1992). Students at metropolitan universities: viewing involvement through different lenses. *Metropolitan University* 2(3): 64–74.
Schunk, D. (1991). *Learning Theories: An Educational Perspective*. New York: Macmillan.
Sevetson, M. (1993, July 8). Grant would help WSU bond with neighborhood. *Wichita Eagle* pp. A1, A8.
Seyffert, M. G. (1975). The university as an urban neighbor. In T. P. Murphy (ed.), *Universities in the Urban Crisis*. New York: Dunellen.
Shaffer, R. H. (1959). Effect of large enrollments on student personnel services. *Personnel and Guidance Journal*, 626–32.
Skardon, A. W. (1983). *Steel Valley University: The Origin of Youngstown State*. Youngstown, OH: Youngstown State University.
Smartt, S. H. (1981). *Urban Universities in the 80s: Issues in State-wide Planning*. Atlanta: Southern Regional Education Board. (ed 202 407)
Smith, B.L., and MacGregor, J. (1992). What is collaborative learning? In A. Goodsell, M.

Maher and V. Tinto (eds.), *Collaborative Learning: A Sourcebook for Higher Education* (pp. 9–22). University Park: National Center on Postsecondary Teaching, Learning and Assessment, The Pennsylvania State University.

Spaights, E. (1980). Toward a definition of an urban university. *Urban Education* 15: 369–374.

Starke, M. C. (1985). A research practicum: Undergraduate as assistant in psychological research. *Teaching of Psychology* 12: 158–160.

Stevens, J. (1986). *Applied Multivariate Statistics for the Social Sciences*. Hillsdale, NJ: Lawrence Erlbaum Associates.

Stewart, S. S. (ed.) (1983). *Commuter Students: Enhancing Their Educational Experiences*. New Directions for Student Services, No. 24. San Francisco: Jossey-Bass.

Sussman, H., Gollattsheck, J., MacIntyre, D., and Shilt, A. (1981). *Connections: Newsletter of the Urban College and University Network* 3(5): 3–6.

The Landscape: The changing faces of the American college campus (1993). *Change* 25(4): 57–60.

The Study Group on the Conditions of Excellence in American Higher Education (1984). *Involvement in Learning*. Washington, DC: United States Department of Education.

Vesper, N., and Kuh, G. D. (April 1993). Institutional conditions and student behaviors associated with student learning at metropolitan universities. Presented at the annual meeting of the American Educational Research Association, Atlanta.

Waetjen, W. B., and Muffo, J. A. (1983). The urban university: Model for actualization. *The Review of Higher Education* 6: 207–215.

Whitt, E. J. (1994). Encouraging adult learner involvement. *NASPA Journal* 31: 309–318.

Williams, D., and Cowley, W. H. (1991). *International and Historical Roots of American Higher Education*. New York: Garland.

Wilson, E.K. (1966). The entering student: Attributes and agents of change. In T. Newcomb and E. Wilson (eds.), *College Peer Groups* (pp. 71–106). Chicago: Aldine.

Wingspread Group on Higher Education (1993). *An American Imperative: Higher Expectations for Higher Education*. Racine, WI: Johnson Foundation.

Wright, R. S., Jr. (1961). They fought for urban renewal. *College and University Business* 30: 76–81.

Applications of Generalizability Theory in Higher Education Assessment Research

Gary R. Pike
University of Missouri–Columbia

Both Banta (1988b) and Terenzini (1989) observed that assessment has become an integral part of American higher education. Recent surveys report that more than 80 percent of American colleges and universities are actively engaged in assessment, or are in the process of implementing assessment programs (El-Khawas, 1991). Furthermore, assessment is a high-stakes enterprise. Students' scores on cognitive and affective measures are used for advising and placement, admission to special programs of study, and certification and licensure (Bradley, Draper, and Pike, 1993). Group-level assessment data are used to evaluate programs for accreditation and resource allocation within institutions (Ewell, 1991). In some instances, assessment data partly determine state appropriations for higher education (Banta, 1988a).

Given the importance of the decisions that are made on the basis of assessment data, it is essential that researchers and assessment professionals carefully examine the dependability of the measures they use and account for measurement error (Millman, 1988). Traditionally, higher-education researchers, program evaluators, and measurement specialists have relied on methods derived from classical test theory to evaluate the dependability of their measures (Cronbach, 1984). Although these methods are useful, several authors argue that generalizability theory, rather than classical test theory, should be used to evaluate the dependability of assessment measures (Erwin, 1988; Pike and Phillippi, 1989; Steele, 1989; Sundre, 1992).

The purpose of this chapter is to provide an introduction to generalizability theory in the context of higher-education assessment. It will outline practical applications, rather than advance statistical theory. While some discussion of the statistical underpinnings of generalizability theory is included, all that is required for understanding is a basic knowledge of research design and analysis of variance (ANOVA). This chapter *does not* represent an exhaustive treatment of generalizability theory. Topics related to the estimation of universe scores and confidence intervals are discussed briefly, while other topics, such as assessing generalizability in designs with unequal cell sizes and multivariate generalizability theory, are not covered.

In order to provide a context for discussing generalizability theory, the chapter begins with a review of recent trends in higher-education assessment, along with a discussion of the basic measurement assumptions underlying assessment. Next, the tenets of classical test theory and generalizability theory are outlined. This discussion is followed by several examples of how generalizability theory can be and is used in assessment research. The chapter concludes with a review of what generalizability theory can and cannot do to improve assessment practice.

Higher-Education Assessment Activities

In the past, the American public accepted at face value the claims made by colleges and universities about the quality of higher education (Pascarella and Terenzini, 1991). However, the increasing cost of a college education, state budget crises, and declines in economic competitiveness at home and abroad during the 1980s made uncritical acceptance of these claims unlikely (Graham and Cockriel, 1989). McClenney (1993) noted that American higher education ''has permanently lost its place as a sacred priority in public funding'' (p. 1). Indicative of the environment in which colleges and universities must operate, McClenney reported that only 25 percent of the American public currently express a great deal of confidence in higher-education leadership, down from 61 percent in 1960.

Reflecting public disaffection with higher education, several blue-ribbon advisory panels issued reports criticizing the quality of postsecondary education and calling on colleges and universities to assess student progress toward institutional objectives as a means of improvement (Association of American Colleges, 1985; Boyer, 1987; National Governors' Association, 1986; National Institute of Education, 1984). In response, states, the federal government, and accrediting associations began requiring that colleges and universities assess students' learning and development in order to improve the quality of higher education (Ewell, 1991). Recent surveys indicate that more than 80 percent of colleges and universities have established, or are establishing, assessment programs (El-Khawas, 1991; Johnson, Prus, Andersen, and El-Khawas, 1991).

While colleges and universities generally acknowledge the need for assessment, there is little agreement on what should be assessed or how it should be assessed. Ewell (1991) proposed a taxonomy that can be used to classify current assessment efforts. The taxonomy, which is presented in Figure 1, is a two-dimensional matrix. The horizontal axis represents the two underlying purposes of assessment, improvement and demonstration (i.e., accountability); these purposes reflect the age-old distinction between formative and summative evalua-

Unit of Analysis	Purpose of Assessment	
	Improvement (formative)	Demonstration (summative)
Individuals	Diagnosis/ Feedback	Certification/ Gatekeeping
Groups	Evaluation/ Self-study	Accountability/ Quality Assurance

FIGURE 1. A Taxonomy of Higher Education Assessment Activities.
(Adapted, with permission, from Ewell, 1991)

tion. The vertical axis represents the two primary units of analysis in assessment research, individuals and groups.

The first cell in the matrix represents assessment activities that provide diagnostic data for individual improvement. Examples of these types of assessment activities include the basic skills testing program in New Jersey (College Outcomes Evaluation Program Council, 1987). Other activities within this cell include assessment of learning styles and other noncognitive characteristics, such as the TRAILS project at Saint Louis University (Kalsbeek, 1989), and assessments of students' critical-thinking and problem-solving skills at Alverno College (Alverno College Faculty, 1979).

The second cell in the taxonomy, accountability-based (i.e., summative) assessment of individual performance, includes a variety of activities related to certification and gatekeeping. Assessment activities in this domain include Florida's *College Level Academic Skills Test* (Postsecondary Education Planning Commission, 1988), tests required for admission to special programs of study (Osterlind and Schmitz, 1993), and certification and licensure examinations in the professions (Ewell, 1991).

The third cell in the assessment taxonomy includes a variety of activities designed to provide formative data about institutional performance. According to Ewell, these data are most often used to guide internal improvement efforts.

Examples include the assessment programs at Alverno College (Mentkowski and Loacker, 1985), Kings College (Farmer, 1988), Miami-Dade Community College (McCabe, 1983), Northeast Missouri State University (McClain and Krueger, 1985), and the University of Tennessee, Knoxville (Banta, 1985).

The final cell in the matrix represents some of the most controversial aspects of higher-education assessment. The activities included in this cell are designed to provide summative data about program and/or institutional performance. These assessments frequently are carried out in response to state mandates and are typified by certain aspects of the Tennessee performance funding program (Banta, 1988a) and the New Jersey assessment of general intellectual skills (College Outcomes Evaluation Program Council, 1990).

Assessment as Educational Measurement

Irrespective of whether the goal is formative or summative evaluation, or whether individuals or programs are the primary units of analysis, assessment efforts rest on the assumption that it is possible to make inferences about the presence or absence of unmeasurable qualities, such as subject-matter knowledge, critical-thinking skills, learning styles, or institutional effectiveness, based on samples of observations. In fact, this assumption is the cornerstone of all testing and evaluation research (Gregory, 1992; Stufflebeam and Webster, 1983). As Cronbach, Gleser, Nanda, and Rajaratnam (1972) observed:

> The decision maker is almost never interested in the response given to the particular stimulus objects or questions, to the particular tester, at the particular moment of testing. Some, at least, of these conditions of measurement could be altered without making the score any less acceptable to the decision maker. That is to say, there is a universe of observations, any of which would have yielded a usable basis for the decision. The ideal datum on which to base the decision would be something like the person's mean score over all acceptable observations, which we shall call his "universe score." The investigator uses the observed score or some function of it as if it were the universe score. That is, he generalizes from sample to universe. *The question of "reliability" thus resolves into a question of accuracy of generalization, or generalizability.* (p. 15)

In assessment research, generalizations are made over a variety of different types of samples. Assessment instruments may be administered to samples of college applicants, enrolled students, alumni, or non-returning students. The instruments may contain samples of test questions or rating scales. Data collection designs may include a sampling of raters, prompts, or points in time. In addition, assessment researchers may be interested in the performance of samples of programs within an institution, across a state, or across the nation.

When the objective of assessment is individual improvement or certification (i.e., the first two cells of the matrix), assessment researchers may be required to generalize over samples of items, rating scales, raters, prompts, and/or occasions. When the goal of assessment is to make inferences about programs or institutions (i.e., the third and fourth cells in the taxonomy), the dependability of group means is at issue. Assessment researchers are required to make generalizations over persons *and* some combination of items, raters, prompts, or occasions. Several authors have argued that the dependability of inferences about group means is generally greater than the dependability of inferences about persons (Linn, 1981; Millman, 1988). However, when there is substantial variability in responses across individuals, the dependability of group means may be less than the dependability of individual scores (Kane, Gillmore, and Crooks, 1976; Millman, 1988).

The costs of not being able to accurately generalize from samples to universes vary, depending on the cell of the assessment taxonomy within which evaluation efforts are classified. For the first cell of the taxonomy, the costs of not making dependable generalizations may be relatively small because students can ignore recommendations based on the assessment. However, erroneous advice may result in students taking some courses that are less beneficial than others, taking longer to graduate, and paying for unnecessary courses (Millman, 1988). When assessment for individual improvement includes mandatory placement, the costs of inaccurate generalizations can include additional time to graduation, increased education costs, and higher dropout rates (Schmitz and DelMas, 1990).

When individual-level assessment serves a gatekeeping or certification function, the costs of not being able to make dependable generalizations can be high. Students may be denied admission to upper-division courses or special programs of study (Millman, 1988). They also may be denied admission to their chosen profession. Because licensure and certification requirements are established to protect the public by ensuring that licensees possess sufficient knowledge and skills to discharge their duties appropriately, improper generalizations can present a danger to the public welfare. Not surprisingly, the *Standards for Educational and Psychological Testing* developed by the American Educational Research Association, the American Psychological Association, and the National Council on Measurement in Education (1985) states that ensuring the dependability of certification and licensure decisions is of paramount importance, both for the individual and society.

The inability to make accurate generalizations about program quality and institutional effectiveness can have serious consequences at all levels. When the objective of program evaluation is improvement, inaccurate generalizations can result in a misallocation of scarce institutional resources. When the objective is accountability, inappropriate generalizations can have even greater costs (Pike, 1992). For example, in Tennessee, millions of performance-funding dollars depend on accurate group-level generalizations (Banta, 1988a).

In summary, the inability to generalize from samples to the universes from which they are drawn can have serious consequences, whether or not the units of analysis are individuals or groups and whether the goals of assessment are formative or summative evaluation. As a general rule, the costs of an inability to generalize are greatest when assessment focuses on accountability, by controlling access or determining the allocation of funds. However, inaccurate generalizations can also have serious consequences when assessment is used for improvement, by placing students in developmental programs or influencing the allocation of institutional resources. Given the importance of being able to make dependable generalizations, the issue thus becomes *what method is most appropriate for evaluating the dependability of assessment measures*?

AN OVERVIEW OF GENERALIZABILITY THEORY

Generalizability theory provides a mechanism for educational researchers, assessment professionals, and policy makers to identify the limits of the inferences that they can draw from their samples (Shavelson and Webb, 1991). Consequently, it can be used to improve the accuracy and appropriateness of the inferences made, as well as actions taken, on the basis of assessment data. Generalizability theory represents a superior alternative to traditional approaches of evaluating the dependability of measures (Cronbach et al., 1972). In order to appreciate the advantages of generalizability theory, it is helpful to review the basic tenets of classical test theory and then focus on how generalizability theory differs from it.

Classical Test Theory

Much of what is called classical test theory has its origins in Gulliksen's (1950) seminal work on mental tests. In classical test theory, the dependability of a measure is represented by two indices: the *reliability coefficient* and the *standard error of measurement* (Feldt and Brennan, 1989). Both indices are based on two assumptions about test scores. The first assumption is that a person's score on a measure (x_p) is composed of a true score (τ_p) and measurement error (ε_p).

$$x_p = \tau_p + \varepsilon_p \tag{1}$$

The term "true score" can be misleading. In this context, a true score is the expected value (i.e., the arithmetic mean) of observed scores from an infinitely large number of administrations (Stanley, 1971). Consequently, a true score is a dependable measure, although not necessarily a valid measure (Feldt and Brennan, 1989).

Measurement error represents the tendency of individuals on some occasions to answer incorrectly questions they know and, at other times, to answer correctly questions they do not know (Gulliksen, 1950). Mathematically, error of measurement is defined as the deviation of observed scores about the true score (Feldt and Brennan, 1989). This definition can be represented by a simple rearrangement of the terms in equation [1].

$$\varepsilon_p = x_p - \tau_p \qquad (2)$$

The second assumption underlying classical test theory is that errors of measurement are randomly distributed (Feldt and Brennan, 1989). If the number of items/scores is sufficiently large and normally distributed, the mean of the measurement errors will be zero, and true scores and measurement errors will be unrelated (Brennan, 1983). These principles are represented in equations [3] and [4].

$$\mu(\varepsilon) = \frac{\sum_{i=1}^{\infty} \varepsilon_i}{n_i} \qquad (3)$$

$$cov[\tau,\varepsilon] = 0 \qquad (4)$$

When a measure is administered to a group of persons, or administered to one individual several times, a researcher obtains a set of observed scores, each comprised of a true score and measurement error. If the true scores and measurement errors are unrelated (i.e., if equation [4] is true), it can be shown that the variance in observed scores ($\sigma^2(x)$) can be partitioned into true score variance ($\sigma^2(\tau)$) and error variance ($\sigma^2(\varepsilon)$).

$$\sigma^2(x) = \sigma^2(\tau) + \sigma^2(\varepsilon) \qquad (5)$$

Using the assumptions of classical test theory, statisticians and researchers have developed a variety of methods for calculating reliability coefficients. These methods can be classified as measures of (1) stability, (2) equivalence, (3) stability and equivalence, and (4) internal consistency (Feldt and Brennan, 1989; Mehrens and Lehman, 1987). Cronbach (1984) noted that all four types of reliability coefficients represent the dependability of a measure as the ratio of true-score variance to observed-score variance (i.e., true-score variance plus error variance). This ratio can be expressed mathematically as

$$r_{xx} = \frac{\sigma^2(\tau)}{\sigma^2(x)} = \frac{\sigma^2(\tau)}{\sigma^2(\tau) + \sigma^2(\varepsilon)} \qquad (6)$$

From equation [6] it follows that if the proportion of variance in observed scores attributable to measurement error is small, then the scores will be highly reliable, and the reliability coefficient will approach 1.00. Conversely, when measurement error is responsible for a substantial proportion of the observed-score variance, the reliability of scores will be low, and the reliability coefficient will be nearer 0.00. Because reliability coefficients are expressed as the ratio of true-score variance to observed-score variance, changes in the score metric (i.e., the mean and/or the variance of the scores) do not influence the magnitude of the reliability coefficient. As a result, reliability coefficients can be used to compare the dependability of several different measures of a construct (Feldt and Brennan, 1989).

The scale-free nature of reliability coefficients is a disadvantage when researchers wish to express the dependability of a measure in terms of the scale of the observed scores. In that case, the standard error of measurement is more appropriate than the reliability coefficient. Feldt and Brennan (1989) defined the standard error of measurement as the standard deviation of within-person variation over an infinite set of replications. Since that within-person variation is assumed to be the product of measurement error, the standard error of measurement is actually the standard deviation of measurement error. As such, the standard error of measurement provides an index of the potency of measurement error expressed in the metric of the observed scores. The standard error of measurement is defined mathematically as

$$S.E.(x) = \sigma(x)\sqrt{1 - r_{xx}} \tag{7}$$

The standard error of measurement is useful in establishing confidence intervals about observed scores. In classical test theory, confidence intervals bound observed scores with a probabilistic statement, identifying the score range likely to contain the true score some percent of the time. For example, the 67 percent confidence interval is define as $\pm$ 1.00 $S.E.(x)$, while the 95 percent confidence interval is defined as $\pm$ 1.96 $S.E.(x)$.

It should be apparent from the preceding discussion that classical test theory does not differentiate among sources of measurement error. To be sure, it does acknowledge that any number of different factors can contribute to errors of measurement. However, these different sources of error are subsumed by a single value (Feldt and Brennan, 1989). When individuals are administered a series of multiple-choice questions, the unitary representation of measurement error can adequately describe the dependability of a person's score. Likewise, classical test theory adequately describes the dependability of a holistic writing score obtained by averaging the scores of several raters, or the scores of a single rater for several different prompts or occasions. When the objective of an assessment program is to evaluate a group mean on a test containing several items, or to evaluate a student's writing performance using the scores of several raters on several prompts, the unitary view of measurement error does not adequately describe the dependability of the scores (Erwin, 1988).

Generalizability Theory

Generalizability theory represents an extension and liberalization of, rather than a dramatic departure from, classical test theory (Feldt and Brennan, 1989). From the perspective of an assessment professional or educational researcher, the most important difference between generalizability theory and classical test theory is that generalizability theory eschews the concept of undifferentiated measurement error in favor of a multifaceted representation (Shavelson and Webb, 1991). The ability to account for multiple sources of error provides assessment researchers with more appropriate dependability indices and allows them to identify how changes in an assessment design influence the dependability of measurement (Erwin, 1988; Webb, Rowley, and Shavelson, 1988).

Generalizability theory assumes that an observed score represents performance on a sample of items or observations at a given point in time (Webb, Rowley, and Shavelson, 1988). Were a different set of measures used, it is almost certain that the observed score would be slightly different. As Cronbach et al. (1972) noted, the ideal would be to base decisions on the average score over all possible items or observations. In most cases, however, the ideal is not attainable. Consequently, assessment professionals must generalize from limited samples to the universe of possible observations (Feldt and Brennan, 1989). The generalizability coefficient provides an index of the dependability of generalizing from an observed score, based on a sample of observations, to a mean score derived from all acceptable observations (Cronbach et al., 1972). Cronbach and his colleagues used the term *universe score*, rather than *true score*, because they believe that the goal of measurement is to make generalizations about a universe based on data from a sample or samples.

Generalizability theory distinguishes between the *object of measurement*—that aspect of the measurement situation about which generalizations are to be made—and *facets of measurement*—those characteristics of the measurement situation that may contribute to error (Brennan, 1983). Drawing on Fisher's (1925) work on the analysis of variance, generalizability theory seeks to partition observed-score variance into variance that is attributable to the object of measurement (i.e., universe-score variance) and variance components that represent the facets of the measurement situation (i.e., error variance). Implicit in the concept of generalizability is an assumption that the attribute being measured is in a steady state. That is, differences among scores are due to various sources of error, rather than to systematic changes in the object of measurement (Shavelson and Webb, 1991).

In generalizability theory, a distinction is also made between *G* (generalizability) and *D* (decision) studies. Brennan (1983) explains that *G* studies are designed to represent the universe of admissible observations and to provide estimates of the variance components for that universe, while *D* studies incorporate the specifics of a research design and provide the basis for estimating and interpreting the dependability of specific measures. Although the literature on generalizability theory treats *G* and *D* studies as separate entities, it is sometimes impractical to conduct two separate studies. In such cases, the same data may be used for both studies (Webb, Rowley, and Shavelson, 1988). The practical applications of *G* and *D* studies can best be understood in the context of actual assessment designs.

ONE-FACET PERSON-BY-ITEM DESIGNS

An assessment measure containing multiple observations (items) administered to a group of students (persons) is a typical one-facet design. The assessment measure may be an objective test, a performance appraisal consisting of multiple observations by a single rater, or a performance assessment in which several raters make judgments about a single performance. For this discussion of one-facet designs, observations are students' responses to questions on the *College Basic Academic Subjects Examination* (*College BASE*). *College BASE* is a criterion-referenced achievement test focusing on the degree to which students have mastered particular skills and competencies consistent with the completion of general education coursework (Osterlind, 1989). The test measures achievement in four subject areas: English (41 items), mathematics (56 items), science (41 items), and social studies (42 items). A composite score, representing the average of the four subject scores, is also provided.

College BASE is calibrated and scored using item response theory (IRT) (Osterlind and Merz, 1990). Because IRT-based tests are not amenable to generalizability analyses (Bejar, 1983), dichotomous item responses (1 = correct, 0 = incorrect) are analyzed here. Subject-area and composite scores are assumed to be reported as either the mean or total number of items answered correctly. Because the data reported in this chapter are not consistent with the true scoring of the test, these results should not be taken as indices of the dependability of *College BASE* scores.

In the examples of one-facet designs that follow, decisions are to be made about individual students. That is, students (persons) are the object of measurement. Since *College BASE* questions (items) are a sample from the universe of acceptable observations, these items are the facet of the measurement situation. In the examples that follow, the goal of the generalizability analyses is to determine the extent to which observed *College BASE* scores can be generalized to hypothetical scores based on all of the items in the universe of acceptable observations.

Figure 2 depicts a one-facet person-by-item ($p \times i$) design consistent with the administration of *College BASE* to a group of students. In the figure, the symbol P is used to represent persons, with individual students being identified by the subscripts $1, 2, \ldots, p, \ldots, n$. Test items are represented by the symbol I, with individual questions having the subscripts $1, 2, \ldots, i, \ldots, k$. Responses for each person on each item are identified by the symbol x, and the response of an unspecified person on a given item is designated x_{pi}.

	I_1	I_2	I_3	...	I_i	...	I_k
P_1	x_{11}	x_{12}	x_{13}	...	x_{1i}	...	x_{1k}
P_2	x_{21}	x_{22}	x_{23}	...	x_{2i}	...	x_{2k}
P_3	x_{31}	x_{32}	x_{33}	...	x_{3i}	...	x_{3k}
...	...	...	...	...	...	...	...
P_p	x_{p1}	x_{p2}	x_{p3}	...	x_{pi}	...	x_{pk}
...	...	...	...	...	...	...	...
P_n	x_{n1}	x_{n2}	x_{n3}	...	x_{ni}	...	x_{nk}

FIGURE 2. A One-Facet Design.

If x_{pi} represents the score of a person on any item from the universe of acceptable observations, then the expected (mean) value of a person's score on all items in the universe is

$$\mu_p = \underset{i}{E} x_{pi} = \frac{\sum_{i=1}^{k} x_{pi}}{k} \tag{8}$$

In equation [8], the symbol E is an expectation operator, and i is the factor over which the expectation is to be taken (in this case items). The symbol k represents the number of items in the universe of acceptable observations. Using the same notation, the formula for the population mean (expectation) for an item is

$$\mu_i = \underset{p}{E} x_{pi} = \frac{\sum_{p=1}^{n} x_{pi}}{n} \tag{9}$$

The expectation over both the universe of acceptable observations (items) and all objects of measurement (persons), the grand mean, is

$$\mu = \underset{p}{E}\underset{i}{E}x_{pi} = \frac{\sum_{p=1}^{n}\sum_{i=1}^{k} x_{pi}}{nk} \tag{10}$$

Obviously, it is seldom possible to obtain a person's responses to all of the items in the universe of acceptable observations. Similarly, it is not likely that an item will be administered to all persons in the population. However, an observed score for a person on a given item can be defined using the parameters μ, μ_p, and μ_i.

$$x_{pi} = \mu + (\mu_p - \mu) + (\mu_i - \mu) + (x_{pi} + \mu - \mu_p - \mu_i) \tag{11}$$

According to the equation, a person's score on an item (x_{pi}) consists of the grand mean (μ), a person effect ($\mu_p - \mu$), an item effect ($\mu_i - \mu$), and the person-by-item interaction ($x_{pi} + \mu - \mu_p - \mu_i$). Because there is only one observation per cell in the design, the residual (error) term is confounded with the person-by-item interaction.

G Study Variance Components

For each of the effects in equation [11] there is an associated variance, termed a *variance component*. Variance components are the key building blocks in generalizability analyses. For the one-facet design in Figure 2, the variance components for the person, item, and person-by-item effects are defined by the formulas:

$$\sigma^2(p) = \underset{p}{E}(\mu_p - \mu) \tag{12}$$

$$\sigma^2(i) = \underset{i}{E}(\mu_i - \mu) \tag{13}$$

and

$$\sigma^2(pi) = \underset{p}{E}\underset{i}{E}(x_{pi} + \mu - \mu_p - \mu_i) \tag{14}$$

These variance components allow the total observed-score variance ($\sigma^2(x_{pi})$) to be decomposed as follows:

$$\sigma^2(x_{pi}) = \sigma^2(p) + \sigma^2(i) + \sigma^2(pi) \tag{15}$$

Although equations [12], [13], and [14] represent the definitions of the *G* study variance components appropriate for a one-facet design, the presence of population parameters in the formulas means that they cannot be used to calculate those components. Instead, traditional analysis-of-variance (ANOVA) procedures must be used to estimate the variance components (Brennan, 1983).

A two-way random-effects ANOVA of a data matrix corresponding to Figure 2 yields degrees of freedom (*df*), sums of squares (*SS*), and mean squares (*MS*) for three sources: persons, items, and the person-by-item interaction. Using the mean squares from the analysis of variance, along with data from the generalizability study concerning the number of persons tested (n) and the number of items in the test (k), G study variance components can be estimated using the following formulas:

$$\sigma^2(p) = \frac{MS(p) - MS(pi)}{k} \tag{16}$$

$$\sigma^2(i) = \frac{MS(i) \quad MS(pi)}{n} \tag{17}$$

and

$$\sigma^2(pi) = MS(pi) \tag{18}$$

Table 1 presents the G study analysis-of-variance results for the *College BASE* English and mathematics subject-area tests. The data for the G study were obtained from the test developer and consisted of the dichotomized item responses of 1,450 students. Fifty students each from 29 institutions were randomly selected for inclusion in the data set. For this analysis, students' institutional affiliations were ignored.

D Study Variance Components

Once G study estimated variance components have been obtained, they can be used to calculate estimated variance components for the D study. Assuming that the goal of the D study is to evaluate the dependability of generalizing from the

TABLE 1. ANOVA Results for a One-Facet Design Representing *College BASE* English and Mathematics Scores

English			
Source	*df*	*MS*	σ^2
Persons (*P*)	1,449	1.0984	0.0220
Items (*I*)	40	29.7764	0.0204
Persons by Items (*P I*)	49,960	0.1964	0.1964
Mathematics			
Source	*df*	*MS*	σ^2
Persons (*P*)	1,449	1.9330	0.0312
Items (*I*)	55	33.1008	0.0227
Persons by Items (*P I*)	68,695	0.1858	0.1858

samples of items in the English and mathematics parts of *College BASE* to the universes of acceptable items for those subject areas, the following formulas should be used:

$$\sigma_D^2(p) = \sigma^2(p) \tag{19}$$

$$\sigma_D^2(I) = \frac{\sigma^2(i)}{k^*} \tag{20}$$

and

$$\sigma_D^2(pI) = \frac{\sigma^2(pi)}{k^*} \tag{21}$$

Because persons are the object of measurement in the decision study, the *D* study estimated variance component for persons is identical to the *G* study estimated variance component for persons (see equation [19]). In equations [20] and [21], the symbol representing items has been capitalized (*I*) to indicate that items are a facet of measurement (i.e., source of error) in the decision study. The *D* study estimated variance components in equations [20] and [21] are calculated by dividing the corresponding *G* study estimated variance components by the number of items (symbolized by k^*) in the *D* study English and mathematics tests. Asterisks (*) are included in the formulas to indicate that the English and mathematics tests used in the decision study are *not* required to contain the same number of items as the tests in the *G* studies.

Once *D* study estimated variance components have been derived, calculation of generalizability coefficients can proceed. Cronbach et al. (1972) defined the generalizability coefficient as the ratio of universe-score variance to *expected* observed-score variance. Stated differently, the generalizability coefficient represents the ratio of universe-score variance to itself plus error variance. Determining what constitutes error variance depends, in part, on the type of score judgment to be made.

Generalizability Coefficients for Relative Judgments

When test results are used in academic advising, the student and the advisor most likely are interested in the student's relative performance. For *College BASE*, attention might well focus on a student's relative performance on the English and mathematics subject-area tests. The defining characteristic of relative judgments is that a student's score is *not* considered in isolation. Rather, it *is interpreted in relation to the scores of other students*. Specifically, the student's mean score is interpreted as a deviation from the grand mean of the other students taking the exam ($\bar{x}_p - \bar{x}$).

Whether the student or the advisor realize it, they are using the student's observed scores as proxies for unmeasured constructs. In the case of the *College BASE*, English and mathematics subject scores are used to make inferences about the student's English and mathematics abilities. These unmeasured constructs are students' English and mathematics scores had they answered all questions in those two universes of acceptable observations. Consequently, relative judgments are concerned with universe score deviations ($\mu_p - \mu$), and the generalizability coefficient is an index of the extent to which observed score deviations ($\bar{x}_p - \bar{x}$) can be used to make inferences about universe-score deviations ($\mu_p - \mu$) (Brennan, 1983).

Cronbach et al. (1972) demonstrated that universe-score variance for relative judgments in a person-by-item design consists of the estimated variance component for persons, while relative error variance ($\sigma^2(\mathrm{d})$) consists of the *D* study estimated variance component for the person-by-item interaction. If all students have taken the same form of the exam, or strictly parallel forms of the exam, the *D* study estimated variance component for items is not considered to be a source of error. Thus, the appropriate formula for calculating the generalizability coefficient ($E\rho^2$) for relative judgments in a one-facet person-by-item design is

$$E\rho^2 = \frac{\sigma^2(p)}{\sigma^2(p) + \sigma^2(\delta)} = \frac{\sigma^2(p)}{\sigma^2(p) + \dfrac{\sigma^2(pi)}{k^*}} \tag{22}$$

Combining the data in Table 1 with equation [22] produces generalizability coefficients for relative judgments about *College BASE* English and mathematics scores of 0.82 and 0.90, respectively. It is significant that these values are identical to alpha (α) reliability coefficients derived from classical test theory (Brennan, 1983; Cronbach et al. 1972).

Because the number of items in the English and mathematics subject tests (k^*) are used to calculate *D* study estimated variance components for the person-by-item interactions (i.e., relative error variance), evaluating the effects of changes in test length on the generalizability of scores is a simple matter of altering k^* to correspond to the desired test length. Figure 3 displays the effects of varying the length of *College BASE* English and mathematics subject tests from 10 to 100 items in increments of 5 items. As indicated by the graph, the generalizability coefficients for English and mathematics scores are quite low (0.53 and 0.63, respectively) when each subject test contains only 10 items. The generalizability of scores increases substantially when test length is increased to 40 items (0.82 for English and 0.87 for mathematics). Beyond 40 items, improvements in the generalizability of scores are more modest. For hypothetical *College BASE* English and mathematics subject tests each containing 100 items, the generalizability coefficients are 0.92 for English and 0.94 for mathematics.

When relative judgments are being made about a person's score, the appro-

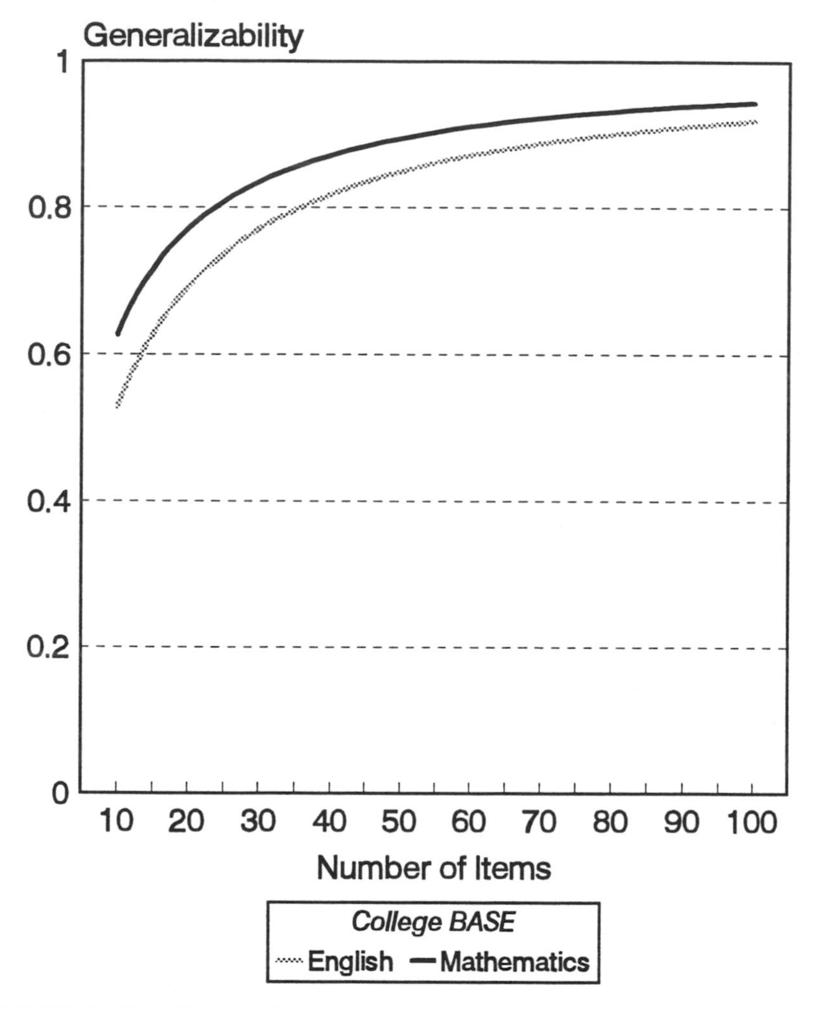

FIGURE 3. The Effects of Test Length on the Dependability of *College BASE* English and Mathematics Scores.

priate standard error is the square root of the relative error variance ($\sigma(\delta)$). The standard errors for *College BASE* English and mathematics subject tests are 0.07 and 0.06, assuming test lengths of 41 and 56 items, respectively. These standard errors presuppose that English and mathematics scores are reported as means. Converting estimated variance components to reflect summed scores simply entails pre-multiplying the estimated variance components by the square of the number of items on the test (Brennan, 1983). While the change from a mean-score metric to a total-score metric does not affect the magnitude of generalizability coefficients, it can have a profound effect on the magnitude of the standard errors. In the case of relative judgments about *College BASE* English and mathematics subject scores, the standard errors for the total-score metrics (i.e., 0 to 41 for English and 0 to 56 for mathematics) are 2.84 and 3.23, respectively.

As with classical test theory, standard errors can be used to establish confidence intervals about scores. The calculation of confidence intervals using generalizability theory is identical to the method used in classical test theory. Thus, the 67 percent confidence interval is defined as ± 1.00 standard error. Unlike classical test theory, the confidence intervals derived through generalizability theory are used to bound universe scores, rather than observed scores. Using confidence intervals to bound universe scores reflects the opinion of Cronbach et al. (1972) that the objective of research is to make inferences about a person's performance had they been administered the universe of acceptable observations.

The estimation of universe scores is a complex issue (see Brennan, 1983; Cronbach et al., 1972) and will only briefly be dealt with in this chapter. The most direct method of calculating a person's universe score is the use of point-estimation procedures (Brennan, 1983). For the person-by-item design, point estimation can be accomplished using the following formula:

$$\mu_p = E\rho^2\overline{x_p} + (1 - E\rho^2)\bar{x} \tag{23}$$

In equation [23], $E\rho^2$ represents the generalizability coefficient for a given test, $\bar{x}_p$ represents a person's observed score on the test, and $\bar{x}$ represents the grand mean of scores from a sample of persons taking the test (e.g., the sample of persons used in the *G* study). For the purpose of illustrating point estimation of universe scores, assume that a person correctly answered 28 out of the 56 items on *College BASE* mathematics subject test. The mean score for this person would be 0.50. Further assume that the *G* study sample mean for the mathematics test was 33.60 on the total-score metric and .60 on the mean-score metric. Given a generalizability coefficient of .90 for the mathematics test, the hypothetical person's universe score would be 28.56 for the total-score metric and 0.51 for the mean-score metric. The appropriate 67 percent confidence intervals for the mathematics universe score would be from 25.33 to 31.79 (28.56 ± 3.23) for the total-score metric and from 0.45 to 0.57 (0.51 ± 0.06) for the mean score metric. The substantive interpretation of these universe score and confidence intervals is that, given a universe score of 28.56 on the *College BASE* mathematics subtest, observed scores, based on random samples of 56 items from the universe of acceptable observations, will range from 25.33 to 31.79 approximately 67 percent of the time.

Generalizability Coefficient for Absolute Judgments

In some instances, an assessment researcher may be interested in a person's absolute score performance on a criterion- or domain-referenced test. In the case of *College BASE*, data about the number (or proportion) of items a student correctly answered could be useful in advising that student about future coursework in English or mathematics. In this instance, the objective would be *to generalize from a student's performance on a sample of items ($\bar{x}_p$) to the student's performance on the universe of items* representing either English or mathematics achievement (μ_p). Unlike relative judgments, absolute-score judgments are made without reference to the performance of other students (Brennan, 1983).

Evaluating the generalizability of a student's absolute score makes use of the same research design, as well as the same *G* and *D* study variance components, as does an evaluation of the generalizability of relative-score judgments. The difference between evaluating the generalizability of relative and absolute scores lies in the definition of error variance used in calculating generalizability coefficients and standard errors (Cronbach et al., 1972). When calculating the generalizability of relative scores, error variance ($\sigma^2(\delta)$) consists of the *D* study variance component for the person-by-item interaction. Error variance for absolute scores ($\sigma^2(\Delta)$) includes the *D* study variance component for the person-by-item interaction *and* the *D* study variance component for items.

In evaluating the generalizability of relative-score judgments, all persons are administered the same form of a test, or strictly parallel forms of the test.[1] Thus, the variability associated with sampling items does not influence the generalizability of a person's score relative to the scores of other persons who have taken the same test. This is not the case when evaluating the generalizability of absolute performance. When a sample of items is drawn from the universe of acceptable items, the sample will, by chance alone, likely be easier or more difficult than the universe of items. This variability due to the sampling of items represents a confounding influence on the generalizability of absolute scores that can be accounted for by including the item variance component in the error term (Cronbach et al., 1972). Thus, the appropriate formula for assessing the generalizability of a person's absolute score is

$$E\rho^2 = \frac{\sigma^2(p)}{\sigma^2(p) + \sigma^2(\Delta)} = \frac{\sigma^2(p)}{\sigma^2(p) + \dfrac{\sigma^2(i)}{k^*} + \dfrac{\sigma^2(pi)}{k^*}} \tag{24}$$

Substituting the data from Table 1 in equation [24] produces generalizability coefficients of 0.81 and 0.89 for *College BASE* English and mathematics absolute-score judgments. The standard errors for absolute English and mathematics scores are 0.07 and 0.06 assuming a mean-score metric, and 2.98 and 3.42 assuming a total-score metric. These values are very similar to the values for

[1]If the assumption that all students have been administered the same form, or strictly-parallel forms, of a test cannot be met, Cronbach et al. (1972) recommend that $\sigma^2(\Delta)$ be used to estimate error variance when calculating generalizability coefficients and standard errors.

relative judgments because the magnitude of the *D* study variance components for items are quite small, relative to the magnitude of the *D* study variance components for persons and the person-by-item interaction. The *D* study variance component for items in the English test is approximately 0.0005, compared to *D* study variance components of 0.0220 for persons and 0.0048 for the person-by-item interaction. For the mathematics test, the *D* study variance component is 0.0004, compared to variance components of 0.0312 for persons and 0.0033 for the person-by-item interaction.

Generalizability Coefficients for Certification Tests

In some instances, an assessment researcher may be interested in comparing a person's score on a criterion- or domain-referenced test to an established performance standard. This type of judgment is consistent with the second cell of the assessment typology. Use of *College BASE* for admission to teacher-education programs in Missouri is one example of this type of certification or mastery testing (Osterlind and Schmitz, 1993).

In the context of generalizability theory, the objective of certification or mastery testing is to make inferences about the deviation of a person's universe score about a given criterion ($\mu_p - C$), with the certification standard being expressed as a proportion of the items in the universe of acceptable items that must be answered correctly. For example, the certification standard for both *College BASE* English and mathematics scores in Missouri is approximately 0.50. In developing their index of dependability for certification tests, Brennan and Kane (1977a) observed that the objective of certification testing is similar to the objective in norm-referenced testing, in which a researcher makes inferences about a person's universe score relative to the performance of other persons taking the test. They concluded that the generalizability of a certification score should be defined in a manner consistent with the definition of generalizability for relative judgments.[2]

Brennan and Kane (1977a) also noted that the generalizability of certification tests is confounded by item variance. As with absolute judgments, the sampling

[2]The similarity of relative and certification judgments is evident in the definitional formulas for the generalizability of the two types of decisions. The definitional formula for the generalizability of relative judgments is

$$E\rho^2 = \frac{\underset{p}{E}(\mu_p-\mu)^2}{\underset{pI}{EE}(x_{pI}-\mu_I)^2} \qquad (n1)$$

while the definitional formula for the generalizability of certification decisions is

$$M(C) = \frac{\underset{p}{E}(\mu_p-C)^2}{\underset{pI}{EE}(x_{pI}-C)^2}\,. \qquad (n2)$$

of items from the universe of acceptable observations almost certainly produces a test that is either easier or more difficult than the universe of items. Thus, it is necessary to include the variance component for items in estimates of the generalizability of certification tests. Brennan and Kane (1977a), therefore, proposed an index of dependability for certification tests that incorporated elements of the formulas for absolute and relative score judgments.

$$M(C) = \frac{\sigma^2(p) + (\mu - C)^2}{\sigma^2(p) + (\mu - C)^2 + \frac{\sigma^2(i)}{k^*} + \frac{\sigma^2(pi)}{k^*}} \tag{25}$$

Because the expectation over the universe of items and population of persons (i.e., the grand mean, μ) is included in equation [25], this formula cannot be used to calculate the dependability of a certification test. However, Brennan and Kane (1977a) demonstrated that an unbiased estimate of *M(C)* can be obtained using the formula:

$$M(C) = \frac{(\overline{x_{PI}} - C)^2 + \frac{(n-1)\sigma^2(p)}{n} - \frac{\sigma^2(i)}{k^*} - \frac{\sigma^2(pi)}{k^*}}{(\overline{x_{PI}} - C)^2 + \frac{(n-1)\sigma^2(p)}{n} + \frac{(n-1)\sigma^2(pi)}{nk^*}} \tag{26}$$

In equation [26], $\bar{x}_{\mathrm{PI}}$ represents the observed mean score for the sample of persons in the generalizability study over all items on the certification test, and C represents the certification standard. In equation [26], n represents the number of persons in the generalizability study, while k^* represents the number of items on the certification test. (An asterisk has been added to the term representing test length to indicate that this value varies.)

Combining the estimates of variance components in Table 1 with equation [26], it is possible to evaluate the dependability of using scores from *College BASE* English and mathematics subject tests to make certification decisions. Assuming that the English and mathematics passing scores for entry into teacher education in Missouri are 0.50, and assuming that the G study observed score means are 0.70 for the English subject tests and 0.60 for the mathematics test, the generalizability of certification decisions would be 0.85 for English and 0.84 for mathematics.

As previously noted, Brennan and Kane (1977a) argued that the appropriate error variance for calculating the standard errors and confidence intervals of certification tests is $\sigma^2(\Delta)$. Thus, the appropriate standard errors for *College BASE* English and mathematics subject tests, using a mean-score metric, are 0.07

and 0.06, respectively. Assuming that a person's universe score is precisely at the cutting score (i.e., 0.50), one would expect that the person's observed English score would range from 0.43 to 0.57 approximately 67 percent of the time. For the mathematics test, observed scores would range from 0.44 to 0.56 approximately 67 percent of the time. If admission to teacher-education programs in Missouri were based on the performance standard of 0.50, it would be prudent for assessment researchers to establish ranges about the observed cutting score which correspond to either the 67 percent or 95 percent confidence intervals. For students whose scores fell within the confidence intervals, additional data should be consulted before making decisions about admission to teacher education.

While the dependability of relative and absolute judgments is influenced by test length, the dependability of certification examinations also is influenced by other factors. These factors include the cutting-score value and the value of the observed-score mean in the *G* study (Brennan and Kane, 1977a). Figure 4 depicts plots of the generalizability coefficients for the *College BASE* English and mathematics subtests at several different cutting-score values. It is interesting to note that the dependability of a certification measure is lowest when the passing score is identical to the observed-score mean of the *G* study. When the cutting score for the English test is set at 0.70, the generalizability coefficient is 0.62. When the cutting score for the mathematics test is 0.60, the dependability index is 0.80. Dependability is much greater when the certification standard is substantially different from the *G* study observed-score mean. When the passing scores for English and mathematics are 0.05, the generalizability of certification decisions is 0.98 for both English and mathematics.

The dependability of certification decisions is influenced by test length. Figure 5 presents plots of the generalizability coefficients for a *College BASE* English test at lengths of 10, 25, 50, and 100 questions. In this example, the *G* study observed-score mean is assumed to be 0.70, and the certification standard is allowed to vary from 0.05 to 0.95. For a test consisting of 10 questions, the dependability of certification decisions is generally quite low. If the passing score is identical to the *G* study score mean (0.70), the dependability of certification decisions is 0.01. Only when the certification standard is set at 0.20 or lower does the generalizability coefficient exceed 0.85.

Substantial improvement in dependability occurs when the test is lengthened to include 25 questions. For an English test of this length, the generalizability coefficient is 0.45 when the passing score is 0.70. To achieve a generalizability coefficient of 0.85 or greater, the cutting score for a test containing 25 items would have to be 0.40 or less. A test of 50 items produces a generalizability coefficient of 0.68 when the cutting score is 0.70, and generalizability coefficients of 0.85 or greater can be obtained when the cutting score is 0.50 or less, or when the cutting score is 0.90 or greater. A test containing 100 questions produces a generalizability coefficient of 0.83 when the cutting score is identical

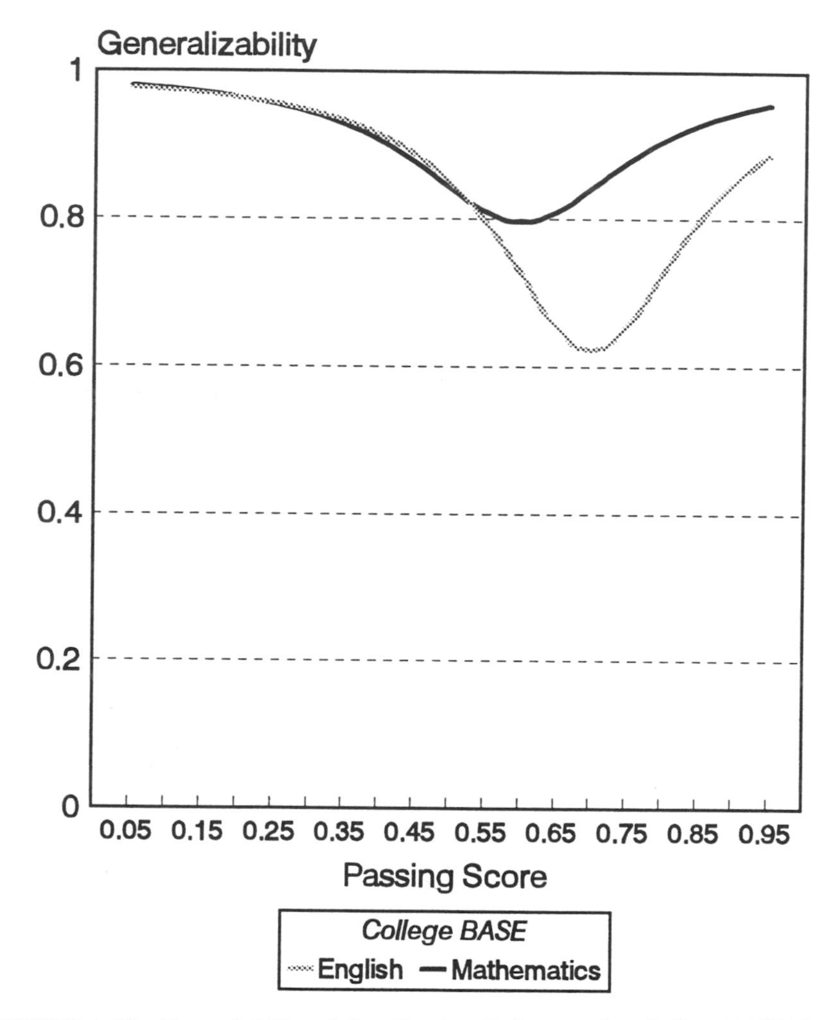

FIGURE 4. The Dependability of Certification Judgments for *College BASE* English and Mathematics Scores Given Different Passing Scores.

to the observed-score mean, while cutting scores of 0.60 or less and 0.80 or greater produce a generalizability coefficient of approximately 0.85.

TWO-FACET DESIGNS

Reliability estimates derived from classical test theory can be calculated for all of the one-facet designs presented in this chapter. The reliability of relative-score

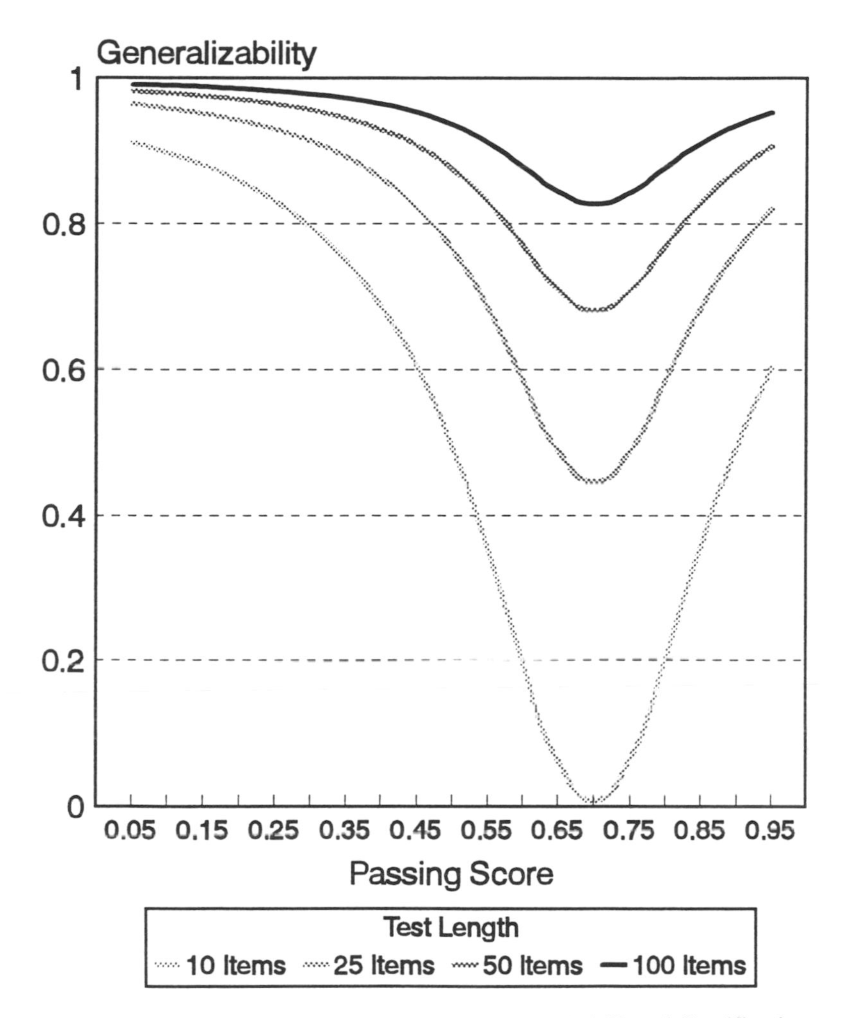

FIGURE 5. The Effects of Test Length on the Dependability of Certification Judgments for *College BASE* English Scores Given Different Passing Scores

interpretations can be evaluated using *alpha* reliability, or *KR-20* if item responses are dichotomous. Also, Livingston's (1972) coefficient *kappa* (k) is similar to the generalizability coefficient for certification tests proposed by Brennan and Kane (1977a). As a general rule, however, the values of k will be somewhat greater than estimates based on $M(C)$ (Brennan and Kane, 1977a). While the dependability of absolute-score judgments cannot be estimated directly using classical test theory, Brennan and Kane (1977b) demonstrated that $\sigma^2(\Delta)$ parallels Lord's (1957) formula for the standard error of measurement of a person's score. The primary advantage of generalizability theory, the ability to identify and account for multiple sources of error, is only apparent in designs with two or more facets.

Institutional Means on a Standardized Test

A typical two-facet design can be found in an assessment-research program that administers a multiple-item test to a group of students and then combines students' scores to produce an institutional mean. The institutional mean may be used in evaluation studies for either institutional improvement or accountability. In Tennessee, several public institutions administer *College BASE* to samples of their students as part of the state's performance-funding program. A mean composite score is calculated for each institution and then the institutional means are compared to the national mean for students at similar institutions (Tennessee Higher Education Commission, 1993).

The objective of the performance-funding standard is to use the deviation of an institution's observed-score mean about the observed mean of the national (i.e., comparable-institution) sample to draw inferences about deviations of an institution's universe score about the universe score of the population of students. In this assessment design, the college is the object of measurement, while samples of students and items are facets of the measurement situation (Pike and Phillippi, 1989). Given the fact that millions of dollars in supplemental appropriations rest on the results of this assessment, the generalizability of scores is of critical importance (Pike, 1992).

Figure 6 presents a *G*-study design that is appropriate for evaluating the generalizability of institutional means. In this design, samples of persons at several different colleges are administered a sample of items. In ANOVA terminology, persons are nested within colleges, while colleges and persons within colleges are crossed with items. Colleges are represented by the symbol C, and individual colleges are identified by the subscripts $1, 2, \ldots, c, \ldots, j$. Persons within each college are represented by the symbol P, with individual persons identified by the subscripts $1, 2, \ldots, p, \ldots, n$. Items are represented by the symbol I, with individual items identified by the subscripts $1, 2, ..., i, ..., k$. A person's score on an item is symbolized by x. Consequently, the score of an unspecified person from a college on a given item is x_{pilc}.

There are six components in the score of a person from a particular college on a given item (x_{pilc}): the grand mean (μ), an effect for colleges ($\mu_c - \mu$), an effect for persons within colleges ($\mu_{\text{plc}} - \mu$), an effect for items ($\mu_i - \mu$), the interaction between colleges and items ($\mu_{ci} + \mu - \mu_c - \mu_i$), and the interaction between persons within colleges and items ($x_{\text{pilc}} + \mu_c - \mu_{\text{plc}} - \mu_{ci}$). Because there is only one observation per cell in this design, the residual (error) term is confounded with the

		I_1	I_2	I_3	...	I_i	...	I_k
C_1	P_1	x_{111}	x_{112}	x_{113}	...	x_{11i}	...	x_{11k}
	P_2	x_{121}	x_{122}	x_{123}	...	x_{12i}	...	x_{12k}
	...	...	...	...	...	...	...	...
	P_p	x_{1p1}	x_{1p2}	x_{1p3}	...	x_{1pi}	...	x_{1pk}
	...	...	...	...	...	...	...	...
	P_n	x_{1n1}	x_{1n2}	x_{1n3}	...	x_{1ni}	...	x_{1nk}
...	...	...	...	...	...	...	...	...
C_c	P_1	x_{c11}	x_{c12}	x_{c13}	...	x_{c1i}	...	x_{c1k}
	P_2	x_{c21}	x_{c22}	x_{c23}	...	x_{c2i}	...	x_{c2k}
	...	...	...	...	...	...	...	...
	P_p	x_{cp1}	x_{cp2}	x_{cp3}	...	x_{cpi}	...	x_{cpk}
	...	...	...	...	...	...	...	...
	P_n	x_{cn1}	x_{cn2}	x_{cn3}	...	x_{cni}	...	x_{cnk}
...	...	...	...	...	...	...	...	...
C_j	P_1	x_{j11}	x_{j12}	x_{j13}	...	x_{j1i}	...	x_{j1k}
	P_2	x_{j21}	x_{j22}	x_{j23}	...	x_{j2i}	...	x_{j2k}
	...	...	...	...	...	...	...	...
	P_p	x_{jp1}	x_{jp2}	x_{jp3}	...	x_{jpi}	...	x_{jpk}
	...	...	...	...	...	...	...	...
	P_n	x_{jn1}	x_{jn2}	x_{jn3}	...	x_{jni}	...	x_{jnk}

FIGURE 6. A Two-Facet Design.

person-by-item interaction within colleges. The score of an unspecified person from a particular college on a given item is defined by the formula

$$x_{pi|c} = \mu + (\mu_c - \mu) + (\mu_{pi|c} - \mu) + (\mu_i - \mu) + (\mu_{ci} + \mu - \mu_c - \mu_i) + (x_{pi|c} + \mu_c - \mu_{p|c} - \mu_{ci}) \quad (27)$$

For each of the effects in equation [27] there is a G study variance component that can be calculated using a random-effects ANOVA.[3] Combining the mean squares produced by the analysis of variance with information about test length (k), the number of colleges (m), and the number of persons from each college (n) in the G study, a researcher can calculate G study variance components for each source of variance in the analysis of variance. For the research design presented in Figure 6, the appropriate formulas for calculating G study variance components are

$$\sigma^2(c) = \frac{MS(c) - MS(p|c) - MS(ci) + MS(pi|c)}{nk} \tag{28}$$

$$\sigma^2(p|c) = \frac{MS(p|c) - MS(pi|c)}{k} \tag{29}$$

$$\sigma^2(i) = \frac{MS(i) - MS(ci)}{mn} \tag{30}$$

$$\sigma^2(ci) = \frac{MS(ci) - MS(pi|c)}{n} \tag{31}$$

and

$$\sigma^2(pi|c) = MS(pi|c) \tag{32}$$

Table 2 presents the ANOVA results for the *College BASE* data set provided by the test developer. As previously noted, this data set contained dichotomous item responses for 50 students each from 29 institutions. Sources of variance, degrees of freedom (df), mean squares (MS), and G study estimated variance components for the English and mathematics subject tests, as well as for the composite score, are given.

Translating the results in Table 2 into generalizability analyses requires a clear delineation of the appropriate measure of error variance. As indicated previously, the Tennessee performance-funding standards, and most other group-level assessment designs, require that researchers make norm-referenced (i.e., relative) judgments. That is, an institution's mean performance is evaluated relative to the grand mean for the population of students taking the test. For this model, the variance component for colleges represents the universe-score variance, while the variance component for colleges plus relative error variance ($\sigma^2(\delta)$) represents expected observed-score variance.

[3]The discussion of two-facet models assumes a balanced ANOVA design. For information concerning the use of generalizability theory with unbalanced designs, the reader should consult Brennan, Jarjoura, and Deaton (1980) and Llabre (1980).

TABLE 2. ANOVA Results for a Two-Facet Design Representing *College BASE* English, Mathematics, and Composite Scores

English			
Source	*df*	*MS*	σ^2
Colleges (*C*)	28	8.5343	0.0037
Persons within Colleges (*P*/*C*)	1,421	0.8635	0.0164
Items (*I*)	40	33.1941	0.0227
Colleges by Items (*CI*)	1,120	0.3109	0.0024
Persons by Items within Colleges (*PI*/*C*)	56,840	0.1917	0.1917
Mathematics			
Source	*df*	*MS*	σ^2
Colleges (*C*)	28	19.4867	0.0064
Persons within Colleges (*P*/*C*)	1,421	1.5842	0.0251
Items (*I*)	55	33.7416	0.0231
Colleges by Items (*CI*)	1,540	0.3039	0.0025
Persons by Items within Colleges (*PI*/*C*)	78,155	0.1809	0.1809
Composite			
Source	*df*	*MS*	σ^2
Colleges (*C*)	28	49.7966	0.0052
Persons within Colleges (*P*/*C*)	1,421	2.8988	0.0150
Items (*I*)	179	32.6024	0.0223
Colleges by Items (*CI*)	5,012	0.3091	0.0023
Persons by Items within Colleges (*PI*/*C*)	254,359	0.1950	0.1950

Kane and Brennan (1977) and Kane, Gillmore, and Crooks (1976) noted that the *D* study variance components representing relative error variance include the effect for persons within colleges ($\sigma^2(P/c)$), the interaction between colleges and items ($\sigma^2(cI)$), and the interaction between persons within colleges and items ($\sigma^2(PI/c)$). As was the case for relative judgments based on one-facet designs, the current model assumes that all students have been administered the same items (i.e., the same form of a test). Thus, the variance component for items ($\sigma^2(I)$) is not a source of error. If multiple forms of a test are administered to students, those forms should be strictly parallel. If the multiple forms are not strictly parallel, Brennan (1983) recommends that the researcher conduct separate generalizability studies for each form of the test and then calculate mean *G* study variance components across test forms before proceeding to the *D* study.

For *D* study variance components, the appropriate divisor of the persons-within-college effect is the number of persons tested at a given college (n^*), while the divisor for the college-by-item interaction is the number of items on the test (k^*). The appropriate divisor for the interaction between persons within colleges and items is the product of the number of persons tested at a college and the number of items on the test (n^*k^*). Thus, the appropriate formula for evaluating the generalizability of institutional means on the *College BASE* is

$$E\rho^2 = \frac{\sigma^2(ci)}{\sigma^2(c) + \frac{\sigma^2(p|c)}{n^*} + \frac{\sigma^2(ci)}{k^*} + \frac{\sigma^2(pi|c)}{n^*k^*}} \tag{33}$$

Given the variance components in Table 2, and assuming that 50 students at a college are tested, the generalizability coefficients for the English and mathematics subject tests are 0.89 and 0.91, respectively. The generalizability coefficient for the group mean composite score is 0.94. The standard error for a *College BASE* mean composite score is 0.02. Interestingly, the standard errors for the English and mathematics subject-area tests also are approximately 0.02. For most uses, these score means would be considered very dependable.

As with one-facet *D* studies, it is possible to vary aspects of the sampling design in order to determine what effect different sampling strategies will have on the generalizability of measurements. For the two-facet (group-mean) design, a researcher can examine the effects of changes in test length and/or testing more or fewer students on the generalizability of group means. Most significant, the researcher can examine the interaction between changes in test length and changes in the number of students tested. Table 3 provides group-mean generalizability coefficients for sample sizes ranging from 25 to 500 student for *College BASE* English subtests containing 10, 25, 50, or 100 items.

An examination of the data in Table 3 reveals that group means based on 25 persons are not particularly dependable. For an English test consisting of 10 items, the generalizability coefficient is only 0.69, while for tests containing 25, 50, and 100 items, group-mean generalizability coefficients are 0.76, 0.81, and 0.83, respectively. Depending on the intended uses of the data, these coefficients may be sufficiently high (i.e., approximately 0.70 or greater) for decision mak-

TABLE 3. Group-mean Generalizability Coefficient for *College BASE* English Scores Given Various Numbers of Persons and Items

Number of Persons	*Number of Items*			
	10	25	50	100
25	0.69	0.76	0.81	0.83
50	0.80	0.85	0.89	0.90
75	0.84	0.89	0.92	0.93
100	0.86	0.91	0.94	0.95
150	0.89	0.93	0.95	0.96
200	0.90	0.94	0.96	0.97
250	0.91	0.94	0.97	0.97
500	0.92	0.96	0.98	0.98

ing. However, in high-stakes assessments, a researcher may demand greater generalizability (i.e., 0.80 or 0.90) for decision making.

If the number of persons in the sample is increased to 50, substantial improvements in generalizability are evident. An English test consisting of 10 items produces a generalizability coefficient of 0.80, while the group-mean generalizability coefficients for tests containing 25, 50, and 100 items are 0.85, 0.89, and 0.90, respectively. Gains in the generalizability of group means are somewhat less substantial when the number of persons tested is increased from 50 to 100. Coefficients for means based on 100 persons are 0.86, 0.91, 0.94, and 0.95 for tests containing 10, 25, 50, and 100 items. respectively. Generalizability coefficients for tests containing 10, 25, 50, and 100 items are 0.90, 0.94, 0.96, and 0.97 when the number of students tested is 200. When the number of students tested is increased to 500, generalizability coefficients are 0.92, 0.96, 0.98, and 0.98 for tests containing 10, 25, 50, and 100 items, respectively.

Recently, Marcoulides (1993) identified generalizability procedures for maximizing the power of a test, given budget constraints. An adaptation of Marcoulides' approach can be seen in the following example. By simply rearranging the terms in equation [33], an assessment researcher can can obtain a formula for identifying the number of persons (n) that must be tested in order to achieve a given level of group-mean generalizability ($E\rho^2$) for tests of various lengths (k^*). This formula is

$$n = \frac{\sigma^2(p|c) + \dfrac{\sigma^2(pi|c)}{k^*}}{\dfrac{\sigma^2(c)}{E\rho^2} - \sigma^2(c) - \dfrac{\sigma^2(ci)}{k^*}} \quad (34)$$

Assuming that an assessment researcher determined that a group-mean generalizability coefficient of 0.90 was needed for decision making, using equation [34] and the estimated variance components for the *College BASE* English subject test in Table 2 would identify configurations of test length and number of persons to be tested capable of producing mean scores of acceptable dependability. Table 4 presents the results of just such an analysis. As indicated by the results in Table 4, an English test containing 10 items would produce an acceptable group mean ($E\rho^2 = 0.90$) if at least 208 students were tested.[4] Only 77 students would need to be tested if the examination contained 25 items, and 56 students would have to be tested to produce a dependable mean if the *College BASE* English test contained 50 items. Very little reduction in sample size (i.e., the number of

[4]If the value for test length (k^*) is set to 5, equation [34] produces an impossible value (-795) for the number of students to be tested (n). This is due to the fact that the generalizability coefficient for a *College BASE* English test containing 5 items is *always* less than 0.90.

TABLE 4. Number of Students Required for Dependable (0.90) Group Means Given Various Test Lengths

Number of Items	*Number of Students*
10	208
15	117
20	90
25	77
30	69
40	60
50	56
75	50
100	47

persons tested) could be achieved by increasing the length of the test beyond 50 items. For a test containing 100 items, 48 students would have to be tested to achieve a dependable group mean. One of the most efficient designs, from the perspective of minimum test length and fewest students tested, would be the administration of a *College BASE* English examination containing 40 items to approximately 60 students.

As Marcoulides (1993) and the preceeding example show, generalizability can be extremely useful in identifying assessment designs that maximize the power of research within established resource and/or decision-making constraints. This advantage of generalizability theory, along with the facility to evaluate the dependability of complex assessment designs, flows directly from the ability to identify multiple sources of error in assessment research.

HIGHER-ORDER DESIGNS

Although the examples presented to this point in the chapter have focused on objective (i.e., multiple-choice) tests, generalizability theory is appropriate for evaluating the dependability of performance assessments. In fact, both Erwin (1988) and Sundre (1992) argued that the use of performance assessment demands increased reliance on generalizability theory due to the complexity of the research designs underlying performance assessments.

Assume, for example, that an institution wishes to assess the quality of its writing program. As part of the assessment, a sample of students is required to write three essays, each representing a different mode of expression (e.g., personal narrative, expository, and persuasive). Each essay is evaluated by three raters using holistic scoring procedures. A student's score is the mean of three raters' evaluations of three essays, while the institution's score is the mean of the students' scores. In this example, the researcher is interested in making a judgment about the group's performance relative to the performance of students at other institutions who responded to the same prompts. (Instead of comparing the scores of a group of students with those of students at *other* institutions, the researcher might be interested in comparing the group's scores to the scores of students at the *same* institution who responded to the prompts on previous occasions.) For simplicity, assume that the same three raters evaluated the essays of all students.

Figure 7 presents the data matrix for the hypothetical writing assessment. In analysis-of-variance terminology, this is a one between- two within-subjects design (Kennedy and Bush, 1985). Persons are nested within colleges, while raters and writing samples are crossed with colleges. Raters and writing samples also are crossed with each other, as well as with students within colleges. In the figure, colleges are represented by the symbol (C), with individual institutions being identified by the subscripts 1, 2, . . . , c, . . . , j. Persons are represented by the symbol P, and individual students are identified by the subscripts 1, 2, . . . , p, . . . , n. Raters are represented by the symbol R, with individual raters identified by the subscripts 1, 2, . . . , r, . . . , k. Writing samples are represented by the symbol W, with essays identified by the subscripts 1, 2, . . . , w, . . . , m. The rating of a student's essay is represented by x, and the rating of a specific writing sample from an unspecified person at a college is x_{prwlc}.

There are 11 sources of variance in a given rating (x_{prwlc}). Between subjects, the sources of variance are the effect for colleges (C) and the effect for persons within colleges (P/C). Within subjects, the sources of variance are the effect for raters (R), the interaction between colleges and raters (CR), the interaction between persons and raters within colleges (PR/C), the effect for writing samples (W), the interaction between colleges and writing samples (CW), the interaction between persons and writing samples within colleges (PW/C), the interaction between raters and writing samples (RW), the three-way interaction among colleges, raters, and writing samples (CRW), and the interaction among persons, raters, and writing samples within colleges (PRW/C). The presence of only one observation in each cell means that residual variance is confounded with the interaction among persons, raters, and writing samples within colleges.

Although determining appropriate expected mean squares is essential for calculating G study variance components, procedures for generating them are not well documented. Table 5 presents the sources of variance and expected mean squares for the G study of college writing effectiveness just described. The expected mean squares were generated using procedures described by Kennedy and Bush (1985, pp. 343–349). These procedures are outlined in the appendix to this chapter.

By substituting mean squares for the variances in Table 5, it is possible to

				R_1			...			R_k		
		W_1	...	W_w	...	W_m	...	W_1	...	W_w	...	W_m
C_1	P_1	x_{1111}	...	x_{111w}	...	x_{111m}	...	x_{11k1}	...	x_{11kw}	...	x_{11km}
	P_2	x_{1211}	...	x_{121w}	...	x_{121m}	...	x_{12k1}	...	x_{12kw}	...	x_{12km}
	...	...	...	...	...	...	...	...	...	...	...	...
	P_n	$x_{1n1'1}$	...	x_{1n1w}	...	x_{1n1m}	...	x_{1nk1}	...	x_{1nkw}	...	x_{1nkm}
...	...	...	...	...	...	...	...	...	...	...	...	...
C_c	P_1	x_{c111}	...	x_{c11w}	...	x_{c11m}	...	x_{c1k1}	...	x_{c1kw}	...	x_{c1km}
	P_2	x_{c211}	...	x_{c21w}	...	x_{c21m}	...	x_{c2k1}	...	x_{c2kw}	...	x_{c2km}
	...	...	...	...	...	...	...	...	...	...	...	...
	P_n	x_{cn11}	...	x_{cn1w}	...	x_{cn1m}	...	x_{cnk1}	...	x_{cnkw}	...	x_{cnkm}
...	...	...	...	...	...	...	...	...	...	...	...	...
C_j	P_1	x_{j111}	...	x_{j11w}	...	x_{j11m}	...	x_{j1k1}	...	x_{j1kw}	...	x_{j1kk}
	P_2	x_{j211}	...	x_{j21w}	...	x_{j21m}	...	x_{j2k1}	...	x_{j2kw}	...	x_{j2km}
	...	...	...	...	...	...	...	...	...	...	...	...
	P_n	x_{jn11}	...	x_{jn1w}	...	x_{jn1m}	...	x_{jnk1}	...	x_{jnkw}	...	x_{jnkm}

FIGURE 7. A Three-Facet Design.

generate simplified equations for calculating *G* study variance components. The equations needed to calculate variance components for the writing assessment example are

$$\sigma^2(c) = \frac{MS(c) - MS(p|c) - MS(cr) - MS(cw) + MS(pr|c) + MS(pw|c) + MS(crw) - MS(prw|c)}{kmn} \tag{35}$$

TABLE 5. Expected Mean Squares for Sources of Variance in the Three-Facet Design

Source	*Expected Mean Square*
C	$\sigma^2_{prw\mid c} + m\sigma^2_{pr\mid c} + k\sigma^2_{pw\mid c} + n\sigma^2 crw + km\sigma^2_{p\mid c} + mn\sigma^2_{cr} + kn\sigma^2_{cw} + kmn\sigma^2_{c}$
P/C	$\sigma^2_{prw\mid c} + m\sigma^2_{pr\mid c} + k\sigma^2_{pw\mid c} + km\sigma^2_{p\mid c}$
R	$\sigma^2_{prw\mid c} + m\sigma^2_{pr\mid c} + n\sigma^2_{crw} + jn\sigma^2_{rw} + mn\sigma^2_{cr} + jmn\sigma^2_{r}$
CR	$\sigma^2_{prw\mid c} + m\sigma^2_{pr\mid c} + n\sigma^2_{crw} + mn\sigma^2_{cr}$
PR/C	$\sigma^2_{prw\mid c} + m\sigma^2_{pr\mid c}$
W	$\sigma^2_{prw\mid c} + k\sigma^2_{pw\mid c} + n\sigma^2_{crw} + jn\sigma^2_{rw} + kn\sigma^2_{cw} + jkn\sigma^2_{w}$
CW	$\sigma^2_{prw\mid c} + k\sigma^2_{pw\mid c} + n\sigma^2_{crw} + kn\sigma^2_{cw}$
PW/C	$\sigma^2_{prw\mid c} + k\sigma^2_{pw\mid c}$
RW	$\sigma^2_{prw\mid c} + n\sigma^2_{crw} + jn\sigma^2_{rw}$
CRW	$\sigma^2_{prw\mid c} + n\sigma^2_{crw}$
PRW/C	$\sigma^2_{prw\mid c}$

$$\sigma^2(p\mid c) = \frac{MS(p\mid c) - MS(pr\mid c) - MS(pw\mid c) + MS(prw\mid c)}{km} \tag{36}$$

$$\sigma^2(r) = \frac{MS(r) - MS(cr) - MS(rw) + MS(crw)}{jmn} \tag{37}$$

$$\sigma^2(cr) = \frac{MS(cr) - MS(pr\mid c) - MS(crw) + MS(prw\mid c)}{mn} \tag{38}$$

$$\sigma^2(pr\mid c) = \frac{MS(pr\mid c) - MS(prw\mid c)}{m} \tag{39}$$

$$\sigma^2(w) = \frac{MS(w) - MS(cw) - MS(rw) + MS(crw)}{jkn} \tag{40}$$

$$\sigma^2(cw) = \frac{MS(cw) - MS(pw\mid c) - MS(crw) + MS(prw\mid c)}{kn} \tag{41}$$

$$\sigma^2(pw\mid c) = \frac{MS(pw\mid c) - MS(prw\mid c)}{k} \tag{42}$$

$$\sigma^2(rw) = \frac{MS(rw) - MS(crw)}{jn} \tag{43}$$

$$\sigma^2(crw) = \frac{MS(crw) - MS(prw\mid c)}{n} \tag{44}$$

and

TABLE 6. ANOVA Results for the Writing-Assessment Design

Source	*df*	*MS*	σ^2
c	19	10.5614	0.0173
P/c	49	1.0453	0.0501
R	2	21.3700	0.0007
cR	38	1.0970	−0.0001
PR/c	1,960	0.2898	0.3233
W	2	46.9700	0.0090
cW	38	2.2407	0.0061
PW/c	1,960	0.4972	0.1015
WR	4	18.6575	0.0176
cWR	76	1.0203	0.01655
PWR/c	3,920	0.1928	0.1928

$$\sigma^2(prw|c) = MS(prw|c) \tag{45}$$

Table 6 contains synthetic analysis-of-variance results for the hypothetical three-facet writing assessment. In the hypothetical example, 50 students each from 20 colleges were administered a writing assessment. As part of the assessment, students wrote on three prompts, and the prompts were evaluated by the same three raters.

Included in the table are the sources of variance, degrees of freedom, mean squares and estimated *G* study variance components produced by the analysis of variance. An examination of the magnitude of the variance components in Table 6 reveals that the variance in scores attributable to difference in modes of expression (i.e., writing samples) is substantially greater than the variability in scores attributable to differences among the raters. As will be shown later, these differences have significant implications for attempts to improve the dependability of judgments about writing ability.

As with one- and two-facet designs, the dependability of relative judgments for the three-facet design is represented by the ratio of universe-score variance to itself plus relative error variance. Because the researcher is interested in institutional performance, the variance component for colleges ($\sigma^2(c)$) represents estimated universe score variance. Relative error variance ($\sigma^2(\delta)$) is represented by several components, including the *D* study estimated variance component for persons within colleges ($\sigma^2(P/c)$), the interaction between persons and raters within colleges ($\sigma^2(PR/c)$), the interaction between persons and writing samples within colleges ($\sigma^2(PW/c)$), and the interaction among persons, raters, and writing samples among colleges ($\sigma^2(PRW/c)$).

Because differential effects for raters and writing samples across colleges represent a confounding influence on judgments about differences among colleges, the D study variance components for the college-by-rater ($\sigma^2(cR)$), college-by-writing sample ($\sigma^2(cW)$), and college-by-rater-by-writing sample ($\sigma^2(cRW)$) interactions are included in the estimate of relative error variance. Because the raters and writing prompts used in the study were the same for all students, the variance components $\sigma^2(R)$ and $\sigma^2(W)$, as well as the variance component for the rater-by-writing sample interaction ($\sigma^2(RW)$), are not included in estimates of relative error variance.[5] The appropriate D study variance components are combined in equation [46] to provide a formula for evaluating the generalizability of mean writing-assessment scores for an institution.

$$E\rho^2 = \frac{\sigma^2(c)}{\sigma^2(c) + \frac{\sigma^2(p|c)}{n^*} + \frac{\sigma^2(cr)}{k^*} + \frac{\sigma^2(pr|c)}{k^*n^*} + \frac{\sigma^2(cw)}{m^*} + \frac{\sigma^2(pw|c)}{m^*n^*} + \frac{\sigma^2(crw)}{k^*m^*} + \frac{\sigma(prw|c)}{k^*m^*n^*}} \quad [46]$$

Assuming the 50 students participate in the writing assessment and respond to three prompts that are scored by three raters, the group mean generalizability coefficient is slightly less than 0.74. Depending on the uses of the data, this level of dependability may or may not be acceptable. For monitoring internal improvement efforts, decision makers may be willing to accept a 0.74 level of generalizability. However, if the allocation of state funds for higher education depends on this group mean, decision makers would want a more dependable measure. Ways of improving the dependability of the group writing-assessment means include increasing the numbers of persons, raters, and/or writing samples in the design.

The generalizability coefficients in Table 7 identify the effects of varying the number of persons, raters, and writing prompts in the D study research design on the dependability of relative judgments about institutional means. If a 0.80 level of generalizability was required, 200 students would have to be assessed using three raters and three prompts. If the number of raters was increased from 3 to 4, between 100 and 150 students would have to be assessed, and if 5 raters were used, between 75 and 100 students would be required.

If the number of writing prompts was increased from 3 to 6, between 50 and 75 students would have to be assessed by three raters to achieve a level of generalizability of 0.80. For this scenario, it was assumed that researchers would want to balance the number of narrative, expository, and persuasive writing prompts. Consequently, increases in the number of writing samples would occur in increments of three. Somewhat less than 50 students would required to achieve

[5]In the description of the three-facet writing-assessment design, it is assumed that all students responded to the same prompts (or strictly parallel prompts) and that the essays were scored by the same raters. If these conditions cannot be met, separate generalizability studies should be conducted for all possible combinations of prompts and raters, and the variance components should then be averaged to produce a set of variance components similar to those in Table 6.

TABLE 7. Group-Mean Generalizability Coefficients Given Various Numbers of Writing Samples, Raters, and Persons

	Writing Samples = 3				
	Number of Raters				
Number of Persons	2	3	4	5	6
25	0.63	0.67	0.69	0.70	0.71
50	0.70	0.74	0.76	0.77	0.78
75	0.73	0.76	0.78	0.79	0.80
100	0.74	0.77	0.79	0.81	0.81
150	0.75	0.79	0.81	0.82	0.83
200	0.76	0.80	0.81	0.83	0.83
250	0.76	0.80	0.82	0.83	0.84
500	0.77	0.81	0.83	0.84	0.85
	Writing Samples = 6				
	Number of Raters				
Number of Persons	2	3	4	5	6
25	0.69	0.73	0.75	0.77	0.77
50	0.75	0.79	0.81	0.82	0.83
75	0.77	0.81	0.83	0.84	0.85
100	0.78	0.82	0.84	0.86	0.86
150	0.80	0.83	0.85	0.87	0.88
200	0.80	0.84	0.86	0.87	0.88
250	0.81	0.84	0.86	0.88	0.89
500	0.81	0.85	0.87	0.88	0.89

dependable group means ($E\rho^2 > 0.80$) with 4 or more raters. These findings reinforce the results in Table 6, showing that writing samples had a greater influence on score variability than raters.

In some instances, simply increasing the number of persons, raters, or writing samples in the *D* study may not be a viable option. For example, if the required level of dependability were 0.90, the *D* study would have to include more than 500 persons responding to 6 writing prompts scored by 6 raters. These requirements would be extremely labor intensive and beyond the capabilities of many institutions. Confronted with a similar problem at James Madison University, Sundre (1992) reported that efforts were made to revise the writing prompts, the scoring rubrics, and the training of raters to achieve more dependable results.

Given the finding that differences in writing prompts had the most substantial effect on score variability, modifying the writing prompts is likely to have the greatest effect on improving the dependability of group writing-assessment means. For example, the assessment researcher might consider using prompts that require the same mode of writing (i.e., either personal narrative, expository, or persuasive). Dunbar (1988) suggests that assessment researchers not include different response modes in their writing-assessment designs because of substantial variability in individual performance across modes of expression. Instead, he suggests the use of multiple writing samples within the same mode of expression. If decision makers insist on an evaluation of multiple modes of expression, profile scores, which include separate scores for each mode of expression, can be developed. If profile scores are used, multivariate generalizability theory should be used to assess the dependability of the profiles (Cronbach et al., 1972).

SUMMARY AND CONCLUSIONS: WHAT GENERALIZABILITY THEORY CAN AND CANNOT DO

This chapter identified several advantages of using generalizability theory in assessment research. The first advantage is that it forces researchers to focus on the underlying purpose of their research, namely making inferences from a set of observations to higher-order constructs or universes. By definition, inferences from the observed to the unobserved are tentative. Unfortunately, researchers too often forget this fact, attributing precision to their conclusions that is not warranted.

As Cronbach et al. (1972) noted, generalizability theory attaches probabilistic statements to inferences based on observed phenomena, and the probabilistic statements can serve to temper the certainty of researchers' claims. Forcing researchers to explicitly consider the limitations of their conclusions is particularly appropriate for higher-education assessment, where the consequences of decisions based of a set of observed scores are significant for individuals, institutions, and society. Sundre's (1992, p. 8) description of assessment at James Madison University illustrates this particular advantage of generalizability theory: "While the results of the performance ratings were used to inform program evaluation discussions, the knowledge of generalizability of the ratings served to temper the dialogue." Sundre concludes that a better understanding of generalizability theory made the faculty more aware of the importance of reliability in the interpretation of assessment results.

The other advantages of generalizability theory are practical. These advantages stem from the ability to identify multiple sources of error in research designs. The first practical advantage of generalizability theory is its flexibility. As the examples presented in this chapter demonstrate, generalizability theory can provide dependability estimates for a variety of research designs, ranging from simple designs involving a single source of potential error to complex designs containing multiple sources of error. In addition, generalizability theory represents a flexible approach with respect to the decisions that are to be made based on the data. Indices of dependability can be calculated for situations that call for either relative or absolute decisions. Indicies of dependability can also be calculated for situations requiring mastery decisions. The importance of a flexible, multifaceted approach cannot be overestimated. As the *Standards for Educational and Psychological Measurement* states:

> Fundamental to the proper evaluation of a test are the identification of major sources of measurement error, the size of the errors resulting from these sources, the indication of the degree of reliability to be expected between pairs of scores under particular circumstances, and the generalizability of results across items, forms, raters, administrations, and other measurement facets. (American Educational Research Association, American Psychological Association, and National Council on Measurement in Education, 1985, p. 10)

A second practical advantage of generalizability theory is that it can be used to identify how changes in an assessment design can improve the dependability of decisions. Assessment researchers are seldom confronted with a situation in which one, and only one, design is appropriate for obtaining needed data. By modifying the parameters of *D* study variance components, assessment professionals can identify those designs that provide the most dependable data for making inferences about the quality of student learning and the effectiveness of academic programs. Since many institutions are confronted with limited resources for assessment, the ability of generalizability theory to identify designs that provde acceptable data within specified resource constraints is a tremendous benefit.

The practical advantages of multifaceted generalizability theory go beyond making minor modifications to a assessment design. As both Erwin (1988) and Sundre (1992) pointed out, generalizability theory can be used to evaluate fundamental aspects of an assessment program. Among the positive outcomes associated with using generalizability theory in assessment research at James Madison University were improved rating scales and rater training, as well as better understanding of what constituted acceptable levels of performance.

While generalizability theory offers several advantages over classical test reliability, it is not without its limitations. As Cronbach et al. (1972) noted, generalizability theory is a "weak" statistical theory. That is, generalizability theory does not require strong measurement assumptions. In one sense, this is an advantage of generalizability theory, allowing it to be applied in almost any measurement situation. However, the absence of assumptions about the distribution of measurements makes it difficult to clearly identify relationships between observed scores and universe scores (Brennan, 1983).

Closely related to the weakness of generalizability theory is the indefiniteness of its results (Cronbach et al., 1972). Estimated variance components in generalizability theory are just that, estimates. While the estimates apply to all observations that might be drawn from a particular universe, they do not apply perfectly for any particular person or any particular set of observations (Cronbach et al., 1972). The inherent variability in estimated variance components has been described as the "Achilles' heel" of generalizability theory (Shavelson and Webb, 1981).

A third limitation of generalizability theory is the assumption of a steady state of measurement. That is, variability in scores is assumed to be the result of various facets of the measurement situation (i.e., measurement error), and not to true changes. As a result of the steady-state assumption, the applicability of generalizability theory to situations of change is limited. As Cronbach et al. (1972, p. 364) noted: "The whole concept of a universe score is of dubious value if the universe stretches over a period when the person's status is changing regularly and appreciably."

Perhaps the most important limitation of generalizability theory is that it is not a substitute for sound research practice. Generalizability theory can identify weaknesses in a measurement design and, in some cases, suggest ways in which those weaknesses can be minimized. However, it *cannot* overcome an inappropriate or poorly executed research design. The key to good assessment research does not lie in a particular psychometric model. Likewise, generalizability theory is of little use if the research questions are ill-concieved or trivial. The key to good assessment lies in the thoughtfulness of the researcher and the care with which the assessment is carried out. As Cronbach (1976, p. 199) observed: "*G* theory enables you to ask your questions better; what is most significant for you cannot be supplied from the outside."

Acknowledgments. I would like to thank Eve Tolan and Jeff Moran for their assistance in the preparation of the manuscript.

APPENDIX

The algorithm developed by Kennedy and Bush (1985, pp. 343–349) involves three preliminary steps. First, all sources of variance in the ANOVA model are listed in order of their complexity from least to most complex. Thus the effect for college (*C*) is the first source of variance in the list, and the interaction among persons, raters, and writing samples within colleges (*PRW/C*) is the last source of variance.

The second of the preliminary steps is to identify the components in the sources of variance that are random (i.e., represent samples from universes). In Table 5, all components are considered to be random, hence all are underlined. The third preliminary step in the process is to identify the expected value for the basic error term in the model. Because there is only one observation per cell in the writing-assessment design, the basic error term corresponds to the most complex effect (*PRW/C*). The expected value of this terms is its variance (i.e., $\sigma^2(PWR/C)$). This expected value is included in the second column of Table 5.

Once the preliminary steps have been completed, the researcher can proceed to generate expected mean squares. Beginning at the bottom of the list of sources of variance, first identify all other sources of variance that contain all of the components (i.e., letters) of the source in question. Since the expected mean square for the most complex component was derived in the first preliminary step, attention focuses on the next source of variance (i.e., *CRW*). For the three-way interaction among colleges, raters, and writing samples, only one other source of variance contains all of the components. That source of variance is the most basic term, *PRW/C*.

Having identified the appropriate sources of variance, the researcher next determines if the components not included in both sources (in this case *P*) are fixed or random. This is the second step in the algorithm. For the three-way *CRW* interaction, the component not included in the *PRW/C* interaction, *P*, is random. As a result, the variance component comprising the expected mean square for *PRW/C* ($\sigma^2(PRW/C)$) is included in the expected mean square for *CRW*. If *P* had been fixed, the expected mean square for *PRW/C* would not have been included in the expected mean square being generated. No other sources of variance contain all of the components in the *CRW* interaction.

The third step in the algorithm is elimination of all duplicate terms. After eliminating duplicate terms, the fourth step involves adding the term representing the null hypothesis of the source in question to the expected mean square being generated. In the case of the *CRW* interaction, the null hypothesis term is $n\sigma^2(CRW)$. As can be seen in Table 5, the expected mean square for the *CRW* interaction is $\sigma^2(PRW/C) + n\sigma^2(CRW)$.

Consider a second example. In the case of the interaction between raters and writing samples (*RW*), two sources of variance, *CRW* and *PRW/C*, contain all of the components in *RW*. Combining the terms for the expected mean squares of these sources ($\sigma^2(PRW/C)$ and $n\sigma^2(CRW)$) with the term for the null hypothesis of *RW* ($jn\sigma^2(RW)$), produces the expected mean square for the *RW* interaction that is included in Table 5.

REFERENCES

Alverno College Faculty. (1979). *Assessment at Alverno College*. Milwaukee, WI: Alverno Publications.

American Educational Research Association, American Psychological Association, and the National Council on Measurement in Education. (1985). *Standards for Educational and Psychological Measurement*. Washington, DC: American Psychological Association.

Association of American Colleges. (1985). *Integrity in the College Curriculum: A Report to the Academic Community*. Washington, DC: Association of American Colleges.

Banta, T. W. (1985). Use of outcomes information at the University of Tennessee, Knoxville. In P. T. Ewell (ed.), *Assessing Educational Outcomes* (New Directions for Institutional Research No. 47.) San Francisco: Jossey-Bass.

Banta, T. W. (1988a). Assessment as an instrument of state funding policy. In T. W. Banta (ed.), *Implementing Outcomes Assessment: Promise and Perils* (New Directions for Institutional Research No. 59.) San Francisco: Jossey-Bass.

Banta, T. W. (1988b). Editor's notes. In T. W. Banta (ed.), *Implementing Outcomes Assessment: Promise and Perils* (New Directions for Institutional Research No. 59.) San Francisco: Jossey-Bass.

Bejar, I. I. (1983). *Achievement Testing: Recent Advances* (Sage University Paper Series on Quantitative Applications in the Social Sciences No. 36.) Beverly Hills: Sage.

Boyer, E. L. (1987). *College: The Undergraduate Experience in America*. New York: Harper and Row.

Bradley, J. L., Draper, G. W., and Pike, G. R. (1993). Assessment Measures. *Assessment Update: Progress, Trends, and Practices in Higher Education* 5(1): 14–15.

Brennan, R. L. (1983). *Elements of Generalizability Theory*. Iowa City, IA: ACT Publications.

Brennan, R. L., Jarjoura, D., and Deaton, E. L. (1980). *Some Issues Concerning the Estimation and Interpretation of Variance Components in Generalizability Theory* (ACT Technical Bulletin No. 36.) Iowa City, IA: American College Testing.

Brennan, R. L., and Kane, M. T. (1977a). An index of dependability for mastery tests. *Journal of Educational Measurement* 14: 277–289.

Brennan, R. L., and Kane, M. T. (1977b). Signal/noise ratios for domain-referenced tests. *Psychometrika* 42: 609–625.

College Outcomes Evaluation Program Council. (1987). *Report to the New Jersey Board of Higher Education from the Advisory Committee to the College Outcomes Evaluation Program*. Trenton, NJ: Department of Higher Education, State of New Jersey.

College Outcomes Evaluation Program Council. (1990). *Report to the Board of Higher Education on the First Administration of the General Intellectual Skills (GIS) Assessment*. Trenton, NJ: Department of Higher Education, State of New Jersey.

Cronbach, L. J. (1976). On the design of educational measures. In D. N. M. de Gruijter and L. J. T. van der Kamp (eds.), *Advances in Educational and Psychological Measurement*. New York: Wiley.

Cronbach, L. J. (1984). *Essentials of Psychological Testing*. New York: Harper and Row.

Cronbach, L. J., Gleser, G. C., Nanda, H., and Rajaratnam, N. (1972). *The Dependability of Behavioral Measurements: Theory of Generalizability for Scores and Profiles*. New York: Wiley.

Dunbar, S. J. (1988). States of art in the science of writing and other performance assessments. In C. Adelman (ed.), *Performance and Judgment: Essays on Principles and Practice in the Assessment of College Student Learning*. Washington, DC: US Government Printing Office.

El-Khawas, E. (1991). *Campus Trends, 1991* (Higher Education Panel Report No. 81.) Washington, D C: American Council on Education.

Erwin, T. D. (1988). The analysis of ratings using generalizability theory for student outcomes assessment. Paper presented at the annual meeting of the Association for Institutional Research, Phoenix, Arizona, May 1988.

Ewell, P. T. (1991). To capture the ineffable: New forms of assessment in higher education. In G. Grant (ed.), *Review of Research in Education* Volume 17. Washington, DC: American Educational Research Association.

Farmer, D. W. (1988). *Enhancing Student Learning: Emphasizing Essential Student Competencies in Academic Programs*. Wilkes-Barre, PA: Kings College.

Feldt, L. S., and Brennan, R. L. (1989). Reliability. In R. L. Linn (ed.), *Educational Measurement* Third Edition. New York: Macmillan.

Fisher, R. A. (1925). *Statistical methods for research workers*. London: Oliver and Bond.

Graham, S. W., and Cockriel, I. (1989). College outcomes assessment factors: An empirical approach. *College Student Journal* 23: 280–288.

Gregory, R. J. (1992). *Psychological Testing: History, Principles, and Applications*. Boston: Allyn and Bacon.

Gulliksen, H. (1950). *Theory of Mental Tests*. New York: Wiley.

Johnson, R., Prus, J., Andersen, C. J., and El-Khawas, E. (1991). *Assessing Assessment: An In-Depth Status Report on the Higher Education Assessment Movement in 1990* (Higher Education Panel Report No. 79.) Washington, DC: American Council on Education.

Kalsbeek, D. H. (1989). Linking learning style theory with retention research: The TRAILS project. *Air Professional File* (No. 32.) Tallahassee, FL: Association for Institutional Research.

Kane, M. T., and Brennan, R. L. (1977). The generalizability of class means. *Review of Educational Research* 47: 267–292.

Kane, M. T., Gillmore, G. M., and Crooks, T. J. (1976). Student evaluations of teaching: The generalizability of class means. *Journal of Educational Measurement* 13: 171–183.

Kennedy, J. J., and Bush, A. J. (1985). *An Introduction to the Design and Analysis of Experiments in Behavioral Research*. Lanham, MD: University Press of America.

Linn, R. L. (1981). Measuring pretest-posttest performance changes. In R. A. Berk (ed.), *Educational Evaluation Methodology: The State of the Art*. Baltimore: Johns Hopkins University Press.

Livingston, S. A. (1972). A criterion-referenced application of classical test theory. *Journal of Educational Measurement* 9: 13–26.

Llabre, M. M. (1980). Estimating variance components with unbalanced designs in generalizability theory. Paper presented at the annual meeting of the American Educational Research Association, Boston, April, 1980.

Lord, F. M. (1957). Do tests of the same length have the same standard error of measurement? *Educational and Psychological Measurement* 17: 510–521.

Marcoulides, G. A. (1993). Maximizing power in generalizability studies under budget constraints. *Journal of Educational Statistics* 18: 197–206.

McCabe, R. H. (1983). *A Status Report on the Comprehensive Educational Reform of Miami-Dade Community College*. Miami, FL: Office of the President, Miami-Dade Community College.

McClain, C. J., and Krueger, D. W. (1985). Using outcomes assessment: A case study in institutional change. In P. T. Ewell (ed.), *Assessing Educational Outcomes* (New Directions for Institutional Research No. 47.) San Francisco: Jossey-Bass.

McClenney, K. M. (1993). Assessment in an era of empowerment. *Assessment Update: Progress, Trends, and Practices in Higher Education*, *5*(1): 1–6.

Mehrens, W. A., and Lehman, I. J. (1987). *Using Standardized Tests in Education*. New York: Longman.

Mentkowski, M., and Loacker, G. (1985). Assessing and validating the outcomes of college. In P. T. Ewell (ed.), *Assessing Educational Outcomes* (New Directions for Institutional Research No. 47.) San Francisco: Jossey-Bass.

Millman, J. (1988). Designing a college assessment. In C. Adelman (ed.), *Performance and Judgment: Essays on Principles and Practice in the Assessment of College Student Learning*. Washington, DC: US Government Printing Office.

National Governors' Association. (1986). *Time for Results: The Governors' 1991 Report on Education.* Washington, DC: National Governors' Association.

National Institute of Education, Study Group on Conditions of Excellence in American Higher Education. (1984). *Involvement in Learning: Realizing the Potential of American Higher Education.* Washington, DC: US Government Printing Office.

Osterlind, S. J. (1989). *College Basic Academic Subjects Examination: Guide to Test Content.* Chicago: Riverside.

Osterlind, S. J., and Merz, W. R. (1990). *College BASE Technical Manual.* Columbia, MO: Center for Educational Assessment, University of Missouri-Columbia.

Osterlind, S. J., and Schmitz, C. D. (1993). *College BASE* versus *American College Testing* as a predictor variable for *National Teacher's Examination* and grade point average. *Journal of College Student Development* 34: 187–190.

Pascarella, E. T., and Terenzini, P. T. (1991): *How College Affects Students: Findings and Insights from Twenty Years of Research.* San Francisco: Jossey-Bass.

Pike, G. R. (1992). *A Generalizability Analysis of the College Basic Academic Subjects Examination.* Knoxville, TN: Center for Assessment Research and Development, University of Tennessee, Knoxville.

Pike, G. R., and Phillippi, R. H. (1989). Using generalizability theory in institutional research. Paper presented at the annual meeting of the Association for Institutional Research, Baltimore, Maryland, May 1989.

Postsecondary Education Planning Commission. (1988). *College Level Academic Skills Test Review.* Tallahassee, FL: Postsecondary Educational Planning Commission, State of Florida.

Schmitz, C. C., and DelMas, R. C. (1990). Determining the validity of placement exams for developmental college curricula. Paper presented at the annual meeting of the American Educational Research Association, Boston, April 1990.

Shavelson, R. J., and Webb, N. M. (1981). Generalizability theory: 1973–1980. *British Journal of Mathematical and Statistical Psychology* 34: 133–166.

Shavelson, R. J., and Webb, N. M. (1991). *Generalizability Theory: A Primer.* Newbury Park, CA: Sage.

Stanley, J. C. (1971). Reliability. In R. L. Thorndike (ed.), *Educational Measurement* Second Edition. Washington, DC: American Council on Education.

Steele, J. M. (1989). *A Generalizability Analysis of the COMP Objective Test (Form 9).* Iowa City, IA: College Outcome Measures Program, American College Testing.

Stufflebeam, D. L., and Webster, W. J. (1983). An analysis of alternative approaches to evaluation. In Madaus, G. F., Scriven, M. S., and Stufflebeam, D. L. (eds.), *Evaluation Models: Viewpoints on Educational and Human Services Evaluation.* Boston: Kluwer-Nijhoff.

Sundre, D. L. (1992). The application of generalizability theory for improvement of an academic program assessment. Paper presented at the annual meeting of the American Educational Research Association, San Francisco, April 1992.

Tennessee Higher Education Commission. (1993). *Performance Funding Standards.* Nashville: Tennessee Higher Education Commission, State of Tennessee.

Terenzini, P. T. (1989). Assessment with open eyes: Pitfalls in studying student outcomes. *Journal of Higher Education* 60: 644–664.

Webb, N. M., Rowley, G. L., and Shavelson, R. J. (1988). Using generalizability theory in counseling and development. *Measurement and Evaluation in Counseling and Development* 21: 81–90.

Policy Models and Policy Instruments in Higher Education: The Effects of Governmental Policy-Making on the Innovative Behavior of Higher Education Institutions

Frans A. van Vught
University of Twente, The Netherlands

INTRODUCTION

Government regulation has become an increasingly important issue. Much of the attention to government regulation has been focused on private sector regulation. Economists have widely analyzed the effects of government regulation on the affected market sector (for instance: Kahn, 1971; Stigler, 1975).

The effects of public sector regulation have also attracted some attention. In disciplines like public administration and policy analysis, public sector regulation has fruitfully been studied as an issue of compliance or noncompliance. The literature on implementation processes in particular has offered some interesting results with respect to the identification of factors explaining why specific government policies have or have not succeeded (Pressman and Wildavsky, 1973; Dunsire, 1978; Rein and Rabinovitz, 1978; Bardach, 1979; Barrett and Fudge, 1981; Mazmanian and Sabatier 1981; O'Toole, 1986). With respect to the implementation of higher education policies the study by Cerych and Sabatier (1986) should be mentioned.

Generally speaking, regulation has to do with the influencing of behavior, i.e., with trying to steer the decisions and actions of others according to certain objectives and by using certain instruments. Mitnick has defined "regulation" as "the intentional restriction of a subject's choice of activity, by an entity not directly part to or involved in that activity" (Mitnick, 1980, p. 5). Government regulation can be described as the efforts of government to steer the decisions and actions of specific societal actors according to the objectives the government has set and by using instruments government has at its disposal. There are three basic categories of rationale for government regulation: efficiency (usually pertaining to correcting market failures), distribution, and stimulating or protecting social and cultural objectives (Skolnik, 1987, p. 60).

Government regulation can be interpreted as a "framework of rules within which other decision units can make decisions without the high transaction costs of maintaining private force for the purpose of protecting their belongings or of maintaining threats to enforce the carrying out of agreed upon contracts. As a framework, the government simply delineates the boundaries within which other units determine substantive choices, the government making its own forces available to defend the established boundaries" (Sowell, 1980, p. 145).

In this chapter I will focus on these frameworks used by government in the policy field of higher education (Van Vught, 1991). I will especially discuss the general orientations that appear to guide the sets of rules that together form the frameworks of government regulation.

When designing and implementing specific policies, governments are guided by general assumptions and points of view. For these assumptions and points of view I will use the term "policy models." "Policy models" are the sets of general postures, assumptions and guidelines that appear to be followed when governments formulate their frameworks of regulation. "Policy models" are what Dror has called "megapolicies: a kind of master policies, clearly distinct from detailed discrete policies" (Dror, 1971, p. 63).

In the following sections first two general policy models will be explored: the **model of rational planning and control**, and the **model of self-regulation.** These two models will then be specified in the policy context of higher education. Next, an overview will be presented of the policy instruments that can be used by governments with respect to public sector regulation. It will be argued that specific categories of policy instruments show a better fit with a specific policy model.

In the second part of this chapter the policy models and policy instruments will be evaluated from the perspective of their capacity to stimulate innovations in the field of higher education.

POLICY MODELS

Premfors (1992) has indicated that, when we accept the point of view that in policy analysis we should at least aim at a certain level of rationality, policy models like the "garbage can model" (March and Olsen, 1976) should not be considered to be part of policy analysis. Nevertheless, says Premfors, there is "a wealth of [what he calls] models of policy processes to choose from" (Premfors, 1992, p. 1908). He mentions models like "bounded rationality" (Simon, 1957), "mixed scanning" (Etzioni, 1968) and "the normative optimum model" (Dror, 1968). Other models in the literature are the "incremental model" (Braybrooke and Lindblom, 1963), the "systems model" (Jantsch, 1972), the "communicative model" (Van Gunsteren, 1976) and the "transactive model" (Friedmann, 1973) (see Maassen and Van Vught, 1992 for an overview).

I argue that when the basic assumptions of the various models that are presented in the literature are studied, only two clearly different models appear to remain. The other models that are found in the literature can all be seen as specific (and often quite interesting) variations or combinations of these two more or less fundamental Models.

The Policy Model of Rational Planning and Control

An extreme case of a governmental approach to public sector regulation is one in which the knowledge of the object of regulation is assumed to be firm, the control over the object of regulation is presumed to be complete, and the self-image of the regulating subject is holistic. I will name this conception the policy model of rational planning and control.

A fundamental assumption of this model is that it should be performed as the normative ideal of the rationalist perspective on decision-making suggests: by comprehensively evaluating all conceivable consequences of all conceivable alternatives.

The authors who can claim to have stated this strategy first in the literature are probably Meyerson and Banfield (Meyerson and Banfield, 1955). However, from their publications it also can be concluded that they want to see the model of rational decision-making as basically a normative ideal which is worthwhile to pursue but which cannot completely be realized in reality (Banfield, 1959; Meyerson, 1956):

> . . . no choice can ever be perfectly rational, for there are usually a great—perhaps an infinite—number of possible actions open to the actor and the consequences of any one of them would ramify ad infinitum. No decision-maker could have the knowledge (or the time!) to evaluate even a small fraction of the actions open to him. It is possible, however, to be more or less systematic in the canvass of alternatives and consequences, so that the conception is not an entirely useless one. For practical purposes, a rational decision is one in which alternatives and consequences are considered as fully as the decision-maker, given the time and other resources available to him, can afford to consider them. (Banfield, 1959, p. 364)

Lindblom especially has strongly criticized this model, variously called by him the rational-deductive or the synoptic ideal (Lindblom, 1959; Lindblom, 1965; Braybrooke and Lindblom, 1970). Lindblom argues against the rational decision-making ideal from the assertion that it cannot be followed in actual practice and that attempts to do so distract decision-makers from a more feasible strategy (called by him the strategy of "disjointed incrementalism"). He argues that the "synoptic ideal" is not adapted to man's limited intellectual capacities, nor to his inadequacy of information or the costliness of analysis.

> In actual fact, therefore, no one can practice the rational-comprehensive method for really complex problems, and every administrator faced with a sufficiently complex problem must find ways drastically to simplify. (Lindblom, 1959)

Perhaps the most crucial aspect of Lindblom's criticism is his conviction that, given the limited knowledge a (governmental) policy-maker can acquire, comprehensive control of an object of regulation should not be strived after. A complete or nearly complete control cannot avoid harming the object of regulation and will eventually result in imposing decisions and commanding their implementation. Rather, according to Lindblom, decisions should be taken by a large number of decision-making units, each of them free to pursue its own interests. It is this conviction that leads Lindblom to speak of "disjointed" incrementalism.

> Analysis and evaluation are disjointed in the sense that various aspects of public policy and even various aspects of any one problem or problem area are analyzed at various points, with no apparent co-ordination and without the articulation of parts that ideally characterizes subdivision of topic in synoptic problem solving. . . . Disjointedness has its advantages . . . chief among them the advantage of preserving a rich variety of impressions and insights that are liable to be "co-ordinated" out of sight by hasty and inappropriate demands for a common plan of attack. (Braybrooke and Lindblom, 1963, pp. 105, 106)

It may be concluded from Lindblom's criticism that the policy model of rational planning and control not only is based on the assumption of the rationalist perspective on decision making, but also implies the centralization of the decision-making process and a large amount of control both over the actual choice to be made and over the implementation of the chosen policy. The model of rational planning and control takes its point of departure in the ideal of rational decision-making, but confronted with the limitations of this ideal in actual practice, it takes refuge in confidence in centralization and control.

The model of rational planning and control is an approach to governmental regulation in which much confidence is put in the capabilities of governmental actors and agencies to acquire comprehensive and true knowledge and to take the best decisions. Also, it is an approach in which these governmental actors try to steer an object of regulation by using stringent rules and extensive control mechanisms. When government designs and implements operational policies using the general policy model of rational planning and control, it sees itself as an omniscient and omnipotent actor that thinks itself able to rightfully steer a part of society according to its own objectives.

The Policy Model of Self-Regulation

The policy model of self-regulation is basically the opposite of the model of rational planning and control. Instead of the assumption that the knowledge of the object of regulation can be firm, comes the recognition that such knowledge is highly uncertain. Instead of the wish to control the object of regulation as completely as possible, comes the conviction that such control should to a large extent be avoided. Instead of a holistic self-image of the regulating subject, comes the assertion that an atomistic self-image offers important advantages.

The policy model of self-regulation is not so much based on the ideal of rational decision-making. It rather incorporates the logic and the assumptions of the cybernetic perspective on decision-making (Ashby, 1956). It puts emphasis on the principles of monitoring feedback variables. It accepts the idea that a decision-maker should only pay attention to a small set of ''critical variables'' which he should try to keep within tolerable ranges. And perhaps most importantly, it underlines the assumption that the fragmentation of complex decision-making processes offers the benefits of a high level of robustness, a high level of flexibility, a high level of innovativeness, and a low level of information, transaction, and administration costs (Steinbrunner, 1974).

From the field of management sciences Beer has indicated that a choice for the cybernetic perspective on decision-making is a choice for the strategy of self-regulation.

> Every manager, whether he runs the family business or a small department in a firm, whether he runs the firm itself or a major department of government, whether he runs the country or an aspect of international affairs, faces an identical problem. He faces, that is, the need to maintain a viable system far more complicated than he personally can understand. And the beginning of wisdom for management at any level is the realization that viable systems are, in large measure, self-regulating and even self-organizing.(Beer, 1975, pp. 105, 106).

Beer makes it clear that the cybernetic perspective on decision-making implies the idea of self-regulation. A cybernetic decision-making unit is able to regulate itself. When the feedback loops are working and when a repertory of operations is available, a decision-making unit hardly needs regulation from outside. Moreover, a complex system with many interrelated decision-making units, is able to realize a high level of stability. Such a system has the capacity of ''homeostasis,'' i.e., the capacity to hold the critical variables at the level of the overall system within acceptable ranges. Confronted with such a system, the task for an external (governmental) regulator is only to monitor these critical variables making sure that they do not exceed the tolerable ranges, and to evaluate the criteria by which the critical variables and the tolerable ranges are chosen.

In the policy model of self-regulation, the role of an external regulating agency or actor is a role at another, higher level: ''. . . the role . . . is to remain above the homeostatic fray, and to consider what is happening in terms of a higher level understanding'' (Beer, 1975, p. 112). Beer explains this higher level role with the following illustration from the world of games.

> Suppose that as a higher manager you have the responsibility to ensure that team A wins in a game which is already being played between team A and team B, where the scoring is already even. You could dress yourself in the appropriate regalia and charge

> onto the field of play. The players would recognise you. Your own side might defer to your tactics . . . while the other side would do their level best to put you out of action. This is not the way to behave at all . . . the clever action would be to change the rules of the game so that your side must win it. (Beer, 1975, p. 112).

In the model of self-regulation emphasis is put on the self-regulatory capacities of decentralized decision-making units. The complex interrelations between these units are respected. The external regulating activities are limited to monitoring the performance of the overall system of the interrelated self-regulating decision-making units and to evaluating (and if judged necessary, changing) the rules which to a large extent define this performance.

Compared with the model of rational planning and control, the model of self-regulation is far more modest. It acknowledges the limitations of acquiring knowledge and exercising control over an object of regulation which, in itself, already consists of a complex set of mechanisms of decision-making. It tries rather to incorporate the benefits of this complex set of mechanisms by limiting itself to setting broad frameworks and by providing facilities for the behavior of decentralized units.

When government uses the policy model of self-regulation, it sees itself mainly as an arbiter. In this model government is the actor who watches the rules of a game played by relatively autonomous players and who changes these rules when the game is no longer able to lead to satisfactory results.

POLICY MODELS IN HIGHER EDUCATION

Looking at the characteristics of the various higher education systems in the world the two general policy models that have just been distinguished can clearly be recognized. Generally speaking, from the perspective of governmental policy-making with respect to higher education two models can be distinguished that are clearly related to the two general policy models presented before. I will call these policy models in higher education: the state control model and the state supervising model (Van Vught, 1988; Van Vught, 1992).

The State Control Model

The state control model is traditionally found in the higher education systems of the European continent. The so-called ''continental model''—to use Clark's label—(Clark, 1983a), is a combination of the authority of state bureaucracy and faculty guilds.

The higher education systems of the European continent traditionally have been ''relatively pure state systems'' (Van de Graaff and Furth, 1978). These systems are created by the state and almost completely financed by it. The state very often also is the overarching and highly powerful regulator of the system.

A clear example is the French higher education system which is characterized by a centralized bureaucratic control exercised by the national ministry of education. In such systems the state controls, at least formally, nearly all aspects of the dynamics of the higher education system. The national ministry of education regulates the access conditions, the curriculum, the degree requirements, the examination systems, the appointment of academic staff, etc. An important objective of this detailed government regulation is the standardization of national degrees, which are often awarded by the state rather than by the higher education institutions. In federal systems (like the Federal Republic of Germany and the United States) state control is usually exercised at the subnational level.

In the continental model the overwhelming power of the state is combined with a strong authority at the level of the senior chaired professors, who hold considerable power at the lower level of the system. As has become most visible in the nineteenth century German higher education system, the chair holders are able to exercise strong collegial control within the faculties and the institutions.

The result of the combination of authority of state bureaucracy and faculty guilds is a power structure which expresses the interests of two groups: state officials and senior professors (Clark, 1983a, p. 126). The level of institutional administration is rather weak and in effect often bypassed when systemwide decisions are taken (Glenny, 1979). The power distribution of the continental model is characterized by a strong top (the state), a weak middle level (the institutional administration), and a strong bottom (the senior chair holders) (Clark, 1983a, p. 127).

The continental higher education model offers the clearest example of the state control model. Especially when the state controls the appointments of the chair holders, it is obvious that the state exercises a major influence on the system. In these cases the state often uses the higher education system for its professional manpower needs. Both the manpower needs of the governmental bureaucracy itself and the assessed needs at the nation's labor market are expected to be fulfilled by the higher education system. The state then finds its legitimization for the detailed control of the higher education system in the self-proclaimed task to steer the nation's economy.

The State Supervising Model

The state supervising model has its roots both in the U.S. higher education system and in the traditional British higher education system. The "American and British models"—to use again Clark's labels (Clark, 1983a)—show far less governmental influence on higher education than the continental model. In the British and certainly in the American model the state plays only a minor role. Although things have changed rather drastically during the last decade in British higher education (see, for instance, Walford, 1991), the traditional British model can still serve as a conceptual tool to describe a limited state influence. The traditional British model of higher education is a combination of the authority of faculty guilds and a modest amount of influence of trustees and administrators (vice-chancellors) at the institutional level. In this traditional model, British universities are chartered corporations, responsible for their own management. Each individual university and college is allowed to decide upon its admission, its curricula, and the hiring of its faculty. In the traditional British model there is no formally organized system of national governmental control. And although during the development of British higher education the funding became largely a governmental task, the budget allocation remained (until the policy changes of the Thatcher government) in the hands of the senior professors (in the University Grants Committee).

During the last decade, things have changed dramatically in British higher education. The higher education budget has been severely cut, a businesslike management style has been introduced, an approach of quality monitoring by means of performance indicators has been developed and the University Grants Committee has been abolished. British government apparently wants to ''privatize'' higher education. A hierarchical businesslike organizational structure has been introduced and the influence of industry on higher education has been increased (Scott, 1988; Walford, 1991). It could be argued that the traditional British state supervising model has recently changed into a ''non-British'' state control model.

The U.S. higher education model shows a rather limited government regulation. The U.S. model is a combination of the authority of faculty guilds and institutional trusteeship and administration. But compared with the traditional British model, the influence of the institutional trustees (or regents) and administrators is stronger (Van de Graaff et al., ch. 7). Like the British universities, the American institutions are established as chartered corporations. But the boards of trustees and the institutional administrators (presidents) play a more important role than their British colleagues. The trustees generally appoint the university president who to a large extent has authority over the strategic and financial policies of the institution. In the U.S. the professors do not have the power of the chair holders, but the authority of the faculty is nevertheless substantial (especially in the academically stronger institutions).

The influence of government is rather limited. There is hardly any power at the federal level. The authority at the state level has been growing during the last few decades (Newman, 1987), but this increase of state authority is moving toward ''adaptations of market control mechnisms'' like outcomes assessment legislation and performance funding (Dill, 1992, pp. 53, 54). Compared with the level of state influence in the continental model, the U.S. state authority in higher education is still rather weak. The U.S. state level regulation largely concerns the mechanisms for the organization of quality assessment and the regulation of the right to award degrees (Berdahl and Millett, 1991).

The traditional British and the U.S. models offer examples of what has been called here the state supervising model. In this policy model the influence exercised by the state is weak. The state sees its task of supervising the higher education system only in terms of assuring academic quality and maintaining a certain level of accountability. Government does not intrude into the higher education system by means of detailed regulation and strict control. Rather, it respects the autonomy of the higher education institutions and it stimulates the self-regulating capabilities of these institutions. The state sees itself as a supervisor, steering from a distance and using broad terms of regulation.

It may be clear from the presentation of the two models of state influence on higher education (the state control and the state supervising model), that each of these two models is related to one of the two general policy models of public sector regulation that were introduced before. The state control model is largely based on the general governmental strategy of rational planning and control. The state supervising model is a specialization of the policy model of self-regulation. Further on I will explore the effects of each of the two models on the innovative behavior of higher education institutions. But first, let us see what categories of policy instruments governments can use in each of the two general policy models (the model of rational planning and control and the model of self-regulation).

POLICY INSTRUMENTS

In principle every government has a number of instruments at its disposal to perform the tasks that have been assigned to it. If government wants to "produce" certain outcomes, it employs certain tools. Without such tools governmental policies would be no more than abstract ideals or fantasies.

In the policy sciences literature the concept of policy instruments recently has attracted renewed interest. Important theoretical concepts have already been developed in the classical publications of Dahl and Lindblom (1953) and Etzioni (1968). Dahl and Lindblom distinguished four sociopolitical processes which, in their opinion, should be used by "any society intelligently bent on using its resources efficiently" (Dahl and Lindblom, 1976, p. 172). These four processes are: the price system (control of and by leaders), hierarchy (control by leaders), polyarchy (control of leaders), and bargaining (control among leaders). Etzioni makes a distinction between three types of social relationships: coercive, utilitarian, and normative relationships. According to Etzioni, in any concrete case there is a mixture of these three forms, leading to different kinds of social interaction (Etzioni, 1978).

Mitnick (1980) takes Dahl and Lindblom's analysis as a starting point to develop a categorization of the instruments of government. A crucial distinction in his work is the one between "regulation by directives" and "regulation by

Regulation by directives	public enterprise (extreme case) common law administrative rules or standards
Regulation by incentives	tax incentives effluent/user charges subsidies promotion campaign laissez faire (extreme case)

FIGURE 1. Mitnick's categorization of governmental instruments. (Source: Mitnick, 1980, p. 346.)

incentives.'' Regulation by directives is defined as ''the interferences that occur by circumscribing or directing choice in some area—i.e., making rules for behavior that may be transmitted as instruction.'' Regulation by incentives is described as ''the interferences that occur by changing the perception of the nature of the alternatives for action subject to choice—i.e., changing the relative attractiveness of alternatives'' (Mitnick, 1980, pp. 342, 343). Mitnick develops an overview of ''some common regulatory means'' which he classifies in his two broad instrumental categories. Figure 1 contains this overview.

It seems that Mitnick's presentation of governmental instruments is based on the criterion of the level of restriction by government of the behavior of societal actors. Directives are more restrictive than incentives, and strong incentives are more restrictive than weak incentives.

Several other authors have pointed at the importance of policy instruments for policy analysis. Several studies of policy implementation emphasize the need to further analyze the effects of the various categories of instruments (Ingram and Mann, 1980; Mazmanian and Sabatier, 1981). Bardach (1979) points to the importance of the behaviorial characteristics of policy instruments. Salamon (1981) asks for a reorientation in the implementation literature toward the comparative effectiveness of policy instruments.

The literature also shows various alternative categorizations of policy instruments. Bardach (1979) proposes to distinguish four categories of instruments: prescription, enabling, positive incentives, and deterrence. Elmore (1987) and McDonnell (1988) indicate that they favor a categorization in: mandates (providing constraining rules), inducements (providing financial resources to encourage certain activities), capacity (providing financial resources to enable actors to take certain actions), and instruments of system change (that alter the arrangement of agencies in a policy network). Schneider and Ingram (1990) distinguish authority tools, incentive tools, capacity tools, symbolic and hortatory tools, and learning tools. "Authority tools are simply statements backed by the legitimate authority of government that grant permissions, prohibit, or require action under designed circumstances." Incentive tools are instruments "that rely on tangible payoffs, positive or negative, to induce compliance or encourage utilization. . . . Capacity tools provide information, training, education, and resources to enable individuals, groups, or agencies to make decisions or carry out activities." Symbolic and hortatory tools

> seek to change perceptions about policy-preferred behavior through appeals to intangible values . . . or through the use of images, symbols and labels. . . . Policy tools that promote learning provide for wide discretion by lower-level agents or even the target groups themselves, who are then able to experiment with different policy approaches. Agents are required to draw lessons from experience through formal evaluations, hearings and institutional arrangements that promote interaction among targets and agencies. (Schneider and Ingram, 1990, pp. 514–522)

For an overview of policy instruments I will follow Hood's *The Tools of Government* (1983). Hood distinguishes four categories of governmental instruments. The categories vary depending on the "basic resources" used by government in trying to reach the objectives set. For each category of "basic resources" a specific set of instruments can be indicated. For the sake of understanding the broad scale of policy instruments, a slightly modified interpretation of Hood's categorization is presented here (see Figure 2).

The first category of instruments concerns the provision of *information*. From its specific position in society, government has the advantage of being "a store of information." Compared with other institutions, governmental agencies often have extra possibilities to develop rather broad, panoramic overviews of societal conditions. Hence, government can use the information it has at its disposal to try to reach its policy objectives.

There are various ways government can "send out" information. It can provide informed responses tailored to questions from outside; it can direct standard messages without being asked to specific groups ("targeting information"); it can send out general messages to the broad public. What type of information outlet government uses depends on various factors such as the size of the informed population, the degree of attention manifested by the informed population, and, of course, the content of the message. A crucial factor is the political and legal framework government operates in.

In general, it can be said that the providing and propagating of information offers government a set of instruments with rather low or even nonexisting

Instruments of information	responses messages
Instruments of treasure	contracts bounties transfers bearer-directed payments
Instruments of authority	certificates approvals conditionals enablements constraints
Instruments of action	operational activities

FIGURE 2. An overview of the instruments of government. (Modified from Hood, 1983.)

"authority costs." When information-oriented instruments can be used, government does not have to lay its authority on the line. It can send out the information judged to be necessary or significant, and it can wait and see if the information is accepted.

A second category of policy instruments concerns "the power of *treasure*." Treasure is what enables government to buy favors, to court popularity, to hire mercenaries, etc.; the power of treasure is the power of signing checks. Hood therefore speaks of the instruments of "checkbook government."

Government can use its treasure in two main ways. It can "exchange" it for some good or service. Or it can "give it away"; that is, it can transfer payments without requiring any "quid pro quo."

According to Hood, the two main instruments of the exchange of treasure are "contracts" and "bounties." Contracts are governmental payments made to specific individuals or organizations, under the condition that the recipient supplies a specified product or service. Contracts are payments "with strings attached." A governmental contract payment is only made when the recipient of such a payment accepts the conditions which government requires. Like contracts, bounties also are payments made in exchange for some quid pro quo, but in the case of bounties the individual or organization which is to provide that ''quid pro quo'' is not specified. A bounty is awarded to anyone who produces the product or service asked for. Bounties are assumed to be especially useful to encourage or discourage specific types of societal behavior.

The two main governmental instruments of the other method of using the power of treasure (the ''give it away'' option) are ''transfers'' and ''bearer-directed payments.'' Transfers are exchanges of treasure without a requirement of a quid pro quo; transfers are ''gifts,'' made to specific individuals or organizations for specific purposes or reasons. Bearer-directed payments also do not involve a clear quid pro quo. But, unlike transfers, bearer-directed payments are made to all those who, by some token, are eligible for them.

The instruments of ''checkbook government'' can be used directly by government or indirectly through intermediaries. Intermediary organizations are an often used alternative for direct governmental allocation of resources, especially when government wants to avoid getting too closely involved in highly specialized budget decisions.

In general, the instruments of ''checkbook government'' are costly, in the sense that financial resources can only be spent once and the renewal of treasure implies the use of the mechanism of taxation. On the other hand, as has been argued many times before, treasure is an elegant category of instruments, often capable of achieving the kind of societal behavior government sets out to create.

The third category of policy instruments is formed by the instruments of *authority*. The instruments of authority are intended to command and to forbid, to commend and to permit.

Instruments of authority vary depending on the degree of restriction they seek to introduce into the behavior of the targeted subjects. Least constraining in this sense are ''certificates'' and ''approvals.'' Certificates are authoritative declarations by government about the properties of a specific individual or object. Approvals are authoritative declarations in a general sense; approvals apply to the world at large or to whomever it may concern. Both certificates and approvals are instruments requiring no compulsive action at all from government.

A subcategory requiring more (but still not extreme) compulsive action is formed by the instruments called ''conditionals'' and ''enablements.'' Conditionals are the promises by government to act in a certain way when certain conditions arise. A well-known example is the governmental guarantee that is provided as a kind of safety net for certain circumstances. Enablements are the tokens that permit certain activities. Modern governments use a large variety of enablements. Licenses, quotas, warrants, coupons, vouchers, and permits are all types of enablements. They all allow (but do not compel) the undertaking of certain activities.

The instrument of authority that asks for compulsive action is the instrument called ''constraint.'' Constraints, in contrast to certificates, approvals, conditionals, and enablements, demand or prohibit certain activities. Constraints can be positive (commanding) and negative (forbidding). In both cases, they imply a compulsory restriction by government of societal behavior.

Generally speaking, the instruments of authority depend on the willingness of the public to accept them. A low level of respect for and acceptance of government can make these instruments rather ineffective. As history has shown, governments sometimes in these cases take refuge in the authority instruments with the highest level of constraint. On the other hand, when government is widely respected and accepted, the low-constraint instruments of authority may be very effective in producing the outcomes government thinks to be relevant.

Hood's fourth and final category of policy instruments is the category of (direct) *action*. Within this category fall all kinds of operational activities by government that directly influence the citizens, their property, or their environment. Government can use "its own" individuals, buildings, equipments, and stocks of lands to directly produce certain outcomes or to perform certain tasks. It can for instance act as a national banker; it usually operates a system of involuntary detention; it sometimes holds a monopoly on the production of a certain good; and it of course often takes care of defending the country, controlling crime, treating sewage, controlling traffic, lighting streets, controlling floods, etc.

The instruments of action to a large extent are related to the traditional monopoly on the use of violence and the enforcement of law. As such these instruments tend to be restricted to some specific areas of governmental control. Next to these areas the instruments of action are often used for providing "collective goods" (like defense and dikes).

In general, it should be noted that the governmental instruments of direct action are rather expensive. They should be reserved for the governmental monopoly on the use of violence, for emergencies, and for activities that might otherwise not be performed.

It may be concluded that, as is the case in several other categorizations, Hood's presentation of policy instruments is to a large extent based on the criterion of the level of restraint the instruments try to produce with respect to the behavior of societal actors.

The instruments of information are hardly at all restrictive. They are used without the explicit goal to directly limit the range of behaviorial options of other actors. The objective of the use of information instruments is to try to influence the behavior of others by providing them with significant information.

The instruments of treasure are more restrictive. In particular when government acts as the most important funding agent of the activities of other actors, these actors may be strongly influenced to adapt their behavior to the ideas and wishes of government. "Checkbook government" in this sense can be very restrictive, although the restraining potential is often used in an indirect way. The power of treasure offers governmental agencies the opportunity to design and implement financial incentives and disincentives, strongly urging actors to behave according to government's wishes.

The instruments of authority range from mildly restrictive to completely restraining. The "certificates" and "approvals" are only mildly restrictive. These specific instruments provide governmental agencies with the ability to approve or disapprove. As such they can limit the behaviorial options of other actors. Especially when the approval of government is sought after (e.g., because such an approval offers the right to acquire financial resources), these mildly restrictive instruments may become very effective in influencing the behavior of nongovernmental actors. The instruments called "conditionals" and "enablements" have a higher level of restrictive potential. They allow or do not allow actors to behave in a certain way, usually by providing or denying financial resources or licenses. The instruments called "constraints" are extremely restrictive. These are the instruments a government can use to command and forbid and by using them government can compel other actors to behave completely according to its wishes.

The instruments of direct (governmental) action are also, generally speaking, rather restrictive. Because these instruments are based either on the governmental monopoly on the use of violence, or on the political decision that government should provide a certain collective good, these instruments tend to strongly influence the other actors' behavior.

However, Hood's presentation seems to imply more than one criterion for the categorization of policy instruments (the level of restraint). A second criterion concerns the distinction between the particular and the general use of instruments. "Particular applications are those that are directed at specific and named individuals, organizations or items. . . . General applications are those that are beamed at the world at large and thus apply to whomever it may concern" (Hood, 1983, p. 17). Other criteria that seem to be important in Hood's categorization are the question whether societal actors should or should not themselves try to obtain the benefits of a certain instrument, the question whether societal actors have or have not to provide a quid pro quo and the level of permanence of an instrument (for instance the instruments of authority are more durable than the instruments of treasure).

The presentation of the instruments of government has made it clear that these instruments vary according to the level of restraint they try to produce with respect to the behavior of societal actors. This variation in the level of restraint allows us to relate some specific categories of instruments to the two general policy models that were distinguished before. Generally speaking, it may be expected that the instruments that are highly restrictive are more easily applied in the policy model of rational planning and control, while the less restrictive instruments are more appropriate in the policy model of self-regulation.

In the model of rational planning and control a government sees it as its task and its capability to influence other societal actors according to its own objectives. In this model government judges it to be its prerogative to restrain the behaviorial options of other actors in order to reach the goals that are thought to be relevant. In such an approach, highly restrictive instruments will be assumed to be the most effective. The highly restraining instruments of authority (''constraints') or the indirect but nevertheless often rather restrictive instruments of treasure will be applied to give concrete form to the confidence in centralized control.

In the policy model of self-regulation government puts its confidence in the self-regulatory capacities of decentralized decision-making units. Governmental activities are limited to gathering information so as to be able to watch the overall system of activities and to providing and, if judged necessary, changing the broad frameworks that enable and stimulate such a system. The instruments that may be expected to be relevant in this policy model are the instruments of information (responses and messages) and the mildly restrictive instruments of authority (certificates and approvals). A special set of instruments may be formed by the indirect instruments of treasure that may be applied at the systems level to install mechanisms that may influence actors to change their behaviorial patterns without reducing their self-regulatory capacities.

It should be stressed that policy instruments are seldom used in isolation. The categories of instruments that have been presented above can only be distinguished analytically. In reality governmental instruments are used in combination and through all kinds of linkages. An example is the combination of ''enablement'' (a specific instrument of authority) and ''bearer-directed payment'' (a specific instrument of treasure): the license for a certain activity may immediately make a person eligible for a certain transfer of payment without a quid pro quo.

Nevertheless, every specific combination of instruments has its own characteristics, which will influence its effectiveness and efficiency. Also, every specific combination of instruments may lead to different results, depending on the context in which it is used.

One of the most crucial questions in present-day public sector regulation is how governmental policy models and instruments can be matched to the circumstances in which they are applied. In the second part of this chapter I will address this question by exploring the appropriateness of the policy models and policy instruments that were presented before for producing innovations in higher education systems and institutions.

THE STUDY OF INNOVATION

Innovation is a concept that has attracted much attention in the social sciences. In the 1950s and the 1960s there was a strong belief that the construction of a comprehensive theory and methodology of innovation would only be a matter of time. There existed a certain optimism and enthusiasm about the possibilities and the usefulness of such a theory and methodology. The general social theory of innovation would soon enable planners and policy-makers to design and implement successful changes and to create a happier society.

Since then doubt and disappointment have grown. The comprehensive theory and methodology did not arise. The growing number of empirical studies offered a picture of extreme variance among its findings. The conceptual frameworks remained vague. As Downs and Mohr concluded in 1976:

> . . . the record in the field of innovation is beyond interpretation. In spite of the large amount of energy expended, the results have not been cumulative. This is not to say that the body of existing research is useless. . . . Perhaps the most straightforward way of accounting for this empirical instability and theoretical confusion is to reject the notion that a unitary theory of innovation exists. (Downs and Mohr, 1976, p. 701).

The literature on innovation is very extensive and covers several disciplines. In the field of organizational behavior, research is underway to try to identify some important variables which are related to the tendency in organizations to adopt innovations. Variables like ''degree of decentralization,'' ''degree of formalization,'' ''degree of specialization,'' and ''complexity'' are frequently mentioned (Hage and Aiken, 1967). In the field of social psychology several variables are suggested, which are assumed to be related to the development of an innovation process. These variables include the level of motivation of the innovator, the degree of compatibility with existing values and practices, and the level of organizational support (Davis et al., 1982).

In the literature on higher education the concept of innovation has also received some attention. Several rather creative and elegant analyses have been performed from which some interesting insights about innovation processes and outcomes in higher education systems can be deduced (e.g., Levine, 1980; Cerych and Sabatier, 1986). I will use these studies to formulate some insights about the relationships between policy models and policy instruments used by governments, and the innovations that take place in higher education systems and institutions.

The conceptual approaches to innovations and innovation processes are numerous. Besides, it is not always clear how these various conceptual approaches can be related in order to try to gain some increasing understanding of the state of the art in the literature on innovation.

Dill and Friedman (1979) have tried to identify the major theoretical frameworks in the conceptual approaches to innovations and innovation processes, with a special focus on the study of higher education. Reviewing these frameworks, they come to the conclusion that the theoretical and methodological problems related to the study of innovation processes are still quite large. The theoretical frameworks appear to be both too complex and insufficiently specified to enable researchers to undertake clear analyzes. Measuring the many variables mentioned in the frameworks and paying attention to their validity and reliability is an enormous task. Dill and Friedman suggest focusing attention on the developments of less comprehensive theories.

In the remainder of this chapter I will follow this suggestion. I will limit myself to an exploration of the relationships between governmental policy models and policy instruments directed towards creating and stimulating innovations in higher education systems and institutions, and the processes and outcomes of these innovations. To be able to do this, I will first discuss some of the fundamental characteristics of higher education Institutions.

Fundamental Characteristics of Higher Education Institutions

Kerr has pointed out that, looked at from without and comparatively, higher education institutions (especially research universities) have hardly changed at all during the past centuries:

> About eighty-five institutions in the Western world established by 1520 still exist in recognizable forms, with similar functions and with unbroken histories, including the Catholic church, the Parliaments of the Isle of Man, of Iceland and of Great Britain, several Swiss cantons, and seventy universities. Kings that rule, feudal lords with vassals, and guilds with monopolies are all gone. These seventy universities, however, are still in the same locations with some of the same buildings, with professors and students doing much the same things, and with governance carried on in much the same ways. (Kerr, 1982, p. 152).

This striking permanence of higher education institutions has to do with some of the most fundamental characteristics of higher education. As in the first medieval universities of Bologna, Paris, and Oxford, higher education can still be seen as a social system in which the handling of knowledge is the most crucial activity. In higher education systems knowledge is discovered, conserved, refined, transmitted, and applied (Clark, 1983a, p. 12). If there is anything fundamental to systems of higher education, it is this handling of knowledge.

The primacy of the handling of knowledge is related to some other fundamental characteristics, which can be found within higher education institutions.

A primary characteristic concerns the authority of the academic professional experts. In higher education institutions many decisions can be made only by these professional experts. These are the decisions regarding the detailed knowledge-oriented academic activities of research and teaching. In all those specialized knowledge fields, which are held together in a higher education institution, decisions on what and how to investigate, and on what and how to teach come, to a large extent, under the direct supervision of the academic experts. Only they are able to oversee their specialized fields. Only they are able to stimulate the enthusiasm of students for specific objects of study. This is why professional autonomy is so important in higher education institutions and this is why these institutions are called ''professional bureaucracies'' (Mintzberg, 1979).

Clark makes it clear how the professionals in higher education organization work with and upon knowledge:

> The factory floor in higher education is cluttered with bundles of knowledge that are attended by professionals. The professionals push and pull on their respective bundles. If they are doing research, they are trying to increase the size of the bundle and even to reconstitute it. If engaged in scholarship other than research, they are conserving, criticising, and reworking it. If teaching, they are trying to pass some of it on to the flow-through clientele we call students, encouraging them to think about its nature, how it may be used, and perhaps take up a career devoted to it. If engaged outside the ''plant'' as advisors, consultants, or lecturers, academics further disseminate knowledge to try to draw out its implications for practical use. (Clark, 1983b, p. 20)

Of course, not all decisions in higher education institutions are taken by professionals. There is a category of purely ''administrative'' decisions (for example, regarding financial administration and support services) which to a large extent is beyond the professional influence. There is also a category of decisions that are mainly taken by ''clients'' (students, research contractors). And there is an important category of decisions mainly taken by ''outsiders'' (government, funding agencies, evaluating committees). Nevertheless, the influence of the professional experts on the decision-making processes in higher education institutions is extensive. In many decisions taken at these institutions professionals play an important role.

A second important characteristic is the organizational principle that in higher education institutions the knowledge areas form the basic foci of attention. The knowledge areas are the ''building blocks'' of a higher education organization and without some institutionalization of these knowledge areas a higher education organization cannot exist. This principle leads to the typical organizational structure of higher education institutions. Fragmentation is abundant in these organizations. Throughout the organization specialized cells exist that are only loosely coupled. Higher education institutions are ''loosely coupled systems'' (Weick, 1976). The crucial knowledge-oriented activities take place within the rather autonomous cells. Specialists in specific knowledge fields group together to teach and undertake research. To a large extent insulated from the rest of the organization, these specialists use their autonomy and expertise to perform the basic activities of the higher education institution.

> . . . specialized professionals have little need to relate to one another within the local shop. . . . They can produce on their own. . . . Producing separately for the most part, the many groups become an extreme case of loosely-linked production. The university

> is a gathering place for professionalised crafts, evermore a confederation, a conglomerate, of knowledge-bearing groups that require little operational linkage. (Clark, 1983b, p. 21)

According to Clark it is this organizational fragmentation that explains the miraculous adaptability of higher education institutions. This adaptability consists of "the capacity to add and subtract fields of knowledge and related units without disturbing all the others." Clark argues that "it is the peculiar internal constitution of universities that allow them . . . to bend and adapt themselves to a whole variety of circumstances and environments, thus producing diversity among universities . . . and, at the same time, to maintain an appearance of similarity that allows us to recognise them in all the guises which they take." (Clark, 1983a, pp. 186, 187)

A further fundamental characteristic of higher education institutions is the extreme diffusion of the decision-making power. In an organization where the production processes are knowledge-intensive, there is a need to decentralize. When besides that, such an organization is also heavily fragmented, the decision-making power will be spread over a large number of units and actors. A higher education institution therefore becomes a federal system; "semi-autonomous departments and schools, chairs and faculties act like small sovereign states as they pursue distinctive self-interests and stand over against the authority of the whole." (Clark, 1983a, pp. 266, 267)

A final characteristic, which is typical for higher education institutions based on the continental or the traditional British model, is the way authority is distributed within these institutions. Traditionally in these models, this authority has been (and in many occasions still is) located at the lower levels of the organization; that is, with the academic professionals (see before). At the level of the institutional administration authority is rather weak. Institutional administrators only have a very limited capacity to steer "their" organization.

Reviewing the fundamental characteristics of higher education institutions just mentioned, it may be concluded that the context of higher education confronts government with some specific problems when it wants to develop and implement a policy directed toward influencing higher education institutions. The extreme professional autonomy within these institutions and the rather limited administrative authority, as well as the organizational fragmentation and the diffusion of the decision-making power, make it very difficult to completely control these institutions from an external position. Higher education institutions appear to be very complex associations of largely autonomous cells. Besides, in higher education institutions the traditional guild culture, rooted in the Middle Ages, is still very much alive. Higher education institutions cherish the traditional norms and values of the "republic of science" (Polanyi, 1962), which enable them to perform their highly professional tasks.

The fundamental characteristics of higher education institutions suggest that these institutions can be controlled from outside only when the organizational variety is greatly reduced and when the professional autonomy is largely restrained. However, it should be realized that when such an external control is imposed, the professional tasks these institutions perform may be severely damaged. Confronted with detailed regulation and with an extreme restriction of their behavior, the scientists and teachers within the higher education institutions may feel the disillusionment of not being able to explore the paths their professional consciousness stimulates them to go. They may become uninterested in new developments, get bored by the routine activities they have to perform, and lose their interest in innovations.

Innovations in Higher Education

Having explored the processes of innovation in general and more specifically in the context of higher education, I will now try to develop some theoretical insights about the relationships between governmental policy models and policy instruments (directed towards the creation of innovations) on the one hand, and innovation processes in higher education systems and institutions on the other hand.

To present the theoretical insights I will classify the rather extensive literature on innovation processes in two broad categories. These categories can be described as "the organizational variables assumed to be related to success or failure of innovations" and "the characteristics of successful innovations." I will discuss the present state of the art in the higher education literature regarding both these categories.

Organizational Variables Related to Success of Innovations

In their impressive research overview of the principal organizational variables that have appeared to influence the success or failure of innovation processes in organizations, Hage and Aiken (1970) offer seven factors that are related to the rate of change in an organization. These factors can be described as follows:

- the greater the formalization (i.e., the greater the degree of codification of jobs, the greater the number of rules specifying what is to be done, and the more strictly these rules are enforced), the lower the rate of organizational change;
- the higher the centralization (i.e., the smaller the proportion of jobs and occupations that participate in decision-making and the fewer the decision-making areas in which they are involved), the lower the rate of organizational change;
- the greater the stratification (i.e., the greater the disparity in rewards such as salaries and prestige between the top and bottom ranks of an organization), the lower the rate of organizational change;

- the greater the complexity (i.e., the greater the number of occupations/specialties of an organization and the greater the degree of professionalism of each), the greater the rate of organizational change;
- the higher the volume of production (i.e., emphasis on quantity versus quality in organizational outputs), the lower the rate of organizational change;
- the greater the emphasis on efficiency (i.e., concern with cost or resource reduction), the lower the rate of organizational change;
- the higher the job satisfaction, the greater the rate of organizational change.

Hage and Aiken's factors are discussed by Levine (1980) in the context of innovations in higher education. Levine suggests that higher education organizations are low in formalization, low in centralization, low in stratification, high in complexity, high in the emphasis on quality of outputs, low on efficiency, and high on job satisfaction. The author therefore comes to the conclusion that ''institutions of higher education might be classified as low in innovation resistance relative to organizations in general.'' (Levine, 1980, p. 173)

The discussion of the fundamental characteristics of higher education institutions (see before) seems on the one hand to lead to the same conclusion. The high autonomy of the professionals within these organizations, the organizational fragmentation, the diffusion of the decision-making power, and the limited administrative authority indicate that higher education organizations are *not* very formalized, centralized, stratified and directed towards efficiency, but *are* very complex and by their specific nature offer possibilities for a strong emphasis on quality of production and a high level of job satisfaction.

However, as has been indicated by Kerr and many others, it should also be remembered that higher education institutions by nature are conservative and that in these organizations innovations are not likely to occur. According to Hefferlin (1969), for instance, innovations will occur in higher education institutions only when the level of instability in these institutions is high, i.e., when conditions arise like changing faculties because of expansion or turnover, low rates of tenure, rotating department chairpersons, etc.

It seems that we are confronted with two contradicting theoretical observations. Let us look at this subject from another perspective.

Clark (1983a) has argued that change is far more crucial in higher education institutions than conventional wisdom would suggest.

> Despite the belief of many observers that academic systems change significantly only when pressured by external forces, such systems increasingly exhibit innovation and adaptation among their bottom lines. Invention and diffusion are institutionalized in the work of the departments and counterpart units that embody the disciplines and professions. . . . Such change is widely overlooked. . . . It occurs in segments of the

> operating level. . . . In a bottom-heavy knowledge institution, grassroots innovation is a crucial form of change. (Clark, 1983a, pp. 234, 235)

Clark points once more at the characteristics of higher education institutions. Innovations take place through the professional activities in the various semi-autonomous units in the organization.

Kerr (1982) seems to agree with this point of view. According to him a distinction should be made between a perspective from within and a perspective from without. "Looked at from within, universities have changed enormously in the emphases on their several functions and in their guiding spirits, but looked at from without and comparatively, they are among the least changed of institutions" (Kerr, 1982, pp. 152, 153).

Bok (1986) makes clear how the two theoretical observations, which seem to be contradictory, can be combined. He underlines Levine's conclusion that, because of their fundamental characteristics, higher education institutions in principle are low in innovation resistance. However, he also points out that these very factors make it difficult to keep innovations alive.

> Universities are large, decentralized, informal organizations with little hierarchical authority over teaching and research. These characteristics favor innovation by making it easy for any of a large number of faculty members to experiment in search of better ways of educating students. Unfortunately, the very factors that aid experimentation make it harder for successful initiatives to spread throughout the institution or from one institution to another. (Bok, 1986, p. 176)

Innovations are created easily within higher education organizations and (as Clark indicates) they may even spread among their bottom levels. But this diffusion of innovations only takes place by virtue of the professional belief that certain innovations are worthwhile. Faculty members will only adopt innovations when they judge them to be worthwhile for their own activities. As Bok observes, ". . . the most promising innovations can languish unless some effective force causes them to be emulated widely" (Bok, 1986, p. 176). And the most effective force is probably the conviction of professional colleagues that an innovation is an effective solution to a common problem.

This point of view leads to an important conclusion: innovations in higher education institutions may arise easily and often, but their diffusion will be difficult and will mainly take place through communication between colleagues.

Clark points at another aspect of the processes of change within higher education institutions. He indicates that innovations in higher education institutions are mainly incremental adjustments, building up to larger flows of change. Major, sudden and comprehensive changes are rare in higher education institutions. Exactly because of the fragmentation of tasks and the diffusion of power such changes are extremely difficult to effect.

It should be realized that the ideology of the academic profession incorporates a basic resistance to comprehensive changes, especially when these are launched "from above." The organizational fragmentation and the diffusion of the decision-making power demand that a relatively large number of people and groups with a wide variation in values and opinions tend to discuss a launched comprehensive reform, the result of which will often be that the reform strands in debates and political fights. Becher and Kogan (1980) argue that, because of the fundamental characteristics of higher education systems, innovation processes are localized and specific.

> . . . we are not dealing with a hierarchical system, where change can be decreed from above, but rather with a negotiative one, in which individuals, basic units and institutions each regard themselves as having the right to decide what is best for them. It follows that any innovative proposal has to be finally sanctioned by those who are in a position to put it into effect. (Becher and Kogan, 1980, p. 121)

This argument has brought many authors to the conclusion that, generally speaking, government-initiated reforms in higher education systems must fail. Referring to the study of Cerych and Sabatier (1986) (see below), Kerr (1987), for instance, comes to the conclusion that "intentional changes" have sometimes perhaps been partially successful, but most often have been a failure. Curricular reforms and changes of governance, generally speaking cannot be called a success (Kerr, 1987, p. 185).

A possible explanation for this observation can again be found in the fundamental characteristics of higher education institutions. Kerr (1982) stresses that most decisions concerning the dynamics of a higher education system are taken outside the formal system of governance.

> Most decisions about teaching, about curriculum, about research topics and methods, about amount and form of public service are made by individual faculty members. Most decisions made about majors selected, courses taken and time spent on study are made by individual students. (Kerr, 1982, p. 178)

Besides, Kerr indicates, when intense competition exists among higher education institutions (as in the U.S.), specific arrangements of governance have only minor implications.

Also, Bok points out that educational reforms in higher education institutions are seldom the result of external influences (including governmental policies). According to him, external pressures can only be successful when they link up with initiatives or opinions inside a higher education institution.

> . . . no external influence offers a reliable way of initiating constructive change or eliciting new ideas to improve the quality of education. The vital task ultimately rests within the university itself. (Bok, 1986, p. 183)

Becher and Kogan (1980) have presented an elegant analysis of innovation processes in higher education systems by differentiating between four levels of these systems: the system as a whole, the institution, the basic unit (within the institution), and the individual. According to these authors innovative attempts often fail because they are unable to accommodate to existing structural constraints.

> Academic structures and regulations for the most part evolve to protect the legitimate interests of researchers and teachers. They help to define, and also defend, the main areas of professional concern within an institution. But once established, they can prove surprisingly intractable. Even when an innovative idea is generally accepted on intellectual grounds, it may face severe difficulty if it appears to conflict with conventional practice, or to cut across some existing organizational arrangement. (Becher and Kogan, 1980, pp. 146, 147)

Becher and Kogan therefore also put a heavy emphasis on the specific organizational characteristics of higher education institutions as important barriers to innovation. They argue that the often mentioned conservatism of higher education institutions ''mainly stems from contextual, rather than from personal factors'' (Becher and Kogan, 1980, p. 147).

Others have tried to take up the challenge of the ''policy failure theme'' in higher education. Referring to his analysis of the Swedish higher education policy which led to the reforms of 1975–1977, Lane (1985) has argued that policy-driven changes in a higher education system are possible. But, like the authors just mentioned, he also points out that, to be able to be successful, reform policies should pay attention to the basic characteristics of higher education institutions.

> Indeed organizational transformation of higher education work and higher education institutions is feasible, as long as basic features of the differentiation of work and the structure of authority inherent in the conduct of higher education activities are not threatened. Whereas public policy may effect institution-building and redefinition, it cannot do away with the bottom-dominated nature of the organization of higher education life. (Lane, 1984, p. 107)

Premfors (1984) disputes Lane's ''optimism,'' but he does not conclude that the Swedish higher education reform policy was a complete failure.

> . . . Swedish higher education policy is a mixed bag of success and failure when judged in terms of the initial intentions of central policy-makers. . . . To an important extent . . . these outcomes have been predicated on basic features of higher education organization in Sweden. (Premfors, 1984, pp. 47, 48)

The same kind of conclusion (in a broader perspective) is drawn by Cerych and Sabatier (1986), who studied a number of policy-driven reforms in higher education systems in Europe. Cerych and Sabatier examined the levels of success and failure of nine rather comprehensive reforms which were all largely initiated and developed by government and implemented in a higher education system through the interaction between governmental organizations and higher education institutions. In their comparative analysis Cerych and Sabatier present a general picture from which it can be concluded that both successes and failures can be distinguished.

This differentiated picture appears to underline Premfors' conclusion about the Swedish higher education reforms. Apparently reforms initiated and developed by government can be judged as "mixed bags of success and failure." An important question of course concerns the factors that might influence the levels of success and failure of these reforms.

Characteristics of Successful Innovations

In a study that has become widely known in the field, Rogers and Shoemaker (1971) have analyzed more than 1500 studies regarding the characteristics that determine an innovation's success or failure. The authors present five critical characteristics:

- the compatibility of a new idea (i.e., the degree to which an innovation is perceived as consistent with the existing values, past experience and needs of the receiver) is positively related to its rate of adoption;
- the relative advantage of a new idea (i.e., the degree to which an innovation is perceived as being better than the idea it supersedes) is positively related to its rate of adoption;
- the complexity of an innovation (i.e., the degree to which an innovation is perceived as relatively difficult to understand and use) is *not* related to its rate of adoption;
- the triability of an innovation (i.e., the degree to which an innovation may be experimented with on a limited basis) is positively related to its rate of adoption;
- the observability of an innovation (i.e., the degree to which the results of an innovation are visible to others) is positively related to its rate of adoption. (Rogers and Shoemaker, 1971, pp. 350–352)

In Levine's analysis (1980) (see before) some important observations can be found concerning the importance of these general characteristics in the context of higher education. This study especially focused on the "institutionalization or termination stage" of innovation processes. This stage is supposed to follow the stages of "recognition of the need for change," "planning an innovation" and "implementing the innovation." In the institutionalization or termination stage attention is concentrated on "the ways in which innovations prosper, persist, decline and fail after they have been adopted" (Levine, 1980, p. 10).

Levine has developed a theoretical model of the ways innovations can be handled in an organization. He suggests that in principle two mechanisms can be used. The first mechanism is called *boundary expansion*: ". . . an acceptance by the host [organization] of some or all of the innovation's differences." This mechanism essentially indicates a process of acceptance (which may be more or less comprehensive). Levine indicates that this acceptance can involve diffusing the innovation through the organization or establishing it as an enclave. "Diffusion is the process whereby innovation characteristics are allowed to spread through the host organization, and enclaving is the process whereby the innovation assumes an isolated position within the organization."

The other mechanism of handling an innovation in an organization is called *boundary contraction*: ". . . a constriction of organizational boundaries in such a manner as to exclude innovation differences." This mechanism labels an innovation as illegitimate or deviant. Again, two forms can be distinguished. "Resocialization occurs when the innovative unit is made to renounce its past deviance and institute the acceptable norms, values and goals. . . . Termination occurs when the innovation is eliminated" (Levine, 1980, pp. 14, 15).

Which of the four possible outcomes of the institutionalization/termination stage of innovation processes (diffusion, enclaving, resocialization, termination) will occur depends, in Levine's theoretical model, on two variables: compatibility and profitability. Like Rogers and Shoemaker, Levine sees compatibility as the degree to which the norms, values, and goals of an innovation are congruent with those of the organization which has to adopt the innovation. Profitability is a subjective concept, rather similar to Rogers and Shoemaker's "relative advantage." It indicates the degree to which an innovation satisfies the adopter's needs or satisfies him better than the existing mechanisms.

Levine's conclusions are that compatibility and profitability are both crucial variables for explaining the success or failure of the adoption of an innovation. An innovation appears to fail (i.e., is resocialized or terminated) when the levels of compatibility and profitability of the innovation decline. Profitability is an especially important variable. When the profitability of an innovation is not disputed, an innovation can still get accepted, even when the compatibility of such an innovation is low. However, when the profitability is seriously questioned, an innovation will fail, even when the compatibility is high.

The argument that the compatibility of an innovative idea is positively related to the rate of adoption of an innovation is frequently found in the literature. We already noticed that for instance Bok (1986) stresses this point. Becher and Kogan (1980) argue that structural reforms of a system as a whole can only succeed when they relate to the fundamental values in higher education (Becher and Kogan, 1980, p. 125).

Concerning the relationship between compatibility and rate of the adoption of an innovation Cerych and Sabatier (1986) introduce an interesting amendment.

Cerych and Sabatier propose a three-dimensional framework for the conceptualization of the "scope of change."

> *Depth of change* indicates the degree to which a new policy goal implies a departure from existing values and practices of higher education. . . . *Functional breadth of change* refers to the number of functional areas in which a given policy is expected to introduce more or less profound modifications: admission, teacher qualifications, internal structures, curriculum, and so forth. . . . *Level of change* indicates the target of the reform: the system as a whole; a particular sector or segment of the system (group of institutions); a single institution or an institutional sub-unit.

Reviewing the various comprehensive reforms that were the object of their analysis, Cerych and Sabatier draw several conclusions. Regarding the interconnection between depth of change and functional breadth of change they claim that reforms that postulate a radical departure of existing rules and values, can nevertheless be successfully implemented when they are limited to a few functional areas (of the higher education institution or of the higher education system as a whole) and if at the same time most other prevailing traditions and standards are rigorously accepted. With respect to the level of change, the authors conclude that, generally speaking, a reform succeeds more easily if it affects an institutional or sub-institutional process, rather than a system as a whole (Cerych and Sabatier, 1986, pp. 244–247).

It appears that Cerych and Sabatier, although they agree with the general conclusion of Rogers and Shoemaker that the more a reform is consistent with existing values the more likely it will be implemented, also notice that a low level of compatibility does not necessarily mean that an innovation cannot be successfully implemented. An important question then is what other factors may stimulate or hamper innovations.

We already noticed that Levine has suggested that the concept of profitability is of crucial importance for the explanation of the acceptance of innovations in higher education institutions. The concept of profitability is also often mentioned in the literature as an important variable positively related to the rate of adoption of an innovation. Becher and Kogan underline their view that externally initiated innovations can be successful in higher education, provided that they are acceptable in terms of intellectual substance (compatibility) and that they establish their merits (e.g., in terms of student recruitment) (profitability) (Becher and Kogan, 1980, p. 132). With regard to the analysis of the outcomes of innovation processes, Clark uses the metaphor of a seesaw, "a long board on which reform-supporting and reform-opposing groups sit at different points in relation to the center of balance." According to this author, a decision as to whether an innovation will or will not be accepted is the result of the distribution of power among the groups involved in the decision-making process. And the behavior of each group and individual in the decision-making process is guided by the subjective interpretation of self-interest.

> Innovations typically "fail" because the innovators cannot acquire enough power fully to protect their new ways. They are allowed to start, even to acquire a clientele, but unless they attach the interests of various groups to their own interests and persuade potential opponents at least to be moderate in their resistance, they can be tightly bounded—resocialized or terminated—as others raise their own level of concern, clarify their own self-interest with respect to the reform, and increase the bearing of their own weight. (Clark, 1983a, pp. 226, 227)

Clearly, like Levine, both Becher and Kogan and Clark combine the concepts of compatibility and profitability. In both their analytical interpretations of the potential success of an innovation the two concepts are interrelated.

The concepts of compatibility and profitability offer us the possibility of formulating some further insights about the appropriateness of governmental policy models with respect to higher education. If we follow the conclusions of the studies just discussed and if we take into account that the higher education context is characterized by a large professional autonomy, a large organizational fragmentation, a diffusion of the decision-making power, and a limited administrative authority, we may expect that governmental reform policies that pay attention to compatibility and profitability will be more effective in creating innovations than policies in which these concepts are not taken into account.

The discussion of innovation characteristics that are supposed to determine the success or failure of an innovation has so far concentrated on two of the five characteristics presented in the survey of Rogers and Shoemaker: compatibility and profitability (relative advantage). However the authors mentioned three other factors: complexity, triability, and observability.

Concerning the complexity of innovation, Rogers and Shoemaker themselves suggest that no relationship exists with the rate of adoption. According to them the degree to which an innovation is perceived to be difficult to understand or use does not really influence the process of acceptance or refusal of an innovation.

However, in the field of higher education another conclusion appears to be drawn. Cerych and Sabatier argue that a reform that is both "deep and broad" will tend to fail (Cerych and Sabatier, 1986, p. 145). When complexity is defined as the combination of the degree to which an innovation is a departure from existing values and practices with the number of functional areas aimed at by innovation, the level of complexity of an innovation process in higher education may be expected to be negatively related to the rate of adoption of the innovation. The more complex an innovation, the less successful that innovation will be in getting adopted.

The observability of an innovation is another factor presented by Rogers and Shoemaker as having a positive relationship with the rate of adoption: the more the goals and results of the innovation are visible and clear, the more likely it is that the innovation will be accepted.

In the field of higher education research Becher and Kogan (1980) come to the conclusion that the observability of an innovation is indeed of some influence. Taking the same position as Cerych and Sabatier (1986) with respect to depth and breadth of innovations (see before), they argue that

> innovations which manage . . . to challenge certain accepted ideas while reinforcing others have a fair chance of success, provided that they also meet two other prerequisites: that their merits are reasonably visible and that they do not appear seriously to undermine the existing patterns of freedom and control. (Becher and Kogan, 1980, p. 146)

Becher and Kogan's second prerequisite can be translated in terms of profitability. It may be interpreted as the inclination to guard the self-perceived interests of academic groups, often expressed as the conservation of the academic definitions of legitimate activities. The first prerequisite has to do with observability: to be able to be successful the merits of innovations have to be visible.

Cerych and Sabatier also suggest that in theory a high level of clarity and consistency of the objectives of an innovation facilitates the implementation of innovations. However, from their case studies they also conclude that in practice vagueness and ambiguity of objectives appear to prevail, especially because otherwise a consensus on the proposed innovation would not have occurred (Cerych and Sabatier, 1986, pp. 13, 14, 243).

Taking the arguments by Becher and Kogan and by Cerych and Sabatier into account, it can be argued that observability as such can hardly be called an important factor for the success or failure of an innovation. At most the level of observability of the objectives and expected results of an innovation is a strategic element in presenting an innovation as compatible with existing values or as profitable for certain groups and interests. Following Levine (1980) it could be concluded that when the objective is to guarantee that others have an accurate or positive picture of an innovation, this factor has more to do with compatibility and profitability than with observability per se. Guaranteeing an accurate or positive picture implies preventing the innovation from appearing incompatible and/or unprofitable (Levine, 1980, p. 187).

This leaves us with triability as a last innovation characteristic which is supposed to be positively related to the rate of adoption. Triability concerns an organization's ability to try an innovation within a limited period and on a limited scale. Moreover, it has to do with the condition that if, after trying an innovation, the conclusion is that the results are disappointing, the situation is reversible without severe damage.

Cerych and Sabatier have found that the assumptions on which reforms are based often are erroneous. This should not surprise us. As is the case with every process of policy design, so too the process of the design of innovations in higher education has to face the basic human impotence in accurately foretelling the future. Our knowledge can only be incomplete and things may change while a policy is designed and implemented (Van Vught, 1987).

Triability is a prudent strategy for those who do not want to overrate the level of knowledge incorporated in the assumptions which form the basis of a certain reform policy or innovation. This is especially the case in higher education because it may be expected that scientists and scholars are particularly skeptical about these kinds of assumptions. It is because of this that Bok (1986) pleads for implementing innovations in higher education institutions by means of experiments. Referring to an example of the Harvard Medical School he argues:

> This tactic has obvious advantages. It relies entirely on volunteers and hence makes few, if any demands on unwilling faculty members. It costs less than an institution-wide reform. It minimizes the risks of failure by leaving traditional programs intact. These virtues are often decisive in holding open the chance of making a substantial change. (Bok, 1986, pp. 187, 188)

The major problem with the experimental strategy is of course the spreading of a successful experiment through the entire institution. As was noticed before, the diffusion of an innovation will only take place by virtue of the professional belief that an innovation is worthwhile. Regarding this issue the concepts of compatibility and profitability have provided us with some insights. Nevertheless, a strategy of experimenting with innovations must be judged to be especially suited to higher education. Therefore, governmental policies that pay attention to triability may be expected to be more successful in creating innovations in higher education institutions than policies in which the idea of triability is absent.

Reviewing the points of view and analyses of the various authors mentioned above an important conclusion should be that government-initiated innovations in higher education institutions and systems can be successful only when certain conditions are met. These conditions have to do with the specific characteristics of higher education institutions. Innovations in higher education institutions can only be brought about by governmental policies, when attention is paid in these policies to the basic values and mechanisms of academic life.

It also can be concluded that an innovative policy can be expected to be more successful when in such a strategy attention is paid to the compatibility and the profitability of the innovation. The compatibility of an innovation (i.e., the degree to which the innovation is perceived to be consistent with existent values and practices) is, generally speaking, positively related to the rate of adoption of the innovation. However, a reform that implies a radical departure from existing values and practices can nevertheless be successful when the ''functional breadth of change'' is limited; that is, when the reform is limited to a few functional areas while at the same time some other prevailing values and practices are rigorously accepted.

The profitability of an innovation is also positively related to the rate of adoption of the innovation. The relative advantage of the innovation (compared with the idea or practice it supersedes) should be clear to those who are supposed to accept it. The behavior of each group and individual confronted with an innovation is guided by the subjective interpretation of self-interest. The outcome of an innovation process to a large extent depends on the distribution of power among the self-interested actors involved in the decision-making process regarding the innovation.

The complexity of an innovation was found to be negatively related to the rate of adoption of the innovation. When complexity is defined as the combination of the degree to which an innovation is a departure from existing values and practices with the number of functional areas aimed at by the innovation, it may be concluded that the higher the level of complexity of an innovation, the less likely it is that the innovation will be accepted.

With respect to the observability of an innovation (i.e., the degree to which the objectives and expected results are clear) it was argued that this factor should be interpreted as a strategic element in presenting an innovation in terms of compatibility or profitability.

The triability of an innovation (i.e., the degree to which an innovation may be experimented with) was judged to be of great importance in higher education. Experimenting with innovations is a prudent strategy, especially because the professionals in higher education institutions will be particularly skeptical about the policy assumption on which these innovations are based.

CONCLUSION

In the beginning of this chapter it was argued that the policy model of rational planning and control on the one hand and the policy model of self-regulation on the other vary in a rather fundamental way with regard to the assumptions they are based on. The model of rational planning and control is founded on the basic assumption of the rationalist perspective on decision-making. In every practical decision-making situation it strives after the objective of trying to select the best alternative from a set that should be as complete as possible. But confronted with the limitations of this ideal, in practice the strategy of rational planning and control takes its refuge in confidence in a strong centralization of decision-making processes and a large amount of control over these decision-making processes as well as over the implementation of the chosen policy.

The policy model of self-regulation is based on the cybernetic perspective on decision-making. It tries to make use of the self-regulatory capacities of decentralized decision-making units. It limits the role of government to the monitoring of a set of "critical variables" and to the analysis and, if judged necessary, the influencing of the framework of rules guiding the behavior of decentralized actors.

With respect to governmental policies in the field of higher education two models were introduced: the state control and the state supervising model. The state control model is largely based on the policy model of rational planning and control. The state supervising model reflects the policy model of self-regulation.

In the first part of this chapter also an overview was presented of the various policy instruments governments may use when they set themselves the task to influence activities and processes in the public sector.

The questions which I will try to answer in this concluding section are: Which of the two higher education policy models (state control and state supervision) is best suited to stimulate innovations in higher education systems and institutions? And, What policy instruments may be expected to be successful in that context?

It may be hypothesized from the analysis presented above that when the basic objective is to stimulate the innovativeness of the higher education institutions, the model of state control, generally speaking, is less successful than the model of state supervision. The model of state control appears to be based on assumptions that are at odds with some of the fundamental characteristics of higher education institutions. The model of state control ignores the fundamental features of higher education institutions that are found in characteristics like the high level of professional autonomy, the large organizational fragmentation and the large diffusion of the decision-making power.

The state supervising model appears to be better suited to the context of higher education. It acknowledges the fundamental characteristics of higher education institutions and it tries to make use of some of these characteristics to stimulate the innovativeness of the whole system of higher education. By limiting itself to only global forms of steering and by putting its confidence in the self-regulatory capacities of the professionals and the basic units of the higher education institutions, this model has the potential to become an effective paradigm for successful operational policies with respect to higher education in many countries (Neave and Van Vught, 1991).

Along the same lines it may be expected that a combination of mildly restrictive policy instruments will be more successful in stimulating innovations in higher education than a combination of extreme compulsive instruments. Compulsive instruments will overrestrict the behavior of the professional scholars in higher education institutions and, by doing so, create disillusion and apathy, rather than enthusiasm and innovativeness. It may be assumed that the fundamental characteristics of higher education institutions add up to a context in which government cannot execute compulsive actions without also bringing about some negative side-effects of these actions. Using Hood's categorization of policy instruments, it may be concluded that the instruments of information (responses and messages), the mildly restrictive instruments of authority (certificates and approvals) and the "give it away" instruments of treasure (transfer and bearer-directed payments) may be expected to be the most effective in the context of higher education.

With respect to higher education Clark (1983b) especially has asked the question of "governance fit":

> What governance arrangements are "naturally" generated? What structures of governance help this or that function to operate well? What governance "fits"? (Clark, 1983b, p. 27)

Clark comes to the conclusion that

> fit is a matter of balance among alternative forms for effecting national governance. Too much emphasis in any one direction, for example on state command, produces an imbalance that leads to a "fit" in a different meaning of the term!—a sudden and violent attack of a disorder, a convulsion, an exacerbation of troubles perhaps leading to prolonged sickness. (Clark, 1983b, 27)

In this chapter an issue has been explored which is very much related to Clark's question of governance fit. My conclusion was that the state supervising model appears to fit better than the state control model and that mildly restrictive instruments fit better than compulsive instruments.

Clark argues that differentiation should be the name of the governance game in higher education. He indicates (among other things) that diverse structures accommodate the conflicting tasks of higher education better than simple structures, that diverse structures allow status differentiation and sector diversification and that diverse structures stimulate flexibility and innovation (Clark, 1983b, pp. 31–37). Along the same lines I have tried to show that the state supervising model (because of its foundation in the cybernetic perspective on decision-making) offers the advantages of flexibility and innovation, of experimenting and robustness, of self-determination and responsibility. At the same time this model is relatively low in the costs of information, transaction, and administration.

The problems with which the model of state control is confronted in higher education can to a large extent be carried back to the basic differences between this model and the fundamental characteristics of the higher education context. The adherents of the state control model tend to see higher education more as an object than as a complex set of subjects (Trow, 1980; Neave, 1985). Besides, they see a higher education system as an object which can be controlled from outside and which can be moulded to the wishes of government.

The state control model puts its confidence in centralization and a large amount of control. But by doing so, it alienates itself from a societal sector like higher education, which above all else is characterized by a large amount of autonomy and differentiation. Speaking of the "unitary approach" Clark (1983b) formulates the same conclusion:

> Surely what we fear most about the unitary approach is the way it cramps a multiplicity of approaches and increases the likelihood of the arbitrary dictate and the large error. Nearly every time we plan centrally we eliminate some options of the operators. In each reform we add structures that constrain future choices. If we do not want things to escape our eyes, we systemize some more, generating a rule book that clogs formal channels and in turn stimulates underground activity for getting things done. (Clark, 1983b, p. 38)

It should not be surprising that the model of state control cannot be called a good fit for an innovation-oriented higher education system. The state control model overlooks the crucial issue of the costs of acquiring knowledge for the sake of creating innovations. It forgets that in a multilevel system general knowledge is usually more economically acquired by higher level decision-making units, while specific knowledge is more easily and more cheaply acquired by lower level units. And it forgets that, by introducing rigid and detailed procedures of hierarchical control, it cuts itself off from the possible knowledge advantages of the lower level decision-making units and thereby loses a large innovative potential.

> . . . the effectiveness of hierarchical subordination varies with the extent to which the subordinate unit has knowledge advantages over the higher unit. In those cases where the subordinate unit has better information, then in terms of the whole decision-making process the knowledge is one place and the power is another; the quality of decisions suffers as a result. Moreover, subordination itself becomes illusory to the extent that the lower level unit can use its knowledge to evade, counteract, or redirect the thrust of orders from its nominal superiors. (Sowell, 1980, pp. 13, 14)

Compared with the model of state control, the state supervising model seems to offer a better fit. This model seems to be better equipped to be used as a general incitement toward innovations in a higher education system. It addresses these systems while taking the fundamental characteristics of higher education institutions seriously. It leaves sufficient room for the (semi-)autonomous professionals and basic units and it does not try to coordinate the large variety of a higher education system in a limited set of rules.

By enlarging the autonomy of the higher education institutions and by limiting itself to monitoring some "critical" system variables and to (not too often and not too drastically) adapting some general "rules of the game," government may find in this model an important approach which may both stimulate the innovativeness of a higher education system and secure its basic values and practices.

REFERENCES

Ashby, W.R. (1956). *An Introduction to Cybernetics.* London: Chapman and Hall.

Banfield, E.C. (1959). Ends and means in planning. *International Social Science Journal* 11(3): 361–368.

Bardach, E. (1979). *The Implementation Game.* Cambridge Mass.: MIT Press.

Barret, S.C., and Fudge, C. (eds.) (1981). *Policy and Action: Essays on the Implementation of Public Policy.* London: Methuen.

Becher, T., and Kogan, M. (1980). *Process and Structure in Higher Education.* London: Heinemann.

Beer, St. (1975). *Platform for Change.* New York: John Wiley.

Berdahl, R., and Millett, J. (1991). Autonomy and accountability in U.S. higher education. In G. Neave and F.A. van Vught (eds.), *Prometheus Bound.* London: Pergamon.

Bok, D. (1986). *Higher Learning.* Cambridge: Harvard University Press.

Braybrooke, D., and Lindblom, Ch.E. (1963). *A Strategy of Decision: Policy Evaluation as a Social Process.* New York: Free Press.

Cerych, L., and Sabatier, P. (1986). *Great Expectations and Mixed Performance: the Implementation of Higher Education Reforms in Europe.* Trentham: Trentham Books.

Clark, B.R. (1983a). *The Higher Education System.* Berkeley: University of California Press.

Clark, B.R. (1983b). Governing the higher education system. In M. Shattock (ed.), *The Structure and Governance of Higher Education.* Guildford: Society for Research into Higher Education.

Dahl, R.A., and Lindblom, Ch.E. (1976, orig. 1953). *Politics, Economics and Welfare.* Chicago: University of Chicago Press.

Davis, R.H., Strand, R., Alexander, L.T., and Hussain, N.M. (1982). The impact of organizational and innovation variables on instructional innovation in higher education. *Journal of Higher Education* 53 (5): 568–586.

Dill, D.D. (1992). Quality by design: toward a framework for academic quality management. In J. Smart (ed.), *Higher Education: Handbook of Theory and Research* Vol. VIII. New York: Agathon Press.

Dill, D.D., and Friedman, Ch.P. (1979). An Analysis of Frameworks for Research on Innovation and Change in Higher Education, *Review of Educational Research* 49(3): 411–435.

Downs, G.W., and Mohr, L.B. (1976). Conceptual issues in the study of innovation, *Administrative Science Quarterly* 21: 700–714.

Dror, Y. (1968). *Public Policymaking Re-examined.* San Francisco: Chandler.

Dror, Y. (1971). *Design for Policy Sciences.* New York: Elsevier.

Dunsire, A. (1978). *Implementation in a Bureaucracy.* Oxford: Martin Robinson.

Elmore, R.F. (1987). Instruments and strategy in public policy. *Policy Studies Review* 7 (1): 174–186.

Etzioni, A. (1968). *The Active Society.* New York: Free Press.

Friedmann, J. (1973). *Retracking America: A Theory of Transactive Planning.* New York: Garden City.

Glenny, L.A. (ed.). *Funding Higher Education: A Six-Nation Analysis.* New York: Praeger.

Hage, J., and Aiken, M. (1967). Program change and organizational properties: a comparative analysis. *American Journal of Sociology* 72(5): 503–519.

Hage, J., and Aiken, M. (1970). *Social Change in Complex Organizations*. New York: Random House.

Hefferlin, J.B. (1969). *Dynamics of Academic Reform*. San Francisco: Jossey-Bass.

Hood, Chr. C. (1983). *The Tools of Government*. London: Macmillan.

Ingram, H., and Mann, D. (1980). *Why Policies Succeed or Fail*. Beverly Hills: Sage.

Jantsch, E. (1972). *Technological Planning and Social Futures*. London: Cassel/Associated Business Progammes.

Kahn, A.E. (1971). *The Economics of Regulation: Principles and Institutions* (2 vols). New York: John Wiley.

Kerr, C. (1982). *The Uses of the University* (third ed.). Cambridge: Harvard University Press.

Kerr, C. (1987). A critical age in the university world: accumulated heritage versus modern imperatives. *European Journal of Education* 22(2): 183–193.

Lane, J.E. (1984). Possibility and desirability of higher education reform. In R. Premfors (ed.), *Higher Education Organisation*. Stockholm: Almqvist and Wiksell.

Levine, A. (1980). *Why Innovation Fails: the Institutionalization and Termination of Innovation in Higher Education*. Albany: State University of New York Press.

Lindblom, Ch.E. (1959). The science of muddling through. *Public Administration Review* 19(2): 79–99.

Lindblom, Ch.E. (1965). *Intelligence of Democracy*. New York: Free Press.

Maassen, P.A.M., and Van Vught, F.A. (1992). Strategic planning. In B.R. Clark and G. Neave (eds.), *The Encyclopedia of Higher Education,* Vol. 2: 1483–1494. London: Pergamon.

March, J.G., and Olsen, J.P. (1976). *Ambiguity and Choice in Organisations*. Bergen: Universitetsforlaget.

Mazmanian, D.A., and Sabatier, P.A. (1981). *Effective Policy Implementation*. Toronto: Lexington Books.

McDonnell, L. (1988). Policy design as instrument design. Paper presented at the 1988 annual meeting of the American Political Science Association. Washington D.C.

Meyerson, M. (1956). Building the middle-range bridge for comprehensive planning. *Journal of the American Institute of Planners* 22(2): 58–64.

Meyerson, M., and Banfield, E.C. (1955). *Politics, Planning and the Public Interest*. Glencoe: Free Press.

Mintzberg, H. (1979). *The Structuring of Organizations*. Englewood Cliffs: Prentice-Hall.

Mitnick, B.M. (1980). *The Political Economy of Regulation: Creating, Designing and Removing Regulatory Reforms*. New York: Columbia University Press.

Neave, G. (1985). Higher education in a period of consolidation: 1975–1985. *European Journal of Education* 20(2): 109–124.

Neave, G., and Van Vught, F.A. (eds.) (1991). *Prometheus Bound: The Changing Relationship Between Government and Higher Education in Western Europe*. London: Pergamon .

Newman, F. (1987). *Choosing Quality: Reducing Conflict Between the State and the University*. Denver: Education Commission of the States.

O'Toole, L. (1986). Policy recommendations for multi-actor implementation: an assessment of the field. *Journal of Public Policy* 6(1): 21–48.

Polanyi, M. (1962). The republic of science: its political and economic theory. *Minerva* 1: 54–73.

Premfors, R. (1984). *Higher Education Organisation*. Stockholm: Almqvist and Wiksell.

Premfors, R. (1992). Policy analysis. In B.R. Clark and G. Neave (eds.), *The Encyclopedia of Higher Education,* Vol. 3, 1907–1916. London: Pergamon.
Pressman, J.L., and Wildavsky, A.B. (1973). *Implementation.* Berkeley: University of California Press.
Rein, M., and Rabinovitz, F. (1978). Implementation: a theoretical perspective. In Burnham, W.D., and Weinberg, W.W. (eds.) *American Politics and Public Policy.* Cambridge Mass.: MIT Press.
Rogers, E.M., and Shoemaker, F.F. (1971). *Communication of Innovations.* New York: Free Press.
Salamon, L.M. (1981). Rethinking public management: third party government and the changing forms of government action. *Public Policy* 29(3): 255–275.
Schneider, A., and Ingram H. (1990). Behavioral assumptions of policy tools. *Journal of Politics* 52(2): 510–530.
Scott, P. (1988). *The British Universities' Response to Institutional Diversification.* Paris: OECD/IMHE.
Simon, H.A. (1957). *Administrative Behavior,* 2nd ed. New York: Macmillan.
Skolnik, M.L. (1987). State control of degree granting: the establishment of a public monopoly in canada. In C. Watson (ed.), *Governments and Higher Education: The Legitimacy of Intervention.* Toronto: Higher Education Group, The Ontario Institute for Studies in Education.
Sowell, T. (1980). *Knowledge and Decisions.* New York: Basic Books.
Steinbrunner, J.D. (1974). *The Cybernetic Theory of Decision: New Dimensions of Political Analysis.* Princeton: Princeton University Press.
Stigler, G.J. (1975). *The Citizen and the State: Essays on Regulation.* Chicago: University of Chicago Press.
Trow, M. (1980). *Dilemma's of Higher Education in the 1980's and 1990's.* Montreal: Conference of Learned Societies.
Van de Graaf, J.H., Clark, B.R., Furth, D., Goldschmidt, D., and Wheeler, D.F. (1978). *Academic Power: Patterns of Authority in Seven National Systems of Higher Education.* New York: Praeger.
Van Gunsteren, H.R. (1976). *The Quest for Control: A Critique of the Rational-central Rule Approach in Public Affairs.* New York: Wiley.
Van Vught, F.A. (1987). Pitfalls of forecasting: fundamental problems for the methodology of forecasting from the philosophy of science. *Futures, the Journal of Forecasting and Planning* 19(2): 184–197.
Van Vught, F.A. (1988). A new autonomy in European higher education? An exploration and analysis of the strategy of self-regulation in higher education governance. *International Journal of Institutional Management in Higher Education* 12(1): 16–27.
Van Vught, F.A. (1991). Public administration. In B.R. Clark and G. Neave (eds.), *The Encyclopedia of Higher Education,* Vol. 3, 1932–1943. London: Pergamon.
Van Vught, F.A. (1992). Autonomy and accountability in government-university relationships. Paper presented at the World Bank Worldwide Senior Policy Seminar on Improvement and Innovation of Higher Education in Developing Countries. Kuala Lumpur: June 30–July 4, 1992.
Walford, G. (1991). The changing relationship between government and higher education in Britain. In G. Neave and F. van Vught (eds.), *Prometheus Bound.* London: Pergamon.
Weick, K.F. (1979). Educational organizations as loosely coupled systems. *Administrative Science Quarterly* 21(1): 1–19.

Reframing Policy Research: A Critical Examination of Research on Federal Student Aid Programs

Edward P. St. John
and
Richard J. Elliott
University of New Orleans

I. INTRODUCTION

The process of framing policy research—deciding on the research questions, conceptual bases, and analytic techniques that will guide the inquiry—generally receives precious little attention by applied policy researchers. Instead, these decisions are often made tacitly (Argyris, Putnam, and Smith, 1987; Rhoades, 1992), based on the researchers' education and training, the political contexts in which they work, and the particular interests that are driving the research—the interests of policy makers, funding agencies, or powerful constituents. Thus, the assumptions policy researchers make when framing policy situations are seldom acknowledged, much less critically examined.

In order to probe the process policy researchers use to frame their work, it is necessary to distinguish between the framing process and the policy process in which policy researchers are enmeshed. In the 1960s and 1970s, there was a great debate between two schools of thought about policy analysis, between those who advocated rational systems and methods (e.g Schultz, 1968) and those who adopted a more incremental approach (e.g. Braybrook and Lindblom, 1963). In the past decade there was a breakdown in the liberal progressive consensus underlying this debate (Simsek and Heydinger, 1992; White, 1992), which has fueled the development of ideological approaches to policy analysis from the left and right.

Our concern here is with the framing process used by applied policy researchers, those in government and closely associated with government who undertake technical analyses aimed at informing policy deliberations. Such research is typically conducted by researchers in evaluation, planning, and budget offices (applied think tanks) in government agencies, and, in the case of higher education, university systems; researchers in private firms and independent consultants whose profession it is to supplement the analytic capacity of these government think tanks; researchers in, and consultants to, nongovernment think tanks funded by associations, foundations, and other philanthropic or advocacy groups; and university researchers who are interested in applied policy problems. This chapter focuses on building a better understanding of the influence of framing assumptions on policy research. It first proposes a meta framework for examining the ways policy researchers frame their research, then uses the meta framework to examine critically policy research on federal student aid programs. Based on this critical examination of the process, a developmental scheme is proposed for examining the policy researchers' reframing process.

II. A META FRAMEWORK

The processes policy researchers use to frame their research are influenced by their own experiences, interests, and values, as well as by the experiences, interests, and values of policy makers whose interests and requests usually influence, if not shape, the research agenda of applied policy researchers. Since specifying all possible variables that could influence these framing decisions would be impossible, we identify three dimensions of the researchers' prism: the particular *historical moment* (and policy context) in which the policy researcher works and the researcher's interpretation of that moment; the *basic theory*—or set of theories—that are used to shape the analytic method used by the researcher[1]; and the *reflective process* used by the researchers.

A. Understanding Policy Contexts

Applied policy researchers respond to particular concerns that emerge within a historical moment. Yet at any given moment, their knowledge about the context is imperfect. Therefore, when they frame their research, they are making interpretations about the particular context in which they work. How they interpret the specific events that influence their work has an influence on their work. According to Kneller (1984, p. 67), Heidegger calls this basic disposition ''primordial'' understanding. Kneller (1984) argues that to *understand* something is to grasp its

[1]In his review of this chapter, James Hearn pointed out that it can be argued that the choice of a theoretical perspective can be so integral to the framing process that the other two aspects cannot practically be separated from this choice. Herein lies an issue for all researchers to consider: that is, the choice of a theoretical perspective may contain within it a whole set of research assumptions. Our purpose here is to help policy researchers build awareness of the assumptions embedded in the choices they make about theoretical frames. Thus, while we agree that the choice of a theoretical perspective is integral to many other aspects of the process of framing policy research, by distinguishing choices about theory as a distinct aspect of the process, we hope to build awareness of the implications of these choices.

meaning or significance; to *interpret* something is to apprehend what it signifies from a certain standpoint. Further, people understand things in the light of their purposes and hence from their standpoints or situations: ''Thus, understanding, at heart, is interpretive.'' (Kneller, 1984, p. 67). Since texts or events stand in a tradition formed by past interpretations that have been handed on, policy researchers do not approach events with a completely open mind.

Modern hermeneutics aims at understanding discourse from the perspectives of those who are engaged in it. Policy makers and researchers bring their interpretations of previous events—interpretations that are influenced by their direct and vicarious experiences—to their interpretations of new events. Thus, the meaning of an event is not limited to its original significance—an interpretation that would be a blind acceptance of the past. The text or event has a structure that each generation and each individual interprets afresh in the light of new individual experiences and a new historical situation. Consider also that if we are not fully attentive, an interpretation may be distorted. For example, if we face and interpret an event one day and the next day there is an historical happening, such as the fall of the Iron Curtain, then we might need to reinterpret our previous interpretation.[2] Therefore, the process of interpretation is limitless and each successive interpretation is different. Thus, the meaning of a text goes beyond the author, which is why understanding is not merely a reproduction, but a productive attitude as well (Gradmar, 1979).

On the surface, it seems that most researchers have an awareness of their historical moment. There are three specific aspects of the historical moment that usually are considered by the policy researcher: the history of the policy or issue that is to be the focal point of the analysis; the particular events and/or policy outcomes that are thought to be critical to the analysis; and the interests of those requesting or funding the research. Most policy research explicitly focuses on the first two of these, as they are integral to the research. And most academic and applied policy journals and other publishers require acknowledgment of the funding source, which implicitly recognizes the potential influence of funding sources. Indeed, there is a long history of this standard in the academic community. These practices illustrate that a superficial acknowledgement of these influences is generally accepted.

However, there is also a deeper level on which policy researchers should be

[2]Indeed, the end of the ''Cold War'' has a profound influence on the way we think about public policy. For example, it can be argued that the federal role in student aid emerged *because* of the Cold War (e.g. the National Defense Education Act, which created the National Defense Student Loan program, was a response to the Cold War). If one holds this assumption—that student aid was necessary to win the Cold War—then one could question whether we need student aid in this ''new world order.'' (The quotation marks are added to ''Cold War'' and ''new world order'' to illustrate the transition in common language about global politics.)

aware of their role in the process of policy discourse and the role their tacit assumptions play in this discourse. According to Cherryholmes (1988):

> Truth is the goal of discourse, and it is a consensus about what is the case. The process by which consensus is brought about is designed to guard against distortions by the exercise of power. What any individual believes to be true may be in error, because we may do something other than what we think we are. (p. 89)

Habermas states how crucial discourse is in similar terms: ''The meaning of the truth or untruth of a statement does not consist in the conditions guaranteeing the objectivity of our experience but in the possibility of argumentative corroboration of a truth claim which is falsifiable in principle'' (Habermas, 1973, p. 166). This creates a paradoxical situation for most policy researchers: their research seems aimed at building a rational understanding of the consequences of policy choices, while their tacit decisions about how to contend with political forces, including the interests and ideologies of policy makers, would seem to preclude falsification of certain assumptions and, thus, to violate the principles of free discourse.

Habermas' falsification principle is designed to minimize distorting influences of commitments, interests, ideologies, and power arrangements. As Cherryholmes noted:

> [C]ritical discourse—between, for example, practitioners and researchers—theorists—must be symmetrical; and nondominated. All parities may initiate comments, challenge assertions, and question not only theoretical formulations but also metatheoretical and metaethical ones. It cannot be bound; it must be radically free, with only the best argument pursued. Strategic behavior, turning the search for truth into a conflict or competition, is not permitted; winning or losing is not the outcome of discourse. No votes are taken. The pursuit of the best argument is what is sought. (Cherryholmes, 1988, p. 89)

Unfortunately, this ideal circumstance seldom exists in the policy arena, therefore our interpretations of policy research should consider the prospect of external influences on researchers. While it is evident that Habermas and Cherryholmes recognize problems in arriving at truth, and they are committed to a discursive means to get to truth, it is Foucault, however, in a poststructuralist analysis, who warns us that truth is rooted in discourse and discourses are historically situated; therefore, truth cannot be spoken in the absence of power and each historical arrangement of power has its own truths. Foucault summarizes this relationship between truth and power in the following passage:

> Truth is a thing of this world: it is produced only by virtue of multiple forms of constraint. And it induces regular effects of power. Each society has its regime of truth, its ''general politics'' of truth: that is, the types of discourse which it accepts and makes function as true; the mechanisms and instances which enable one to distinguish

> true and false statements, the means by which each is sanctioned; the techniques and procedures accorded value in the acquisition of truth; the status of those who are charged with saying what counts as true. (Foucault, 1980, p. 131)

Policy makers and researchers who do not wish to reproduce what is in place in the name of change or progress, must be aware of the origins of discursive practices. Since the ideal conditions for discourse cannot normally be attained in a practical political environment, policy researchers require means for reflecting on these deeper forces and how they influence the framing of their policy Research.

B. Basic Theories

There are, of course, a range of basic theories that can be, and frequently are, used in policy research, depending on the policies or programs under consideration. There are two broad categories of theories typically used in applied policy research[3]; analytic/empirical and historical/hermeneutic (Argyris, Putnam, and Smith, 1987).

Most applied policy research is rooted in analytic/empirical research tradition. To a large extent, economic theories underlie the development of applied policy models. A variety of other discipline orientations can also be adapted to applied policy studies. For example, sociological attainment models and economic human capital models are frequently used in student aid research and other education policy research. The analytic/empirical tradition also can be adapted to the development of systematic policy models, such as planning, programming, budgeting systems, or zero-based budgeting. And, of course, there are many analytic techniques typically used in policy studies, including cost-benefit and cost-effectiveness analyses.

The second research tradition focuses on understanding what actually happens and what policies mean for recipients of program services. These studies tend to be more historical, philosophical, or ideological in their orientation. These approaches can also be used to develop models for policy analysis and implementation, such as political incrementalism (e.g. Braybrook and Lindblom, 1963). Over a decade ago, Lindblom and Cohen (1979) argued that policy analysts should take more of an advocacy position. To a large extent there has been an infusion of ideological perspectives in applied policy analyses in the past decade. However, researchers engaged in this new type of ideological policy research seldom apply the falsification principle to their own framing assumptions.

Most policy analysts are reasonably clear about the theories they use to frame

[3]By applied policy research, we are referring to studies that relate directly to policy decisions. On the state and federal levels, many studies are conducted by or for planning, budget, and evaluation offices. These studies typically either evaluate the outcomes of former policies or programs, or produce information that can be used in redesigning these policies and programs. This applied research is distinct from basic research which often does not have direct policy implications.

their research. However, when researchers apply theory in an instrumental way, they do not critically examine the assumptions embedded in the theories they use (Argyris, Putnam, and Smith, 1987; Habermas, 1984, 1987; Schon, 1983, 1987), which can seriously limit the quality, if not the practical utility of their analyses.

To develop a better understanding of the processes used by policy researchers when assessing historic policies and future policy options, it is necessary to identify and critically examine the theoretical assumptions they use to frame their policy studies. This topic is seldom investigated, either by policy analysts or social scientists who study the policy process. Yet these assumptions have a substantial impact on the ability of researchers to understand the embedded policy issues and to identify alternative policies that could transform replicating social problems.

C. Reflecting on Framing Assumptions

To develop an understanding of the consequences of their framing assumptions, policy researchers must reflect on the way they frame their work. In our view, the development of reflective skills by policy analysts has received too little attention. We propose a developmental perspective that can be used to examine the reflective dimension of policy research. Our developmental scheme is based on three theoretical arguments.

First, in his *Theory and Communicative Action*, Habermas (1984, 1987) distinguishes between two major types of action: *strategic* action, which is oriented toward the pursuit of goals; and *communicative* action, which is oriented toward understanding and communicating about the consequences of choices about purposes and actions. He further distinguishes between strategic action that is *instrumental*, in the sense of merely applying externally imposed goals, and *open strategic* action that emphasizes openly choosing goals and action strategies. He argues that critical discourse is the appropriate means of promoting communicative action. In subsequent work, Habermas (1991) argues that the process of evolving from instrumental to communicative forms of action is developmental, analogous to the process of moral development. It should be further noted that Habermas (1984, 1987) critically examines—deconstructs and reconstructs—theories that are in both the empirical and hermeneutic traditions in his development of the theory of communicative action.

Second, Argyris, Putnam, and Smith (1987) argue that basic research, regardless of the research tradition in which it is framed (empirical or hermeneutical), is of little use to policy makers since these theories usually focus on explanations that are out of the control of policy makers. In contrast, they argue, applied researchers essentially scan a range of possible theories to identify the theory, or set of theories, that can be adapted to the problems facing policy makers. Accordingly, applied policy researchers and consultants may take the policy makers' goals as a given and try to analyze how alternative forms of action by the policy makers might help them to achieve their policy goals. Finally, they argue that action scientists aim to understand the replicating functional and dysfunctional forms of action (theories in use) and identify ways of transforming the dysfunctional patterns. They argue that action science requires a method that combines the analytical/empirical and historical/hermeneutic traditions.

Third, we adapt a developmental perspective on reflective choice making (St. John, 1990a; St. John and Burlew, 1993). Based on an examination of Carl Jung's concept of individuation, St. John and Burlew (1993) proposed four stages of reflective choice making: a basic stage in which the individual oscillates between feelings of being in control, as though his/her personal theories help him/her to understand and cope with his/her experience, and feelings of being out of control, or at the mercy of chaos; a strategic stage in which the individual learns to adapt to new conditions that develop, by thinking about and choosing situational goals and strategies; a communicative stage in which the individual discovers the need to communicate with others about the choice of goals and strategies and build a shared understanding of mutual experience; and a transformational stage in which the individual begins to discover replicating patterns, or archetypes, and to envision new forms of action that promote transformation.

In this paper we develop a four-stage model of reflective choice making by policy researchers that integrates these three lines of argument. First, the *basic* stage is essentially an instrumental application of a particular basic theory to an applied policy problem. When the basic orientation is used, the assumptions of the theory are not routinely subjected to the falsification principle. The *strategic* stage involves adaptations of these basic techniques based on the researchers' efforts to understand how policy makers can best pursue their aims. Adaptations are made to build a new understanding of the likely consequences of policy choices, but the framing assumptions made by these researchers still are not critically examined. The *communicative* stage involves inquiry into both the selection of aims and of strategies. Adaptations are made to build a new understanding of the likely consequences of policies and of the replicative nature of policy choices. In this stage, the critical examination of framing assumptions is considered essential to building new understandings. Finally, the *transformational* stage aims to transform patterns that are dysfunctional by publicly testing assumptions about how new policies might influence practice. This mode of inquiry not only tests assumptions about the world as it is now (the status quo), but also considers mechanisms for testing assumptions about how future policies might influence practice.

This review of student aid policy research identifies and critically examines the framing assumptions of a diverse range of student aid policy studies. Student aid is a worthwhile area for the study of policy research because: 1) it is the most direct area of federal involvement in higher education; 2) many states and institutions use student aid as an integral part of their strategy to finance higher education; and 3) there has been extensive research from a diverse range of theoretical perspectives.

D. The Policy Researcher's Prism

Policy researchers are confronted by a myriad of necessarily moral choices. To the extent that they make these choices tacitly, in adherence to a theoretical perspective, or without reflection on underlying assumptions, they will be unaware of possible long-term consequences of their choices. The poststructural or postmodern perspective helps us toward this end, by making us more aware of certain voices that have been marginalized. But even these new insights, by themselves, are not enough to inform policy researchers' choices about framing their research. Beyer and Liston state the practical limitations of postmodernism and poststructuralism as follows:

> As educators [or policy researchers] we are always and necessarily moral actors, at whatever level we teach [or inquire] we are confronted daily with myriad choices that call for the development of reasons to support one course of action over another, the result of which may have profound long-lasting consequences. A postmodern orientation seems ill-equipped to handle these deliberative failures of educational life (Beyer and Liston, 1992, p. 390). [Our comments in brackets]

Since Habermas' communicative discourse represents a postmodern ''ideal'' that cannot be readily achieved in the daily practice of policy research, policy researchers need ways of understanding how the assumptions they make not only influence their work, but also influence the course of policy.

Our thesis is that the prisms policy researchers use to examine policy issues are framed by three types of assumptions. First, assumptions about the historical moment influence the way policy researchers interpret previous policy developments and program consequences, as well as how they look forward to assess the likely consequences of alternative policy choices. Second, the assumptions embedded in the basic theory, or theories, used to design policy studies also influence the ways researchers organize and interpret historic events and predict future developments. Finally, the decisions policy researchers make about the public testing of these framing assumptions serve as an indicator of their reflective orientation.

In the analysis of student aid research, we critically examine the assumptions embedded in this research and reconstruct the theoretical framework based on this research. In the process we identify practices that might promote more public testing not only of assumptions about current and past policies, but also of assumptions about the impact of new policy choices. Thus by critically examining student aid policy research, we hope to illustrate the way policy researchers can reframe their research to better inform policy choices.

TABLE 1. Framework for Critically Examining Policy Research: The Student Aid Case Study.

Aspects of the Framework	Related Student Aid Policy Research
I. Historical Dimension	
A. Legislation	Generally available (Title IV of the HEA) Specially directed (military, health, etc.)
B. Funding	Budget history
C. Intended outcomes	Participation rates
II. Theoretical Dimension	
A. Analytic/empirical	Economic (human capital) models Sociological (educational attainment) models Hybrid models Student choice models
B. Historical/hermeneutical	Political incrementalism Neo-conservatism Neo-Marxism
III. Reflective Dimension	
A. Basic	Instrumental application of base theories
B. Strategic	Adaptations of base theories that address policy issues
C. Communicative	Critical analyses examining basic assumptions
D. Transformative	Recursive models (using research to reframe policy choices)

III. A CRITICAL EXAMINATION OF STUDENT AID POLICY RESEARCH

Student financial aid, the direct subsidy of students' costs of attending postsecondary institutions, is the primary means for federal support of higher education in the United States. As a result of the size of federal student aid programs, an estimated $22.3 billion in fiscal year (FY) 1990 (College Board, 1992), these programs receive the attention of policy researchers using diverse applied policy perspectives. The application of our meta framework to this field of policy research is summarized in Table 1. This critical review of policy research on federal student aid programs has three parts: a brief historical overview of the federal student aid programs, which is intended to illustrate the influence of assumptions made about policy contexts (historical moments); a summary of basic theories used in research on student aid and related topics; and an analysis of the framing assumptions made by policy researchers, using the developmental stages proposed above.

A. Historical Perspectives on Federal Programs

When policy researchers turn their attention to federal student aid programs, they do so within a specific historical context. The assumptions they make about policy contexts—their historical moment—influence the way they interpret data. This overview considers three aspects of the historical context: the legislative history, focusing on the evolving intent of federal student aid programs; program funding, focusing both on the sources of aid (i.e. generally available or specially directed) and on types of aid (i.e. grants, work, loans); and the outcomes of the programs, focusing on intended outcomes.[4] We consider this brief background necessary to build an understanding of how the assumptions researchers make about policy contexts can influence their analyses.

Legislative History

When researchers distinguish among historical periods, they make tacit assumptions that influence their analyses. In this analysis we distinguish between three periods: prior to 1965, a period during which the foundations for current federal programs were established and a dual federal system of specially directed and universally available aid was developed; 1965 to 1978, a period when the federal role in promoting equal opportunity evolved and this intent was frequently used as a criterion for analyzing the consequences of these programs, which usually meant focusing on changes in participation rates for the historically disadvantaged; and post 1978, a period in which a major restructuring has taken place, forcing analysts to reconcile the original equal opportunity goal with the emergent goals of universal opportunity (middle-income access) and program efficiency.

The identification of these three periods as distinct was influenced by our consideration of shifts in the target populations for federal student aid programs. Therefore we did not use the same breakpoints as some other researchers. For example, many researchers focus on 1972 as pivotal, both because there were major program changes at that time and because the overall goal of promoting equal opportunity was made explicit (e.g. Gladieux and Wolanin, 1976). Others might treat 1980 as a crucial turning point because of the election of Ronald Reagan (e.g. Kramer, 1982). Thus the reader of this text should be aware that our distinction between these three major periods, explained below, has an influence on all of our subsequent analyses.

[4]We also recognize that there are unintended consequences of student aid programs. Further, we recognize that explicit consideration of unintended consequences can be very useful in the policy process. Unfortunately, we lack the space to deal with these other consequences in text. Therefore, we use footnotes to acknowledge these connections.

The modern federal role in student aid can be traced to the emergence of specially directed student aid programs after World War II. The initial veterans benefit program, known as the *GI Bill of Rights*, provided direct subsidies to veterans who returned to college (Finn, 1978). The next major development in the federal role in supporting students was the *National Defense Education Act of 1958* (NDEA), which created National Defense Student Loans (NDSL, now Perkins Loans), the first major program generally available to all qualified applicants.

In the early 1960s, new federal laws created major new student aid programs that were both specially directed and generally available. The *Equal Opportunity Act of 1964* created the college work study program, which continues today as a generally available program. And the *Social Security Amendments of 1965* created the Social Security Survivors Educational Benefits program, a specially directed grant program for children of deceased workers.

Programs to Promote Equal Opportunity: 1965–1978. The passage of the *Higher Education Act* (HEA) of 1965 marked the formal commitment of the federal government to fund students as a means of promoting equal opportunity in higher education. Between 1965 and 1978, the generally available programs, created under Title IV, eventually became dominant.[5] Title IV of the HEA reauthorized the NDSL and CWS programs as well as created two new programs: a new Equal Opportunity Grant program (now Supplemental Equal Opportunity Grants or SEOGs); and the Guaranteed Student Loan program, which both reinsured guaranteed loans programs in states that already had programs (the GSL portion of the initial program) and initiated Federally Insured Student Loans (FISL) to insure loans for student in states that did not have state guarantee agencies. The HEA of 1965 established the federal role in promoting equal opportunity through student aid.

The debates over the 1972 reauthorization of the HEA addressed basic issues over the future of the federal role in higher education finance. Responding to different political interests, the Senate and House included different program developments. The two versions of the bill represented competing interests in the higher education community: most institutional associations were advocating for a major new institutional subsidy program, which was incorporated into the House of Representatives' bill, under a new Title I; while a group of economists were arguing for a major new grant program, which was included in the Senate's version of the bill, as the Basic Educational Opportunity Grant (BEOG) program (now Pell) under Title IV. The compromise bill, the *Education Amendments of 1972*, included the Senate Title IV with the BEOG program, and the House's

[5]Frequently, policy analysts who assess the effects of the federal student aid programs authorized under Title IV ignore specially directed programs. Our assumption is that students are influenced by the amount of aid they receive, regardless of its source. Therefore, we are concerned here with all federal student aid. The implications of this broader assumption are considered.

Title I, although the Title I program was never funded (Gladieux and Wolanin, 1976).

Throughout the period between the initial passage of the HEA in 1965 and the passage of the *Middle Income Student Assistance Act of 1978* (MISAA), the federal government increased its commitment to student aid programs aimed at promoting equal educational opportunity. While there was some institutional discretion allowed in the packaging of the campus-based programs—work study, SEOG, and Perkins (formerly NDSL)—all of the programs funded under Title IV were directed primarily at the low income, with an explicit interest in equalizing opportunity between the historically disadvantaged and middle- and upper-income students. Throughout this period, however, there was growing advocacy among the middle and upper income for some form of relief for their college costs (Carlson, Farmer, and Weathersby, 1974).

Responding to New Priorities: 1978–present. President Carter's administration responded to the demands of the middle class for relief with college costs by pushing MISAA, a major revision of HEA Title IV programs, aimed at making access to higher education universal. MISAA removed the income cap for the GSL program, made middle-income students eligible for the Pell program, and expanded eligibility to the Campus-Based Programs. Immediately after passage of MISAA, Congress was confronted by a set of programs that it literally could not afford to fully fund (St. John and Byce, 1982). Thus Congress was caught between meeting the educational needs of either middle-income students or lower-income students. The Carter administration responded to this dilemma by proposing elimination of the Social Security Education Benefits Program and reducing other specially directed forms of student aid. Carter's attempt to cut the Social Security Education Benefits Program was unsuccessful and Congress was left to reconcile the competing interests of the two groups through the budget process.

In contrast to Carter, Reagan was successful in eliminating the Social Security Education Benefits Program and introducing an Income Contingent Loan Program, which was never fully funded. The annual battle over the budget became the arena for dealing with these competing priorities. The growing national debt and the neo-conservative antagonism toward programs for the lower income heightened the political nature of the budget process.

Budget History

When assessing federal student aid programs, policy researchers can focus exclusively either on HEA Title IV programs, which are generally available, or on all federal student aid, which includes subsidies provided through the specially directed programs as well as Title IV programs. Since specially directed programs have provided access to special populations, we feel it is necessary and appropriate to examine both sources. However, the discussion of program impact

TABLE 2. Trends in Financial Aid Awarded Through Federal Student Aid Programs, FYs 1971, 1976, 1981, 1986, 1991 (in thousands of 1990 dollars)

	70–71	75–76		80–81		85–86		89–90	
	$	$	% chng.	$	% chng.	$	% chng.	$	% chng.
I. Generally Available Student Aid (HEA, Title IV)									
A. *Grants*									
Pell	$ 0	$ 2,301	NA	$ 3,755	63%	$ 4,469	19%	$ 5,116	14%
SEOG	458	494	8	579	17	514	−11	478	−7
SSIG	0	48	NA	114	138	95	17	77	−19
Subtotal	$ 458	$ 2,843	521%	$ 4,448	57%	$ 5,078	14%	$ 5,671	12%
B. *Work*									
CWS	780	725	−7	1,039	43%	822	−21%	712	−13
C. *Loans*									
Perkins	825	1,130	37	1,090	−3	881	−19	968	10
ICL	0	0	NA	0	NA	0	NA	6	NA
Guaranteed	3,482	3,113	−11	9,757	213	11,073	13	13,038	18
Subtotal	$ 4,307	$ 4,243	−1%	$10,847	156%	$11,954	10%	$14,012	17%
II. Specially Directed Student Aid (Other Legislation)									
A. *Grants*									
Social Sec.	1,712	2,686	57	2,962	10	0	−100	0	NA
Veteran	3,846	10,270	167	2,697	−74	1,082	−63	848	−22
Military	221	238	8	316	33	429	36	391	−9
Other	55	155	182	192	24	84	−56	118	40
Subtotal	$ 5,834	$13,349	129%	$ 6,167	−54%	$ 1,595	−74%	$ 1,357	−15%
B. *Loans*									
Other	144	111	−28%	98	−12%	467	377%	381	−18%
III. Total Federal Student Aid									
A. *Available Funds*									
Grants	6,292	16,192	157	10,615	−34	6,673	−37%	7,028	5
Work	780	725	−7	1,039	43	822	−21	712	−13
Loans	4,451	4,354	−2	10,045	151	12,421	13	14,393	16
Total	$11,523	$21,271	85%	$22,599	6%	$19,916	−12%	$22,133	11%
B. *Composition of Funds*									
Grants	55%	76%		47%		34%		32%	
Work	7%	3%		5%		4%		3%	
Loans	39%	21%		48%		62%		65%	

Source: Calculated from College Board, 1992

below considers both vantages in order to illustrate the consequence of this framing assumption.

Trends in the amounts of funds available through all federal programs between FY 1970–71 and FY 1989–90 are presented in Table 2. First, when only the Title IV programs (Part I of Table 2) are examined, it appears that the growth in student aid has been constant and substantial. The total aid available through the Title IV programs increased throughout the period. In FY 1970–71, the funding for Title IV loans was substantially higher than for the grant program. However by FY 1975–76, the amount of grant aid awarded had increased substantially, but the loan aid had decreased slightly. Both grant and loans dollars awarded increased in the late 1970s, although loans grew more rapidly. In the 1980s, both grant and loan programs increased at more moderate rates. These trends illustrate a steady pattern of growth in Title IV aid, in spite of budget deficits.

Second, when these trends are examined from the perspective of the specially directed programs (Part II of Table 2), most of which were in existence before the HEA, a different story emerges. The funding for specially directed programs increased substantially in the early 1970s, a period when funding for Title IV grant programs also expanded, then declined substantially in subsequent years. Viewed from this perspective, it seems that the growth in Title IV programs during the 1980s was more than offset by reductions in these specially directed programs.[6]

Finally, if we examine these trends from the perspective of the total amount of funds made available to students through federal student aid programs (Part III, Table 2), then we get a more complete view of changes in federal student aid programs. Viewed from this perspective, it becomes apparent that the total amount of student aid available increased in the early 1970s, but remained stable thereafter. Moreover, it should be noted that the total amount of grant aid dropped substantially between FY 1975–76 and FY 1989–90, while the total amount of loan aid increased substantially.[7]

Two facts related to this shift should be considered by the reader. First, loans

[6]In our view, if policy analysts focus exclusively on Title IV funding, they will miss the fact that total federal student aid did not increase in the 1980s. It could perhaps be argued that the tacit decision to shift funds from specially directed programs to generally directed aid increased the cost effectiveness of aid dollars. However, since this issue is seldom considered by policy analysts, this argument has not been made or tested publicly.

[7]The issue of whether specially directed student aid can or should be treated in the same way as generally available federal student aid can be debated. Our argument is that the increased availability of funds makes higher education more accessible, which is consistent with arguments originally made by Becker (1964). Thus, if researchers control for financial need, then it is possible to assess the effects of different types (and amounts) of aid, regardless of their source. The alternative argument is that only generally available programs should be considered since they are administered based on need. The problem with this approach, while it is theoretically more consistent, is that it ignores the practical reality that all forms of aid can influence student choice. Analysis that considers only Title IV could be distorted as a result of the fact that specially directed programs may also influence access.

cost less than grants because they are subsidized rather than fully funded[8]. Thus, given the budget constraints of the 1980s, federal student aid programs became a source of overall savings, rather than a resource drain. Second, some low-income students respond better to grants than to loans (Leslie and Brinkman, 1988; St. John, 1990b). The redistribution of aid from grants to loans could have had a negative influence on equal opportunity. An irony created by these conditions—that the form of student aid that was potentially most beneficial to low-income students began to decline in the late 1970s, a period when middle-income students were intentionally included in the eligibility criteria for the Title IV grant programs—should not be overlooked.

Intended Outcomes[9]

Promoting equal opportunity in postsecondary education has historically been defined as the primary goal of the HEA Title IV programs (Gladieux and Wolanin, 1976). The simplest way of investigating the "effectiveness" of federal student aid programs is to examine the relationship between funding and participation rates, an approach that does not take into an account the many other forces that could influence student participation rates.[10] In spite of the many limitations with this approach, the relationship between funding levels and participation rates is considered as a means of examining whether researchers should consider total federal student aid or just Title IV student aid when they consider these trends.

Twenty-year trends in participation rates for traditional college-age students (18- to 24-year-olds) are summarized in Table 3. These trends indicate an improvement in participation rates by African-Americans and Hispanics[11] during the early 1970s, but a decline in their participation rates in the late 1970s and early 1980s. Since African-Americans and Hispanics are historically disadvantaged compared with whites, their participation rates are often viewed as an indicator of success or failure of federal student aid programs (e.g. Leslie and Brinkman, 1988).

Between 1970 and 1975, there was a substantial (521 percent) increase in spending on Title IV grant programs, due largely to the creation of the Pell program. Total federal grants also increased during the period (by 157 percent). However, loans from both Title IV and specially directed programs decreased

[8]Fifty cents on the dollar is generally accepted as the cost of Title IV loan programs (St. John and Masten, 1990).

[9]The unintended outcomes of federal student aid programs include direct effects on institutions (McPherson, Wagner, and Willie-Schiff, 1989). Additionally, prices and price subsidies influence participation by adults (Tynes, 1993), a population seldom considered in policy studies.

[10]It should be noted that this approach tacitly uses assumptions of human capital theory, i.e. that people make their educational choice based on a rational assessment of the costs and benefits. These assumptions are more explicitly examined in section IIB below.

[11]Participation rates by Hispanics were not collected in fall 1970.

TABLE 3. Trends in participation rates (percent currently enrolled) by 18- to 24-year-olds, by ethnicity, falls 1970, 1975, 1980, 1985, 1989.

	Fall 1970	Fall 1975	Fall 1980	Fall 1985	Fall 1989
All Races	29.9%	30.2%	30.4%	32.2%	37.1%
Whites	30.9%	30.1%	30.7%	32.7%	37.7%
African-American	22.7%	29.8%	26.9%	26.9%	31.7%
Hispanics	NA	28.4%	23.1%	24.8%	24.2%

NA: Not available

Source: Calculated from Current Population Surveys, Series P-20. U.S. Department of Commerce, Bureau of the Census, 1971, 1976, 1985, 1989, 1991.

*Students enrolled in any type of school included in enrolled.

slightly during the period. During the five-year period the participation rate for African-Americans increased substantially (from 22.7 percent in fall 1970 to 29.8 percent in fall 1975), to a rate nearly equal to whites. Therefore, from this evidence it would seem possible to attribute some of the gains in participation rates by African-Americans and Hispanics to growth in Title IV and/or total grants.

Between 1975 and 1980, participation by Hispanics dropped by over five percentage points, while the participation rate for African-Americans[12] dropped (to 26.9 percent) and participation for whites increased (Table 3). If we consider aid provided by Title IV programs only, then these results seem incongruent, since Title IV programs increased during the period (see Part I, Table 2). If, on the other hand, we consider total aid available through federal student aid programs, then we must consider the fact that total grant dollars declined during the late 1970s, while loan dollars increased. It seems, therefore, that the decline in the total amount of grant aid available provides a plausible explanation for the drops in minority participation.[13] Additionally, it should be noted that there was a shift in grant dollars from low-income to middle-income during the period (St. John and Byce, 1982), which could further explain the differential changes in partic-

[12]When the annual participation rates are examined, it is further apparent that participation rates by African-Americans were higher in 1976 and 1978 than in either 1975 or 1980 (Mingle, 1987; Pelavin and Kane, 1987).

[13]This distinction between Title IV funding and total federal grants seems important when assessing the effects of federal student aid programs. Hansen (1983), for example, examined the relationship between Title IV funding and participation rates by high school seniors in 1972 and 1980, using the longitudinal data bases. He concluded that there was no relationship between funding and participation. However, had he used total federal grants, he might have reached a different conclusion. This issue, which has been addressed by others (Leslie and Brinkman, 1988), illustrates the crucial nature of the researcher's interpretation of the historical moment.

ipation rates for African-Americans and Hispanics (both of which declined) and whites (which increased).

Between 1980 and 1985, the overall participation rate and the participation rate for whites improved; the participation rate for Hispanics improved slightly, but remained lower than in 1975; and the participation rate for African-Americans did not change and remained below the 1975 level (Table 3). During this period there was an increase in total loans, but a decrease in total grants (Part III, Table 2), as well as a slight increase in Title IV grants and loans (Part I, Table 2). If we use total aid as a base, then we might attribute the change in participation by whites to expansion of loans, which have a greater influence on middle-income students. The same explanation would hold if we considered Title IV only.

Finally, there was an increase in the overall participation rate and the participation rates for whites and African-Americans between 1985 and 1989 and a slight drop for Hispanics (Table 3). The participation rates for whites and African-Americans increased by about five percentage points. What explains these leaps? During the period there was an increase in total grants (by 5 percent) and Title IV grants (by 14 percent). It is plausible that the growth in grants, especially growth in Pell, could explain the growth in African-American participation. Total federal and Title IV loans also increased during the five-year period, which could explain the increase in participation by whites, since middle-income student are more responsive to loans (Carlson, 1975; St. John, 1990b). Additionally, the redistribution of grant dollars from middle-income to low-income students, a recent policy development (Hearn, 1993), could have positively influenced African-American participation rates. However, given the extent of the increase in participation rates for African-Americans and whites, it would appear that other forces, possibly growth in the returns to education or other changes in the labor market, also influenced the increase in participation rates. Nevertheless, it appears from this limited information that Congress and the Bush administration may have successfully developed a strategy that simultaneously addressed the needs of both the low-income and middle-income populations. If this were the case,[14] then it would appear that competing interests of the middle and lower

[14]We cannot reach any conclusions about causal linkages from these trend analyses. Many student aid researchers do not put much stock in participation rate studies because they do not control adequately for other factors that influence student enrollment decisions, a line of argument summarized well by Leslie and Brinkman (1988). However, since studies have been given attention in the past (e.g. Hansen, 1983), we decided we needed to examine critically the role of this approach. Nevertheless, the reader is reminded that such analyses are overly simplistic and may completely miss other forces. For example, the amount of student aid awarded could have gone up in the late 1980s because labor market changes influenced students to enroll, rather than because of changes in federal student aid policy. Thus, growth in aid expenditures could be influenced by growth in enrollment, rather than the reverse.

classes were being balanced, a major accomplishment given the history of Title IV programs.[15]

Gaining Perspective

The historical moment is but one dimension of the policy researcher's prism—one of the tacit lenses used in policy research. This summative review of the history of the federal student aid programs has had two purposes. First, the role of historical assumptions in the framing of policy analyses was illustrated. Specifically, we distinguished among three historical periods, based on the assumption that these periods illustrated major shifts in the intended target population for federal programs. Further, we assumed that all types of aid could influence participation rates. Our analysis of trends considered how these assumptions influenced our conclusions and how these differed from other researchers.

Second, this brief history of federal student aid programs also provides a reference point—an interpretive perspective—for our critical examination of selected policy studies below. Thus, the historical periods of the student aid programs, program funding history, and changes in postsecondary participation rates during this period provide reference points for subsequent analyses.

B. Basic Theories

In our meta framework (Section I), we characterized two dominant research traditions—the empirical/analytical and the historical/hermeneutical. This section examines the assumptions of the basic theories in both traditions typically used in this type of research.

The Empirical/Analytical Tradition

Most policy research on student aid uses basic theories from the empirical/analytic tradition. Since the analysis of trends does not provide an indication of whether fluctuations in enrollment were caused by, or caused, fluctuations in expenditures on student aid, we need better ways to assess these linkages. More sophisticated statistical models provide a tool; but a more complete theory is needed to guide the choice of variables to include (and control for) in assessments of the effects of student aid. Economic theory on human capital and sociological theory on educational attainment are most frequently used for this purpose. Research in these traditions addresses the basic question of whether student aid

[15]Issues related to the tradeoffs between the middle class and the lower class have seldom explicitly been examined using this broad framework. Instead the assumption has usually been made that the effectiveness of Title IV programs can best be measured by participation rates for students from low-income families (e.g. Hansen, 1983). This assumption does not fully recognize that: 1) the intent of federal programs shifted to include middle-income students in 1978 and funds followed this shift in intent (St. John and Byce, 1982); or 2) that other types of student aid, including specially directed federal programs, can also influence enrollment.

influences enrollment and persistence. The assumptions and applications of these theories, as well as the emergence of hybrid approaches, are explored below.

Human Capital Theory: Human capital theory (Becker, 1964, 1975) provides a conceptual base that can be, and indeed frequently has been, used in research on student aid. According to human capital theory, individuals and society make rational choices about their investments in education. Accordingly, individuals weigh the costs—the direct costs of attending, foregone earnings, and psychic costs—against the benefits, both economic and psychic, when they make their decisions to attend college.[16] Society's decisions to invest in education are also based on weighing the direct costs of educational subsidies against the economic returns—the gains in tax revenues from gains in production and individual earnings. In his initial book, Becker (1964) speculated that student loans could be viewed from this framework.

The original studies applying human capital theory focused on the impact of prices and price subsidies on student enrollment decisions. There have been several reviews of these "student demand" studies (e.g. Jackson and Weathersby, 1975; Leslie and Brinkman, 1988; McPherson, 1978). Some of these studies were cross-sectional, using a sample of prospective students to assess the impact of prices, net prices, or aid offers on whether students attend. The most noted example of this type of economic analysis is Manski and Wise's *College Choice in America*, which used an assessment of the impact of student aid on the enrollment decisions by students in the high school class of 1972 (which entered college the year before the Pell grant program was implemented) to estimate the impact the Pell program would have had on enrollment (Manski and Wise, 1983). They used an analysis of the enrollment rates of students in the high school class of 1980 to assess the reasonableness of their estimates. Others use historical information, in econometric trend analyses,[17] to assess how changes in prices influence enrollment (e.g. Corazzini, Dugan, and Grabowski, 1972). The most notable recent study using this method was McPherson and Schapiro's *Keeping College Affordable* (1991). Their study established that both changes in tuition and changes in student aid influence enrollment rates. The overwhelming conclusions from these analyses are that there is a link between prices and enrollment.

The human capital paradigm has also been used for research on the returns to public decisions to invest in higher education. Research on individual returns consistently indicates that college graduates earn more than high school graduates (Leslie, 1990; Leslie and Brinkman, 1988; Pascarella and Terenzini, 1991). Some economists have argued that the costs of benefits of vocational and post-

[16]The term "psychic" is derived directly from Becker (1964).

[17]These studies typically use regressions that consider the effects of a range of economic variables that could influence enrollments. Thus they use more sophisticated techniques than trend studies that compare trends in aid dollars with trends in enrollment rates.

secondary programs can be assessed using tax revenue returns derived from increases in educational attainment attributable to public expenditures (e.g. Friedman, 1962; Levin, 1983). In fact, Friedman (1962) has argued that tax revenue returns should be the basis on which the public makes its decisions to invest in postsecondary education. Based on Friedman's argument, St. John and Masten (1990) assessed the influence student financial aid had on the educational attainment of students in the high school class of 1972, then estimated the future federal tax revenue returns attributable to these gains and the actual costs of the subsidies provided. They concluded that the tax revenue returns to the federal government were more than four times the costs, a ratio that does not take into account the indirect gains, such as reduced social welfare costs. While this line of inquiry indicates the federal returns on its investment in student aid are substantial, there are no doubt refinements that can be made to the estimation methods used in this study.

In sum, research studies that use the human capital assumptions usually find a linkage between student aid and student enrollment (Leslie and Brinkman, 1988). However, these studies generally do not consider the range of social background variables that should be considered when the effects of student aid are examined.

Educational Attainment: Sociological research on educational attainment usually assumes that educational attainment is a function of parental background, student ability and achievement, school characteristics and achievement (e.g. Alexander and Eckland 1975; Blau and Duncan, 1967; Wolfle, 1985). This line of inquiry, which is more likely to use causal models that examine both the direct and indirect effects of social variables, has been particularly useful in building an understanding of the effects of socioeconomic status and ethnicity on first-time college attendance and college attainment (Pascarella and Terenzini, 1991).

In recent years this line of inquiry has been particularly germane to addressing issues related to minority attendance rates. In particular, understanding how ethnicity, family socioeconomic status, and ability/achievement combine to influence first-time college attendance. This line of research consistently finds that African-Americans are more likely to attend college than whites when high school grades and standardized test scores are included in the equation (e.g. Hearn, 1988). When the emphasis is placed on attainment research, analysts may conclude that high school grades and test scores, which are lower on average for African-Americans than for whites, explain why participation rates are lower for African-Americans than for whites. This assumption frequently leads to a conclusion that the way federal government can best improve college attendance by African-Americans is to improve the quality of elementary and secondary schools (e.g. Chaikind, 1987; Pelavin and Kane, 1988).

A recent study using the High School and Beyond senior cohort (students who were high school seniors in 1980) provides more insight into how these background variables combine to influence postsecondary attendance. Hearn (1988) examined the influence of ethnicity (African-American, Hispanic, Asian), genders, siblings, high school program and grades, and test scores on whether this cohort attended college at two points in time (fall 1980 and fall 1981). He found that the direct and indirect influence of being African-American, as well as of most other background variables, increased between the fall of 1980, when 46 percent of the sample attended college (and 53 percent attended any postsecondary), and the fall of 1981, when 51 percent attended college (and 62 percent attended any postsecondary). Hearn's study reveals that the variables that have an influence on college attendance directly after high school, have an even stronger direct influence on college attendance a year after high school. Hearn's research suggests that the measurable disadvantages of African-Americans compared with whites may decrease when broader definitions are used.[18]

Sociological studies on educational attainment consistently confirm a linkage between social background and postsecondary attendance, which is not as consistently and completely considered in economic studies. However, these studies usually do not explicitly consider the influence of student aid on postsecondary attendance or attainment (persistence), which limits their utility in the policy arena.[19] Thus, they provide insight into the general causes of inequity, but do not explicitly consider whether government intervention actually mitigates these inequities. Therefore, research that explicitly considers both the economic human capital paradigm and the sociological educational attainment paradigm was needed to more fully examine these relationships.

Hybrid Studies: Jackson (1977, 1978) was one of the first researchers to explicitly consider both the sociological and economic research before framing the inquiry into students' college attendance decisions.[20] Jackson's research established a framework for considering the influence of a more complete set of variables, including student aid, on access, choice, and persistence. His research not only confirmed the linkage between student aid and college attendance, but it also documented the fact that students' aspirations have an influence on their prospects of attending college.

In a more recent study, St. John and Noell (1989) examined how social

[18]This finding further illustrates the crucial role of tacit framing assumptions. Specifically, Hearn (1988) illustrates that the specification of outcome variables—an action necessary in quantitative policy studies—can influence research findings.

[19]It could also be argued that the utilitarian orientation of economic theories lend themselves to instrumental uses that can be destructive to the very policies and programs that economists are supposed to plan for and evaluate. Thus, while economic approaches have more direct policy applicability, they can also easily be misused, an issue discussed below.

[20]Manski and Wise (1983) also used the National Longitudinal Study of the High School Class of 1972 and considered a similar range of variables. Jackson's research is emphasized in this section because: 1) his research predated the work conducted by Manski and Wise; and 2) his work was widely read in the higher education research community, perhaps because it originally appeared in the *Journal of Higher Education*, rather than in economic or sociological journals.

background variables influenced the decision by high school seniors to apply to college and the decision by applicants to attend college. They also examined the influence of aid offers on attendance by college applicants, which had a consistently positive influence, consistent with Jackson's findings (Jackson, 1978, 1988). St. John and Noell (1989) found that African-Americans were more likely to apply to college, but African-American applicants were less likely to attend. In a follow-up study, St. John (1991c) used one set of sequential logistic regressions to examine how background variables and aspirations interacted to influence college attendance by high school seniors and another set to assess how these variables and student aid interacted to influence first-time attendance by college applicants. Based on these analyses he suggested that there were three ways policy makers could influence postsecondary attendance by underrepresented minorities: improvements in elementary schooling for at-risk youth could possibly improve postsecondary attendance if they improved academic preparation; postsecondary information aimed at middle school students could improve postsecondary attendance if it positively influenced students' aspirations; and the targeting of student aid can influence postsecondary attendance by minority students.

There have also been a few studies that used the combined sociological attainment and economic paradigms to examine the influence of student aid on persistence. Terkla (1985) was one of the first to develop a workable model for national research on the effects of student aid on persistence. She found that aid had a positive direct influence on long-term persistence to college graduation.[21] In addition to social background, high school experience, ability/achievement, and aspirations, her study explicitly considered the influence of college characteristics and student aid. St. John (1989) used NLS and HSB to examine how aid packages influenced year-to-year persistence by students who entered college in 1972, 1980, and 1982. This research seemed to untangle unresolved issues about how different types of student aid influence persistence. It discovered that loans had a negative association with first-to-second-year persistence by college students from the high school class of 1972, but not for students in the high school class of 1982.[22] This finding was consistent with prior research by Astin (1975) that found a negative association between loans and persistence by students who enrolled in the 1960s. With the exception of this anomaly, student aid had a

[21]Astin (1975) had previously conducted a national study of the influence of student aid on persistence, but did not use a regression or causal model, which is the case with the studies cited here. Terkla's path model represented an improvement to the extent that she carefully selected the set of variables that would need to be considered in order to assess the influence of student aid on persistence using a national data base.

[22]St. John (1989) concluded that there may have been a change in the ways students viewed loans. However, based on an analysis of the influence of federal budget decisions on enrollment (St. John, 1993), it also would seem possible that the shift could be related to changes in the population receiving loans as the only form of aid.

positive association with persistence in both the 1970s and 1980s (St. John, 1989).

These newer hybrid studies reconcile some of the policy limitations of using either the educational attainment or human capital paradigms. They confirm sociological studies that conclude social background has a substantial influence on attainment (e.g. Alexander and Eckland, 1975; Eckland and Henderson, 1981; Hearn, 1988) and economic research that suggests a linkage between aid and attainment (e.g. Leslie and Brinkman, 1988; McPherson and Schapiro, 1991).

Student Choice: Inquiry into the factors that influence students to choose one college over an other has implications for student aid policy research, as well as for enrollment management. Student choice first emerged as an objective for federal student aid programs as a result of the *Education Amendments of 1972*, which created Pell as a portable grant program that could promote choice of college (Gladieux and Wolanin, 1976).

National research on student choice began in the late 1970s, as part of a federally funded evaluation study that reexamined issues related to whether student aid was more effective than institutional subsidies (Weathersby, Jacobs, Jackson, St. John, and Tingley, 1977). In a report written for that study, Jackson (1977) conceptualized student choice of college as a process that began in high school, when the predisposition to attend college is formed and students select an initial choice set. Jackson's research established that aid offers have an influence on choices among schools in the initial choice set, a finding later confirmed by M.L. Tierney (1980a and 1980b). Jackson's conceptualization of the choice process influenced subsequent models of the student choice process (Hossler, Braxton, and Coopersmith, 1989; Hossler and Gallagher, 1987) and was integral to the development of theory and practice in the field of enrollment management (Hossler, 1984, 1987; Hossler, Bean, and Associates, 1990).

Other more recent research on student aid and student choice has the potential of extending, possibly even transforming, the assumptions embedded in the economic and sociological paradigms. First, there is substantial evidence that the redistribution of aid from grants to loans in the 1980s influenced a shift of low-income students to lower- cost four-year and two-year colleges. This conclusion was reached by recent studies that examined longitudinal data bases (Grubb, 1990; Pascarella, Smart, and Smylie, 1992). Pascarella, Smart, and Smylie (1992) found that price increases in the 1980s not only influenced the distribution of students but also their early social attainment. Further, based on their time-series analysis, McPherson and Schapiro (1991) found middle-income students shifted to less expensive institutions in the 1980s, as a consequence of the price increases. This conclusion, about the effects of redistributing aid from grants to loans, was at least partially confirmed in a recent analysis that considered the effects of actual changes in tuition and aid awards by sector on enrollment distributions (St. John, 1993).

Second, a couple of recent studies on the influence of variables related to choice of college on persistence by college students seem to open new avenues for assessment of aid programs. Fine (1992) analyzed the effects of sets of variables related to student social and economic background, high school experience, college choice, and college experience, aspirations, and prices on within-year persistence by traditional college-age students enrolled in private colleges using the National Postsecondary Student Aid Survey of 1986–87 (NPSAS-87).[23] He used sequential logistic regressions to examine the interactions among each set of variables. He found that: 1) two college choice variables were significant—whether the college was close work was positively associated with persistence and field of study was negatively associated with persistence—before prices and price subsidies were entered into the equation; 2) when current aspirations were entered into the logistic model (the step before prices and price subsidies), being close to work shifted from having a positive (and significant) to a negative (and significant) association with persistence (apparently because students with short-term goals chose a college because of its location); 3) none of the student choice variables remained significant when prices and price subsidies were entered into the equation; and 4) when prices and price subsides were entered into the final logistic regression, the amount of variance explained by the model more than doubled (based on change in the pseudo R^2). Fine's study not only confirms that there is a linkage between college choice and persistence, but indicates there is an interaction between the reasons students choose a college and the way they respond to tuition charges and student subsidies.

In another recent study using a similar logistical model, Tynes (1993) used NPSAS-87 to examine the influence of college choice on within-year persistence by nontraditional college-age students (adults over 25 years of age) at four-year colleges. She found that four choice variables had an influence on persistence by adults: choosing a college because of the course of study and because of low costs were both significant and negatively associated with persistence, while choosing a college because of student aid and because they could live at home were significant and positively associated with persistence. None of these college choice variables were significant in Tynes' study when college experience was considered without prices and price subsidies. In combination, these studies indicate that there is an interaction between the reasons why students of all ages choose to attend a college and the way they respond to the prices and subsidies they face.

This line of inquiry expands the potential ways of viewing the effects of student aid. Further studies exploring the relationship between college choice and persistence could provide insight into how changes in government student aid

[23]Fine (1992) adapted a persistence model that St. John, Oescher, and Andrieu (1992) had previously used to examine the effects of student aid on within-year persistence in public and private four-year colleges.

and institutional pricing policies influence students' college choices and their persistence in college.

Competing or Compatible Paradigms? Within the empirical/analytical tradition, there is a tendency to work within a basic set of assumptions. And, typical of researchers working within a paradigmatic community (Kuhn, 1970), the dominant researchers within each of the three communities of inquiry described above tend to communicate within their own scientific communities. Researchers working within the human capital paradigm tend to publish in economics journals, researchers working within the sociological attainment paradigm tend to publish in sociology journals, and researchers dealing with the hybrid models and student choice tend to publish in higher education journals. In these academic discourses, the underlying assumptions within these research communities can go unquestioned for extended periods.[24] Therefore, these four ways of assessing the effects of student aid could be viewed as competing paradigms.

Alternatively we can construct a broader communicative discourse that critically examines the underlying assumptions of the various theories that are germane to the study of student aid policy. When we use this broader perspective, we find that there are assumptions related to each of these lines of inquiry that appear verifiable, and, therefore, merit consideration in new reconstructions of theory regarding the effects of student aid.

The Historical/Hermeneutic Tradition

In the education community in general, research in the historical/hermeneutic tradition has become a dominant force (e.g. Apple, 1985; Liston, 1990). And there is a growing number of studies in higher education that attempt to build an understanding of how and why change happens in the policy arena (e.g. Rhoades, 1992; Slaughter, 1991; W.G. Tierney, 1990, 1991, 1992). Three lines of inquiry are of particular relevance to this case study: investigations that attempt to examine the forces that shape evolution of student aid programs without taking a particular ideological perspective; investigations into student aid and higher education finance that maintain neo- conservative assumptions; and critical inquiries into higher education policy that essentially hold neo-Marxist assumptions. These particular lines of inquiry were chosen because their inherent positions are crucial to the understanding of the current discourse about student aid and other federal programs.

Political Incrementalism: The concept of political incrementalism emanates from the work of Lindblom (1977) and Wildavsky (1979). Researchers working in this tradition attempt to maintain an objective point of view, but do not assume

[24]For example, W.G. Tierney (1992) argues that the assumption of social integration is not only commonly accepted (Stage, 1990) but also seldom questioned. Holding this assumption, treated in the discussion of the hermeneutical research tradition below, could limit our ability to identify factors that inhibit minority retention or strategies that could transform them.

a rational basis for policy decisions. Rather, they generally try to assess objectively whether these decisions are rational, without making the positivist assumption that society is continually evolving toward a better, more rational state. Thus researchers working in this tradition make no attempt to rationalize policy developments in terms that emphasize general progress or goal attainment. Rather they attempt to untangle the forces and interests that influence policy decisions. A few studies have examined the policy process in student aid, including a recent study by Hearn (1993),[25] which provides an insightful argument about the convergence of rational intentions and political forces.

Hearn (1993) identifies a paradox in the growth of federal student aid programs. On the one hand, there has been substantial growth in funding for the Title IV programs since the passage of HEA. On the other, these programs have lacked both the ideal, and even the usual "philosophical, managerial, political, fiscal, and demographic bases for such growth" (Hearn, 1993, p. 94).[26] After examining the history of Title IV programs and the possible explanations for the paradox, Hearn concludes that Wildavsky's (1979) argument about rationality within political constraints, may explain the paradox: "Placed in the context of federal student aid, Wildavsky's idea of dual modes may help inform our understanding of the paradox. It seems reasonable to argue that the paradox stems from an excessive domination of the social interaction mode over the cognition mode" (p. 143).[27]

Another issue that emerges from Hearn's analysis merits attention in the policy research community. In the epilogue to his chapter, Hearn addresses the Bush administration's attempt to redirect funds in the Title IV programs from middle-income students to low-income students. There is another paradox embedded in

[25]Hearn's chapter provides an extensive review of this literature on student aid policy as an incremental political process. Therefore, no attempt is made to review that literature in this chapter.

[26]This paradox takes on different dimensions depending on the vantage we choose relative to the budget for student aid programs. If we consider only the budget for Title IV (Part I, Table 2), then the paradox seems quite formidable. However, if we consider the entire federal budget for student aid programs (Part III, Table 2), then the magnitude of the issues is quite different— the focus might naturally shift to the reasons for the transfer of funds from specially directed programs to generally available programs. Further, total federal expenditures probably decreased, given the lower cost of loans compared to grants. If we use this broader assumption, then it would seem that the generally available programs (Part I, Table 2) would have a more "rational" base than the specially directed programs (Part II, Table 2). Thus, if viewed from this vantage, it appears there could be some underlying rational base to the incremental political decisions that created and expanded the Title IV programs. However, from Hearn's analysis it is also evident that such rationality (the cognition mode) was not explicitly considered in the political process.

[27]If we hold the broader interpretation of the paradox, that total student aid funds should be considered, then this analysis could be recast. Since there appears to be some rationality in shifting funds from specially directed programs to Title IV programs, it could be argued that there has been a relative balance between the social interaction mode and the cognition mode in the political decisions about federal student aid programs. However, there remains a paradox, considered here, as well as by Hearn (1993), relative to the recent shift in the amount of aid awarded from low-income to middle-income students.

this action, given the history of student aid policies during the past 15 years. On the one hand, officials of the Reagan and Bush administrations had redirected grant funds from SEOG, which has been used for middle-income students since the passage of MISAA (St. John and Byce, 1982), to the Pell program, which is more targeted on low-income students. These actions were taken through the budget process, however, rather than the legislative process.[28] On the other hand, the political rhetoric of the Reagan and Bush administrations favored the middle-income students and actions were taken to exclude some low-income aid recipients.[29] These policies seem to have both redistributed students across institutional sectors, with more low-income students moving to two-year colleges and more upper-middle-income students moving to private colleges, and to have pushed some low-income students out higher education, especially in the middle 1980s (e.g. Pascarella, Smart, and Smylie, 1992).

Thus the political incremental perspective provides a way of further untangling the political forces that influence the creation and evolution of student aid programs.[30] However, explicit consideration of the ideological positions of various analysts is also needed if we are also to build a more complete understanding of how political influence is used in the framing of policy analyses.

Neo-Conservative Analyses: Habermas (1992) argues that the new conservatives assume that there has been an erosion of social values and that social policy should be aimed at returning society to an earlier state. Thus neo-conservatism can be distinguished from the historic conservative position, which essentially argued against government intervention in social affairs, by its emphasizing moving backwards to a prior state. In higher education policy, the arguments of neo-conservatives (e.g. Bennett, 1987; Finn, 1988a, 1988b) were very influential in the 1980s. Therefore, these arguments merit scrutiny when examining ways of framing student aid policy research.

One argument made by neo-conservatives was that federal student aid fueled price increases in colleges and universities and, therefore, that constraining student aid budgets was an appropriate way to constrain prices (Bennett, 1987). This

[28]Certainly Congress also influenced this shift since they set the level of funding in annual budget process. However, the Reagan budget bills consistently tried to reduce funding for SEOG, and budget analysts in the U.S. Department of Education's Office of Planning, Budget and Evaluation, routinely analyzed the income levels of aid recipients in their budget models. Therefore, senior administration officials had visibility into this issue when they put together the budget bill each year.

[29]Specifically, the Reagan and Bush administrations' policies on loans and on loan defaults created problems for low-income, first-time college attenders and for institutions that served them. Research indicates that social background rather than institutional loan practices are the cause of default (Wilms, Moore, and Bolus, 1987). Yet, the Reagan and Bush administrations made numerous efforts to eliminate institutions with high default rates.

[30]It should be noted that a policy analyst could use neo-conservative or neo-rational assumptions to examine incremental changes. Hearn, as Wildavsky, tends to seek a ''neo-rational'' (or ideologically neutral) base for his analysis rather than an ideological basis. Nevertheless the three categories of hermeneutic research described here could be overlapping.

line of argument assumes that institutions use revenues from federal student aid programs to offset tuition increases (McPherson and Schapiro, 1991). However, trend analyses do not support this line of argument (McPherson and Schapiro, 1991). Further, the regulations for the Pell Grant program—the combination of maximum awards and 60 percent of cost provisions—would seem to preclude this possibility for most private institutions. In fact, it appears that private institutions used their own tuition revenues to offset losses from federal grants during the 1980s (St. John, 1992), which would seem to support those who argued that reductions in federal student aid fueled increases in tuition charges (Hauptman, 1988; Hauptman and Hartle, 1987), which was the reverse of Bennett's argument.

There seems to be at least one special circumstance in which institutions can realize some gain in revenues from federal student aid programs by increasing tuition. Hearn and Anderson (1989) examined the impact of changes in state financing strategies in Minnesota, where the state government purposely raised tuition and grants. Thus, if more public institutions adopted this strategy, which has been widely advocated (McPherson and Schapiro, 1991; Wallace, 1992), they could realize some marginal revenue gain from federal student aid programs. However there are probably limits to the viability of this approach because of the Pell regulations already discussed. Once institutions increase beyond the level at which most of there needy students have maximum Pell awards, there may be more to lose than to gain from continuation of this strategy (Lopez, 1993).

A second argument frequently made by neo-conservatives is that excessive administrative expenditures drove tuition higher in the 1980s (Finn, 1988a, 1988b). To critically examine this argument, it is necessary to move beyond the mere analysis of trends in administrative expenditures to explore the possible causal link between growth in administrative expenditures and increases in tuition charges. Analyses of trends in administrative expenditures clearly indicate that administrative expenditures increased faster than instructional expenditures in the early 1980s (Kirshstein, Tikoff, Masten, and St. John, 1990). It is evident from trend analyses that there was an escalation in professional positions in administration, as well as in the salaries of administrators (Kirshstein, et al., 1990). Thus, there is reason to be concerned about controlling costs (e.g. Basset, 1983). However, when these patterns are deconstructed through the examination of case studies, the assumed causal linkage running from administration to prices does not hold. Instead, it appears that growth in administrative expenditures was related to growth in total revenues, but not to increases in tuition charges (St. John, 1992). When revenues go up, administrative expenditures rise. However, tuition often goes up when other revenue sources go down, especially in public institutions where tuition increases are routinely used to offset reductions in state support. Therefore, tuition charges can go up when total revenues and administrative expenditures remain stable or decline.

Thus, while there may be reasons to be concerned about rising administrative expenditures and other higher education costs, it does not appear that there is a causal linkage running from increases in administrative expenditures to increases in tuition. Further, it should be noted that some areas of administrative expansion are intended to increase other revenue sources (and therefore may not only pay their own costs but also constrain tuition increases). For example, the development function is intended to raise revenue from gifts, while enrollment management is intended to increase the number of students and total amount of tuition collected. The increased capacity of these units to raise revenue could, in fact, serve to mitigate future tuition increases. Thus the linkage between tuition charges and administrative expenditures is complex and may, in fact, be quite different from the relationship hypothesized by the neo-conservatives.

There is also some circumstantial evidence that the neo-conservative intent of moving backwards on social programs took precedence over the rational pursuit of policy objectives in the 1980s. The sequence of events surrounding the funding and eventual publication of a study of the returns to the federal investment in student aid serves as an illustration. In the middle 1980s, the U.S. Department of Education commissioned a study of the returns on the federal investment in student aid. Friedman's (1962) argument that the federal investment in higher education should be made based on tax revenue returns was used as the rationale for the request for proposal. When the study concluded that net present value of future tax revenues was far in excess of the costs of providing aid (St. John and Masten, 1988), the report was, in effect, shelved. When the principal investigator of the study left the consulting business, he published an article based on the report (St. John and Masten, 1990), thus disseminating the findings to the student aid community.[31] In this instance, the political interests that influenced the funding of the study had expected the opposite finding. But when the study, which used consistently conservative assumptions,[32] did not support their basic tenets (that student aid was ineffective and should be cut), it was not disseminated.

These examples illustrate a limitation of using an ideological argument as the basis for policy analysis. It can reduce policy analysts to putting together a case to support an ideological position, rather than objectively assessing the assump-

[31]For professional consultants there is an implicit threat that if they take action to publish findings without the appropriate political agreements, they will lose the opportunity for future funding. In the case of the study of the returns on the federal investment in student aid, the findings were unexpected by the funding agency. The assumption apparently had been made that federal expenditures on student aid would have low direct (tax revenue) returns, in which case the study could be used along with others that concluded that student aid was ineffectual (e.g. Hansen, 1983), in support of arguments to reduce spending on federal student aid programs.

[32]For example, no attempt was made to estimate the indirect returns, such as reductions in welfare or prison costs. Yet it is the indirect returns that are used for cost-benefit ratios for some other social programs, such as Head Start. Additionally, adjustments were made to allow for the influence of ability even though these adjustments were not necessary because the regressions used to estimate the model had already considered (and controlled for) the influences of this variable.

tions embedded in these arguments. This seems to have been the case with the neo-conservative analyses of student aid and college prices. The sole criterion used to filter through the evidence seems to have been whether the evidence supported the political position of the administration. Therefore, the policy community needs to exercise extreme caution about the ideological arguments embedded in the policy literature, which is an issue that is getting increasing attention in the policy research community (e.g. Fischer and Forester, 1987).

Neo-Marxist Interpretations: The primary neo-Marxist assumption is that a class dialectic, with the implicit upper class oppression of the lower class, permeates social systems. According to Habermas (1992), many critical theorists hold Marxist assumptions. Habermas argues that while the Marxist assumptions of the class dialectic seem to hold when they are critically analyzed, critical theorists who use Marxist assumptions need to test these assumptions using the falsification principle.

The problem of not testing implicit assumptions was evident in the critical examination of the neo-conservative arguments above. Therefore, those who make ideological arguments need means for testing their assumptions. Liston (1990) argues that neo-Marxists should not rest their arguments on the mere coincidental occurrence of phenomena. For example, Liston points out that the argument that ''[a]bility grouping in public schools occurs because such practices supply capitalists with a skilled and compliant work force'' (p. 88) may be spurious because of the implicit causal linkage. In other words, the use of ability grouping in schools may be compatible with the labor force needs of an industrial society, but both phenomena could have the same underlying cause and may not be causally linked.

In higher education, there have been recent critical analyses that use the Marxist dialectic as an analytic base (e.g. W.G. Tierney, 1991). However, no prior neo-Marxist studies explicitly deal with federal student-aid programs,[33] we do not take on the task of critically reexamining these studies here. There is, however, evidence that the class dialectic may be a useful lens[34] for examining recent developments in student aid policy.

Federal policy on student loans in the 1980s exhibited substantial evidence of a bias against the lower class. The shift in emphasis between grants and loans during the late 1970s and 1980s was evident from the review of program funding history (Table 2). There were also budget proposals to require aid administrators to use a new ''self- help'' packaging philosophy, which would require that work

[33]W.G. Tierney's study (1992) of administrators' perceptions of social integration in persistence by Native Americans, is germane to the overall purpose of this paper and was examined as part of section II.C. However, since he does not deal explicitly with the issues related to student aid, his article is not discussed in this section.

[34]We are distinguishing here between using theory as a ''lens'' and the policy researcher's ''prism,'' which includes multiple dimensions. Our concept of prism is much broader than a ''lens'' provided by a particular theory or set of theories.

study and loans be packaged before grants. While this requirement was never specifically legislated, due to a lack of Congressional support, these arguments apparently did have an influence on the redistribution of federal student aid from grants to loans. With the growth in federal loans and the limitations on the Pell maximum award, most aid administrators packaged loans in offers to low-income students. At about the same time, the administration released papers that emphasized the effectiveness of federal loans.[35] The timing of the release of these papers indicates an intent to influence policy on loans.

Unfortunately the new policies on loans and grants did not favor the low-income population.[36] For example, the assumption of neo-conservative policy makers that consumer fraud and institutional abuse were the causes of high default rates seems to have influenced policies aimed at reducing default, such as eliminating program eligibility for colleges with high default rates. These policies were promoted, even when quality control studies did not indicate widespread evidence of fraud (Advanced Technology, Inc. and Westat, Inc., 1987), and published research indicated that default was attributable to social and economic background rather than institutional practices (Wilms, Moore, and Bolus, 1987).

This created incongruity between the assumptions held by policy makers and the consequences of these policies they developed. Their policy changes had an unintended impact, in spite of a belief to the contrary. A problematic situation emerged for low-income students and institutions that served them. Loans were given to high-risk students and when they defaulted, the institutions that served these students were penalized. As a result, opportunities for low-income students were reduced through two mechanisms: 1) some institutions that served low-income students lost program eligibility; and 2) other institutions ceased giving loans to students with high prospects of defaulting, if they could.[37] Thus, low-

[35]Specifically, a paper written collaboratively by a contractor and government analyst (St. John and Noell, 1988) was publicly released by the Department of Education. At the same time, informal permission was given to publish papers that indicated that loans were not problematic for minority students (e.g. St. John and Noell, 1989). However, the principal investigator was not given informal permission to publish findings that were legally available through the sunshine laws (since they had been submitted as reports under federal contracts), when they included findings that raised questions about the efficacy of loans for low-income students. When the principal investigator left the consulting business for academe, he published these papers (St. John, 1989, 1990b, 1990c, 1991c; St. John and Masten, 1990). These events illustrate the moral dilemma inherent in the power imbalance between policy makers and researchers.

[36]We recognize that by 1989 there was an increase in the participation rate of African-Americans (Table 3). However, it should also be noted that: 1) changes in the labor market (i.e. the recession) could influence initial enrollment; and 2) federal aid alone was not sufficient to promote within-year persistence in the late 1980s (St. John, Oescher, and Andrieu, 1992).

[37]Actually, proprietary schools (and other postsecondary institutions with high default rates) were in a legal double bind, a Catch 22. If their students went to lending agencies and got loans, then they could not refuse these new loans. Yet, if they accepted too many risky loans, they faced an increased

income students lost some opportunities for access and, perhaps more importantly, seem to have lost sufficient resources to persist.[38] Further, there is also evidence that higher education institutions are becoming even more economically segregated (Pascarella, Smart, and Smylie, 1992), possibly as a result of these policies.

It could be argued by analysts holding neo-Marxist assumptions that the dominant class deliberately undertook these policies to hold down the working class, to maintain a supply of unskilled labor. Carried to an extreme, one could argue such policies would contribute to urban riots (the modern equivalent of proletariat revolt). However, these more extreme claims cannot be tested from available evidence. Nor are these assumptions that should necessarily be deliberately tested. Our purpose here is not to make the case to support neo-conservative or neo-Marxist political agendas, but rather to illustrate how these perspectives can be used as an analytic tool. From this analysis, it appears that changes in policy during the 1980s did not favor the lower income. Such an understanding has direct implications for future student aid policy.

This brief treatment of how the neo-Marxist perspective could be used in an analysis of federal student aid programs indicates that such a perspective has merit, providing the embedded assumptions are critically examined. However, this treatment of the issue is too brief and superficial to reach firm conclusions in this regard.[39]

Understanding Politics and Ideology: Policy analysts should reflect on the political nature of the policy process and the impact of ideologies on their work, whether they work in the policy community or academe. The facts that there are underlying political forces and that rationality does not predominate in the student aid policy arena seem quite evident from all three streams of research considered. This poses a problem for policy researchers.

There are strong and persuasive arguments that true objectivity may not be possible in any research (Foucault, 1980; Habermas, 1991), as well as that the struggle to find an objective position is nevertheless necessary (Taylor, 1985). But regardless of the position the researcher takes on this philosophical issue, policy researchers need to be aware of the implicit assumptions made in their research.

probability of losing their program eligibility. More than 800 proprietary schools were in the process of losing their Title IV eligibility due to high default rates according to one report (Zook, 1993).

[38]There are a series of recent studies of the NPSAS-87 data base that seem to indicate that persistence in some postsecondary institutions is inhibited by federal policies (e.g. St. John, Oescher, and Andrieu, 1992; St. John and Starkey, 1994).

[39]For example, we have not addressed the implicit moral issue about whether this treatment of low-income students is unjust. To address this issue we need better ways of assessing policy choices. The next section suggests a framework that could be used to consider such choices.

Toward Communicative Understanding

Theory and ideology are very basic aspects of the prisms researchers use to guide their inquiry. Yet an understanding of how theoretical assumptions and political ideologies influence the practice of policy research is not easy to acquire. In fact, it has been argued that a researcher never acquires such objectivity (Aladjem, 1991). Therefore, policy researchers are left with a dilemma about how to acquire an understanding of the influence of political ideologies, as well as of theoretical assumptions they apply in the framing of their policy studies, while they are enmeshed in a policy process that is highly politicized and provides limited opportunities to test their framing assumptions. These conditions create an environment where policy analysts must aim toward building a personal communicative understanding, if they are to avoid being part of the replicative process.

C. Reflective Orientations

There are many who argue that the reflective capacity of the individual practitioner is developmental (Argyris, 1990; Schon, 1983, 1987; Habermas, 1991; Van Manen, 1977). A particular approach to examining this dimension of the policy researcher's prism was proposed in section II. Specifically, four stages of reflective practice were proposed, which are explored below.

Basic Orientations[40]

The basic orientation to policy research is linear in its approach and instrumental[41] in its use of assumptions. The linear orientation—with its emphasis on long- and medium-range objectives and operational controls[42]—is highly compatible with classic models of planning and policy. In higher education, linear methodologies—including master planning (Halstead, 1974), and planning, programming, and budgeting systems (PPBS) (Balderston and Weathersby, 1972)—predominated throughout the 1970s. And the PPBS approach (Schultz, 1968) predominated in the federal policy arena when the higher education programs were first formulated.

The PPBS approach was highly compatible with economic theory on human capital. PPBS involved identifying social and economic goals, designing and legislating programs aimed at achieving those goals, acquiring funding for pro-

[40]This section focuses on the logic of the reflective orientation to policy analysis. Some of the basic research studies were reviewed above.

[41]It appears that any new methodology would probably be learned in an instrumental way because the process of learning new skills often requires adherence to the perceived assumptions of the method. After gaining skill, practitioners may learn to make workable adaptations, which represents the emergence of the strategic orientation. Once researchers reach this point in one situation, they may find it easier to make adaptations in future situations.

[42]From a postmodernist perspective this is where the implicit ''progressive'' assumptions come into play. By using the goals as a basis for accessing policy, we limit our understanding of unintended consequences. (Keep in mind this analysis has been limited to the direct effects of student aid and has not considered the indirect effects.)

grams, using the implementation process to achieve efficiency in the delivery of the program, and using evaluation strategies to refine legislative and budgetary strategies. Consonant with this approach, the HEA created a set of student aid programs aimed at promoting access to higher education.

Cost effectiveness is implicit in the evaluation and research methodologies used in this basic mode (e.g. Levin, 1983). The cost side of the ratio is typically measured by expenditures, either on programs or individuals receiving funds through programs. The ''effectiveness'' part of the equation was traditionally assessed relative to enrollment gains given the costs. This basic ratio can be constructed either on a program basis, in which case the focus is on gains in enrollment relative to the level of funding (e.g. Hansen, 1983; McPherson and Schapiro, 1991), or on the basis of individual responses to aid offers and packages (Jackson, 1977; Manski and Wise, 1983). Both approaches have limitations. The cross-sectional approach ignores the influence of labor-market fluctuations and other external forces, while the time-series approach ignores entirely the fact that the effects of prices and aid can change over time.

In this basic mode, the researcher not only accepts the program goals as a given, but also tends to operate within a basic research paradigm, such as human capital, educational attainment, or a hybrid approach. In this sense, the research—and the researcher—can be viewed as an instrument of current policy.[43] Reflection of the purposes of the programs or the bases on which they are evaluated are not required.[44]

The problem that consistently confronts linear methodologies is that the policy process does not behave according to rational models (e.g. Hearn, 1993). Experienced government bureaucrats learn to adapt to new systems, as they develop. Political interest groups find new ways to advocate for program features that favor their interests.

Strategic Orientations[45]

Strategic planning and management methodologies differ from traditional linear approaches to planning and management in two respects: they emphasize orga-

[43]Because of the unequal power relationships, the applied policy researcher is generally in an ''advisory'' role. In such an environment, the policy researcher literally cannot avoid being an instrument.

[44]This is not to imply that researchers using these basic approaches have not reflected both on the goals of programs and the methods they use to evaluate them.

[45]It should be noted that policy researchers frequently make strategic adaptations within basic research paradigms in order to address policy issues. The hybrid enrollment and persistence models discussed above were essentially strategic adaptations of economic (human capital) and sociological (attainment) models. Additionally, McPherson and Schapiro (1991) made adaptations in econometric methods so that they could address a complex of interrelated issues related to the consequences of federal, state, and institutional financing strategies. These adaptations also represent the type of strategic thinking about policy issues that is the topic of this particular section of the chapter.

nizational adaptation to changing environment conditions; and/or they incorporate interpretive symbols aimed at conveying new strategies. Strategic methodologies began to emerge in business in the late 1960s and early 1970s (Anthony, 1965; Steiner, 1979) and gained popularity in higher education during the 1980s (Chaffee, 1985, 1989; Hearn, 1987; Norris and Poulton, 1989). Strategic methodologies were also widely used in the student aid policy arena during the 1980s, although there was evidence of strategic methodologies in the 1970s.

One aspect of the shift from classical rational policy models involved the use of adaptive methods of policy analysis to address short-term policy issues. In the strategic mode, analysts survey possible theories to identify those that can be used to address the issues of concerned policy makers. One of the first national studies to use a strategic methodology was the National Commission on the Financing of Postsecondary Education (NCFPE). The Congressional mandate for the study in the *Education Amendments of 1972* required an analysis of the tradeoffs between institutional subsidies and student grants. The study team derived price-response coefficients from the early student-demand studies, then used these measures to assess the relative effectiveness of student grants and institutional subsidies in promoting equal opportunity. In its final report, the NCFPE concluded that student grants would be more effective (National Commission on the Financing of Postsecondary Education, 1973) and the institutional subsidy program was never funded (Gladieux and Wolanin, 1976).

This process of using policy analysis to facilitate adaptive program changes increased in frequency during the 1980s. The Reagan administration introduced numerous program changes through the budget and regulatory processes, as the locus of higher education policy shifted from the legislative process to the budget process.[46] The budget process was used to propose major program changes, including the self-help concept and regulations to limit program eligibility for postsecondary institutions with high default rates. Additionally the quality control studies suggested corrective actions, such as verification of aid applications (Advanced Technology, Inc. and Westat, Inc., 1983), that were introduced through regulatory changes. Thus policy analysis became an integral part of this shift to strategic and adaptive approaches to policy.

States and institutions also began to use adaptive strategies to adjust to changes in federal student aid and other external conditions. States adapted to shortfalls in state tax revenues by reviewing their financing strategies and making incremental adjustments (Hines, 1988). Private institutions adapted to changes in aid policy and student preferences by developing new pricing strategies, including the allocation of a larger portion of tuition revenue to scholarships and grants

[46]This shift in the locus of policy authority is consonant with the widespread emergence of adaptive strategic approaches. The budget process could be used to make adaptive changes, such as increasing the emphasis on loans.

(Hauptman, 1990a, 1990b). These shifts placed a greater emphasis on short-term analyses by state and institutional researchers, planners, and budget analysts.

Another dimension of the introduction of strategic methodologies was the integration of ideological arguments into the policy process, an issue discussed above. Ideological arguments have no doubt long been part of the political process. For example, Slaughter (1991) points out that college presidents have historically used human capital and social equity arguments to advocate for their proposals before Congress. In the 1980s, however, there was a breakdown in the liberal progressive consensus (White, 1992), which influenced the broad acceptance of neo-conservative arguments (Bloland, 1992). Under these conditions, analysts in the Department of Education and in private firms with contracts to do policy research were required to develop analytic support for the administration's positions.

In this neo-conservative strategic environment, which began to take shape in the late 1970s, the role of analysts shifted from conducting planning, budget, and evaluation studies in support of legislated program goals (e.g. equal opportunity), to conducting quick turnaround analyses aimed at addressing short-term political concerns (St. John, 1982). When the linear mode had predominated, there was also a tacit consensus among both political parties that human capital and equal opportunity were the goals of student aid programs, and the role of the policy analyst was to assess progress and propose incremental policy changes. In the new environment, new ideological perspectives dominated. The desire to cut student aid pervaded the policy arena. Consultants were funded to conduct studies that documented the virtues of loan programs (e.g. St. John and Noell, 1988) and identified fraud, waste, and abuse in the administration of student aid programs (e.g. Advanced Technology, Inc. and Westat, Inc. 1983, 1987).

In this context, policy analysts may have an opportunity to exercise a greater degree of creativity in framing the way they address research questions, but they remain instruments of ideological points if they do not have the freedom to determine what the questions are or to openly question the ideological assumptions of those funding the research. Even when strategic analyses were conducted in what seemed a purely adaptive mode, there were ideological points of view embedded in the theories they used in their analyses. For example, some of the research that found that loans had a positive influence on equal opportunity (e.g. St. John and Noell, 1988) were commissioned by neo-conservative policy makers who were advocates of expanding loan programs because they cost less than grant programs. This emphasis on loans led to some innovations in the methods used to measure the effects of student aid, adaptations of basic research methodologies described above in the section on hybrid models. Such political interests give the researchers an opportunity to be innovative, at the cost of being an instrument of an ideological point of view. Thus the strategic policy environment presents a perplexing situation for policy analysts.

Communicative Orientations

In the communicative mode, the focus shifts from the pursuit of goals to seeking understanding of the underlying problems (Habermas, 1987). This involves critically examining the assumptions embedded in action, a process that is still relatively unusual in the higher education policy context. In fact, critical analyses of student aid policy are quite rare. Therefore, a cursory analysis of the theory underlying student aid policy research is undertaken below. We first use critical analyses by Dresch (1975) and W.G. Tierney (1992) to illustrate the process of deconstructing theories used in student aid research; then, based on their work and the review above, we reconstruct the theoretical basis for student aid policy research.[47]

Habermas' theory of communicative action (1984, 1987) is used to frame our analysis. Habermas critically analyzes—deconstructs and reconstructs—both rational theorists, such as Max Weber and Talcott Parsons (Habermas, 1984), and social and phenomenological theorists, such as Emile Durkheim and George Herbert Mead (Habermas, 1987), in the development of his theory of communicative action. He argues that communicative action should integrate an understanding of both the life world and the systems world in which people communicate.

Deconstructing theory: Federal student financial aid programs are firmly entrenched in the human capital paradigm. A commonly held assumption of analysts working in this paradigm is that enrollment and persistence decisions can be influenced by prices and price subsidies, an assumption supported by the research reviewed above. However, there are other tacit assumptions in the human capital model, as it has been perpetuated in student aid policy research, that still merit critical examination. Two studies merit consideration.

First, Dresch (1975) undertook a critical analysis of the National Commission on the Financing of Postsecondary Education's model. He identified fundamental problems with the assumptions[48] of the logical models and the research on which they were based. First, the original demand studies, the research upon which the NCFPE model was based, did not consider the range of factors, such as student

[47]One additional study that exhibits a critical orientation was identified. Hearn and Longanecker (1985) deconstructed and partially reconstructed price-response theory when they developed their rationale for a high-tuition/high-aid public finance strategy. However, since this work is discussed below, it is not specifically considered here. Their analysis represents a partial reconstruction within the empirical/analytic tradition. They questioned some of the assumptions of human capital theory, but did not use a hermeneutical lens or critique many of the implicit assumptions embedded in human capital theory.

[48]The National Commission on the Financing of Postsecondary Education (1973) assumed that students respond to a single price and that the measures of price response could be standardized to develop a universal measure of student price response, an assumption that was consistent with the discussion of the effect of prices in *Human Capital Theory* (Becker, 1964).

background and ability, that should be examined when the effects of prices and student aid are assessed. Second, these original demand studies did not include student aid, but only tuition. (Therefore analysts using these studies tacitly assumed students' responses to tuition and grants were identical). Third, major changes in the labor market, a force that is totally outside of cross-sectional studies used to develop the original price-response measures, were not considered in the original research or in the analyses, and the influence of labor market changes were ignored in these models. Fourth, the effects of prices and price subsidies can change over time as a result of changes in policy, such as the creation of federal grant and loan programs, a possibility totally overlooked in these models. Subsequent research, reviewed briefly above, has at least partially addressed the first two issues.

Recent research that has more extensive controls finds that there are differences in the ways students from different economic backgrounds respond to prices and price subsidies (e.g. McPherson and Schapiro, 1991; St. John, 1990c). Further, the price-response measures derived from these recent studies are lower than those derived from the standardization of price-response measures derived from averaging across multiple studies over time (e.g. Leslie and Brinkman, 1988). During the past 18 years, there were a succession of efforts aimed at refining the methods used to standardize price-response measures (Jackson and Weathersby, 1975; Leslie and Brinkman, 1988; McPherson, 1978). However, these price-response coefficients have not adequately predicted enrollments (Leslie and Brinkman, 1988). It is possible that the alternative of using price-response measures that differentiate both for income and for prices and subsidies (St. John, 1993) could improve marginally on the quality of enrollment estimates.

Unfortunately, these developments do not test Dresch's assertion that the effects of prices and subsidies can change over time, due to changes in the labor market, student aid programs, and institutional pricing behavior. This is especially problematic given evidence that the influence of prices, as measured by price-response measures, apparently changed in the 1980s: price-response measures for price subsidies developed from research on students enrolled in the late 1980s (St. John, Oescher, and Andrieu, 1992) are lower than those developed from studies conducted on students enrolled in the early 1980s (St. John, 1990c). Since there are many possible reasons for these differences, we cannot reach a definitive conclusion about how (or if) changes in policy influenced changes in price-response measures, although it would appear this is the case.

Thus, based on Dresch's criticism and more recent inquiry, there is an obvious need to continually monitor the effects of prices and price subsidies on student enrollment and persistence decisions in different settings and at different points in time. Further, deliberate caution should be used when interpreting any analyses of the effects of policy alternatives developed using these measures. Indeed, more experimentation with alternative ways of reconstructing price-response measures[49] seems necessary.

Second, W.G. Tierney's (1992) critical analysis of student participation in college raises questions about underlying assumptions about social integration that have implications for the equal opportunity goal of student aid programs.[50] Tierney identifies the commonly held assumption by researchers (Stage, 1990; Tinto, 1982, 1987) and administrators that students must socially integrate in order to persist in college. He then identifies four problems with the integrationist approach. First, social integration theory extracts the anthropological concept of "ritual" from its cultural foundations. Rather than using the term as a functionalist definition of integration into a native culture, persistence models tacitly apply it to the integration of students from minority cultures into the dominant culture. Second, the definition of departure from college as a "ritual" is problematic because in traditional culture, rites of passage do not have embedded notions of failure. Third, the conceptualization of social integration at the individual level rather than at a collective one is problematic because of the implicit assumption that conformity is the norm and it is the responsibility of the individual. Finally, the fact that there is an implicit bias in the social integration model of " 'native' studying 'native rituals' " (W.G. Tierney, 1992, p. 610) is not adequately acknowledged. These criticisms are similar to Habermas' criticism of Durkheim's concept of social integration (Habermas, 1987) on which Tinto's theory of persistence is based.

Thus the tacit assumptions about social integration made by researchers and administrators are problematic for analyses of student aid programs because they point to inherent inequities for ethnic minorities that might limit opportunity, even if student aid was sufficient. If these inequities exist, then it is not possible to achieve the longstanding goal of equalizing opportunity for the historically disadvantaged through price subsidies alone. W.G. Tierney concludes that "an alternative model is to conceive of universities as multicultural entities where difference is highlighted and celebrated" (1992, p. 604). This alternative conceptualization merits consideration in the reconstruction of student aid policy.

W.G. Tierney's argument that the social integration assumption can, in effect, discriminate against students from diverse cultures seems consonant with our examination above of the ideological influence on student aid policy. Specifically, there appears to be a discriminatory aspect of loan policies that reduces the overall effectiveness of student aid policy, due to limitations in the instrumental

[49]Specifically, institutional researchers and state and federal budget analysts should experiment with new ways of constructing price-response measures. Clearly, the assumption that students respond to a single price does not seem to hold when it is critically examined. However, a generally accepted alternate approach has not yet emerged.

[50]Specifically, federal student aid policy tacitly assumes that finances alone can equalize opportunity. However, if social integration mechanisms also create barriers, then changes in finances alone cannot equalize opportunity.

quality control techniques used in student aid programs, particularly punitive policies related to defaults. These analyses suggest a fundamental reframing is needed, one that focuses on how institutions and government student aid programs can promote multicultural attainment, rather than on how efficiencies can be realized in the current integration model.

In combination, these critical studies illustrate the limitations of the human capital model that has predominated student aid policy. More extensive critical work in these areas would be a fruitful line of inquiry. Based on these studies, coupled with the review above, a partial reconstruction of theory pertaining to student aid policy is attempted below.

Reconstructing theory: Given these criticisms, along with the conclusions from the review above, the concept of equal opportunity as the basis of federal student aid programs as currently organized, is problematic. Not only is the concept of equity ambiguous as it applies to social programs (LeGrand, 1991), but it is difficult to rationalize in the face of neo-conservative criticisms of the efficacy of student aid programs and the widely held public doubts about efficiency in higher education. Therefore, we propose a reconstructed basis for analyzing, designing, and assessing student aid policies. Before attempting to reconstruct the theoretical basis for investigating federal student aid programs, it is important to reconsider both the evolution of program intent and outcomes. The initial intent of federal student aid programs was to promote equality of opportunity, which was usually interpreted as meaning a narrowing gap in the participation rates for whites and African-Americans (or between students from lower-income and upper-income families). There seems to have been some progress on this measure in the early 1970s. However, in the late 1970s, the intent of Title IV programs shifted to include the middle income and grant dollars were shifted to middle-income families (St. John & Byce, 1982). There were subsequent gains in middle-income participation rates. However, many policy analysts persisted in using equal opportunity goals—and participation rates by the historically disadvantaged—to assess the effectiveness of student aid. Clearly, there is a need to consider systematically the effects of student aid and prices on middle-income students, as well as on lower-income students. Further, given the changes in college charges in the past decade (Hauptman, 1990a, 1990b), there appears to be a need to consider the effects of prices and price subsidies on both groups.

Specifically, the freedom of all students to make informed educational choices seems integral to student aid programs. However, since the student choice process begins as early as middle school (Stage and Hossler, 1989), consideration should be given to the message communicated to the public by the debates about student aid programs. Providing information to students as early as middle school can influence their aspirations for college (Hossler and Stage, 1992; Stage and Hossler, 1989). It has been persuasively argued that a communicative understanding in social and organizational processes is most appropriately based on the principle of "free and informed choice" by all individuals (Argyris, Putnam, and Smith, 1987). Additionally, there are other forces in addition to prices that influence postsecondary attendance and persistence: W.G. Tierney's argument about multicultural approaches merits consideration in the federal policy arena. Policies that promote free and informed choice for all students, including students from diverse ethnic backgrounds, should be integral to the design of federal student aid programs.[51] Specifically, federal student aid programs can be assessed regarding their impact on student educational choices (e.g. percentage attending, types of schools attended, levels of attainment, and so forth).

Further, the public's concern about tax burden and efficiency should be integral to the frameworks used to assess federal student aid programs and other pricing policies. The quality control studies identified some waste in federal programs. However, beyond improvements in verification and financial aid office operations, the potential monetary gains from such technical changes are limited. Unfortunately, the issues of waste got intertwined with public doubts about the effectiveness of federal student aid programs in the 1980s. This fueled both the shift in emphasis from grants to loans and systematic efforts to reduce defaults, which put poor students and the institutions that serve them into double jeopardy, a situation which has already been discussed. Unfortunately, this combination of policies seems to have forced more low-income students into less expensive institutions or out of higher education. Further, the systematic use of loans in proprietary schools, coupled with the high default rates, which are attributable primarily to individuals' backgrounds, have essentially eliminated future postsecondary opportunities for some prospective students.[52] This unintended consequence would seem to have high long-term costs since the prospect that students caught in this bind will eventually pay taxes is substantially reduced. Therefore, these concerns about program costs should be judged based on their probable long-term consequences.

The locus of neo-conservative criticisms of student aid programs and higher education pricing policies also needs to be considered. While many of the neo-conservative assumptions do not hold when critically examined, public doubts about the efficacy of student aid and the excessiveness of institutions need to be taken into account. The concept of investment, assessing the returns on student aid and other social programs, seems to have gained public acceptance. It could

[51] Based on LeGrand's (1991) discussion of choice sets, we stop short of arguing that opportunity truly be equalized (e.g. Haveman, 1988). We say this because those with great wealth will always have choices that the public cannot afford to make generally available. The costs of sending low-income students to the most expensive institutions may be too much for the debt-burdened public sector to bear. On the other hand, research indicates that the extreme limitations of choice embedded in current policy may be excessively unjust and uneconomical. Therefore, policy makers and researchers should give explicit consideration to the extent of choice that merits public subsidy.

[52] The reader is reminded that loan defaulters are not eligible for federal student aid if they have a prior default.

provide a basis for reconciling public concerns about efficiency with a deeper concern about the long-term effects of policies and programs. However, there are limits to the amount of money the public is willing to invest—the extent to which they will allow taxation—that also need to be considered.[53] Thus the simplistic approach to thinking about return on investment as a fixed ratio should be replaced by more refined approaches that critically examine ways of constraining costs, as well as maximizing returns.

Thus, federal student aid policy decisions can be assessed in their capacity to balance between two compatible goals: choice and investment. The extent to which the choice goal is achieved can be assessed in terms of economic and social returns. Viewed from this perspective, the policy questions become: How much choice can society afford, given its current tax revenues on one hand, and its need for future tax revenues on the other hand? And what combination of program funding levels have the greatest potential for promoting choice? On the one hand, public concerns about the federal debt may influence limits on the extent of investment in student aid. On the other, these short-term constraints would need to be balanced against the potential for future tax revenue gains when the longer-term investment perspective is used. Thus the reconstructed framework can be conceived of as a basis for examining how best to promote choice in economical ways.

This reconstruction leads to a range of policy alternatives not routinely considered. For example, loans may be a more economical strategy than grants, as neo-conservatives have argued, but loan forgiveness in some circumstances[54] may be necessary to achieve choice (and long-term economic returns). Further, strategies that appear economical in the short term, such as forcing schools with high default rates out of federal loan programs, would seem to be foolish over the long term, because they eliminate high-need (and potentially high-return) recipients from student aid programs. Clearly, such a fundamental rethinking of federal student aid policy is needed.[55]

Transformational Orientations

This reconstruction of the theories used to frame student aid policies leads to a range of new ways of conceiving of policy options. However, to avoid the trap

[53]However, we also need to consider the fact that student aid has a high enough return to merit taking on more public debt.

[54]We think that three forms of forgiveness merit consideration: a partial reduction in debt (and payment) based on eventual earnings; forgiveness of the debt in cases of academic failure; and forgiveness for certain forms of service.

[55]Notice that we do not suggest an ideal strategy. We suspect that any specific strategy we or other policy analysts can suggest would need to be assessed using this framework. Further, there are at least two logical points for assessing policy choices: before the choice is made, when the prospective returns can be assessed; and after a reasonable pilot test period, when the actual returns can be compared to the prior estimates of the effects on student choices and related returns.

of continually seeking "the ultimate solution," we also need to reconstruct the way we view the policy implementation process. The fact that the policy process is incremental is well established. Additionally, it would appear there is no one ideal way of constructing federal student aid programs, or any other social programs for that matter. Rather, the design and redesign of programs can be viewed as a recursive process (Longstreet, 1982) of discovering ways of improving policy and adjusting to new conditions as they develop.

In this context, policy researchers and policy makers can be viewed as practitioners in a natural experimental process, with policy researchers engaged in articulating alternative experiments and evaluation designs, while the policy makers are engaged in choosing experimental strategies.[56] If we hold this view, then it seems desirable to conceive of new policies as experiments that openly test assumptions about future policies. This "ideal" form of policy inquiry is explained further below, first by reviewing a few recent policy experiments, then suggesting ways of reframing policy issues.

Recursive models: The static nature of most policy research limits its direct applicability in the policy decision process. Longstreet (1982) argues that action research studies should be recursive in their approach: ". . . constantly calling upon their results or elements for development of new results or elements" (p. 148). Integrating this concept of recursion into the policy research domain would mean that policy researchers and policy makers would jointly engage in the processes of deconstructing and reconstructing theory (policy agendas) and of using applied research findings (evaluation of pilot tests) to inform future policy decisions.

Our review of student aid policy literature suggests two examples of the use of recursive approaches to policy research and policy decisions: Minnesota's implementation of cost-centered pricing; and Indiana's implementation of early information about postsecondary opportunities for middle school students. Both of these experiments appear consonant with our preliminary theory on reconstruction.

First, the Minnesota experiment with state financing strategies enabled the state to work through a dysfunctional problem. In 1977, Minnesota decided to cap its funding in order to avoid severe cutbacks when enrollments eventually declined. This "bulge" policy proved problematic for the state university and community college systems, both of which continued to grow. This situation was further complicated when the state cut funding, due to tax revenue shortfalls. In a review of state financing strategies, Hearn and Longanecker (1985) developed a rationale for a high-tuition high-aid strategy, which was eventually adopted in Minnesota (St. John, 1991a). The state developed an average-cost strategy that

[56]The conception recognizes the roles of the two parties, but potentially transforms the asymmetrical power relationsships.

involved subsidizing two-thirds of educational costs, with the remaining third coming from tuition (Berg and Hoenack, 1987). The state also increased funding for its grant program. Assessments of the new policy indicate that access was maintained or improved, in spite of the tuition increase (Hearn and Anderson, 1989).

Rather than viewing this policy experiment as confirmation that high-aid high-tuition works in all instances, it is more appropriate to view it as a recursive experimental process. If the former conclusions were held as an assumption, then the strategy of continuing increases in tuition and aid would appear reasonable in Minnesota. However, there is evidence in the state college system, at least, that such a continuation of policy could severely limit access.[57] Thus, future choices about financing strategies in Minnesota need to proceed with caution, based on open inquiry. Presumably, the state should continue to assess the consequences of further incremental policy changes. And other states should adopt a deliberate approach in assessing the consequences of their choices, rather than adopting a strategy because it worked in Minnesota.

Second, the state of Indiana is currently engaged in an early information experiment aimed at improving access. Like many states, Indiana identified low minority participation as a policy issue in the 1980s. With foundation support, Indiana designed an early postsecondary information program for middle school students. Early research on the program indicates that early information has an influence on postsecondary aspirations (Hossler and Stage, 1992; Stage and Hossler, 1989). By using research as an integral part of the program (Hossler, Schmit, and Bouse, 1992), the Indiana project seems to exemplify the process of deliberate social experimentation.

These examples seem to illustrate a more general strategy proposed by Levin (1991). He argues that colleges and universities can use an inquiry process that involves faculty, to identify experimental strategies for increasing productivity. He suggests that not only should faculty be involved in planning decisions about teaching loads and class size, but that it would be appropriate to tie their compensation increases to gains in productivity. This possibility certainly merits consideration as a long-term strategy to containing costs and tuition charges.

Reframing policy: There is a tendency for policy makers to make claims that their proposals will solve social problems. Further, policy researchers tend to design research that supports policy makers' claims without questioning the tacit assumptions embedded in these claims, a situation that is especially true when the policy research is subsidized by those who agree with the policy maker's agenda. The experiments described above appear to be exceptions to this general pattern. Such deliberate public experimentation should be widely adopted.

[57]The original conception of Minnesota's high tuition/high aid strategy assumed students could fund half their costs through self-help (St. John, 1991a). If this cost got too high or if their were barriers to loans, then this strategy would break down, if the self-help philosophy were maintained.

TABLE 4. A developmental perspective for reframing policy research.

	Dimensions	
Stages	*Theoretical* (Framing)	*Interpretive* (Understanding)
Basic	Instrumentally applies base theories	Tacit framing and interpretation
Strategic	Adapts base theories to address policy makers' concerns	Reframes assumptions to address policy issues
Communicative	Generates new theoretical perspectives based on new understanding (reconstructs theory)	Critically examines framing assumptions
Transformational	A dynamic interaction between theoretical and practical understanding of behavioral patterns	Builds understanding of recursive patterns and transformative processes

IV. REFRAMING POLICY RESEARCH

The critical examination of policy research on student aid can enhance our understanding of policy research as a developmental process. Toward this end, a developmental perspective on the policy researcher's reframing process is presented in Table 4.

These generalized patterns of framing and reframing policy research are potentially applicable more generally than student aid policy research. The framework integrates the three dimensions of the policy researcher's prism into four distinct developmental stages. It views the policy researcher's framing process from a developmental perspective, with the insights gained in one stage providing a basis for the next. The theoretical dimension essentially moves from being static and instrumental to being dynamic and practical, while the interpretive dimension moves from being more tacit and unaware to being more focused on building understanding and awareness of patterning processes. The developmental (or reflective) dimension of the framework is evident in the evolving awareness, or consciousness, of these framing assumptions from one stage to the next. Thus, the integration of these three dimensions of the framing process provides a way of understanding the development of the prisms policy researchers use to frame their inquiries.

In the basic stage, policy researchers instrumentally apply theory and learn to interpret results consonant with their emerging theoretical understanding. However, the assumptions and ideological biases embedded in their work remain largely tacit and untested. This basic stage is considered a necessary initial stage of learning the craft of policy research.

Once researchers are grounded in a theory (or set of theories) and have some experience interpreting study findings, they may begin to make adaptations, so that their results can inform ongoing policy decisions. At this ''strategic'' stage, the results are more directly applicable to the types of decisions policy makers actually face.[58] These adaptations permit policy makers to make strategic adjustments to their policy decisions. Thus a symbiotic relationship can develop between policy makers and policy analysts, or policy analysts may become policy makers in part because of the power of their ideas.[59] This strategic stage has become more visibly evident in the policy research literature.

During the third stage, policy researchers take a step back from the ideological and political battles that shape policy deliberations; they try to understand the underlying course of policy actions and outcomes. The reconstruction of theory and the reframing of policy issues are crucial to this stage of inquiry. We seem to have entered a period where this type of reflective inquiry and theory reconstruction is needed. Such reconstructive theoretical work has been limited in student aid research (e.g. Dresch, 1975; Hearn and Longanecker, 1985), but it seems vital to building an understanding of the consequences of the emerging financial strategy of raising tuition without adequate consideration of the financial needs of all students. Additionally, we suspect that this type of deconstruction and reconstruction is needed in a wide range of policy arenas.

Finally, the ultimate stage of policy research would involve policy researchers and policy makers in a recursive inquiry process that builds theoretical understanding through analyses of practical experience, by explicitly considering both the intended and unintended consequences of policy choices. In the student aid arena there are a couple of examples that appear, from available evidence, to have these qualities: the Minnesota financing experiment and the Indiana student information experiment. These experiments merit scrutiny not only from the student aid community, but also from policy researchers in other arenas who are interested in developing ''transformational'' strategies.[60]

Thus, in our view the ultimate aim of policy researcher is not to evolve toward

[58]Once these adaptive techniques have been developed (e.g. the use of SPRCs in planning models), they can be instrumentally applied by policy researchers who remain largely instrumental in their orientations.

[59]In the case of federal student aid programs, the leading neo-conservative critics (e.g. Bennett and Finn) were in key policy positions where they could influence policy decisions as well as shape the policy research agenda of the Department of Education and its contractors.

[60]According to this point of view, transformation is not a single transition from one state or form to another, but rather an ongoing recursive and enlightened process.

any particular political agenda, but rather to evolve a perspective that can create new understandings as new conditions evolve. Thus, the "ideal" is an enlightened recursive process in which policy researchers and policy makers critically examine their assumptions through experimental processes, with an intent of developing better policies and programs. Such an ideal may be easiest to realize during periods of time when there is a need for new forms of action based on a fundamental rethinking of the course of policy and human action.

V. CONCLUSIONS

This paper has explored three propositions. The first is that policy analysts have tacit prisms they use in their analyses. These prisms are derived from assumptions they make about a particular set of policies at a particular point in time, based on a basic theory (or set of theories) that pertains to the programs these policies are concerned about, as well as their capacity to reflect on these forces and assumptions and to use these reflections in framing and reframing their work. To the extent that policy researchers make these assumptions tacitly, without critically examining and reflecting upon them, their work runs the risk of being an instrument of policy makers and political ideologies. In contrast, to the extent that researchers reflect on these tacit framing decisions, test their assumptions using available evidence, and reframe their work based on an understanding of what really needs to be done in a particular situation, they can generate information that can not only inform, but also potentially transform, dysfunctional tendencies in social programs.

A case study of policy research on federal student aid programs was used to discern and actually examine these tacit framing decisions. This review illustrated the difficulties researchers face in assessing the effects of current programs and in envisioning viable alternative approaches. When reflecting on his work on student aid and pricing in Minnesota, James C. Hearn observed:

> Along those lines, you are right in your interpretation . . . of what Dave Longanecker and I were trying to do in our article, and right in your assumption that we (Longanecker, Hearn, Sano, Urahn, etc.) at least *thought* we were working out of a rational (or neo-rational) theoretical frame. In a way, we were saying in poker terms that "we'll see your rational theory and raise you." That is, we sought to evaluate traditional price-response and policy-planning models on rationalist terms extending beyond, but consistent with, the rationalist terms outlined in those original theories. In fairness, though, any linking of my post-Longanecker work (e.g., the Hearn, Sano, and Urahn monograph; the Hearn and Anderson article) to direct policy action in Minnesota is probably overdrawn. We were a step behind the policies' formation, merely questioning, testing, validating, etc. rather than leading. Later, I heard a couple of people at the HECB [Higher Education Coordinating Board] and in the legislature say they were familiar with the work, and were fans of it, so its main role was probably to help

> prevent a few folks from "jumping ship," rather than to help create new policy directions.[61]

Hearn's comment illustrates that reframing the process is not always fully understood by the researcher when he or she is engaged in the process. Rationality plays a role, but the process itself does not always appear rational, at least in retrospect.

The second proposition that has guided this inquiry is that the capacity to reflect on tacit framing decisions develops as a result of skill and practice. This argument is based both on the critical analyses by Habermas and Argyris, as well as on an understanding of developmental processes. The case study illustrates the developmental dimension by critically examining a diverse set of studies, as well as by tracing the development and use of new approaches. A limited set of studies was identified that exhibited the qualities of the communicative and transformational orientations, the more highly evolved ways of framing policy research. However, our assumption that the capacity to reflect is developmental cannot be considered "confirmed" from such a literature review.[62] Nevertheless, we hope the developmental perspective provides a useful framework for experienced and aspiring researchers who are interested in reflecting on their work.

Finally, another proposition of this analysis has been that timely *and* objective analysis is probably an impossibility in the policy arena. The goal of providing timely analysis may limit analysts' ability to be objective, given the large number of assumptions that must be made when predicting future conditions. This analysis has focused on the assumptions researchers make and whether available evidence appears to support these assumptions. Two general types of assumptions were discussed: assumptions made when framing research on extant programs; and assumptions made when identifying and assessing alternative solutions. The first type of assumption can be openly tested as part of the post hoc research process, a practice we strongly recommend. The second type of assumption can only be tested through action experiments, a process we also recommend.

Further, we argued that the process of framing and testing assumptions about how to transform practice should be the ultimate aim of policy research. This deliberate experimental approach could also be widely applied in higher education and other fields. For example, such a deliberative experimental process seems applicable in a range of areas from financial reform to curriculum reform in schools as well as colleges. Implicit in the orientation is a set of value choices. In the student aid arena, these value choices can be characterized as a set of dual goals: promoting free and informed educational choices; and promoting sound public investment decisions. We assume these objectives are interrelated because

[61]Correspondence from James C. Hearn to the authors, dated December 1, 1992, in response to our proposal to write this chapter.

[62]Rather, it would seem appropriate to develop and analyze case histories of individual researchers to test this proposition.

there are public returns to individual educational attainment, an assumption that seems reasonable based on our understanding of extant research.

Finally, based on this understanding, we have proposed a reconstructed framework for viewing the reframing of policy research as a developmental process. In any event, since the prospect that a policy researcher can extract himself or herself from making framing assumptions is simply not possible, the processes researchers use to make framing assumptions merit serious attention, scrutiny, and reflection. At the very least, we hope we have given those who are engaged in—or who are considering—policy research as a career something to ponder.

REFERENCES

Advanced Technology, Inc., and Westat Research, Inc. (1983). *Preliminary Report on Assessment of 1982–83 Pell Grant Program*. Reston, VA: Advanced Technology, Inc.

Advanced Technology, Inc., and Westat Research, Inc. (1987). *Title IV Quality Control Study, Stage 2, Final Report, Executive Summary*. Reston, VA: Advanced Technology, Inc.

Aladjem, T.K. (1991). The philosopher's prism, Foucault, feminism, and critique. *Political Theory* 19: 277–291.

Alexander, K.L., and Eckland, B.K. (1975). Basic attainment processes: a duplication and extension. *Sociology of Education* 48: 457–495.

Anthony, R.M. (1965). *Planning and Control Systems*. Boston: Harvard Business School, Division of Research.

Apple, M.W. (1985). *Education and Power*. New York: Routledge and Kegan Paul, ARK edition.

Argyris, C. (1990). *Overcoming Organizational Defenses: Facilitating Organizational Learning*. Boston: Allyn & Bacon.

Argyris, C., Putnam, R., and Smith, D.M. (1987). *Action Science*. San Francisco: Jossey-Bass.

Astin, A.W. (1975). *Preventing Students from Dropping Out*. San Francisco: Jossey-Bass.

Balderston, F.E., and Weathersby, G.B. (1972). *PPBS in Higher Education: From PPBS to Policy Analysis*. Berkeley, CA: Ford Foundation Program in University Administration, University of California, Report P-31.

Basset, W.B. (1983). Cost control in higher eduction. In J. Froomkin (ed.), *The Crisis in Higher Education*. New York: The Academy of Political Science.

Becker, G.S. (1964). *Human Capital: A Theoretical and Empirical Analysis with Special Reference to Education*. New York: National Bureau of Economic Research.

Becker, G.S. (1975). *Human Capital: A Theoretical and Empirical Analysis with Special Reference to Education*, Second Edition. New York: National Bureau of Economic Research, Distribution: Columbia University Press.

Bennett, W. (1987). Our greedy colleges. *New York Times* (February 18): A31.

Berg, D.J., and Hoenack, S.A. (1987). The concept of cost-related tuition and its implications at the University of Minnesota. *Journal of Higher Education* 58: 276–395.

Beyer, L.E., and Liston, D.P. (1992). Discourse or moral action? A critique of postmodernism. *Educational Theory* 42(4): 371–393.

Blau, P.M., and Duncan, O.D. (1967). *The American Occupational Structure*. New York: Wiley.

Bloland, H.G. (1992). Higher education in the new lobbying system: old and new policies.

Paper presented at the Association for the Study of Higher Education Annual Meeting, Minneapolis, MN.

Braybrook, D., and Lindblom, C.E. (1963). *A Strategy of Decision: Policy Evaluation as a Social Process*. New York: Free Press.

Carlson, D.E. (1975). A Flow of Funds Model for Assessing the Impact of Alternative Student Aid Programs. Menlo Park, CA: Stanford Research Institute.

Carlson, D.E., Farmer, J., and Weathersby, G.B. (1974). *A Framework for Analyzing Postsecondary Financing Policies*. A Staff Report for the National Commission on the Financing of Postsecondary Education. Washington, DC: U.S. Government Printing Office.

Chaffee, E.E. (1985). The concept of strategy. In J.C. Smart (ed.), *Higher Education: Handbook of Theory and Research*, Vol. 1. New York: Agathon.

Chaffee, E.E. (1989). Strategy and effectiveness in higher education. In J.C. Smart (ed.), *Higher Education: Handbook of Theory and Research*, Vol. 5. New York: Agathon.

Chaikind, S. (1987). *College Enrollment Patterns by Black and White Students*. Prepared for the Planning and Evaluation Service, U.S. Department of Education, Washington, DC: DRC.

Cherryholmes, C. (1988). *Power and Criticism: A Poststructural Investigation in Education*. New York: Teachers College Press.

College Board. (1992). *Trends in Student Aid: 1982 to 1992* New York: College Board.

Corazzini, A.J., Dugan, D.J., and Grabowski, H.G. (1972) Determinants and distributional aspects of enrollment in U.S. higher education. *Journal of Human Resources* 7: 39–59.

Dresch, S.P. (1975). A critique of planning models for postsecondary education: current feasibility, potential relevance, and a prospectus for future research. *Journal of Higher Education* 46(3): 246–286.

Eckland, B.K., and Henderson, L.B. (1981). *College Attainment Four Years After High School*. Research Triangle, NC: Center for Educational Research and Research Triangle Institute.

Fine, P. (1992). The influence of college choice variables on persistence by traditional college-age students in private colleges. University of New Orleans. Unpublished manuscript.

Finn, C.E. (1978). *Scholars, Dollars, and Bureaucrats*. Washington, DC: Brookings Institution.

Finn, C.E. (1988a). Judgment time for higher education. *Change*: 35–38.

Finn, C.E. (1988b). Prepared statement and attachments. Hearing before the Subcommittee on Postsecondary Education of the Committee on Education and Labor, House of Representatives, One Hundredth Congress, First Session, Hearing Held 15 September 1987, Serial No. 100–47, U.S. Government Printing Office.

Fischer, F., and Forester, J. (eds.). (1987). *Confronting Values in Policy Analysis: The Politics of Criteria*. Newbury Park, CA: Sage.

Foucault, M. (1972). *The Archeology of Knowledge: The Discourse of Language*. New York: Pantheon.

Foucault, M. (1980). *Power/Knowledge*. New York: Pantheon Books.

Friedman, M. (1962). *Capitalism and Freedom*. Chicago: University of Chicago Press.

Gadamer, H. (1979). The problem of historical consciousness. In Rabinow, P.R., and Sullivan, W. (eds.), *Interpretive Social Science: A Reader*. Berkeley and Los Angeles: University of California.

Gladieux, L.E., and Wolanin, T.R. (1976). *Congress and the Colleges*. Lexington, MA: Heath.

Grubb, W.N. (1990). *The Causes of Enrollment in Postsecondary Education: Evidence from the National Longitudinal Study of the High School Class of 1972*. Final Report. Berkeley, CA: Institute for the Study of Family, Work and Community.

Habermas, J. (1973). A postscript to knowledge and human interests. *Philosophy of Social Science* 3: 157–189.

Habermas, J. (1984). *The Theory of Communicative Action, Volume 1: Reason and the Rationalization of Society*. Trans. T. McCarthy. Boston: Beacon Press.

Habermas, J. (1987). *The Theory of Communicative Action, Volume 2: Lifeworld and System: A Critique of Functionalist Reason*. Trans. T. McCarthy. Boston: Beacon Press.

Habermas, J. (1991). *Moral Consciousness and Communicative Action*. Trans. C. Lenhardt and S.W. Nicholsen. Cambridge, MA: MIT Press.

Habermas, J. (1992). *The New Conservatism: Cultural Criticism and the Historians' Debate*. Trans. S. B. Nicholsen. Cambridge, MA: MIT Press.

Halstead, D.K. (1974). *Statewide Planning in Higher Education*. Washington, DC: U.S. Government Printing Office.

Hansen, W.L. (1983). Impact of student financial aid on access. In J. Froomkin (ed.), *The Crisis in Higher Education*. New York: Academy of Political Science.

Hauptman, A.M. (1988). Prepared Statement. Hearing before the Subcommittee on Postsecondary Education of the Committee on Education and Labor, House of Representatives, One Hundredth Congress, First Session, Hearing held 15 September 1987.

Hauptman, A.M. (1990a). *The College Tuition Spiral*. New York: Macmillan.

Hauptman, A.M. (1990b). *The Tuition Dilemma: Assessing New Ways to Pay for College*. Washington, DC: Brookings Institution.

Hauptman, A.M., and Hartle, T. (1987). Tuition increases in 1970: a perspective. *Higher Education and National Affairs*, Newsletter of the American Council on Education, 23 February.

Haveman, R. (1988). *Starting Even: An Equal Opportunity Program to Combat the Nation's New Poverty*. New York: Simon and Schuster.

Hearn, J.C. (1987). Strategy and resources: economic issues in state planning and management in higher education. In J.C. Smart (ed.), *Higher Education: Handbook of Theory and Research*, Vol 4. New York: Agathon.

Hearn, J.C. (1988). Determinants of postsecondary education attendance: some implications of alternative specifications of enrollment. *Education Evaluation and Policy Analysis* 10(2): 171–185.

Hearn, J.C. (1993). The paradox of growth in federal aid for college students: 1965–1990. In J.C. Smart (ed.), *Higher Education: Handbook of Theory and Research*, Vol. 9. New York: Agathon.

Hearn, J.C.,and Anderson, M.S. (1989). Integrating postsecondary education financing policies: the Minnesota model. In R.H. Fenske (ed.), *Studying the Impact of Student Aid on Institutions*, New Directions for Institutional Research, No. 62.

Hearn, J.C., and Longanecker, D. (1985). Enrollment effects of alternative postsecondary pricing policies. *Journal of Higher Education* 56(5): 485–508.

Hines, E.R. (1988). *Higher Education and State Governments: Renewed Partnership, Cooperation, or Competition?* (ASHE-ERIC Higher Education Report) Washington, DC: Association for the Study of Higher Education.

Hossler, D. (1984). *Enrollment Management: An Integrated Approach*. New York: College Entrance Examination Board.

Hossler, D. (1987). *Creating Effective Enrollment Management Systems*. New York: College Entrance Examination Board.

Hossler, D., Bean, J.P., and Associates. (1990). *The Strategic Management of College Enrollment*. San Francisco: Jossey-Bass.

Hossler, D., Braxton, J., and Coopersmith, G. (1989). Understanding student choice. In J.C. Smart (ed.), *Higher Education: Handbook of Theory and Research*, Vol. 5. New York: Agathon.

Hossler, D., and Gallagher, K.S. (1987). Studying student college choice: a three phase model and implications for policy makers. *College and University* 2?(3): 207–221.

Hossler, D., Schmit, J., and Bouse, G. (1991). Family knowledge of postsecondary costs and financial aid. *Journal of Student Financial Aid* 21(1): 4–17.

Hossler, D., and Stage, F.K. (1992). Family and high school experience influences on postsecondary plans of ninth grade students. *American Educational Research Journal* 29(2): 425–51.

Jackson, G.A. (1977). Financial aid to students and the demand for higher education. Unpublished Doctoral Dissertation, Harvard Graduate School of Education.

Jackson, G.A. (1978). Financial aid and student enrollment. *Journal of Higher Education* 49(6): 548–574.

Jackson, G.A. (1988). Did college choice change during the 1970s? *Economics of Education Review* 7(1): 15–27.

Jackson, G.A., and Weathersby, G.B. (1975). Individual demand for higher education. *Journal of Higher Education* 46(6): 623–652.

Kirshstein, R., Tikoff, V.K., Masten, C., and St. John, E.P. (1990). *Trends in Institutional Costs*. Prepared for the Office of Planning, Budget, and Evaluation, U.S. Department of Education. Washington, DC: Pelavin Associates.

Kneller, G.F. (1984). *Movements of Thought in Modern Education*. New York: John Wiley & Sons.

Kramer, M. (ed.) (1982). *Meeting Student Aid Needs in a Period of Retrenchment*. New Directions in Higher Education, No. 40. San Francisco: Jossey-Bass.

Kuhn, T.S. (1970). *The Structure of Scientific Revolutions*, Second Edition. Chicago: University of Chicago Press.

LeGrand, J. (1991). *Equity and Choice: An Essay in Economics and Applied Philosophy*. London: Harper Collins Academic.

Leslie, L.L. (1990). Rates of return as informer of public policy: with special reference to the World Bank and third world countries. *Higher Education* 20: 271–286.

Leslie, L.L., and Brinkman, P.T. (1988). *The Economic Value of Higher Education*. San Francisco: Jossey-Bass.

Levin, H.M. (1983). *Cost Effectiveness: A Primer. New Perspectives in Evaluation*, Vol. 4, Beverly Hills: Sage.

Levin, H.M. (1991). Raising productivity in higher education. *Journal of Higher Education* 62(3): 241–262.

Lindblom, C.E. (1977). *Politics and Markets: The World's Political and Economic Systems*. New York: Basic Books.

Lindblom, C.E., and Cohen, D.K. (1979). *Usable Knowledge: Social Science and Social Problem Solving*. New Haven: Yale University Press.

Liston, D.P. (1990). *Capitalist School: Explanation and Ethics in Radical Studies of Schooling*. New York: Routledge, Chapman, and Hall.

Longstreet, W.S. (1982). Action research: A paradigm. *The Educational Forum* (Winter) 46(2): 135–158.

Lopez, M. (1993). High tuition, high aid won't work. *The Chronicle of Higher Education*, (April 7): B1–B2.

Manski, C.F., and Wise, D.A. (1983). *College Choice in America*. Cambridge, MA: Harvard University Press.

McPherson, M.S. (1978). The demand for higher education. In D.W. Breneman and C.E.

Finn (eds.), *Public Policy and Private Higher Education*, Washington, DC: Brookings Institution.

McPherson, M.S., and Schapiro, M.O. (1991). *Keeping College Affordable: Government and Educational Opportunity*. Washington, DC: Brookings Institution.

McPherson, M.S., Wagner, A.P., and Willie-Schiff, N.A. (1989). Student financial aid and institutional behavior: how institutions use and benefit from student aid. In J.C. Smart (ed.) *Higher Education: Handbook of Theory and Research*, Vol. 5. New York: Agathon.

Mingle, J.R. (1987). *Focus on Minorities: Trends in Higher Education Participation and Success*. A joint publication of the Education Commission of the States and the State Higher Education Executive Officers, Denver, CO.

National Commission on Financing Postsecondary Education. (1973). *Financing Postsecondary Education in the United States*. Washington, DC: Government Printing Office.

Norris, D.M., and Poulton, N.C. (1987). *A Guide for New Planners*. Ann Arbor, MI: Society for College and University Planners.

Pascarella, E.T., Smart, J.C., and Smylie, M.A. (1992). College tuition costs and early socioeconomic achievement: do you get what you pay for? *Higher Education* 24: 275–290.

Pascarella, E.T., and Terenzini, P.T. (1991). *How College Affects Students*. San Francisco: Jossey-Bass.

Pelavin, S.H., and Kane, M.B. (1988). *Minority Participation in Higher Education*. Washington, DC: Pelavin Associates.

Rhoades, G. (1992). Beyond the "state": interorganizational relations and state apparatuses in post–secondary education. In J.C. Smart (ed.), *Higher Education: Handbook of Theory and Research*, Vol. 8. New York: Agathon Press.

St. John, E.P. (1982). *The Policy Process in Higher Education: A Strategic Approach*. Armidale, NSW, Australia, Institute of Higher Education, Monograph No. 2–1981, University of New England.

St. John, E.P. (1989). The influence of student aid on persistence. *Journal of Student Financial Aid* 19(3): 52–68.

St. John, E.P. (1990a). A developmental perspective on transformative leadership. Paper presented at the Mid-South Educational Research Association Annual Meeting, New Orleans, Louisiana.

St. John, E.P. (1990b). Price response in enrollment decisions: an analysis of the high school and beyond sophomore cohort. *Research in Higher Education* 31(2): 161–176.

St. John, E.P. (1990c). Price response in persistence decisions: an analysis of the high school and beyond senior cohort. *Research in Higher Education* 31(4): 387–403.

St. John, E.P. (1991a). A framework for reexamining state resource-management strategies in higher education. *Journal of Higher Education* 62(3): 263–287.

St. John, E.P. (1991b). The impact of student financial aid: a review of recent research. *Journal of Student Financial Aid* 21(1): 18–32.

St. John, E.P. (1991c). What really influences minority attendance? Sequential analyses of the high school and beyond sophomore cohort. *Research in Higher Education* 31 (4): 387–403.

St. John, E.P. (1992). Changes in pricing behavior during the 1980s: an analysis of selected case studies. *Journal of Higher Education* 63(2): 165–187.

St. John, E.P. (1993). Untangling the web: using price- response measures in enrollment projections. *Journal of Higher Education* 64(6): 676–695.

St. John, E.P., and Burlew, L.D. (1993). A developmental perspective on reflective prac-

tice: an application of Jung's theory of individuation. *Louisana Journal of Counseling* (4)1: 9–24.
St. John, E.P., and Byce, C. (1982). The changing federal role in student financial aid. In M. Kramer (ed.) *Meeting Student Aid Needs in a Period of Retrenchment.* New Direction in Higher Education, No. 40, San Francisco: Jossey-Bass.
St. John, E.P., and Masten, C.L. (1988). *An Analysis of Return on Investment for Federal Student Aid Programs: final Report.* Prepared for the Office of Planning, Budget, and Evaluation, U.S. Department of Education. Washington, DC: Pelavin Associates.
St. John, E.P., and Masten, C. (1990). Return on the federal investment in student financial aid: an assessment of the high school class of 1972. *Journal of Student Financial Aid* 20(3): 4–23.
St. John, E.P., and Noell, J. (1988). Student loans and higher education opportunities: evidence on access, persistence, and choice of major. *Fourth Annual NASSGP/NCH-ELP Research Network Conference Proceedings,* Vol. I, June 3–5, 1987.
St. John, E.P., and Noell, J. (1989). The impact of financial aid on access: an analysis of progress with special consideration of minority access. *Research in Higher Education* 30(6): 563–82.
St. John, E.P., Oescher, J., and Andrieu, S.C. (1992). The influence of prices on within-year persistence by traditional college-age students in four-year colleges. *Journal of Student Financial Aid* 22(1): 17–26.
St. John, E.P., and Starkey, J.B. (1994). The influence of costs on within-year persistence by traditional college-age students in two-year colleges. *Journal of Research and Practice* 18(2): 201–214.
Schon, D. (1983). *The Reflective Practitioner.* New York: Free Press.
Schon, D. (1987). *Educating the Reflective Practitioner.* San Francisco: Jossey-Bass.
Schultz, C.E. (1968). *The Politics and Economics of Public Spending.* Washington, DC: Brookings Institution.
Simsek, H., and Heydinger, R.B. (1992). An analysis of the paradigmatic shift in the evolution of U.S. higher education and its implications for the year 2000. Paper presented at the Association for the Study of Higher Education Annual Meeting. (ERIC # ED352923).
Slaughter, S. (1991). The official "ideology" of higher education: ironies and inconsistencies. In W. G. Tierney (ed.) *Culture and Ideology in Higher Education.* New York: Praeger.
Stage, F.K. (1990). Research on college students: commonality, differences, and direction. *Review of Higher Education* 13: 249–258.
Stage, F.K., and Hossler, D. (1989). Differences in family influence on college attendance plans for male and female ninth graders. *Research in Higher Education* 30(3): 301–315.
Steiner, G.A. (1979). *Strategic Planning: What Every Manager Must Know.* New York: Free Press.
Taylor, C. (1985). *Philosophy and Human Sciences: Philosophical Papers 2.* New York: Cambridge University Press.
Terkla, D.G. (1985). Does financial aid enhance undergraduate persistence? *Journal of Student Financial Aid* 15(3): 11–18.
Tierney, M.L. (1980a). Student matriculation decision and student aid. *Review of Higher Education* 3 (Winter): 14–25.
Tierney, M.L. (1980b). The impact of student financial aid on student demand for public/private higher education. *Journal of Higher Education* 45(1): 89–125.
Tierney, W.G. (ed.). (1990). *Assessing Academic Cultures.* New Directions in Institutional Research, No. 68. San Francisco: Jossey-Bass.

Tierney, W.G. (ed.). (1991). *Culture and Ideology in Higher Education: Advancing a Critical Agenda*. New York: Praeger.

Tierney, W.G. (1992). An anthropological analysis of student participation in college. *Journal of Higher Education* 63(6): 603–618.

Tinto, V. (1982). Limits of theory and practice in student attrition. *Journal of Higher Education* 52: 687–700.

Tinto, V. (1987). *Leaving College: Rethinking the Causes and Cures of College Attrition*. Chicago: University of Chicago Press.

Tynes, S.F. (1993). *The Relationship of Social, Economic, Academic and Institutional Characteristics to Persistence by Nontraditional-Age Students: Implications for Counselors*. Unpublished doctoral dissertation, University of New Orleans.

U.S. Department of Commerce, Bureau of the Census. (1971). School enrollment: October 1970. *Current Population Reports, Population Characteristics*, Series P-20, No. 222.

U.S. Department of Commerce, Bureau of the Census. (1976). School enrollment—social and economic characteristics of students: October 1973. *Current Population Reports, Population Characteristics*, Series P-20, No. 303.

U.S. Department of Commerce, Bureau of the Census. (1985). School enrollment—social and economic characteristics of students: October 1981 and 1980. *Current Population Reports, Population Characteristics*, Series P-20, No. 400.

U.S. Department of Commerce, Bureau of the Census. (1989). School enrollment—social and economic characteristics. *Current Population Reports, Population Characteristics*, Series P-20, No. 426.

U.S. Department of Commerce, Bureau of the Census. (1991). School enrollment—social and economic characteristics of students: October 1989. *Current Population Reports, Population Characteristics*. Series P-20, No. 452.

Van Manen, M. (1977). Linking ways of knowing with ways of being practical. *Curriculum Inquiry* 6(3): 205–228.

Wallace, T.P. (1992). Public higher education access and affordability. *Journal of Student Financial Aid* 22(1): 39–41.

Weathersby, G.B., Jacobs, F., Jackson, G.A., St. John, E.P., and Tingley, T. (1977). The development of institutions of higher education: theory and assessment of four possible areas of federal intervention. In M. Guttentage (ed.), *The Evaluation Studies Review Annual*, Vol. 2. Beverly Hills: Sage.

White, S.K. (1992). *Political Theory and Postmodernism*. New York: Cambridge University Press.

Wildavsky, A. (1975). *Budgeting: A Comparative Theory of Budgetary Processes*. Boston: Little, Brown.

Wildavsky, A. (1979). *Speaking Truth to Power: The Art and Craft of Policy Analysis*. Boston: Little, Brown.

Wilms, W.W., Moore, R.W., and Bolus, R.E. (1987). Whose fault is default? A study of the impact of student characteristics and institutional practices on guaranteed student loan default rates in California. *Educational Evaluation and Policy Analysis* 9(1): 41–45.

Wolfle, L.M. (1985). Postsecondary educational attainment among whites and blacks. *American Educational Research Journal* 22(4): 501–525.

Zook, S. (1993). 900 institutions could be dropped from student aid programs for high default rates: 55 are non-profit colleges. *Chronicle of Higher Education* (September 1) 60(2): A36.

Educational Paradigms in the Professional Literature of the Community College

John H. Frye
Triton College

INTRODUCTION

Education's role in social class mobility is frequently discussed, particularly in the writings of conflict theorists (e.g., Bowles and Gintis, 1976; Brint and Karabel, 1989b). The same is not true for the issue of status conflict between groups of professional educators. Much like the name of an ancient god too terrible to be spoken, the existence of status and hierarchy among educators is seldom discussed. Yet it pervades literature about American education and influences its direction, affecting how problems are defined and what evidence is selected. We see this particularly in the literature on the two-year college. The reluctance of American educators to name and discuss status conflicts among groups of educators stems from an ideology that is profoundly meritocratic. The impact of this ideology is discussed in this chapter as a prologue and conceptual framework for a discussion of the literature of the two-year college. This article is not an attempt to evaluate individual research efforts, but rather an attempt to understand how major themes and issues of concern relate to the changing patterns in education and how professional writers react to these changes.

Two conditions affect the presentation of the literature on the two-year college. First, the uncertain place of the two-year college in the system of higher education colors many of the issues expressed. Second, the changing paradigm of higher education in the United States influences the debate on issues relating to the community college. To develop this thesis, the paper will be divided into two principal sections after an introduction that examines the role of paradigms in the literature. One section builds a framework for understanding education as a complex social system. The second section examines major themes in the literature of the two-year college to show their relationship to the problems posed by place in this social system and the effects of a changing paradigm of post-secondary education. As a practical consideration, the literature review will concentrate on recent literature, especially that published since the appearance of Cohen, Palmer, and Zwemer's *Key Resources on Community Colleges* (1986).

Paradigms in Education: The Purposes of Higher Education

Making sense of a large body of professional literature is always a challenge. The literature on the two-year or community college is no exception. Those familiar with its content know the themes and issues that dominate its pages, but constructing a framework for this literature is a complex task. Looking at education as a social system and utilizing the paradigms of such a system help to frame the literature in a meaningful context.

Paradigms are exemplars or ideal images of what a social group's activities and beliefs are about. A natural outgrowth of group interaction because they produce a sense of coherency and order for group activities, paradigms are based on a complex interplay of perceived conditions, experience, goals, and shared traditions (e.g., Geertz, 1973). As Thomas Kuhn argues in *The Structure of Scientific Revolutions* (1970), paradigms undergo pressure as social and intellectual conditions change and threaten the models upon which the paradigms are based.

Higher education operates under a paradigm, largely shared by professional educators, regarding its principal purpose. This paradigm is peculiarly American with respect to the primacy which we place on individual interests. Young people are presumed to prepare themselves for future responsibilities during a dedicated period of study. Higher education is thought to be meritocratic: it is assumed to serve the public need for various technical skills and knowledges by allocating social position to students based on their achievement. Achievement is equated with merit or natural ability. Hence, in theory, the system is fair and egalitarian. This is a hierarchical model and makes a dual assumption: 1) critical and prestigious social positions are limited in number, and 2) those capable of filling those positions are also limited in number. Another implicit assumption is that most people are not capable of filling all or most prestigious positions. This paradigm is a traditional one and has dominated United States higher education to some degree since its colonial beginnings but especially since the late 19th century.

It would not be an exaggeration to say that higher education in the United States is in ferment. This ferment derives from the threat to this paradigm from social conditions external to the educational system itself. From the growth of postdoctoral work to the growth of part-time enrollment, the increase in nontraditional students, and the proportion of money spent by businesses on training employees, to the return to education of currently employed and displaced workers, the traditional paradigm is under growing pressure. The structure of employment is changing and this in turn alters the demands on higher education.

The Paradigm and the Community College

Presumably a new paradigm of higher education will emerge as changes in social conditions are absorbed, defined, and produce institutional adaptation. In the meantime, the literature is filled with contradictory calls. Return to the traditional curriculum. Revolutionize teaching through technology. Respond to student needs. Educate for world competitiveness. Teach information-processing skills. Teach students how to learn and work in groups (e.g., Almeida, 1990; Cross and Fideler, 1989; Gollattscheck, 1988; Jacobson, 1992; Meyer, 1988; Wattenbarger, 1987).

The literature on the two-year college reflects the confusion that results from problems in the traditional paradigm of higher education. These conflicts, by their nature, do not result in a clear, linear, coherent path in the literature. Rather, the literature reflects a complex interplay of social group interest, traditional values, inertia, and innovation. Education that brings personal development is praised in the same article that also praises education for producing socioeconomic development (California, 1989). Calls for teaching methodologies appropriate for multicultural enrollments appear in works calling for higher standards (e.g., Rendon, 1991; McGrath and Spears, 1991; Grubb, 1992). Claims that the two-year college represents a new thrust for democratic education are paired with expressions of concern that community colleges are leaving higher education (Clowes and Levin, 1989). Apparent contradictions between concepts are denied by assertions that they are one and the same if rightly understood (California, 1989, p. 5).

The pattern of these conflicting perspectives suggests what Thomas Kuhn identifies as a paradigm shift (Kuhn, 1970). The outline of the new paradigm is as yet unclear while the older paradigm has its vigorous, outspoken defenders. The older paradigm, which is not in itself very old—that higher education is for the select, those individuals with the special cognitive and personal talents necessary to make a significant contribution to society through their leadership and other skills —is still strong. But many of the current realities of higher education in general and community colleges in particular appear to have only a weak reflection in this paradigm. While new models are tried out, the current paradigm is beset by unresolved contradictions with emergent social and political conditions. The paradigm has not been able to deal effectively with the change from an industrial-manufacturing base to an information-financial system. It has not been successful in dealing with political and social demands of oppressed minorities and women as these groups have gained political leverage. And it struggles under the burden of the academic structure it helped produce: an educational system based on subject disciplines, whose status structure drives its members into more and more remote and isolated corners of specialization.

The paradigm produces dissonance in the two-year college more powerfully than in the university for two reasons. First of all, the place of the two-year college in the hierarchy of education provides it with an ambiguous position. It is between high school and college but it is also the first two years of college. What's more, practitioners in the two-year college tend to have a pragmatic focus. This pragmatism gives primacy to problem solving rather than theory and philosophical considerations. Hence, subordination to the university and a focus on making things work, leave the literature of the two-year practitioners weak on issues of broader scope, so the problems posed by inconsistencies in the paradigm are often not addressed.

Theoretical and practical problems in research into the community college, two-year college, or junior college, are symbolized by the confusion over its name. These *nomina dubia* symbolize the current and historic lack of agreement as to the institution's purposes or functions, its role in the educational system, descriptions of its programs, and both summative and formative evaluations of its effectiveness. Since its inception, the institution has been fulsomely praised as a high-minded venture in the American tableau (Hutchins, 1933, pp. 154–155) and routinely criticized as a high school with ashtrays (Zwerling, 1976) or a mechanism of class repression (Brint and Karabel, 1989). Legislatures have viewed it as the key to a competitive world-class work force (Mensel, 1989), and those with a social reconstructionist outlook have seen it as democracy's college (Cohen, 1989; Cohen and Brawer, 1991; Gleazer, 1980; Labaree, 1991).

Paradigms and the Community College Literature

The professional literature on the two-year college, by which is meant refereed journals, conference proceedings, doctoral dissertations, and professional monographs, is generally considered poorly developed, with exceptions in certain areas such as finance and instruction. The absence of dominant foundational works, comprehensive theoretical analysis, and definitive treatments has frustrated more than one researcher. By and large the professional literature is diffuse, lacks focus, and does not display the theoretical grounding more common in the elementary and secondary school literature and present to some degree in the balance of the higher education literature on the baccalaureate college and the university (Cohen, Palmer, and Zwemer, 1986).

This character of the two-year college literature has persisted over the 90-year history of the institution. While this confusion reflects a formless and splintered debate about its nature and mission in the literature, the two-year college itself has prospered and evolved. The numbers are impressive by any standard: some 1,200 two-year institutions sharing 5 million students, 43 percent of all students in higher education (AACJC, n.d.). Two-year colleges, particularly public ones, appear genuinely popular with local populations and continue to grow and to diversity their programs. National associations arising from the two-year college, most notably the American Association of Community Colleges (formerly the AACJC), tend to ignore theoretical questions and, in the nature of trade associations, focus on securing resources for solving institutional problems.

Many of the perceived weaknesses in the two-year-college literature are present in the literatures of the larger educational system. Especially in the literature of American education, less so in the educational literature of other countries, there is a breadth of approach, of topic selection, and of style of analysis that defies easy categorization (Clark, 1984, 1985; Teichler, 1988; Trow, 1991). That this problem confronts the educational literature of other countries to a lesser degree is instructive about American education. The relationship of American education to a variety of social and political goals has often been noted (e.g., Button, 1983; Herbst, 1992). Assumptions about education in other countries tend to be more restricted and hence more manageable from a theoretical point of view.

If an analysis of the two-year college literature, then, is to be helpful, certain conceptual problems must be handled first. Categories that are commonly used such as students, instruction, administration, and finance, while often useful, tend to mask larger issues operating between society and the community college.

Models, Paradigms, and Ways of Seeing

In general, the written educational literature of the United States is positivist and rationalistic in approach. That is, things are taken as they appear, measurement and quantification are taken to be the key to understanding, and actors are assumed to be rational; or at least institutions are assumed to be rational (Papagiannis, 1982). Scientific method is the model of study and comment, and objectivity is the preferred quality of discourse. It is assumed that educational institutions meet social goals or that they should do so.

Another assumption is that society's needs for knowledge and skills require formal, separate educational institutions to be effectively met. On its most general level, these needs form the basis of citizenship. Here a difference in emphasis can be noted in the literature as to what these social needs are. The most popular perception stems from the social value Americans place on independence, individualism, equality, and opportunity. In contemporary literature, little attention is given to the potential for conflict among these values, but before World War II concern in the literature over too much individualism and opportunism was fairly common (e.g., Thwing, 1896; Courtis, 1936). Today, however, the emphasis on individual needs and opportunity is not directly challenged. The idea is powerfully articulated that education serves the individual's need to develop her talent and achieve a maximum potential. When the educational system is perceived to have done less, it is considered to have failed or at least failed to meet a standard (Kaestle, 1983; Ravitch, 1974, 1983).

A second view is a variation on the first. It emphasizes the labor needs of the society and stresses the role of a productive work force. The two views are not thought to be contrary for the most part, and the two views can be equally emphasized by the same speaker in different contexts or even the same context (e.g. AACJC, 1991b). Interestingly, the human resource model is more commonly identified in European literature, quite likely because of the closer relationship between university and government in Europe than in the United States (Clark, 1984; Teichler, 1988; Trow, 1991).

There are exceptions to these dominant expressions of educational purpose. One is a neo-Marxist criticism that the educational system perpetuates class distinctions (Bowles and Gintis, 1976). In one sense, this point of view is not different from the first; it merely suggests that the real purpose of education has been perverted or is covert. Again, it is interesting that in the European literature on education this issue receives little emphasis suggesting rather significant differences in the perceived role of education in society between European and American educators. In countries where class issues are more explicit and socialists or communists are powerful, one might expect this to be a major issue, but the literature on this issue is more muted than in the United States or absent altogether (Rubinson, 1986; Teichler, 1988).

Alternative and hypothetical interpretations of American education can be advanced. Such views may be objectionable on several grounds, but they serve the purpose of putting the dominant ideology and its paradigms in perspective. One alternative view sees the principal function of the American educational system as being anti-religious and specifically anti-Christian. The perception is that by being strictly secular and emphasizing science, as opposed to faith, the school system attacks the basis of religious belief and produces an agnostic population (Buckley,1951; Hubner, 1944; Noll, 1942). Although this interpretation might be considered a fringe view and certainly is not significantly represented in the professional literature, much evidence can be adduced to support the view. While this view may be dismissed as hopelessly naive, the fact that this subject is invisible in the professional literature begins to show the limits of discussion imposed by the ideology of educational professionals.

Yet another interpretation of the purposes of schooling in industrial societies might hold that its function is simply to take up excess time (Hitch, 1933). Because increased productivity may result in excess labor, education is extended so that there is a progressive delay in students' entry into the work force. During the Great Depression this delay in the form of additional schooling was promoted as a formative policy (Judd, 1933). Related issues have been studied, but this explanation does not hold a prominent position in the literature.

Another interpretation of educational function which might be proposed is even more extreme. In this view the chief purpose of the American educational system is the elimination of gender differences in the American population. One could argue that through the opening of all curriculums to both sexes and the providing of all instruction to mixed classes, the goal has been to eliminate or reduce all social gender distinctions. Again considerable evidence could be marshaled to defend the theses that this is the main goal of American education (Tyack and Hansot, 1990). Of course, many objections could also be raised. The nature of these potential objections is revealing of paradigmatic limitations.

First of all, this perception is so unusual that it is not clear whether someone taking this point of view would take this function as a positive or a negative one. In a society where sexual differentiation is a major concern, for example certain Muslim societies, this function would be objectionable. In contemporary America this would not likely be the case. In fact, objections to this proposed interpretation from feminists in the United States can be anticipated. Feminists might argue that, indeed, the opposite is the case, that the school system operates to denigrate women, is male-dominated and tracks females out of high prestige occupations, and that the increase in women teachers was stimulated by a disadvantageous wage differential rather than an attempt to benefit female students. It might be argued that the measurable differences between the social position of women in 1900 and today derives from other social forces and has little or nothing to do, positively, with the educational system.

Educators will recognize that schooling as a mechanism to eliminate social gender differences, for example, is not a mainstream interpretation even though the many related issues have been dealt with in the literature (Tyack and Hansot, 1990). It is difficult to see how such an issue could arise in the United States because, unlike a traditional Muslim society, the concerns that might give rise to such an emphasis are not part of our social reality. Yet the absence of these minority views from the approved body of educational debate should suggest that there is a dominant point of view among professional educators. As David Tyack tells us, such paradigms allow us to ''see'' in certain ways, but one way of ''seeing'' is, at the same time, a way of ''not seeing'' (Tyack, 1976).

Interpretations of education that might argue that its function is to eliminate religion, or to oppose social gender differences, or to consume excess labor do not need to be considered seriously to allow us the perception that the current ideology and research paradigms in education limit the scope of research and the possible interpretations of educational purposes. There may be little reason to dispute the dominant interpretation of education as a process for providing needed skills and knowledge to serve individual and social needs. However, an analysis of a professional literature needs to take account of the limiting qualities of professional paradigms if the strengths, as well as the weaknesses, of the literature are to be assessed. Understanding education as a social system, rather than from a more limited institutional perspective, assists in revealing the content of a literature as it reflects the structural problems arising from the social interactions of systems. This is a particularly important process in the investigation of the two-year college, because of its position as a relatively recent entry in an educational system already structurally developed from kindergarten through graduate school.

PART I. THE EDUCATIONAL SYSTEM AS A SOCIAL SYSTEM

Using a Social Science Model

An alternative approach is to look at education as a social system and to relate its literature to the operations of education as a social subsystem with its various divisions. This approach has several advantages for the analysis of the two-year college. First of all, forcing the literature review into the context of the larger social system helps to overcome the tendency of professional specialists to narrow the focus of their research. Second, a social systems approach emphasizes the relatedness of subsystems to each other. This is particularly important when considering the place of the two-year college within the larger system of education. Third, a social systems approach places a focus on individuals and collectivities as systematic actors who fulfill a social role with reciprocal rights and responsibilities. Lastly, with the social system approach, students and other publics can be seen as participants in many subsystems outside of education and active participants in the educational system, not passive clients of educational institutions.

An understanding of the two-year college literature can benefit from a perspective that sees the institution not in an isolated institutional form, but as a dynamic system representing interest groups which in turn are impacted by social forces outside education altogether. In order to develop a social systems perspective, I will propose a process based on a schema presented by Parsons in another context (Parsons, 1991). Since the written literature is the focus of this study, it should be understood that that in itself limits the nature of the analysis and restricts conclusions to a certain class of actors. There is, for example, an oral literature on the two-year college, as there is for any other institution. Characterization of the two-year college as, for example, ''a high school with ash trays'' (Zwerling, 1976) is rarely found in the written literature; such sentiments are more frequently expressed over coffee and in hallways during conferences. The context of such a statement carries powerful meaning in an informal setting that differs remarkably in quality, force, and implication from critical comments posed in more academic written style used in professional journals. But such an offhand comment is no less part of the literature of the two-year college when we understand literature to be the body of communications dealing with an institution's meaning and operation, in this case an oral literature.

Sociological theory deals with social operations in terms of social roles of both individuals and collectivities. Social roles are reciprocal and bounded by rules. Social roles and institutions have boundaries; that is, definitional limits of what is within and outside the social role. Social status attaches to social roles, and status is a defining and rewarding quality for the individuals within the social system. Generally, the higher the status, the greater the social rewards in terms of power and deference. Hence, members of society tend to seek higher status (Merton, 1957).

Institutions are collectivities of roles in which members share a set of goals or purposes. In order to establish and maintain boundaries of their institutions, participants engage in a set of activities to achieve definition and operational scope. Institutions must respond to external influences, establish meaningful goals, achieve and maintain internal order, and establish values that qualify goals and describe appropriate standards of processes. Parsons (1991) refers to these aspects as adaptive, goal-attaining, integrative, and value-patterning. These elements operate to achieve and maintain the status of the institution in relation to other social systems. When considering a professionally dominated organization, such as an educational institution, the professional literature will reflect this social system aspect. Conceptual constructs used by professionals as well as the descriptive literature that analyzes particular institutions and problems will reflect these sociological categories. Their positions on these sociological categories can be understood as the professional ideology. It should also be clear that from this perspective that the two-year college has built-in contradictions in terms of its goal establishment and relationship to other educational institutions. In several respects it is now, and has been from the beginning, a duplicative institution in terms of traditional educational structures and paradigms. This by itself makes boundary issues central to the institution and raises clear definitional and programmatic problems.

As in other social groups, professional educators develop paradigms that meet the need for shared values, integration, goal-attainment, and boundaries. Paradigms emerge that become the accepted positions from which institutional issues are viewed. Institutions resist both internal challenges to these paradigms and external attack in order to maintain stability and to retain their social position. One would not expect a professional educator to conduct a study whose results suggested that too much public funding was allocated to schools. Similarly, there are few studies in the literature of higher education on the adverse effects of poor classroom teaching. Although objectivity would suggest random or even-handed selection of issues, the professional literature is tightly focused on issues that are thought to meet the needs of the system. Scholars or outsiders who take unconventional and potentially threatening perspectives in their writing become targets of criticism in education just as they would in other social institutions. There are many formal and informal ways that professional groups provide sanctions against those who violate the paradigm. (Sykes, 1988)

Viewing educational institutions as subsystems of a larger educational system, which is itself a subsystem of the larger community, helps put the content, as well as the lacunae, of the professional literature in a larger perspective. This perspective helps explain why administrative problems play such a large role in the literature and student values do not. It helps explain why teaching methodology is a critical concern at the secondary level but receives scant attention in higher education, since teaching has much less to do with the social system in higher education. In the educational paradigm in the United States, the student is seen in the role of pathogen, a subject on whom the educational system must operate. Hence, the student's home and peer value systems outside of education are not considered of much significance as compared with curriculum concerns of educators. Student learning is generally considered a function of student ability rather than of student values. The paradigms of education, then, give the literature its structure and determine what is included and what is left out.

In order to develop a social systems approach to the analysis of the two-year college literature, it will be necessary to review the historical development of the two-year college because its evolution reflects both the constraints placed on its conceptualization by the larger system of education and the influence of non-educational social systems such as students themselves and the founding communities where two-year colleges were established.

The Two-Year College as a Subsystem of the Educational System

One question to be considered in an historical interpretation of the community college is why there are two-year colleges at all in the United States. The pattern of four-year baccalaureate institutions and public education through secondary school was fairly well established by 1900. And, although the situation was certainly less clear and clean in 1900 than it appears in retrospect a century later, there appears to be no overriding reason why two-year colleges should have emerged. There were collegiate institutions of various kinds with various terms of study from less than a year to three years and more. These included business schools, trade schools, normal schools, a variety of seminaries, and many others. In fact, two-year general colleges, both public and private, played a very small role in the educational system until after 1945.

The picture is further complicated by a regional pattern in the evolution of the two-year college. Numerous private collegiate institutions of two-year term existed in 1900. Many were religious in focus or origin and their various missions are almost too diverse to classify. All were small. After 1890, two-year public colleges grew in the Mississippi Valley and the western states. Unlike four-year private schools, however, which dominated higher education in the United States until after World War II and continue a powerful role in higher education, private two-year colleges shrank to relative insignificance in both number and enrollment by the middle of the 20th century (Frye, 1992). Like private four-year schools, private two-year schools dominate in the east, while public two-year schools dominate in the western states.

In the first 20 years of the 20th century, two principal rationales are found in the literature justifying or promoting the two-year college. One view has been characterized as an expression of the "great-man" theory of history (Ratcliff, pp. 154–155). In this literature, figures such as Harper, James, and Folwell promoted the two-year college based on presumed modeling from a German system. The model separated the research and scholarship functions of the university from the lower divisions of college work, sometimes described as secondary. As enrollment in universities grew, the two-year college was sometimes seen as a mechanism for preserving the mission of the university by keeping the mass of undergraduates in a separate institution if not on a separate track (Cohen and Brawer, 1991).

The second rationale had a very different origin and focus, although the literature then as now frequently mixes two or more distinct explanations without a hint of conflict. The second rationale is most clearly articulated in California. There, in a large state with little available in private higher education and only one state university in 1900, an argument developed for extending the high school curriculum to a 13th and 14th year to maximize the availability of higher education (McLane, 1913). In part the argument saw the "junior college" as a stimulus to university access. Others, such as some eastern university leaders, saw the same junior college as a brake on access, an institution that should weed out undesirables from university access (Cousens, 1934).

It must be stressed again that understanding these two positions as definitive and categorical opposites is to read into the texts of 1900–1920 the social conflicts of the 1980s. Presentism does not illuminate this issue; it only obfuscates the differences and nuances. By 1920, a significant variation emerged in a literature increasingly dominated by professional educators who had devoted their careers to junior college education. The American Association of Junior Colleges was created in 1920 and served as a focus for this group (Brick, 1964). Reflecting the views of neither high school superintendents nor university leaders, these junior college experts represent the national trend toward specialization and narrow concentration among professionals in all fields including education (Bledstein, 1976). This group of men developed a focus that created a new, more explicit rationale for two-year colleges. They generally argued that new modes of labor created the need for specialized mid-level training for occupations which they labored mightily to define as the semiprofessions. They often argued, on the basis of then current concepts of intelligence, that most students did not have the mental ability for a four-year degree but that the economy required that large numbers be educated beyond the high school level. By this argument the professionals, focused in the American Association of Junior Colleges, created a presumption that most, or at least many, high school students should go to a two-year college but not to a four-year college. Their own needs as a professional group were clearly served by such an argument. Acceptance of their position created a potentially large student body for the junior college and avoided possible conflict with powerful university leaders who increasingly expressed hostility toward the two-year college and feared enrollment competition (Frye, 1992).

These three views enjoyed expression and development in a period of growth and expansion for the two-year college. The three interpretations and numerous adumbrations co-existed in an environment where there was little need for critical analysis of the various approaches to definition. Ironically, the development of actual junior colleges proceeded almost in isolation from the visions outlined in the professional literature. Generally speaking, public junior colleges were created by local high school superintendents or other local luminaries who tapped into the enthusiasms of chambers of commerce, Rotary, and other influential community organizations. These moves often failed, but when they succeeded, the junior college reflected in curriculum and structure the needs of local professional educators and the social mobility aspirations of students and especially their parents. The local junior college program modeled as closely as possible the lower division program of the state university and as much of the "ideal" collegiate atmosphere as could be achieved given local resources and culture (Frye, 1992). Such colleges were often created in the absence of or contrary to state laws (Ratcliff, 1987). Most were the expression of small town America in the midwest and west. Where public junior colleges appeared in large cities, such as Los Angeles and Chicago, there were significant differences in curriculum but often a similar aping of "college life" insofar as was possible. Municipal junior college systems usually reflected powerful outside control such as city councils and municipal school boards.

In the post-World War Two period, the United States underwent a complex social and political revolution, the depths of which have yet to be fully understood. Expectations rose as social and political movements revolutionized relationships of race and gender, and broke down a variety of cultural stereotypes concerning the handicapped, sexual preference issues, marital relations, and family definitions. While the roots of these changes clearly date back to before World War Two, after 1945 changing social attitudes affected a broad range of social interactions including political rhetoric, social welfare, economic relations between social groups, and, of course, education.

The two-year college was in an enviable position to find institutional advantage in the evolving social environment. Being community-based, lacking the disciplinary focus of other higher education, and already emphasizing access and opportunity, the two-year college flourished in an age in which individual interests tended to overshadow social ones. As an institution the two-year college already had an internal culture that emphasized growth. Less trammeled than four-year schools by traditional commitments to disciplines and comparatively indifferent to student social origins, the two-year college found itself on a path of explosive growth. First, the two-year college absorbed rising numbers of nontraditional European-American college-age students from modest socioeconomic background. These increases were followed by growing enrollment among older students and those from minority populations and other ethnic groups. Responding to local needs and focusing on growth drove two-year colleges to provide access to part-time students. This commitment alone provided college admission to large numbers of students who would have been denied access to residential colleges.

The sporadic support for rapid growth of the two-year college that appeared in the literature of the 1950s and 1960s is best represented by Edmund Gleazer, president of the American Association of Junior Colleges. In *The Community College: Values, Vision, and Vitality* (1980), Gleazer promoted a concept of community education that was, in fact, so broad in scope as to exclude little in the way of potential educational services.

Growth in two-year colleges was indeed enormous—exceeding even the rapid expansion of other institutions of higher education—and occasioned outpourings of self-congratulation on the part of community college writers. Foundational issues and definitional, structural, and organizational problems tended to be ignored in the general euphoria until enrollments became stabilized and then began to decline in the 1970s and 1980s.

Contraction of enrollment growth and more difficult access to financial resources forced the two-year college into a difficult confrontation with issues that had been happily ignored earlier. Dale Parnell, succeeding Gleazer as president of the AACJC, responded as Gleazer had earlier to a different environment, with a book aimed at staking out a safe position in the educational hierarchy. In *The Neglected Majority*, he argued for a tie to high schools and a limited focus on social mobility by proposing a two-plus-two program that would direct a large number of middling students into middle-level occupations. The position harks back to Eells' construction of the semiprofessions concept in the 1930s (Eells, 1941). Like other two-year college leaders, Parnell did not suggest restricting access to the higher status degree, but his approach clearly reflected the fear that in an era of competition for students with other higher education institutions, the welfare of the community college was jeopardized. Adverse economic conditions that degraded the relative position of the United States in world trade also appeared to support Parnell's approach to strengthening middle- level technical occupational training.

As with many educational "reforms," the effect of Parnell's proposal is difficult to gauge. A limited number of programs were showcased in the AACJC *Journal*, but there seems to have been little impact on a nationwide scale and the approach was vulnerable to attacks by critics who alleged the institution was tracking minority students out of higher prestige occupations (e.g., Pincus, 1980, 1986). As Parnell approached retirement as president of AACJC, his emphasis on two-plus-two was quietly reduced although not repudiated.

While Gleazer's emphasis on broad-based community services and Parnell's push for a non-baccalaureate emphasis in programming dominated the literature of two-year college professionals, something very different was transforming the two-year college nationwide. The number, intensity, and sophistication of developmental programs increased steadily, while emphasis on completing a two-year academic program of any kind declined (Cohen and Brawer, 1991). Although enrollment in colleges expanded rapidly, enrollment in second-year courses declined, prerequisites tended to be lost, and acquisition of the associate degree as a percentage of enrollment plummeted. The cause as well as the effects of these changes are still obscure. But the discordance between the rhetoric of the national leadership and the activities of local colleges is again brought into clear focus by this dichotomy.

The literature on the two-year college produces a bewildering variety of views and interpretations. A satisfactory picture of the two-year college, its programs, purposes, procedures, and definitions does not emerge. This brief historical survey serves only to set the framework for an analysis of this literature. This cacophonous literature can be examined more meaningfully if it is seen in the context of the social systems from which it arises. In particular, the literature needs to be understood as reflecting the needs of the social groups it represents and the functions inherent in any social organization.

PART II. THE LITERATURE OF THE TWO-YEAR COLLEGE

The literature of any field can be understood as expressions of the interests, needs, and values of individuals and groups or collectivities in that field. This is true of the literature on sociology as a discipline, the fast-food industry, or golfing as a sport or business. These literatures reflect the diversity of groups within these fields, not abstract monolithic visions. For example, there are coaches of high school golf, sports writers on professional golf, those who write on the concerns of golf equipment manufacturers, and so on. Such categories are not always exclusive, mutually incompatible, or diverse in their values and attitudes, but they may be; moreover, their differences will generally be obvious in the literature.

Professional Writers on the Two-Year College

Preliminary analysis could identify at least three major sources of the literature on the two-year college: advocates, practitioners, and external specialists. Advocates are defined as those whose role in the system positions them to advocate and promote the interests and development of the two-year college nationwide.

The most obvious advocacy group is the AACC, but other organizations such as the League for Innovation fulfill a similar function. The AACC does, in fact, support a variety of staff positions, programs, and publications to this end. While the association staff is small, there is a strong network of community college presidents and former presidents now located in university programs related to community colleges. Community college presidents in this role usually come from some of the larger or more prestigious two-year institutions.

Practitioners form the second group of writers on the two-year colleges. By far the largest of the three groups, its members are people who teach or work as administrators or in some other professional capacity in a two-year college. This group also includes a substantial number of staff people within state or other governmental bureaucracies that have direct responsibilities for community colleges. Practitioners generally focus on one aspect of the two-year college. If rhetoric teachers, they may write on developmental English; if vice presidents for development, they may make contributions to the literature on college foundations. Although the contributions of this group to the traditional print literature may not be proportional to their numbers, the unique nature of the ERIC database makes many of their papers, research reports, and proposals available to a wide audience.

External specialists, exemplified by the university professoriate in higher education, represent the type of specialization in scholarship and research that has dominated higher education in the 20th century. Members of this third group have an analytical interest in the two-year college by virtue of their discipline of education, sociology, or another field. As a group, its members are very different in training, background, and outlook from those professors of community college education who obtain university positions at the end of a long and perhaps distinguished career as community college administrators.

The division of professional writers on the two-year college into three groups is somewhat arbitrary but not capricious. It will give some focus for understanding the authorship of the literature as reflecting a social organization within education. The three groups—advocates, practitioners, and specialists—have different motives for writing, different audiences, and different standards. The social outlook of each group provides a framework from which they define and respond to issues. While idiosyncratic motives and purposes may be present, writers in each of these groups tend to be dominated by group interests, usually thought of as professional.

The university professoriate, the external specialists, is the easiest group to review because their literature production is considered central to their role as faculty. High standards in scholarship are inherent in their position. But subjects considered appropriate for writing tend to be limited by the previous literature. How a subject, as well as the approach used, fits into the previous literature is one of the many standards by which a work is judged. While the intended audience may be diverse, the most critical audience component are peers who have power to influence career and future prospects, financial and otherwise. Scientific rationalism and objectivity set further criteria for peer judgment and hence limit the possible approaches.

The advocates are generally college presidents or members of associations related to the two-year colleges. Their literature often has a very different purpose and audience than that of the university professoriate. Generally, their literature production is central neither to their professional responsibilities nor to their future prospects, unlike the university professoriate. As a group they are likely to benefit marginally from improving morale among two-year college staff, improving public perception of the two-year colleges, or enhancing the prospect of favorable policy or funding decisions on the part of state or local agencies.

The third group, the practitioners, is more difficult to deal with in terms of its literature because of the group's diversity. For some, their duties as professionals responsible for research may require publication. For many, the prestige acquired by publication in any form is a motivation. In many cases, publication results from professional interest in a subfield of the two-year college such as developmental English or the uses of educational technology. Publication may be, or may be thought to be, important in career advancement. In general, the framework is narrow and the scope of perception limited. Broader conceptual issues tend to be received from elsewhere, uncritically, with little direct reference, since a report on the use of a specific mediated instructional program, for example, must assume a broad range of foundational arguments and theoretical explanations.

Given this foundation for the different authoring groups, the literature will be examined to provide an interpretation as to how the literature reflects differing interests among groups of educators. Two broad categories will be examined: the community college student and the institutional organization of the two-year college. This second category includes staff—faculty, administrators, counselors—as well as issues relating to organizational function—structure, financing, and governance.

The Concept of Student in the Two-Year College Literature

The concept of student is so basic to the idea of institutional education it would seem at first blush not to require significant time for analysis. However, if we keep in mind the patterns of thought that tend to dominate professional groups, we would expect educators to use the concept of student in ways that meet the needs of their group. Teachers think of students in terms of learning problems; administrators may think of students in terms of marketing, retention, and recruitment. Counselors will have another set of perspectives. McGrath and Spears (1991) and Pulliams (1988) illustrate the inherent conflict between the perspectives of counselors and teachers.

The evolution of the literature on students in the United States is dominated by writing on the elementary and secondary student. Since in the first half of the 20th century, many teachers and administrators of the two-year colleges arose from secondary experience and training, the public school perspective on students tended to be carried into the two-year college. Until World War II the literature on students in higher education in general was comparatively light, as can be seen in various sources such as *Education Index* and the *Journal of Higher Education*. Before World War II, the content of the student literature in higher education typically had a more humanistic and qualitative focus than literature on students in the lower schools. These differences were stimulated by the growing emphasis on quantitative studies in the literature on primary and secondary students. After the war, as postsecondary enrollments increased dramatically and the federal role in higher education expanded, quantitative studies on higher education also increased.

These two elements, the development of the research methods first in lower grades and the emphasis on quantification, dominate the conception of student in the educational literature. For example, there are numerous materials produced on primary and secondary student learning and relatively few studies on higher level student or adult learning. The problems inherent in this have come to light by a back door; namely, the difficulties experienced by minority and non-native students at college level (Mercado, 1988; Rendon, 1991). A more general problem presents itself. What is a student and how does the literature look at her/him?

Because of the institutional nature of education, educational professionals tend to write as if the distinction between student and non-student in unproblematic. Persons enrolled are students; persons not enrolled are non-students. This perspective is reinforced by the evolutionary history of the research model growing out of the primary and secondary systems. A research paradigm based on students using a coercive enrollment model of the lower public schools is likely to be very different from a research model arising first in a voluntary enrollment system such as higher education.

Although enrollment in college is voluntary, for most people the mental image of a college student is likely to be a youth in residence at a four-year institution, whose goal is automatically taken to be graduation. This traditional view has added strength in the literature because most educational specialists live and work in a university environment where the model appears to dominate. The rising age of students, the growing proportion of part-time students, increasing rates of leaving and returning, and a growing pattern of returning for professional growth based on personal needs or mandates for continuing education in various fields such as health, do not fit the traditional model of student. And yet there is no other model because of the historical evolution of the research paradigm and the structure of the educational profession.

Two-year college personnel will immediately see the inappropriateness of this model. A full-time Harvard University male, working on a program in international relations, is a student. If he leaves Harvard for a year to join his parents in Europe because his father has been appointed an ambassador, he is no longer a student. The two-year college student, in a program with the same title, who leaves for a semester to work in his father's business is also not a student. The state university residential student who ''flunks-out'' and the two-year college student who drops out to have her third child are also non-students. The Stanford student in business management and the Illinois fireman taking a required refresher course in emergency medical training at a two-year college are both students. Distinctions need to be made among these students and non-students, but the research model does not lend itself to this level of diversity when it produces studies of students. Quantification techniques in particular are limited by such a large number of variables (Papagiannas, 1991, pp. 269–270).

The research model of students and their definition as those enrolled is powerfully related to the social purposes of higher education: the allocation of merit-based rewards. Considering that the percentage of American population enrolled in higher education has gone from a few percent in 1900 to 25 percent in 1992, one might reason that a population change of that magnitude would raise warning flags about the statistical applications relevant to the cohort in terms of its definition. This has not happened, and a student is still an enrollee in quantification studies.

Problems of student body complexity and the diversity of individual motives, institutional mission, program goals, and the like are clearly seen in the literature. Three major research efforts will be reviewed to demonstrate the effect of student definition on the research literature. Brint and Karabel's *Diverted Dream* (1989) raises major historical and social issues about the origins and social effects of the two-year college. Their work has been widely cited. A study by Lee and Frank (1990) attempts to review the social effects of two-year colleges in terms of their impact on social mobility by once again applying rigorous statistical tests to determine the effect on students. Adelman's *The Way We Are* (1992) introduces a further commentary on the issues by an analysis of the 1972 NLS material. Each of these studies casts a somewhat different light on the issue of the impact of the two-year college on students. In combination, they illustrate the uncertain conceptual ground on that the research paradigm is based. While all three studies work from the model of student as enrollee, Adelman's work in particular raises the specter that the idea of higher education is undergoing significant shift in conceptualization.

Brint and Karabel's book is the culmination of a long line of social criticism of the effect of the two-year college, most prominently begun by Zwerling in 1976 (see also Pincus, 1980; Karabel, 1972). The basic premise is an attack on the assertions of two-year college proponents that the institution is ''democracy's college,'' that it promotes access and opportunity for social advancement. On the contrary, argue Brint and Karabel, the effect of the two-year college is to limit opportunity, and the institution works to maintain class divisions through social reproduction of the status system in the United States. This attack is based on quantification studies that show a small number of two-year college enrollees ever transferring to the university and fewer still graduating with baccalaureate degrees (Grubb, 1991). In particular, *Diverted Dream* argues that the promotion of occupational programs in the two-year college over transfer programs demonstrates the institutional motives underlying this trend.

Brint and Karabel represent a theoretical perspective, largely Marxist in approach, that understands social life to be dominated by conflict between social groups over power. Social classes and interest groups compete for social position and struggle over the control of social institutions to promote or protect their interests. For Brint and Karabel, then, the two-year college is a tool that assists the dominant classes in blunting the demands of lower social orders by diverting potential competitors from paths toward prestigious and powerful social occupations. This view has taken on a special quality because of the disproportionate numbers of lower socioeconomic groups and minorities in the two-year college.

Numerous criticisms of Brint and Karabel, both their general perspective and the details of their research, have been made (e.g., Adelman, 1992). Nonetheless, their criticism is an effective and powerful attack on the two-year college if one accepts the dominant paradigm of higher education and its conceptualization of student. One assumption is that higher education is a path to social mobility. This, of course, is a premise not only of the two-year college proponents, but of higher education in general. An ancillary perspective is that students, as research subjects, enter "college" to maintain or improve their relative social status. Conflict theorists and other educators conclude on the basis of this model that students who enter the baccalaureate track are failures if that goal is not reached. Opinions may differ as to whether the failure is an individual one or an institutional one, but the structure of the current paradigm forces this perspective on the research model.

If society is composed of competing interest groups and if students enter college to improve their chances in the conflict, then Brint and Karabel's analysis has considerable force. Their thesis has problems if one of these two premises is wrong; if either their conflict theory of society is in error because it does not accurately reflect social dynamics or the model of student is in error. Rather than being wrong, one or both of these views could merely be too simplistic. The problems of an overly simplistic view would tend to be accentuated by some quantification methodologies. This is not the place to argue the nature of human society, but the concept of student is central to the educational literature and fundamental to an analysis of that literature. Brint and Karabel's work is carefully grounded in statistical analyses of students and their path through the two-year college system. The recent work of Lee and Frank demonstrates both the strengths and limits of this quantification approach.

Lee and Frank's (1990) study utilizes the *High School and Beyond* study to establish a random sample of 2,500 students from the senior year of 1980 who attended a two-year college (p. 180). After a thorough review of earlier studies, Lee and Frank ask if the ''decreased social stratification'' (p. 178) made available by the community college through ''relaxed *access criteria*'' (emphasis Lee and Frank, p. 180) is an illusion because of ''trivial proportions'' (p. 180) who actually transfer. Sophisticated statistical techniques are applied to a limited range of student characteristics. These include social class, race, sex, high school behaviors such as academic rank, parental interest, GPA, and a variety of measures of college experience: GPA, semesters of math and science, and full-time/part-time comparisons. The results confirm the results of numerous earlier studies of factors that appear to be related to tendencies of failure or success in transfer. High GPA, high social class, and selection of math and science courses increase the likelihood of transfer. Being African-American, Hispanic, or having low grades decreases the likelihood of success.

However, the structure of Lee and Frank's research design, a form of path analysis, allows them to draw a variety of more general conclusions on direct and indirect effects on student transfer. Their study shows that the two-year college operates as a filter. Higher proportions of white males come out the end of the tunnel than enter. Racial minorities and women are disproportionately filtered out. Their path analysis places this process in a broader social context:

> It is social disadvantage that impedes community college students from transferring, through the effect of social class on virtually all the academic behaviors associated with transferring. While social class is strongly and positively associated with almost all such behaviors, race/ethnicity is related only to a few after social class is held constant. . . . Being a minority student, per se, is not a hindrance to persistence in higher education. (p. 191)

The level of complexity illustrated in Lee and Frank's study is confirmation of a variety of studies exemplified by Rendon (1991) that illustrate the complexity of cultural factors that affect student behavior.

In concluding their study, Lee and Frank answer their opening question, ''Do community colleges increase equity in higher education?'' by saying, ''Yes and no'' (p. 191). The two-year college offers access for a wider social range of students than four-year schools, but appears to have little effect since it is the ''better'' (p. 191) students who are likely to succeed in transfer. ''Family background and advantage'' (p. 191) confer the most likely combinations for success, and the two-year colleges do not ''change individuals much.'' (p. 191)

This is a criticism that proponents of the two-year college have invited by the use of extravagant and ill-considered claims about the opportunities presumably offered by two-year colleges. Two factors stimulate the use of extravagant rhetoric on the part of two-year-college supporters. First, their own professional interests in growth and financial support limit the appeal of rhetorical modesty. But the powerful value placed on self-improvement and upward mobility in the United States creates an audience that wants to hear enthusiastic support for access and upward mobility. When such value-laden visions combine with the traditional model of a ''student'' in higher education—a college-ready youth, at a residential four-year college with graduation as a goal—the reality is often disappointing.

In *The Way We Are*, Clifford Adelman looks at the NLS 1972 data and suggests that the problem is more complex than the research model currently in use will allow. Adelman examines the NLS 1972 data for two-year college effects. The period covered comprises 14 years from 1972 to 1986. In that period about 25 percent of the 1972 graduates had attended a community college. As Adelman points out, this does not mean they were community college students (pp. 4–6). This figure includes those who attended the two-year college right after high school and those who attended the community college after earning their bachelor's degree. It includes those who earned over 60 hours at the two-year college and those who took one course. Adelman's purpose is to ask ''who these people were, how they used the community college, and what happened to them in economic life, . . .'' (p. v). In order to accomplish this, Adelman reviewed the actual transcripts of student activities as well as their self-reported goals and activities. His conclusion, after reviewing the complex patterns of activity and the failure of the data to answer critical questions, is that ''the way we are as a learning society is best understood by the way we use community colleges'' (p. V). Illustrating a trend that brings into question the usual research approaches of student models, Adelman's study indicates that the social patterns of use in higher education do not clearly reflect the hierarchical social-allocation paradigm currently in use among professionals of higher education.

Adelman notes that the community college is used ''in a variety of 'occasional' roles'' (p. v). It is used for remediation by students, for experimentation, exploration, specific knowledge and skill goals, as well as the first two years of higher education. Moreover, the population using the two-year college is more representative of American society than the four-year college student body or the group that stops at high school. Like other researchers, Adelman finds the associate's degree to be a ''weak force'' (p. vi). It is the goal of few students and is attained by only 20 percent of community college attendees. The study shows no clear connection between any college attendance and occupational outcomes either in the two-year or four-year school. This important question has been overlooked in most of the literature. The career path from academic program to occupation is not a ''linear'' one in many cases (Adelman, p. vi). Finally, the earning of any degree, either associate's or bachelor's, does make a difference in terms of income, home ownership, and other measures.

When the three studies are taken together—the social criticism of Brint and

Karabel, the cautious data of Lee and Frank, and the in-depth transcript analyses of Adelman—a troubling picture emerges of a research literature that does not serve the educational profession well. More than the specific criticism of particular data bases or style of argument (Adelman, pp. 27–29), the shortcomings suggest a fundamental problem with the research concept of ''student.'' For example, Monk-Turner (1990) has produced a study in which she concludes that after all ''relevant'' factors are held constant, the effect of the two-year college is to retard and degrade the social expectation of a student who begins there instead of at a four-year school. The ''relevant'' (p. 724) data to which she alludes are a restricted list of socioeconomic factors in which significant characteristics such as cultural influences are ignored and a variety of populations are submerged in a vortex of general labels. What are the conclusions of critics such as Monk-Turner and Karabel (1972)? Is their conclusion that an entering class at a two-year urban college, if magically transported to be the entering class at Harvard University, would enjoy the same social success as a regular entering class at Harvard? Such a hypothesis reveals the shallowness of the data used to draw conclusions on the effects of two-year college education (e.g., Bers, 1992; Bauer, Mitchell, and Bauer, 1991; Kajstura and Keim, 1989).

Another example of the limits imposed on student research is seen in the use of ethnic and racial categories. These categories are identified not on any objective basis, but are a reflection of current political conditions and the current focus of those who do research. The most common categories used are White, Black, Hispanic, and, sometimes, Asian-American. Before 1950, these categories were rarely used, while there were concerns about Jewish students and white ethnics (e.g., Shuttleworth, 1951). Today the white ethnic category of student has disappeared. Religious divisions are also absent generally speaking. Rural and urban origins are rarely used as a concept to study cohort differences. What would be the result of studies similar to Monk-Turner's, Lee and Frank's, Pincus', and others, if they focused on Catholic, fundamentalist, and main-line Protestant student cohorts? Would significant statistical differences emerge in terms of community college effects? What if the studies examined Italian-Americans, Arab-Americans, English-Americans, or even the students who are children of Irish and Italian-American mixed marriages contrasted to the children of European-American and Asian-American marriages? It is tempting to carry this permutation of categories farther, but the point is clear that categorization of students for study is not, as is often assumed, an objective affair, but is, rather, a social construct. If some of these different categories were used, it seems probable that significant differences would be apparent among the groups. And what would that tell us?

Although the concept of ''student'' has been refined to include divisions into gender, race, SES group, and a few other categories, the basic problem with the conceptualization of student is still present. The problem is not in the students themselves: it is in the assumptions that educators impose on the cohort, that college student means a recent high-school graduate, full-time in college, aiming for the bachelor's degree to prepare for entry into high-status occupations usually thought of as professional.

Since two-year colleges offer enrollees not only this option but programs aimed at employment after two years, educators have utilized the concept of ''track.'' There are transfer tracks and career or occupational tracks. Among his other criticisms, Adelman argues that the idea of a track makes sense to educators, but examination of the transcripts of thousands of students suggests that ''tracking'' is a term of little meaning to students (pp. 18–19). Again the reality of how the population uses education contradicts the educational paradigm.

Another effect of the current paradigm is apparent in the literature on the two-year college. Since the model is assumed to include the baccalaureate degree, two-year college students are held up against this achievement. But studies of two-year college student success rates rarely compare four-year college student success rates in terms of completion by ''native'' students (i.e., those drawn from the local area). In 1989 for example, 93.3 percent of Harvard's entering class completed their bachelor's degree in four years. But at the University of Massachusetts only 57.9 percent completed their degrees in four years. At Chicago State University only 8.1 percent graduated in four years. At the University of Illinois at Urbana, 76.2 percent completed in four years while at the University of Illinois at Chicago, only 26.1 percent did so (*Chronicle*, 1991, pp. A39–A44). In other words, those four-year institutions that more closely parallel the social environment of the community college (i.e., being less residential and more commuter oriented, having easy access, and being more culturally diverse) are also more likely to fare badly when measured by the standards that elicit criticism of the two-year college. The influence of the traditional paradigm of what college is, then, not only adversely affects perception of the two-year college but other non-elitist, open-access institutions as well.

A further difficulty with the higher education paradigm is the assumptions made about social mobility (see Adelman, pp. 27–31). In a culture such as ours, where issues of social mobility play such a dominant role, it is understandable that proponents of higher education would make a strong connection between higher education and social mobility. In fact the data make clear that earning a bachelor's degree or higher is strongly correlated with higher social status in terms of occupation and other measures of status (Adelman, p. vi). In the literature, however, careless rhetoric confuses correlation with cause. Studies seldom compare social status of, say father's occupation, with child's status to see if real upward mobility has occurred. Monk-Turner, for example, in her discussion appears to assume that the bachelor's degree is the cause of the higher status rather than family influence.

This problem is critical because this assumption ignores complex family background issues that relate to the question of life success. These background issues are difficult to extract and statisticians must rely on gross measures of socioeconomic status in which the backgrounds of Hispanic families and Asian-American cultural influences are lost. This paradigm causes studies of the two-year college student to focus almost exclusively on the transfer issue, since the baccalaureate is the presumed standard. And while studies compare the results of education in terms of some gross measure such as income, they rarely compare family origin to postgraduation occupation of offspring. For example, Monk-Turner judges a native four-year college graduate to be more successful than a baccalaureate graduate who began in a two-year college because the former's average income is higher. This is done without any comparisons between the family of origin of the two kinds of students with the exception of gross SES data.

The power of the paradigm of college student has another effect that reveals its limitation. Most of the research studies focus on the transfer issue when considering the social mobility effects of the community college. When researchers are sensitive to the role of the community college in two-year programs (which is not always the case), the effects of these programs on social mobility are usually ignored, with Adelman again being an exception. For an Hispanic youth whose family has never had a high school graduate let alone a college graduate, a job as an auto mechanic, whether obtained after an associate's degree or only appropriate course work at a two-year college, may be a significant social advance. Some studies such as Pincus (1986) would suggest that the two-year college has retarded this youth's potential for upward mobility.

There is a further complication with the issue of social mobility. Both left-wing social critics and community college proponents often sound as if the two-year college does or should elevate the poor and minorities to higher social positions in society. To have social mobility, however, you must have a stratified society. There is no logic in moving up in a society where everyone is essentially equal. Community college enthusiasts cannot be elevating social classes, only individuals. Expressions in the literature to the contrary result from careless rhetoric. The left-wing critics, on the other hand, usually have a more egalitarian society as a goal. This conundrum adds further confusion to the discussion of this issue.

Student Models: Conclusion

If Lee and Frank are correct that the family of origin has more to do with success in college than race or ethnicity, the implications are profound. If success in college is largely a by-product of social origins, then the role of college in achieving social status is minimal. This contradicts the paradigm that assumes that a college education is fundamental to achieving high status. This question relates to the operations of social organizations outlined by Parsons (1991). Two goals of every social organization are to define mission and establish boundaries.

Enrollees are defined as within the boundaries of higher education—the appropriate subjects of teaching and research. One element of the mission of educators, as seen in the literature, is to improve or maintain the social status of students. If the role of education in allocating social status is minimal as compared with family background, then more questions are raised about the paradigm currently in use among the higher education community. The structure and operations of the two-year college bring this problem into focus.

As Adelman (1992) suggests, the model of student within the higher education paradigm is eroding. As in most paradigm shifts (Kuhn), the models need to erode before new paradigms are able to emerge. The literature on the student relating to the two-year college is an example of this process of erosion.

Professional educators in the United States are invested in the student model. The rhetoric of the literature provides two goals for students as seen by professional writers: satisfaction of personal needs for occupational access and consequent status allocation, and the satisfaction of labor needs for a skilled work force. American ideology requires that this process be assumed to work on meritocratic principles. The question of how well two-year college students satisfy this predictive model is central to the literature on students. The paradigm tells educators that students who go to college and do not succeed in improving their status by conventional research measures have either failed personally or have been betrayed by the system.

The structure of the educational system with its professional class has created a paradigm that is being challenged by the reality of uses to which the institution is being put by society at large. The above section illustrates some of these conflicts that appear in the literature on students. Further evidence of this conflict is apparent in the literature on other two-year college topics.

Professional Staff and Institutional Status

For the two-year college the definition of student is a boundary issue. This problem is central to most of the issues relating to the two-year college. Its answer defines the function of the two-year college, expresses the level of status for its faculty, guides program design, and justifies public finance and charitable largess. The multiple functions of the two-year college bring the disjunctions of the national paradigm into bold relief. Because the two-year college educates for both the baccalaureate and the occupational degree, and because it has increasingly taken a role in remediation and serves an "adult education" function, it confronts the dual purpose of higher education with a set of incongruities.

While the higher education paradigm provides education for social mobility opportunities as well as for work force needs, the two-year college exhibits features that challenge the meritocratic assumptions in the higher education paradigm. Open access threatens ideas that access to higher education is based on merit. Remediation raises the possibility that the educational system does not operate equitably. Career education, resulting in two-year degrees, implies tracking or purposeful allocation into ''inferior'' social occupations. ''Adult'' or continuing educational services imply that a need exists which is unmet by the current structure of K-12 through graduate school. The increase in part-time students threatens traditional ideas of collegiate education. Easy access and drop-in, drop-out patterns further erode the tradition of the specialness of higher education. Apparent adverse effects on mobility expectations of racial, ethnic, and gender minorities again threaten meritocratic assumptions and raise the specter of racism at the same time. The responsiveness of two-year colleges to perceived market and allowing a high level of curriculum, program, and course choice also produces stress in the higher education paradigm. How responsive should higher educational institutions be to student demands?

The problem of conflict between the paradigm and actual practice is also apparent in nearly all aspects of the two-year college literature, whether the topic is faculty, finances, organization, or leadership. The literature expresses the needs of any organization to adapt to external pressure, to achieve consistency and stability, to set goals, and to achieve success. But as new paradigmatic elements emerge in a literature, there continues to be a defense of the older paradigm that often produces complicated and inconsistent patterns of argumentation. This pattern of shifting focus, multiplex criticism, and inconsistency is well illustrated in the two-year college literature. One issue often present in the literature is sensitivity to status issues relating to professional staff. The quest for status is a motif in the two-year college literature produced by both the advocate group and the practitioners. While university specialists may question with impunity the value of the two-year college and even benefit from a critical approach, advocates and practitioners speak to different audiences and have different needs, especially in regard to institutional and professional status.

Adaptive Approaches in the Two-year College Literature

Adaptive themes in the professional literature promote the interests of the group and seek to maintain or improve its status position. Status for institutions, as well as individuals, defines more than simply a sense of well-being and satisfaction. Status describes relative position in a hierarchy and identifies the deference and power which external elements grant to the status in question. One has only to think of the associate professor searching for a publisher for yet another book, laboring to squeeze out another article, or struggling to obtain appointment to a prestigious association committee to appreciate the desire for and benefits of status. Physicians are a classic example of a profession with high status and the benefits that accrue to this status. Financial rewards may not even be the greatest of these.

Neither is the quest for status a demeaning activity. It should not suggest a false value system nor the dominance of self-interest or financial greed. The status of physicians, for example, derives from highly valued social service and exacting standards of performance. Sensitivity to status questions does not denigrate the professional educator's commitment to research, love of teaching, nor sincere devotion to personal student growth and society's needs for an educated population. Nonetheless, status issues are power issues and power describes the subjects ability to achieve goals.

The peculiarly vulnerable position of the two-year college in the American educational system produces a literature that brings the status issue closer to the surface than, say, in the university literature or that of the graded schools. Analysis of status issues in the community college literature is not only an illuminating approach for that literature, but provides further insight into the American social system as a whole. Recent community college literature will be analyzed from this point of view. Representative materials will be examined. Four principal areas will be explored: the place of the two-year college in higher education; the primacy of growth as a theme; the emphasis on innovation; and perspectives on faculty in the two-year college.

The University as a Model in the Two-Year College Literature

Two recent works eloquently illustrate the status issue in the two-year college literature. They are Kevin Dougherty's paper "The Community College at the Crossroads" (1991) and George Vaughan's and James Palmer's *Enhancing Teaching and Administration Through Scholarship* (1991). Although these works have radically differing themes, they both use the university model in an attempt to solve problems in the two-year college. Implicit in both works is a quest for the status inherent in the operations of university models. Neither work actually examines the operations of universities but assumes certain ideal characteristics of those institutions. Also characteristic of the two-year college literature, both works qualify their university models by certain traditional values associated with two-year colleges. This quality is more apparent in Vaughan and Palmer than in Dougherty.

Kevin Dougherty's article reviews the critical literature on the ability of community college students to effect transfers. He concludes that the community college has an undeniable "negative institutional effect" (p. 312) on transfer. Other things being equal, students who begin higher education in the two-year college are less likely to obtain a bachelor's degree than if they begin at a four-year college. While Dougherty's argument is open to criticism, his proposed solutions to this problem are of interest here. His solution to this presumed weakness is, in effect, to eliminate the community college by means of one of two alternatives: either make them four-year colleges or make them branch campuses of universities. These proposals are rather baldly stated and their consequences are not significantly explored, but Dougherty presumes that either change would improve the completion rate of entering students.

For Dougherty, the power of the baccalaureate institution as a model is so great that it is not necessary to examine actual four-year colleges. For example, the article makes no distinction among four-year colleges. Differences between urban universities and exclusive state and private universities are not taken into account. From Dougherty's article, one could conclude that all four-year institutions are uniformly more successful than all two-year colleges. Dougherty asserts that "the community college has failed to provide lower-division baccalaureate preparation of equal quality to that of four-year colleges" (p. 320). His evidence for this stems from largely anecdotal evidence from disparate articles by Nunley and Breneman (1988), Anderson (1984), Velez (1985), Astin (et al 1982), and others. Even if the assertion is true, there is little reason to believe that the structural changes proposed would materially alter this relationship. But the prestigious ideal of the baccalaureate school/university is so strong, the viability of these solutions is not doubted.

Dougherty spends little time discussing the other functions of the two-year college such as occupational education. He does note that "occupational education is no longer an absolute barrier to transfer" (p. 317). This statement reveals a primary assumption that educators make but students do not about occupational education. In the United States, occupational education has never been an "absolute" prohibition to transfer either in the distant past or recent history (Frye, 1992; Adelman, 1992). But the paradigm of higher education and the status of the university at its apex are so powerful that educators continue to make assumptions based on this model which affect policy and policy proposals.

Dougherty's proposal is not new. The relationship between two-year and four-year schools has been debated since the inception of two-year schools. The creation of independent two-year schools was a result of economic and geographic factors as well as professional needs of educators (Frye, 1992). But the persistence of the debate and its rebirth in Dougherty's proposal is a result of status problems as well as structural ones. Dougherty notes that two-year colleges do not always have high enough standards (p. 318) and that four-year institutions often do not willingly accept transfers from two-year colleges (pp. 316–317). Implicitly these failures would be removed or reduced by enhancing the status as well as the control of two-year colleges by transmogrification into four-year colleges or administratively attaching them to higher-status institutions. The performance of real community colleges is criticized, while the ideal standards of the baccalaureate institutions are accepted as real and contrasted to the reality of the two-year college. It is apparent that the high status of the four-year institution has played a powerful role in the formulation of Dougherty's proposals.

One might ask, what is the success rate of native students at the four-year college? Is it the same for Northeastern Illinois University and the University of Illinois at Urbana? If not, should Northeastern become an administrative appendage of some more "successful" institution? These questions are not considered in this context because Dougherty is working with the status disparity between two-year and four-year schools, not between different four-year schools. While the subordination of two-year institutions to four-year makes sense on one level, the subordination of one four-year institution to another will be recognized as an entirely different problem. This is because the hierarchy of status between levels in higher education is a fundamental part of the paradigm. Discrimination between institutions on the same level is not.

The subject of Vaughan's and Palmer's work is entirely different. It is focused on administrators and faculty in the two-year college and the emphasis the two-year college has always placed on teaching. They note that "scholarship" is often actively discouraged in the two-year college and argue that this is a weakness that should be corrected (pp. 6, 7). At the university, of course, scholarship is the sine qua non of status. A productive scholar on the faculty normally has higher status than an administrative staff member. Scholarship is usually thought of in the restricted sense of research and especially published research. Scholarly publication means, however, appearance in a limited range of outlets such as books or specialized journals meeting rigorous professional standards. Faculty and administrators in the two-year college produce few such works. The origin of this pattern requires some exploration because it is fundamental to the issue of status in the educational hierarchy.

The research university is the epitome of the educational system and its operations mark the status criteria. The emphasis on research is well known and the conflict between teaching and research is a common subject of discussion in the literature. Lower division teaching is often left to less prestigious members of the faculty and frequently is avoided by university faculty (Bywater, 1990). The evolution of the two-year college, its definition as a lower division, and its roots in the secondary system condemn its operation to this lower status position.

Power relationships in the two-year college also give administrative staff more authority and prestige relative to the faculty than is typical of the university. This is true not only because of the affinity with secondary schools, but because the two-year college tends to explore program variations that benefit by the application of management principles more than scholarly values. Disciplinary ties of the two-year college are weak, and the commitment to disciplinary specialization is one of the factors that provides the university professoriate with a powerful measure of protection from university administrators. Administrators at the two-year college tend to view scholarship by their faculty as frivolous and potentially counterproductive to the purposes of their colleges (Vaughan and Palmer, pp. 6, 7). Teaching loads and other factors militate against research in the community colleges.

Why then is there a concern in the community college literature for promoting scholarship in the two-year college? First of all there is an assumption that scholarship benefits teaching (p. 4). It is also argued that scholarship results in ''informed judgments,'' a quality needed by administrators (p. 73). It is significant that in Vaughan and Palmer's work the need for scholarship among administrators is given more space, energy, and emphasis than for the faculty (e.g., p. 75).

Palmer (1991) notes that the ''increased attention'' to scholarship is ''reassuring'' because it reinforces the community college's roots ''in higher learning.'' At the same time, he finds this trend troubling because it suggests that scholarship in the two-year college has been ''viewed with indifference or disparagement'' (p. 69). Vaughan (1991) reports a survey in which community college presidents identified ''publications'' last in a list of 17 items as important for themselves and for those administrators who report to them (p. 6). He notes that new faculty hires at the community college are made to understand that ''they are not joining a community of scholars'' (p. 4). To meet the needs of two-year college staff and protect the values of the two-year college, Vaughan is careful to define scholarship in a way that covers a wide range of activities. Scholarship is ''precise observation, organization, and recording of information in the search for truth'' (p. 5). Its manifestations include art productions, scholarly articles other than research-based, computer programs that are subject- or content-based, and research on teaching (p. 6). At the same time Vaughan makes it clear that he does not want to import the university principle of ''publish or perish'' (p. 6).

The conclusion is clear that the two-year college will be strengthened by an increasing commitment to scholarship, yet this agenda should not go too far according to Vaughan and Palmer. Programmatic benefits of research should be harvested, but promotion and advancement should not be made to depend on ''scholarship.'' This approach indicates the power of the university model in terms of status achievement. The two-year college will be taken more seriously as it approaches the behavior and values of the university. At the same time scholarship is made palatable to community college staff by emphasizing its practical benefits in teaching and especially its material decision-making benefits for the more powerful administrative group. Dougherty's solution to the transfer problem is to convert the two-year into a four-year school or, at least, make it organizationally a part of the higher-status institution. Vaughan and Palmer call upon two-year college staff to increase their commitment to activities highly valued in the university. The power of the university model is apparent. Neither article considers the reality of baccalaureate institution or university life, because the ideals of these institutions and their institutional status are what is sought. The status of the two-year college will be enhanced by the implementation of these proposals.

The Importance of Growth and Innovation in the Two-Year College

The concepts of growth and innovation are closely related in the two-year college. For an institution at the bottom of the higher education system, isolated from the principal source of high status at the university, namely research and publication, the areas of growth and innovation, as well as teaching, provide substantial opportunities for achievement, in contrast to the university model. Growth is seldom the explicit subject of the literature, but it is commonly embedded in the issues discussed (e.g., Gardner, 1988; Macomb Community College, 1991). Innovation is the explicit subject of a large and popular literature on the two-year college.

In an institution that has experienced periods of striking growth, it should not be surprising that the concept is popular and powerful. The emphasis on growth was and is encouraged in many states by the system of state reimbursements. In many states credit hours are reimbursed at a set rate so that the more enrollment the greater the income from the state treasury as well as from tuition. These increases often provide more cash that creates more options.

Interest in growth is not restricted to head count. In general, it is considered advantageous to have a large number of certificate and degree programs, of non-credit programs, and of remedial programs. The literature describing new programs often indicates that the community is consequently being better served. Recent examples in the literature are Pohrte (1990), Miranda and Rita (1989), Jacobs (1988), and Schubert (1989). The connection between program growth and enrollment growth is usually apparent.

While the dramatic enrollment growth of earlier years has stopped, the literature contains numerous subjects that relate directly to growth and maintenance of enrollment. Concern with retention has to do not only with service to students but also with maintaining a high level of credit-hour generation. In an institution where stopping and starting again is a common student practice, reducing the drop-out rate can have a major stabilizing influence on enrollment.

Retention of minorities is another area of recent concern. Minority generally means African-American and Hispanic although others can be included. A dual concern exists because of the lower transfer rate of minority students but also because in general, drop-out rates for these students are higher than for the majority white population. *Rekindling Minority Enrollment* by Angel and Barrera (1991) represents the concerns characteristic of this literature. The social demands for fair service are noted on a national scope, and equal note is made of the fact that a rising proportion of the college age population will be composed of these groups. Robert Atwell, President of the American Council on Education, observes in an introduction that minority education is "one of the most important goals of American higher education" (p. 1). After recounting the standard facts of minority enrollment, its disproportionately low level, and the social need for enhancing minority enrollment, one of the editors, Dan Angel, forcefully captures the urgency in a three-bullet conclusion:

> We have the need.
> We have the knowledge.
> Now is the time for action. (p. 6)

Serving minorities has not only the benefit of enrollment maintenance and growth but serves the traditional image that two-year college professionals have of themselves in serving the educational needs of those without special advantage (Velez, 1985, p. 91). The egalitarian theme is powerful in the two-year college literature.

The concept of quality in programs and services has likewise gained prominence because of the presumed positive effect on marketing. Quality in the literature is used to denote a performance level that not only achieves institutional and program goals, but creates a positive public image that attracts and retains enrollment (Cross, 1993). The use of quality in the literature acts as a stimulus and a support for growth.

For ''the lower end of higher education'' (Bywater, 1990), growth becomes a purpose in itself. The community college cannot compete with the main source of status within the system of higher education: the creation of new knowledge. Therefore growth serves as a standard of worth in the two-year college. While numbers of students and numbers of programs may not, in themselves, constitute a sufficient measure of status, many factors in the environment of the two-year college provide powerful motives that elevate growth to a prominent place in the model. Growth is a sign of popularity. Growth suggests a broadening or democratization of higher education which is a potent theme from the earliest origins of the two-year college in the Progressive Era (Koos, 1925). And not least important, financial systems that reward growth strengthen this model.

The literature of the two-year college clearly reflects the high value placed on growth. The concept of growth serves as an adaptive mechanism within the system of education. The goal also serves the practical needs of a professional class whose options increase with growth and markedly decline with enrollment and program shrinkage. In order to advance the institution, promotional organizations such as the AACC use the traditions of growth at every opportunity that presents itself (AACC, 1991).

The concept of innovation serves a similar function in the literature. In a mass consumption society things that are new and different serve a powerful economic function, and the concept of new and different as being better has a life of its own in American cultural traditions. Beyond general cultural attitudes, however, ideas of innovation in the two-year college literature hold a special place. It is not an accident that one of the most prestigious community college associations is named The League for Innovation. The idea that the two-year college was new and different and consequently not bound by the dead hand of tradition is found in the earliest literature of the two-year college and is common in the earliest years of the *Junior College Journal*. The powerful appeal of the idea can be seen in such works as B. Lamar Johnson's surveys of innovations. These works have the grandiose, almost spiritual titles of *Islands of Innovation* (1964) and *Islands of Innovation Expanding*. (1969)

A contemporary work by Terry O'Banion continues this tradition. *Innovation in the Community College* (1989) opens with a clear declaration of the importance of the concept among community college professionals:

> Administrators, faculty, board members, and support staff will find here the exciting ideas and programs that make the community college a significant force in American society. (pp. ix-x)

O'Banion recalls the "tremendous" period of the innovations of the 1960s and laments the decline of the innovative spirit in the 1970s and early 1980s as a variety of difficulties, including financial and enrollment declines, presumably stopped the innovation drive (p. ix). He then notes that the book will not highlight the definitions and processes of innovation although "the careful reader" will find them. Earlier innovations were access-driven for O'Banion, that is, focused on growth (p. 5). Currently innovations are focused on "new demographics" (p. 11). This is also a growth and maintenance issue as discussed above. O'Banion is concerned about contemporary innovations building networks with other institutions, business and industry, secondary schools, economic development, and a broad range of institutions.

O'Banion provides a sample list of innovations identified with the community college. Individualized instruction, management by objectives, experimental colleges, encounter groups, and "a host of others" are mentioned. These innovations may seem pallid after the build-up, and actually none of them originated in the two-year college. Since a definition of innovation is not provided, and the list of innovations is so broad, it appears that innovation means any program change. No criteria regarding significance, scope, or effectiveness are identified. The approach impels O'Banion to introduce the qualifying concepts of "new innovations" (p. 17) and "refurbished innovations" (p. 14).

The power of this image, the idea of innovation, is clear from the rhetorical approach taken by O'Banion. Like the idea of growth, the idea of change or innovation enhances the distinctiveness and defines the place of the two-year college in higher education. Neither are growth and innovation simply rhetorical flourishes. Their role in the two-year college literature clearly mark them as central goals and motivational elements. They serve to promote consistency and stability within the individual institutions as well as the literature. The broad appeal of these concepts tends to maintain internal harmony within particular institutions and within the larger system of two-year colleges. Although validity studies are not present in the literature, it may well be true that the two-year colleges are more innovative than other areas of higher education and that overall the impact of "innovations" has been beneficial. It is certainly true that the high portion of Americans in higher education at any one time, compared with other industrialized states, is, in part, a function of growth in the two-year college. Whatever the objective measures of these concepts show, they are crucially important concepts in the definition of the two-year college and the self-concept of its professional staff. Since 1902 ideas of growth and change have played a dominant role in the conceptualization of the two-year college.

Even though ideas of growth and change are powerfully evident in community college literature, they are not concepts that play a large role in the paradigm of higher education. High standards in higher education tend still to be measured by quality rather than quantity. And, in general, the concept of "innovation" in higher education has a different focus than in the two-year college. In disciplines and research conducted at the university level, innovation, in the sense of new knowledge, is central. But institutional and program innovation are suspect at the university because the disciplines, not the institution, are the central focus. Consequently, two-year college professionals get little mileage from the idea of innovation from the university professoriate.

The ideas of growth and innovation are value-laden in the two-year college literature. They are useful internally in integrating specific institutional cultures. They are useful concepts in dealing with the local district community and state legislators and state agencies. But they do not solve, for the two-year college, the problem of status within the system of higher education. The paradigm of higher education, its focus on individual learning and status allocation, is remote from these more material and public values. This dichotomy is seen more clearly in the literature that deals with professional personnel, faculty and administrators, in the two-year college. In this literature, contradictory images of staff emerge depending on the author's perspective and the methodology employed.

Two-Year Faculty and Staff: A Literature at War with Itself

Studies of two-year college faculty are relatively few compared with studies of students, instruction, and administration. The major qualitative studies are dominated by a dark view of the community college faculty. The faculty are usually described as frustrated, demoralized, and overwhelmed by ill-prepared students and insensitive administrators. The works of McGrath and Spear (1991), Seidman (1985), and Zwerling (1976) fit this pattern. These studies rely on personal experience, interview methodology, and often, anecdotal evidence. Unsurprisingly, these authors all have humanities or social science backgrounds in the liberal arts. These authors tend to see community college faculty as lacking a scholarly outlook, having lost connection with their disciplines, and lacking the youthful idealism that initially motivated them to seek a community college position. More quantitative studies utilizing large samples show the two-year college faculty in a very different light. (Carnegie, 1990; Keim, 1989) Such studies frequently suggest that two-year college faculty are satisfied with their work, more content than other higher education faculty, and reluctant to leave their positions even when alternatives are available. The differences in these two types of studies are significant and reveal again the influence of the higher education paradigm that delimits and defines the boundaries of discourse and identifies acceptable models in the field.

Seidman's work, *In the Words of the Faculty* (1985), is based on intensive interviews with faculty at a variety of two-year colleges. Seidman identifies "the problems that now confront community college faculty," and the burden of "student centeredness" (p. x). Community college faculty are oppressed by administrators who do not deal with what is "really important" (p. x) The dichotomy between teaching and research has narrowed the definition of scholarship to the point that two-year faculty engage in neither research nor other forms of scholarship (p. 252). This loss of scholarship lowers "aspirations" and plagues their teaching by undermining "their intellectual energy" (p. 253).

For McGrath and Spear (1991), who frequently refer to Seidman, the problem is "the steady erosion of intellectual life in the open-access college" (p. 11). The introduction to their work provides a series of descriptions of rude student behavior, students unprepared for class, and students forcefully and publicly objecting to the teacher's methods and content in class. McGrath and Spear fear the "remedialization" of the community college and the resultant vulnerability to charges by "left critics" and "educational effectiveness critics" (pp. 46–47, 53). Their hope is that community colleges "may yet . . . form themselves into powerful instruments for social equality and mobility . . ." (p. 7). To achieve this, the two-year college must "bridge the gulf between nontraditional students and academic life" (p. 88). To do so the "teachers of the traditional academic disciplines" must be rescued from their "role ambiguities" and the disengagement from disciplines." They must be rescued "from anemic practices" and be returned to "rigor" (p. 142).

The prescriptions of Seidman and McGrath and Spear for the necessary reforms are similar in tone and specifics. Seidman lists 15 recommendations while McGrath and Spears want to stress the criterion of the doctorate for two-year college teachers. Seidman's list and McGrath and Spear's recommendations both reflect adherence to the traditional value system of the university and its student paradigm.

Seidman's first item is to demand a moratorium on "new vocational programs." Like McGrath and Spear, Seidman is deeply suspicious of the influence of vocational education and vocational educators in the two-year college (Seidman, pp. 176–77; McGrath and Spear, p. 142). It is presumed that the background of vocational teachers differs greatly from liberal arts teachers and that their standards have a negative effect throughout the institution. Seidman further promotes traditional collegiate activities such as narrative writing, high expectations, and high esteem for the faculty and their authority (pp. 277–279). He wants holders of the doctorate to be affirmed and scholarship to be supported and recognized (pp. 280–281).

The prescription of McGrath and Spear is less wide-ranging if more insistent. They require that the certificate for teaching two-year-college "introductory or survey courses" in academic subjects be the doctorate (p. 145). "Faculty . . . who are relatively undereducated" and "professionally disconnected," without ongoing research interests, are unlikely to "represent their disciplines intelligibly to nontraditional students, to interpret its intellectual structures, theoretical models, and vocabulary . . ." (p. 145).

These prescriptions represent traditional paradigmatic models in higher education. These views reinforce the perspective that two-year college faculty are inferior to four-year faculty. This view reinforces the traditional value and status system of higher education. It speaks to the power of the paradigm and confronts the dissonance present in the weakened paradigm of higher education as a provider of student intellectual development and consequent status allocation and social mobility.

Broad-based studies of two-year college faculty present a different picture. A national survey of faculty in higher education reveals significant differences between two-year faculty and university faculty in certain categories, while responses to other questions, especially attitudinal ones, show substantial similarities in many areas. Salaries for two-year faculty are less than those for other categories of higher education except for baccalaureate colleges, but not remarkably less. The average 1991 salary for community college faculty was $37,760, compared with $51,080 for faculty at doctoral institutions, $43,440 at comprehensive universities, and $37,260 at baccalaureate granting institutions (CHE, 1992, p. 28). Women comprise a larger percentage of two-year college faculty compared with other institutions, but surprisingly, the percentage of minority faculty is smaller than the average for all types of institutions. Considering the large percentage of minority students in two-year schools this statistic is remarkable. Only 17.5 percent of community college faculty have doctorates, while all other types of institutions show more than 50 percent of their faculty with that degree. Research was viewed by only 25 percent of the community college faculty as "essential or very important," while more than 50 percent of faculty at other institutions did so. In other respects, community college faculty attitudes on many issues are remarkably similar to those of all higher education faculty (CHE, 1992, p. 30).

In terms of job satisfaction, 52 percent of two-year college faculty expressed themselves satisfied or very satisfied compared with 44.5 percent of all faculty. On overall satisfaction 74 percent of two-year versus 69 percent of all faculty expressed strong satisfaction. Satisfaction with the quality of students was lower for the two-year college faculty (30 percent to 37.5 percent for all faculty). The following percentages compare two-year college faculty opinion with the average opinion for all faulty. These are the percentages that agree strongly or somewhat strongly:

	Community College	All
Interested in student problems	84.9%	73.8%
Sensitive to minorities	73	69.1
Much racial conflict on campus	5.4	11.8
Different ethnic and racial groups get on well together	69.7	59
Feminist perspectives included	31.1	28.8
Students well prepared	20.3	27.4

Other questions revealed that two-year college faculty are somewhat more politically conservative than their four-year colleagues (CHE, p. 30). The Carnegie Foundation reported that 47 percent of two-year college faculty were "more enthusiastic" about their work than when they began, while the same question elicited a 43 percent response rate for four-year faculty (Carnegie, p. 25). Only 13 percent of the two-year faculty, but 16 percent of the four-year faculty, report that they would not become college teachers if they "had it to do over again" (p. 25). And 46 percent of the four-year faculty reported their jobs a "source of considerable strain," compared with 38 percent in the two-year college. In an unrelated study, Marybell Keim found faculty at the two-year college were generally satisfied with their positions (Keim, p. 39).

While there are indeed notable statistical differences between two-year and four-year faculty, the differences do not appear to support the cataclysmic visions in the qualitative literature. On the other hand, the differences in these two types of literature are what one would expect in a complex social system undergoing paradigmatic shift. Like the perception of students and the perception of mission, the picture of faculty offers diverse alternatives for interpretation. From one perspective, they have drifted from their moorings; that is, the model of what a higher education faculty should be and do. That this view is not a consensus is an understatement, given the perception that the community college faculty represents "A Sector with a Clear Purpose" (Carnegie, p. 23). This dissonance is less apparent in the four-year institution because that is the seat of the paradigm and the two-year college is effectively subordinate. However, as Kuhn (1970) observes, paradigms erode first around the edges, not at the center (pp. 64–65, 67).

CONCLUSION: "ARROGANT CARPING" AND THE EROSION OF THE PARADIGM

The literature of the two-year college raises questions for which there are no generally accepted answers. What should be the role of remediation in the two-year college? Does the low level of transfer mean that the community college has failed? Should two-year college faculty be required to have a doctorate to teach liberal arts subjects? If both career and transfer programs are appropriate, what should be the balance between them? Should two-year colleges be autonomous or branches of universities? Should faculties have more authority in the management of community colleges? Many other questions could be added as well as countless permutations of these questions.

The first point to note is that many players have a hand in answering these questions. Local boards of control play a role. College presidents have power in these decisions. Faculty do as well, but it is important to recognize the complex sources of faculty attitudes, divided as they are into career and transfer, labor union and academic senate, developmental teachers, librarians, counselors, and both traditional disciplinary departments and nontraditional departments and divisions. State agencies play a role in deciding these questions, as do governors and legislators. The local electorate and the general public influence these questions by their votes and support or lack of it. Not least, students by their choices, enrollment or non-enrollment, pressure institutions on these and other issues. Universities affect these decisions in a variety of ways, both directly and indirectly.

Contributors to the literature of the two-year college represent only a small sampling of these players. Like the contributors to other professional literatures, they tend to be members of certain social groups writing for specific audiences. To understand such a literature, it is necessary to understand the functions of social groups. These include the need to defend interests, define goals, integrate member activities, and achieve outcomes that legitimate the organization. These functions revolve around paradigms shared by group members but also shared, to some degree, by those outside the organization. When paradigms are not shared or when their meaning is undergoing a shift, communications suffer. This condition characterizes the two-year college literature. Those in community colleges and those who write about them are beset by a social environment that is pressuring the meaning of higher education.

The problem of shifting paradigms dominates the literature of the two-year college. When the community college is understood as a part of a much larger social system of education, the problem in the literature becomes clearer. Since the current paradigm of higher education assumes that higher-education institutions play a role in allocating social position and status, a problem is created in the research literature when the two-year college does not appear to succeed in this arena. When students at the community college do not resemble the model of "college student," more difficulties appear. When two-year college faculty do not practice scholarship at a level comparable with other higher education faculty, something needs to be explained. When growth and program innovations are selected as centering devices in the culture of the two-year college, values are being expressed that are aberrant, to some degree, to the premier values of other institutions in higher education.

Does postsecondary education significantly determine what happens to the future of its students? In *Academic Crisis . . .* , McGrath and Spear certainly wish to believe that it does (p. 7). This is a powerful assumption throughout higher education. If this presumption of higher education is incorrect for the two-year college, there is a serious paradigmatic problem. Paradigms operate in such a way that their truth is seldom challenged. It does not much matter whether the paradigm is true for universities; it is accepted as the model. If family background is the primary cause of success and college education is only a corollary, the integrity of the two-year college is still not safe because the relationship of college education and success is paradigmatic throughout higher education.

In a book review published in *Educational Studies*, James Wattenbarger (1992), a long-time specialist on the community college, referred to some criticism of the two-year college from university personnel as ''arrogant carping'' (p. 227). His remark was made in passing, and although such sentiments can be often heard in the informal talk of higher education professionals, it is rare to see such opinions in print. It is not hard to find reasons for such reticence, but such expressions do illustrate some of the frustrations felt by two-year college professionals. In terms of a social organization, the university model is still the epitome of status in higher education. The two-year college, highly successful from many perspectives, finds its position threatened by a model which the two-year college cannot match in many important respects even in the limited range of operations assigned to it. That actual universities may not succeed when judged by this paradigm is not, perhaps, a successful defense for the community colleges failure to succeed, because the traditional paradigm is still the ideal. Numerous social factors have begun to erode the traditional paradigm of higher education. Writers on the two-year college reflect the traditional paradigm and its weaknesses, both by what they defend and what they attack, by what they propose and what they ignore. In this respect the two-year college literature, because of the vulnerable nature of the institution, provides insight into the future problems and directions of all of higher education.

REFERENCES*

Adelman, C. (1992). *The Way We Are*. Washington, DC: GPO.

Almeida, D. A. (1991). Do underrepresented students and those with lower academic skills belong in the community colleges? A question of policy in light of the ''mission.'' *Community College Review* 18(4): 28–31.

American Association of Community and Junior Colleges (1991). *Information Brief 1991*. AACJC.

American Association of Community and Junior Colleges (1991). *Public Policy Agenda*. AACJC.

American Association of Community and Junior Colleges (n.d.). *A Summary of Selected National Data Pertaining to Community Technical and Junior Colleges*. AACJC.

*Includes works not cited in the text.

Anderson, K. (1984). Institutional differences in college effects. Boca Raton, FL: Atlantic University (ERIC Documentation Reproduction Service No. ED 256204).
Astin, A., Astin, H.S., Green, K.C., Kent, L., McNamara, P.R., and Williams, M.R. (1982). *Minorities in American Higher Education.* San Francisco: Jossey-Bass.
Angel, D., and Barrera, A. (eds.) (1991). *Rekindling Minority Enrollment.* (New Directions for Community Colleges, No. 74.) San Fransisco: Jossey-Bass.
Bauer, K., Mitchell, F. R., and Bauer, P. F (1991). Students' perceptions of selected academic and personal characteristics acquired at community colleges. *College and University* (Fall): 65–71.
Bers, T. H. (1992). Yet another look at transfer: Oakton students and bachelor's degree recipients at Illinois public universities. Oakton Community College, Oakton Office of Research.
Bledstein, B. J. (1976). *The Culture of Professionalism.* New York: W. W. Norton.
Bowles, S., and Gintis, H. (1976). *Schooling in Capitalist America.* New York: Basic Books.
Brick, M. (1964). *Forum and Focus for the Junior College Movement: The American Association of Junior Colleges.* New York: Teacher's College Press.
Brint, S., and Karabel, J. (1989). American education, meritocratic ideology, and the legitimation of inequality: the community college and the problem of American exceptionalism. *Higher Education* 18: 725–735.
Brint, S., and Karabel, J. (1989). *The Diverted Dream: Community Colleges and the Promise of Educational Opportunity in America, 1900–1985.* New York: Oxford University Press.
Buckley, W. F. (1951). *God and Man at Yale.* Chicago: Regnery.
Budd, J. M. (1988). A bibliometric analysis of higher education literature. *Research in Higher Education* 28: 180–190.
Budd, J. M. (1990). Higher education literature: characteristics of citation patterns. *Journal of Higher Education* 61: 85–97.
Button, H. W., and Provenzo, E. (1983). *History of Education and Culture in America.* Englewood Cliffs: Prentice- Hall.
Bywater, T. R. (1990). The lower end of higher education: freshmen, sophomores, the research university, and the community college. In Feroza Jussawalla *Excellent Teaching in a Changing Academy: Essays in Honor of Kenneth Eble* (New Directions for Teaching and Learning, No. 44): 73–81.
California Community Colleges. Office of the Chancellor (1989). *California Plan for Career-Vocational Education. Part I: Policy Directions.* ERIC ED 301 277.
Carnegie Foundation for the Advancement of Teaching (1990). Community colleges: a sector with a clear purpose. *Change* (May/June): 23–26.
Chronicle of Higher Education (1992). *Almanac* 39:1 (August 26, 1992).
Chronicle of Higher Education (1991). Graduation rates of athletes and other students at division I colleges. (March 27, 1991): A39–A42.
Clark, B. R. (ed.) (1984). *Perspectives on Higher Education: Eight Disciplinary and Comparative Views.* Berkeley: University of California Press.
Clowes, D. A., and Levin, B. H. (1989). Community, technical, and junior colleges: are they leaving higher education? *Journal of Higher Education* 60: 349–355.
Cohen, A. M. (1989). The case for community colleges. ERIC ED 308 920.
Cohen, A. M., and Brawer, F. (1991). *The American Community College.* San Francisco: Jossey-Bass.
Cohen, A. M., Palmer, J. C., and Zwemer, K. D. (1986) *Key Resources on Community Colleges.* San Francisco: Jossey-Bass.

Courtis, S. A. (1936). The evolution of individualism. *Educational Method* 15: 291–298.
Cousens, J. A. (1936). President Cousens' Opinions. *Junior College Journal* 4: 371–372.
Cross, K. P. (1993). Involving faculty in TQM. *AACC Journal* 63: 15–20.
Cross, K. P., and Fideler, E. F. (1989). Community college missions: priorities in the mid-1980s. *Journal of Higher Education* 60: 209–216.
Dougherty, K. J. (1991). The community college at the crossroads: the need for structural reform. *Harvard Educational Review* 61: 311–336.
Dougherty, K. J. (1988). The politics of community college expansion: beyond the functionalist and class-reproduction explanations. *American Journal of Education* 96: 351–393.
Eells, W. C. (1941). *Why Junior College Terminal Education*. Washington, DC: AAJC.
Frye, J. H. (1992). *The Vision of the Public Junior College, 1900–1940 Professional Goals and Popular Aspirations*. New York: Greenwood Press.
Gardner, J. W. (1988). Developing leadership in community colleges. *Education Digest* 53: 56–58.
Geertz, C. (1973). *The Interpretation of Cultures*. New York: Basic Books.
Giroux, H. A., Simon, R. I., and contributors (1989). *Popular Culture, Schooling, and Everyday Life*. Massachusetts: Bergin and Garvey.
Gleazer, E. J. (1980). *The Community College: Values, Vision, and Vitality*. Washington, D.C.: AACJC, 1980.
Gollattscheck, J. F.(1988). The AACJC and curriculum reform. In D. B. Wolf and M. L. Zoglin (eds.), *External Influences on the Curriculum* (New Directions for Community Colleges No. 64) San Francisco: Jossey-Bass.
Grubb, W. N. (1991). The decline of community college transfer rates. *Journal of Higher Education* 62: 194–222.
Grubb, W. N. (1992). Finding an equilibrium: enhancing transfer rates while strengthening the comprehensive community college. *Transfer* 3(6): 1–11.
Herbst, J. (1992). The American people's college: the lost promise of democracy in education. *American Journal of Education* May: 275–297.
Hitch, A. M. (1933). Opportunity of the junior college—a challenge. *Junior College Journal* 4: 1–2.
Hubner, Sister M. (1944). Professional attitudes toward religion in the public schools of the United States since 1900 (Dissertation, Catholic University of America). Washington, DC: Catholic University of America Press.
Hutchins, R. M. (1933). Education and the public mind. *School and Society* 38: 161–165.
Jacobs, J. (1988). Training for new manufacturing technologies. *Community Technical Junior College Journal* 59: 38–42.
Jacobson, R. L. (1992). Role of community colleges questioned by research on five state systems. *Chronicle of Higher Education* (November 11): A30.
Jaeger, R. M. (1988). *Complementary Methods for Research in Education*. Washington, DC: AERA.
Johnson, B. L. (1964). *Islands of Innovation*. Occasional report no. 6. Junior College Leadership Program. Los Angeles: UCLA.
Johnson, B. L. (1969). *Islands of Innovation Expanding: Changes in the Community College*. Beverly Hills, CA: Glencoe Press.
Judd, C. H. (1933). Quoted in *Junior College Journal* 4: 153.
Kaestle, C. F.(1982). Ideology and American educational history. *History of Education Quarterly* Summer: 125–136.

Kajstura, A., and Keim, M. (1989). Reverse transfer students in Illinois community colleges. *Community College Review* 20:2 39–44.

Karabel, J. (1972). Community colleges and social stratification. *Harvard Educational Review* 42: 521–562.

Keim, M. (1989). Two-year college faculty: A research update. *Community College Review* 17: 34–43.

Knoell, D. (1990). *Transfer, Articulation, and Collaboration Twenty-Five Years Later.* Washington, DC: AACJC.

Koos, L. V. (1925). *The Junior College Movement.* New York: AMS Press.

Kuhn, T. (1970). *The Structure of Scientific Revolutions.* Chicago: University of Chicago Press.

Labaree, D. F. (1990). From comprehensive high school to community college: politics, markets, and the evolution of educational opportunity. *Research in the Sociology of Education and Socialization* 9: 203–240.

Lee, V. and Frank, K. (1990). Students' characteristics that facilitate the transfer from two-year to four-year colleges. *Sociology of Education* 63: 178–193.

Macomb Community College (1991). The top ten issues facing America's community colleges. ERIC ED 327 248.

Martorana, S. V., and Garland, P. H. (1991). *State Legislation and State-Level Public Policy Affecting Community, Junior, and Two-Year Technical College Education, 1989.* (A Report to the National Council of State Directors of Community and Junior Colleges). University Park: Pennsylvania State University.

McGrath, D., and Spear, M. B. (1991). *The Academic Crisis of the Community College.* Albany: State University of New York Press.

McGrath, D., and Spear, M. B. (1988). A professoriate is in trouble and hardly anyone recognizes it. *Change* (January/February): 26, 53.

McLane, C. L.(1913). The junior college or upward extension of the high school. *School Review* 21: 161–170.

Mensel, F. (1989). The Ford bill: creating a world-class work force. *Community, Technical, and Junior College Journal* 59: 12–13.

Mercado, O., et al. (1988). *Successful Teaching Strategies:* Instruction for Black and Hispanic Students in the California Community Colleges. ERIC ED 319 421.

Merton, R. K. (1957). The role-set: problems in sociological theory. *The British Journal of Sociology* 8: 106–120.

Meyer, M. W. (1988). A case of incomplete institutionalization. In D. B. Wolf and M. I. Zoglin (eds.), *External Influences on the Curriculum.* (New Directions for Community Colleges No. 64, Winter) San Francisco: Jossey-Bass.

Miranda, S. and Rita, E. S. (1989). Developmental minicourses. *Journal of College Student Development* 30: 270–271.

Monk-Turner, E. (1990). The occupational achievements of community and four-year college entrants. *American Sociological Review* 55: 719–725.

Noll, J. F. (1942). *Our National Enemy No.1 Education without Religion.* Huntington, IN: Our Sunday Visitor Press.

Nunley, C. R., and Breneman, D. W. (1988). Defining and measuring quality in community college education. In J. Eaton (ed.), *Colleges of Choice.* New York: Macmillan.

O'Banion, T. (1989). *Innovation in the Community College.* New York: Collier Macmillan.

Palmer, J. (1991). Nurturing scholarship at community colleges. In Vaughan and Palmer, *Enhancing Teaching and Administration Through Scholarship.* (New Directions for Community Colleges, No. 76) San Francisco: Jossey-Bass.

Papagiannis, G. J., Klees, S. J., and Bickel, R. N. (1982). Toward a political economy of educational innovation. *Review of Educational Research* 52: 245–290.
Parnell, D. (1985). *The Neglected Majority*. Washington, DC: The Community College Press.
Parsons, T. (1991). The Marshall lectures—the integration of economic and sociological theory. *Sociological Inquiry* 61: 10–59.
Pelavin, S. H., and Kane, M. B. (1990). *Minority Participation in Higher Education*. ERIC ED 334 931. Washington, DC: Pelavin Associates.
Pincus, F. L. (1980). The false promises of community colleges. *Harvard Educational Review* 50: 332–361.
Pincus, F. L. (1986). Vocational education: more false promises. in L. S. Zwerling, *The Community College and Its Critics*. San Francisco: Jossey-Bass.
Pohrte, T. W. (1990). *Telecourses: instructional Design for Nontraditional Students*. (New Directions in Community Colleges, No. 69) San Fransico: Jossey-Bass.
Pulliams, P. (1988). The emerging role of community college counseling. Community College of Philadelphia. ERIC ED 300 739.
Ratcliff, J. L. (1987). "First" public junior colleges in an age of reform." *Journal of Higher Education* 58: 151–180.
Ravitch, D. (1974). *The Great School Wars*. New York: Basic Books.
Rendon, L. (1991). Qualitative indicators of Hispanic student transfer. Paper presented at the annual meeting of the Association for the Study of Higher Education, Boston.
Richardson, R. C. Jr. (1990). Community colleges: democratizing or diverting? *Change* (July/August, 1990): 52–53.
Richardson, R. C. Jr. (1990). *Minority Achievement Counting on You*. ERIC ED 326 261.
Rubinson, R. (1986). Class formation, politics, and institutions: schooling in the United States. *American Journal of Sociology* 92: 519–48.
Schubert, R. (1989). Community colleges pool resources to improve training in industry. *Engineering Education* 79: 494–495.
Seidman, E. (1985). *In the Words of the Faculty* San Francisco: Jossey-Bass.
Shuttleworth, F. K. (1951). Discrimination in college opportunities and admissions. *School and Society* 74: 398–402.
Smith, B. M. (1990). The personal development of the commuter student: what is known from the comparisons with resident students? an ERIC review. *Community College Review* 17: 47–56.
Smith, K., and Bers, T. H. (1989). Parents and the college choice decisions of community college students. *College and University*, 64: 335–348.
Sykes, C. J. (1988). *ProfScam: Professors and the Demise of Higher Education*. Washington, DC: Regnery Gateway.
Teichler, U. (1988). Higher education and work in Europe. In John C. Smart (ed), *Higher Education: Handbook of Theory and Research* Vol. IV. New York: Agathon.
Thwing, C. F. (1896). Drawbacks of a college education. *The Forum* September: 483–492.
Tierney, W. G. (1992). An anthropological analysis of student participation in college. *Journal of Higher Education*. 63: 603–618.
Trow, M. (1991). American higher education: Exceptional or just different. In B. Shafer, *Is America Different? A New Look At American Exceptionalism*. Oxford: Clarendon Press.
Tyack, D. B. (1976). Ways of seeing: an essay on the history of compulsory schooling. *Harvard Educational Review* 46: 355–389.
Tyack, D., and Hansot, E. (1990). *Learning Together: A History of Coeducation in American Schools*. New Haven: University Press.

Vaughan, G. B. (1991). Scholarship and the community college professional: focusing the debate. In Vaughan and Palmer, *Enhancing Teaching and Administration Through Scholarship*. (New Directions for Community Colleges, No. 76) San Francisco: Jossey-Bass.

Vaughan, G., and Palmer, J. (1991). *Enhancing Teaching and Administration Through Scholarship* (New Directions for Community Colleges No. 76, Winter). San Francisco: Jossey-Bass.

Velez, W. (1985). Finishing college: the effects of college type. *Sociology of Education* 58: 191–200.

Velez, W., and Javalgi, R. (1987). Two-year college to four-year college: the likelihood of transfer. *American Journal of Education* (November): 81–94.

Wattenbarger, J. L. (1982). Junior and community college education. In H. E. Mitzel (ed.), *Encyclopedia of Educational research* 2:982–989.

Wattenbarger, J. L. (1992). Review of T. W. Fryer and J C. Lovas: *Leadership in Governance: Creating Conditions for Successful Decision Making in the Community College. Educational Studies* 23: 226–229.

Wattenbarger, J. L. (1983). Research as a basis for improving the community college. *Community College Review* 10: 58–62.

Zwerling, L. S. (1976). *Second Best.* New York: McGraw-Hill.

Logistic Regression Analysis in Higher Education: An Applied Perspective*

Alberto F. Cabrera
School of Education, SUNY—Albany

Deciding to attend college, choosing a particular institution over another, dropping out before completing a degree, majoring in a particular academic discipline, and transferring from one institution to another are examples of some college outcomes educational researchers constantly deal with when addressing issues affecting higher education institutions. As the seasoned educational researcher already knows, how well one answers these research questions can substantially affect how effective institutional programs will be in addressing such college behaviors as enrollment and retention (Hossler, 1991). In dealing with these behaviors, however, the researcher faces two main problems. First, college outcomes are the product of an array of factors in which both student characteristics and those of the institution interact among themselves (Pascarella and Terenzini, 1991). Second, many college outcomes are dichotomous in nature. There are no interval scales to describe such behaviors. Either an individual attends college or not, majors in hard sciences or not, stays or leaves the institution, or obtains a bachelor degree or not.

While a growing number of conceptual frameworks can assist the researcher in identifying what factors are relevant to the particular college behavior under consideration (see Pascarella and Terenzini, 1991), the task of quantifying the effect these factors have may be constrained by the nature of the college behavior under consideration. Although several statistical techniques are available, only a few of them conform to the specific dichotomous nature of outcome measures such as enrollment, persistence, and degree attainment. These include: structural modeling for dichotomous dependent variables (e.g., Bentler, 1989; Jöreskog and Sörbom, 1988; Muthén, 1988), log-linear analysis (e.g., Christensen, 1990; Hinkle, Austin and McLaughlin, 1989; Marascuilo and Serlin, 1988), discriminant analysis (e.g., Marascuillo and Levin, 1983), probit regression and logistic regression (e.g., Fienberg, 1983; Hanusheck and Jackson, 1977).

*The author would like to thank Maria B. Castañeda, SUNY-Albany, Barbara Zusman, University of Illinois Research Laboratory, Amaury Nora, University of Illinois at Chicago, W. Paul Vogt, SUNY-Albany, and Ernest Pascarella, University of Illinois at Chicago, for their invaluable comments and suggestions.

The application of logistic regression in higher education to deal with dichotomous dependent variables is not new. Its use can be traced back to the late '60s and early '70s. During these decades efforts were made at developing econometric models to explain college choice (see Manski and Wise, 1983). Bishop (1977), for instance, employed this technique to study college enrollment decisions and how responsive these decisions were to tuition and student aid programs. Likewise, Manski and Wise (1983) relied on multivariate logistic regression in addressing the role of the Basic Educational Opportunity Grant (BEOG) in facilitating college choice and enrollment for the high school class of 1972. More recently, St. John (1990, 1991) and St. John and Noell (1989) relied on logistic regression to address the role of tuition on college attendance and to estimate the effect of student aid in facilitating college attendance on the part of minorities. The application of logistic regression has not been restricted to college enrollment. Behaviors such as college persistence, transfer decisions, and degree attainment have also elicited the use of this technique.

Stage (1989), for instance, used a combination of logistic regression and LISREL for validating Tinto's (1975, 1987) model of college persistence. Stampen and Cabrera (1986, 1988) used logistic regression for aggregate data in exploring the extent to which student aid equalized opportunities to persist in college. St. John, Kirshstein and Noell (1991) utilized logistic regression to document the effects of financial aid on year-to-year college persistence for the 1980 high school senior cohort. Cabrera, Stampen and Hansen (1990) used this method to explore the effects of ability to pay on the persistence process. Dey (1991) relied on logistic regression to explore determinants of persistence to graduation for a national sample of college students.

The purpose of this chapter is to provide a basic introduction to the use of logistic regression. The chapter was written with a specific audience in mind: educational researchers seeking basic information about how logistic regression can be used in addressing policy questions involving dichotomous outcomes[1]. The focus of the chapter is not on the mathematical foundations underlying logistic regression. These foundations are discussed in detail by Aldrich and Nelson (1986), Backer and Nedler (1988), Christensen (1990), Collett (1991), Fienberg (1983), Freeman (1987), Hanusheck and Jackson (1977), and Maddala (1987), among others. Rather, the emphasis is on the practical applications of logistic regression. The chapter is organized into three sections. Section I introduces the reader to the underlying assumptions associated with the logistic re-

[1]Logistic regression need not to be confined to the analysis of dichotomous dependent variables. Weiler (1987), for instance, relied on nested multinomial logistic regression to model the effect of factors affecting decisions of nonattendance, attendance at a four-year college or university, attendance at a community college, or attendance at a technical institute. Examples on the use of multinomial logistic regression can be found in Aitken, Anderson, Francis and Hinde (1990) and in Aldrich and Nelson (1984).

gression model. Section II presents a step-by-step illustration of the use of logistic regression. This section also introduces the reader to two statistical packages that handle logistic regression: the Generalised Linear Interactive Modelling (GLIM) and SPSS-X (Backer and Nedler, 1988; Norusis, 1990). In illustrating the results, particular effort is placed on discussing methods available for assessing alternative models, indicators of goodness of fit, procedures for testing the statistical significance of variables, and interpretation of the results in practical terms. Finally, Section III briefly summarizes the controversy surrounding the use of Ordinary Least Square (OLS) over Logistic regression.

I. ASSUMPTIONS UNDERLYING THE USE OF LOGISTIC REGRESSION

There are two main assumptions underlying the use of logistic regression. The first deals with the nature of the distribution associated with the binary outcome; the second deals with the nature of the relationship between the outcome variable (e.g., persistence) and the independent variable(s) (e.g., financial aid).

Under the first assumption, it is presumed that each of the potential values of the outcome variable Y (0 or 1), has a corresponding expected probability that varies as a function of the values that the independent variable(s) can take for each subject. Statistically this statement can be expressed as follows:

$$\mathrm{E}[Y_{\mathrm{ith}} = 1 / \mathrm{X} = \mathrm{x}] = \mathrm{P}(Y_{\mathrm{ith}} = 1)$$

where $\mathbf{P}(Y_{\mathrm{ith}} = 1)$ represents the probability of observing the condition of success (i.e., persisting) for the ith subject given a particular value of X. These probabilities are assumed to follow a binomial distribution (see Plane and Oppermann, 1977). A unique characteristic of this type of distribution is that although the probability distribution has an overall mean referred to as P (i.e., the proportion of subjects that meet the criterion of success), the variance changes as a function of the subject under consideration. The variance for each subject ($\mathrm{V}(_{\mathrm{ith}})$) is expressed as follows:

$$\mathrm{V}(_{\mathrm{ith}}) = \mathrm{P}(Y_{\mathrm{ith}} = 1) * [1-(\mathrm{P}_{\mathrm{ith}} = 1)]$$

where $\mathrm{P}(Y_{\mathrm{ith}} = 1)$ represents the probability of observing the condition of success, say persisting, for the ith subject and $[1-(\mathrm{P}_{\mathrm{ith}} = 1)]$ represents the probability of not observing the condition of success, say dropping-out, for the ith subject.

As far as the nature of the relationship between a binary outcome and a given independent variable is concerned, the logistic regression model presumes that this association can be accounted for by a logistic function (Collett, 1991; Hanusheck and Jackson, 1977). In the case of one independent variable, the logistic function takes the following form:

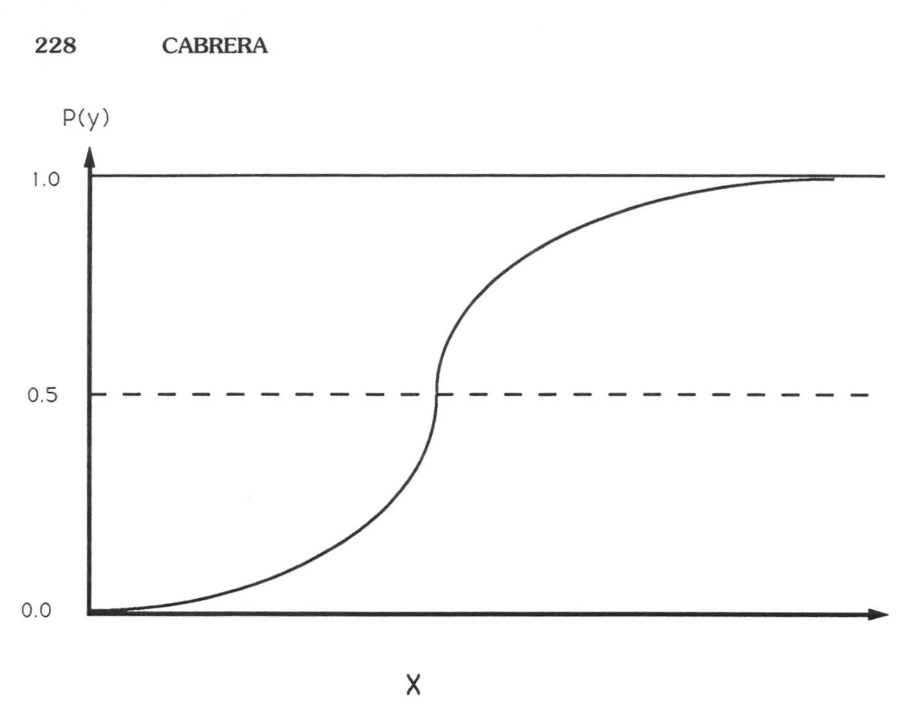

FIGURE 1. The logistic distribution.

$$L = \ln \frac{P(Y)}{1 - P(Y)} = B_0 + B_1\, X_1 \qquad (1)$$

where L is called the logit or the natural logarithm of the odds ratio, B_0 and B_1 refer to the familiar intercept and beta weight and $P(Y)$ stands for the expected probability of Y across different values of X. Since probabilities are the focus of analysis, equation (1) can be restated as follows:

$$P(Y) = \frac{\exp(B_0 + B_1\, X_1)}{1 + \exp\,(B_0 + B_1\, X_1)} \qquad [2]$$

As shown by Aldrich and Nelson (1986), the logistic distribution is *S*-shaped and has values ranging from .0 to 1.0 as $B_1\, X_1$ changes from negative infinity to positive infinity. Figure 1 displays a logistic distribution function.The estimation of the equation's parameters (intercept and betas) rests upon a method called Maximum Likelihood (ML). ML basically assumes that the underlying relationship between an independent variable and a dichotomous dependent variable (Y) follows a probability function (also called likelihood function)[2] which is

[2]A detailed discussion of the nature of the probability or likelihood function and its properties can be found in Christensen (1990), Collett (1991), Hanusheck and Jackson (1977) and Fienberg (1984).

S-shaped in nature (see figure 1). There are two types of probability distributions that can be employed to study the relationship between the dichotomous dependent variable *Y* and the independent variable(s). These are the probit distribution and the logistic distribution (Hanusheck and Jackson, 1977). Of the two, the logistic distribution is the most frequently used[3]. Analyses based upon the logistic distribution are usually referred to as logistic regression. Based on the assumption that the relationship between the dichotomous dependent variable and an independent variable can be represented by a logistic distribution (see Figure 1 and equation 1), the probability of the dependent variable (P) is estimated for each group (in the case of grouped data) or for each subject (in case of individual data). The natural logarithm of the odds (logit) is employed to transform the probability estimates into a continuous variable. Next, the ML approximation to logistic regression seeks to assess the effects of the independent variable upon the probability function. This is accomplished through an iterative process of estimation whereby estimates for the intercept and for betas are chosen so as to maximize the likelihood of reproducing the observed probability value for *Y*. Thus, the principle underlying ML approximation can be simply summarized as deriving those estimates for the intercept and the slopes that would make the *likelihood* of having observed *Y* the highest (Hanusheck and Jackson, 1977).

As noted by Aldrich and Nelson (1984), the principle followed by ML for estimating parameters for the intercepts and the slopes is quite similar to that employed by the Ordinary Least Squares (OLS) regression model, with a major conceptual difference. While OLS is concerned with choosing those parameter estimates that would minimize the sum of the squared errors between the observed and predicted *Y*s, ML estimation seeks to choose those estimates that would yield the highest probability or likelihood of having obtained the observed probability *Y*.

Several computer programs are available to handle logistic regression models. These programs rest on different approximations to the Maximum Likelihood method and consequently are likely to yield slightly different results. The most popular are GLIM and SPSS-X[4]. These programs are available for both main frame and PC environments. The illustration of the use of logistic regression for individual data will be based on GLIM version 3.77 (Backer and Nedler, 1988) and on SPSS-X version 4.0 (Norusis, 1990) both for the PC environment.

[3]The probit distribution and the logistic distributions are very similar. The difference between the two functions shows up in the tails of the distributions with the probit distribution approaching the axes faster than the logistic distribution does (see Hanusheck and Jackson, 1977). The logistic approximation is usually preferred over probit given its convenient mathematical properties (Hanusheck and Jackson, 1977; Norusis, 1990).

[4]Options to handle the logistic regression model are also available in SAS and in BMDP.

II. HANDLING OBSERVATIONS: A MICRODATA APPROACH

The logistic regression model is quite flexible as to the unit of analysis it can handle (Christensen, 1990; Hanusheck and Jackson, 1977). The logistic regression model can be employed when the unit of analysis is the individual subject, or in those circumstances in which the group[5], rather than the individual subject, is the unit of analysis. The application of logistic regression for individual observations (also called logistic regression for microdata) is adaptable to the metric of the independent variable under consideration. The microdata approach can be applied where the independent variables are truly categorical, such as gender, ethnicity, type of major, or where the variable has been categorized, such as low, middle and high income, or where continuous and categorical variables are mixed together such as type of major and GPA[6].

Several examples can be found in the literature that include applications of these two approaches in higher education. Manski and Wise (1983), for instance, employed the aggregate approach to study the effect of SAT (broken down into two categories), family income (two categories), region (two categories), ethnicity (two categories), and being a high school leader (two categories) on the likelihood of applying for and being admitted to college, for a representative sample of the high school class of 1972. More recently, St. John (1991) employed the microdata approach to study the effect of academic preparation, academic ability, region, social background, and degree aspirations on the probability of attending college for a representative sample of the high school class of 1982. Moreover, St. John's study provides an excellent illustration of how logistic regression for microdata data can bring together continuous and categorical variables in attempting to predict a dichotomous dependent variable.

There are several procedures that can be utilized for model testing, assessing the fit of a given model, estimating the statistical significance of the parameters and selecting alternative models. The reader familiar with OLS will find that these procedures bear a striking resemblance to those employed for assessing models under the OLS approach. These methods, as they apply to microdata, will be illustrated with a data base on the outcomes of doctoral work.

An Illustration

Background. This illustration utilizes a data base on graduate students created by a major midwestern doctoral granting institution. The data base is the product of an ongoing project aimed at studying determinants of graduate related behaviors (see Baird and Smart, 1991; Ethington and Bode, 1992; Smart, Baird and

[5]The reader interested in the use of logistic regression for aggregate data is referred to Fienberg (1984), Freeman (1988) and Christensen (1990). Aitken et al. (1990) also provide several illustrations.

[6]For a comprehensive discussion of the differences between the two approaches, see Collett (1990) and Hanusheck and Jackson (1977).

Rode 1991). The doctoral student subsample employed by Nora, Cabrera and Shiville (1992) for testing a model of engagement in graduate related behaviors will be employed. The specific focus of the example is one of those behaviors, namely, determinants of research engagement.

Variables. The dependent variable under study is research engagement, this is a dichotomous variable; doctoral students who indicated that they participated with faculty or peers in research projects were coded as 1. Those who indicated otherwise were coded 0. Consequently, the dependent variable Y had two potential values. In order to facilitate the illustration of logistic regression only eleven of the independent variables employed in the Nora et al. (1992) study were analyzed. Two indicators were employed to measure background variables. These were father's education, an ordinal variable made up of five levels ranging from 1 = high school diploma or less to 5 = PhD or advanced degree, and gender (1 = female, 2 = male). Pre-Commitments were measured through the Pre-institutional commitment scale, a composite averaged across two items, and Pre-professional commitment, made up of a single item measured in a Likert scale ranging from 1 (not important) to 5 (very important). Academic Contacts with Faculty, a composite scale averaged across five items, and Interactions with Peers, a composite scale averaged across four items, provided measures of a student's integration with the academic and social components of the department in which the doctoral student was enrolled. Final vocational and professional commitments were measured through a single Likert-scaled item. Academic growth and development was measured via a Conceptualizing Skills scale, a composite averaged across six items, and a Research Skills scale, a composite averaged across four items. These scales basically measure the extent to which students reported gains in conceptualization and research skills resulting from experiences with their respective academic departments. Using the Biglan's subject matter classification scheme (Biglan, 1973a, 1973b), students were also classified as either majoring in soft majors (major = 1) or majoring in hard majors (major = 2). This variable was included to account for the effect that a particular discipline may have on scholarly behaviors. Table 1 displays summary statistics and alpha reliabilities for each variable.

Creating the Data Base. Preparing data bases for individual cases for GLIM and SPSS-X is similar to the process employed for other canned programs. Columns are used to represent variables while rows stand for individual cases across variables. Table 2 displays the case number, the columns representing the respective variable, values for each independent variable (X_1 throughout X_{11}) and the observed probability of conducting research (Y).

Coding Schemes for Categorical Variables. In GLIM, the specification of categorical and ordinal variables is quite simple, for the program contains options allowing the researcher to specify the categorical variable with its respective levels. In GLIM, such a categorical variable as Father's education can be iden-

TABLE 1. Descriptive Statistics and Marginal Distributions

Variables	Count	Cell %	Mean	S.D.	Alpha
Dependent Variable:					
Research Engagement (RENG)					
1. Yes	263	49.4	–	–	–
0. No	269	50.6	–	–	–
Independent Variables:					
Father's Education (FAED)					
1. High School or less	224	42.1	–	–	–
2. Some college	79	14.8	–	–	–
3. Bachelor's degree	95	17.9	–	–	–
4. Master's or equivalent	55	10.3	–	–	–
5. Ph.D. or advance	79	14.8	–	–	–
Sex					
1. Female	284	53.4	–	–	–
2. Male	248	46.6	–	–	–
Pre-Commitments					
Pre-Institutional (PINT)	–	–	2.33	0.87	0.864
Pre-Professional (PPRF)	–	–	3.31	0.84	–
Integration:					
Faculty (FACU)	–	–	3.47	0.98	0.848
Peer	–	–	3.04	0.99	0.627
Final Commitments:					
Professional (PROF)	–	–	4.50	0.89	–
Vocational (VOCA)	–	–	3.72	1.25	–
Academic Growth:					
Conceptualizing Skills (CSKL)	–	–	2.91	0.59	0.811
Research Skills (RSKL)	–	–	3.01	0.68	0.748
Major (MJR)					
1. Soft	282	53.0	–	–	–
2. Hard	250	47.0	–	–	–

tified by a single variable made up of five categories. Unlike SPSS-X, the use of the coding 0 and 1 in GLIM is reserved for the dependent variable, while categorical variables can be represented by any digit provided that 0's are not included. In the case of the variable *MAJOR*, for instance, the code 1 represents those subjects majoring in soft disciplines while code 2 represents those subjects majoring in hard disciplines. For the dependent variable, the code 1 represents students that reported being engaged in research ($y = 1$) while 0 is reserved for those students who indicated otherwise ($y = 0$). Displayed in Table 1 is the coding system employed for analyzing the data in GLIM.

In SPSS-X, two-category variables—also called dummy or indicator variables—are coded as 0 or 1 to signify the presence or absence of the classification

TABLE 2. Layout of Data for Logistic Regression

Case #	FAED (*X*1)	SEX (*X*2)	PINT (*X*3)	PPRF (*X*4)	FACU (*X*5)	PEER (*X*6)	PROF (*X*7)	VOCA (*X*8)	CSKL (*X*9)	RSKL (*X*10)	MJR (*X*11)	RENG (*Y*)
1	3.00	1.00	3.00	3.00	4.00	4.67	5.00	4.00	3.00	3.50	1.00	0.00
2	1.00	2.00	2.00	3.00	3.60	2.00	5.00	2.00	3.17	3.50	1.00	1.00
3	1.00	2.00	2.00	4.00	1.00	2.67	5.00	5.00	3.67	3.75	2.00	0.00
4	1.00	1.00	3.00	2.00	2.60	2.67	4.00	3.00	3.17	3.50	1.00	1.00
.	.	.	.	.	.	.	.	.	.	.	.	.
.	.	.	.	.	.	.	.	.	.	.	.	.
.	.	.	.	.	.	.	.	.	.	.	.	.
.	.	.	.	.	.	.	.	.	.	.	.	.
532	2.00	1.00	2.00	1.00	3.20	4.33	3.00	3.00	4.00	4.00	1.00	1.00

condition. In the case of the variable *MAJOR*, for instance, the code 0 represents those subjects majoring in soft disciplines while the code 1 represents those subjects majoring in hard disciplines. When the categorical independent variable under consideration is made up of more than two categories, new variables need to be created to represent the categories. In SPSS-X, the handling of the five-level Father's education variable involves the creation of four dummy variables. These are: *COLLEGE* = 1 for students whose father has some college and 0 otherwise, *BACHELOR* = 1 for students whose father has a bachelor degree and 0 otherwise, *MASTER* = 1 for students whose father has a master degree and 0 otherwise, and *PHD* = 1 for those students whose fathers have a Ph.D. degree or equivalent and 0 otherwise (see Table 4). Since the categorical independent variables were created to meet GLIM specifications, these variables were recoded to meet SPSS-X requirements as shown in Table 4.

Reading the Data Base. There are two procedures to supply GLIM and SPSS-X with the data. The first is iterative; that is, the data can be provided once GLIM or SPSS-X is invoked. The second procedure relies on creating an ASCII file and storing it under the directories containing the GLIM and SPSS-X programs. The latter is recommended particularly in those cases where large data bases are in place. The complete set of GLIM commands for reading and performing the series of logistic regressions employed in this illustration is displayed in Table 3. The equivalent SPSS-X commands are listed in Table 4.

GLIM uses the terminology "**$UNITS**" to refer to cases or individuals. The command **$UNITS 532 $** instructs GLIM that information on 532 subjects is to be processed. The command **$FACTOR** identifies the categorical independent variables along with their respective number of categories. As noted, the command identifies three categorical variables; namely, Father's education (FAED), Gender (SEX) and Major (MJR). In the case of FAED, the command

TABLE 3. Commands for Logistic Regression Using GLIM

```
$UNITS 532 $
$FACTOR FAED 5 SEX 2 MJR 2 $
$VARIATE PINT PPRF FACU PEER PROF VOCA CSKL RSKL $
$FORMAT FREE $
$DATA FAED SEX PINT PPRF FACU PEER PROF VOCA CSKL RSKL MJR
RENG $
$DINPUT 13 $
  File name? PHD.DAT
$CALC N = 1.0 $
$YVARIATE RENG $
$ERROR B N $
$LINK G $
$FIT FAED+SEX $
$DISPLAY D E R $
$FIT FAED+SEX+PINT+PPRF $
$DISPLAY D E R $
$FIT FAED+SEX+PINT+PPRF+FACU+PEER $
$DISPLAY D E R$
$FIT FAED+SEX+PINT+PPRF+FACU+PEER+PROF+VOCA $
$DISPLAY D E R$
$FIT FAED+SEX+PINT+PPRF+FACU+PEER+PROF+VOCA+CSKL+RSKL $
$DISPLAY D E R$
$FIT FAED+SEX+PINT+PPRF+FACU+PEER+PROF+VOCA+CSKL+RSKL+MJR $
$DISPLAY D E R $
$FIT SEX+PINT+PPRF+FACU+PEER+PROF+VOCA+CSKL+RSKL+MJR $
$DISPLAY D E R $
$FIT 1 $
$DISPLAY D $
$STOP
```

identifies a categorical variable made up of five values or levels. The command **$VARIATE** specifies the continuous independent variables; namely, Pre-Institutional Commitment (PINT), Pre-Professional Commitment (PPRF), Interactions with Faculty (FACU), Interactions with Peers (PEER), Professional Commitment (PROF), Vocational Commitment (VOCA), Conceptualization Skills (CSKL) and Research Skills (RSKL). The command **$DATA** identifies the particular order in which information for each variable was stored. In this case: FAED, SEX, PINT, PPRF, FACU, PEER, PROF, VOCA, CSKL, RSKL, MJR, and RENG. In GLIM, like in SPSS-X, data may be read in either fixed or free format. In either mode, the data are read by GLIM on a row basis. Under the **FIXED** format, Fortran commands are used to identify the specific number of variables and their location in the file. If a **FREE** format is used, it is advisable that the variables be separated at least by one space. The command

TABLE 4. Commands for Logistic Regression Using *SPSS-X*

```
DATA LIST FILE 'PHD.DAT' FREE /FAED SEX PINT PPRF FACU PEER PROF
                                    VOCA CSKL RSKL MJR RENG.
COMPUTE COLLEGE = 0.
COMPUTE BACHELOR = 0.
COMPUTE MASTER = 0.
COMPUTE PHD = 0.
IF (FAED EQ 2) COLLEGE = 1.
IF (FAED EQ 3) BACHELOR = 1.
IF (FAED EQ 4) MASTER = 1.
IF (FAED EQ 5) PHD = 1.
COMPUTE NSEX = 0.
IF (SEX EQ 2) NSEX = 1.
COMPUTE NMJR = 0.
IF (MJR EQ 2) NMJR = 1.
LOGISTIC REGRESSION RENG WITH COLLEGE BACHELOR MASTER PHD
NSEX /CASEWISE = PRED RESID ZRESID.
LOGISTIC REGRESSION RENG WITH COLLEGE BACHELOR MASTER PHD
NSEX PINT PPRF/CASEWISE = PRED RESID ZRESID.
LOGISTIC REGRESSION RENG WITH COLLEGE BACHELOR MASTER PHD
NSEX PINT PPRF FACU PEER/CASEWISE = PRED RESID ZRESID.
LOGISTIC REGRESSION RENG WITH COLLEGE BACHELOR MASTER PHD
NSEX PINT PPRF FACU PEER PROF VOCA/CASEWISE = PRED RESID ZRESID
LOGISTIC REGRESSION RENG WITH COLLEGE BACHELOR MASTER PHD
NSEX PINT PPRF FACU PEER PROF VOCA CSKL RSKL/CASEWISE = PRED
RESID ZRESID.
LOGISTIC REGRESSION RENG WITH COLLEGE BACHELOR MASTER PHD
NSEX PINT PPRF FACU PEER PROF VOCA CSKL RSKL NMJR/CASEWISE =
PRED RESID ZRESID. LOGISTIC REGRESSION RENG WITH NSEX PINT.
PPRF FACU PEER PROF VOCA CSKL RSKL NMJR/CASEWISE = PRED RESID
ZRESID.
FINISH.
```

$DINPUT 13 $ instructs GLIM that the raw data file is located under the directory containing the GLIM programs and prompts GLIM for a file name. In this case, **PHD.DAT**. The **$YVARIATE** directive identifies the dependent variable; namely, Research Engagement (RENG).

The specification of the data for SPSS-X is varied and simpler as compared with GLIM. The data can be read from a file already defined for SPSS-X—the SPSS-X system file—through the command **GET FILE** or from an ASCII file via the command **DATA LIST FILE**. In the example (see Table 4), the command **DATA LIST FILE** indicates that the data are to be read on a **FREE** format basis from a file named **PHD.DAT** whose variables are listed in the sequence identified in the command. That is, FAED SEX PINT PPRF FACU PEER PROF VOCA CSKL RSKL MJR RENG (see Table 4).

Model Testing. To fit logistic regression models to binary dependent variables in GLIM, it is necessary to establish that the probability distribution associated with the dependent variable is binomial (B). In turn, the binomial distribution depends on both n, number of trials in which $Y = 1$ is observed and p, the observed probability. The commands **$CALC N = 1.0 $** and **$ERROR B N $** meet these two objectives; that is, the identification of n for which the observed probability is to be computed, the value of n for which the condition in the dependent variable is met ($Y = 1$) and the underlying distribution associated with the dependent variable (B or Binomial). The command **$LINK G $** makes reference to the likelihood function to be employed in estimating the slopes and the intercept. In this particular case, **$LINK G $** instructs GLIM to use the ML for logistic distributions[7]. In GLIM, the **$FIT** command is employed in specifying the models to be estimated. In this example, seven alternative models were specified. For each model under estimation, the **$DISPLAY** command specifies the output. The **D** command prints the scaled deviance and degrees of freedom for the model. Option **E** displays the estimates of the parameters and the standard deviations for each parameter[8]. Option **R** lists for each subject the observed probability of engaging on research activities, the predicted probability of engaging on research activities, and the standardized residual (see Table 3). The standardized residuals are obtained by scaling the difference between observed probabilities and predicted probabilities under the model[9]. Standardized residuals provide an indication of how well the model fits the data. In general, standardized residuals greater than two (2) in absolute value signify that the model produced a poor prediction for the particular observation under consideration (see Aitkin et al., 1990; Fienberg, 1984). The use of these options will become evident as the results of the logistic models are discussed.

[7]There are two possibilities that the educational researcher can use to define the relationship between the independent and the categorical dependent variable. These are **G** for the logit model and **P** the probit model. For a technical discussion of the available models see Backer and Nedler (1988) and Aitken et al. (1990).

[8]There are many options that the user can employ when estimating a logistic model. Option **S**, for instance, requests for standardized residuals and fitted values which are particularly useful when assessing the extent to which the model under or over-predicts the observed frequencies for the dependent variable. For a detailed discussion of these options see Backer and Nadler (1988).

[9]The formula to compute the standardized residuals is as follows:

$$e_{\text{ith}} = \frac{\text{Y}_{\text{ith}} - \text{P}_{\text{ith}}}{\text{P}_{\text{ith}} * (1 - \text{P}_{\text{ith}})}$$

where e_{ith} represents the standardized residual for the ith subject, Y_{ith} the observed probability for the ith subject and P_{ith} the predicted probability under the logistic model for the ith subject. The expression $\text{P}_{\text{ith}} * (1-\text{P}_{\text{ith}})$ represents the variance.

The equivalent GLIM program for SPSS-X is listed in Table 4. Fitting logistic regression models in SPSS-X is accomplished with the command **LOGISTIC REGRESSION**[10]. In this command, the dependent variable is listed first while the independent variables are specified after the directive **WITH** (see Table 4). By default, SPSS-X treats variables coded as either 0 or 1 as dummy variables. The options **DEVIATION**, **CATEGORICAL** and **CONTRAST** within the SPSS-X's procedure **LOGISTIC REGRESSION** can be used to identify independent dummy variables originally coded with values other than 0 and 1 or to handle categorical variables made up of more than two categories or levels[11] (see Norusis, 1990). In the example, categorical variables originally coded with values other than 0 or 1 were recoded to meet the SPSS-X default option for categorical variables (see lines 3 through 13 in Table 4). The command **CASEWISE** in SPSS-X is employed to specify options to examine the adequacy of the resulting logistic regression models. The options **PRED RESID ZRESID** estimate for each subject the observed probability of engaging on research activities, the predicted probability of engaging on research activities, and the standardized residual[12].

Hierarchical Testing of Models

Testing Alternative Models. In OLS, testing alternative models basically rests on assessing whether or not adding or deleting variables accounts significantly for changes in the proportion of variance in the dependent variable (Pedhazur, 1982). Such tests basically rest on a comparison between the coefficients of determination (R^2) associated to each model under consideration, and an assessment of the statistical significance of any observed change in R^2s.

A similar test is available for assessing alternative logistic regression models. The core of this test rests on the maximum likelihood function (usually referred to as G^2 or scaled deviance[13]) associated with a particular logistic regression model (Aldrich and Nelson, 1986; Collett, 1990; Fienberg, 1983; Freeman, 1987). The maximum likelihood function statistics (G^2) provides an overall

[10]To estimate probit regression models, the **PROBIT** command is also available.

[11]Care should be exercised when using these options. By default, these options can create new classification schemes that may not conform to the classification scheme originally intended by the researcher. Furthermore, these different classification schemes can generate different regression coefficients that can lead the researcher to reach incorrect conclusions as to the effect of the variables under consideration (see Norusis 1990, pp. 52–56).

[12]The output generated by this program is available upon request.

[13]The manner in which the maximum likelihood function is reported varies. Some of the terms most commonly used are: the -2 Log L (Aldrich and Nelson, 1984; St. John, 1991), the -2 Log-likelihood value (Manski and Wise, 1983; Norusis, 1990), and the G^2, also called ''scaled deviance'' (Christensen, 1990; Collett, 1991; Feinberg, 1984; Freeman, 1987). In GLIM, the maximum likelihood function is reported as ''scaled deviance'' while in SPSS-X this measure is reported as -2 Log Likelihood.

indication of how well the estimates for the parameters in the model fit the data[14]. Nevertheless, unlike the R^2, the maximum likelihood function per se has little value in judging whether or not the model is a valid one. Unlike the R^2 in OLS, the maximum likelihood function does not represent the proportion of variance explained in the dependent variable. As already noted, the focus of analysis in logistic regression is not the matrix of interrecorrelations among the dependent and independent variables but, rather, the probability of a given outcome, and finding those estimates for the slope and the intercept that maximize the likelihood of reproducing the observed probability. Therefore, the utility of the maximum likelihood function statistics lies on assessing alternative models (Fienberg, 1984; Collett, 1991).

The test basically involves a comparison of the likelihood function between two alternative models. In logistic regression, the best fitting model is the one that yields a significantly smaller G^2. This test is carried on by comparing the differences in G^2s between two given models to a Chi-square distribution table with degrees of freedom equal to the difference in degrees of freedom between two alternative models[15]. In logistic regression, reductions in G^2 with an associated p-value less than .05 indicate that the model accounts for a significant improvement of fit.

Forward and Backward Stepwise Processes. As in OLS, the estimation of alternative models in logistic regression can follow a forward stepwise process or a backward stepwise process (Pedhazur, 1982). Under the forward stepwise approach, individual variables or groups of variables are added in a sequential manner, and the validity of the added variables is judged in terms of significant improvements of fit. The backward stepwise process basically consists of deleting groups or individual variables and assessing the extent to which their deletion significantly worsens the model (Fienberg, 1983). Both approaches have been applied to study dichotomous dependent variables in higher education (see St. John, 1991; Cabrera et al., 1990; Mallete and Cabrera, 1991).

The use of the forward stepwise approach is illustrated in Table 5[16]. Each column displays the parameter estimates for the specific model under consideration. For each model, the scaled deviance G^2 and corresponding degrees of freedom are also presented. As shown in Table 5, six models, referred as steps, were sequentially estimated. The sequence of this testing was dictated by the

[14]By convention, a good fit is evidenced when the maximum likelihood function is close to the degrees of freedom for the respective model (see Cabrera et al., 1990; Mallette and Cabrera, 1991; St. John, 1991).

[15]The chi-square test is used based on the fact that the difference in G^2s follows a Chi-square (X^2) distribution (see Feinberg, 1984).

[16]This table is based on results generated by GLIM. The interested reader will notice that SPSS-X produces slightly different results. These differences are attributable to the fact that the programs take different approaches to the maximum likelihood solution.

TABLE 5. Effects of Background, Prior Commitments, Integration, Academic Growth, and Major on Research Engagement

Factor	Step 1 (Beta)	Step 2 (Beta)	Step 3 (Beta)	Step 4 (Beta)	Step 5 (Beta)	Step 6 (Beta)
Father's Education:						
Some College	0.3007	0.3169	0.2770	0.2906	0.3248	0.2322
Bachelor	0.3989	0.3529	0.3440	0.3462	0.3613	0.2562
Master	0.4049	0.3963	0.3416	0.3475	0.4728	0.2847
Ph.D.	0.0669	0.0335	−0.0720	−0.0691	0.0302	0.0495
Gender (Male)	0.4478**	0.4173**	0.5134**	0.5182**	0.5356**	0.3980*
Pre-Institutional		−0.1753	−0.2639**	−0.2675**	−0.2968**	−0.2867**
Pre-Professional		−0.0028	−0.0770	−0.0821	−0.0649	−0.0966
Faculty			0.4172**	0.4128**	0.3278**	0.3361**
Peer			0.2313**	0.2255**	0.1869*	0.1553
Professional Comit.				0.0624	0.0633	0.0758
Vocational Comit.				−0.0048	−0.0475	−0.0475
Conceptualization					−0.2325	−0.1831
Research					0.7712**	0.7276**
Major (Hard Major)						0.6314**
Intercept	−0.3991	0.0444	−1.6690	−1.8790	−2.9890	−3.0960
G^2	727.070	724.170	696.120	695.770	673.610	663.290
df	526.000	524.000	522.000	520.000	518.000	517.000
G^2/df	1.382	1.382	1.334	1.338	1.300	1.283
"R^2"	0.019	0.024	0.072	0.073	0.107	0.122
PCP	56.02	57.33	59.4	59.77	63.16	64.85
X^2, *df*	10.37, 5	13.27, 7	41.32**, 9	41.67**, 11	63.83**, 13	74.15**,14

* = $p < .05$ ** = $p < .01$

pattern suggested in the model advanced by Nora et al. (1992). Model 1 (step 1) represents the effect of background characteristics on the likelihood of engaging in research activities. Model 2 represents the added effect attributable to Pre-Commitment factors while Model 6 represents the incremental effect on the outcome variable attributable to major while taking into account background characteristics, pre-commitments, interactions with faculty and peers, and academic growth.

As shown in Table 5, the addition of the groups of variables in each of the six steps appears to increase the ability to predict research engagement. This is suggested by the reduction in the G^2 across the six models. At this point, however, the G^2 associated with model 6 only provides an indication that this model appears to fit the data better than its predecessors. A more rigorous test of the statistical significance of the alternative models is displayed in Table 6.

TABLE 6. Effects of Adding Factors on the Fit of the Model

Model	df	G^2	Change in df	Change in G^2	Improvement of Fit p-value
1. Background Only	526	727.07			
2. Adding Pre-Commitments	524	724.17	$df_1 - df_2 = 2$	$G^2{}_1 - G^2{}_2 = 2.90$	.2466
3. Adding Integration	522	696.12	$df_1 - df_3 = 4$	$G^2{}_1 - G^2{}_3 = 30.95$	.0005
4. Adding Commitments	520	695.77	$df_1 - df_4 = 6$	$G^2{}_1 - G^2{}_4 = 31.30$	.0005
5. Adding Academic Growth	518	673.61	$df_1 - df_5 = 8$	$G^2{}_1 - G^2{}_5 = 53.46$	.0005
6. Adding Major	517	663.29	$df_1 - df_6 = 9$	$G^2{}_1 - G^2{}_6 = 63.78$	.0005

Column 1 in Table 6 represents the model under estimation. Columns 2 and 3 display the degrees of freedom and scaled deviance (G^2) for the respective model while columns 4 and 5 represent changes in degrees of freedom and in G^2s between a given model, say Pre-Commitments, and the alternative model (Background only). In logistic regression, it is customary to use the first model (the Background only model in this case) as the *baseline* model or null model when comparing alternative models (see Feinberg, 1983).

As indicated in Table 6, results of the hierarchical inclusion of variables suggest that the variable Major contributed the most to the model's fit followed by Academic Growth and Final Commitments. Results also indicate that the addition of Pre-Graduate Commitments variables, as a group, made a small and nonsignificant contribution to the fit of the model (p-value = .25). Comparisons across models need not be merely constrained to the background model as the only reference model. This strategy can be used to compare models among themselves. For instance, results indicate that model 6 gives a more plausible representation of the data than model 5 (observed $X^2 = G^2{}_5 - G^2{}_6 = 673.61 - 663.29 = 10.32$; $df = df_5 - df_6 = 518–517 = 1$; p-value = .001). Likewise, results suggest that model 5 constitutes an improvement in relation to model 4 (observed $X^2 = G^2{}_4 - G^2{}_5 = 695.77 - 673.61 = 22.16$; $df = df_4 - df_5 = 520 - 518 = 2$; p-value = .0005). However, no evidence is found as to the relative improvement of model 4 over model 3 (observed $X^2 = G^2{}_3 - G^2{}_4 = 696.12 - 695.77 = .35$; $df = df_3 - df_4 = 522 - 520 = 2$; p-value = .8187).

Judging alternative models under the backward elimination test rests on the extent to which deleting variables actually worsens the fit of the model. The test is accomplished by estimating a model in which a group of variables is deleted

TABLE 7. Reduced Model

Factor	Beta	S. E.	Change in P
Gender (Male)	0.3755*	0.1929	0.0930
Pre-Institutional	−0.2918**	0.1138	−0.0723
Pre-Professional	−0.0901	0.1138	−0.0225
Faculty	0.3397**	0.1102	0.0843
Peer	0.1560	0.0967	0.0390
Professional Comit.	0.0711	0.1088	0.0178
Vocational Comit.	−0.0490	0.0791	−0.0122
Conceptualization	−0.1818	0.2033	−0.0453
Research	0.7178**	0.1739	0.1728
Major (Hard Major)	0.6834**	0.1921	0.1651
Intercept	−2.9650	0.7749	
Baseline P_o: .494			

G^2, $df = 664.91$, 521; X^2, $df = 72.53$**, 10; $G^2/df = 1.276$;
pseudo $R^2 = 0.120$; PCP = 64.85%

*$p < .05$ **$p < .01$

and the G^2 of the reduced or trimmed model is compared against the G^2 for the original model. An inspection of Table 5 indicates that the variable Father's education had no significant effect across the six models. It stands to reason, then, that the exclusion of this variable would not affect the predictive power of the models. In order to test this hypothesis a new model (model 7), in which the variable Father's education was eliminated from model 6, was estimated. Results support this expectation. The reduction of parameters ($df_7 - df_6 = 521 - 517 = 4$) did not significantly worsen the fit of the model (observed $X^2 = G^2_7 - G^2_6 = 664.91 - 663.29 = 1.62$; p-value = .8088). The resulting trimmed model (Model 7) will be kept to continue illustrating the interpretation of the output. Results for Model 7 are displayed in Table 7.

Goodness of Fit

Several indicators are available for assessing the goodness of fit of a given logistic regression model. Some of them are: the pseudo "R^2", the proportion of cases correctly predicted (PCP) by the model, the G^2 / df ratio and The X^2 statistics for overall fit. As in hierarchical modeling, most of these tests rely on the maximum likelihood function associated with a particular model. *The pseudo "R^2".* An equivalent formulation of R^2 is also available in logistic regression. This indicator is usually referred as the pseudo "R^2". In the OLS context, the coefficient of determination (R^2) has the interesting property of providing an indicator of how well a set of independent variables explains the variance observed in the dependent variable (Draper and Smith, 1981). No equivalent interpretation, however, is available in the logistic regression context. As demonstrated by Christensen (1990) and by Aldrich and Nelson (1986), the pseudo "R^2" represents, at most, the proportion of error variance that an alternative model reduces in relation to a null model. As a standard practice, the null model is usually specified as the one in which all the slopes with the exception of the intercept are set to zero. In GLIM, this model is specified by the following command **$FIT 1 $**. In SPSS-X the maximum likelihood function for the null model is produced by default and it is referred as the "Initial Log Likelihood Function."

Several formulas are available to estimate the pseudo "R^2" (see Aldrich and Nelson, 1986; Christensen, 1990; Maddala, 1987; Mare, 1980; Taylor, 1983). Aldrich and Nelson recommend the following formula:

$$\text{pseudo } R^2 = \frac{X^2}{(\mathrm{N} + X^2)} \qquad [3]$$

where X^2 is the chi-square statistic for the overall fit for the model as described below, and N is the total sample size. As is the case of the OLS' R^2, this formula produces values ranging from 0 to 1, and produces a conservative estimate of the reduction in error variance. As shown in Table 5, each successive model accounted for a reduction in unexplained variance. In the case of Model 7 (see Table 7), the corresponding pseudo R^2 indicates that the model accounted for a 12 percent reduction in error variance [$R^2 = 72.53/(532+72.53)$].

Regardless of the method employed in the computation of the pseudo "R^2", the reader is cautioned against relying on this indicator as the sole criterion in judging the validity of a particular model. As noted above, the pseudo "R^2" has no equivalent interpretation to the R^2 in OLS. Moreover, controversy exists as to the most appropriate formula to be employed in the computation of the pseudo "R^2" (see Maddala, 1987; Aldrich and Nelson, 1986). Furthermore, there are no tests to assess the statistical significance of this measure (Maddala, 1987). This controversy is also compounded by the fact that different formulas can yield large or small pseudo R^2s. In view of these problems, Aldrich and Nelson (1984) recommend that different measures of fit be simultaneously taken into account when judging the fit of a particular model, while Fienberg (1983) encourages that the selection of models be also based on the hierarchical testing procedures already described.

Proportion of cases correctly predicted (PCP). Aldrich and Nelson (1983) note that the proportion of cases correctly predicted (PCP) by the logistic model provides an overall indicator of fit much in line with the OLS' R^2. This measure basically involves a comparison between the number of cases that the model predicted as being either 0 (i.e., not engaged in research activities) or 1 (i.e., engaged in research activities) against the total sample size. In GLIM, predicted probabilities are obtained by the following command: **$DISPLAY R $** (see Table 3). In SPSS-X, the option **PRED** accomplishes the same purpose (see Table 4). Since predicted probability values range from 0 to 1, cut-off scores are employed to identify correctly predicted cases. Subjects are usually identified as correctly predicted by the model whenever the model predicts a probability .5 or greater (see Aldrich and Nelson, 1984). Using this criterion, results indicate that Model 7, for instance, yielded correct predictions for 65 percent of the subjects (see Table 7). By default, SPSS-X produces the classification tables needed in the computation of PCPs.

As is the case in the pseudo "R^2", no known procedures can be found to assess the statistical significance of this indicator of overall fit. Furthermore, the manner in which the cut-off score is set can substantially increase or decrease the estimates of the proportion of cases correctly predicted under the model (see Aldrich and Nelson, 1984). In view of these problems, it would be advisable that judgments on the validity of this indicator be based on PCPs reported by the extant literature applicable to the particular outcome under consideration. For instance, Dey (1991) reported PCPs for college enrollment, dropout and degree attainment obtained from a large national data base. Dey's estimates, then, can assist the educational researcher in judging institutional based models dealing with similar college behaviors. In the absence of such a literature, PCPs associated to alternative models can aid in such an evaluation. As noted in Table 6, the PCPs increased as groups of variables were added. The highest is the one associated with Model 6 (PCP = 65%). Deleting the variable Father's education, as shown in Table 7, did not substantially worsen the proportion of cases correctly predicted (PCP = 65%).

The G^2/df ratio. Similar to chi-square (X^2) tests for LISREL models (see Stage, 1990), the ratio of the G^2 to its degrees of freedom provides an additional indicator of how well the model fits the data (see Cabrera, Stampen and Hansen, 1990; Mallette and Cabrera, 1991; St. John, 1991). The degrees of freedom are given by the following formula: df = sample size − # of parameters fitted. The degrees of freedom for model 7, for instance, are 521 since we are estimating eleven parameters for a sample of 532 PhDs ($df = 532 - 11 = 521$). Since there are no known procedures to test the statistical significance of the G^2/df ratio, rules of thumb such as those suggested by Stage (1990) for LISREL can also be applied to the logistic regression context. Stage (1990) recommends that a particular model be accepted whenever the G^2/df ratio is less than 2.5. Model 7 meets such a criterion ($G^2/df = 1.28$; see Table 7).

The X^2 statistic for overall fit. In OLS, the F ratio for the regression equation is commonly employed to assess the omnibus hypothesis that the independent variables as a group have no effect on the dependent variable (Pedhazur, 1982). The X^2 statistic for overall fit plays the same role in logistic regression. Aldrich and Nelson (1984) recommend the following formula:

$$X^2 = G^2_o - G^2_a \text{ [17]} \quad (4)$$

where G^2_o represents the scaled deviance associated with a model in which only the intercept is fitted (also referred as the null model), and G^2_a represents the scaled deviance for the full model (also referred as the alternative model). In GLIM, the scale deviance for the null model (G^2_o) can be estimated by the following command: **$FIT 1 $.** In SPSS-X, the X^2 statistic for overall fit is produced by default and it is referred as **"Model Chi-Square."** SPSS-X also automatically estimates the degrees of freedom and corresponding significance level for this indicator.

Support for the full model will be evidenced whenever there is a substantial reduction in the X^2. Furthermore, unlike the measures of fit described so far, there are procedures to assess whether the X^2 statistics for overall fit is statistically significant. This test is based on the fact that the difference in G^2s follows a X^2 distribution (see Feinberg, 1984). The degrees of freedom for the X^2 statistics for overall fit are K-1; where K-1 represents the number of coefficients constrained to be zero under the null model (see Aldrich and Nelson, 1984; Collett, 1991). The test, then, involves comparing the computed "X^2" to a critical value drawn from a X^2 distribution with K-1 degrees of freedom at a given significance level. For model 7 (see Table 7), the observed $X^2 = 737.44 - 664.91 = 72.53$ with corresponding $df = 10$ yielded a p-value less than .01 which indicates that the model fits the data.

Testing Individual Regression Coefficients

Individual Coefficient Estimates. Table 7 presents the beta weights and corresponding standard errors for the model under consideration. There are several similarities between OLS and logistic regression concerning the estimation of individual coefficients (Aldrich and Nelson, 1986). As in OLS regression analysis, one of the purposes of logistic regression is to estimate the relationships between a set of independent variables and the dependent variable as well as the statistical significance of such relationships. These relationships, as in OLS, are expressed in terms of beta weights associated with each independent variable. The ML approximation to logistic regression also estimates standard errors for each coefficient which can be employed for testing the null hypothesis that a particular coefficient, say B_{major}, has no effect on the dependent variable. Resembling the test employed in OLS for assessing the significance of individual parameters, the test employed in logistic regression is defined as a t-test. This test

[17]Statistical packages differ in terms of the reported statistics for this joint hypothesis test. Some of them report the equivalent statistics $-2\log(L_0/L_1)$. Aldrich and Nelson (1984) provide a detailed description of alternative ways in which this test is reported.

is obtained by the ratio of the estimated parameter over its standard error (i.e., t-test = B_{major}/SE_{major}). As shown in Column 1 in Table 7, the t-test reveals that only five variables in Model 7 were found to exert a significant effect at a p-value $< .05$.

As in OLS, the sign associated to the beta weights indicates the direction of the effect that a particular independent variable has on the dependent variable. In the case of categorical variables, the interpretation of the coefficients is a function of the excluded category. For instance, the positive sign associated to the beta weight for the variable Hard Major indicates that students majoring in hard sciences are more likely to engage in research activities than those majoring in soft sciences, even after controlling for gender, pre-institutional commitments, interactions with faculty and peers, final commitments and academic growth measures.

The analogy between the logistic regression and OLS concerning beta weights stops at this point. In contrast to OLS, the interpretation of the coefficients is rather troublesome. Unlike OLS, the metric of the individual coefficients under logistic regression is expressed in terms of logits rather than in terms of the original scale of measurement. This problem is particularly accentuated for categorical variables since the corresponding beta weights represent contrasts among categories summarized in terms of differences in logits (see Hanusheck and Jackson, 1977; Freeman, 1987). In other words, Model 7 (see Table 7) predicts that students majoring in hard majors are .68 logit units more likely to conduct research than are students majoring in soft sciences. To overcome the problem of conveying the logistic regression results to the practitioner in a meaningful manner, several methods are available that illustrate the effects of the independent variables on outcome measures.

Interpretation of Results

Two methods are available to illustrate the effect that the predictor variables have on the outcome variable. One method attempts to estimate the overall change a given variable has on the outcome variable. The other attempts to illustrate how responsive the dependent variable is to changes in different independent variables. The former is usually accomplished by measures of overall change, while the latter is usually done via tables and graphs displaying estimated probabilities.

The Delta-p statistics. Petersen (1985) recommends the use of the Delta-p statistics[18] as the most suitable method to estimate the overall change in the dependent variable. The Delta-p can also be employed for assessing the relative size of these changes across variables provided that the variables are measured in a similar unit. St. John (1991) warns that such comparisons should be approached with care in those cases where the independent variables have a different metric.

[18]St. John and associates (St. John, 1990a, 1990b, St. John et al., 1989) pioneered the use of Delta-p to illustrate the results of logistic regression for higher educational outcomes.

Petersen's formula to compute changes in the probability resulting from a unit change in the dependent variable is as follows:

$$\text{Delta-}p = \exp(L_1) / [1 + \exp(L_1)] - P_o \quad (5)$$

where P_o is the sample mean of the dependent variable. As shown in Table 7, the probability of engaging in research for the whole sample is .494 ($P_o = 0.494$). The expression $L_1 = L_o+B$ represents the logit after the unit change in the variable under consideration. L_o represents the natural logarithm of $[P_o /(1-P_o)]$.

For Model 7 (see Table 7), the incremental effect attributable to Major can be illustrated as follows:

$$L_o = \ln [P_o / (1 - P_o)] = \ln [0.494 / (1-.494)] = -0.024$$

$$L_1 = L_o + B_{major} = -0.024 + .6834 = .6594$$

Thus, the logit before the change is $L_o = -0.024$, and after the unit change the logit is $L_1 = .6594$. Using the equation for Delta-*p* in (5) establishes the rate of change in terms of probabilities. In the present example, the Delta-*p* for Major yields the probability value of .1651. As in the case of beta weights for categorical variables, Delta-*p*s are to be interpreted in terms of the excluded category. **In other words, the model predicts that majoring in hard sciences increases the probability of engaging in research activities by 16.5 percentage points over majoring in soft sciences.** In the case of continuous variables, Delta-*p* represents the incremental effect on the outcome variable resulting from a unit change in the dependent variable. **For instance, the model predicts that a unit increase in interactions with faculty increases the probability of engaging in research activities by 8.4 percentage points while a unit increase in research skills increases such a probability by 17.3 percent points.** The last column in Table 7 displays estimates of changes in probabilities in the outcome variable for each independent variable under consideration. Echoing recommendations by St. John (1991), it would be advisable that the use of Delta-*p*s be constrained to those parameters found significant in the model since there are no known procedures to estimate the statistical significance of Delta-*p*s.

Tables and Graphs of Predicted Probabilities. As in OLS, one of the major applications of logistic regression is to predict how likely it is that subjects will engage in the particular outcome under consideration. Predicted probabilities provide the practitioner with basic information about how the variables under consideration can be used to forecast such a behavior and to illustrate how responsive such a behavior is to changes in a given variable. Predicted probabilities, then, can provide the practitioner with basic information when implementing and evaluating intervention strategies. In logistic regression, predicted probabilities for each subject can be obtained by multiplying the values in each variable by its corresponding beta weights and adding the resulting products. The logistic equation in Table 7 can be displayed as follows:

$$\text{Logit}_{ith} = \frac{P}{1-P} = -2.965 + .3755\text{MALE} - .2918\text{PINT} - 0.0901\text{PPRF} + .3397\text{FACU} + .1560\text{PEER} + .0711\text{PROF} - .049\text{VOCA} - .1818\text{CSKI} + .7178\text{RSKL} + .6834\text{MJR} \quad [6]$$

where Logit_{ith} represents the predicted natural logarithm value or logit for the ith subject. The predicted logit value for the last subject in our example (case number 532 in Table 2), for instance, is .33408. By undoing the arithmetic of the logit transformation under the formula displayed below, this logit value corresponds to a predicted probability for engaging in research of .583[19].

$$P_{532} = \frac{\exp(.33408)}{1 + \exp(.33408)} = .583$$

It is also possible to estimate probabilities attributable to a particular variable that may be of interest to the educational researcher. Consider the example in which the researcher is interested in assessing the effects of interactions with faculty across type of major and gender. Such an assessment can be accomplished by estimating the corresponding logistic regression equations for different types of major and gender while holding the rest of the independent variables constant[20].

The next step is to choose those values for the independent variables that would make it possible to estimate the effects due to changes in interactions with faculty, multiplying this value by the corresponding beta weight, adding these products to obtain logits and estimating the corresponding predicted probability. Manski and Wise (1983), for instance, selected the mean as the value to hold constant the effect of the variables under consideration. Using the same criterion[21], Table 8 displays the estimated probabilities across major and gender. Figures 2 and 3 illustrate the predicted effects of interactions with faculty on the probabilities of engaging in research across males and females while holding constant the rest of the variables at their mean value.

As shown in Table 8 and in Figures 2 and 3, Model 7 predicts that increasing interactions with faculty also raises the likelihood of engaging in research independently of a student's major and gender. As shown in Table 8, a unit increase in the interactions with faculty scale, say from 2.2 to 3.2, increases the likelihood of conducting research between .073 to .085 across gender and major. The reader

[19]In GLIM, the predicted probabilities across all subjects are obtained by the following command: **$DISPLAY R $** (see Table 3). In SPSS-X, the option **PRED** within the LOGISTIC REGRESSION command accomplishes the same purpose (see Table 4).

[20]The logistic regression equations are available upon request.

[21]The means are provided in Table 1.

TABLE 8. Estimated Probabilities of Research Engagement: Effects of Interactions with Faculty

Interactions with Faculty	Hard Major		Soft Major	
	Male	Female	Male	Female
1.00	0.4253	0.3370	0.2720	0.2042
1.20	0.4420	0.3524	0.2857	0.2155
1.40	0.4588	0.3680	0.2997	0.2272
1.60	0.4757	0.3840	0.3142	0.2394
1.80	0.4927	0.4002	0.3290	0.2519
2.00	0.5096	0.4166	0.3442	0.2650
2.20	0.5266	0.4332	0.3596	0.2784
2.40	0.5435	0.4499	0.3755	0.2923
2.60	0.5603	0.4668	0.3915	0.3065
2.80	0.5770	0.4837	0.4078	0.3211
3.00	0.5935	0.5007	0.4243	0.3361
3.20	0.6097	0.5177	0.4410	0.3515
3.40	0.6258	0.5346	0.4578	0.3671
3.47	0.6313	0.5405	0.4637	0.3726
3.60	0.6416	0.5515	0.4747	0.3830
3.80	0.6570	0.5682	0.4917	0.3992
4.00	0.6722	0.5848	0.5086	0.4156
4.20	0.6870	0.6012	0.5256	0.4322
4.40	0.7014	0.6174	0.5425	0.4489
4.60	0.7154	0.6333	0.5593	0.4658
4.80	0.7290	0.6489	0.5760	0.4827
5.00	0.7423	0.6642	0.5925	0.4997

will notice that this rate of change matches closely the one estimated by Delta-*p* (Delta-*p* = .0843 in Table 7).

Rows in Table 8 can be used to estimate the change in probabilities induced by changes in the independent variable, columns can be employed to study the moderating effects of gender and major. For each value of the interactions with faculty scale and within each major, males have higher chances of conducting research than females have; these differences range from .07 to .09. On the other hand, regardless of a student's gender, majoring in hard sciences yields higher probabilities of conducting research as compared with majoring in soft sciences; these probabilities range from .13 to .16. Again, the reader would notice that these differences match closely the estimates produced by Delta-*ps* for gender and major (Delta-*ps* = .093 and .165; respectively. See Table 7).

In sum, it is recommended that the reader adopt a comprehensive approach in judging a particular logistic model. A careful analysis of the statistical significance of the individual parameters coupled with a thorough analysis of the

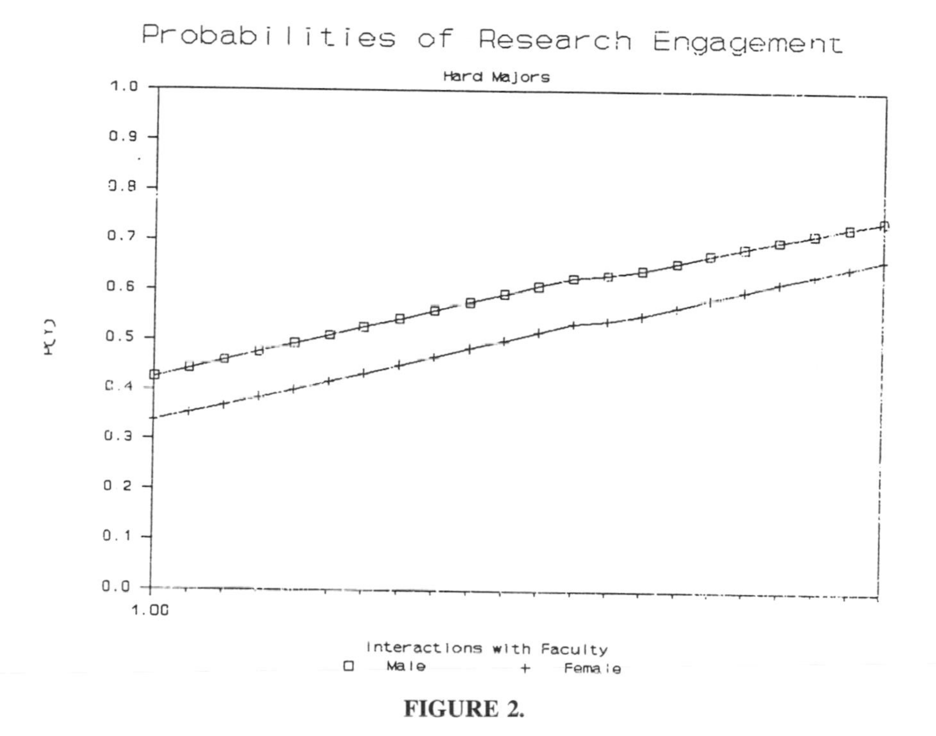

FIGURE 2.

indicators of fit along with an examination of standardized residuals produced by the model should assist the researcher or the practitioner in judging the validity of the model. Hierarchical analyses, individual parameters and the indicators of goodness of fit all suggest that Model 7 is a good representation for the data. This conclusion is further strengthened by the fact that Model 7 yielded only four out of 532 standardized residuals greater than two[22], a pretty low ratio (.75%).

III. CONCLUDING REMARKS

The use of logistic regression in higher education is not without controversy. The debate centers around the use of OLS over logistic regression. Advocates of OLS basically argue that linear regression models: a) are more commonly known, b) the results are easier to explain, c) the method can be used to analyze nonlinear relationships when the variables are properly transformed, and d) it is easier to implement given the increasing availability of statistical programs (Jackson 1980, 1988; Dey, 1991). These arguments are further strengthened by some

[22]These correspond to observations 74, 93, 311 and 386. The complete SPSS-X and GLIM outputs are available upon request.

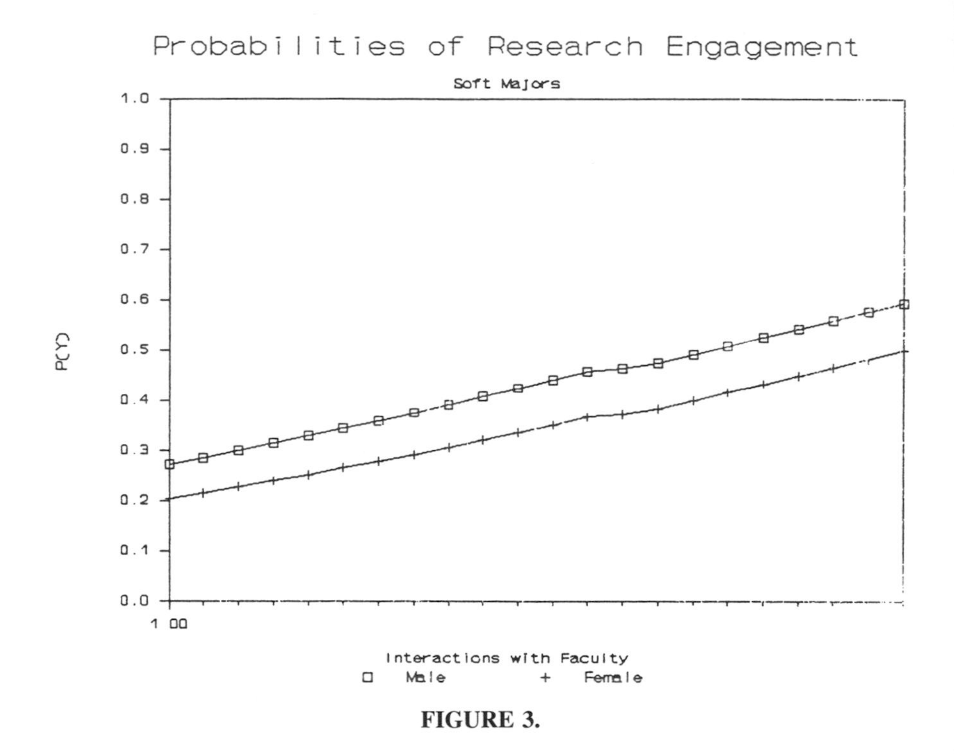

FIGURE 3.

studies finding the application of linear regression models to binary outcomes yielding comparable results to those produced under logistic regression strategies (Jackson, 1981). Dey (1991), for instance, reported that when the dependent variable was moderately distributed, with corresponding splits of .29/.71, .49/.51 and .54/.46, linear regression models replicated the logistic regression's findings concerning the direction of the effect, the ability to predict the statistical significance of the beta weights and the proportion of cases correctly identified as persisting upon graduation for a subsample of the CIRP data base.

On the other hand, advocates of the use of logistic regression argue that the straightforward application of OLS to binary outcomes essentially violates each of the assumptions upon which OLS rests (Hanusheck and Jackson, 1977; Aldrich and Nelson, 1986). Only under very unique circumstances, would the OLS approximation yield results equivalent to those produced under logistic regression (Aldrich and Nelson, 1986; Goodman, 1977; Hanusheck and Jackson, 1977).

At the core of this argument is the different way the two methods approach the functional form underlying the relationship between an outcome variable and an independent variable. Under OLS, the dependent variable is presumed to be

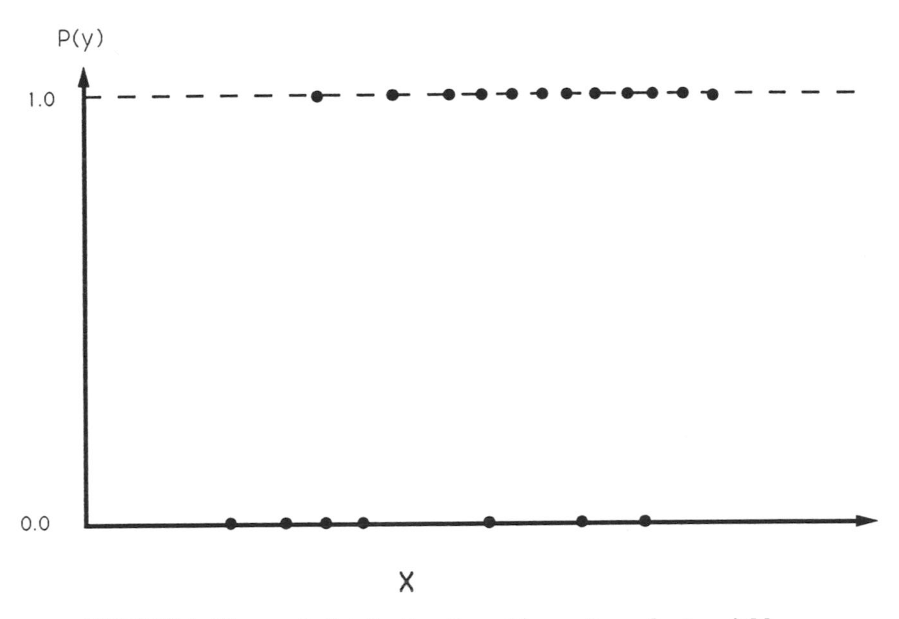

FIGURE 4. Observed distribution for a binary dependent variable.

continuous while the relationship between the outcome variable and, say, an independent variable is supposed to be expressed by a straight line. Neither condition is met when the dependent variable is binary. As shown in Figure 4, the dependent variable is not continuous. Observations lie flat on the X axis depending upon which value the variable assumes (0 or 1 with no other values in between).

Although several transformations can be attempted when the relationship between an independent variable and a dependent variable is not linear, ". . . the dichotomous nature of the dependent variable renders most of these ineffective" (Hanusheck and Jackson, 1977, p. 185). As noted by Hanusheck and Jackson (1977), the logistic approximation is the most appropriate transformation for dichotomous outcomes since empirical studies have shown that the relationship between binary dependent variables and continuous independent variables indeed resembles the already familiar *S* pattern (see Figure 1).

Figure 5 illustrates the effect of using the linear approximation to estimate a logistic distribution. Between x′ and x″, the linear approximation would overestimate the true probabilities while the contrary is true for that region corresponding to x′ and x‴. Moreover, the linear approximation is likely to yield such nonsensical estimates as negative probabilities when the equation is estimated below x′, and probabilities greater than one when the equation is estimated

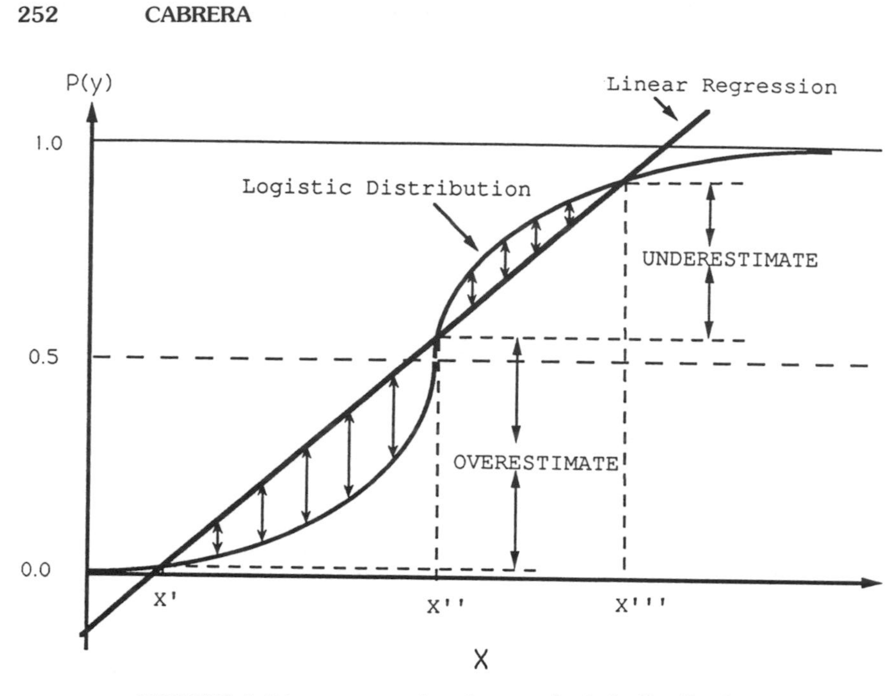

FIGURE 5. Linear approximation to a logistic distribution.

beyond x‴. Only on those points when the regression line intercepts the logistic function would the linear regression produce correct predictions.

Advocates of the logistic regression approach do acknowledge the fact that OLS can approximate the logistic function (Aldrich and Nelson, 1986; Hanusheck and Jackson, 1977). It is also noted that such an approximation may hold under two conditions; and both are sample driven. The first condition is met when the dependent variable is moderately distributed, with splits from as low as .25/.75 (see Goodman, 1977) to .50/.50. As shown in Figure 6, the linear solution would approximate the true relationship in the central part of the distribution. Accordingly, the linear regression approach would correctly identify significant effects while generating predicted probabilities closely resembling the true ones. Only in the extremes of the distribution, would the linear approximation yield incorrect estimates (Hanusheck and Jackson, 1977; Goodman, 1977).

The second condition is met when the sample fails to reproduce the potential range of values in the domain of the independent variable (Aldrich and Nelson, 1986). Figure 7 displays ranges for the independent variable corresponding to three hypothetical samples. As shown in Figure 7, the linear approximation would yield correct estimates in each of the three samples under consideration. This situation is reversed, however, when the linear approximation is applied to

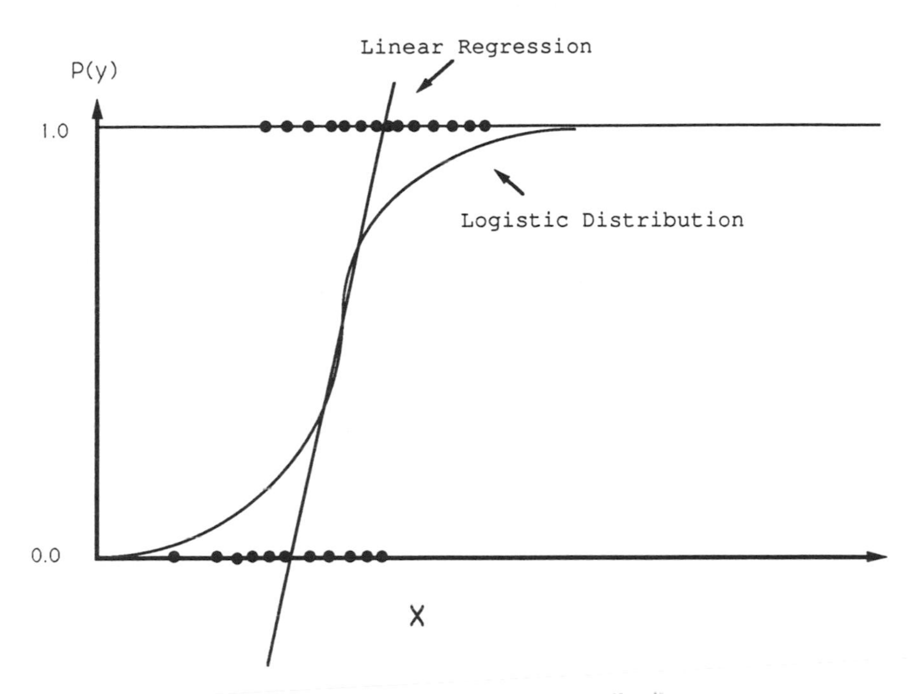

FIGURE 6. Linear approximation to a moderately distributed Y variable.

samples capturing the full range in the independent variable as illustrated in Figure 5.

OLS presumes that the variance around the straight line is constant across all observations in the independent variable (Marascuilo and Serlin, 1988). To the extent that this condition holds, OLS would generate sampling estimates for the beta weights that are both unbiased [in the sense that the sampling beta weights approach the true values in the population] and efficient [in the sense that the sampling beta weights have the smallest sampling variance] (see Pedhazur, 1982). In turn, these efficient sampling variances play a key role when testing hypotheses about the statistical significance of the estimated beta weights (t-tests). When estimating a logistic distribution the error term is all but constant. As noted above, the variance for each predicted Y value changes as a function of the sample size and the value that X happens to assume. Aldrich and Nelson (1986) have demonstrated that the OLS approximation to logistic distributions may produce unbiased sample beta weights whose sign resembles the ones estimated under the logistic regression approximation. Yet, the lack of homoscedasticity in the error term leads to the incorrect estimation of the sampling variances. Consequently, ". . . any hypothesis tests (e.g., the t and F tests) or

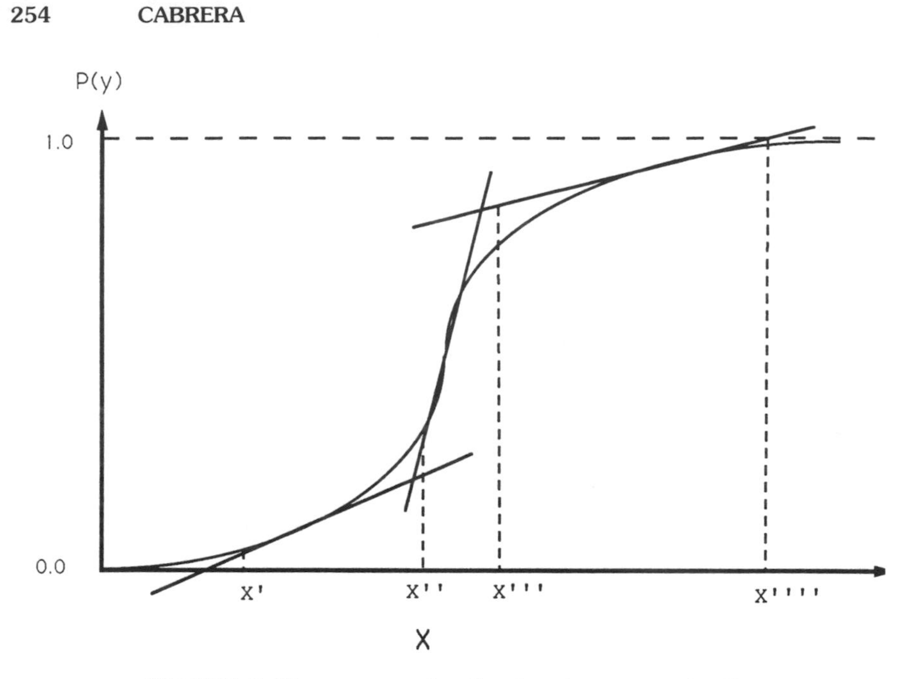

FIGURE 7. Linear approximation for given ranges in X.

confidence intervals based on these sampling variances will be invalid, even for very large samples'' (Aldrich and Nelson, 1986, pp. 13–14).

Ordinary least square regression analysis remains a powerful technique. Nevertheless, it is a technique that operates under very stringent assumptions regarding the nature of the dependent variable and the relationship that such a variable has with a given set of independent variables. Unlike OLS, logistic regression conforms with the probability function underlying the relationship between a dichotomous outcome and corresponding independent variables. Factors such as familiarity with the technique and easiness in its use should not dictate the choice of the estimation procedure. Rather, the nature of the phenomenon under consideration should dictate such a choice.

REFERENCES

Aitkin, M., Anderson, D., Francis, B., and Hinde, J. (1990). *Statistical Modeling in GLIM* (rev. ed). England. Oxford: Clarendon, Press.

Aldrich, J. H., and Nelson, F. D. (1986). *Linear Probability, Logit and Probit Models* (3rd edition). Beverly Hills, CA.: Sage Publications.

Backer, R. J., and Nedler, J. A. (1988). *The Generalised Linear Interactive Modeling* (release 3.77). England, Oxford: Numerical Algorithms Group.

Bentler, P. M. (1989). EQS: *Structural Equations Program Manual*. Los Angeles, CA.: BMDP Software.

Baird, L. L., and Smart, J. C. (1991, November). Graduate students and their academic and professional development: A study of interactions among personal characteristics, life circumstances and graduate school experiences. Paper presented at the annual meeting of the Association for the Study of Higher Education. Boston. Mass.

Biglan, A. (1973a). The characteristics of subject matter in different academic areas. *Journal of Applied Psychology* 57(3): 195–203.

Biglan, A. (1973b). Relationships between subject matter characteristics and the structure and output of university departments. *Journal of Applied Psychology* 57(3): 204–213.

Bishop, J. (1977). The effects of public policies on the demand for higher education. *Journal of Human Resources* 12: 285–307.

Christensen, R. (1990). *Log-linear Models*. New York, NY.: Springer-Verlag.

Cabrera, A. F., Stampen, J. O., and Hansen, W. L. (1990). Exploring the effects of ability to pay on persistence in college. *Review of Higher Education* 13(3): 303–336.

Collett, D. (1991). *Modelling Binary Data*. England, London: Chapman and Hall.

Dey, E. (1991, April). Statistical alternatives for studying student retention: a comparative analysis of logit, probit and linear regression. Paper presented before the 1991 annual meeting of the American Educational Research Association. Chicago, IL.

Ethington, C. A., and Bode, R. (1992, April). Differences in the graduate experience for males and females. Paper presented at the annual meeting of the American Educational Research Association. San Francisco, CA.

Fienberg, S. E. (1983). *The Analysis of Cross Classified Categorical Data* (rev. ed.). Cambridge, MA: Massachusetts Institute of Technology.

Freeman, D. H. (1987). *Applied Categorical Data Analysis*. New York: Marcel Dekker.

Goodman, L. A. (1977). The relationship between modified and usual multiple-regression approaches to the analysis of dichotomous variables. In D. R. Heise (ed.), *Sociological Methodology*. San Francisco: Jossey-Bass.

Hanusheck, E. K., and Jackson, J. E. (1977). *Statistical Methods for Social Scientists*. New York: Academic Press.

Hinkle, D. E., Austin, J. T., and McLaughlin, G. W. (1989). Log-linear models: Applications in higher education research. In J. C. Smart (ed.), *Higher Education: Handbook of Theory and Research*, Vol. V. New York: Agathon Press.

Hossler, D. (1991). *Evaluating Student Recruitment and Retention Programs*. (New Directions for Institutional Research, Vol. 70). San Francisco: Jossey-Bass.

Jackson, G. A. (1980). The case of the dependent dichotomy: practical approaches to college choice models. In *Proceedings of the American Statistical Association*. Washington, DC: American Statistical Association.

Jackson, G. A. (1981). Linear analysis of logistic choices, and vice versa. In *Proceedings of the American Statistical Association*. Washington, DC: American Statistical Association.

Jackson, G. A. (1988). Did college choice change during the seventies? *Economics of Education Review* 7: 15–27.

Jöreskog, K. G., and Sörbom, D. (1989). *LISREL 7*. Mooresville, IN: Scientific Software.

Maddala, G. S. (1987). *Limited-Dependent and Qualitative Variables in Econometrics* (rev. ed.). Cambridge, MA.: Cambridge University Press.

Mallette, B. I., and Cabrera, A. F. (1991). Determinants of withdrawal behavior: an exploratory study. *Research in Higher Education* 32(1): 179–194.

Manski, C. F., and Wise, D. A. (1983). *College Choice in America*. Cambridge, MA.: Harvard University Press.

Marascuilo, L. A., and Levin, J. R. (1983). *Multivariate Statistics in the Social Sciences: A Researcher's Guide*. Monterey, CA.: Brooks/Cole Publishing Co.

Marascuilo, L. A., and Serlin, R. C. (1988). *Statistical Methods for the Social and Behavioral Sciences.* New York: W. H. Freeman and Company.
Mare, R. D. (1980). Social background and school continuation decisions. *Journal of the American Statistical Association* 75(370): 295–305.
Muthén, B. O. (1988). *LISCOMP: Analysis of Linear Structural Equations with a Comprehensive Measurement Model.* Mooresville, IN.: Scientific Software Inc.
Nora, A., Cabrera, A. F., and Shiville, P. (1992). Graduate student involvement in scholarly behavior: a structural model. Paper presented before the 1992 AERA annual meeting. San Francisco.
Norusis, M. J. (1990). *SPSS Advanced Statistics.* Chicago, IL: SPSS Inc.
Pascarella, E. T.,and Terenzini, P. T. (1991). *How College Affects Students.* San Francisco: Jossey-Bass.
Pedhazur, E. J. (1982). *Multiple Regression in Behavioral Research: Explanation and Prediction.* San Francisco: Holt, Rinehart and Winston.
Petersen, T. (1985). A comment on presenting results from logit and probit models. *American Sociological Review* 50(1): 130–131.
Plane, D. R.,and Oppermann (1977). *Statistics for Management Decisions.* Dallas, TX.: Irwin-Dorsey.
Smart, J. C., Baird, L. L., and Bode, R. (1991, November). Discipline differences in the learning demands of doctoral programs. Paper presented at the annual meeting of the Association for the Study of Higher Education. Boston, MA.
St. John, E. P. (1990a). Price response in enrollment decisions: An analysis of the High School and Beyond Senior Cohort. *Research in Higher Education* 31(2): 161–176.
St. John, E. P. (1990b). Price response in persistence decisions: An analysis of the High School and Beyond Senior Cohort. *Research in Higher Education* 31(4): 387–403.
St. John, E. P. (1991). What really influences minority attendance? Sequential analyses of the High School and Beyond Sophomore Cohort. *Research in Higher Education* 32(2): 141–158.
St. John, E. P., Kirshstein, J. R., and Noell, J. (1991). The effects of financial aid on persistence: A sequential analysis. *Review of Higher Education* 14(3): 383–406.
St. John, E.P., and Noell, J. (1989). The effects of student aid on access to higher education: An analysis of progress with special consideration of minority enrollment. *Research in Higher Education* 30(6): 563–581.
Stage, F. K. (1988). University attrition: Lisrel with logistic regression for the persistence criterion. *Research in Higher Education* 29: 343–357.
Stage, F. K. (1990). LISREL: An introduction and applications in higher education. In J. C. Smart (ed.), *Higher Education: Handbook of Theory and Research*, Vol. VI. New York: Agathon Press.
Stampen, J. O., and Cabrera, A. F. (1988). The targeting and packaging of student aid and its effect on attrition. *Economics of Education Review* 7(1): 29–46.
Stampen, J. O. and Cabrera, A. F. (1986). Exploring the effects of student aid on attrition. *Journal of Student Financial Aid* 16(2): 28–40.
Taylor, D. G. (1983). Analyzing qualitative data. In P. H. Rossi, J. D. Wright, and A. B. Anderson (eds.), *Handbook of Survey Research.* San Diego: Academic Press.
Tinto, V. (1975). Dropout from higher education: A theoretical synthesis of recent research. *Review of Educational Research* 45: 89–125.
Tinto, V. (1987). Leaving college: *Rethinking the Causes and* Cures of Student Attrition: Chicago: University of Chicago Press.
Weiler, W. C. (1987). An application of the nested multinomial logit model to enrollment choice behavior. *Research in Higher Education* 27(3): 273–282.

Integrating General Education, Wellness, and Athletics: A Conceptual, Historical, and Reform Agenda

Lester F. Goodchild, Sheila M. Arredondo,
and
Robin B. Glaser
University of Denver

To this day, the relationship between intercollegiate sport and the purposes of higher education in America remain ill-defined, and the translation of education philosophy into sporting reality remains unrealized at the big-time levels of play.
—Donald Chu, Jerry O. Segrave, and Beverly J. Becker
Sport and Higher Education (1985, p. 2)

Calls for reform of the undergraduate curriculum, especially general education (Association of American Colleges, 1985; Bennett, 1984; Boyer, 1987; Boyer and Levine, 1981; Cheney, 1988, 1989; Katz, et al., 1988; Levine and Weingart, 1973; Study Group on the Conditions of Excellence in American Higher Education, 1984), and collegiate athletics (DiBiaggo, 1991, 1992; Gilley, et al., 1986; Knight Commission, 1991) have pervaded higher education during the past ten years. Yet, their interrelatedness has barely been acknowledged, except perhaps as a detriment to one another. Consistent with their evolution in American undergraduate life, this disassociation underscores their historic antipathy: the intellectual purposes of higher learning espoused by the faculty and even, in its loftier moments, the administration contrast sharply with the student extracurriculum. Such disjunctive thinking represents the mind of the academic professional attuned to a compartmentalized worldview of the campus.

It does not correspond to the unitive experience of undergraduate student life. Ernest Boyer in *College: The Undergraduate Experience in America* (1987) and the Carnegie Foundation in *Campus Life: In Search of Community* (1990) as well as George D. Kuh, John H. Schuh, Elizabeth J. Whitt, and others in *Involving Colleges: Successful Approaches to Fostering Student Learning and Development Outside the Classroom* (1991) understand this reality and advocate integrating formal structures of higher learning with educational experiences outside the classroom. In reflecting on this issue for *The Modern American College* (1988), Theodore K. Miller and John D. Jones wrote poignantly:

> . . . out-of-class education cannot be viewed merely as supplementary to the curriculum in carrying out the educational mission of the American college but rather must be seen as an integral part of its educational program. More and better linkages are needed between the formal and the informal portions of this total program—between the credit curriculum and noncredit extracurricular activities. Only as such linkages are created will we be able to offer students a comprehensive educational environment designed to be responsive to all their educational and developmental needs . . . (p. 658)

However, only a few higher education scholars have investigated the relationships between undergraduate education and athletics (Boyer, 1987; Chickering, 1969; Chu, 1989; Thelin and Wiseman, 1989). They suggest how athletics and undergraduate education may be understood as having an innate coherence. Most current reform efforts have not reconceptualized what may be perceived as this innate contemporary interdependence between learning and health. Indeed, a more enlightened, 21st-century student-oriented perspective undoubtedly will show them as integral to a successful completion of the undergraduate experience. How might this be so?

While collegiate reform efforts have taken a formal academic direction, reconceptualizing the purpose of American undergraduate education also from a student perspective enables the interdependency of these academic and athletic dimensions to be readily discerned. Academics redefined as the art of learning and athletics recast as the art of wellness constitute several arts to be mastered within an integrated curriculum for the next century. Wellness is a crucial art to be achieved, if learning is to occur satisfactorily. One cannot normally accomplish one without the other. Such integration has often been presumed, yet a more comprehensive undergraduate curriculum requires their explicit interrelatedness to be discerned, to be enhanced, and to be fused. A postsecondary learner who has mastered these arts is prepared for future graduate studies or occupational demands. This thesis undergirds the structure of this chapter.

Our purpose here is to offer a conceptual proposal linked to a historical analysis and a reform agenda for integrating wellness and its various manifestations (such as, physical education, sports, athletics, etc.) within undergraduate education. While aspects of this proposal have been made before within the history of American higher education, an argument for their natural coherence in assisting the undergraduate attain the knowledge and skills of a successful graduate seem obvious today. This chapter has six parts: (1) a conceptual discussion centering on the art of wellness and its relationship to undergraduate education; (2) a short historical review of the importance given to athletics from the ancient Greeks to the rise of physical culture and gymnastics in 19th-century colleges in the United States; (3) a longer historical assessment of the governance struggles involving the rise of intercollegiate sports as initial amateurism, linked to student and faculty control, which gave way to the commercialization of athletics under administrative purview; (4) an analysis of the athletic reform efforts during this century pointing out the enduring problems of big-time athletics; (5) an exploration of the student-athlete ideal and the ethical requisites facing college and university administrations; and (6) a practical discussion outlining the recommendations for integrating wellness within undergraduate education, faculty involvement, and National Collegiate Athletic Association (NCAA). Through this conceptual, historical, and programmatic analysis, a reform agenda for collegiate athletics may be offered.

I. GENERAL EDUCATION AND WELLNESS

Reforming the Contemporary American College

Recently, undergraduate education has received extensive criticism from many quarters. Two major reform dimensions center on the problems of the undergraduate curriculum and athletics. However, rarely are they treated as two interrelated aspects of the same overall problem, namely the problematic condition of the entire undergraduate experience. We intend to explore their connections and to suggest that all athletics be understood and acknowledged as part of general education. This recommendation also restores the historic role faculty have played in maintaining student activities and assuring their educational quality.

Amid the flurry of works and reports on undergraduate education during the 1980s, Ernest Boyer's *College: The Undergraduate Experience in America* (1987) stands out as the most sympathetic to this chapter's thesis. Unlike other works, after the usual condemnation of big-league sport, he espouses the expansion of intramural and wellness programs:

> Most encouraging is the emerging emphasis on wellness. More and more colleges see health and body care as an important educational objective. This, in our opinion, should be a high priority on every campus. . . .
>
> We urge that all students be helped to understand that wellness is a prerequisite to all else. They should be taught about good food, exercise, and should begin to understand that caring for one's body is a special trust. (pp. 186–187)

While seeking to reform sports to profit the individual athlete rather than the institution, Boyer's endorsement does not link athletics, intramurals, and wellness programs specifically to general education nor does he argue how physical education should be balanced with more academic subjects, except to endorse a "quality undergraduate experience" (p. 187). In *Campus Life* (1990), the Carnegie Foundation again alludes to how these activities might promote a caring community or how ''intercollegiate athletics must enrich the academic mission'' in a celebrative campus community (pp. 54, 59). Unfortunately, a more comprehensive philosophy of undergraduate education or actual reform proposals are absent.

Other major undergraduate reform reports (Association of American Colleges, 1985; Bennett, 1984; Boyer and Levine, 1981; Education Commission of the States, 1986; Katz, et al., 1988; Newman, 1985) fail to consider sufficiently or at all how athletics, physical education, or wellness may be connected to learning and campus life (Kimball, 1986). This absence is hardly surprising, given the fragmented divisions of our colleges and universities. A review of contemporary general education literature (Gaff, 1983; Martin, 1982; Mayhew, Ford, and Hubbard, 1990) reveals again little interest in the interrelationships between the academic and athletic divisions on campus. Only accrediting groups have sought in a limited fashion to restrain ''big-time sports'' which ''are out of control'' (Boyer, 1987, p. 185). Since 1977, the Southern Commission included the assessment of this area under student services (Thelin and Wiseman, 1989). However, major efforts at controlling athletics never seriously revived after the Big Ten thwarted North Central Association's attempt to regulate athletic scholarships in the early 1950s (Semrow, et al., 1992).

In the student development literature, Arthur W. Chickering in *Education and Identity* (1969) suggested seven vectors which comprised essential tasks during the collegiate experience: (1) developing competence, (2) managing emotions, (3) developing autonomy, (4) establishing identity, (5) freeing interpersonal relationships, (6) clarifying purposes, and (7) developing integrity. In exploring the competence vector, Chickering noted how athletics provided college students with an opportunity to demonstrate physical competence, but its association with intellectual and other activities remained ''unclear'' (p. 27). (These vectors were further refined in Chickering and Thomas, 1984.) Recently, Barr, Upcraft, and associates concluded that Chickering ''would take into account our more complete understanding of nutrition, exercise, and other wellness concepts'' today (1990, p. 52). Important as this thought might be to understanding collegian development, again any direct association with general education was not perceived.

However, one major campus group was particularly concerned about how these activities related to collegiate life. In reviewing the collegiate athletics literature, more focused proposals may be found. Six types appear in relationship to the topic of undergraduate reform: (1) higher education works which examine the academic and athletic nexus (Andre and James, 1991; Chu, 1989; Chu, Segrave, and Becker, 1985; Thelin and Wiseman, 1989); (2) histories of collegiate athletics (Park, 1987; Smith, 1988); (3) reporting of athletic scandals and problems (Bailey and Littleton, 1991; Funk, 1991; Sperber, 1990); (4) ethical inquiries about athletics in higher education (Kliever, 1990); (5) governance discussions often linked to presidential action and the National Collegiate Athletic Association (Frey, 1982); and (6) financial analyses of athletics (Atwell, 1991). For our purposes, three works provide an essential foundation for understanding the collegiate dimensions of athletics. Judith Andre and David James in their *Rethinking College Athletics* (1991) most comprehensively explore the history of athletics, conditions related to the players on American campuses, and recommendations for reform. Donald Chu in his *The Character of American Higher Education and Intercollegiate Sport* (1989) best investigates the educational nexus between undergraduate education and athletics. John Thelin and Lawrence Wiseman in their *The Old College Try: Balancing Academics and Athletics in Higher Education* (1989) provides the best overview of the fiscal, governance, and policy aspects of collegiate athletics.

Unfortunately, most of these commentaries have not offered a substantive solution to this crisis in collegiate life. No positive comprehensive conceptual framework for resolving difficulties—other than minor adjustments, such as incremental curricular change or piecemeal rule changes—has been forthcoming. Therefore, additional works are needed which specifically inquire about how general education, the undergraduate curriculum, wellness, health promotion, intramurals, and athletics might be related to the undergraduate experience. In large part, this state of affairs has occurred because of the overall intellectual muddle about the purposes of undergraduate education, except for the agreement on basic skill development, general knowledge, and specialization through the major. Yet, even this concurrence is hampered by the passive learning orientation left from the older pedagogical models of recitation and lecture. Our current undergraduate curricular model owes its origins to Harvard President A. Lawrence Lowell's attempt to contain the thoroughgoing electivism practiced under Eliot's masterful administration. In 1909, Lowell ordered Harvard's curriculum to contain general education, concentration, and elective components (Grant and Riesman, 1978; Levine, 1978). Unfortunately, his philosophical foundation for liberal education, espoused in 1915, has long since been forgotten. If we recall his undergraduate cultural ideal at all, our images center on ancient classics and character. It was more than that.

> Culture, therefore, does not mean the possession of a body of knowledge common to all educated men, for there is no such thing today. It denotes rather an attitude of mind than a specific amount of information. . . . Such a mind goes, we say, easily to the root of the matter. This is an art that can be learned, but like other arts it can be learned only by practice, that is by getting to the root of something.
>
> The art, or the habit, of getting to the root of things is essentially an attitude of mind. (Lowell, 1934, pp. 117, 120)

The Harvard president believed the undergraduate curriculum enabled the student to develop the intellectual art of inquiry. Each component of the baccalaureate course furnished the learner with a different approach to this objective.

While we have no agreed-upon common purpose for the American undergraduate experience, we might find Lowell's pedagogical strategy useful in devising a meaningful method to revitalize the undergraduate curriculum: namely, creating multiple postsecondary learning opportunities both in and outside of the classroom. For with the coming of a telecommunicated multimedia age, there is no longer a clear differentiation between the curriculum and the extracurriculum. The challenge is to orchestrate a coherent structure to an undergraduate environment filled with rich possibilities for reflective learning. Students thus may develop, for example, the art of inquiry when faculty, staff, and students fully embrace collaborative or service learning with this objective in mind.

What undergraduate curricular model might be best suited to such an enterprise? While there have been many experiments during this century after Lowell set the basic structure of undergraduate education, one general strategy has particular merit for our proposal: the integrated curriculum. At least four different patterns of integration have appeared this century: (1) the general education movement, (2) the telic undergraduate movement, (3) the integrated undergraduate curriculum, and (4) the competence-based liberal arts curriculum. First, the general education movement began in earnest with Columbia's civilization course in 1919, resulting in some 100 such courses across the country by 1928 (Rudolph, 1977). This interdisciplinary development attempted to bring coherence to the first part of undergraduate education. Similar themes might be found in special course requirements, central subjects, core courses and programs, survey courses and programs, and sometimes entire experimental colleges (Carnegie Foundation, 1979, pp. 173–179; Josephs, 1981). Characterized as integrative learning experiences, such efforts provided an interdisciplinary structure to general education.

Second, Grant and Riesman (1979, p. 17) argue that many innovative educators created undergraduate colleges as alternatives to the typical research university college where departmental faculty sought to socialize students into their own disciplines. They propose that four curricular types constituted this telic movement: neoclassical, aesthetic-expressive, communal-expressive, and activist-radical. The progenitor of this movement may be seen at St. John's College in 1937. Its Great Books curriculum, unlike its 19th-century predecessor, provided a coherence to all learning in this four-year endeavor. On the other hand, they designated Vassar, Bryn Mawr, Smith, Mount Holyoke, Mills, Bennington, Sarah Lawrence, and Black Mountain as aesthetic colleges. More communal approaches appeared at Johnston College at the University of Redlands and Kresge College at the University of California–Santa Cruz. Finally, Antioch College since the 1960s and the College of Human Services in New York sought to provide revolutionary activist designs to curricular forms.

Third, another approach to the integrated curriculum introduced a particular theme, philosophy, or ideology throughout the undergraduate course. This curriculum began in the 1930s when Catholic college administrators sought structurally to integrate Thomistic philosophy and theology in their undergraduate curricula. This effort at coherence reached its zenith 20 years later as Roy J. Deferrari, dean of the Catholic University of America's School of Education, described in his four related works: *Integration in Catholic Colleges and Universities* (1950), *Discipline and Integration in the Catholic College* (1951), *The Curriculum of the Catholic College (Integration and Concentration)* (1952), and *Theology, Philosophy, and History as Integrating Disciplines in the Catholic College of Liberal Arts* (1953). In this case, ideology was wedded to curricular structure to create a thoroughly Catholic college—not until the Second Vatican Council in 1962 did a decoupling occur which freed faculty from anchoring the disciplines to a religious orientation. A more recent attempt to espouse an integrated curriculum for the college based on character development can be seen in Warren Bryan Martin's *College of Character: Renewing the Purpose and Content of College Education* (1982).

Fourth, the integrated competence-based curriculum in liberal arts colleges is a relatively recent approach to undergraduate education, although its roots extend from vocational and professional education. Gerald Grant and others have provided the most comprehensive assessment of this type of curriculum in their work, *On Competence: A Critical Analysis of Competence-Based Reforms in Higher Education* (1979). They traced its contemporary origins to Alverno College in 1973 (Ewens, 1979). At the same time in Chicago, DePaul University launched the School for New Learning which was a competence-based college for working adults (Apps, 1988). Other programs across the country experimented with this form of curriculum in less comprehensive patterns, such as at Justin Morrill College at Michigan State, Florida State, Grand Valley State Colleges, College of Public and Community Services at University of Massachusetts–Boston, Mars Hill College, Our Lady of the Lake University, Bowling Green State University, and Sterling College (Ewens, 1979, pp. 167–168; Pottinger and Goldsmith, 1979). These coherence efforts have remained essentially tied to formal classroom instruction, although the granting of credit through portfolios for life experiences has been added at a few colleges (Nickse and McClure, 1981).

Yet, many calls for undergraduate reform seek a broader integration of all undergraduate learning experiences. Recently, Jerry Gaff in his work, *New Life for the Undergraduate Curriculum* (1991), stated:

> What is needed is to develop a college of integrity in regard to general education. A college of integrity says what it does and does what it says, not just in the curriculum but in *all* of its activities. It backs up the official rhetoric about general education with a strong, comprehensive, and coherent curriculum and with an organization that solidly supports it. It embeds the curriculum within a coherent academic culture to make general education permanent and central to the education of students and to the operations of the institution itself. (p. 233)

Without an expansive concept of general education aimed at the education of the whole individual, undergraduate reform will never achieve its comprehensive goal. Rather, conflicting philosophies about the purposes of such education and competing faculty disciplinary interests will continue to work at cross purposes.

We can assert from this overview, therefore, that reform of the undergraduate curriculum and of athletics are interrelated. Each aspect of student life would be advanced if there were greater coherence and integration with the general and particular espoused purposes of the college mission. Specifically, at least one integration pattern, namely, a competence-based liberal arts curriculum, within the waves of undergraduate reform during this century (Boyer and Levine, 1981; Goodchild, 1991) offers a most serviceable option to accomplish this endeavor, because its competence structure provides a better way to evaluate many learning experiences. This option may be chosen as the most appropriate means to integrate athletics within the general education and may provide the way for true lasting reform.

Expanding the Scope of General Education

To lessen the separation between formal undergraduate instruction and the learning related to athletics requires not only returning to the older whole person conceptualization of liberal education but also revitalizing this ideal to conform with our contemporary understanding of human development. Reestablishing a renewed holistic collegiate educational philosophy within the American college enables administrators and faculty to use the entire undergraduate experience as an opportunity to facilitate advanced learning.

What are some specific reasons for expanding the scope of general education to include all aspects of athletics? First, the American college student is in poorer physical health than college students of past eras, especially when compared with the 1920s. Second, this development has occurred because administrators and faculty have continued to lessen the requirements for physical education since the turn of the century. Third, amateurism, especially in individual sports activities, has declined in relative importance and financial support with the rise of big-time team sports. This quasi-professionalism has resulted in Division I teams being very costly and rarely assisting substantially the financial condition of the institution. Following this trend, the importance of physical education has declined in favor of professionalized sports goals for collegiate teams. Fourth, the quasi-professionalization of college athletics has stifled efforts toward reform during the past 20 years. However, several developments have significantly improved collegiate athletics. Title IX of the 1972 Education Amendments of the Higher Education Act has forced colleges to confront equity issues for women athletes. In 1983, Proposition 48 restored basic academic standards for collegiate athletes. Yet, much more remains to be done as athletic scandals still embroil many colleges and universities each year. Fifth, a proactive approach to health requires institutions to encourage students to adopt supportive lifestyles which aid learning and development during the collegiate years. Similar to academic assessment, students who understand and adopt a wellness orientation will enhance their learning success. Sixth, the rising interest in aerobic exercise and strength training has pointed to the physical need for vigorous workouts to promote healthy lifestyles throughout life. Early physical education efforts would promote lifelong learning. Finally, seventh, the rise of health risks on college campuses from communicable diseases, alcoholism, smoking, personal violence, rape, and so forth point to the need for greater prevention. In short, these reasons demonstrate a clear rationale for integrating health and wellness more completely with general education.

Declining Physical Education Requirements

Eight physical education surveys conducted since 1955 provide a clear picture of the dramatic changes regarding the place of physical education in general education (Oxendine, 1961, 1969, 1972; Oxendine and Roberts, 1978; Trimble and Hensely, 1984, 1990, as cited by Trimble and Hensely, 1990). During the late 1950s, 90 percent of all public colleges and universities surveyed structured their general education course requirements to include basic physical education. However, 30 years later, only 60 percent of colleges and universities have required their students take such courses. Moreover, these requirements may often be substituted for other ''personal choices from the curricular offerings'' (Trimble and Hensley, 1990, p. 64). Even where physical education is compulsory on campuses, the number of hours required is anemic. Only one or two credit hours for the entire undergraduate degree are required at approximately 50 percent of the studied institutions. Only ten percent of the colleges and universities demanded five or more hours. Comparatively, during the 1960s, most institutions had adopted eight hours for the first two years. The compulsory courses represented a significant commitment to physical education as part of general education. However, since 1984, there has been a slight increase in required hours and compulsory programs across the country in large part because of the interest in fitness activities and wellness programs (Miller, Dowell, and Pender, 1989).

Currently, these activities as a group constitute the major part of physical education course offerings for those institutions surveyed: individual and team sports comprise 42 percent, while fitness activities, aquatics, dance, gymnastics, outdoor skills, combatives, and others represent 58 percent. Some of this change has occurred because faculty have encouraged interdisciplinary linkages which promote physical education enrollments from various departments.

> The most commonly cited interdisciplinary relationships are shown here; the number in parentheses represents the number of times mentioned. Drama majors are required or recommended to take: dance (18), figure skating (1), fencing (13), and rhythmic

> exercise (1). ROTC students are recommended or required to take: swimming (18), sailing (1), physical conditioning (12), orienteering (2), boxing (1), wrestling (2), weight training (9), rifle (6), pistol (1), and concept of fitness (19). Thirty-four different interdisciplinary relationships were cited, from Agriculture (horseback riding) to Women's Studies (self-defense). (Trimble and Hensley, 1990, p. 73)

In retrospect, the most important curricular change during this period has been the substitution of specific sports courses for multidimensional courses which comprise such wellness activities as exercise science, movement fundamentals, nutrition, stress management, substance abuse, leisure awareness, environmental sensitivity, and self-responsibility (Trimble and Hensley, 1990, pp. 69–71). These dramatic shifts during the last three decades disclose the need to reevaluate the role that physical education plays in general education, especially as the adoption of wellness and multidimensional courses clearly indicates a way to incorporate athletics into more formal postsecondary learning opportunities.

Exploring the Art of Wellness

The convergence of these general and specific trends regarding the condition of undergraduate education, college physical education and athletics, and student development accentuates the urgency to reconceptualize the place of athletics in undergraduate education. Early efforts to remedy this situation have seen student service professionals advancing the concept of wellness within the context of health promotion on campus. Giving this ideal greater intellectual and formal learning content requires introducing wellness as an essential art to be mastered within liberal education.

By adopting a new expanded conceptual design for general education, faculty and administrators may designate the art of wellness in all its many forms as a requirement for completing the undergraduate degree. Understanding wellness as an integral part of a liberally educated individual encourages a lifelong learning pattern supporting the ideal of a productive, healthy citizen for a democratic society. In addition to this expanded philosophy, a competence-based curriculum could be adopted which would provide an implementation structure suitable to what has been designated physical education. Yet, the art of wellness goes beyond the current expectations of physical education by broadening its scope to include more personal behaviors and by integrating it more closely with formal postsecondary learning.

The formal concern and study of student health may be traced to two 19th-century movements in educational institutions. Schools pursued hygiene as a major issue for principals and teachers. On the other hand, collegiate faculty and students adopted gymnastics, physical culture, and later physical education interests as significant components of a holistic concern for learning. These movements resulted in the establishment of physical education as an academic department, especially at land-grant universities, since the 1920s. However, the decline in compulsory courses and administrative funding of this area of study recently fostered a dramatic shift in the direction of comprehensive health promotion on campus.

The Concept of Wellness

In the late 1950s, Halbert L. Dunn (1961) launched the idea of wellness in a series of lectures at a Washington, D.C. Unitarian church. He believed wellness was "an integrated method of functioning that is oriented toward maximizing the potential of the individual within his or her environment" (Leafgren and Elsenrath, 1986, p. 4; Sivik, et al., 1992, p. 136). Rather than emphasizing physical health alone, Dunn addressed the comprehensive needs of the individual in society (Hart and Sechrist, 1970). In 1975, John Travis, a medical doctor, opened the first public clinic for wellness education and services. Two years later, Don Ardell became the national herald for this idea in his work, *High Level Wellness: An Alternative to Doctors, Drugs, and Disease* (1977). Ardell defined "wellness as a positive approach to health that concerns five dimensions of living: fitness, stress management, responsibility, nutrition, and environmental sensitivity" (Montgomery and Dalton, 1986, p. 44). This pivotal book expanded the concept of health beyond more medically oriented considerations and concentrated on how daily activities contributed or challenged personal wellness. In large part, the interest in stress reduction, especially among corporate managers, pointed to the potential health hazards for middle level management. Greater interest arose in how appropriate health care "encourages individuals to seek lifestyles which enable them to achieve their highest potential for well-being" (Pelletier, 1979, as cited by Warner, 1984, p. 32). These developments in sports and business also affected higher education.

Meanwhile, at the University of Wisconsin–Stevens Point, William Hettler, M.D., began a wellness program for members of the university community in the early 1970s. His efforts in developing the National Wellness Conference and National Wellness Institute enabled the university to pioneer the national movement on college campuses. Most importantly, in 1980, he wrote "Wellness Promotion on a University Campus." This article in *Family and Community Health* discussed six dimensions of wellness which have become the foundation for the current wellness movement. They are: (1) emotional development, (2) intellectual development, (3) physical development, (4) social development, (5) occupational development, and (6) spiritual development (Leafgren and Elsenrath, 1986). The addition of the spiritual dimension (Ryan, 1986) represents a restoration of an essential component within liberal education which was eliminated with the coming of the Enlightenment and the rise of positivism in Europe during the 18th century: namely, the contemplation of God, a divine being, an ultimate force, or an ultimate value (Goodchild, 1989). Recent assessments of human development also have pointed to spirituality as being one of the more enlightened stages of consciousness (Alexander and Langer, 1990). Each dimension of wellness became a focused concern for student and staff at those campuses which joined the movement.

In 1981, S. R. Ryan and John Travis wrote the all important *Wellness Workbook*. In its foreword, Dorothy Jongeward, the president of the International Transactional Analysis Association, said: "Health comes when we are total, whole people; when we have achieved a level of integration between mind, body, emotions, and spirit; when we allow ourselves to balance." It was clear that wellness had become a comprehensive concept. Moreover, it gained moral force when Travis claimed: "Wellness is the right and privilege of everyone" (p. 2, as cited by Leafgren and Elsenrath, 1986, p. 7).

Yet, advocates of the wellness movement struggled to promote their concept and approach in the face of older groups, especially health educators, who warned rather that they should remain on the sound theory and research base within the field of physical education (Timmreck, Cole, James, and Butterworth, 1987). Nevertheless, persons concerned about wellness and physical education chose to ally themselves with this important developing effort.

The Two Philosophies of Wellness

Initially wellness programs provided services on a voluntary basis for campus members. However, as the societal and personal costs of poor health have become more recognized, various advocates sought a more proactive stance. Ruth P. Saunders's "What is Health Promotion?" (1988) describes this major juncture in the wellness movement. Advancing a more aggressive wellness approach, proponents have chosen *health promotion* as a new ideal. It emphasizes program development directed at changing personal behavior to adopt more healthy lifestyles through the use of "any combination of educational, organizational, economic, and environmental supports" (Green and Johnson, 1984, p. 6, as cited by Saunders, 1988, p. 14). In 1985, J. P. Opatz in *A Primer of Health Promotion: Creating Healthy Organizational Cultures* similarly claimed that wellness is "the process of adopting patterns of behavior that lead to improved health and heightened life satisfaction" (DeGuire North and Munson, 1990, p. 106). Saunders (1988, p. 14) perceived this orientation again in M. P. O'Donnell's (1986a, p. 4) definition: "Health promotion is the science and art of helping people change their lifestyle to move toward a state of optimal health." O'Donnell (1986b) further clarified this new direction in health promotion by designating three interrelated approaches: (1) awareness, (2) lifestyle change, and (3) supportive environment or maintenance (Saunders, 1988, p. 17). Most texts on this subject (Edlin and Golanty, 1992; Greenberg and Pargman, 1989) have employed these techniques. The rationale for adopting this more proactive approach in colleges and universities may be understood from Keeling's (1992) perspective, which argues for health promotion on campus because knowledge in and of itself—so much associated with the initial voluntary wellness efforts—did not cause behavioral change. While these two philosophies of wellness characterize all such programs across the country, health promotion appears to be displacing wellness as more institutions establish these types of programs.

Current Campus Wellness Programs and Courses

Campus health programs incorporate both wellness and health promotion most often under the legitimate role of student services, although many institutions are introducing these ideas and programs as part of general education. Currently, health education programs have adopted the most proactive philosophy of wellness. ''Over 100 colleges and universities offer some type of academic program for health promotion professionals''; the ''oldest and most well-established are those at American University, the University of Georgia, Loma Linda University (Calif.), Purdue University, Springfield College (Mass.), and the University of Wisconsin–Stevens Point'' (DeGuire North and Munson, 1990, p. 109). Besides these academic degree programs, support programs have been established at 55 campuses for faculty, staff, and students (DeGuire North and Munson, 1990, p. 113). A recent commentary (McMillan, 1986) notes that 20 percent of all postsecondary institutions have some type of wellness program for at least one major group on campus (Sivik, et al., 1992, p. 137). Yet, knowing what specific campuses among the 3,500 have these programs remains more difficult to determine, at least from the literature. The oldest ones have been identified and described: the University of Wisconsin–Stevens Point in 1972, James Madison University in 1978, St. Cloud State University in 1978, University of Virginia in 1982, University of Maryland–Baltimore County in 1982, and University of South Carolina in 1982 (Warner, 1984). To these first six universities may be added another 16 institutions (Ball State University, Baylor University, Boston University, California Polytechnic University, University of Illinois, Illinois State University, University of Miami–Ohio, Michigan State University, Central Missouri State University, University of Nebraska, New York State University College of Technology–Utica, University of North Carolina–Charlotte, Northern Illinois University, Regis University, University of Wisconsin–Stout, University of Wisconsin–Whitewater) and the Texas university system (Carlson, et al., 1991; Leafgren and Elsenrath, 1986, pp. 3–4; Montgomery and Dalton, 1986, p. 63; Robbins, Powers, and Rushton, 1992; Zevin, 1992). The most comprehensive list is available from the National Wellness Association at Stevens Point.

In a recent survey of wellness programs at major postsecondary institutions, Sivik, Butts, Moore, and Hyde (1992, pp. 140–141) describe two basic courses—not surprisingly representing the two philosophies of wellness and health promotion. Many courses may be characterized as fitness programs, including aerobic dance, cycling, jogging/running, walking, water exercise, and weight training. Other educational wellness programs evince more of a health promotion stance by focusing on AIDS, drug/alcohol problems, eating, fitness, healthy back exercises, high blood pressure, nutrition, smoking, stress management, and weight loss (Carlson, et al., 1991; Keeling and Engstrom, 1992; Robbins, Powers, and Rushton, 1992).

On the other hand, wellness programs for nontraditional students emphasize how "wellness is seen as the responsibility of the individual" (Hybertson, et al., 1992, p. 50). In their study of 356 students (two-thirds were 25 years or older), Hybertson, Hulme, Smith, and Holton (1992) found that nontraditional students identified the social dimension (involving marital and family relationships, friendships, helping others) as affecting their wellness more than any other. Using Hettler's (1980) typology, they ranked in order of importance: social, physical, emotional, intellectual, occupational, and spiritual. "Programmatically, the results suggest that the wellness approaches of health education, substance abuse prevention, physical fitness, leisure opportunities, and personal counseling must include strong programs in time and stress management" (p. 54). Whereas traditional students ranked physical, emotional, social, occupational, intellectual, and spiritual dimensions as more important to them. It is not surprising that adolescents believed physical health as being most valuable, while adults considered social wellness as being the most crucial. These findings may assist administrators in creating appropriate programs for various individuals and in taking one more step toward developing authentic learning communities.

An Ethical Imperative for Creating Campus Community

Creating a learning community on campus requires that all of its members—whether students, staff, administration, or faculty—are healthy. Both wellness and health promotion programs encourage greater opportunities for advancing the moral development of students (Bok, 1982) who as a result may monitor their behavior not only to further their own well-being but also that of other learners (Bok, 1990, pp. 87–90). While not attempting to restore *in loco parentis* (Hoekema, 1990), administrations may assist in creating student wellness communities through these programs which seek to support the greatest good for all. Improving all six dimensions of wellness (Hettler, 1980) provides a foundation for establishing a wellness community. This imperative advances the Carnegie Foundation's suggestions in *Campus Life: In Search of Community* (1990) by expanding the concepts of celebratory and caring community on campus. It only mentions campus sports in its athletics orientation and group support through various organizations, respectively. Unfortunately, this work does not mention how current campus wellness and health promotion programs have been one of the major forces to achieve the goal of creating campus community. The concept of a healthy community—a necessary seventh dimension which should be added to purposeful, open, just, disciplined, caring, and celebrative—would include three elements: health education, wellness, and health promotion; intramurals; and athletics. Each plays an important role in creating a healthy campus community. Adding integration and coherence to the mission of the college, this lifelong learning art would demonstrate the holistic role of general education. Given these developments and rationales, the art of wellness as a general education competence represents a legitimate addition to a new integrated undergraduate curriculum for the 21st-century American college.

II. EDUCATION AND SPORTS: A HISTORIC RELATIONSHIP

> A Sound Mind in a sound Body, is a short, but full Description of a Happy State in this World: He that has these Two, has little more to wish for; and he that wants either of them, will be but little the better for any thing else. Men's Happiness or Misery is most part of their own making. He, whose Mind directs not wisely, will never take the right Way; and he, whose Body is crazy [i.e., frail] and feeble, will never be able to advance it.
>
> —John Locke, *Some Thoughts Concerning Education* (1705; Axtell, 1968).

Contrary to the contemporary reform agenda for collegiate athletics, the major problem inhibiting any lasting systematic change has not been widely recognized. The underlying difficulty is a basic conflict between two opposing philosophies of athletics. Each has roots three millennia old. The Greeks believed in both individual and team competition. American collegiate athletic traditions adopted these patterns from their more recent 19th-century European progenitors. Linked to the heritage of Cambridge and the colonial colleges, English team sports (Mangan, 1981) provided a model for student extracurricular activity in the antebellum era. On the other hand, German emigrants in the 19th century introduced a more individualistic pattern of athletics tied to gymnastics and physical culture. Until the turn of the 20th century, administrators contested these philosophies. Only after team sports proved so lucrative did team athletics win the wholehearted endorsement of college presidents. Its abuse provoked the football excesses of 1905 where deaths and injuries littered playing fields (Smith, 1988). While the formation of the Intercollegiate Athletic Association and the National Collegiate Athletic Association (NCAA) did eliminate the worst defects, team sport held center stage. However, during the 1890s, 1920s, and 1960s, individual interests and college requirements made physical education a significant component of college life. The integration of these two philosophies with general education has yet to occur (see Table 1). This resolution within the contexts of wellness and health promotion would clarify the educational aspects associated with college athletics.

This section reviews the foundations of modern collegiate athletics by describ-

TABLE 1. The Two Philosophies of Collegiate Athletics in Each Century

Century	Philosophies	Corresponding Programs
18th	Naturalism	Exercise—walking
	Sport	Blood Sports—bear baiting, campus football
19th	Physical Culture and Physical Education	Gymnastics and Hygiene
	Athleticism	Intercollegiate team contests (amateur and professional)
20th	Physical Education and Health Promotion	Gymnastics, Intramural, and Wellness Programs
	Sports	Intercollegiate individual and team contests (quasi-professional)

Sources: Review of these programmatic developments may be seen for physical culture, physical education, and health promotion in Dyreson, 1989, Etheredge, 1958; Grover, 1989, Leafgren, 1986; Lee, 1983; Park, 1987, 1989, 1991; and Welch and Lerch, 1981. On the other hand, the rise of sports and intercollegiate athletics may be reviewed in Andre and James, 1991; Chu, 1989; Chu, Segrave, and Becker, 1985; Guttmann, 1985; Rudolph, 1962; Ryan, 1929; Savage, 1929; and Smith, 1988.

ing the ancient Greek philosophies and ideals of sports and 18th-century European proponents of education and health. How these ideas affect college athletics will be reviewed in the third section of this chapter.

Ancient Philosophies of Athletics

Ancient Greece enthroned the athletic ideal as a way of life. Out of the rivalry between Sparta and Athens came the Olympic Games spanning half a millennium from B.C.E. 776 until 394 A.D. The Greek ideal of *agon* involved a contest or struggle for excellence which reflected the Homeric sacred traditions. Just as the gods struggled for power and influence in their pantheon, mortals also gained in their worldly contests whether as merchants, warriors, or athletes. Athletics entailed a physical competition for excellence; this new ideal of sport represented a ''ritual sacrifice of human energy'' (Sansone, 1988, p. 75). Those persons who succeeded achieved a heroic and sacred ideal (Robinson, 1955). Yet this ideal was not divorced from daily life. Greeks perceived ''athletics was a part of Greek education, the belief being that here one could learn about something important about life, even about reality'' (Hatab, 1991, p. 31). Many philosophers contended that education was both mental and physical. In the *Republic* (III, 401–404), Plato believed that the guardians of the republic must be trained in both music and gymnastics. Such intellectual education encouraged the adoption of discipline (i.e., virtue) which was also required to embrace exercise for the body (Hamilton and Cairns, 1969, pp. 646–649). In this way, wisdom included physical training. In his *Politics* (VII, 1323 a, b), Aristotle considered a person's happiness to consist of intellectual, physical, and material goods; all three were necessary (McKeon, 1968, p. 1277). In writing about the art of gymnastics, he contended that it required both mental and physical training (*Politics*, IV, 1288b; McKeon, 1968, p. 1205). In short, Greeks believed that athletics taught persons the abilities of physical training, competition, and cooperation which were necessary for an exemplary life (Hatab, 1991, pp. 32–37).

Athletic contests, moral behavior, political life, and even business provided arenas for the citizen to demonstrate goodness. The Greek idea of an educated person is centered on the concept of *arete*: a person of virtue. While different groups proposed ideals for this virtuous person, Isocrates provided a useful definition. "This is my definition of an educated man. First, he is capable of dealing with the ordinary events of life; by possessing a happy sense of fitness and a faculty of usually hitting upon the right course of action." Second, he behaves properly. Third, he has mastery over his pleasures. Fourth, he is not egotistic, yet takes pleasure in the products of his own talents and intelligence. Fifth, he is a wise and perfect man. In the Homeric stories, persons become heros or heroines after succeeding through a struggle or contest. In this sense, an enlightened person has demonstrated *arete* through *agon*. A truly educated person thus demonstrated his or her virtue through disciplining the mind and body.

With the decline of the Roman empire and the rise of Christianity, survival and combat-related contests replaced most organized athletic activities until after the Reformation. However, aristocratic sports included "hunting, horsemanship, horse racing, rowing, swimming, archery, dancing, and games similar to football, cricket, tennis, and golf." Common sports seem most prevalent in medieval England where university students and entire towns played "loosely organized" games of football (Lee, 1983, p. 9). Not until the Renaissance and the rediscovery of Greek and Roman patterns of education and leisure did an appreciation of the interrelationship between learning and sports reappear.

Modern Philosophies and Practices of Education

The modern foundation for athletics and education came from England, France, Germany, and the United States in the 18th century. Five continental philosophers and educators provided the principles linking exercise and education. The most articulate advocate of what became physical culture and education was John Locke (1632–1704). In *Some Thoughts Concerning Education* (1705), he encouraged discipline of the body through exercise as one of the chief aims for the education of children along with an emphasis on increasing the mental and moral powers of the mind (Axtell, 1968, p. 58). Locke introduced dancing, fencing, and horsemanship into school programs. Based on Greek and Roman ideas, his treatise began a new era in education by espousing the pedagogical foundation for physical education. In France, Jean-Jacques Rousseau (1712–1778) in his

Emile believed that education was the "art of forming men" (p. 33). Its natural aspects provided a foundation for later development. In his later writings which followed the ideas from Plato's *Republic*, he argued that education should make them men and citizens. This included teaching about one's nation state and the building of gymnasiums to incorporate physical exercises (Boyd, 1911/1963, pp. 217–224).

These ideas enabled leading German educators to create schools which adopted such practices. Johann Basedow (1723–1790) founded the Philanthropinum in 1774 where children were allowed to use games as a form of education. "Basedow's institution was the first to give physical education an important place in the school, with the realization of the importance of play and body activity for the potential intellectual and moral as well as physical values. In his school, the out-of-door life and the process of instruction were closely related" (Cowell and France, 1965, p. 201). In this growing educational reform effort, Johann Friederick Gutsmuths created the first physical education manuals. Friederich Ludwig Jahn (1778–1852) created gymnastic exercises and apparatus that launched the 19th-century gymnastic movement. Their work following Greek ideals led to gymnastic societies and athletic contests (Cowell and France, 1965, p. 202). Fitness and education complemented each other. These developments greatly shaped postsecondary physical education in the United States.

III. THE RISE OF COLLEGIATE ATHLETICISM: STUDENT, FACULTY, AND ADMINISTRATIVE STRUGGLES TO CONTROL SPORTS

> I believe in the development of wholesome games and sports, particularly those that are conducted out of doors. . . . I believe that the chief aim of college athletics should be the physical and moral improvement of the entire group. . . . We must believe in all sincerity . . . that physical education, including competitive sports, is an essential part of the obligation of the college, and in no sense a mere excrescence, to be confined to the casual outsider or the transient apprentice. We must recognize that it stands in the closest possible relation to moral education, which we often pronounce one of the prime duties of the college, . . . We must believe unreservedly in sports for the whole college community, and competitive group sports as far as possible.
>
> —James R. Angell (Ryan, 1929, p. xviii).

The Invisible Players: Faculty and Sports on Campus

While Angell's sentiment characterized the administrative view of collegiate sports, competing voices among student and faculty as to who should control athletics arose in the 19th-century college. Unexplored is the pivotal role faculty played in the evolution of collegiate athletics—largely by their noninterference. Yet, if one believes that faculty are at the heart of the academic enterprise (Bowen and Schuster, 1986; Weimer, 1990; Jarvis, 1991), then one might justifiably ask: What has been the faculty role in either helping or hindering those forces which might have brought campus sports to a more positive state of affairs? Is it true that "higher education cannot control the cultural forces into which college sports have evolved and are evolving still" (Bailey and Littleton, 1991, p. 10)? Must one fear that academics are powerless to confront the problems historically besetting campus sports and those "behavioral patterns of selfishness, yuppie-greed, self-enrichment, and instant gratification characteristic of the 1970s and 1980s" (Lasch, 1989, p. A23)? Is it fair to say that faculty have simply not pursued the "potentially infectious causes that their own educational purposes and ethical commitments should have led them to confront and reject" (Bailey and Littleton, 1991, p. 26)?

This section addresses these poignant questions by examining the role of faculty vis-à-vis campus sports in light of the societal context confronting colleges and universities. Whether for better or worse, American institutions of higher education have always been uniquely responsive to societal influences in a lively give-and-take relationship (Boyer, 1987; Bok, 1982; Birnbaum, 1991). The action of the faculty can only be appreciated through a historical perspective. Accordingly, faculty and sports are examined by century, with the full understanding that this approach remains an artificial construct to analyze this complex phenomena. Each section begins with an overview of the nation to capture the major trends molding the new republic and follows with an explanation of faculty actions—or inactions—within the world of campus athletics.

The 18th-Century College: Prayer Versus Sport

Institutions of Higher Learning in the Colonies

In colonial America, privileged sons of the wealthy went to Harvard, Yale, and Princeton (and later six other small denominational colleges) to become the new generation of community leaders (Bowen and Schuster, 1986; Pfnister, 1990; Rudolph, 1962). Students adopted a civilized lifestyle, which conflicted with the sometimes barbaric conditions of those times (Morison, 1936). Many studied ministry; others became lawyers, doctors, and learned men of the community. Instruction consisted of Latin, Greek, Hebrew, logic, and rhetoric—the classical curriculum (Cremin, 1970).

Puritan society dwelled on the virtues of industry to assure the salvation and survival of soul and body in both real and spiritual terms. "Their divinity studies tested their wills but not their bodies . . . games and play were carnal pleasures and frivolous diversions from devotion, survival, and salvation" (Sojka, 1985, p. 18). The Puritan antipathy to sports was rooted in the belief that it diverted honest men from realizing their "calling" or true purpose for being on earth. The Sabbath was strictly observed. Traditional village recreations were frowned upon, unless free-time pursuits could be shown to glorify God. "To the Puritans, play often stimulated the passions, leading to deceit, feasting, dancing, gambling, sexual immorality, and the neglect of one's calling" (Rader, 1983, pp. 10, 12). It was desirable only to be a moral athlete (Perry, 1964). The Protestant temperament went diametrically against the growth of colonial sports. The evangelical revivals of the mid-18th century further bolstered religious zeal, which had begun to ebb. The absolute submission of self to parents and an omnipotent God made sporting in public difficult at best and severely punishable at worst.

In these small colonial colleges, presidents kept faculty on a short leash. Generally, tutors were most often themselves bright graduates of the colonial colleges. Their responsibilities entailed pedagogical, pastoral, and custodial duties (Finkelstein, 1983). Tutors remained with their charges 24 hours a day and shared sleeping quarters. They took heed not to indulge in the luxury of moral transgressions—actions which would gravely offend presidential sensibilities, anger Puritan lay boards, and bring swift reprisal. Being at the beck and call of the president, these faculty often did not stay long in what constituted a revolving door existence (Pfnister, 1990).

Enacting the will of the president, tutors truly acted *in loco parentis*, that is, "functioning in the place of parents" (Levine, 1978, p. 526). Moore (1976) reports that "much effort was expended in attempting to reform student offenders" (p. 72), but adds that cases of student misconduct were actually not numerous, at least not in the 17th century. This is not so surprising, considering that offenses were punished in a draconian manner. A student public confession was often followed by shaming techniques, not to exclude corporal punishment and expulsion. It is clear that faculty in colonial days would not have and could not have officially sanctioned campus sporting events. Such frivolous activities would have gnawed at the very moral fibers on which the colleges were founded. Tutors were in an adversarial position, being at all times the role models which students were expected to emulate, at least in theory.

Colonial students knew of the sporting traditions of Oxford and Cambridge, after which the colonial colleges were modeled, as well as those of English town life. These traditions continued in the colonies, including such diverse entertainments as boating, cricket, horse racing, hunting, tennis, boxing, cudgel-playing, fishing, handball, football, and swimming (Smith, 1988, pp. 4–12). Blood sports, such as bull-baiting, cock-fighting, dog-fighting, and bear-baiting, excited local townspeople—many of which authorities in England declared illegal by the 1850s (Guttmann, 1985). Simpler pleasures also engaged village commoners who, at the risk of incurring the ire and wrath of Puritanical authorities, played "games of chance, games of skill, individual games, team games . . . stool-ball, footraces, quoits (in which a contestant attempted to throw an iron ring over a peg), skittles, and ninepins (both forms of bowling)'' (Rader, 1983, pp. 8–9). Yet, faculty restrained student participation in these activities.

As a consequence, a state of friction between faculty and students existed. Students eagerly sought out any activity that might free them from the ''rigid and staid curriculum and a suffocating college life dictated by the institution's faculty'' (Smith, 1988, p. x). However, while students sought avenues of escape from their pressure-cooker environments, 18th-century educators were engrossed with instilling ''reason'' into their charges to combat the numerous perils of passion—''ambition, envy, covetousness, pride, selfishness, vanity, and indulgence'' (Vine, 1976, p. 71). Rarely did faculty openly and generously embrace sporting activities on campus. To do so in this theocracy would have evinced being in league with the devil. Such pent-up hostility occasionally resulted in food fights in the refectory and campus riots—called routs—during commencement revelries (Moore, 1976).

The confines of Puritan and Calvinist educational traditions did not, however, prevent continental ideas of education and exercise from taking root in the new American soil. Early colonial schooling consisted of basic education and some physical activities. Benjamin Franklin and Samuel Moody, headmaster of the Dummer Grammar School in Bayfield, Massachusetts, both advocated these types of instruction (Lee, 1983). Having read the ancient classics and contemporary French treatises on education, Thomas Jefferson included a gymnasium in his plan for the University of Virginia. He believed that such exercise was ''a proper object of attention for every institution of youth.'' It consisted of military training, manual arts, and dancing. Above all, Jefferson advocated walking as the most important exercise for youth (Arrowood, 1930, pp. 153, 163). These philosophies and practices provided a foundation for physical education at developing collegiate institutions during the next century.

The 19th-Century College: Gymnastics Versus Athleticism

The new century saw a commercial-urban-industrial revolution through harnessing steam as an energy source, building vast rail networks, creating improved communications through the telegraph, encouraging western expansion, and establishing a new economic order based on manufacturing. Technological advances, coupled with the Victorian credo of hard work, temperance, frugality, and punctuality, led to an ever larger segment of society realistically hoping for a higher standard of living for themselves and their children. ''The revolution in material aspirations also undermined older social restraints'' (Rader, 1983, p. 29). Fittingly, President Jackson ushered in the ''egalitarian spirit of the age.'' Frontiers were pushed back, cities flourished, and massive mobility characterized Americans who President Lincoln declared were, after all, ''created equal.'' An emotional disengagement from the past was made possible by the new economic realities. The diminished roles of an established elite class, the church, or even the homogeneous geographical community provided the impetus for Americans to develop their robust sense of individualism.

As business opportunities expanded, there was a call for supervisors and mid-level managers who needed collegiate training to function well in an increasingly complex work environment. Colleges and universities stepped in to help provide this cadre of potential managers. Colleges also began to absorb a greater number of middle and upper-class urban youth preparing for professional roles. These were youngsters who, because of the technological advances of a manufacturing society, could no longer find work on the farm, in cottage industries, or in self-sufficient nuclear family economies. Institutions of higher education were also challenged to provide practical answers for a technologically more sophisticated society (Lang, 1978) and were called upon to provide insight into newly recognized social problems (Hoeveler, 1976). The German university model promised hope that the advancement of knowledge through research would pave the way for a social Darwinism that would explain, if not solve, most of humankind's problems—as well as explain the world of natural phenomena.

The country's new urban industrial base provided for more leisure time and wealth. Both poor and rich took full advantage of sporting opportunities. Urban laborers found their ticket at the saloons. These had evolved from the colonial taverns and inns, which had always functioned as social centers for entertainment and thirst-quenching libations. Laborers found in the saloon an antidote to the Victorian virtues of hard work, temperance, and frugality. They fully enjoyed such pastimes as ". . . gambling, crime, prostitution, speculative ventures, entertainment, and sport" (Rader, 1983, p. 25). The middle and upper-class Victorians, whose youth had many idle hours to kill, were busy forming numerous voluntary associations and sporting clubs. Sporting fraternities sprang up for all income levels and soon added social functions to their raison d'être. To belong to one or several elite sporting fraternities or country clubs provided a gateway to social acceptance and entry into the social registry. "By 1850, the Victorians had even begun to develop a positive sporting ideology, one that defended the playing of certain sports as useful for improved health, as a respite from work, as a surrogate for the vices of the city, and as an instrument for the nurture of proper character traits among the young" (Rader, 1983, p. 26). Not only had it become acceptable to participate in sports, but it also became chic to be spectators at large sporting events. The tradition of spectator sports was a reinvention of what southern gentry had been doing for decades anyway—in their dissolute pastimes of horse racing and gambling. By 1823, crowds of 100,000 gathered at the Union Course on Long Island to witness horse racing. In 1835, a foot race there attracted some 20,000 enthusiastic spectators (Rader, 1983). The rabble contented themselves with billiards and violent prize fighting (Johnston, 1947), while the richer set absorbed themselves in horse racing, yachting, foot racing, rowing, and football games. A sign of the times was that by 1860 baseball teams could charge admission to their games and that by 1876 the National League was organized to manage the growing commercialization of the sport.

Institutions of Higher Learning

Americans with resources sent their prodigy to colleges and universities as never before and institutions sprang up around the country. The multitude of educational settings was uniquely American, as institutions attempted to meet the desires of diverse constituencies with financial resources. Colleges became useful pathways to successful careers, corporate magnets to attract capital investment, and political images to aspiring communities (Boorstin, 1965). Modern research universities as success-oriented enterprises prepared individuals for competition with curricula and programs to meet everyone's needs (Veysey, 1965). Not surprisingly, institutions were dominated by communities with governance structures highly responsive to external constituencies (Frey, 1982). The educational scene was marked by a diversity which continues to this day.

Such diversity required institutional competition for survival. Chu, Segrave, and Becker (1985) succinctly point out factors leading to a lack of consensus as to what American higher education in the 19th century should be. Few institutions had clearly defined missions. Most were proud of the autonomy guaranteed by courts and the federal constitution. While states regulated colleges by granting institutional charters, there were few historical precedents to emulate. Institutions freely invented themselves, not being bound by traditions. Scarcity marked dependable financial revenues. A high degree of individuality marked campuses, as the country lacked a state church or national education ministry to set the tone. An emerging private sector often created the impetus for seeding institutions. Colleges used highly creative financing schemes to stay alive, and institutions generally had faculty with little influence. Administrators, eager to rise above other institutions, sought ways to stimulate boosterism (Potts, 1977). Athletics and sporting events clearly fit the bill.

> Without an established "charter," college leaders were relatively unhampered in making decisions concerning programs which might draw resources to their schools. Without clear understandings in the minds of the public, students, administrators, money bearing groups, and faculty at their own and other schools, the business-minded leaders were not constrained from bringing intercollegiate athletics formally into the education institution, nor from using sport for its resource-drawing capabilities. (Chu, Segrave, and Becker, 1985, p. 45)

In reviewing the evolution of collegiate athleticism during the early 19th and 20th centuries, three distinct periods may be discerned. First, from 1820 to 1850, collegians found exercises and gymnastics to be the most popular activity, often sponsored by faculty interest. However, the thrill of intercollegiate team sports following English school traditions soon overwhelmed this generally individualistic competition. During the second period from 1850 to 1890 team sports quickly moved from student to administrative control, and in the process colleges adopted professional strategies to produce team winners at any cost. In its wake, gymnastics, revitalized as physical culture, moved to the sidelines. Yet, this turn to violent sports eventually brought revulsion from the faculty in the 1880s and then from the administration in 1905. Reform efforts during a third period from 1890 to 1930 recast collegiate athletics. A fourth era with even greater reforms appears in the late 20th century—to be explored in the next part of this chapter.

Early Gymnastics, 1820 to 1850

With the sporting mentality deeply embedded in society's psyche, it should come as no surprise that sporting activities including both team sports and gymnastics flourished on campuses across the nation. As blood sports waned in England and the United States during the first part of the century, other more republican sports became popular. Continuing the medieval traditions of violent village football games, Harvard students' ''kick ball'' on ''Bloody Monday'' became an annual event by 1820. This hallowed occasion consisted of sophomores crushing and demolishing freshmen in a bloody free-for-all on the greens for control of an animal bladder (Hardy and Berryman, 1982; Smith, 1988). The event served as a hazing, sporting contest, and rite of passage.

In the early 19th century, emigration introduced a sports ideal more attractive than any group or team athletics. A German gymnastic spirit took hold during this first period. As early as 1826, the emigré innovator Charles T. Follen (1796–1840), who had been one of Jahn's disciples, established collegiate gymnastics in the Harvard dining hall and eventually erected outdoor facilities. Other outdoor gyms soon followed at Yale, Amherst, Williams, Brown, Bowdoin, and Dartmouth. Such demonstrations produced faculty advocates. In the same year, William Russell launched the *American Journal of Education* with an editorial claiming how ''physical education . . . formed habits and stamped the character'' of students (Park, 1989, p. 135). Numerous articles and books appeared during the next 20 years led by a translation of Jahn's *Die Deutsche Turnkunst* (1816), which launched gymnastics as the main thrust of the physical culture craze. Reaction was very enthusiastic.

> Observing that men needed to take regular exercise in forms where the mind ''may be occupied at the same time as the body,'' the reviewers noted that pedestrian excursions, running, climbing, jumping, exercises on the horizontal and parallel bars, wrestling, skating, swimming, the use of dumbbells, and dancing were appropriate for men until they reached the ages of 16 or 17. Older men needed activities such as vaulting, fencing, riding, boxing, and driving. (Park, 1989, p. 136)

On the other hand, Catharine Esther Beecher (1800–1878), who was at Hartford Female Seminary, wrote *A Course of Calisthenics for Young Ladies* (1831) as ''the first manual of physical education,'' and created specific gymnastic exercises for women (Lee, 1983, pp. 27, 46). She continued to preach the benefits of an active lifestyle in *Treatise on Domestic Economy* (1841), and recommended at least two hours of strenuous, total body exercise daily in a 1855 work *Letters to the People on Health and Happiness* (Guttmann, 1991, p. 91). This work was followed by *Physiology and Calisthenics for Schools and Families* (1856) which claimed that ''no program of education for women was complete without attention to physical development'' (Cowell and France, 1965, p. 209). This movement continued to gain popularity on college campuses.

Intercollegiate Athletics, 1850 to 1890

However, after mid-century, team sports began to rival physical culture. Fired on by Thomas Hughes' best-seller, *Tom Brown's School Days* (1857), a glorification of campus sporting life in England, American collegians organized intramural baseball and cricket matches, as well as other impromptu sporting events. Sports on the Harvard campus became so disruptive that President Felton (1860, p. 22) lamented to the Overseers that students ''imply that muscular development is identical with moral, intellectual, and religious progress. It seems to be thought the panacea for all the evils under which humanity labors'' (Rader, 1983, p. 72). Clubs cropped up on the campuses whose uniform goal was ''geared toward molding championship teams'' (Hardy and Berryman, 1982, p. 18).

With the railroad as a new means of transportation, intramural college teams expanded their field of operations to compete with neighboring schools. The first intercollegiate contest, a race between the crew teams of Harvard and Yale, took place on Lake Winnepesaukee in New Hampshire in 1852. ''Neither winning nor potential profits motivated the early rowers. They took up rowing principally for exercise and recreation'' (Rader, 1983, p. 71). There were no trainers, no coaches, no systematic training schedules. The students ran the show. Yet the event occurred only because a small New England railroad sponsored the match to promote railroad travel by paying customers. This might well be the first instance where hidden financial interests were a driving force—a harbinger of things to come. By 1870, as many as 16 colleges participated in regattas. In addition to providing a vehicle for reducing campus boredom, sport allowed American institutions to develop a pride in their athletic accomplishments which mirrored American society's increasing enthusiasm for sport (Chu, 1989; Smith, 1988). On July 1, 1859 Amherst and Williams played the first intercollegiate baseball game. On November 6, 1869, the Princeton-Rutgers game inaugurated American football (Smith, 1988, p. 219). Faculty and students joined together to play in the games, as eligibility was yet to become an issue (Rudolph, 1962, pp. 154, 373–374). Team sports gained wide acceptance among northeastern academies and colleges. Through the 1870s ''the students organized clubs, scheduled the contests, managed the finances (such as they were), and determined the rules of the game'' (Rader, 1983, p. 75). With no professional coaches, student team captains called the shots. They decided on playing eligibility, strategy, and preparation for a game.

What the students did not expect was the overwhelming enthusiasm with which spectators would embrace their sporting efforts, especially when it came to football, the darling of the spectator sports. By the 1890s more than 40,000 fans gathered to watch college Thanksgiving Day football championships in New York (Rader, 1983). An 1889 Yale-Princeton game brought in more than $25,000 in cash receipts! Nelson (1982) describes the ambiguity with which faculty and administrators, especially presidents, approached the situation, ''like the family member locked in a room and fed under the door, intercollegiate athletics was tolerated because they had to be some place since the demand from students was high'' (p. 49).

For many students, victory meant more than their studies. Clubs went all-out to win. The words of Senator Henry Cabot Lodge in 1896 sum up the mind-set of an influential segment of American society. ''The time given to athletic contests . . . and the injuries incurred on the playing field are part of the price which the English-speaking race has paid for being world-conquerors'' (Mrozek, 1983, p. 28). Sports laid the groundwork for upwardly mobile young men to gain the moral qualities which would later serve them well in all of life's aspects. Men came to college to achieve social standing, make connections, and prepare themselves for a social position in tandem with their family wealth (Rudolph, 1962).

There was often little common ground between faculty and sports-minded students. Horowitz (1987) reports that ''college men forged a peer consciousness sharply at odds with that of the faculty. They created college life'' (p. 23). The dominant modus operandi was defined by faculty-student dissonance. Students reasserted themselves and reclaimed paradise lost. Gone were the days of the early Republic when ''the prescribed student role was to pay, pray, study, and accept'' (Horowitz, 1987, p. 26). In essence, presidents and faculty won the battle, but lost the war. Administration quelled student unrest on the surface, but students went underground, organized, and found their fullest expression in campus sports. Here were energy-venting student activities that faculty perhaps disliked as much as unwelcome dinner guests, but there was nothing they could do (Huk, 1993).

In summary, team sports thus created a new arena of student life on campus in several ways. First, students in 19th-century America rebelled against a legacy of straitjacket-type control by presidents and faculty. Second, students organized among themselves and produced a sporting culture which in no small way acted as a pressure release to institutional demands and stresses. Third, the student sporting movement found wide acceptance in a society already heavily invested in leisure-time activities, gambling, and spectatorship. Fourth, many students no longer approached collegiate life merely as an opportunity for education, but mainly as a rite of passage to social connectedness and standing. Fifth, students found their sporting events to be vehicles for recognition, pride, as well as income. And finally, little understanding and empathy occurred between faculty and students—except in one area.

Since mid-century, educators, influenced by biologists, introduced physical education as a way to achieve hygiene and educational goals. First public schools included physical education. Children had exercise periods two or three times a week for approximately 20 minutes (Lee, 1983, p. 86). At the collegiate level, gymnastics entered the collegiate curriculum. Amherst College led the way. To address the health of undergraduates, Amherst established the first Department of Hygiene and Physical Education in 1860 (Rudolph, 1962, pp. 151–153). In 1861, Edward Hitchcock also required physical education through Amherst's intramural activities (Lee, 1983, p. 87). At Harvard, Dudley Allen Sargent, director of the Howard Hemenway Gymnasium, formally adopted the ideal of bodily culture by promoting German, English, and French practices of exercise. Calisthenics, gymnastics, physical training, outside pursuits, and competitive athletics provided a new strategy for occupying students' attention. Again, women's colleges played prominent roles. Eliza Monsher at Vassar and later the University of Michigan as well as Amy Morris Homans at the Boston Normal School incorporated women's gymnastics into baccalaureate education (Lee, 1983, p. 101; Guttmann, 1991, pp. 112–116). Collegiate gymnastics had become a national phenomenon. Tremendous enthusiasm created the American Association for the Advancement of Physical Education (AAAPE) in 1885. It became the vehicle which challenged the growing attraction of college athletics. In the following year at a major presentation of the AAAPE, Edward M. Hartwell, director of the Johns Hopkins gymnasium, contended that ''gymnastics were more comprehensive in their aims, more formal, elaborate, and systematic in their methods, and . . . productive of more solid and considerable results'' than athletics (Park, 1989, p. 131). Most of his colleagues concurred. During the next five years, Hartwell lessened this endorsement somewhat, but still held to gymnastics' superiority, unless team sports achieved true ''*educational* ends'' (Park, 1987, p. 48). In 1889, Charles Kendell Adams, president of Cornell, furthered the gymnastic ideal by claiming these sports promoted moral development among students. Five years later, he claimed that gymnastics was a liberal art (Park, 1989, pp. 127–130). This physical culture philosophy of college athletics anchored the student-athlete ideal of academics and athletics to amateurism.

However, between 1880 and 1890, commercialism and professionalism of team athletics directly challenged this amateur ideal. College presidents soon replaced student managers of athletics with coaches and administrative coordinators (Nelson, 1982; Smith, 1988). Administrators had perceived how these contests could be revenue enhancing activities for their institutions.

> Professionalism has done much within the past five years to bring discredit upon college sports; and by professionalism we mean the purpose to win a game by any means, fair or foul. Athletic honors are sometimes—not generally, but more and more frequently in recent years—sought by collegians through the use of dishonorable means. . . . When college men are willing to travel with professional ball-players, and especially under assumed names, it is time for college authorities to recognize and regulate college athletics. (Hartwell, 1885, as cited by Ryan, 1929, p. xxi)

Yet, college and university presidents saw in athletics creative inroads to new markets. Athletics were to be the honey to assist in fund-raising and student recruitment, while at the same time bringing notoriety and money to their host communities (Chu, 1982, 1985). A college could use athletics as a device to forge community relationships and ''broaden its appeal and perceived relevance'' (Frey, 1982, p. 185). Professionalized college teams, departments of physical education dedicated to athletics, and their coaches provided exciting intercollegiate contests. These brutal struggles heightened the ancient Greek idea of *agon* and attracted many spectators as opposed to the tame gymnastic competitions. Increasingly intercollegiate sports became the means to a specific end, rather than an end in itself (Nelson, 1982; Smith, 1988; Thelin and Wiseman, 1989). Although detractors, the most notable being Harvard's President Charles W. Eliot, emerged, Norman Bignham in his *Book of Athletics and Out of Door Sports* (1895) claimed the ''effects of athletics'' had displaced the good of physical exercise (Park, 1987, p. 31). Toward the end of the decade, the transition from ''gymnastic-centered curriculum to a sport-centered curriculum'' had occurred (Park, 1987, p. 57). The commercialization of college sports marked the turn of the 20th century.

The Faculty as Ineffective Players, 1890 to 1930

In this new era, administrators hired coaches to produce winning teams and athletic directors to coordinate the complex infrastructure of intercollegiate sports. Alumni continued their support, legal and otherwise, of programs ''plagued by weak presidents, disorganized faculties, and powerless students'' (Sojka, 1983, p. 23). Faculty members stood by as the campus sports industry emerged as a gargantuan force not to be denied. Campus athletics were a phenomenon marked by organizational efficiency and a single-minded ''emphasis on winning, which accommodates the democratic tendency to measure and record achievement'' (Bailey and Littleton, 1991, p. 3). Faculty were overwhelmed by the campus sports phenomenon, which became much larger than its individual parts. Though special faculty committees were frequently established on campus, their main focus was not on taking corrective action, but rather to ''prevent the athletic tail from wagging the educational dog'' (Scott, 1982, p. 31). Academicians wanted to keep sports at arms' length and were mostly concerned with curbing programs and formulating prohibitions. ''Not only has control by faculty members failed to curb traditional abuses in athletics, it sometimes appears that the academicians have joined forces with the athletic barbarians to create new abuses'' (Scott, 1982, p. 32). Faculty members had only slim chances of being heard anyway, for they were rarely among the community movers and shakers who decided economic and political issues (Guttmann, 1982).

Complicating the 19th-century faculty role vis-à-vis sports was the fact that faculty had not yet matured into their full professional identity. Not until the 1860s and 1870s did roles for instructors and assistant professors even emerge or was an academic career sequence formalized (Finkelstein, 1983). Given the lack of a clear identity or institutional career track, real decision-making power rested with presidents, who in turn were at the beck and call of business-dominated trustees. Faculty members as a group were a disparate lot, lacking identity and only rarely coming together for concerted action on anything. Since they did not form the American Association of University Professors (AAUP) until 1915, no collective voice sounded the alarm. It seems clear that the faculty was powerless to stop the inevitable commercialization of campus sports. The 19th-century American faculty was an invisible and relatively minor player on the stage of the great play that was unfolding. There is little they could have done to prevent the sowing of those seeds which would grow into the flagrant abuses characterizing campus sports in the 20th century.

The 20th-Century College: Commercialism Versus Reform

The Nation

The United States entered the new century with a boom of prosperity in which anything seemed possible. Manifest destiny dictated a larger role for America politically and the manufacturing base remained strong, fueled by the willing labor of skilled and unskilled immigrants. The nation embraced an activist mood, the hallmark of which was aggressive nationalism. As the century wore on, the United States came out of the relative seclusion guaranteed by the Atlantic and Pacific oceans to fight in two world wars. The wars propelled the United States into world leadership, destined to shape world finances, politics, technology, and military matters. The Cold War only magnified and sharpened America's role as leader of the West—one of two ideological giants dominating world politics.

In terms of societal trends, the importance of manufacturing and mass production assured continued urbanization and economic growth (aside from a temporary lull during the Great Depression and occasional temporary economic downswings). Naisbitt (1984) describes eloquently the major trends which changed (and are changing) 20th-century America. Among the more important trends are: (1) the gradual shift from an industrial society to an information society; (2) the incorporation of ever higher and more complex levels of technology; (3) the movement from national economies to world economies; (4) the shift from seeking short-term solutions to long-term planning; (5) the move to decentralize politics, business, and the other structures defining society; (6) the gradual change from bureaucratic hierarchies to complex networks of experts sharing ideas, information, and resources.

The bureaucratic model served as the blueprint for societal institutions during the greater part of the century (Weber, 1930). Bureaucracy called for a rational ordering of the economy along with rationalization of social relationships from the top down to achieve maximum efficiency. Power no longer resided in the person, but in the office or status occupied. Formal regulations and a pyramidal set of offices assured maximum efficiency. Obedience was a virtue, personal interests were subsumed to corporate interests, hierarchy was all-important, and technical training was the passport to officialdom. Decisions, administrative acts, and rules were eternalized in writing.

Adding to the bureaucratic model, Frederick Taylor superimposed ''scientific management,'' which stressed ''analyzing, planning, and controlling every detail of the entire manufacturing process'' (Bennett and LeCompte, 1990, p. 47). Every aspect of every task was closely examined, standardized, and made to follow rules, laws and formulae. Performance was carefully measured and accordingly rewarded. Bureaucracy and scientific management dealt the death knolls to 19th-century family cottage industries, the extended family economic unit, and many a small-time entrepreneur. It had become a less personal world. People moved to follow their jobs, children left home to get specialized education, material possessions were the currency of success, and cities became the hub of economic activity. Americans were enriched financially, but a lessened quality of interpersonal relationships was the price. ''The efficiency that now characterizes the productive process also characterizes social organization. In their social lives, people are now 'processed' as impersonally and as efficiently as the material resources that are also necessary for production'' (Cuzzort and King, 1989, p. 54).

A Sporting Society

The sports enthusiasm planted in the American national psyche during the 19th century came to full bloom in the 20th. Sustained national wealth, more discretionary leisure time, and a need for escape combined to make the period from 1920 to the present a time that Rader (1983, pp. 171–173) calls ''The Age of the Spectator.'' Lipsky (1981), perhaps better than any other contemporary sports author, gets to the heart of what sports provide in this age of depersonalization and mechanization:

> The game is the garden where the values of the larger society are grown through the ''stylistic subterfuge'' of creating a mythical and unproblematic world. Obstacles that symbolize the barriers of the larger political and social system are dramatically

> resolved. . . . When life offers fewer opportunities for "emotional pay-offs," a vacuum of feeling is created that threatens the ongoing stability of society. The game feeds the emotions and provides a collective strength of purpose that is rarely seen in the real world except during wars and disasters (pp. 31–32).

The sportsworld is a "complete universe that warms the cold bars of our iron cage" (Lipsky, 1981, p. 33). Sports are the substitute for political allegiances and satisfy the nostalgia for simpler times when community was important. During times of dissension and turmoil, sports can provide a feeling of "euphoric togetherness" (Lipsky, 1981, p. 44). Sports provide the counterbalance to the overwhelming advance of technological progress and the crushing bureaucratization inherent in modern civilization.

On the College Campus

The enthusiasm for college team sports on the part of alumni, students, boosters, administrators, and a doting public continued unabated from the 19th century into the 20th. Presidents and administrators continued to view campus athletics as a viable means to recruit students, gain regional and national visibility, court individual and corporate donors, retain alumni loyalties, balance financially stressed budgets, impress trustees, and curry influence with legislators holding the purse strings and fortunes of many an institution (Andre and James, 1991; Smith, 1988; Lapchick and Slaughter, 1989; Frey, 1982; DeVenzio, 1986; Thelin and Wiseman, 1989). Campus sports became such an integral part of the sport consumer's diet that Michener (1976) aptly described universities as being practically under an obligation to provide mass entertainment as part of their legitimate mission.

By the turn of the century "big-time intercollegiate sport became incorporated within the formal structure of American higher education" (Chu, Segrave, and Becker, 1985, p. 48). Gone was the student initiative. There to stay were full-time coaches, scholarship athletes, and contractually obligatory schedules (Savage, 1933). Year-round athletic activities requiring "intense commitments of time and physical and mental energy" (Rader, 1983, p. 53) became de rigueur. As various sports developed, established rules placed controls on this all-pervasive enthusiasm. Yet, football still owed too much to "Bloody Monday" traditions. In 1905, 18 college students were killed and another 159 were injured on the college playing fields (Fleisher, Goff, and Tollison, 1992, p. 39). This tragedy promoted reform efforts with the founding of the Intercollegiate Athletic Association. Whatever faculty control had been attempted with the founding of the Inter College Faculty Representatives concerning player eligibility in 1895 came to naught. These reform efforts—as fully explored in the next section—took the onus of controlling competition, enforcing rules, and monitoring abuses of institutions (Lawrence, 1987). Largely successful in stemming deaths and injuries, big-time college team athletics grew in even greater popularity throughout the century, and eclipsed other forms of sport, especially gymnastics.

This swing also occurred with the endorsement of leading educators. Team sports were claimed to be a superior substitute for gymnastics. In the National Education Society's ninth yearbook, Wood of Columbia and Hall of Clark along with other sociologists approved team sports. In particular, G. Stanley Hall gave respectability to sports because of his ideas on adolescence and games in his 1904 book, *Adolescence* (Chu, 1989, p. 51; Park, 1987, pp. 48–49). Subsequently, universities and colleges made athletics compulsory. The University of Pennsylvania was the first to require all students to take physical education courses all four years. Most colleges followed. By 1920, three hours per week in the first two years of general education became standard (Lee, 1983, pp. 173–179).

Yet, "the Age of Play" and "Big Society" in the 1920s rejected the ideal of physical culture and substituted the new progressive ideal of athleticism. "Play was the true essence of modern sport" (Dyreson, 1989, pp. 144, 261–270). The new spectator sports included baseball, boxing, football, tennis, and golf. Continuance of physical education requirements lasted until the 1960s. Eighty-four percent of all institutions required some physical education: 5 percent had four years; 30 percent had three years, 68 percent had two years, and 25 percent had one year.

Throughout the decades of this century, the pressure to field winning teams has been intense, especially in basketball and football. The laundry list of regularly occurring abuses is lengthy: (1) students enrolling in nonexistent courses or maintaining eligibility by enrolling in "easy" classes unrelated to graduation; (2) booster clubs directing athletic programs and buying coaches and players; (3) disregarding regular admission standards to allow illiterate athletes to play; (4) using community colleges to filter marginal students; (5) falsely promising financial help; (6) subjecting athletes to physical harassment and verbal abuse to increase performance; (7) using fraudulent transcripts to obtain illegal transfer credit; (8) using illegal cash payments, gifts, or sex to motivate star athletes; and (9) luring foreign athletes to campuses with false promises (Nyquist, 1985). To that impressive list, one could add as well: free loans, jobs for athletes, courtesy tickets for family and friends, jock dorms, fast cars, free credit cards, free phone calls and, when needed, courtesy bail bondsman service (Sperber, 1990). There are few institutions which, in a moment of brutal honesty, could have justified many of the practices invoked for the sake of winning. Fewer still could have reconciled their sporting faux pas with institutional mission statements touting lofty ideals, such as morality, honesty, truth, and citizenship. Rooney (1980, p. 134) laments the many prestigious institutions guilty of infractions and who receive multiyear probation—and who ". . . represent only a small percentage of the actual culprits." As difficult as it was and is to tease out institutional fact from institutional fiction, the true violence of campus sports affects the individual student-athlete most of all.

The competitive exploitation of student-athletes by many coaches is the logical conclusion of a situation where ''coaches are paid to win; losing coaches are fired, while winning coaches receive more substantial pecuniary rewards'' (Hart-Nibbrig and Cottingham, 1986, p. 107). Coaches often view their players as mere commodities and means to an end. Coaches are entrepreneurs in their own right and would not enjoy their high salaries, cuts from ticket deals, profits from summer camps, shoe contracts and sporting goods endorsements, their own media shows, car deals and miscellaneous other freebies—if it were not for their Lombardian aggressiveness toward winning at all costs (Sperber, 1990). There is room for doubt that intercollegiate sports build character, leads to better grades, and paves the way to successful careers. In all too many cases student-athletes use up four years of eligibility and are left without a college degree, sometimes functionally illiterate. Schembechler and Albom (1990) speak of coaches who persuade, pressure, and wheel-and-deal young athletes into accepting free education at reputable universities—and describe them as being at best ''pimps.'' Cynicism takes the place of hope as athletes realize they are no more than ''. . . staff members whom the university hires on the basis of their skills to do particular jobs'' (Sperber, 1990, p. 208).

Faculty as Invisible Players

Blackburn and Nyikos (1974) maintain that the weakest link in the governance of intercollegiate athletics has been the faculty. In part this may have occurred because faculty continued to struggle for identity and a firm academic niche. The professionalization of the professorate did not begin till the mid-19th century (Finkelstein, 1983). Not until the mid-1960s did faculty finally ''arrive'' in the full flower of academic power and prestige (Jencks and Riesman, 1968; Bowen and Schuster, 1986). The lengthy road to professionalization was made more rocky by numerous factors which absorbed faculty energies and left little time for such ethereal considerations as the role of sports in academe.

During this century, for example, the faculty dealt with the increasing complexity of the natural and social sciences (Naisbitt, 1984) and an unrelenting information explosion. Ever greater specialization left the faculty disjointed and without a common dialogue. Societal trends brought glory to academics teaching hard core sciences, business, law, computer science, and medicine, but brought grief to the humanities. A shift in the academic interests of students during times of retrenchment left faculty members bitterly divided on two sides of a fence (Bowen and Schuster, 1986).

In recent times faculty hustled to adjust to the (1) new needs of nontraditional students, (2) decreasing academic quality of incoming students, (3) need to serve more than 50 percent of the nation's yearly cohort of 18– to 22–year-olds, (4) dramatic shift of students from private to public institutions, (5) uncertain times of budgetary restraints and retrenchment, (6) greater centralization and administrator power, and (7) emphasis on accountability (Kerr and Gade, 1987). Other issues of concern included faculty autonomy and academic freedom (Slaughter, 1987; McConnell, 1987), the ever expanding intrusion of federal and state governments on campus (Gladieux and Lewis, 1987; Millett, 1987), and increasing legal vulnerability (Hobbs, 1987). Faculty wrestled with undergraduate curriculum reform, while seeking to survive in a publish or perish environment (Jencks and Reisman, 1968). The issues confronting faculty were and still are numerous, complex, and time-consuming. With so much to do and so little time, faculty labored under a siege mentality. They gladly left the Pandora's Box of intercollegiate sports for others to grapple with. "This lack of enthusiasm by faculty to be a major participant in the governance of intercollegiate athletics can be attributed in part to the loose structure for decision-making in higher education" (Bailey and Littleton, 1991, p. 74), a status quo which shifted the onus of responsibility to the president.

In turn, presidents prioritized concerns and actions, given that universities had become enormously complex institutions with multiple priorities and opinions (Kerr, 1963). Presidents became more like politicians and mediators than scholars (Kerr, 1963), especially at institutions increasingly resembling "organized anarchies" with "garbage can" decision-making styles (Cohen and March, 1974). Athletic concerns were most often not the biggest fire to put out and were put on a back burner to take care of themselves. This was especially the case when athletic departments were seen as subcomponents of institutions, loosely coupled (Weick, 1976) and not part of the "real" academic enterprise. Atwell (1979) shares that pessimism about presidential effectiveness, stating that "the more intense, the more visible, and the more costly the athletic program, the less influence the chief executive officer has over it" (p. 367). The apparent lack of presidential control of big-time sports can perhaps be explained by the general dilution of presidential authority on large campuses (Davis, 1979; Nelson, 1982). That presidents have circumscribed powers is evidenced by the ten-year struggle to make inroads in NCAA matters through a "President's Board" (Bok, 1985). To date, efforts have only led to a watered-down NCAA "President's Commission," limited to advising, commissioning studies, and proposing legislation. Athletic directors still comprise the majority of the NCAA general assembly (Sperber, 1990).

Major studies on the control and governance of campus athletics generally omit any mention of faculty (Gilley et al., 1986) and focus instead on presidents, athletic directors, and trustees. When an institution does designate an official NCAA faculty athletics representative (FAR), many end up being administrators holding faculty rank or are themselves athletic directors (Thelin and Wiseman, 1989). Weistart (1987) states that a FAR who is hand-picked by the president and athletic director is often beholden to administration interests and not attuned to faculty concerns (Thelin and Wiseman, 1989). The role of a FAR is further diminished by the many faculty members who "rarely . . . know that their institution has a specific faculty member whose role it is to give academic perspective to athletic programs and decisions'' (Thelin and Wiseman, 1989, p. 88).

To sum up, faculty members have generally been absent from the sports scene due to their involvement with other issues and a general lack of interest. They have exercised little influence on the campus sports movement. For the past three centuries, there have been ample reasons why faculty could not, would not, and did not help shape the governance structure of intercollegiate athletics. In their place stood presidential oversight.

IV. 20TH-CENTURY SPORTS REFORM EFFORTS: RECURRENT THEMES

> Nothing in college life to-day exerts a greater influence for good or bad than athletics. Rightly guided, controlled, and supervised, properly administered, athletics develop many of the finest qualities that a student can possess. Left to run riot, unsupervised, uncontrolled, improperly administered, athletics become a potent force for evil.
>
> —Elmer Berry in W. Carson Ryan, Jr., *The Literature of American School and College Athletics* (1929, p. xx).

A Brief History of the National Collegiate Athletic Association

Although sports and athletic contests have been popular in this country since its founding, it was not until the 20th century that athletics were formally embraced by college and university leaders as part of the legitimate mission of higher education. Society valued the benefits derived from athletic participation. ''The spirit of competition, high ideals, and ambition instilled through'' the college experience were thought to best serve ''the graduate and the nation'' (Chu, 1989, p. 53). Extracurricular activities, formerly tolerated by faculty and administrators, were now viewed with understanding and support. College presidents ''altered previous criticism or apathy toward sport to assume an enthusiastic stance and rationalize the intercollegiate sport program'' (Chu, 1989, p. 60). Intercollegiate athletics became the predominant extracurricular activity pursued by students (Underwood, 1984, p. 9; Eitzen and Sage, 1978).

Once intercollegiate athletics were formally endorsed, winning became paramount (Rudolph, 1962, p. 9). Winning meant prestige for the local community and an enhanced image for the institution (Rooney, 1987, pp. 14–15). Pressures to win, to attract students, and to acquire resources resulted in numerous ''growing pains and critics'' of the maturing empire (Smith, 1988, p. 181). Teams once managed by students were taken over by administrators who hired coaches, arranged competitions, built facilities, managed budgets, and promoted athletic programs (Chu, 1989, p. 57). Instead of becoming highly structured, the system was more chaotic. Because of a lack of rules and regulations, the use of ringers (highly skilled athletes brought in to help teams win specific games) and tramp athletes went unmonitored and became commonplace. Although many people opposed high-level recruitment efforts and subsidization of athletes, no one could effectively do anything about it (Rooney, 1987, p. 18).

Turn-of-the-century collegiate football games characterized this chaos. Primitive techniques and equipment, violence, numerous injuries, and the use of nonstandardized rules were widespread. Various coalitions organized rule committees between the years 1890 and 1905 to address these issues. The result, however, was further confusion among football teams and additional problems (Lawrence, 1987, p. 7). In 1905, 18 deaths and more than 150 serious injuries were recorded in football. College and university leaders suspended programs, abolished programs, or adopted other less threatening sports (Fleisher, Goff, and Tollison 1992, p. 39). This was the only time (until recently) that higher education officials seriously considered abolishing sports on campus (Smith, 1988, p. 181). Scandals in intercollegiate athletics have continued to alternate with reform efforts ever since (Andre and James, 1991, p. 1).

The crisis of 1905 and mounting public protest led to an official response. Theodore Roosevelt invited academic leaders to the White House and pleaded for reform. President Roosevelt called college and university representatives together for a meeting at Murray Hill Hotel in New York on December 8, 1905. Representatives from Columbia, New York University, Stevens Institute, Union College, and the University of Rochester wanted to abolish football, but the majority which represented Fordham, Haverford, Lafayette, Rutgers, Swarthmore, Syracuse, Wesleyan, and West Point voted to reform the sport (Andre and James, 1991, p. 1; Guttmann 1991, p. 20). Thus was established the Intercollegiate Athletic Association of the United States (IAAUS) in 1906. Faculty and other official representatives from 38 competing institutions composed the initial membership of the IAAUS. The association's first president was Captain Palmer E. Pierce, a professional military officer, who is credited with establishing a "mature and stable presence" for the association (Lawrence, 1987, p. 12). The supervision and regulation of college athletics was the original mission of the association. Program control, however, was under the jurisdiction of representatives from the competing institutions (Sage, 1982, p. 132). The membership's first priority was to develop new football rules and eliminate the dangerous play known as the "flying wedge." Unfortunately, early recommendations did not occur in time to prevent a second football crisis. Thirty-three football players died during the 1909 season. On October 16, 1909 during the Navy-Villanova game, Navy quarterback Earl D. Wilson was hit by a flying tackle and died. Administrators, coaches, faculty, and the public once again called for reform or the abolition of football (Falla, 1981, pp. 43–44).

In 1910, the IAAUS membership officially changed names to the National

Collegiate Athletic Association (NCAA) and began to pursue a vigorous reform agenda. The years between 1910 and 1920 were relatively uneventful as the membership was defining the role and responsibilities of the organization. Several trends, however, were evident: (1) the NCAA extended its authority beyond football and added eight more sports; (2) study groups or task forces were formed; and (3) the membership had trouble enforcing the regulations that were passed, so a resolution was adopted in 1919 "to encourage compliance with the rules of eligibility and amateurism" (Fleisher, Goff, and Tollison, 1992, p. 42).

Commercialization and athlete inducements increased dramatically throughout mid-century (Fleisher, Goff, and Tollison, 1992, p. 44). A 1929 Savage report commissioned by the Carnegie Foundation revealed that the quest for glory in intercollegiate competition had made a travesty of the values associated with higher education. Also noted in the report was the presence of an intricate system of recruitment and subsidy, the special treatment of talented athletes, and the widespread problem of commercialization. The author concluded that while colleges and universities were still educational institutions, they had also evolved into commercial organizations which overshadowed academic life. College and university athletes were referred to as professionals in the report because they received money for their athletic endeavors and devoted the majority of their time to sport. The report also alleged (some evidence was provided as well) that numerous NCAA rules violations regarding recruitment and athlete subsidization occurred (Guttmann, 1991, p. 20; Savage, 1929). In 1938, issues of commercialization and professionalism came to the forefront when President Robert M. Hutchins declared that colleges which produced professional athletes were not educational institutions. He proceeded to withdraw Chicago from intercollegiate football in 1939 (Guttmann, 1991, pp. 20–21). The years between 1920 and 1950 are often referred to as the "Golden Age" due to the popularity of college football, which quickly was becoming a nationwide preoccupation (Fleisher, Goff, and Tollison, 1992, p. 42). Comments and concerns, however, regarding the principles of the sport did not cease. Coach Herman Hickman wrote about the football crisis in 1956, stating that the principles of football had long been discarded and the nation was nourishing a monster that would eventually destroy all sport (Guttmann, 1991, p. 21). Attendance at college football games continued to escalate. For example, a record attendance of 20.4 million in 1960 was recorded for 620 member institutions.

To stem this rising tide, the NCAA membership in response adopted a new policy further extending its legislative jurisdictions and terminated its relationship with the Amateur Athletic Union (Falla, 1981, p. 243). Once again, the popularity of intercollegiate athletics grew and so did the amount of negative comments. During the 1970s Indiana basketball coach Bobby Knight frequently commented on the amount of corruption in sport. Many college sport leaders and administrators concluded that the only major for the student-athlete was eligibility.

TABLE 2. NCAA Historical Events

Year	Event
1939	First intercollegiate sports telecast. NBC, Columbia-Princeton baseball game.
1940	First football telecast, Pennsylvania versus Maryland.
1946	Conference of Conferences results in draft of ''Principles for the Conduct of Intercollegiate Athletics,'' held in Chicago.
1954	First telecast of national basketball finals.
1964	Division II football established.
1964	Special Committee on Women's Competition appointed.
1967	Committee appointed to study feasibility of women's intercollegiate athletics.
1968	Television contract guarantees several conferences a specific number of appearances.
1971	Drug Education Committee establishes national program to fight drug use by all students.
1973	Dacia Schileru, Wayne State University diver, first woman to compete in any NCAA championship.
1973	Three Divisions established.
1977	First four-year television contract, football, ABC.
1978	Membership votes to develop Division IA in football.
1980	Members vote to conduct championships in five Division II and III women's sports, commencing 1981–1982.
1981	Members vote to conduct championships in nine Division I women's sports, and cross-Division championships in fencing, golf, and lacrosse, commencing 1981–1982.

Sources: Falla, 1981; Rooney, 1987.

Athletes and athletic sponsors continue to exploit the system. Abundant evidence exists of illegal assistance provided to athletes from coaches, administrators, boosters, trustees, and even presidents (Guttmann, 1991, p. 21; Underwood, 1984).

College sports expanded in the late 1960s and early 1970s with the introduction of women's intercollegiate athletic programs. All NCAA deliberations prior to this time focused almost exclusively on programs for men (see Table 2). Representatives from numerous member institutions desired participation and competition alternatives for their women's athletic programs. Their demands were answered in 1975 when the NCAA membership considered the provision of athletic services and programs for women (Tow, 1982, p. 108). Throughout its history the NCAA has always been a force for reform.

The Role of the NCAA

Numerous scandals led to the call for an entity that would initiate and preserve order among higher education institutions that supported intercollegiate athletic teams (Sage, 1982, p. 131). Essentially, the original and main role of the NCAA was governance of intercollegiate athletics. As previously mentioned, part of the stated purpose of the NCAA was the supervision and regulation of intercollegiate athletics in the United States so that all activities would ''be maintained on an ethical plane in keeping with the dignity and high moral purpose of higher education'' (NCAA Proceedings, 1906, p. 29 as cited in Fleisher, Goff, and Tollison, 1992, p. 41). The membership was to provide advice to institutions, develop strategies for controlling violence, and establish standardized game rules (Sage, 1982, p. 132). Representatives from each of the individual member institutions were responsible for enforcing NCAA rules and regulations. Although most representatives agreed with these objectives and rules, after all they had developed them, few had any incentive to enforce them. Thus the organization often relied upon hearsay and the use of informants to uncover rules violations. The NCAA, however, lacked legal authority to punish transgressors and many escaped due to the numerous loopholes in the regulations (Sperber, 1990, pp. 246–247).

Prior to World War II, the NCAA discovered that an incentive problem existed because resolutions were consistently being violated by member institutions. Association leaders realized that a lack of adequate enforcement mechanisms was the source. These frustrations helped direct the NCAA to move toward considering active enforcement practices. According to Lawrence (1987, p. 26), the adoption of an enforcement function was hastened by four events: (1) the Carnegie Foundation's report, (2) the Great Depression, (3) increased football revenues, and (4) ''the failure of a comprehensive but voluntary 1934 code'' concerning the recruitment and subsidization of athletes. Thus World War II marked the occasion when the association was poised ''to change from consultative rules committee to a regulatory body with power to control and discipline'' members (Lawrence, 1987, pp. 21, 31).

During the 1950s the traditional role of consultant and advisor took a backseat as policies and programs were designed to enforce members' adherence to NCAA rules and regulations. The association assumed an inspection and monitoring role. Sanctions were employed when member institutions violated NCAA policies. As the commercialization of intercollegiate athletics increased dramatically, so did the size and power of the NCAA expand. A complex administrative network now began to develop with its own set of rules, laws, system of justice, and bureaucrats (Sage, 1982, p. 132).

Although the NCAA remained active in rule making and the organization of championship tournaments, it also took steps that have been associated with the establishment of a cartel (Lawrence, 1987, p. 38). A conscious decision had been made to evolve from a rule-making body into a trade-controlling cartel by subtly assuming greater powers (Fleisher, Goff, and Tollison, 1992, p. 35). According to economists, the NCAA is a cartel: an association of colleges and universities that was established to control marketing, production, and competition in intercollegiate athletics. Its unique administrative structure and reputable public image have allowed for the exploitation of numerous student-athletes. Rules and regulations are designed to benefit management and are frequently detrimental to student-athletes (Sage, 1982, p. 131). Policies effectively ''restrict output and restrict competition for inputs'' (Fleisher, Goff, and Tollison, 1992, p. 5). The NCAA has the power to set labor prices, regulate output quantity and quality, aggregate and distribute profits, and enforce sanctions for inappropriate behavior. The association enhances its public image and authority by ensuring competitive equality among member institutions (Frey, 1982, p. 106). For example, recruitment and financial aid regulations effectively transfer rewards from athletes to coaches and institutions. Simply stated, such regulations function as agreements ''among buyers to restrict competition for inputs'' (Fleisher, Goff, and Tollison, 1992, p. 5). Thus the organization of championship sporting events (see Table 3) has become the primary function of this highly effective conglomerate.

The National Collegiate Athletic Association is the oldest, best-known, most powerful, and most prestigious national organization that regulates intercollegiate athletics. More than 880 institutions, organizations, and conferences belong to this voluntary association. The association provides a forum for college and university representatives to discuss and develop strategies for addressing athletic issues at a national level (Tow, 1982, p. 108). Income is generated from four primary sources: television rights; gate receipts from national championships; grants, royalties, investments, and publishing; and membership dues and foundation profits. The annual operating budget for 1992–1993 was over $175–million (*Chronicle of Higher Education*, September 22, 1993).

Notwithstanding this extensive economic role, the association's current enforcement program is highly effective for a voluntary membership organization. Allegations of rules violations are referred to an investigative staff which conducts a preliminary investigation to determine whether an official inquiry is warranted. Institutional representatives receive prompt notification regarding all charges and may elect to appear on behalf of the institution before the Committee on Infractions (a five-member body consisting of representatives from member institutions). Committee findings and penalties are reported to the institution which may then appeal to the NCAA Council (Tow, 1982, p. 115). This zealous program, however, has also led to cries of unwarranted intrusiveness. Critics state that the NCAA infringes upon institutional autonomy by increasingly encompassing within its purview greater portions of the administrative and academic prerogatives of higher education institutions. The NCAA serves as the guardian of academic, administrative, and admission morals of its member institutions.

Key NCAA Legislation

One of the association's first actions was to establish the Football Rules Committee. The ultimate goal of this group was to eliminate dangerous plays and thus reduce the number of injuries by totally revising all college football rules. The great disparity between players—frequently resulting from the recruitment of

TABLE 3. First NCAA-Sponsored National Collegiate Championships

Year	Sport, Location
1921	Track and Field, Staff Field, University of Chicago
1928	Wrestling, Iowa State College, Ames
1937	Boxing, California Agricultural College, Davis
1937	Swimming, University of Minnesota
1938	Cross Country, Michigan State University, East Lansing
1938	Gymnastics, University of Chicago
1938	Tennis, Marion Cricket Club, Haverford, Pennsylvania
1939	Basketball, Northwestern University
1939	Golf, Wakonda Country Club, Des Moines, Iowa
1941	Fencing, Ohio State University, Columbus
1947	Baseball, Western Michigan University, Kalamazoo
1949	Ice Hockey, Broadmoor Ice Palace, Colorado Springs, Colorado
1954	Skiing, University of Nevada, Reno
1959	Soccer, University of Connecticut, Storrs
1965	Indoor Track, Cobo Hall, Detroit
1969	Trampoline, University of Michigan, Ann Arbor
1969	Water Polo, California State College, Long Beach
1970	Volleyball, University of California, Los Angeles
1971	Lacrosse, Hofstra University, Hempstead, New York
1980	Rifle, East Tennessee State University, Johnson City

Source: Adapted from Falla, 1981, pp. 182–200, 236–251.

ringers—was another aspect of the game requiring immediate attention. Besides contributing to the widespread injury problem, it was simply a matter of fairness and good competition. Thus was developed the first statement on player eligibility in 1906. Labeled the "Amateur Code," this piece of legislation addressed graduate student participation and the amateur-professional question (Lawrence, 1987, pp. 19–22). In 1916 the association adopted a resolution to petition the Carnegie Foundation to survey the current status of intercollegiate athletics. In 1918 the association recommended the recognition of athletic departments as bona fide collegiate departments whose administrators were responsible directly to institutional administration. It also recommended that all students be provided with time for physical training (Falla, 1981, p. 237). The association's popularity decreased among athletes in 1920 when a regulation was passed requiring permission to participate on teams other than those sponsored by the student's institution. Athletes who did not comply with the policy were to be ruled ineligible (Fleisher, Goff, and Tollison, 1992, p. 44).

Articulating a major change in philosophy by expanding upon the "altruistic original purposes," the association revised the constitution in 1921 and regulated conditions of athlete participation (Lawrence, 1987, p. 24). This regulatory role grew decade by decade. The Ten-Point Code, adopted in 1922, limited eligibility to three years, prohibited graduate student participation, and banned competition against non-member teams (Fleisher, Goff, and Tollison, 1992, p. 44). Recruitment and athlete subsidization codes, which were to be locally enforced, were adopted in the 1930s. The constitution was again revised to reflect specific standards for membership and additional executive regulations (Falla, 1981, p. 238). In the 1940, the NCAA added investigative and judicial functions to its legislative powers by enacting the Declaration of Sound Principles and Practices for Intercollegiate Athletics. According to Lawrence (1987, p. 33), these ''detailed and far-reaching'' rules were ''designed to decrease the cost of producing an athletic'' contest ''by limiting competition for student-athletes.'' This was an early attempt to ''control the entire conduct of intercollegiate athletics.'' Probably the best known legislation became the Sanity Code. This 1948 code restricted financial aid to student-athletes. It was the first attempt by the NCAA to couple rules on amateurism, financial aid, and eligibility with an enforcement mechanism by requiring that financial aid to student-athletes flow through the same channels that other students were compelled to follow. Section Five of the Sanity Code prohibited institutional officials from making financial aid offers to prospective athletes based solely upon their athletic ability. It also provided a mechanism for addressing violations (Fleisher, Goff, and Tollison, 1992, pp. 47–48). Section Four of the Sanity Code, which outlined what financial aid could entail (tuition and fees), was repealed in 1951.

In the early 1950s, the association proposed a Twelve-Point Plan. This reform plan provided institutional representatives with some basic strategies to combat negative public opinions about athletics and address pressures in intercollegiate athletics. Its intent was to eliminate abuses in sports and strengthen enforcement policies (Fleisher, Goff, and Tollison, 1992, p. 49). Included within the plan were proposals that limited the dollar amount and total number of athletic scholarships per institution, eliminated improper recruitment procedures and activities, mandated strict compliance to all NCAA rules and regulations, and punished athletes who received any type of subsidy (Lawrence, 1987, p. 50). Because the plan was to serve as the foundation for future legislation, it was reviewed by the presidents of all member institutions. Responses to the Twelve-Point Plan resulted in the adoption of constitutional amendments and additional legislation at the 1952 convention. Key areas included academic standards, conduct, financial aid, and off-season practice in basketball and football. The widespread popularity of television necessitated the establishment of a television committee. In 1952, committee members successfully limited the total number of televised games to 12 and negotiated a contract with a national television network (Fleisher, Goff, and Tollison, 1992, p. 52). It was also during this time that an enforcement committee was established. This committee was responsible for considering all reported charges of rules violations by member institutions. It was the establishment of this committee that marked the formal beginning of the association's enforcement program and additional associated powers (Tow, 1982, p. 115).

The prominent legislation adopted in the 1960s was the Five-Year Rule (1961) which required an athlete to complete three years of eligibility within five years after first entering an institution (Falla, 1981). The Five-Year Rule effectively limited the number of years that an athlete could be supported by scholarships; otherwise the concept of "redshirting" could continue indefinitely (Lawrence, 1987, p. 112). The first attempt to address academic standing occurred in 1965 when a rule passed that required a 1.60 grade point average of all student-athletes (Fleisher, Goff, and Tollison, 1992, p. 57). Although eligibility continued to be a critical issue throughout the 1970s, the primary concern was financial aid. However, the newly established Drug Education Committee addressed the use of recreational and performance enhancing drugs. It launched a national program to combat the use of drugs by all students. Other major legislation focused on freshman eligibility for all NCAA championships, strengthening of the enforcement program, elimination of the 1.60 legislation by adopting a 2.00 grade-point average for Division I athletes, and a resolution calling for the development of women's intercollegiate athletics (Falla, 1981).

A new wave of restrictive legislation combined with greater enforcement mechanisms characterized the 1980s (Fleisher, Goff, and Tollison, 1992, p. 60). For example, a commission composed of 44 presidents collectively developed Proposition 48, which required that all in-coming freshmen have studied a specific core curriculum, achieved an overall high school grade-point average of 2.0, and have a combined score of 700 on the verbal and mathematical sections of the SAT, or a score of 15 on the ACT, to be eligible for competition (Hanford, 1985, p. 368; Lapchick, 1989, p. 16). Freshman were labeled "qualifiers" if they met all of the criteria; "partial qualifiers" if they had a 2.00 grade point average in high school; and "nonqualifiers" otherwise. Never before had one piece of legislation resulted in more controversy and accusations of racial discrimination than were aroused over Proposition 48 (Atwell, 1985, pp. 392–393; Lapchick, 1989, p. 16). Small revisions were eventually made. For example, Proposition 42 was adopted to simplify Proposition 48 by eliminating the category of "partial qualifier." Finally, the quintessential example of increased enforcement powers came with the initiation of the Death Penalty. This legislation allowed the association to suspend an athletic program found guilty of repeated rules violations within a five-year period.

In summary, throughout NCAA history the majority of legislative actions have been focused in four areas: (1) athlete compensation, (2) methods of athlete recruitment, (3) definitions of eligibility, and (4) judicial and enforcement

TABLE 4. NCAA Rules, Regulations, and Reform Initiatives

Year	Legislation/Initiative
1922	10–Point Code. Key points: recommend member institutions organize into sectional conferences, abide by Association's amateur definition, adopt new freshman rule, limit eligibility to three years, end graduate student participation, suppress gambling, prohibit involvement with non-college teams, and maintain faculty control (p. 128).
1934	Code on athlete recruiting and subsidization adopted (p. 238).
1940	Executive committee assumes investigative and judicial responsibilities (p. 131).
1948	Sanity Code adopted. Regulation with enforcement mechanisms. Revised 1951 (p. 133).
1951	12–Point Code. Basis for NCAA's position regarding sport conduct at institutions (p. 135).
1952	Television policy endorsed. Members agree on ''program of limited live television'' to be controlled/directed by NCAA (p. 104).
1960	Letter-of-Intent program initiated.
1961	Five-Year Rule. Student-athletes had five years to complete their eligibility.
1965	1.600 Rule. Establishes academic criteria for award and retention of financial aid, limits practices and game competition, strengthens junior college transfer rule (p. 146).
1973	2.000 Rule. Ends use of prediction tables, sets 2.000 high school grade point average for an athlete to receive grants-in-aid (p. 147).
1974	Adopt resolution for development of women's intercollegiate athletics.
1981	Adopt governance plan to include women's programs. Results of five-year American College Testing Program study indicate that male student-athletes graduate at higher rates than non-athletes at member institutions.
1983	Proposition 48
1990	Knight Commission Report

Source: Falla, 1981, passim.

powers of the association (see Table 4). The main impetus for legislation has been and continues to be the demand for the activities provided by the NCAA as well as widespread rules violations. According to Edwin Cady (1978, pp. 169–170), ''the rules of conferences and the NCAA which govern intercollegiate athletics evolved on the same principles as English Common Law—from precedents established to meet specific cases.'' Although a realistic and widely employed method, it is also a reactive way of conducting business not a proactive one. Without a vision of how athletics should be conducted and governed, this method tends to result in massive code books of flexible, sometimes contradictory, and often meaningless procedures and regulations. It is virtually impossible for one athletic administrator to keep abreast of the legislative literature.

Unfortunately, because so many institutional representatives have and will continue to sidestep the rules, the NCAA will undoubtedly respond as it has in the past by writing more rules. If history is indicative of the impact of additional legislation, it also may be assumed that future rules will have the carefully orchestrated effects of decreasing operating costs while increasing profits, limiting athlete compensation, and further defining academic standards (Lawrence, 1987, p. 111).

Anatomy of the Reform Movement

Historically, whenever crisis, corruption, foul play, and unethical conduct become commonplace, there are calls for reform and moves toward stricter NCAA regulations (Rooney, 1987, p. 1; Tow, 1982, p. 120). For example, Columbia athletics were riddled with corruption in 1902. The dean of the law school, who was also the chair of the faculty committee for athletics, made a report to the president stating that the "illness of the football program was incurable." At the time a secret fund had been established to reimburse players for their expenses and to support an outstanding player that the faculty committee had disqualified (Guttmann, 1991, p. 25). Criticism of intercollegiate athletics continued in 1914 when John Savage voiced his grievances at the NCAA convention. He provided documentation for the alleged violations in the 1929 Carnegie report which to this day provides the most systematic empirical inquiry ever conducted into intercollegiate athletics. Drug abuse, the noneducation of athletes, and booming commercialization were all decried in the report.

Today, the problems and dilemmas of intercollegiate athletics are much the same. Because these problems arise from and affect various parties within the system, it is useful to categorize them based upon their level of origination. For example, commercialization and mass media pressures and distortions are, for the most part, focused at the national level. Whereas, low graduation rates, point-shaving, gambling, antisocial behavior, and use of performance-enhancing and other drugs seem to be focused more at the individual level. Hence, the root of the majority of problems lies at the institutional level. Some of these problems include alumni and booster interference, use of gate receipts and profits from the sale of athletic paraphernalia to construct new buildings, questions regarding racial bias, recruiting violations, low admission standards, grade fixing and transcript doctoring, empty courses created for athletes, inducements and payments to athletes, questionable agent-player relationships, lack of academic integrity, ambiguous status of coaches, and bribery (Fleisher, Goff, and Tollison, 1992, p. 4; MacAloon, 1991, p. 224; Rose, 1985, p. 143).

How did these numerous and troublesome problems arise? Some theorists suggest that it all began when athletics became a source of revenue, support, and visibility for the institution. When revenue and visibility are the goals of athletic participation, the focus shifts from supporting and developing the individual to a win at all costs mentality. The need to recruit top athletes becomes paramount; the means to secure these individuals are of lesser concern. Thus athletic success is placed above educational achievement because of the dramatic effect it can have on an institution's image. Blame, therefore, should be placed not at the individual level, but at the institutional and organizational levels. The numerous problems with intercollegiate athletics cannot be traced to one individual or group; they are the result of a flawed system in which principles and values are neither aligned with the organizational structure nor function as the basis for decision making (Sack, 1982, p. 80). Hardy and Berryman (1982, p. 15) suggest that the scandals that rocked numerous institutions of higher education during the late 1970s and early 1980s (e.g., altered transcripts, empty courses, slush funds) have caused many people to raise questions about the effectiveness of current governance structures and organizational methods. These complaints are not new, however. For more than a century, critics have continually stressed that intercollegiate competition was running afoul, and in addition to suggesting stricter controls, have called for new administrative structures in order to reunite athletics and academics.

The latest environmental force contributing to corruption in intercollegiate athletics is the poor condition of the national economy. The majority of program administrators face dire financial constraints due to tax-limiting legislation, the growth of women's programs, a reduction in the amount of leisure time, and fewer charitable contributions (Frey, 1985). They find themselves competing with television and professional sports for desperately needed revenue and with one another to recruit the most talented athletes essential for building winning teams. Funding shortfalls have contributed to unethical practices involving recruitment, subsidization, and care of athletes. As rules violations increase so do calls for stronger enforcement programs. These recurring circumstances continue to haunt the NCAA, who thought the issue had been addressed after identification in the 1929 Carnegie report, and again during the early 1950s; yet it remains unresolved (Hanford, 1982, p. 44). Given the numerous and widespread allegations of unethical conduct, inequality, racism, discrimination, lack of academic rigor, and illegal financial dealings, it is difficult to support the further development of intercollegiate sport programs (Frey, 1982, p. 115).

In summary, none of the problems that plague intercollegiate athletics today is new. There is ample evidence to demonstrate that the prominent issues of today have been a cause of concern for over a century. The major differences between the issues arising in the 1900s and now stem from the following forces: the introduction of television, the prominence of basketball, the induction of state and junior colleges into the system, and the notion of African-American youths as "special objects of recruitment" (MacAloon, 1991, p. 225). Three issues that have been controversial since the inauguration of intercollegiate athletics will be explored further. These issues are amateurism versus professionalism, athlete exploitation, and cost control. Once these have been addressed, the contemporary athletic scene will be examined.

Amateurism versus Professionalism

''Like certain other aspects of the antique ideal of the gentleman, 'amateurism' was killed by the democratization of the culture. It is now mainly a source of frustration and misplaced rage as applied to American intercollegiate athletics'' (Cady, 1978, p. 215). Edwin Cady (1978, p. 218) continues to berate the notion that amateurism exists in intercollegiate athletics at the Division I level by describing the *Manual of the National Collegiate Athletic Association* as a ''logical phantasmagoria which represents the collective effort, over decades, of earnest, intelligent men, men of deep professional dedication and good will, to design a workable sense for 'amateurism.''' The manual is full of contradictions and absurdities regarding the amateur status of intercollegiate athletes. The time has come to replace the concept of an amateur because it has not been appropriate for more than six decades.

Roger G. Noll (1991) suggests that institutions of higher education be allowed to pay their athletes. He agrees with Cady that the notion of an amateur is not only inappropriate but ludicrous in the 20th century. During the 1800s, when a truer version of the amateur existed, society's elite had time for sports because they did not need to earn a living. In contrast, it was the inferior, lower classes who had no time for sport. Today, everyone must earn a living and employment is a part of the lives of most college students (Andre and James, 1991, pp. 11–12). Therefore it seems ridiculous to maintain this ancient ideal. Institutions could treat their athletes like work-study students or staff and pay them. Senator Bill Bradley is another supporter of paying college athletes who play major sports in top intercollegiate programs. These individuals are professionals, and as such, should be paid to play. They need not be students, but could attend classes if they so desired (Simon, 1991, p. 58). There is, however, a lot of opposition to such proposals because the pressure to compromise academic standards would still exist. This issue could be eliminated by not insisting that athletes be students, and by transforming men's football and basketball into minor league programs. Rooney (1987, p. 176) suggests the development of semiprofessional or minor leagues designed to meet the needs of individuals interested in athletics not academics.

> There is a practical solution to the ethical and economic problems which plague big-time athletics: separate the athletic function, the revenue sports, from the traditional form of university control and allow a select group of collegiate football and basketball teams to become second-order, or minor league if you prefer, professional franchises located in the university communities. . . . By professionalizing big-time

football and basketball and methods of player acquisition, both the distasteful aspects of recruiting and the unethical practices so often associated with maintaining athletes on campus would be eliminated. (Rooney, 1987, p. 178)

Athlete Exploitation

As early as 1890, athletic recruits were characterized as young men who enrolled in college in order to exhibit their athletic talent as opposed to their academic skills. Student-athletes, then and now, became ''media celebrities and valuable pieces of property'' as college athletic programs became dependent upon exposure and positive public relations for profit and ultimately for their survival (Sojka, 1985, p. 25). Unfortunately, ''the fact that fewer African-American student athletes actually earn degrees'' has resulted in charges ''that they are 'paid gladiators' expected to win games and to bring notoriety and money to an institution which excludes them from social life and serious academic pursuits'' (Sojka, 1985, p. 24). For decades athletes have been tempted to enroll in institutions of higher education by coaches, alumni, boosters, and other institutional representatives who extol the value of sports as a ladder for upward economic and social mobility. This argument has been especially successful with African-American athletes, and used to exploit their talents on the field, track, and court. African-American athletes are frequently more vulnerable than white athletes to abusive practices as socialization and racial discrimination continue to contribute to disproportionate representation of African-Americans among top athletes. Although African-Americans comprise only 12 percent of nation's population, they account for 35 percent of all college football and basketball players. Also, success in athletics appears to be more valued in African-American communities because it can provide an escape route from poverty and the ghetto, but only for some (Simon, 1991, pp. 54–56).

Student-athletes continue to agree informally to a contract with the institutions they attend which allows them to exchange athletic performance for an education. Although the athletes usually keep their part of the bargain, the institutions frequently do not. Whereas state support for higher education has been declining, institutions with successful athletic programs continue to build their coffers through revenue sharing, ticket and paraphernalia sales, and charitable contributions which all depend upon the performances of their athletes, of whom a disproportionate number tend to be of African-American descent (Edwards, 1985, p. 373). Institutions of higher education must be accountable for providing all of their student-athletes, especially their minority athletes, with the skills to succeed in society. Positive athletic experiences can provide shelter from culture shock, while simultaneously allowing African-American athletes to remain in touch with their culture. These athletes are students as well, and as such must be equipped to succeed in the mainstream American culture (Cady, 1978, pp. 186–187).

Cost Control

As previously mentioned, intercollegiate athletics are big business. The combination of profits from television rights, football and basketball gate receipts, and sales of brand name paraphernalia can result in revenues that approach $15 to $20 million annually. Many programs benefit from the millions received in alumni contributions. Boosters also raise a great deal of money for athletic departments by soliciting gifts and sponsoring various promotions. These funds are often used to subsidize coaches' salaries, entertain prospective and current athletes, provide cars for coaches and athletes, and influence politicians and media representatives when necessary (Frey, 1985, p. 117). Many head coaches who reportedly receive six-figure salaries earn additional money from outside endorsements and television programs. Thus the possible rewards for successful basketball and football performances are indeed immense. Coaches and other institutional officials face numerous temptations to sidestep rules and regulations. On the flip side, athlete remuneration has remained at the in-kind level of tuition, fees, and room and board. Thus while coaches and institutions prosper, athletes purposefully do not (Fleisher, Goff, and Tollison, 1992, pp. 4–5). Two of the most frequently broken collegiate athetic rules are those that forbid paying athletes and therefore hinder the recruitment and retention of the most talented players, and those that make academic demands on athletes, which limits the potential pool of players to select from (Noll, 1991, pp. 11, 197). Because institutions of higher education are non-profit, academic organizations, many unethical and profit-motivated behaviors remain unnoticed (Fleisher, Goff, and Tollison, 1992, pp. 4–5). During the 1980s, the cost crisis in intercollegiate athletics stemmed from reforms designed to control athletic empires and reunite them with the intellectual community. Numerous steps taken to effect control have also affected program costs. Some of the actions taken to reduce program costs include: (1) limiting the amount and number of athletic grants; (2) abolishing slush funds for coaches, and prohibiting the creation of foundation or other accounts for gift monies in support of athletics—such accounts are now subject to regular institutional procedures of disbursement and reporting; (3) instituting departments of athletics rather than separate athletic divisions—this action usually entailed the abolition or co-optation of the student athletic fees; and (4) requiring all students, including athletes, to pay an athletic fee (Cady, 1978, pp. 197–198). Procedures to control costs were instituted when the NCAA began to offer the services of financial specialists to member institutions for purposes of auditing program expenditures and methods of accounting (Fleisher, Goff, and Tollison, 1992, p. 62).

The Contemporary Scene

Reform discussions that had begun in the 1980s continued with release of the 1990 Knight Commission Report. This relatively biased report (16 of the 22 commission members were either current or former board members or presidents of member institutions) has been described as another attempt at internal reform with the appearance of external validity. The authors of the report cited four primary areas to be targeted for initial movement toward reform. These included: (1) presidential control, (2) academic integrity, (3) fiscal management, and (4) independent certification. The authors specifically recommended that presidents assume greater responsibility for implementing policies and controlling finances, that revenue generated from athletics be deposited into general accounts, that annual audits be conducted, that institutions be accountable for the academic progress of their athletes, that athlete graduation rates be representative of the general student population, that the administration of athletic departments be aligned with institutional mission, and that a new governance structure for intercollegiate athletics be put into place. Overall, the report seems to serve the same basic function as other internal reform efforts: it became a marketing tool. The recommendations in no way began to resolve the issues of athlete eligibility, athlete compensation, or unethical behavior (Fleisher, Goff, and Tollison, 1992, pp. 159–160; Lederman, 1991; Lucas and Smith, 1978).

Representatives from member institutions anticipated that the 1991 convention would result in the enactment of landmark reforms. Presidents and administrators were expected to provide the leadership necessary to produce sweeping reform. Unfortunately, the only changes that occurred were minor and insignificant. Scholarships were reduced by 10 percent, and reductions were made in coaching staffs and paid visits to athletes. Additional restrictions were made on competition departure and return times. Minimum sport participation was increased, minimum financial aid standards were established, restrictions were placed on daily and weekly practice times, incoming freshman were prohibited from receiving summer scholarships, athletic dorms are to be eliminated by 1996, training table meals are to be reduced to one per day by 1996, and members agreed to allow the United States Olympic Committee to pay athletes for training expenses (Fleisher, Goff, and Tollison, 1992, p. 156). Once again bandaids and silver bullets were applied without substantive changes being made. Reformers' dreams of large-scale organizational changes were dashed.

At the 1993 convention, legislation was again proposed to soften Proposition 48. Convention delegates defeated the proposal that would have allowed students who did not qualify under Proposition 48 a fourth season of eligibility. Other convention results included the following: (1) flexible coach/recruit telephone contact legislation, (2) provisions for Division I basketball games on the first Friday after Thanksgiving, (3) prohibitions against athletic department staff acting as recruit consultants or scouts, (4) game limit exemptions for Division I hockey teams in order to scrimmage the U.S. Olympic hockey team, and (5) redefinition of the minimum sports requirements for Division I (*Denver Post*, January 16, 1993, p. 9D). The obvious focus of the legislation is on Division I athletic programs, and the obvious outcome will undoubtedly be more rules violations and a need for greater enforcement strategies. Piecemeal legislation targeted at symptoms rather their their causes reigned once again.

According to Edwin Cady (1978, p. 178) "the true frontier of intercollegiate athletics in our times is sexual. There a revolution has long been churning in the deeps of American women's culture, altering emotions, images, hopes, intention, beliefs." Although slightly premature in his predictions, gender equity undoubtedly will be the major focus of future NCAA conventions. Especially with the numerous court cases regarding program cancellations (Blum, April 28, 1993, p. A35; Lederman, May 5, 1993, p. A38), coaching salaries (Blum, July 7, 1993, p. A45), and other allegations of sex bias (Lederman, April 15, 1992, pp. A43–A44; Lederman, May 26, 1993, pp. A31–A32). The key question to be addressed by athletic directors is: What percentage of the athletic budget should be allocated to women's programs? Presently, most Division I institutions allocate approximately 70 percent of the budget for men's programs, with football being the largest consumer and revenue producer. A special task force has been assigned to prepare legislation that changes the allocation ratios, providing women with a greater share of the funds (*Denver Post*, January 16, 1993, p. 9D). Additional recommendations may include increasing the number of scholarships for women in Division I and II sports, offering more championships for women by reducing the minimum number of sponsoring institutions required before the NCAA establishes a national championship, and clearly defining gender equity as it relates to intercollegiate athletics (*Chronicle of Higher Education*, May 5, 1993, p. A38). In addition to gender equity, issues of racial and ethnic equality are likely to crop up at future conventions. Several African-American coaches are criticizing the system for exploiting the talents of African-American athletes and not providing sufficient opportunities for them in return. Future reforms may continue to address equity from multiple perspectives.

Future Directions

> Efforts to reform intercollegiate sport's abuses have paralleled the record of their improprieties. Rules governing play, recruiting, and eligibility have been adopted with the express purpose of promoting fair and equal playing opportunities within the educational setting. Generally reform efforts have taken place within an extraorganizational setting. Colleges and universities have not, for the most part, been able to autonomously make the changes perceived as necessary for intercollegiate sport. (Chu, Segrave, and Becker, 1985, p. 361)

Can anything be done? For more than 100 years scandals have been documented and reforms have been proposed, yet the number of abuses in intercollegiate athletics continues to grow. Critical issues have never been completely resolved by faculty committees, athletic conferences, the NCAA, regional and voluntary accrediting agencies, or any other entity. Who then, can be relied upon to bring about the long overdue, much-needed reform in intercollegiate athletics? Reform is a professional problem. Similar to other academic problems, it must be initiated by individual experts in the field. For reform to be effective it must be led by administrators and other representatives of competitive sports (Scott, 1982, p. 34). The place to begin is the individual campus. Institutional leaders must ensure that students who are not adequately prepared are not admitted, that eligible athletes are the only ones who participate, that NCAA regulations are strictly observed, and that educational assistance is provided as appropriate (Bok, 1985). Dominance exercised by some alumni and boosters will have to be addressed, if institutional control is to be a reality. This is particularly true for Division I institutions with large athletic operations that demand tremendous amounts of resources because they are frequently dependent upon booster support for survival (Frey, 1985, p. 119). Although reform efforts must begin at the institutional level, they can next be extended to the elementary and secondary school level. The establishment of a required core curriculum for freshman eligibility is a message to secondary educators that higher education officials demand that athletes receive adequate academic preparation. It is imperative that all parties work together to change a system which currently results in the exploitation of young bodies and simultaneous abandonment of their minds (Atwell, 1985, p. 394).

In summary, throughout the history of organized sport in this country various groups have attempted to chip away at the problems underlying intercollegiate competition by applying bandaids and silver bullets. Instead, what is needed is a complete overhaul of the current system (Rooney, 1987). All stakeholders must be involved in a process that results in the creation of an effective structure focused on the development and growth of the individual.

Can Meaningful Reform Be Accomplished?

The desired outcome of legislation passed during the 1980s was the restoration of academic credibility and the control of deviance. The effectiveness of these measures, however, may be limited because intercollegiate athletic leaders have failed to address the underlying fundamental issue, which is the incongruence between the values of higher education and the values of big-time intercollegiate athletics. Additional legislation and stricter enforcement procedures will continue to result in the development of new ways to beat the system. Change will occur only when the value structure of sports is addressed. If intercollegiate athletic leaders are to effectively control deviance in their programs, they cannot depend solely on increased NCAA regulations and expanded NCAA enforcement. They will need to devise and implement strategies that develop and strengthen ethical values at all levels of the intercollegiate athletic organization (Santomier and Cautilli, 1985, pp. 397, 403).

Several theorists have made other suggestions that could be pursued simultaneously. For example, Simon (1991, pp. 59–60) suggests that all institutions conform to Division III rules where athletes do not receive special financial aid packages. Students would select an institution based upon her or his individual educational needs. Institutional representatives would not recruit athletes, and athletic talent would be viewed as only one aspect applicable in the admissions process. In this system, athletes would be viewed as academically qualified students who are expected to make satisfactory progress, and graduate with meaningful academic skills. ''A purely amateur system would represent a purification, a cleansing, and a return to past values'' (Rooney, 1987, p. 175). There are several additional ways to emphasize the priority of educational goals. First would be the abolition of commercial football, which would successfully exclude quasi-professional athletes from campuses. Fans, however, would probably turn their attention to another sport. Second, the establishment of a defined continuum to compensate athletes for their services. This would naturally require a change in NCAA policy. And, third, separation of sports from colleges altogether. Athletic teams could be sponsored by local clubs and existing organizations that could then elect to affiliate with an institution or remain independent (Lawrence, 1987, pp. 144–148). Rooney (1987, p. 164) has also suggested developing an athletics continuum ranging from institutions that do not offer sports, to those in which control has been removed from the institution, to institutions that offer professional programs. Other suggestions include the adoption of regional recruiting formats based upon distance, implementation of need-based aid programs, and the abolition of scholarships for athletes participating in non-revenue sports.

Regardless of agreed-upon reform strategies, it must be recognized that intercollegiate athletics has much to offer participants and non-participants alike. Well-organized programs help students to develop a sound body to accompany a sound mind. ''Athletics partakes of art, teaches courage, informs us of and disciplines us to the price and rewards of excellence. It gives us pleasure, helps us to shape our ideals and our values, and is not incidentally good for our bodies. Let us keep athletics in perspective'' (Atwell, 1985, p. 395). Athletic programs hold a place in the educational enterprise that is not simply legitimate, but essential.

Reevaluation, Reflection, and Restructuring

The majority of ''big-time'' intercollegiate athletic programs are currently in the midst of crisis. Fingers are being pointed at presidents and other institutional leaders for not supporting reform efforts and often ignoring them entirely (Nyquist, 1985, p. 111). Administrators and other officials of ''big-time'' athletic programs need to update themselves regarding the culture and subcultures in which the activities they support are functioning. Programs must be independent from the media and other commercializing entities. A fresh reconciliation between athletics and academe is essential (Cady, 1978, p. 233).

College life is enriched through sports participation. This tends to be the case for the non-revenue-producing sports. However, few college students are involved in these activities. There is also the issue of accessibility and equity. The peculiar features of revenue-producing sports must be reevaluated to determine if they are what college sport is all about (Andre and James, 1991, pp. 2–3). A meaningful reform of intercollegiate athletics will require major changes in national governing legislation to span the gap that currently exists between athletics and academics. These two entities must be reunited; otherwise it is doubtful whether meaningful reform will ever be achieved (Bailey and Littleton, 1991). To accomplish this it will be necessary to conduct an honest strategic planning process that allows individuals to evaluate the current status and future needs required for successful administration of intercollegiate athletic programs.

Administrators of intercollegiate athletic programs have recently been challenged by dramatic increases in popularity, attendance, and revenues. In spite of this renewed support, the future of the NCAA seems tenuous at best. Leaders of member institutions have weakened the NCAA's one-time stable facade. Institutional leaders are looking out for number one. This behavior is becoming more common. It was observed when Oklahoma and Georgia challenged the "one-size-fits-all" television package created by the NCAA. More recently, Notre Dame decided that the network television package provided by the College Football Association was inadequate for the Fighting Irish. All of this behavior demonstrates the weak bonds holding the NCAA together. Additionally, many athletes have decided to leave college prior to graduating. They are accepting illegal payments and dropping out to enter national drafts. Unless college and university officials address these issues, Congress and state legislatures will undoubtedly answer the call. Many legislators have already expressed a desire to remedy intercollegiate athletic issues. Fleisher, Goff, and Tollison (1992, p. 13) attribute the growth of these currents in college athletics to the forces and competition that occur within a cartel. Thus, although reforms have occurred within college athletics, strategies are often developed by members of the association. The lack of participation in decision making by numerous stakeholders has resulted in increased NCAA power and maintenance of its authoritarian position. Unfortunately, reform strategies that have originated from outside constituents seem to have resulted in strengthening of the NCAA's cartel power as well (Fleisher, Goff, and Tollison, 1992, p. 160).

The present structure of the NCAA, with all of its discontinuities, ambiguities, and inadequacies, does not and cannot be made to work. The record of the past century demonstrates that a new start is needed and long overdue in intercollegiate athletics. Therefore, renewal will entail the following activities: (1) clarification of values and intentions; (2) identification of new methods for finding talent and freeing it to lead, manage, and organize sound programs; (3) implementation of a policy review to determine which rules support the desired system and which are detrimental—many may be thrown out entirely (this aspect also includes rewriting charters and constitutions); and (4) restructuring and/or dissolution of present organizations so that they truly serve the client which in the case of intercollegiate athletics is the athlete and not the institution. Those who develop new structures must consider the relationships between sports, "big-time" programs, and academic life (Cady, 1978, pp. 223–224). The reform essays in *Rethinking College Athletics* (1991, pp. 10, 56–57) provide several principles to guide the development of strategies that address intercollegiate athletic problems: (1) the individual must be respected, (2) the distinct aspects of sport must be protected, (3) structures that build upon and enhance an athlete's self-esteem and motivation to achieve at high levels must be established, (4) the educational value of athletic competition must be acknowledged, and (5) the integrity of institutions of higher learning must be upheld. Each of these principles protects something of vital importance in preserving and promoting healthy intercollegiate athletic programs.

V. THE CONTEMPORARY STUDENT-ATHLETE

> Intercollegiate athletics must enrich the academic mission, not negate it, and we found in our study, places where sports do still serve the student, not the other way around. We found institutions where sports are put in the proper perspective and where the predominant attitude toward athletics among the students is one of playfulness.
>
> —Ernest Boyer in *Campus Life: In Search of Community* (1990, p. 59)

More than 20 million young people participate in sport programs in this country. At the high school level, there are 3.3 million male participants (953,506 play football, 505,130 play basketball) and 1.8 million female participants (Lapchick, 1989). According to a National Collegiate Athletic Association (1990) survey of administrators in 780 active member institutions, 171,361 men participated in 23 intercollegiate athletic programs during the 1986–1987 academic year and 82,979 women participated in 20 intercollegiate athletic programs. Clarence Underwood (1984, p. 3) estimates that more than 500,000 students at both two-year and four-year institutions participate in intercollegiate athletic programs each year. Athletic programs provide exposure for institutions; they are a source of institutional pride, and can create campus unity. Although many student-athletes expect to become professional athletes, the majority aspire merely to participate in programs administered by competent coaches in which they can develop to their full potential. The student-athletes at institutions today are representative of every state and territory, including both urban and rural areas. The average age is 20, with a range from 17 to 24. Anglo students comprise the majority of student-athletes, with African-American and other minority group members completing the balance of the population (Underwood, 1984, p. 14).

Since the NCAA rule change in 1973, there has been an increase in the number of "marginal student athletes" (Underwood, 1984, p. 18). The stereotypic marginal student-athlete is generally a male football or basketball player between the ages of 17 and 19 from a major urban area. He is generally of African-American descent and attended a large high school; he is of average intelligence, characterized as an athletic overachiever and an academic underachiever, reads below grade level, has difficulty in classes, and fears exams. He is motivated by the ideal of the professional athlete, believing that his sport will lead to financial rewards, not academic ones. Conversely, the nonmarginal student-athlete is more convinced that participation in his or her sport can provide the opportunity to obtain an education (Underwood, 1984, pp. 3, 14, 17–18). Most marginal student-athletes fail to complete their collegiate athletic careers, are excluded from entering the professional ranks, and lack the knowledge and skills necessary to pursue other endeavors (Lapchick, 1989, p. 12).

Social Aspects

Social development and the acquisition of personal skills necessary for successful living are as much a part of a quality college education as the acquisition of knowledge. Sports are environmentally cultivated and provide opportunities to satisfy the human drives for recognition and achievement. Although many student-athletes (especially football and basketball players) report that they receive special treatment and recognition from the local community, they also report that it is difficult for them to take advantage of many personal growth opportunities (Center for the Study of Athletics, 1989, p. 61). Rader (1983) describes the extreme fatigue and isolation of year-round student-athletes who end up with skewed social lives and jeopardized grades. Sperber (1990) concurs that time constraints make it virtually impossible for most college athletes to also be bona fide students. Reviewing the literature, Chu, Segrave, Becker (1985) found evidence "that athletes are generally less well prepared for college" and performed less well academically, especially in the case of black male scholarship football and basketball players (p. 218). Whereas studies indicate no difference in intellectual capacity between athletes and nonathletes, in general, student-athletes are said to "possess more desirable personality traits and enjoy greater peer status than do nonathletes" (Stevenson, 1985, pp. 252, 253). Researchers who conducted personality studies of student-athletes concluded that they tend to be outgoing, confident, dominant, and tolerant of physical pain. Although more research is needed on the socialization of the student-athlete, "the overall picture pertaining to personality traits is positive" (Underwood, 1984, p. 14).

Stevenson (1985), after a voluminous review of pertinent literature, found no evidence that college athletics have any effect on personality characteristics. Although coaches believe that sports develop certain desirable social values (e.g., kindness, cooperation, truthfulness, courage, loyalty, friendliness) among participating athletes, much controversy exists over whether sports build character (Stevenson, 1985, pp. 249, 255). This may be due to the observation that some of the more talented athletes seem to disregard rules of etiquette, appropriate conduct, and sportsmanship. They do, however, appear to display more discipline, aggressiveness, courage, and competitive spirit than nonathletes (Underwood, 1984, pp. 7–8). Sage (1982, 1985) found that, if anything, sports tend to condition athletes to prevailing social structures and conformism, preparing them for successful living in a bureaucracy. Many coaches view team members "as objects in a machine-like environment who need to be conditioned to perform prescribed, fragmented tasks as instrumental to team performance" (Sage, 1985, p. 278). Andre and James (1991, p. 47) raise the point that athletic competition may not cause positive personality traits to develop and that "it may well be the other way around . . . rather than developing character by participating in sports, those with certain personal characteristics tend to be successful athletes."

Educational Aspects

Reports written for the Carnegie Foundation in 1929 and 1933 stressed the overemphasis of intercollegiate sport which distracted from the legitimate purposes of higher education. Critics argued that "sport was outside of the proper domain of higher education's institutional responsibilities" (Chu, 1989, p. 35). Intercollegiate athletics continue to be rocked by revelations of academic compromises made in the interests of institutions and their athletes. "Abuses and infractions of NCAA rules associated with student-athletes" . . . "are a source of national embarrassment to prominent universities" (Underwood, 1984, p. xi). Some of the unethical practices that have been revealed include falsified transcripts, credit for imaginary courses, and exploitation of student-athletes. At issue is the relationship between sport and the educational process (Purdy, Eitzen, and Hufnagel, 1985, p. 221; Ogilvie and Tutko, 1985).

Purdy, Eitzen, and Hufnagel (1985, pp. 223, 230–231) suggest that student-athletes have a disadvantage educationally due to their sports commitments. They found that over a 10-year period at one major university that athletes were poorly prepared to enter higher education, had lower grade point averages, and graduated in fewer numbers than nonathletes.

> The seamy side of this whole sordid business, of course, is its effect on the young person at issue, and we are now only beginning to understand what might be called the

> plight of the student athlete. Sought out almost entirely for athletic ability alone, seeing his persona reduced in the media to an almost commercial array of statistics, the prospect more often than not will hear little about the educational possibilities and expectations of this or that institution. (Bailey and Littleton, 1991, p. 50)

Historically, it has been the NCAA Division I football and basketball programs that have attracted the most publicity regarding rule violations (Bailey and Littleton, 1991, p. x). Although abuses appear to be more common and serious among Division I NCAA member institutions, violations also occur in Division II and III programs, "where the opportunity for corruption may be enhanced because of relative neglect by NCAA enforcement attention" (Bailey and Littleton, 1991, p. 22). Perhaps Division III institutions are not the last bastion of athletic purity, but they come much closer than Division I institutions in attempting to meet the individual needs of their student-athletes. Academic achievement by athletes in the non-revenue sports is similar to that of the general student population. Additionally, female athletes and nonathletes perform at approximately the same academic level (Purdy, Eitzen, and Hufnagel, 1985, p. 231). Several studies indicate that athletes graduate at rates equal to those of nonathletes. Michener (1976, p. 297) reported that of the 223 male athletes at Stanford who participated during the 1969–70 academic year in baseball, basketball, football, swimming, and track, 88.3 percent graduated compared with 82.5 percent of the total student body. In a 1975 NCAA study conducted by the American College Testing Program, it was determined that the graduation rate of student-athletes was slightly higher than that of nonathletes for the male population that entered higher education institutions in the fall of 1968. Bowlus (1975) conducted a study, using a sample of Indiana University graduates, that focused on the effect of college on both athletes and nonathletes. He found that the athletes surveyed were earning equivalent or higher salaries than were the college nonathletes.

Other studies, however, yield different conclusions. Michigan State released figures which show that only 51 percent of its athletic-scholarship men graduated with their class (Michener, 1976, p. 297). A study conducted at the University of New Mexico (1980) revealed a graduation rate of 21 percent for football players (Purdy, Eitzen, and Hufnagel, 1985, p. 222). NCAA leaders tend to place partial blame for overall low graduation rates on basketball and football athletes who leave school early to pursue professional contracts (Sperber, 1990, p. 299). Although there appears to be a problem with low graduation rates in the sport of basketball, there is a lack of data on this topic. Many institutions keep this information confidential because the results could be used against them in recruiting. African-American athletes, however, appear to suffer the most. Whereas graduation rates for African-American students are approximately 31 percent (which is lower than that of their Anglo counterparts), graduation rates for African-American football and basketball players is around 20 percent. Although popular majors for those achieving degrees include physical education, communications, and athletic administration, there are few jobs available in these fields. Additionally, only 3 to 5 percent of all head coaching positions are held by African-Americans (Lapchick, 1989, p. 13). In summary, it seems that low graduation rates are more likely a greater concern for marginal student-athletes, those that enter professional drafts prior to graduation (Denlinger and Shapiro, 1975), and African-American football and basketball players (Underwood, 1984, p. 29).

Institutional Responsibilities

Many student-athletes report that it is difficult to give top priority to their academic work and get the grades they are capable of achieving due to extreme tiredness or exhaustion. The institution is demonstrating a lack of regard for the welfare of the student-athlete and the centrality of education in its mission when a student-athlete is required to reach his/her full athletic potential without regard to whether the individual has the time or the energy to meet the minimal academic requirements to maintain eligibility. A recent study conducted by the NCAA revealed that basketball and football players spend more time preparing for and participating in their sports than studying for and attending classes. Most athletes cannot spend this amount of time each week on sport and also spend an equal amount of time on academic work. Few will experience success under this type of regimen (Sperber, 1990, pp. 302, 305–306). Additionally, another great disservice occurs when coaches and administrators assist athletes by providing shortcuts and special treatment. At some universities, the student-athletes have someone register them for classes, purchase the required texts, and in some cases even attend classes for them. This perpetuates an attitude of self-importance when student-athletes are not required to follow institutional regulations that pertain to the rest of the student body.

Academic support programs are developing rapidly across the nation. These programs are designed to meet the academic needs of student-athletes (e.g., the University of Texas at Austin requires its student-athletes to enroll in study hours where tutors are present). Tutoring and counseling are the main tools that institutions are using to prepare athletes that are marginal students. Critics of such efforts charge that equitable programs are unavailable for other students, and that favoritism continues to be pervasive when it comes to the student-athlete (Lederman, 1991, p. A1). It is therefore essential that institutional leaders create an environment that features effective communication about policies and regulations regarding support services for students; social and academic development opportunities for students; protection, health, and welfare of students; and respect for the individual (Bailey and Littleton, 1991, p. 87).

Drug use and abuse is another issue requiring the attention of institutional leaders. They must do everything within their means to deter drug use and abuse by student-athletes, indeed by the entire study body. Widespread consumption of alcohol is common on many campuses and serious problems have been known to coincide with alcohol abuse by students. This responsibility also lies with the student-athlete who must resist temptations to use illicit drugs, including those that enhance athletic performance. Ethical behavior and community values must be inherent throughout the institution to promote health and the general welfare of the student-athlete.

Institutional leaders need to provide student-athletes with opportunities to adjust culturally and socially once on campus or it will be difficult to meet their educational needs (Bailey and Littleton, 1991, pp. 51, 90–91, 122). If a student-athlete is allowed to remain at an institution even one year without the institution attempting to improve her or his academic situation, then exploitation is the result. This recently occurred at Creighton University, where Kevin Ross managed to compete on the varsity basketball team for four years, yet was unable to read at a first-grade level. Those in charge of athletic programs must prevent these student-athletes from "walking the streets" uneducated and unemployed once their four years of eligibility are over (Underwood, 1984, p. 27).

Overall, the majority of intercollegiate athletes (those in non-revenue sports and participants at small liberal arts institutions) are truly student-athletes who exhibit the traditional values associated with sport. On the other hand, their counterparts in the big-time sport institutions have been severely compromised in the battle for revenue acquisition. Incidents of unethical conduct have embarrassed representatives of these institutions and will continue to do so until athletic officials reevaluate their responsibilities to students who are also athletes. Athletic administrators seem to be reaching consensus regarding the feasibility of treating athletes just like regular students (Lederman, May 1, 1991, p. A31). They need to collaborate with academic leaders to develop positive, supportive programs that help student-athletes develop the values of loyalty, self-discipline, responsibility, and fairness, in addition to promoting academics and humanistic qualities. Sports must contribute to the central mission of the institution; student-athletes cannot be sacrificed in the name of institutional exposure and revenue acquisition. All athletes should have the opportunity to be students first, not just the those participating in non-revenue sports and small programs. For the sake of the student-athlete, it is time for all institutional leaders to verbalize and model a commitment to simultaneous excellence in academics and athletics.

VI. TOWARD FUNDAMENTAL CHANGE

> The concept of reform certainly isn't a new one in intercollegiate athletics. From abolition of the lethal "flying wedge" formation to contemporary demands for academic integrity, we have seen improvements. But too frequently over the de-

> cades, mere changes in rules have been labeled as reforms when, at best, they have been only refinement or clarifications. At worst, they have obscured understanding and perpetuated the myth that more and more regulations are the answer. We have been tinkering at the margins instead of getting at the core of reform.
>
> —John DiBiaggio, "Our Last, Best Chance for Athletic Reform," *College Board Review* (Spring 1992, p. 26)

The next ten years present a unique opportunity for faculty, administrators, and trustees to shake off the lethargy of inaction and become active change agents in a dynamic process to redefine the role of intercollegiate sports. No longer are game results and end-game statistics the only front page news. Media attention has abundantly revealed the endemic illness within intercollegiate sports. Media coverage has systematically focused on the exploitation of players, the corruption spawned by a billion-dollar commercial enterprise, and the disintegration of traditional academic values based on moral and ethical behavior. Without a doubt "heightened media attention to recent scandals has spurred numerous reforms or induced college presidents to devote more careful administrative attention to college sports" (Hart-Nibbrig and Cottingham, 1986, p. 107). Moreover, there is abundant evidence that college sports, much as 50-ton dinosaurs, are doomed to slow but steady death by their own sheer weight and inability to adapt to new realities.

Nisbet (1979) points out that most athletic programs have ceased to grow and are in a stationary state. Frey (1985) states that "athletic programs are consuming more energy than they are able to generate" and explains why:

> During the last 5 to 7 years, many college athletic programs have fallen on hard times largely because the trends of tax-cutting legislation, mandated growth in women's sports, and large inflationary bites out of the American leisure time and charitable dollar. In addition, revelations of scandal and impropriety, of discrimination and inequality, of education irresponsibility, and illegal financial wizardry have presented additional obstacles to justifying the growth and expansion of athletic programs . . . fewer quality athletes are available to fill the labor pool required to maintain high-level programs. Thus, faced with resource supply problems in the form of labor and capital unlike any previously encountered, college and university athletic decision makers will have to make some hard choices. . . ." (p. 115)

It is clear that intercollegiate athletics as we know them will change or perish. The status quo is untenable. Whether intercollegiate programs remain amateur, become semi-professional, or truly achieve fully professionalized status should not be the bone of contention. What campus leaders should be concerned about is that they become integral and valued players in the ongoing dialogue leading to any number of plausible solutions (Mallette and Howard, 1992).

Recommendations

1. Faculty, administrators, and trustees must restore the student-athlete ideal on campus through wellness and health promotion programs for all students.
2. Faculty, administrators, and trustees must create an institutional mission statement which clearly defines the art of wellness, the requirements of health promotion, and the role of athletics as part of the total integrated undergraduate experience. The mission statement should be a collaborative effort and should be more than rhetorical window-dressing found in student handbooks. It should be a guiding light and the standard against which all programs and administrative actions are measured.
3. Faculty must take a keen interest in the issues affecting campus athletics with the full realization that nothing less than the intellectual integrity of the institution is at stake (Sperber, 1990, pp. 345–349).
4. Faculty must become more ''actively involved as a partner in determining the policies for conduct of intercollegiate athletics'' (Bailey and Littleton, 1991, p. 74), since faculty are the intellectual heart of the university and are ultimately responsible for an ethical campus environment. The avenues for action which suggest themselves are the faculty senate, participation as faculty representatives for athletics, or membership on athletic boards or committees. Bailey and Littleton (1991) believe the faculty senate can be an active voice in the ''development and revision of the institution's position on athletics'' (p. 74), defining the actual operation of the athletic program. A direct link to the administration is crucial. The faculty representative for athletics has a critical oversight and coordinating role to play, often focusing on eligibility issues and compliance monitoring. Faculty athletics policy committees ''may have a great deal to say about sports programs with considerable impact'' (Thelin and Wiseman, 1989, p. 89). Such a committee can provide direction to athletic programs and may even set policy, while at the same time providing support and a broader base of consensus for presidential action (El-Khawas, 1979).
5. Presidents should include athletic departments in the full regional accrediting process. Whether athletic departments are in fact or only in fiction integral and connected parts of the educational enterprise, they would find it difficult to refuse visits to determine minimum standards of propriety. ''Such action would result in public examination of the relationship of athletics to the total university activity, along with activities such as research and student services'' (Bailey and Littleton, 1992, p. 115).
6. Presidents and trustees, by word and action, should support initiatives to integrate student-athletes into the full academic community. The role of the president is difficult, for that individual must adapt a wide, rather than parochial view of responsibilities (Gilley, et al., 1986) and must secure the

cooperation of sometimes intransigent governing boards (Oliva, 1989). Pres idents often find few allies when difficult and unpopular decisions must be made and faculty have as much to lose as anyone if ethical and moral principles are compromised. Thus, "presidents need to find and consolidate this support. And they must involve, inform, and persuade their governing boards that at stake is the erosion of public confidence and trust in higher education" (Thelin and Wiseman, 1991, p. 79). Presidents should press for a comprehensive reform of the NCAA to restore the student-athlete ideal.

CONCLUSION: RESTORING BALANCE

> If the college is indeed an educational institution, then all athletics, whether on the campus or off it, must be regarded as an integral part of the educational program and treated accordingly.
>
> —George E. Dawson in W. Carson Ryan, *The Literature of American School and College Athletics* (1929, p. xviii)

According to Ernest Boyer (1985, p. 410), "the tragedy of big-time athletics is not just the corruption on the campus, but the damaging of students." Because of the Knight Commission, administrators, coaches, and the public have a better understanding of the nature and scope of the problems of intercollegiate athletics. Athletics is not an abstract machine. Athletics is about people. Actions should be directed toward the development of superior student-athletes. Institutional leaders must agressively implement programs that create a balance among the social, physical, and mental capacities of every student. Ideally, they seek to establish a healthy complementarity between the academic curriculum, cocurriculum, and the extracurriculum to enhance the quality of student life. When the environment exudes caring and nurturing qualities, wellness, and health promotion, athletics can provide participants with a feeling of belonging, connection, and personal worth. According to Martin (1982, p. 79), "the college of character has the power to lift our spirits and focus our abilities, to exemplify true character so strongly that students will always have their experiences in the college as a point of reference, to unify a community and make it a model for society." Thus the college of character is a cohesive, supportive, and celebratory community. By sharing common interests, goals, and experiences, student-athletes encounter this type of community "in which the heritage of the institution is remembered and where rituals affirming both tradition and change are widely shared" (Carnegie Foundation, 1990, pp. 2, 7–8). Such a reform agenda cannot take place without a comprehensive collegiate transformation involving the place of wellness in the undergraduate curriculum, the role of the faculty, and the revitalization of the NCAA through presidential and trustee action.

REFERENCES

Alexander, C. N., and Langer, E. J. (eds.) (1990). *Higher Stages of Human Development: Perspectives on Adult Growth.* New York: Oxford University Press.

Altbach, P. G., and Berdahl, R. O. (eds.) (1987). *Higher Education in American Society.* Frontiers of Education. Revised Edition. Buffalo: Prometheus Books.

Andre, J., and James, D. N. (eds.) (1991). *Rethinking College Athletics.* Philadelphia, PA: Temple University Press.

Apps, J. W. (1988). *Higher Education in a Learning Society: Meeting New Demands for Education and Training.* San Francisco: Jossey-Bass.

Arrowood, C. F. (ed.) (1930). *Thomas Jefferson and Education in a Republic.* New York: McGraw-Hill.

Ardell, D. B. (1977). *High Level Wellness: An Alternative to Doctors, Drugs, and Disease.* Emmaus, PA: Rodale Press.

Association of American Colleges. (1985). *Integrity in the College Curriculum: A Report to the Academic Community: The Findings and Recommendations of the Project on Redefining the Meaning and Purpose of Baccalaureate Degrees.* Washington, DC: Association of American Colleges.

Atwell, R. (1979). Some reflections on collegiate athletics. *Educational Record* 60: 367–373.

Atwell, R. (1985). It's only a game. In C. Donald, J. O. Segrave, and B. J. Becker (eds.), *Sport and Higher Education.* Champaign, IL: Human Kinetics.

Atwell, R. (1991). Sports reform: Where is the faculty? *Academe* 77: 10–12.

Axtell, J. L. (1968). *The Educational Writings of John Locke: A Critical Edition with Introduction and Notes.* Cambridge: University Press.

Bailey, W. S., and Littleton, T. D. (1991). *Athletics and Academe: An Anatomy of Abuses and a Prescription for Reform.* New York: American Council on Education/Macmillan.

Barr, M. J., Upcraft, M. L., and Associates. (1990). *New Futures for Student Affairs: Building a Vision for Professional Leadership and Practice.* Jossey-Bass Series in Higher Education. San Francisco: Jossey-Bass.

Bennett, K., and LeCompte, M. (1990). *How Schools Work: A Sociological Analysis of Education.* New York: Longman.

Bennett, W. J. (1984). *To Reclaim a Legacy: A Report on the Humanities in Higher Education.* Washington, DC: National Endowment for the Humanities.

Birnbaum, R. (1991). *How Colleges Work: The Cybernetics of Academic Organization and Leadership.* San Francisco, CA: Jossey-Bass.

Blackburn, R. T., and Nyikos, M. S. (1974). College football and mr. chips: All in the Family. *Phi Delta Kappan* 56 (2): 110–113.

Blum, D. E. (1993, April 28). Appeals court upholds order requiring Brown U. to reinstate women's gymnastics and volleyball. *Chronicle of Higher Education*, pp. A35–A36.

Blum, D. E. (1993, July 7). Howard coach wins sex-bias suit. *Chronicle of Higher Education*, p. A45.

Bok, D. (1982). *Beyond the Ivory Tower: Social Responsibilities of the Modern University.* Cambridge, MA: Harvard University Press.

Bok, D. (1985). Presidents need power within the NCAA to preserve academic standards and institutional integrity. In D. Chu, J. O. Segrave, and B. J. Becker (eds.), *Sport and Higher Education.* Champaign, IL: Human Kinetics.

Bok, D. (1990). *Universities and the Future of America.* Durham, NC: Duke University Press.

Boorstin, D. (1965). *The Americans: The National Experience.* New York: Random House.

Bowen, H., and Schuster, J. (1986). *American Professors: A National Resource Imperiled.* New York: Oxford University Press.

Bowlus, W. C. (1975). How well do our college athletes fare? *Journal of Physical Education and Recreation* 46: 25.

Boyd, W. (1911/1963). *Educational Theory of Jean Jacques Rousseau.* New York: Russell and Russell.

Boyer, E. L. (1985). College athletics: The control of the campus. In D. Chu, J. O. Segrave, and B. J. Becker (eds.) *Sport and Higher Education.* Champaign, IL: Human Kinetics.

Boyer, E. L. (1987). *College: The Undergraduate Experience in America.* New York: Harper and Row.

Boyer, E. L., and Levine, A. (1981). *A Quest for Common Learning: The Aims of General Education.* A Carnegie Foundation Essay. Washington, DC: Carnegie Foundation for the Advancement of Teaching.

Cady, E. H. (1978). *The Big Game.* Tennessee: University of Tennessee Press.

Cahn, S. M. (ed.) (1990). *Morality, Responsibility, and the University: Studies in Academic Ethics.* Philadelphia: Temple University Press.

Carlson, J., Robison, J. Song, W., Heusner, W., and VanHuss, W. (1991). A university health promotion course. *Journal of Nutrition Education* 23: 138C–D.

Carnegie Foundation for the Advancement of Teaching. (1979). *Mission of the College Curriculum: A Contemporary Review with Suggestions.* San Francisco: Jossey-Bass.

Carnegie Foundation for the Advancement of Teaching. (1990). *Campus life: In Search of Community.* Foreword by E. L. Boyer. Lawrenceville, NJ: Princeton University Press.

Center for the Study of Athletics. (1989). *Comments from Students in the 1987–1988 National Study of Intercollegiate Athletics.* Studies of Intercollegiate Athletics, Report No. 6. Palo Alto, CA: American Institutes for Research.

Cheney, L. V. (1988). *Humanities in America: A Report to the President, the Congress, and the American People.* Washington,DC: National Endowment for the Humanities.

Cheney, L. V. (1989). *50 Hours: A Core Curriculum for College Students.* Washington, DC: National Endowment for the Humanities.

Chickering, A. W. (1969). *Education and Identity.* Jossey-Bass Series in Higher Education. San Francisco: Jossey-Bass.

Chronicle of Higher Education. (1993, May 5). NCAA panel agrees on proposals to promote sex equity, p. A38.

Chronicle of Higher Education. (1993, September 22). NCAA Budget, 1992–93 and 1993–94, p. A36.

Chu, D. (1982). The American conception of higher education and the formal incorporation of intercollegiate sport. *Quest* 34: 53–57.

Chu, D. (1985). The American conception of higher education and the formal incorporation of intercollegiate sport. In D. Chu, J. O. Segrave, and B. J. Becker (eds.), *Sport and Higher Education.* Champaign, IL: Human Kinetics.

Chu, D. (1989). *The Character of American Higher Education and Intercollegiate Sport.* Frontiers of Education. Albany, NY: State University of New York Press.

Chu, D., Segrave, J. O., and Becker, B. J. (eds.) (1985). *Sport and Higher Education.* Champaign, IL: Human Kinetics.

Cohen, M., and March, J. (1974). *Leadership and Ambiguity: The American College President.* New York: McGraw-Hill.

Cowell, C. C., and France, W. L. (1965). *Philosophy and Principles of Physical Education.* Englewood Cliffs, NJ: Prentice-Hall.

Cremin, L. A. (1970). *American Education: The Colonial Experience, 1607–1783*. New York: Harper and Row.
Cuzzort, R., and King, E. (1989). *20th-Century Social Thought*. Fourth Edition. Chicago: Holt Rinehart and Winston.
Davis, W. (1979). The president's role in athletics: Leader or figurehead? *Educational Record* 60(4): 420–430.
Deferrari, R. J. (1950). *Integration in Catholic Colleges and Universities*. Higher Education Workshop Proceedings. Washington, DC: Catholic University of America Press.
Deferrari, R. J. (1951). *Discipline and Integration in the Catholic College*. Higher Education Workshop Proceedings. Washington, DC: Catholic University of America Press.
Deferrari, R. J. (1952). *The Curriculum of the Catholic College (Integration and Concentration)*. Higher Education Workshop Proceedings. Washington, DC: Catholic University of America Press.
Deferrari, R. J. (1953). *Theology, Philosophy, and History as Integrating Disciplines in the Catholic College of Liberal Arts*. Higher Education Workshop Proceedings. Washington, DC: Catholic University of America Press.
DeGuire North, J., and Munson, J. W. (1990). Promoting faculty health and wellness. In Schuster, J., Wheeler, D. and Associates (eds.), *Enhancing Faculty Careers*. San Francisco: Jossey-Bass.
Denlinger, K., and Shapiro, L. (1975). *Athletes for Sale*. New York: Thomas Y. Crowell Company.
Denver Post. (1993, January 16). Money, sex and power at issue, p. 9D.
Denver Post. (1993, January 16). Proposition 48 softening voted down, p. 9D.
DeVenzio, D. (1986). *RIP-OFF U.: The Annual Theft and Exploitation of Major College Revenue Producing Student- Athletes*. Charlottte, NC: Fool Court Press.
DiBiaggio, J. (1991). Cosmetic change versus real reform. *Academe* 77: 21–22.
DiBiaggio, J. (1992). Our last, best chance for athletic reform. *College Board Review* 163 (Spring): 26–29, 37.
Dunn, H. L. (1961). *High Level Wellness*. Arlington, VA: R. W. Beatty Company.
Dyreson, M. (1989). The emergence of consumer culture and the transformation of physical culture: American sport in the 1920s. *Journal of Sport History* 16(3): 261–281.
Edlin, G. and Golanty, E. (1992). *Health and Wellness: A Holistic Approach*. Fourth Edition. Boston: Jones and Bartlett.
Education Commission of the States. (1986). *Transforming the State Role in Undergraduate Education: Time for a Different View*. Ps-86–3. Denver: Education Commission of the States.
Edwards, H. (1985). Educating black athletes. In D. Chu, J. O. Segrave, and B. J. Becker (eds.), *Sport and Higher Education*. Champaign, IL: Human Kinetics.
Eitzen, D. S. and Sage, G. H. (1978). *Sociology of American Sport*. Dubuque, IA: W. C. Brown.
El-Khawas, E. (1979). Self-regulation and intercollegiate athletics. *Educational Record* 60(4): 510–517.
Etheredge, M. L. (1958). *Health Facts for College Students*. Philadelphia: W. B. Saunders.
Ewens, T. (1979). Analyzing the Impact of Competence-Based Approaches on Liberal Education. In G. Grant, P. Elbow, T. Ewens, Z. Gamson, W. Kohli, W. Newmann, V. Olesen, and D. Reisman (eds.), *On Competence: A Critical Analysis of Competence-Based Reforms in Higher Education*. Jossey-Bass Series in Higher Education. San Francisco: Jossey-Bass.

Falla, J. (1981). *NCAA: The Voice of College Sports*. Mission, KS: National Collegiate Athletics Association.

Felton, C. (1860). *Annual Report of the President of Harvard College to the Overseers, 1859–60*. Cambridge, MA: Harvard University.

Finkelstein, M. (1983). From tutor to specialized scholar: Academic professionalization in eighteenth and nineteenth century America. *History of Higher Education Annual* 3: 99–121.

Fleisher, A. A., Goff, B. L., and Tollison, R. D. (1992). *The National Collegiate Athletic Association: A Study in Cartel Behavior*. Chicago: University of Chicago Press.

Frey, J. (1985). Boosterism, scarce resources, and institutional control: The future of American intercollegiate athletics. In D. Chu, J. O. Segrave, and B. J. Becker (eds.), *Sport and Higher Education*. Champaign, IL: Human Kinetics.

Frey, J. (ed.) (1982). *The Governance of Intercollegiate Athletics*. West Point, NY: Leisure Press.

Funk, G. D. (1991). *Major Violation: The Unbalanced Priorities in Athletics and Academics*. Champaign, IL: Leisure Press.

Gaff, J. G. (1983). *General Education Today: A Critical Analysis of Controversies, Practices, and Reforms*. San Francisco: Jossey-Bass.

Gaff, J. G. (1991). *New Life for the College Curriculum: Assessing Achievements and Furthering Progress in the Reform of General Education*. San Francisco: Jossey-Bass.

Gilley, J. W., Hickey, A., Barnsback, M., Gerber, E., and Sears, K. (1986). *Administration of University Athletic Programs: Internal Control and Excellence*. Washington, DC: American Council on Education.

Gladieux, L. E., and Lewis, G. (1987). The federal government and higher education. In P. G. Altbach and R. O. Berdahl (eds.), *Higher Education in American Society*. Frontiers of Education. Revised Edition. Buffalo: Prometheus Books.

Goodchild, L. F. (1989). A revisionist addendum to the history of liberal education: The restoration of the religious contribution. Roundtable paper presented at the History of Education Society, Chicago, Illinois, October, 1989.

Goodchild, L. F. (1991). What is the condition of American research universities? *American Educational Research Journal* 28(1): 3–19.

Grant, G., Elbow, P., Ewens, T., Gamson, Z., Kohli, W., Neumann, W., Olesen, V., and Reisman, D. (1979). *On Competence: A Critical Analysis of Competence-Based Reforms in Higher Education*. San Francisco: Jossey-Bass.

Grant, G., and Reisman, D. (1978). *The Perpetual Dream: Reform and Experiment in the American College*. Chicago: University of Chicago Press.

Green, L. W., and Johnson, K. W. (1984). Health education and health promotion. In J. Matarazzo, S. Weiss, J. Herd, N. Miller, and S. Weiss (eds.), *Behavioral Health: A Handbook of Health Enhancement and Disease Prevention*. New York: Wiley.

Greenberg, J. S., and Pargman, D. (1989). *Physical Fitness: A Wellness Approach*. Second Edition. Englewood Cliffs, NJ: Prentice Hall.

Grover, K. (ed.) (1989). *Fitness in American Culture: Images of Health, Sport, and the Body, 1830–1940*. Amherst: University of Massachusetts Press and the Margaret Woodbury Strong Museum.

Guttmann, A. (1982). The tiger devours the literary magazine, or, intercollegiate athletics in America. In J. Frey (ed.), *The Governance of Intercollegiate Athletics*. West Point, NY: Leisure Press.

Guttmann, A. (1985). English sports spectators: The Restoration to the early 19th century. *Journal of Sport History* 12(2): 103–125.

Guttmann, A. (1991). The anomaly of intercollegiate athletics. In J. Andre and

D. N. James (eds.), *Rethinking College Athletics*. Philadelphia: Temple University Press.

Hamilton, F. A., and Cairns, C. J. (1969). *The Greek Life and Its Meaning for Today*. New York: Doubleday.

Hanford, G. H. (1982). Intercollegiate athletics today and tomorrow: The president's challenge. In J. Frey (ed.), *The Governance of Intercollegiate Athletics*. West Point, NY: Leisure Press.

Hanford, G. H. (1985). Proposition 48. In D. Chu, J. O. Segrave, and B. J. Becker (eds.), *Sport and Higher Education*. Champaign, IL: Human Kinetics.

Hardy, S. H., and Berryman, J. W. (1982). A historical view of the governance issue. In J. Frey (ed.), *The Governance of Intercollegiate Athletics*. West Point, NY: Leisure Press.

Hart, E., and Sechrist, W. C. (1970). *Dynamics of Wellness*. Belmont, CA: Wadsworth.

Hart-Nibbrig, N., and Cottingham, C. (1986). *The Political Economy of College Sports*. Lexington, MA: Lexington Books.

Hatab, L. J. (1991). The Greeks and the meaning of athletics. In J. Andre and D. N. James (eds.), *Rethinking College Athletics*. Philadelphia: Temple University Press.

Hettler, B. (1980). Wellness promotion on a university campus. *Journal of Health Promotion and Maintenance* 3: 77–95.

Hobbs, W. C. (1987). The courts. In P. G. Altbach and R. O. Berdahl, *Higher Education in American Society*. Frontiers of Education. Revised Edition. Buffalo: Prometheus Books.

Hoekema, D. A. (1990). Beyond *in loco parentis*? Parietal rules and moral maturity. In S. M. Cahn (ed.), *Morality, Responsibility, and the University: Studies in Academic Ethics*. Philadelphia: Temple University Press.

Hoeveler, D. (1976). The university and the social gospel: The intellectual origins of the "Wisconsin Idea." *Wisconsin Magazine of History* 59: 282–298.

Horowitz, H. L. (1987). *Campus Life: Undergraduate Cultures from the End of the Eighteenth Century to the Present*. Chicago: University of Chicago Press.

Huk, I. P. (1993). The collegiate way: A study of four midwestern universities, 1850–1920. Ph.D. dissertation, University of Chicago.

Hybertson, D., Hulme, E., Smith, W. A., and Holton, M. A. (1992). Wellness in non-traditional-age students. *Journal of College Student Development* 33: 50–55.

Jarvis, D. (1991). *Junior Faculty Development: A Handbook*. New York: Modern Language Association of America.

Jencks, C., and Reisman, D. (1968). *The Academic Revolution*. Chicago: University of Chicago Press.

Johnston, A. (1947). *Ten and Out!* Third Edition. New York: Ives Washburn.

Josephs, M. J. (1981). Curricular Integration: Mortar for the Ivory Tower. In *Current Issues in Higher Education,* No. 2. Washington, DC: American Association for Higher Education.

Katz, J., Bornholdt, L., Gaff, J. G., Hoffman, N., Newman, L. F., Ratner, M., and Wengartner, R. H. (1988). *A New Vitality in General Education: Planning, Teaching, and Supporting Effective Liberal, Learning by the Task Group on General Education*. Washington, DC: Association of American Colleges.

Keeling, R. P. (ed.) (1992). *Effective AIDS Education on Campus*. New Directions for Student Services, no. 57. San Francisco: Jossey-Bass.

Keeling, R. P., and Engstrom, E. L. (1992). Building community for effective health promotion. In *Effective AIDS Education on Campus*. New Directions for Student Services, no. 57. San Francisco: Jossey-Bass.

Kerr, C. (1963). *The Uses of the University*. Cambridge, MA: Harvard University Press.

Kerr, C., and Gade, M. (1987). Current and emerging issues facing American higher education. In P. G. Altbach and R. O. Berdahl (eds.), *Higher Education in American Society*. Buffalo, NY: Prometheus Books.

Kimball, B. A. (1986). *Orators & Philosophers: A History of the Idea of Liberal Education*. Foreword by Joseph L. Featherstone. New York: Teachers College Press.

Kliever, L. D. (1990). Ethical issues in intercollegiate athletics. In William W. May (ed.), *Ethics and Higher Education*. New York: American Council on Education/Macmillan.

Knight Commission. (1991). *Keeping Faith with the Student- Athlete: A New Model for Intercollegiate Athletics*. New York: American Council on Education/Macmillan.

Kuh, G. D., Schuh, J. H., Whitt, E. J., and Associates. (1991). *Involving Colleges: Successful Approaches to Fostering Student Learning and Development Outside the Classroom*. Jossey-Bass Higher and Adult Education Series. San Francisco: Jossey-Bass.

Lang, D. (1978). The people's college, the mechanics of mutual protection and the agricultural college act. *History of Education Quarterly* 18: 295–321.

Lapchick, R. E. (1989). *Pass to Play: Student Athletes and Academics*. Washington, DC: National Education Association.

Lapchick, R. E., and Slaughter, J. (1989). *The Rules of the Game: Ethics in College Sport*. New York: Macmillan.

Lasch, C. (1989, December 27). The I's have it for another decade. *New York Times*, p. A23.

Lawrence, P. R. (1987). *Unsportsmanlike Conduct: The National Collegiate Athletic Association and the Business of College Football*. New York: Praeger.

Leafgren, F. (ed.) (1986). *Developing Campus Recreation and Wellness Programs*. New Directions for Student Services, no. 34. San Francisco: Jossey-Bass.

Leafgren, F., and Elsenrath, D. E. (1986). The role of campus recreation programs in institutions of higher education. In Leafgren, F. (ed.), *Developing Campus Recreation and Wellness Programs*. New Directions for Student Services, no. 34. San Francisco: Jossey-Bass.

Lee, M. (1983). *A History of Physical Education and Sports in the U.S.A.* New York: Wiley.

Lederman, D. (1991, March 27). Knight commission tells presidents to use their power to reform the 'fundamental premises' of college sports. *Chronicle of Higher Education*, pp. A1, A33–34.

Lederman, D. (1991, May 1). Special admissions treatment for athletes widespread at big-sports colleges. *Chronicle of Higher Education*, pp. A1, A31–33.

Lederman, D. (1992, April 15). NCAA officials try to counter chargers of sex-bias in sports. *Chronicle of Higher Education*, pp. A43–44.

Lederman, D. (1993, January 27). Following its sedate 1993 meeting, NCAA anticipates a "Blockbuster" in 1994. *Chronicle of Higher Education*, pp. A36–37.

Lederman, D. (1993, May 5). Appeals court dismisses sex-bias suit against Colgate. *Chronicle of Higher Education*, p. A38.

Lederman, D. (1993, May 26). Abide by U.S. sex-bias laws, NCAA panel urges colleges. *Chronicle of Higher Education*, pp. A31–32.

Levine, A. (1978). *Handbook on Undergraduate Curriculum*. San Francisco: Jossey-Bass.

Levine, A., and Weingart, J. (1973). *Reform of Undergraduate Education*. San Francisco: Jossey-Bass.

Lipsky, R. (1981). *How We Play the Game: Why Sports Dominate American Life*. Boston: Beacon Press.

Locke, J. (1989). *Some Thoughts Concerning Education*. J. W. Yolton and J. S. Yolton (eds.). New York: Oxford University Press.

Lowell, A. L. (1934). *At War With Academic Traditions in America*. Cambridge, MA: Harvard University Press.
Lucas, J., and Smith, R. (1978). *Saga of American Sport*. Philadelphia: Lea and Febiger.
MacAloon, J. J. (1991). Memory, attention, and the communities of sport. In J. Andre and D. N. James (eds.), *Rethinking College Athletics*. Philadelphia: Temple University Press.
MacIntyre, A. (1984). *After Virtue: A Study in Moral Theory*. Second Edition. South Bend, IN: University of Notre Dame Press.
Mallette, B. I., and Howard, R. D. (eds.) (1992). *Monitoring and Assessing Intercollegiate Athletics*. New Directions for Institutional Research, no. 72. San Francisco: Jossey-Bass.
Mangan, J. A. (1981). *Athleticism in the Victorian and Edwardian Public School: The Emergence and Consolidation of Educational Ideology*. Cambridge, England: Cambridge University Press.
Martin, W. B. (1982). *A College of Character: Renewing the Purpose and Content of College Education*. San Francisco: Jossey-Bass.
May, W. W. (ed.) (1990). *Ethics and Higher Education*. New York: American Council on Education/Macmillan.
Mayhew, L. B., Ford, P. J., and Hubbard, D. L. (1990). *The Quest for Quality: The Challenge for Undergraduate Education in the 1990s*. San Francisco: Jossey-Bass.
McConnell, T. R. (1987). Autonomy and accountability: Some fundamental issues. In P. G. Altbach and R. O. Berdahl, *Higher Education in American Society*. Frontiers of Education. Revised Edition. Buffalo: Prometheus Books.
McKeon, R. P. (1968). *Introduction to Aristotle*. Chicago: University of Chicago Press.
McMillan, L. (1986, February 19). Bran muffins at faculty meetings and 5–mile runs at lunch: This college is mecca for fitness buffs. *Chronicle of Higher Education*, p. 23.
Michener, J. A. (1976). *Sports in America*. New York: Random House.
Miller, G. A., Dowell, L. J., and Pender, R. H. (1989). *Journal of Physical Education, Recreation, and Dance* 60: 20–23.
Miller, T. K., and Jones, J. D. (1988). Out-of-class activities. In Chickering, A. W., and Associates (eds.), *The Modern American College: Responding to the New Realities of Diverse Students and a Changing Society*. Foreword by Nevitt Sanford. San Francisco: Jossey-Bass.
Millett, J. D. (1987). State governments. In P. G. Altbach and R. O. Berdahl, *Higher Education in American Society*. Frontiers of Education. Revised Edition. Buffalo: Prometheus Books.
Montgomery, B., and Dalton, J. C. (1986). Promoting wellness through recreation facilities development and programing. In F. Leafgren, F. (ed.), *Developing Campus Recreation and Wellness Programs*. New Directions for Student Services, no. 34. San Francisco: Jossey-Bass.
Moore, K. (1976). Freedom and constraint in eighteenth century Harvard. *Journal of Higher Education* 17(6): 649–659.
Morison, S. (1936). *Harvard College in the Seventeenth Century*. Cambridge, MA: Harvard University Press.
Mrozek, D. (1983). *Sport and American Mentality, 1880–1910*. Knoxville, TN: University of Tennessee Press.
Naisbitt, J. (1984). *Megatrends: Ten New Directions Transforming Our Lives*. New York: Warner Books.
National Collegiate Athletic Association. (1990). *The Sports and Recreational Programs of the Nation's Universities and Colleges, 1956–1987*. Report No. 7. Mission, KS: National Collegiate Athletic Association.

Nelson, D. (1982). Administrator's views of athletic governance. In J. Frey (ed.), *The Governance of Intercollegiate Athletics*. West Point, NY: Leisure Press.

Newman, F. (1985). *Higher Education and America's Resurgence*. Princeton, NJ: Princeton University Press.

Nickse, R., and McClure, L. (eds.) (1981). *Competency-Based Education: Beyond Minimum Competency Testing*. New York: Teachers College Press.

Nisbet, R. (1979). The rape of progress. *Public Opinion* 2: 2–6.

Noll, R. G. (1991). The economics of intercollegiate sports. In J. Andre and D. N. James (eds.), *Rethinking College Athletics*. Philadelphia: Temple University Press.

Nyquist, E. B. (1985). Immorality of big-power intercollegiate athletics. In D. Chu, J. O. Segrave, and B. J. Becker (eds.), *Sport and Higher Education*. Champaign, IL: Human Kinetics.

O'Donnell, M. P. (1986a). Definition of health promotion. *American Journal of Health Promotion* 1(1): 4–5.

O'Donnell, M. P. (1986b). Definition of health promotion: Part II: Levels of Programs. *American Journal of Health Promotion* 1(2): 6–9.

Ogilvie, B., and Tutko, T. (1985). Sport: If you want to build character, try something else. In D. Chu, J. O. Segrave, and B. J. Becker (eds.), *Sport and Higher Education*. Champaign, IL: Human Kinetics.

Oliva, L. (1989). *What Trustees Should Know About Intercollegiate Athletics*. Association of Governing Boards special report. Washington, DC: Association of Governing Boards.

Opatz, J. P. (1985). *A Primer of Health Promotion: Creating Healthy Organizational Cultures*. Washington, DC: Oryn Publications.

Oxendline, J. B. (1961). The service program in 1960–61. *Journal of Physical Education and Recreation* 32(7): 37–38.

Oxendline, J. B. (1969). Status of required physical education programs in colleges and universities. *Journal of Health, Physical Education and Recreation* 40(1): 32–35.

Oxendline, J. B. (1972). Status of general education programs of physical education in four-year colleges and universities: 1971–72. *Journal of Health, Physical Education and Recreation* 43(3): 26–28.

Oxendline, J. B., and Roberts, J. E. (1978). The general instruction program in physical education at four-year colleges and universities: 1977. *Journal of Physical Education and Recreation* 49(1): 21–23.

Park, R. J. (1987). Physiologists, physicians, and physical educators: 19th century biology and exercise, hygienic and educative. *Journal of Sport History* 14(1): 28–60.

Park, R. J. (1989). The second 100 years: or, can physical education become the renaissance field of the 21st century? *Quest* 41: 136–149.

Park, R. J. (1991). Physiology and anatomy are destiny!?: Brains, bodies and exercise in 19th century American thought. *Journal of Sport History* 18(1): 31–63.

Pelletier, K. R. (1979). *Holistic Medicine: From Stress to Optimum Health*. New York: Dell Publishing Company.

Perry, R. (1964). *Puritanism and Democracy*. New York: Harper Torchbacks.

Pfnister, A. (1990). *Challenge and Response: American Higher Education, 1630–1900*. Unpublished manuscript. Denver, CO: University of Denver.

Pottinger, P. S., and Goldsmith, J. (eds.) (1979). *Defining and Measuring Competence*. New Directions for Experiential Learning, no. 3. San Francisco: Jossey-Bass.

Potts, D. B. (1977). "College enthusiasm!" As a public response, 1800–1860. *Harvard Educational Review* 47(1): 28–42.

Purdy, D. A., Eitzen, D. S., and Hufnagel, R. (1985). Are athletes also students? The

educational attainment of college athletes. In D. Chu, J. O. Segrave, and B. J. Becker (eds.), *Sport and Higher Education*. Champaign, IL: Human Kinetics.
Rader, B. (1983). *American Sports*. Englewood Cliffs, NJ: Prentice-Hall.
Robbins, G., Powers, D., and Rushton, J. A. (1992). A required fitness/wellness course that works. *Journal of Physical Education, Recreation, and Dance* 63: 17–21.
Robinson, R. S. (1955). *Sources for the History of Greek Athletics*. Cincinnati, OH: The Author.
Rooney, J. F. Jr. (1980). *The Recruiting Game*. Lincoln, NE: University of Nebraska Press.
Rooney, J. F. Jr. (1987). *The Recruiting Game: Toward a New System of Intercollegiate Sport*. Lincoln, NE: University of Nebraska Press.
Rose, D. A. (1985). The controversy over college sport: Will it ever end? In D. Chu, J. O. Segrave, and B. J. Becker (eds.), *Sport and Higher Education*. Champaign, IL: Human Kinetics.
Rousseau, J-J. (1979). *Emile or On Education*. Allan Bloom (trans.). New York: Basic Books.
Rudolph, F. (1962). *The American College and University: A History*. New York: Alfred A. Knopf.
Rudolph, F. (1977). *Curriculum: The American Undergraduate Course of Study Since 1636*. San Francisco: Jossey-Bass.
Ryan, S. R., and Travis, J. (1981). *Wellness Workbook*. Berkeley, CA: Ten Speed Press.
Ryan, T. (1986). *Wellness, Spirituality and Sports*. New York: Paulist Press.
Ryan, W. C., Jr. (1929). *The Literature of American School and College Athletics*. Foreword by Henry S. Pritchett. Bulletin, no. 24. New York: Carnegie Foundation for the Advancement of Teaching.
Sack, A. L. (1982). Cui bono? Contradictions in college sports and athletes' rights. In J. Frey (ed.), *The Governance of Intercollegiate Athletics*. West Point, NY: Leisure Press.
Sage, G. H. (1982). The intercollegiate sport cartel and its consequences for athletics. In J. Frey (ed.), *The Governance of Intercollegiate Athletics*. West Point, NY: Leisure Press.
Sage, G. H. (1985). American values and sport: Formation of a bureaucratic personality. In D. Chu, J. O. Segrave, and B. J. Becker (eds.), *Sport and Higher Education*. Champaign, IL: Human Kinetics.
Sansone, D. (1988). *Greek Athletics and The Genesis of Sport*. Berkeley: University of California Press.
Santomier, J., and Cautilli, P. (1985). Controlling deviance in intercollegiate athletics. In D. Chu, J. O. Segrave, and B. J. Becker (eds.), *Sport and Higher Education*. Champaign, IL: Human Kinetics.
Saunders, R. P. (1988). What is health promotion? *Health Education* 19(5): 14–18.
Savage, H. J. (1929). *American College Athletics*. New York: Carnegie Foundation for the Advancement of Teaching.
Savage, H. J. (1933). *Economy in Higher Education*. New York: Carnegie Foundation for the Advancement of Teaching.
Schemblecher, B., and Albom, D. (1990, September 3). Here's the real play in sports. *Sports Illustrated*, p. 49–53.
Scott, H. A. (1982). New directions in intercollegiate athletics. In J. Frey (ed.), *The Governance of Intercollegiate Athletics*. West Point, NY: Leisure Press.
Semrow, J. J., Barney, J. A., Fredericks, M., Fredericks, J., Robinson, P., and Pfnister, A. O. (1992). In *In Search of Quality: The Development, Status, and Forecast of Standards in Postsecondary Accreditation*. New York: Peter Lang.

Simon, R. L. (1991). Intercollegiate athletics: Do they belong on campus? In J. Andre and D. N. James (eds.), *Rethinking College Athletics*. Philadelphia: Temple University Press.

Sivik, S. J., Butts, E. A., Moore, K. K., and Hyde, S. A. (1992). College and university wellness programs: An assessment of current trends. *NASPA Journal* 29(2): 136–142.

Slaughter, S. (1987). Academic freedom in the modern university. In P. G. Altbach and R. O. Berdahl, *Higher Education in American Society*. Frontiers of Education. Revised Edition. Buffalo: Prometheus Books.

Smith, R. A. (1988). *Sports and Freedom: The Rise of Big-time College Athletics*. New York: Oxford University Press.

Sojka, G. S. (1985). The evolution of the student-athlete in America: From the divinity to the divine. In D. Chu, J. O. Segrave, and B. J. Becker (eds.), *Sport and Higher Education*. Champaign, IL: Human Kinetics.

Sperber, M. (1990). *College Sports Inc.: The Athletic Department Versus the University*. New York: Henry Holt and Company.

Stevenson, C. L. (1985). College athletics and "character": The decline and fall of socialization research. In D. Chu, J. O. Segrave, and B. J. Becker (eds.), *Sport and Higher Education*. Champaign, IL: Human Kinetics.

Study Group on the Conditions of Excellence in American Higher Education. (1984). *Involvement in Learning: Realizing the Potential of American Higher Education*. Washington, DC: National Institute of Education.

Thelin, J. R., and Wiseman, L. L. (1989). *The Old College Try: Balancing Academics and Athletics in Higher Education*. ASHE-ERIC Higher Education Research Report No. 7. Washington, DC: George Washington University.

Thomas, R., and Chickering, A. W., (1984). Education and identity revisited. *Journal of College Student Personnel* 25: 392–399.

Timmreck, T. C., Cole, G. E., James, G., and Butterworth, D. D. (1987). The health education and health promotion movement: A theoretical jungle. *Health Education* 18(5): 24–28.

Tow, T. C. (1982). The governance role of the NCAA. In J. Frey (ed.), *The Governance of Intercollegiate Athletics*. West Point, NY: Leisure Press.

Trimble, R. T., and Hensley, L. D. (1990). *Journal of Physical Education, Recreation, and Dance* 61: 64–73.

Underwood, C. (1984). *The Student Athlete: Eligibility and Academic Integrity*. East Lansing, MI: Michigan State University Press.

Veysey, L. (1965). *The Emergence of the American University*. Chicago, IL: University of Chicago Press.

Vine, P. (1976). The social function of eighteenth century higher education. *History of Education Quarterly* 16: 409–424.

Warner, J. J. (1984). Wellness promotion in higher education. *NASPA Journal* 21: 32–38.

Weber, M. (1930). *The Protestant Ethic and the Spirit of Capitalism*. New York: Scribners.

Weick, K. E. (1976). Educational organizations as loosely coupled systems. *Administrative Science Quarterly* 21(1): 1–19.

Weimer, M. (1990). *Improving College Teaching*. San Francisco, CA: Jossey-Bass.

Weistart, J. (1983–1984). Legal accountability and the NCAA. *Journal of College and University Law* 10(2): 167–196.

Welch, P. D., and Lerch, H. A. (1981). *History of American Physical Education and Sport*. Springfield, IL: Charles C Thomas.

Zevin, D. (1992). Healthy U. *Walking Magazine* 7: 40–44.

The Matrix Representation System: Orientation, Research, Theory and Application*

Kenneth A. Kiewra
University of Nebraska-Lincoln

Suppose that you are a biology instructor teaching students about human bones. You line several bones across the floor so that students can examine each one carefully. In so doing, students might learn specific information about particular bones (e.g., a rib bone is curved) and general information about all bones (e.g., bones have a white color) but little about the structures that bones form. That bones form the human skeleton in general or that the hands, feet or ribcage in particular is obscured.

Knowing that bones interrelate to form a hand or skeleton is an example of structural knowledge. Structural knowledge is knowledge about the interrelationships among concepts or ideas (Jonassen, Beissner, and Yacci, 1993). Interrelated information is more meaningful than the sum of its parts just as an assembled puzzle is more meaningful than a random collection of its pieces. According to Mandler (1983), ''meaning does not exist until some structure or organization is achieved.''

This chapter is about representing structural knowledge spatially so that the interrelationships among ideas—the entire skeleton, the assembled puzzle—are apparent. Spatial representations present ideas two dimensionally so that relations within and across topics are easily seen. Text and outline representations, although most common, present information linearly, one idea at a time, like bones lined up across the floor. They often separate or conceal important relationships.

This chapter focuses on a single representation system developed by Du Bois and Kiewra (1989) for displaying structural knowledge. Their system, called the

*I greatly appreciate the helpful comments I received from two anonymous reviewers and the editor, Ray Perry, who read an earlier draft of this chapter. Special thanks are also extended to colleagues Daniel Robinson, Mississippi State University, and Nelson Du Bois, SUNY Oneonta, who helped plan and organize the chapter and critiqued earlier drafts of it. Nelson Du Bois should also be recognized as the chief architect of the Matrix Representation System. Last, I appreciate the work of Ken Jensen, who developed the chapter's graphics.

Matrix Representation System, displays structural knowledge spatially using three simple patterns: hierarchy, sequence, and matrix. The matrix is the system's cornerstone because it develops from a hierarchy or sequence representation. Therefore, discussion centers on the matrix representation.

There are other ways to represent structural knowledge. Many of these are detailed by Jonassen et al. (1993). Although this chapter acknowledges and occasionally compares other representation techniques to the Matrix Representation System, its purpose is to orient the reader to this system, and describe its theoretical underpinnings, research evidence, and applications.

ORIENTATION

This section provides an orientation to the Matrix Representation System. First, an example is presented along with a description of general advantages. Second, its structure and construction are discussed. Next, its utility is described. Fourth, its advantages over linear representations are presented. Last, the Matrix Representation System is compared with other spatial representation systems.

Example and General Advantages

Read the following passage about moths and butterflies.

Lepidoptera

> Moths and butterflies are insects belonging to the order Lepidoptera. The moth has two sets of wings that are folded down over its body like a roof when it rests. Moths have feathery antennae and spin a fuzzy cocoon. Moths generally have subdued colors and fly at twilight or night. They go through four stages of development: egg, caterpillar, pupa and adult.
>
> Butterflies are brightly colored. They fly during the day. They have two sets of wings that remain vertical or outstretched at rest. Their antennae are long and thin with knobs at the end. They proceed through four stages of development: egg, caterpillar, pupa and adult.

This passage has a linear, list-like structure. It presents ideas successively. Consequently, a reader focuses on individual ideas (e.g., a moth's antennae are feathery) rather than the information's overriding structure and interrelationships.

Now examine the representation presented in Figure 1. It was developed using the Matrix Representation System. Its two-dimensional structure has several advantages over the passage. First, it presents the information's overriding structure or framework. Two things are immediately apparent. One, the information is organized hierarchically. Subsumed beneath the superordinate concept Lepidoptera are the subordinate concepts moths and butterflies. Two, moths and butterflies are described along several common categories (e.g., wings and rest).

A second advantage is that within-topic (e.g., moths) relations are easily identifiable. Reading down the moths column, for example, the reader might

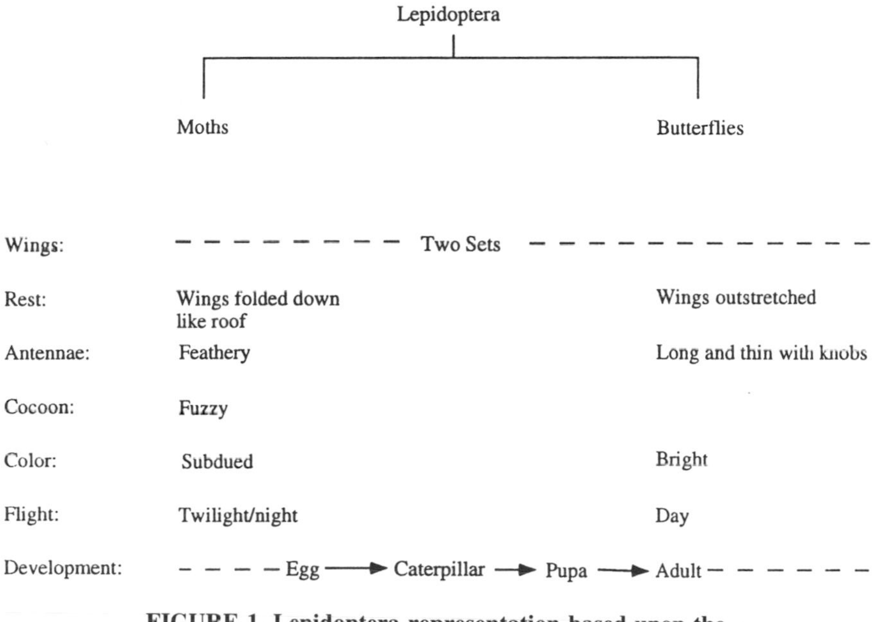

FIGURE 1. Lepidoptera representation based upon the Matrix Representation System.

relate the *feathery* antennae and *fuzzy* cocoon because of their similar texture. Reading down the butterflies column, the reader might relate the butterfly's *bright* colors to its *daytime* flight by reasoning that bright colors are only observable at daytime.

A third advantage is that across-topic relations are apparent. The representation encourages readers to compare and contrast the topics (i.e., moths and butterflies) by reading across the representation. Common elements are the two sets of wings and the four stages of development. Differences pertain to rest, antennae, color, and flight. Examining differences, a major pattern emerges: moths have more subtle characteristics than butterflies. Moths have subdued colors; butterflies have bright colors. Moths fly at night while butterflies fly by day. A moth's wings fold down whereas a butterfly's wings extend outward. The moth's antennae are feathery but the butterfly's are long with knobs. Realizing this general pattern should help in understanding and interrelating facts.

The fourth advantage is that relations within the representation's cells are evident. The developmental stages of moths and butterflies are illustrated in a left-to-right sequence with directional arrows joining the stages. Last, missing information is easily spotted. In a glance it is obvious that information about the butterfly's cocoon is missing.

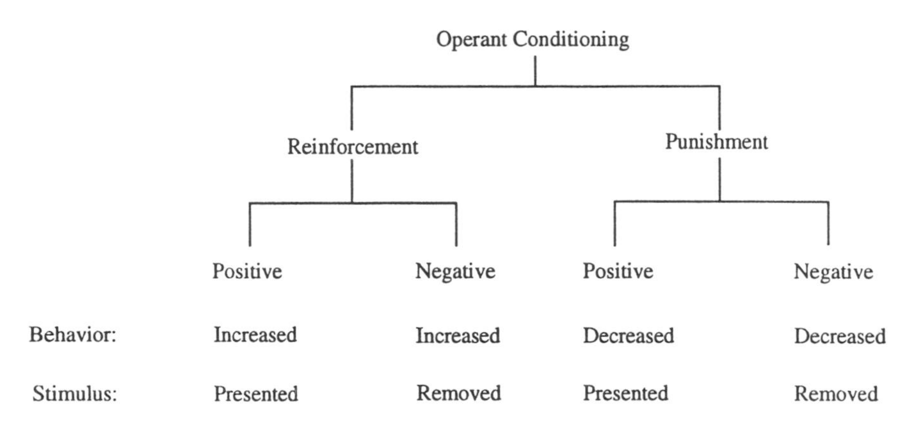

FIGURE 2. Hierarchy extended to form a matrix.

Structure and Construction

As seen in the previous example, the Matrix Representation System depicts four types of structural relations: superordinate-subordinate, temporal, within-topic, and across-topic. These are represented using three simple patterns: hierarchy, sequence, and matrix.

A hierarchy shows superordinate-subordinate relations in a top-down fashion. Types, parts, or characteristics of something are connected with vertical lines to superordinate ideas above. A sample hierarchy from psychology about operant conditioning is shown in the top three rows in Figure 2. It indicates that there are two types of operant conditioning: reinforcement and punishment, and that each of these has positive and negative subtypes.

A sequence shows temporal relations. Steps, events, phases, or changes in a process are depicted in a left-to-right sequence with directional arrows between them. A sample sequence pertaining to operant conditioning is shown in the top two rows of Figure 3. This sequence indicates that positive reinforcement occurs when a behavior is followed by a presented stimulus followed by an increased behavior.

A matrix is a grid or cross-classification table representing information along two dimensions. Column headings designate *topics*; row headings designate *repeatable categories* (or features) common to the topics. Within the intersecting *cells* (or slots) are *details*. Matrices are developed from a hierarchy or sequence representation that is extended downward by adding repeatable categories and details. Return to Figures 2 and 3 and notice that each was extended downward to form a matrix.

In the Figure 2 matrix, the topics are the four operant concepts: positive and negative reinforcement, and positive and negative punishment. The repeatable

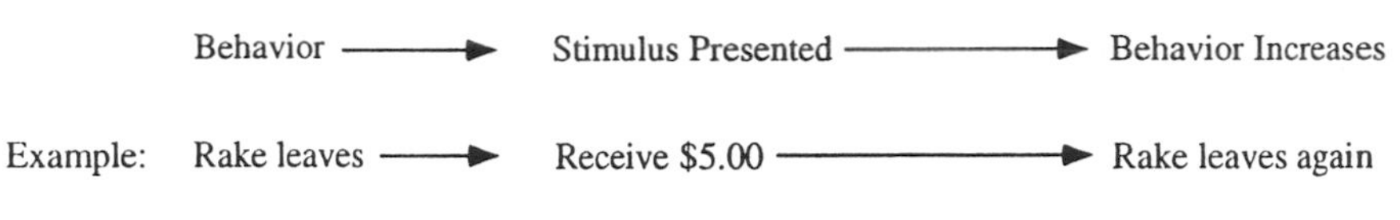

FIGURE 3. Sequence extended to form a matrix.

categories are behavior and stimulus. The details corresponding to the intersection of topics and repeatable categories appear in the matrix cells. Within-topic relations are observed by reading vertically beneath each topic. For instance, positive reinforcement involves both an increase in behavior and the presentation of a stimulus. Across-topic relations are observed by reading horizontally across the topics. Here, two key patterns emerge: reinforcement involves an increase in behavior whereas punishment involves a decrease in behavior; positive techniques involve a presented stimulus whereas negative techniques involve a removed stimulus.

In the Figure 3 matrix, the topics are the steps in positive reinforcement (i.e., behavior, stimulus presented and behavior increases), the repeatable category is example, and the details are the three example parts. Within-topic relations are formed by matching portions of the definition (the steps) to corresponding portions of the example. For instance, raking leaves is an example of behavior and receiving $5 is an example of a presented stimulus. Across-topic relations are formed when the example parts are learned as a sequence of events and not in isolation.

How can a learner tell which representation is appropriate? Certain alert words in lecture or text specify the appropriate representation. Words such as types, parts, components, characteristics, and kinds signal a hierarchical representation. The phrases ''three types of saws,'' ''two characteristics of leaves,'' and ''kinds of cells,'' for example, all signal a hierarchical structure. Words such as steps, stages, phases, next, before, procedure, and period signal a sequential representation. The phrases ''eight phases of the moon,'' ''the next character introduced,'' and ''experimental procedure,'' for example, all signal a sequential structure. Comparative words such as whereas, however, contrast, and similar signal a matrix representation. The phrase ''women on the other hand'' signals a matrix structure comparing women with the previous topic—perhaps men. Adjectives like deciduous and liberal also signal a potential comparison with yet unstated topics. If there are deciduous trees, there must be other types (i.e., evergreens); if there are liberal views, there must be conservative and moderate views too.

It is important to remember that even though the initial representation is a

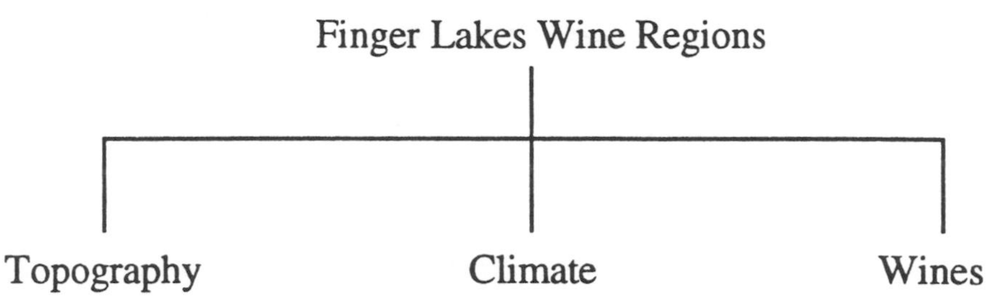

FIGURE 4. Hierarchy representing a descriptive structure.

hierarchy or sequence, all hierarchy or sequence representations can be extended into a matrix representation. Although it is possible that a text only reports the two types of Lepidoptera or the four stages in the development of butterflies, this information is potentially embellished with the addition of repeatable categories and related details. For instance, the wings, antennae, and color are important repeatable categories for comparing moths and butterflies. Similarly, the appearance, activity and location of the butterfly throughout the stages are germane to its development.

Utility

The Matrix Representation System uses three simple patterns to represent structural knowledge. I contend that these three patterns have widespread utility. As evidence, I briefly introduce the five types of content structures proposed by Meyer (1985) through prose analysis (and illustrated by Jonassen et al., 1993) and show that the Matrix Representation System can represent all of them.

The *descriptive* structure focuses on hierarchical relationships. A descriptive text, for example, might describe the Finger Lakes Wine Region with respect to characteristics such as topography, climate, and wines. A hierarchical representation appears in Figure 4.

The *collection plan* structure describes the attributes of a group of topics. The topics might be arranged hierarchically or sequentially. The topics are described along repeatable categories within a matrix framework as shown in Figure 5.

Text arranged by *causation* specifies the antecedent conditions that produce consequences. For example, how varying weather conditions affect wine quality. Such relations are captured using a sequence representation as shown in Figure 6.

Problem/Solution structures are also sequential. The sequential structure is antecedent event, problem, and solution. A sequence representation depicting a problem/solution structure for photography appears in Figure 7.

The *comparison* structure relates two or more topics across several features. The topics are sequentially related or coordinate topics at the same level in a

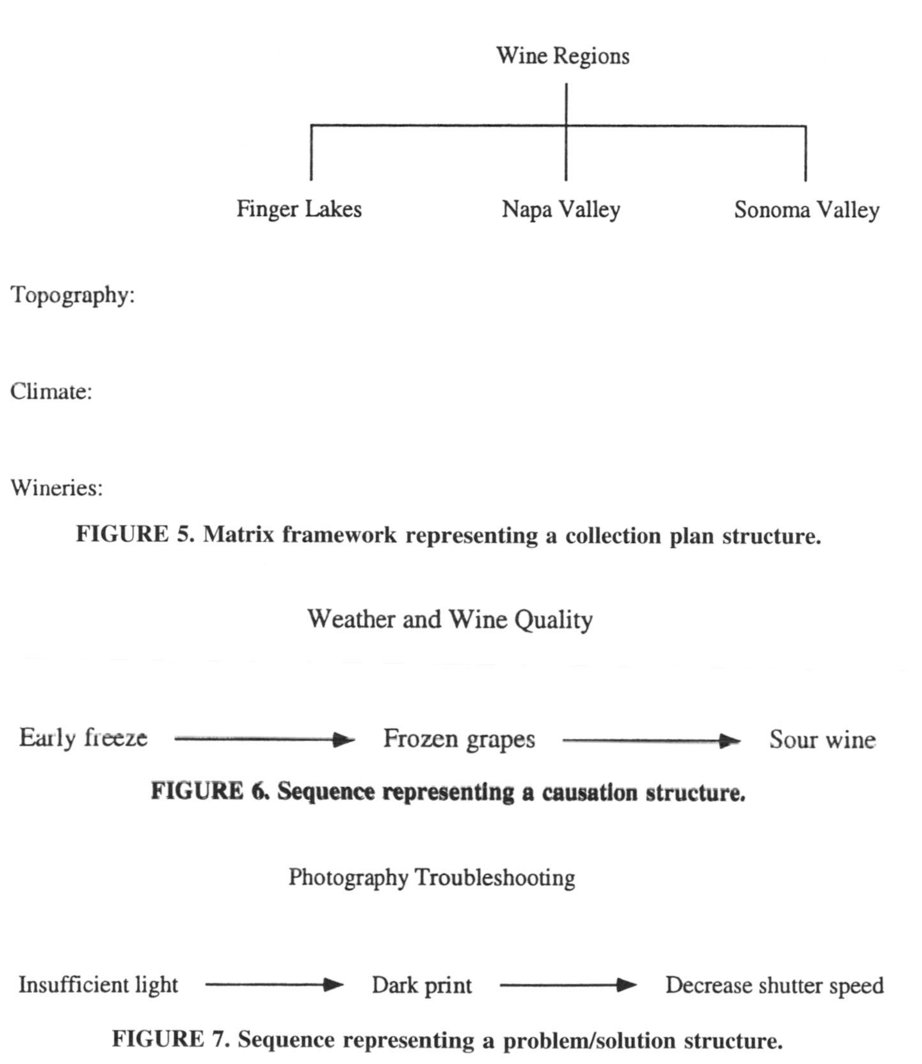

FIGURE 5. Matrix framework representing a collection plan structure.

FIGURE 6. Sequence representing a causation structure.

FIGURE 7. Sequence representing a problem/solution structure.

hierarchy. In either case, their comparative nature is illustrated by developing a matrix representation. A matrix framework for comparing computer models is shown in Figure 8.

How useful is the Matrix Representation System? Musgrave and Cohen (1971), for example, believe that all information has an underlying topic-repeatable category structure. Du Bois and Kiewra (1989) believe that most information ultimately has a topic-repeatable category structure and that information's underlying structure is hierarchical or sequential. It is from these structures that a matrix is potentially developed.

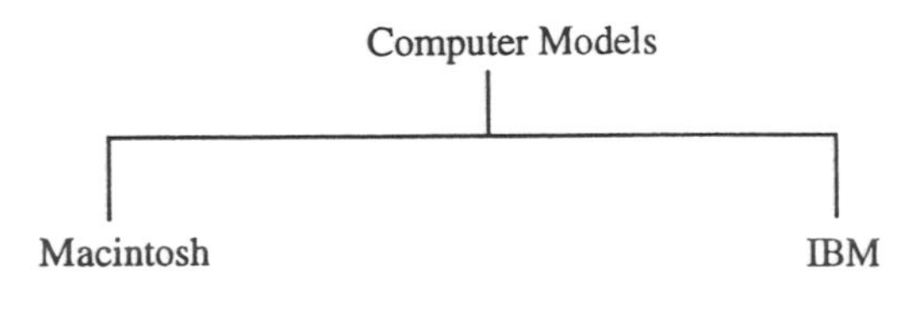

Ease of use:

Software availability:

Cost:

Compatibility:

FIGURE 8. Matrix framework for comparison structure.

Advantages Over Linear Representations

Earlier, the advantages of the Matrix Representation System compared with text were illustrated. In this section its advantages compared with linear representations such as lists or outlines are examined.

Figure 9 is an outline representation of the Lepidoptera passage. Compare it with the matrix representation in Figure 1. In terms of content, they are informationally equivalent (Larkin and Simon, 1987) because they include the same ideas. In terms of structure, however, they are computationally different (Larkin and Simon, 1987) because relational information is drawn more easily from the matrix. In particular, the matrix is more computationally efficient because it: a) reduces clutter by minimizing labels and details, b) localizes information, and c) facilitates perceptual enhancement (Larkin and Simon, 1987).

The outline is more cluttered. It presents each label (e.g., wing and rest) twice. The matrix presents a label (repeatable category) one time. The matrix also requires fewer details within its slots than the outline. Common information (e.g., about wings and development) need only appear once in the matrix. The elimination of repetitive labels and details in the matrix reduces clutter and also emphasizes the shared characteristics between topics.

The matrix localizes related information better than the outline. Notice how information about wings, for example, is adjacent in the matrix but separated by several intervening ideas in the outline. Both representations localize information within topics (e.g., moths) but only the matrix localizes information across topics (i.e., moths and butterflies) making coordinate relations more apparent.

Lepidoptera

I. Moths
 A. Wings - Two sets
 B. Rest - Wings folded down like roof
 C. Antennae - Feathery
 D. Cocoon - Fuzzy
 E. Color - Subdued
 F. Flight - Twilight/night
 G. Development
  1. Egg
  2. Caterpillar
  3. Pupa
  4. Adult
II. Butterflies
 A. Color - Bright
 B. Flight - Day
 C. Wings - Two sets
 D. Rest - Wings outstretched
 E. Antennae - Long and thin with knobs
 F. Development
  1. Egg
  2. Caterpillar
  3. Pupa
  4. Adult

FIGURE 9. Outline representation of Lepidoptera passage.

Perceptual enhancement occurs when the "big picture" (Winn, 1988) or overriding structure is readily apparent. At a glance, it is evident from the matrix that two types of Lepidoptera are compared along seven dimensions. On two dimensions they are similar, on four dimensions they are different, and on one dimension there is missing information. Upon closer inspection an important pattern emerges from the matrix. It appears that butterflies have more pronounced characteristics than moths. The overriding structure and important pattern develop far more slowly, if at all, from the outline. Its one-dimensional structure obscures these pictures.

Turn now to another example about fish represented in outline (Figure 10) and matrix (Figure 11) form. Examine those and determine whether the matrix holds an advantage in terms of reducing clutter, localizing information, and facilitating perpetual enhancement.

The labels for social group, color, size and diet appear a total of 24 times in the outline but only four times in the matrix. If more fish are studied, then the number of labels increases for the outline but not for the matrix. Because some information is identical for certain fish (i.e., size and diet), the matrix reports these details one time. Consequently, it contains less information within its cells than the outline. In this case, six repetitive details are eliminated from the matrix. Of course, reducing labels and details not only reduces clutter but emphasizes the shared characteristics among fish.

In terms of localization, the outline separates related information. For example, when examining fish size, there are three intervening facts (pertaining to diet, social group, and color) between each size designation. This is not true with the matrix where all fish sizes appear together in one row. Because there is no intervening information, the matrix reduces the amount of search necessary to locate information.

The fish matrix facilitates perceptual enhancement more than the outline. Only with the matrix representation does the "big picture" or integrative patterns emerge readily. Examining the matrix vertically, it is immediately clear that fish at 200 feet eat algae, are 150 cm in length, and are dark colored. The outline surrenders this information only with greater search and effort. Examining the matrix both vertically and horizontally, the major patterns emerge. As fish swim deeper they consume larger prey, increase in size, become lighter in color, and tend to swim in larger social groups. Extracting this pattern from the outline involves extensive data manipulation. The pieces of the puzzle are there, but lie scattered and unattached—like bones lined up across the floor. A matrix representation comparing the outline and matrix with regard to informational and computational efficiency appears in Figure 12.

Comparison With Other Spatial Representation Systems

Researchers and practitioners have developed several alternative types of text representations for displaying structural knowledge (see Jonassen et al., 1993). These include, among others, lists, outlines, matrices, tree diagrams, flow charts, concept maps, networks, graphs, numerical tables, topographical maps, pictures and illustrations.

Some of these are isomorphic; they present a representation nearly identical with its source. Topographical maps, illustrations, and pictures are isomorphic representations. These are powerful representations when a visual depiction is

Depth of Fish

I. 200 ft
- A. Lup Fish
  1. Social Group - Small
  2. Color - Black
  3. Size - 150 cm
  4. Diet - Algae
- B. Hat Fish
  1. Social Group - Solitary
  2. Color - Brown
  3. Size - 150 cm
  4. Diet - Algae

II. 400 ft
- A. Arch
  1. Social Group - Solitary
  2. Color - Blue
  3. Size - 300 cm
  4. Diet - Minnows
- B. Bone
  1. Social Group - School
  2. Color - Orange
  3. Size - 300 cm
  4. Diet - Minnows

III. 600 ft
- A. Scale
  1. Social Group - School
  2. Color - Yellow
  3. Size - 500 cm
  4. Diet - Flounders
- B. Tin
  1. Social Group - Small
  2. Color - Tan
  3. Size - 500 cm
  4. Diet - Flounders

FIGURE 10. Outline representation for Depth of Fish.

Depth of Fish	200 ft		400 ft		600 ft	
Fish:	Lup	Hat	Arch	Bone	Scale	Tin
Social Group:	Small	Solitary	Solitary	School	School	Small
Color:	Black	Brown	Blue	Orange	Yellow	Tan
Size:	150 cm		300 cm		500 cm	
Diet:	Algae		Minnows		Flounder	

FIGURE 11. Matrix representation for Depth of Fish.

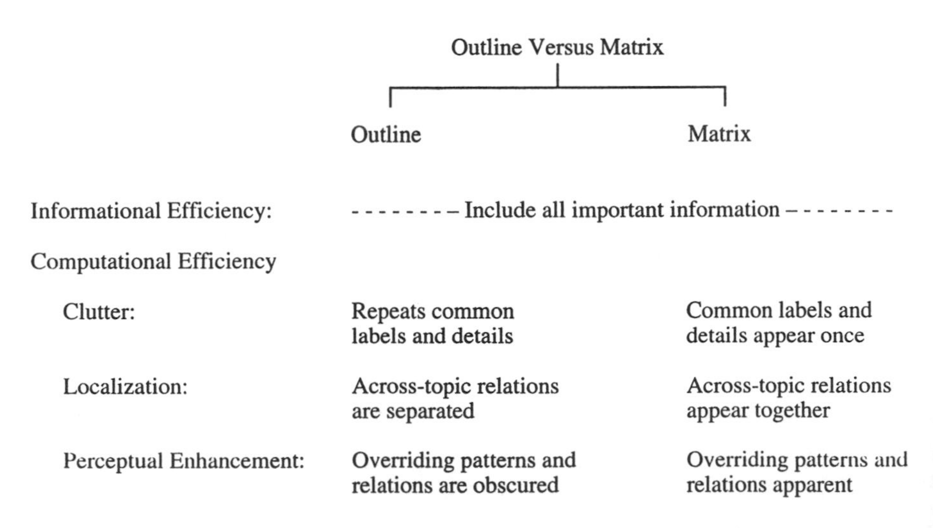

FIGURE 12. Matrix representation comparing outline and matrix.

helpful such as showing the parts of a flower (Kiewra, Du Bois, Weiss and Schantz, 1992), or how brakes operate (Mayer and Gallini, 1990). The others are abstract representations in the sense they comprise the essential qualities of a

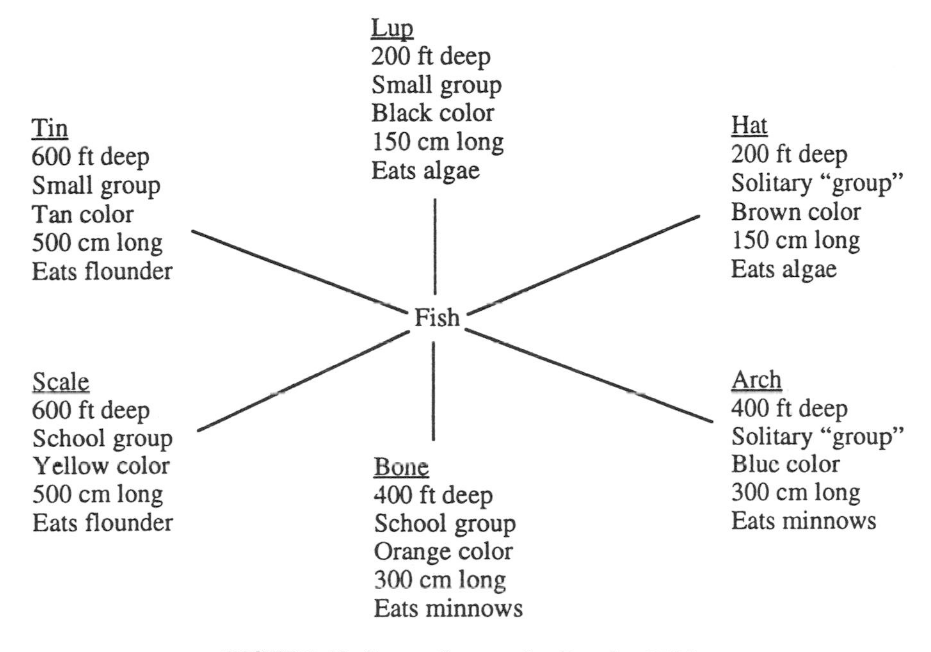

FIGURE 13. Semantic map for Depth of Fish.

larger thing. Some of these are one dimensional such as lists and outlines and are therefore limited, like text, because they present information sequentially. The others present information in a two-dimensional or spatial form. Some of these have highly specific purposes such as graphs and numerical tables which display numerical data. Others, I believe, have limited utility with respect to reducing clutter, localizing information, and facilitating perceptual enhancement. This is demonstrated by examining the three most popular abstract representation systems: semantic maps, concept maps, and networks (see Jonassen et al., 1993) along these dimensions.

Semantic maps represent concepts hierarchically. They position the primary or superordinate concept in the center and subordinate concepts around the primary concept. Related ideas are listed below the corresponding subordinate concept. An example of a concept map for the fish material introduced previously is shown in Figure 13.

The semantic map is informationally equivalent to the matrix in Figure 11. Computationally, it appears more cluttered, less localized, and less perceptually enhancing. The semantic map contains 30 labels versus four for the matrix. Because common information is listed separately for each fish, the semantic map contains 30 details versus 21 for the matrix. In terms of localization, the semantic map physically separates related information (e.g., about diet) whereas the matrix positions related information along the same row. The overriding pattern and relationships readily apparent in the matrix are obscured in the semantic map which fails to provide perceptual enhancement.

Concept maps (Novak and Gowin, 1984) and networks (Holley and Dansereau, 1984; Lambiotte, Dansereau, Cross, and Reynolds, 1989) are similar because both represent concepts and specify the links between concepts. Their primary difference is that the link names are invented by the concept map builder but chosen from a menu of six designated links by the network builder. A concept map/network for the fish material is found in Figure 14.

The same problems inherent in the semantic map are found with the concept map/network. First, 30 labels are used and common details are listed separately. The additional labels and details add clutter and shroud common characteristics between fish relative to the matrix. Second, related information is separated physically rather than located adjacently. Last, the concept map/network does not aid perceptual enhancement. The overriding pattern and interrelationships are hidden.

In summary, neither of these representations appear as effective as the matrix for representing information about fish. Of course, research is needed to determine the relative benefits of representation systems for various learning tasks.

THEORY

Why should the matrix representation system facilitate learning? This question is examined in terms of how information is processed in memory. Two sequential memory processes are necessary for learning: attention and encoding. Each of these have two subprocesses. Attention depends on the sequential subprocesses of pattern recognition and selective attention. Encoding has two components: organization and integration. Figure 15 shows the relations among these processes and subprocesses.

Learning begins when information is received through our senses and identified through pattern recognition. Pattern recognition occurs almost instantaneously and without effort. Familiar concepts are recognized by their physical properties. At a carnival, for example, you might recognize at once a giant ferris wheel, a row of game booths, and a concession area housing several merchants.

During selective attention, attention is focused on selected aspects of the environment. At the carnival, for example, you might attend selectively to the concession area focusing on merchant names, the signs displaying prices, and the lengths of service lines.

Organization occurs when selected ideas are restructured in a coherent manner. Organization is also called building internal connections (Mayer, 1984) because the learner makes logical connections among available ideas. At the carnival you

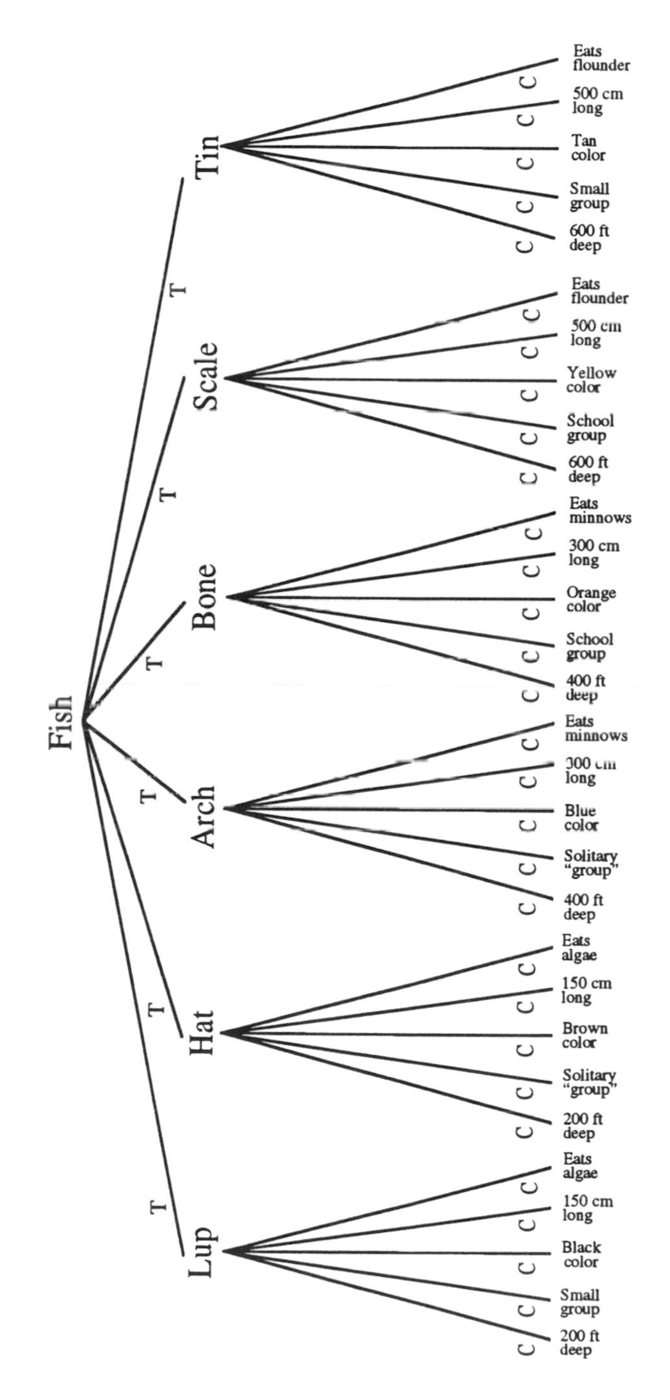

FIGURE 14. Concept map/network for Depth of Fish.

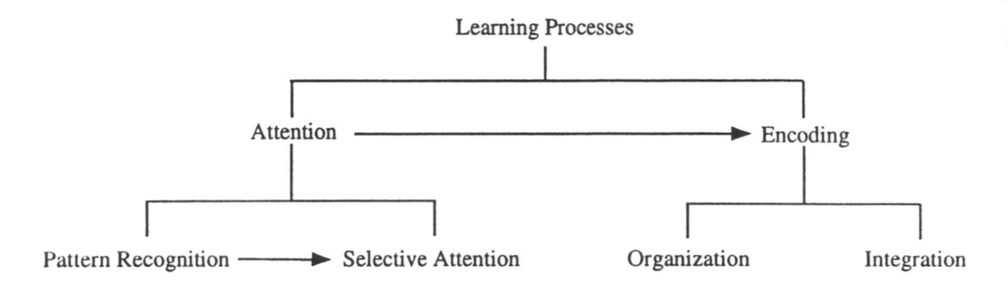

FIGURE 15. Learning processes supporting the Matrix Representation System.

might organize selected ideas regarding food as shown in Figure 16. In this case, your organizing framework is the types of food. Subsumed beneath each food type are the representative merchants. The framework's slots house information about the line length and food prices associated with each merchant. Inherent in this organizational structure are several internal connections. You realize, for example, that prices range from $3.00 to $6.00; that lines are either short or long, but most are long; and that low prices are associated with long lines whereas high prices are associated with short lines.

Integration occurs when new knowledge is related with previous knowledge already in memory. This process is also called *building external connections* (Mayer, 1984) because the learner connects new information with previously acquired knowledge outside the current learning context. In considering what to eat at the carnival, for example, you might recall that you dislike tacos, that pizza from the Pizza Parlor gives you heartburn, and that you disdain long lines. Integration provides a context for new learning and serves to make new knowledge more meaningful.

I believe that the matrix can facilitate information processing with respect to these four subprocesses. Each subprocess is examined in turn.

Pattern Recognition

One advantage the matrix has over an outline or text is that more structural knowledge is available from the matrix upon immediate viewing. Information's structure is at once apparent. It is quickly apparent, for example, whether information is organized hierarchically or sequentially. If it is hierarchical, the numbers of levels, topics, and subtopics are known at a glance. Furthermore, the number of repeatable categories pertaining to the topics is known instantly. The structure of knowledge must be sewn together from a text and even an outline. Initial processing of a matrix representation is simultaneous; initial processing of an outline or text is successive—one idea at a time.

Few attentional resources are necessary to identify a matrix's informational structure just as few resources are necessary to perceive these three dots (∴) as

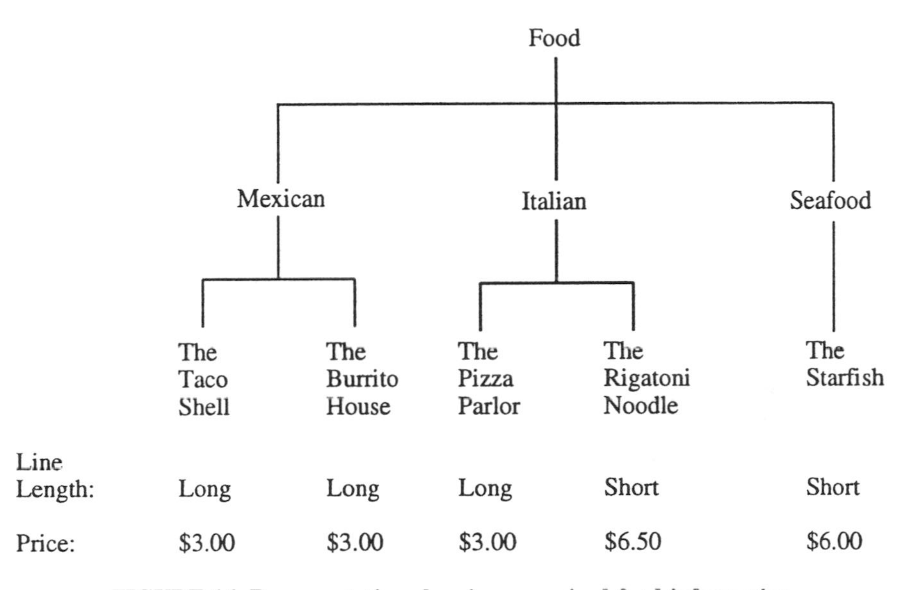

FIGURE 16. Representation showing organized food information.

a triangle. In this sense, the matrix provides valuable information before the learner even sets out to process it. Because minimal mental effort is spent uncovering the information's structure in a matrix or other well designed representation, Waller (1981) contends that such representations present a ''visual argument.'' Through visual argument, ideas are transmitted via a spatial arrangement of words rather than ongoing written language. By ''seeing'' ideas, readers are relieved of the burden of searching and untangling complex relationships embedded in text.

Glance back at the operant conditioning representation in Figure 2. Immediately, the information's structure is apparent. There is a top-level concept (i.e., operant conditioning) subsuming two concepts (i.e., reinforcement and punishment). Each of these subsume two more concepts. These most subordinate concepts are described along two repeatable categories.

Selective Attention

During selective attention, learners focus attention on a few selected ideas. Because the matrix generally contains a subset of the text's ideas, it directs attention better than the text (Kiewra and Sperling-Dennison, 1992). A matrix might also facilitate selective attention better than an outline even though both representations incorporate identical ideas. Recall that only the matrix's streamlined structure reduces repetitive labels and details (see Figures 10 and 11).

Perhaps most importantly, the matrix's structure guides the route of selective

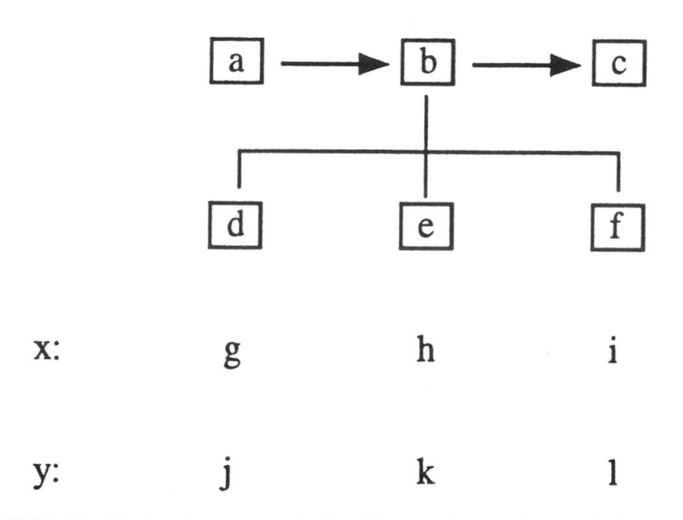

FIGURE 17. Algebraic representation illustrating various relation types.

attention. Its spatial structure encourages students to search for hierarchical, sequential, and coordinate relations. Returning to Figure 2, a student attends to hierarchical relations (e.g., there are positive and negative types of reinforcement) and coordinate relations (e.g., reinforcement results in an increase in behavior, whereas punishment results in a decrease in behavior).

Organization

To paraphrase Tukey (1990), the purpose of a matrix representation is to organize information, not store facts. A matrix should serve more than an attention function, it should aid the learner in connecting ideas. The hallmark of an effective matrix should be its ability to facilitate relational understanding.

There are a variety of types of connections that a student might learn from studying a matrix. These include sequential, hierarchical, within-topic and across-topic (i.e., coordinate). Based on the algebraic representation in Figure 17, sequential relations exist among a, b, and c. Hierarchical relations exist between b and d, e, and f. Across-topic relations exist among d, e, and f as observed among g, h, and i; and j, k, and l. Within-topic relations exist among d, g, and j; e, h, and k; and f, i, and l.

In some instances, a matrix has facilitated organization (Kiewra and Sperling-Dennison, 1992) and in other instances it has not (Kiewra, Du Bois, Staley, and Robinson, 1992). Contradicting findings may be the result of the learner's activities. No matter how well organized or developed a matrix is, internal connections are formed by the learner who searches the matrix in appropriate ways. A matrix that represents across-topic relations is essentially useless if the learner

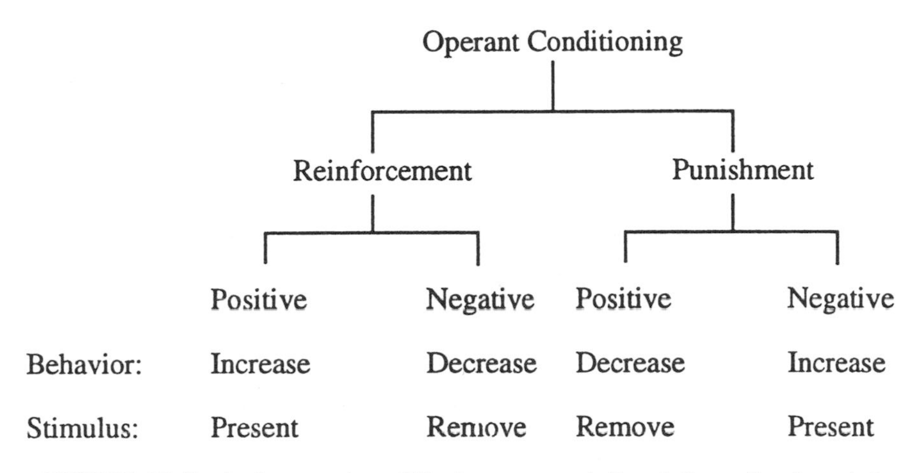

FIGURE 18. Revised operant conditioning representation; information is sorted but generally unrelated.

does not search the rows of the matrix and operate on the information within the rows to form such relations. In other words, the matrix is a tool that facilitates, but does not ensure, internal connections. If the learner, for example, studies the four subordinate concepts in Figure 2 independently by examining the matrix in a vertical fashion only, then he/she would not understand the concepts' interrelationships.

Contradictory findings can also be attributed to the nature of the learning materials. Matrices that merely sort arbitrary information should not be more effective than lists or outlines in building internal connections. Consider the revised operant conditioning representation in Figure 18. This representation merely sorts information. No relationships or patterns emerge when the information is searched horizontally. In this case, the matrix offers little help in building internal connections.

A third factor possibly producing conflicting results is the type of dependent measure used to assess organization. Matrices should primarily affect the learning of across-topic relations. The matrix's two-dimensional structure accents these relations that are ordinarily obscured in linear representations. Organizational tests that fail to tap across-topic relations are, in part, invalid.

Integration

The matrix can support integration in two ways. First, learners can acquire new information more easily if they have an organized structure in memory for assimilating new knowledge. The notion is consistent with Schema theory (Rumelhart, 1980; Rumelhart and Ortony, 1977) which contends that information in memory is organized categorically along various features (as is a matrix). For example, a building schema might include the categories house, school, and office and the features size and location. The schema's slots or cells store new information intersecting the category members and their features (e.g., most houses are located in the suburbs).

Second, integration can occur when a completed matrix is extended or embellished with previously acquired knowledge. A matrix representation can be modified in three ways: horizontally, vertically, or within its cells. As an example, return to Figure 2 (p. 334). Suppose the learner has past knowledge about another operant technique such as extinction. This concept is added by extending the matrix horizontally. The learner's personal examples of behaviors warranting the various techniques are added by extending the matrix vertically and including the repeatable category ''example.'' Previous knowledge that the stimulus should be presented immediately for positive reinforcement is recorded within the matrix cell intersecting positive reinforcement and stimulus. These integrative adaptations are shown in the boxed portion of Figure 19.

REVIEW OF RESEARCH

In this section, research on matrix representations is reviewed versus more linear representations such as text and outlines. The guiding framework is the theoretical ideas presented previously: attention and encoding.

Attention

Attention has two subprocesses: pattern recognition and selective attention. During pattern recognition, the reader rapidly perceives the information's structure. I know of no research investigating pattern recognition for matrix representations. Pattern recognition can be assessed by providing students via computer an outline, text, or matrix representation and inquiring about the information's structure. For example, students might be asked whether the overriding structure is hierarchical or sequential, or about the number of topics, subtopics, features (repeatable categories), and details that appear. Assessing the time needed to respond to such questions can determine if a matrix is previewed more rapidly and accurately than an outline or text.

An experiment, similar in methodology, determined how rapidly different representations are searched during the selective attention phase. Robinson (1994) presented a question to students before they viewed an outline, text, or matrix representation presented by computer. Answering the question depended upon locating two or more details in the representations. For instance, a question might ask which of four snakes is shortest in length. This information was spread over four text paragraphs, four outline sections, or presented within the same matrix row. Students located relevant information and formulated a response

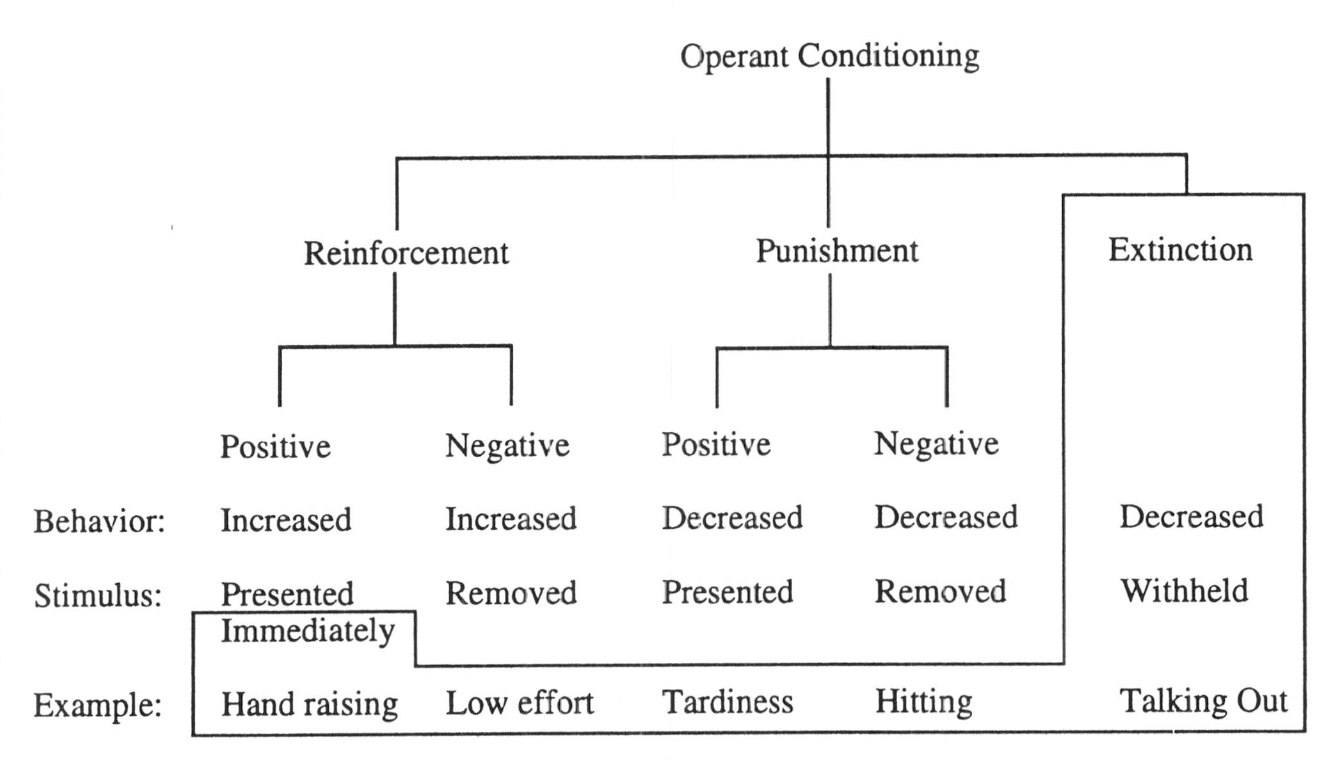

FIGURE 19. Representation including external connections.

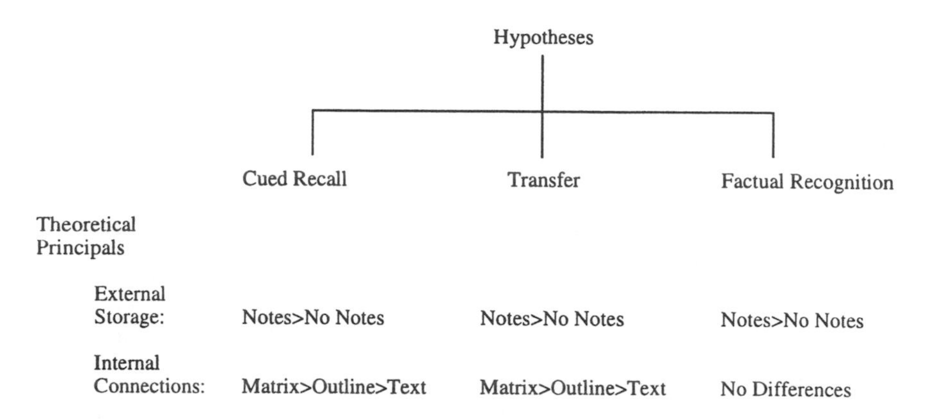

FIGURE 20. Hierarchy/Matrix used by Kiewra and Sperling-Dennison (1992).

more rapidly when viewing the matrix than when viewing the text or outline. This is evidence that selective attention is more rapidly applied to across-topic information in a matrix than a text or outline.

Selective attention was assessed in three experiments conducted by Kiewra and Sperling-Dennison. Their experiments investigated the utility of representations as supplements to a research article. In the first experiment (Kiewra and Sperling-Dennison, 1992), graduate students assigned to one of two groups studied a two-and-a-half page research article for 45 minutes. The article, adapted from the *Journal of Educational Psychology* (1988, *80*: 595–597), pertained to different forms of note taking. One group received only the article; the other group received the article plus four representations. Three of these were hierarchy/matrices; the other was a sequence/hierarchy. One of the representations appears in Figure 20. The others pertained to the experimental method and results described in the research article.

A cued-recall test was administered immediately following the study period. Some items could be answered from the representations (represented items) and some could only be answered from the text (nonrepresented items). Results indicated that students studying the text-plus-representations recalled more represented information. The authors contend that the representations served a selective attention function as evidenced by the superior performance of the representation group on the represented items. Having this information represented outside the text drew students' attention to it.

Experiment 2 (Kiewra and Sperling-Dennison, 1992) was designed to further test representation's selective attention function. A group that received the text with pertinent information underlined (that which appeared in the representations) was added. The research question was whether underlining served as powerful an attention function as representations. A significant group by item type interaction revealed that with respect to represented information the ordering of means wastext-plus-representations > underlined text > text only. With respect to non-represented information, the ordering of means was opposite. This interaction indicates that representations served a superior selective attention function, but at same cost. They produced the least recall for nonrepresented information.

A third experiment (Sperling-Dennison and Kiewra, 1993) added yet another group to the previous groups. Participants in this group studied outlines that were informationally equivalent to the spatial representations. This group was added to assess whether it was the structure of the spatial representations that produced consistent selective attention effects over text and underlined text.

Results indicated that both outline and spatial representation groups outperformed the text only group on represented facts items. For nonrepresented facts items, however, there were no differences among groups. These results indicate that outlines and spatial representations both serve a selective attention function relative to studying the text. However, the outline and matrix proved equal in their ability to aid selective attention.

In summary, spatial representations serve an attention focusing function relative to text or underlined text. They are, however, no more effective than outlines that select and display the same information. In terms of search time, however, a matrix representation is attended to more rapidly than an outline or text.

Encoding

Encoding is the process whereby new information is stored in memory. It is possible to assess whether encoded information is stored as isolated facts, organized structures, or integrated with previous knowledge. Recall tests commonly assess memory for facts. Relational tests or writing tasks assessing coherence measure organization. Problem solving tasks assess integration. Integration produces the meaningful learning necessary to solve new problems (Mayer, 1984). In the following subsections, research is reviewed regarding how matrix representations affect a) memory for factual details, b) relational learning, c) written discourse, and d) problem solving.

Memory for factual details. The fish representations presented as Figures 10 and 11 (see pp. 341, 342) were used in a series of experiments by Kiewra and his colleagues assessing memory for factual details.* In each experiment, participants read or heard a short passage about six fictitious fish. Five different facts were presented about each fish pertaining to its depth, social group, color, length, and diet. The text presented this information in a linear format and did not reveal how this information interrelated. In fact, the passage obscured the similarities

*After the chapter was typeset, Kiewra and his colleagues reclassified their ''memory for factual details'' test as a ''between-concepts relations'' test. Their rationale was that the test measures memory for *related* facts more than for *independent* facts. A sample test item is ''what two fish eat algae?''.

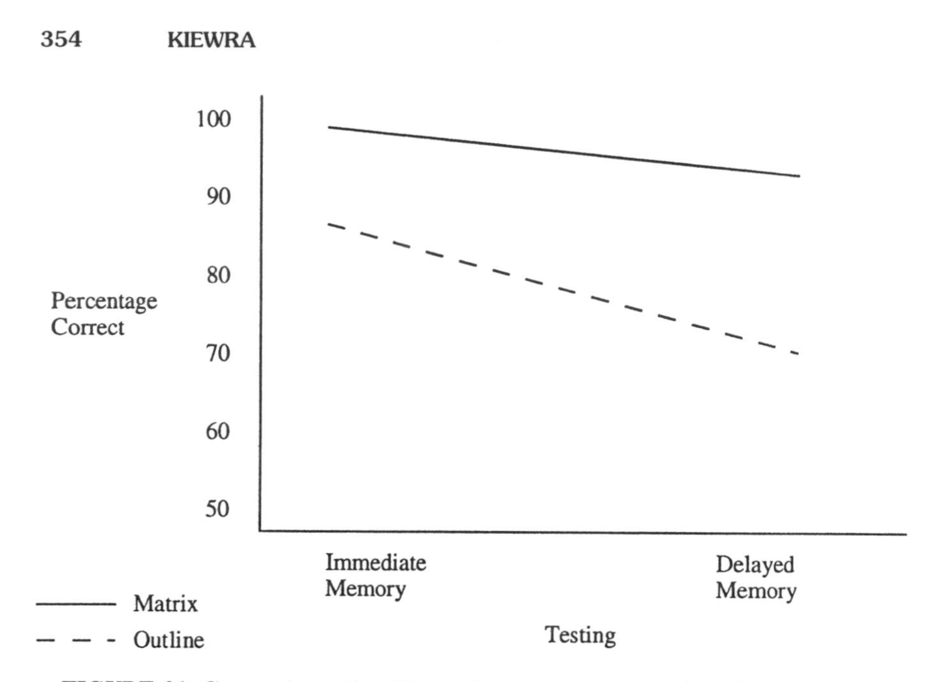

FIGURE 21. Comparison of outline and matrix representations for immediate and delayed memory tests (Kiewra, Du Bois, Staley, and Robinson, 1992).

between fish (e.g., both the Hat and the Lup fish are 150 cm long and eat algae) and the overriding patterns among all the fish (e.g., fish swimming at progressively deeper depths are lighter in color, larger in size, and consume larger prey).

In the first experiment (Kiewra, Du Bois, Staley, and Robinson, 1992), the comparison of interest was between those studying a matrix (Figure 11) versus those studying an outline (Figure 10) for 15 minutes. The representations were informationally, but not computationally, equivalent (Larkin and Simon, 1987). The two-dimensional matrix contained fewer labels, placed like information in closer proximity, and provided greater perceptual enhancement than the outline. The interrelationships or patterns among ideas were more apparent in the matrix.

A memory test was administered immediately following the study episode and again two days later. As seen in the graph in Figure 21, the matrix group outperformed the outline group for both immediate and delayed recall. Performance on delayed testing also declined more for the outline group than for the matrix group. These findings indicate that the matrix produced greater immediate and delayed recall than the outline and that learning from the matrix was relatively resistant to memory loss over a moderate two-day delay

In a second experiment (Kiewra, Du Bois, Staley, and Robinson, 1992), the matrix and outline representations were examined in terms of efficiency and long-term retention. To assess efficiency, participants studied representations for

5, 10, or 15 minutes. It was thought that the matrix, given its perceptual advantages, would have its biggest advantage over the outline at 5 minutes. To assess long-term retention, memory tests were administered immediately after study and again five days later. The matrix proved relatively effective for remembering facts. Students studying the matrix statistically outperformed those studying the text, and descriptively outperformed those studying the outline. The matrix's advantage over the outline was most apparent with delayed testing. This observed advantage following a five-day delay supports and extends the findings from the first experiment where the test was delayed two days. In both experiments the matrix facilitated long-term retention.

Finally, with regard to efficiency, there was mild support favoring the matrix over the outline when study time was brief. Although results were not significant, following a five-minute study period the matrix group averaged 94 percent correct versus 83 percent correct for the outline group. After 10 minutes of study, the groups performed virtually the same (94 percent for the matrix group and 92 percent for the outline group).

A third experiment (Kiewra, Levin, Kim, Meyers, Renandya, and Hwang, 1994) investigated whether a matrix for fish could be enhanced by using pictures or mnemonic pictures in place of verbal descriptions. In the picture conditions, the row headings designated social grouping, the column headings designated depth, and along the bottom appeared a series of rulers against which the fish could be measured. Each fish was drawn to its relative size, and in its appropriate color. Solitary fish were pictured alone; those in small groups were pictured in pairs; those in schools were pictured among several fish. The food for each fish was also drawn to resemble the actual food in appearance and relative size. The mnemonic pictures were drawn to help students recall the names of the fish and associate the names with related characteristics. The Hat fish, for example, was drawn to resemble a dark brown hat. The tin fish looked like a tin can and was colored light tan. The ''mnematrix'' (mnemonic picture matrix) appears in Figure 22.

The three matrix forms (verbal, picture, and mnematrix) were compared with three corresponding outline forms, and to a read-only control group. Groups studied their instructional materials for 10 minutes before taking several memory tests. Results indicated that the mnematrix group outperformed the text-only control group across memory tests. The conventional matrix group also outperformed the control group on a memory test assessing color. Mnemonic pictures proved generally effective. They boosted memory whether they were presented in matrix or outline form. This study showed first that a matrix can incorporate other instructional aids such as pictures and mnemonics, and that the combination of pictures, mnemonics, and matrix is a powerful one under these conditions.

In summary, the following conclusions can be drawn from the memory studies reported here. First, the matrix was superior to the outline for immediate reten-

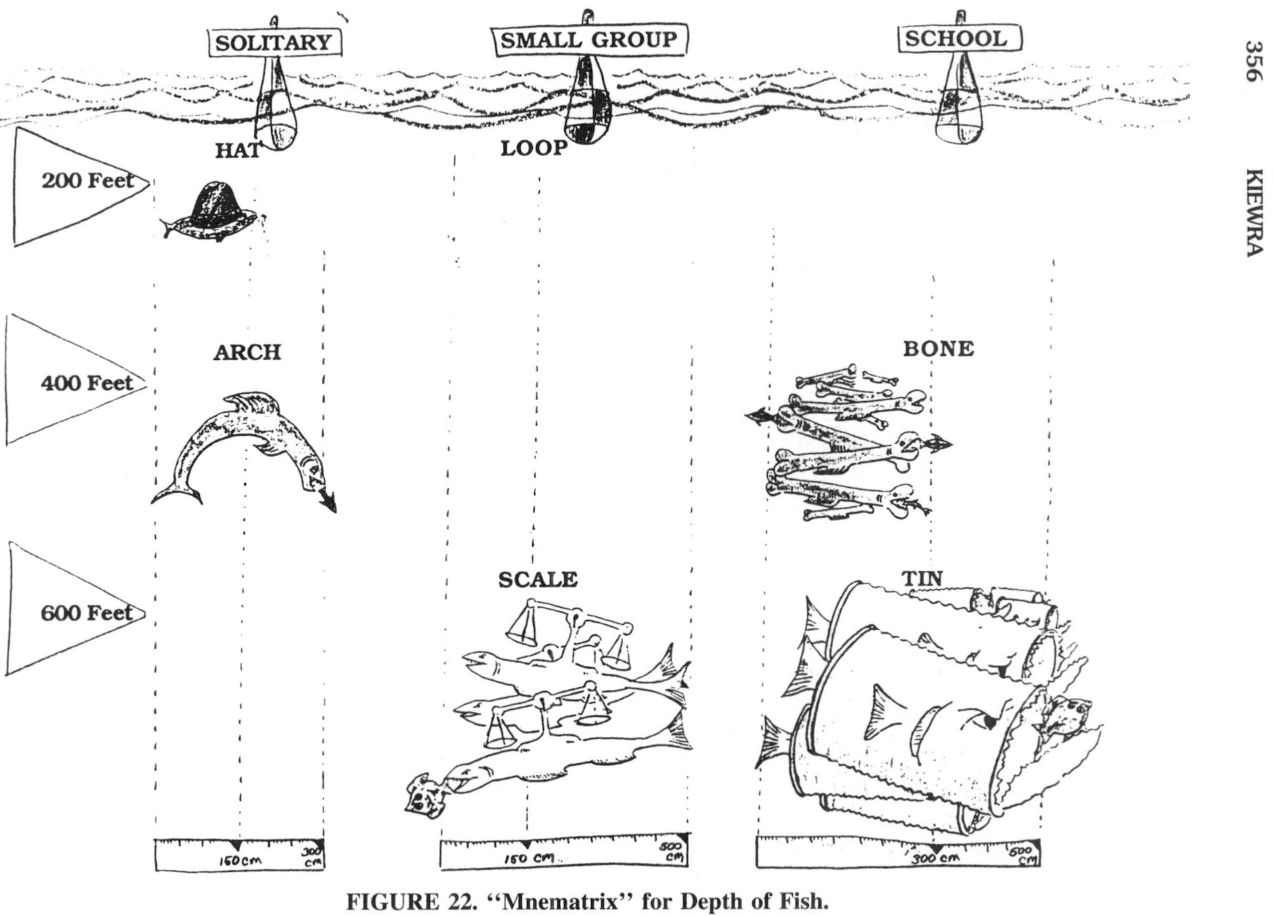

FIGURE 22. "Mnematrix" for Depth of Fish.

tion and particularly long-term retention. Second, the matrix was somewhat more efficient than the outline. More information was learned more quickly from the matrix. Third, the matrix can incorporate pictures and mnemonics that bolster memory performance. Studies by Day (1988), Jones, Amiran, and Katims (1985), and Kiewra, Du Bois, Christian, McShane, Meyerhoffer, and Roskelley (1991) also support the memory advantage of matrix representations versus linear representations or methods.

Memory for relationships. In the experiments reviewed earlier pertaining to learning from a research article (Kiewra and Sperling-Dennison, 1992; Sperling-Dennison and Kiewra, 1993), relational learning was also assessed. Participants were administered tests assessing relationships among ideas. A sample test question was, ''what are the internal connection hypotheses for recall, transfer and recognition tests.'' (See Figure 20.) In general, results indicated that studying the research article plus representations produced higher relational performance than studying the research article only or the research article with important (represented) ideas underlined. However, the outline representations and spatial representations had similar effects on relational learning.

Relational learning was also assessed in experiments involving fish learning (Kiewra, Du Bois, Staley, and Robinson, 1992). Relational items probed the overriding relationships between fish characteristics. One relational question, for example, asked about the relationship between depth and length. In Experiment 1, matrix, outline, and text groups did not differ significantly on relational performance. The practical differences among means, however, was noteworthy. The matrix group averaged 75 percent correct whereas the outline group averaged 65 percent correct, just barely above the text-only control group (62 percent). When study times were varied in Experiment 2, both matrix and outline representations boosted relational performance beyond that of studying the text alone. No relational performance differences were found, however, between outline and matrix studiers.

Two other experiments by Kiewra and colleagues investigated relational learning. In each experiment, participants viewed a 19-minute videotaped lecture about five types of creativity. The lecture contained 1,881 words and 121 idea units, and was delivered at a rate of about 100 wpm. For each type of creativity, nine different features (e.g., definition, motivation, distinguishing characteristics, and myths) were discussed in varying order.

In the first experiment (Kiewra, Du Bois, Christian, and McShane, 1988), college students viewed the lecture and then reviewed either a set of complete notes for 25 minutes or reviewed mentally . Those studying notes either reviewed a verbatim text of the lecture, outline notes, or matrix notes. All materials contained all 121 idea units. The outline contained 758 words; the matrix contained 610 words. The matrix contained 45 cells that were the intersections of the five types of creativity and their nine common features.

Type of Creativity	Expressive	Adaptive	Innovative	Emergentive	School
Definition					
Time Demand to Display Creativity					
Time Demand to Develop Creativity					
Motivation					
Distinguishing Characteristic(s)					
Related Characteristics					
Examples					
Myths					
Myths Expelled					

FIGURE 23. Matrix framework for note taking (Kiewra, Du Bois, Christian, McShane, Meyerhoffer, and Roskelley, 1991).

Following the review period, students were administered a 30-item transfer test. It comprised 10 relational items (e.g., which two types of creativity take a lifetime to develop?) and 20 conceptual items where novel examples of the types of creativity were presented for classification. On the transfer test, only the matrix group (M = 63 percent) significantly outperformed the text group (M = 36 percent). The matrix group scored somewhat higher than the outline group (M = 56 percent). The authors contended that the matrix's advantage for transfer performance occurred because the matrix best facilitated across-topic relations among the five types of creativity. An increased understanding of similarities and differences among creativity types helped students answer relational items (how are types of creativity similar or different?) and concept items whose solution involved making subtle comparisons among the creativity types.

A second study (Kiewra, Du Bois, Christian, McShane, Meyerhoffer, and Roskelley, 1991) introduced the matrix to lecture note taking. College students viewed the 19-minute creativity lecture while either recording notes in an outline framework, a matrix framework, or on lined paper in a conventional manner. The blank outline and matrix frameworks were identical to those used in the study by Kiewra, Du Bois, Christian, and McShane (1988) but contained no details. Instead, blank spaces were provided for students to record ideas. The matrix framework appears in Figure 23.

With respect to relational performance, mean scores did not vary significantly. However, the pattern of scores mirrored those from the earlier study (Kiewra, Du Bois, Christian, and McShane, 1988) and supports the predicted advantage of the matrix for relational performance (*M*s = 73 percent, 68 percent, and 64 percent for matrix, conventional, and outline notes, respectively).

In summary, the results from these studies indicate that the matrix is superior to text for relational learning. Relative to the outline, however, the matrix shows only a trend toward producing higher relational performance. One problem inherent in these studies, however, is that students were not trained in how to study representations. In fact, students in one study (Kiewra, Du Bois, Christian, and McShane, 1988) were actually observed transforming a provided matrix into an outline. As mentioned previously, the matrix's contribution to relational learning depends on a) students seeking internal connections, b) meaningful relationships being presented within the matrix, and c) dependent measures assessing relationships, particularly across topics. Another means for assessing relational learning is by examining the organization of written discourse.

Written discourse. Four experiments were conducted (Benton, Kiewra, Whitfall, and Dennison, 1993) that examined, in part, whether different note forms affect the organizing processes of writing. In all four experiments, college students viewed the 19-minute videotaped lecture about creativity described earlier. In Experiments 1 and 2, participants recorded notes on matrix or outline frameworks or recorded conventional notes or no notes. Following the lecture, students had 25 minutes to write a compare-and-contrast essay about three types of creativity. One half of the students in each note-taking group wrote essays with their notes available, whereas the other half wrote without notes. In Experiment 1, the writing task was administered immediately after the lecture. In Experiment 2, it was administered following a one-week delay. In Experiments 3 and 4, participants listened to the lecture without recording notes. Afterward they completed the essay assignment with or without notes made available by the experimenters. Those writing with notes were provided with one of three sets of complete notes differing only in form: conventional, outline, or matrix. The writing assignment was immediate in Experiment 3 and delayed one week in Experiment 4.

There were two results of interest. In Experiment 1, students with matrix notes wrote essays containing more cohesive ties than students with outline notes. Cohesive ties are a measure of organization. They are words or phrases that correctly compare or contrast one element of text with another (Halliday and Hasan, 1976). Words and phrases like *similar, however, whereas* and *on the other hand* are examples of cohesive ties. The use of cohesive ties is indicative of a cohesive writing style that interrelates information for the reader. It is contrasted with a linear style where ideas are presented sequentially and independent from potentially related ideas.

In Experiment 4, those writing from matrix notes produced more coherent essays than those writing without notes following a one-week delay. Coherence, like cohesive ties, is an indication of organization. Coherence was measured based upon the Bamberg (1983) coherence scale that globally assesses written discourse along a continuum essentially ranging from incomprehensible to fully coherent where the essay clearly identifies topics, flows smoothly, and provides a clean sense of closure.

Although the matrix did not uniformly produce higher quality writing throughout the four experiments, it was the only form of notes that affected the organization of written discourse. These findings support Langer's (1984) finding that the degree to which topic-related knowledge is organized influences writing quality.

The benefit of matrix notes for increasing organization in written discourse was also seen among college students who read a lengthy text about personality disorders and then reviewed outline, matrix, or text materials. Students reviewing matrix materials wrote responses to compare and contrast essay items that contained more comparisons and more cohesive ties than students reviewing outlines (Robinson, 1993).

In summary, matrices facilitate the organization subprocess of encoding as seen through written discourse. Students who use matrices produce essays that are more coherent, comparative, and cohesive.

Problem solving. Effective problem solving depends on effective problem representation. For example, Bovenmeyer Lewis and Mayer (1987) found that students who represent the elements in a word problem generate more correct solutions than those who do not generate a representation. For purposes of this chapter, studies are reviewed where problem solvers use a matrix representation versus another form of representation (e.g., list or hierarchy) in attempts to problem solve. The reported studies show a clear advantage for the matrix across different problem types.

Early investigations of the matrix for problem solving were conducted by Schwartz and his colleagues (Polich and Schwartz, 1974; Schwartz, 1971; Schwartz and Fattaleh, 1972). They presented who-done-it-type deductive reasoning problems for which solvers had to match values along several dimensions by reasoning deductively from sentence clues. In one problem, participants were given a list of statements pertaining to a) the names of men in a hospital, b) their illness, and c) their room numbers. Sentences only presented partial information such as the man in Room 101 has asthma or Mr. Jones has cancer.

The problem entailed determining what disease Mr. Young had. Results showed that when sentence information was represented in a matrix, rather than in a list or hierarchy, problems were solved more accurately. This was particularly true when problem size increased (Polich and Schwartz, 1974) because the matrix permitted the greatest number of relations to be deduced correctly and simultaneously.

	Breakfast	Lunch	Dinner	Bedtime
Lanoxin	✓			
Inderal	✓	✓	✓	
Quinaglute	✓	✓	✓	✓
Carafate	✓	✓	✓	✓
Zantac	✓			✓
Coumadin				✓

FIGURE 24. Matrix medication schedule (Day, 1988).

A study reported by Day (1988) showed how studying a medication schedule represented in a matrix form (Figure 24) produced more accurate problem solving than studying it in list form (Figure 25). The list contained the names of the six drugs in a column with a dosage alongside each drug (e.g., one tablet four times a day). The matrix also listed the drugs in a column but used time designations (i.e., breakfast, lunch, dinner, and bedtime) as repeatable categories. A check mark in the matrix cells indicated when a drug should be taken (e.g., Lanoxin at breakfast). After studying the list or matrix, students were asked problems (e.g., If you leave home in the afternoon and will not be back until breakfast time the next day, how many Inderal should you take along?). Results showed a superior effect for studying the matrix. The matrix was superior, Day concluded, because, unlike the outline, it presented the union of medication and time information.

A matrix representation was compared with a hierarchical representation for problem solving in a study by McGuinness (1986). Participants first memorized a two-level hierarchy or a 4 × 4 matrix showing family relations. The representations contained 16 names of family members. The birth order and nuclear descendants were given for each member.

After memorizing the representations, students were given word problems to solve pertaining to the representations. These had to be solved from memory. Results showed that participants studying the matrix responded to the test items more than twice as fast as those studying the hierarchy. This was true, however, only when problem solution involved searching the matrix in a horizontal manner

Inderal - 1 tablet 3 times a day

Lanoxin - 1 tablet every a.m.

Carafate - 1 tablet before meals and at bedtime

Zantac - 1 tablet every 12 hours (twice a day)

Quinaglute - 1 tablet 4 times a day

Coumadin - 1 tablet a day

FIGURE 25. List medication schedule (Day, 1988).

across topics. In this case the information needed for solution was available in a single package by searching a single matrix row; the same information could be extracted only by searching over many intervening facts throughout the hierarchy. When solution depended on locating information within a single topic, the hierarchy and matrix were equally effective because information was equally accessible within a matrix column or within a single arm of the hierarchy. These results confirm the earlier point that matrix representations particularly facilitate across-topic comparisons.

The matrix has shown transferability across problems (Novick, 1990). Students received a probability problem and a matrix framework (an empty matrix) to aid in problem solution. When they later received a deductive reasoning problem (the patient/room/disease problem described earlier), these students were more likely to generate a matrix to aid solution than were students who had not received the original matrix problem. Although transfer was local (within the same experimental setting), it is encouraging to see that students used the matrix spontaneously and capably without training to solve new problems.

In summary, the matrix proved effective for problem solving. Problem solving is facilitated when meaningful learning—the integration of old and new knowledge—occurs (Mayer, 1984). In each case, the matrix representation allowed learners to see all the data in a meaningful way. John Tukey (1990) said that the greatest possibilities of visual displays lie in their vividness and inescapability of the intended message. A visual display can make you notice what you never intended to see.

MATRIX APPLICATIONS

In this section, how matrices are used to facilitate learning from lecture or text is illustrated. Also demonstrated is how they aid concept and rule learning, and support problem solving, critical thinking, and writing. Last, a method for teaching matrix use and construction is presented.

Learning from Lecture and Text

As a college instructor, I commonly present matrix representations to help students acquire lecture and text information. In lectures about memory, for example, I present a matrix comparing the three memory stores (sensory, short term, and long term) with respect to capacity, forgetting, and storage modality. Another example is a matrix comparing the temporal and capacity limitations of short-term memory in terms of evidence, and strategies for overcoming the limitation.

I also introduce generic matrix frameworks early in the educational psychology course usable throughout the course. Understanding a discipline's structure in advance is instrumental in focusing attention and facilitating encoding. One educational psychology framework organizes research evidence from various studies. All studies have a purpose, method, results, and conclusions. Another framework organizes competing theories. All learning theories have theorists, supporting data, and implications for education.

Generic frameworks exist in all fields. For example, history's structure is always a sequence of events. Cutting across all historical events are the generic repeatable categories: who, what, where, when, why, and so what. In literature, stories are compared along common repeatable categories such as plot, setting, and main characters or the phases of a story: introduction, conflict, climax, and resolution. In physics, all mechanical problems involve a) the external force on the object, b) qualities of the object itself, c) surface features, and d) the resulting movement.

When my educational psychology students read a measurement chapter about distribution of scores, I supply four representations. Two of these are shown in Figures 26 and 27. Figure 26 is a hierarchy that overviews the structure among concepts. Figure 27 is a matrix that develops one arm of that hierarchy by comparing the three measures of central tendency. As you might suspect, the other representations compare the three dispersion concepts (i.e., range, variance, and standard deviation) and the four distribution shapes (i.e., normal, negatively skewed, positively skewed, and bimodal), respectively.

Concept Learning

Concept learning occurs when novel concept examples are correctly identified from among nonexamples (Gagné, 1985). For instance, the concept of triangle is acquired when triangles are identified from among a host of geometric shapes. A

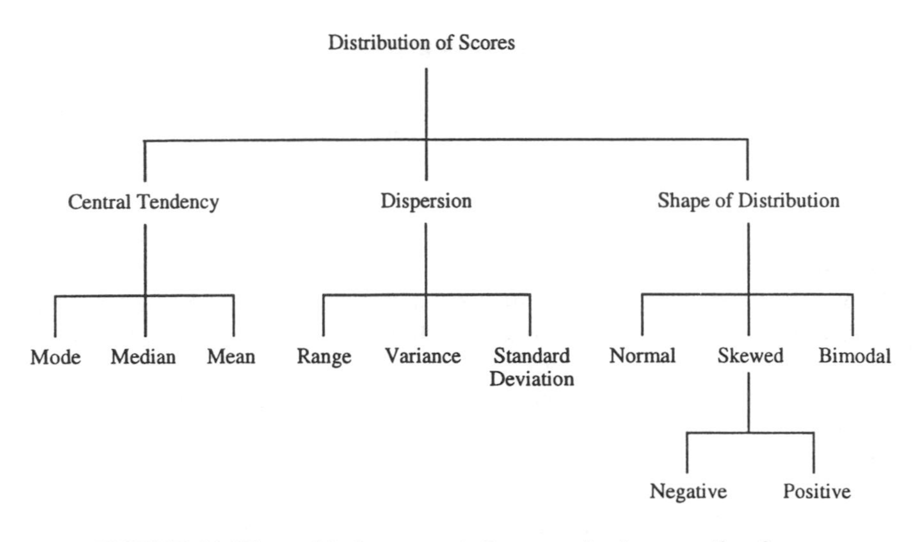

FIGURE 26. Hierarchical representation overviewing a section from a measurement text.

matrix aids concept learning two ways. First, its two-dimensional structure facilitates concept comparison. The geometric shapes matrix in Figure 28, for example, allows easy comparison of characteristics and examples across concepts. Second, a matrix representation can include a diverse range of examples beneath each concept. A range of examples is necessary to promote concept generalization. If a child saw only the single triangle example shown in Figure 28, the child might have difficulty recognizing triangles of different sizes, colors, and shapes (e.g., scalene and right).

The importance of experiencing a range of examples is perhaps best illustrated by a 36-year old doctor friend who had developed a rash he was unable to diagnose. Reluctantly (because he had to pay) he sought the counsel of a dermatologist who made the diagnosis instantaneously: shingles. Throughout medical school and his fledging practice, my friend had seen examples of shingles only in an acute phase among elderly patients (where it most commonly occurs). My friend's diagnostic powers could have been strengthened had a sequence-matrix been used during medical training. The topics are the disease stages from inception to restoration. The repeatable categories are various age levels. Within the matrix cells are pictures (examples) and details describing the disease throughout its progression for varying aged patients.

Rules

Rules are condition-action statements that govern our behavior in a variety of settings (Gagné, 1985). An example is the rule "if the case is objective (condi-

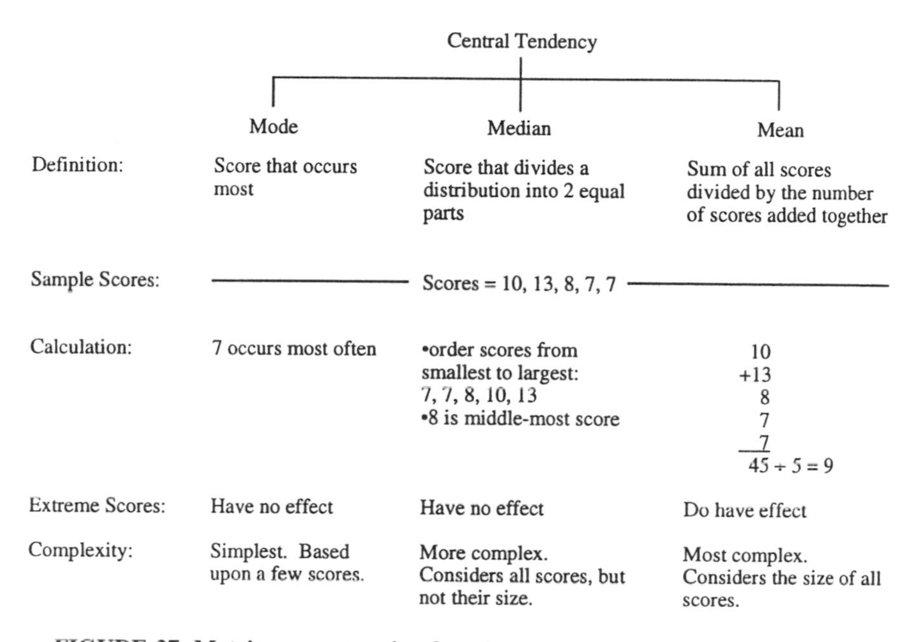

FIGURE 27. Matrix representation focusing on one portion of Distribution of Scores representation.

tion), then use *whom* (action).'' This rule, if properly learned, is generalized to any situation such that a person uses *whom* appropriately in instances where the conditions apply. Another example is the mathematical rule ''if there are parentheses, then do the operation in the parentheses first.'' This rule permits learners to approach correctly all problems like the following by first completing the operation within the parentheses: $6-(7+13) = -14$.

In college instruction, many rules are learned such as the statistical rule ''if a data set contains ordinal data, then a nonparametric (and not a parametric) test is appropriate.'' Students in a physical education class learning tennis may acquire the rule ''if your opponent is at the baseline and hits a short ball, then progress to the net and volley.''

How can the matrix assist in rule learning? Rules, like concepts, are best learned in families. For example, the communitive and associative rules of addition comprise a family of rules. If learned together, students can readily observe and confront similarities and differences between the rules. Because the matrix is effective for displaying coordinate information, it is ideal for presenting rules from within a family. An example follows in Figure 29.

Students often have trouble determining whether to use a comma or a semicolon. The rules for comma and semicolon use are actually better understood

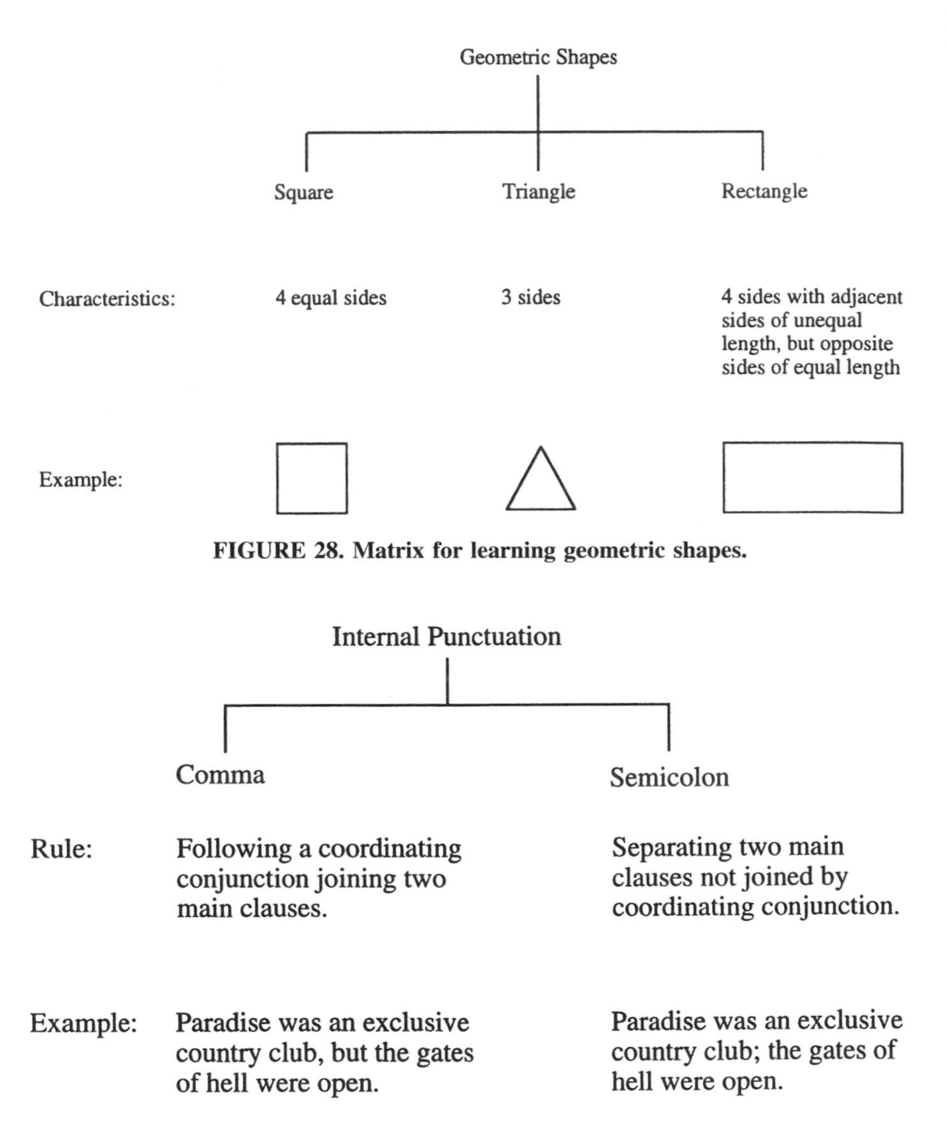

FIGURE 28. Matrix for learning geometric shapes.

FIGURE 29. Matrix for learning comma and semicolon rules.

when presented together along with examples than if presented separately (as is common in most grammar texts). If these rules were learned separately, the learner might have trouble understanding and applying them. The learner might wonder what is meant by a main clause and coordinating conjunction. Presented as a family, with examples, it is evident that main clauses are parts of a sentence

	Train A	Train B	Hawk
Distance:	25 miles	25 miles	?
Rate:	25 mph	25 mph	100 mph
Time:	?	?	?

FIGURE 30. Matrix for solving Trains and Hawk algebra problem.

that can stand alone and that coordinating conjunctions such as *but* join main clauses. It is also apparent how the rules are similar (both include main clauses) and how they are different (the comma is used only with the coordinating conjunction).

Problem Solving and Critical Thinking

Problem solving and critical thinking is facilitated by representing the problem spatially (e.g., Day, 1988). In this section, examples of how a representation aids problem solving and critical thinking are presented.

Try to solve the following algebra problem:

> Two train stations are 50 miles apart. At 1 p.m. on Sunday a train pulls out from each of the stations and the trains start toward one another. Just as the trains pull out from the stations a hawk flies into the air in front of the first train and flies ahead to the front of the second train. When the hawk reaches the second train, it turns around and flies toward the first train. The hawk continues in this way until the trains meet. Assume that both trains travel at the speed of 25 miles per hour and that the hawk flies at a constant speed of 100 miles per hour. How many miles will the hawk have flown when the trains meet?

This is the type of problem that often makes students tremble. In reality it is a rather simple distance/rate/time problem. Once the given information is represented, the problem practically solves itself. The ideal representation for problem solution is a matrix. There are three main topics for comparison: Train A, Train B, and the Hawk. They should be compared with respect to the repeatable categories of distance, rate, and time as shown in Figure 30.

Having developed this representation it is simple to derive the time that the trains traveled and the hawk flew (i.e., one hour). Knowing that the hawk flew

Facial Expressions

	Smile →	Surprise →	Laugh →	Fear →	Shyness →	Anger →	Laugh →	Guilt
Age:	2-3 mo.	4 mo.	4-5 mo.	5-7 mo.	6-8 mo.	8 mo.	1st yr.	2nd yr.
Response Inducement:	adult face	unusual situation	silly adult face	loud noise	new person	take away cookies	at event they cause	bad behavior

FIGURE 31. Matrix representation facilitating critical thinking.

100 mph for one hour, the total distance for the hawk is computed (i.e., 100 miles) and the problem solved. Earlier, it was shown that the matrix is helpful for solving deductive reasoning problems and problems associated with adhering to a medication schedule.

Critical thinking depends on having a complete and organized body of knowledge from which to reason. That body of knowledge must be well understood in order to reason beyond it. For example, recall the information presented earlier about fish (see Figure 11, p. 342). If that information were memorized as discrete facts, but its patterns were unnoticed, then it would be impossible for someone to think critically beyond that information. Only when the inherent patterns are understood could one reason beyond the information and speculate as to what fish are like at the unexplored depth of 1,200 feet. Understanding the existing patterns inherent in the matrix one can speculate that fish at that depth are 800–1,000 cm long, in schools, white-colored, and consumers of prey larger than flounders. This sort of extrapolation beyond existing data is possible only when existing data make sense. The matrix then has the potential to aid local understanding and facilitate reasoning beyond the data.

Consider now the material from a college developmental psychology textbook about the development of facial expressions. Figure 31 is a matrix representation of that material. Upon examination of Figure 31, two trends or patterns that were not specified in the text are apparent. Notice that the first three expressions are positive and the next three are negative. Also notice that before age one, expressions are induced by environmental stimuli; after age one, they are induced by the child. These are perhaps important developmental patterns. Learners can now think critically about these data and speculate why such patterns exist. Is this evidence that children are inherently innocent but learn negative emotions? Does the facial musculature of infants constrain them to form positive expressions which in turn are met by social approval and reinforcement? Are facial expressions governed by cognitive or physical development? These critical issues are only explorable once the patterns of existing knowledge are known.

	Piagetian Stages			
	Sensorimotor ⟶	Preoperational ⟶	Concrete ⟶	Formal
Age of Onset:				
Social Characteristics:				
Cognitive Characteristics:				

FIGURE 32. Matrix framework for writing Piagetian stages essay.

Writing

The planning phase is one of the primary components of the writing process (Flower and Hayes, 1977). However, novice writers often write off the top of their heads. Expert writers, on the other hand, are more planful, often writing from representations they construct. This section includes two examples showing how a matrix facilitates writing.

Suppose students were asked the following essay question on a test in developmental psychology. How could they plan their response?

> Trace the Piagetian stages of development with respect to age of onset, and social and cognitive characteristics.

Many students asked this type of question explode with any or all information available to them about the topic. Again, they are not planful. Developing and completing the matrix framework in Figure 32 can aid the planning and writing processes.

Now consider this essay question from history:

> Christopher Columbus's voyages to the new world were more characteristic of French and British exploration than those of the Spanish. Explain how this is so with respect to goals, methods, and relations with Native Americans.

Having the necessary information available in an organized form (as shown in Figure 33) is certainly important, but does not ensure a well structured essay. How the writer traverses the matrix in responding to the question is also important. In this last example, it is inappropriate for the writer to simply report the contents of each matrix cell or to discuss Columbus's, and the French and British explorations independent of one another. The question calls for a comparison of Columbus's voyages with those typical of other countries. To best answer this question, the writer should first discuss Columbus's goals, how they were similar

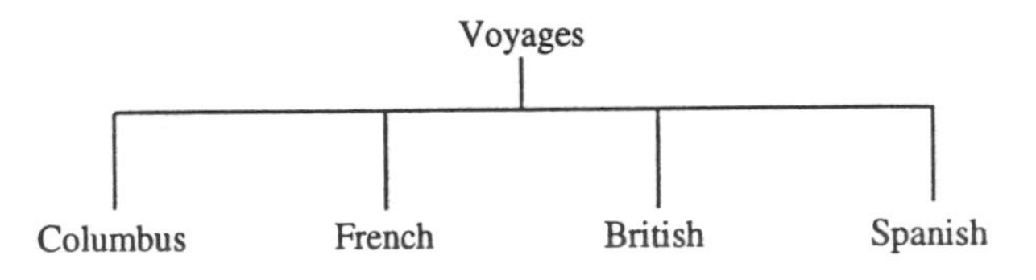

Goals:

Methods:

Relations with
Native Americans:

FIGURE 33. Matrix framework for writing Voyages essay.

to French and British goals, and then how they differed from the Spanish. Next the writer should discuss methods and relations with Native Americans using the same comparative format. There is evidence that students who use a matrix do produce essays that are more coherent and cohesive (Benton, Kiewra, Whitfall, and Dennison, 1993) and include more and better topic sentences (Jones, Amiran, and Katims, 1985).

Teaching Students To Construct Representations

As instructors we can help students learn by providing them with effective learning materials. For example, by providing students with matrix materials about fish (recall Figure 11, p. 342) rather than the passage alone, learning is facilitated. Doing just that, however, is like giving a person a fish to eat for a day instead of teaching him/her how to fish for a lifetime. Certainly instructors should provide the best instructional materials they can, but should also teach students how to learn.

How then are strategies such as the development and application of the matrix taught to college students? One method is through an adjunct course on study skills. An adjunct course, however, separates the strategy from the content areas where it is applicable. The best place for study skills instruction is within content areas. Study skills instruction works best when it makes contact with domain specific knowledge (Perkins and Salomon, 1989). Such training belongs in the math, English, economics, and science curriculums.

Teaching students how to learn, or in this case teaching them to generate and use representations, can and should occur simultaneously with good teaching in the content areas. The process of embedding strategy instruction into content instruction resembles that used by an experienced tradesperson who is training an apprentice. While the tradesperson works, he/she speaks aloud so that personal thoughts and actions become public and explicit for the watchful apprentice.

College instructors can teach students to make and use representations by following a few basic rules that an experienced tradesperson working with an apprentice knows well. First, commonly model the use of representations during instruction. Second, while using representations explain why they are being used (e.g., "to compare several topics or to discern overriding patterns") and how to develop and use them relative to the content being learned (e.g., "because all birds of prey have special weapons for attack, we can make weapons a repeatable category"). This sort of conditional knowledge (Paris, Lipson, and Wixon, 1983) is crucial for strategy instruction. Students must know how and why to use a strategy.

Third, give students opportunities to practice the strategy. This should proceed through successive approximations. After modeling matrix use many times, for example, provide students with a matrix framework prior to a lecture or reading assignment and have them complete it. Later, prompt students to find topics, repeatable categories, and details for a unit of information. Through these types of experiences the skill of generating and using representations is gradually transferred to the students. With practice and feedback they can spontaneously and autonomously generate effective representations.

In summary, an effective instructor teaches the matrix techniques by embedding its use in content instruction. The techniques are modeled, and thoughts and actions are made explicit to students. Multiple opportunities are provided for students to gradually learn and automatize the skills through successive practice and feedback.

REFERENCES

Bamberg, B. (1983). What makes a text coherent? *College Composition and Communication* 18: 417–429.

Benton, S. L., Kiewra, K. A., Whitfall, J., and Dennison, R. (1993). Encoding and external-storage effects on writing processes. *Journal of Educational Psychology* 85: 267–280.

Bovenmeyer Lewis, A., and Mayer, R. E. (1987). Students' misconception of relational statements in arithmetic word problems. *Journal of Educational Psychology* 79: 363–371.

Day, R. S. (1988). Alternative representations. In G. Bower (ed.), *The Psychology of Learning and Motivation* 22: 261–303. New York: Academic Press.

Du Bois, N. F., and Kiewra, K. A. (1989). Promoting competent study skills: Some new directions. Paper presented at the National Conference on the Freshman Year Experience, Columbia, SC.

Flower, L. S., and Hayes, J. R. (1977). Problem-solving strategies and the writing processes. *College English* 39: 449–461.

Gagńe, R. M. (1985). *The Conditions of Learning*, New York: CBS College Publishing.

Halliday, M. A. K., and Hasan, R. (1976). *Cohesion in English*. London: Longman.

Holley, C. D., and Dansereau, D. F. (1984). Networking: The technique and the empirical evidence. In C. D. Holley and D. F. Dansereau (eds.), *Spatial Learning Strategies: Techniques, Applications and Related Issues*. New York: Academic Press.

Jonassen, D. H., Beissner, K., and Yacci, M. (1993). *Structural Knowledge: Techniques for Representing, Conveying, and Acquiring Structural Knowledge*. Hillside, NJ: Lawrence Erlbaum Associates.

Jones, B. F., Amiran, M. R., and Katims, M. (1985). Teaching cognitive strategies and text structures within language arts programs. In J. Siegel, S. Chipman, and R. Glaser (eds.), *Thinking and Learning Skills: Relation to Basic Research* (Vol. 1). Hillsdale, NJ: Lawrence Erlbaum Associates.

Kiewra, K. A., and Sperling-Dennison, R. A. (1991). How supplemental representations affect learning from a research article. Paper presented at the annual conference of the American Educational Research Association, Chicago, IL.

Kiewra, K. A., Du Bois, N. F., Christian, D., and McShane, A. (1988). Providing study notes: A comparison of three types of notes for review. *Journal of Educational Psychology* 80: 595–597.

Kiewra, K. A., Du Bois, N. F., Christian, D., McShane, A., Meyerhoffer, M., and Roskelley, D. (1991). Notetaking functions and techniques. *Journal of Educational Psychology* 83: 240–245.

Kiewra, K. A., Du Bois, N. F., Staley, R. K., and Robinson, D. H. (1992). Outline versus matrix representations: Memory, integration, and application effects. Paper presented at the annual conference of the American Educational Research Association, San Francisco, CA.

Kiewra, K. A., Du Bois, N. F., Weiss, M. E., and Schantz, S. (1992). Abstract and illustrative text supplements. Paper presented at the annual conference of the American Educational Research Association, San Francisco, CA.

Kiewra, K. A., Levin, J. R., Kim, S., Meyers, T., Renandya, W. A., and Hwang, Y. (1994). Fishing for text facilitators: The lure of the mnematrix. Paper presented at the annual conference of the American Educational Research Association, New Orleans, LA.

Lambiotte, J. G., Dansereau, D. F., Cross, D. R., and Reynolds, S. B. (1989). Multirelational semantic maps. *Educational Psychology Review* 1: 331–365.

Langer, J. A. (1984). The effects of available information on response to school writing tasks. *Research in the Teaching of English* 18: 27–44.

Larkin, J. H., and Simon, H. A. (1987). Why a diagram is (sometimes) worth ten thousand words. *Cognitive Science* 11: 65–99.

Mandler, J. (1983). Stories: The function of structure. Paper presented at the annual convention of the American Psychological Association, Anaheim, CA.

Mayer, R. E. (1984). Aids to text comprehension. *Educational Psychologist* 19: 30–42.

Mayer, R. E., and Gallini, J. K. (1990). When is an illustration worth ten thousand words? *Journal of Educational Psychology* 82: 715–726.

McGuinness, C. (1986). Problem representation: The effects of spatial arrays. *Memory and Cognition* 14: 270–280.

Meyer, B. J. F. (1985). Signaling the structure of text. In D. H. Jonassen (ed.), *Technology of Text* (Vol. 2). Englewood Cliffs, New Jersey: Educational Technology Publications.

Musgrave, B. S., and Cohen, J. (1971). The relationship between prose and list learning. In E. Z. Rothkopf and P. E. Johnson (eds.), *Verbal Learning and the Technology of Written Instruction*. New York: Teacher College Press.

Novak, J. D., and Gowin, D. B. (1984). *Learning How To Learn*. New York: Cambridge University Press.

Novick, L. R. (1990). Representation transfer in problem solving. *Psychological Science* 1: 128–132.

Paris, S. G., Lipson, M. Y., and Wixon, K. K. (1983). Becoming a strategic reader. *Contemporary Educational Psychology* 8: 293–316.

Perkins, D. N., and Salomon, G. (1989). Are cognitive skills context-bound? *Educational Researcher* 18: 16–25.

Polich, J. M., and Schwartz, S. H. (1974). The effect of problem size on representation in deductive problem solving. *Memory and Cognition* 2: 683–686.

Robinson, D. H. (1993). The effects of multiple graphic organizers on students' comprehension of a chapter-length text. Doctoral dissertation, University of Nebraska–Lincoln, NE.

Robinson, D. H. (1994). Computational efficiency of graphic organizers: Speed of search. Paper presented at the annual conference of the American Educational Research Association, New Orleans, LA.

Rumelhart, D. E. (1980). Schemata: The building blocks of cognition. In R. J. Spiro, B. C. Bruce, and W. F. Brewer (eds.), *Theoretical Issues in Reading Comprehension: Perspectives From Cognitive Psychology, Linguistics, Artificial Intelligence, and Education*. Hillsdale, NJ: Lawrence Erlbaum.

Rumelhart, D. E., and Ortony, A. (1977). The representation of knowledge in memory. In R. C. Anderson, R. J. Spiro, and W. E. Montague (eds.), *Schooling and Acquisition of Knowledge*. Hillsdale, NJ: Lawrence Erlbaum.

Schwartz, S. H. (1971). Modes of representation and problem solving: Well evolved is half solved. *Journal of Experimental Psychology* 91: 347–350.

Schwartz, S. H., and Fattaleh, D. L. (1972). Representation in deductive problem solving: The matrix. *Journal of Experimental Psychology* 95: 343–348.

Sperling-Dennison, R. A., and Kiewra, K. A. (1993). Studying text supplements: Attention focusing and internal connection effects. Paper presented at the annual conference of the American Educational Research Association, Atlanta, GA.

Tukey, J. W. (1990). Data-based graphics: Visual display in the decades to come. *Statistical Science* 5: 327–329.

Waller, R. (1981). Understanding network diagrams. Paper presented at the annual conference of the American Educational Research Association, Los Angeles, CA.

Winn, W. (1988). Recall of the pattern, sequence, and names of concepts presented in instructional diagrams. *Journal of Research in Science Teaching* 25: 375–386.

New Faculty Socialization in the Academic Workplace

Dana Dunn,* Linda Rouse
The University of Texas at Arlington

and

Monica A. Seff
Bowling Green State University

Recent reviews of the literature on new and junior faculty note that current interest in this subject is due, in part, to demographic changes in the academic workplace (e.g., Boice, 1992; Finkelstein and LaCelle-Peterson, 1992; Schuster, 1990; Smelser and Content, 1980). College enrollment is expected to increase in the late 1990s, just as a large segment of faculty hired in the late 1960s and early 1970s are preparing to retire. A decline in interest among Ph.D. graduates in pursuing careers in higher education, as a result of the depressed academic job market, the failure of academic salaries to keep pace with inflation, and the declining status of the professoriate, has generated concerns about the availability of new faculty to fill position openings. Efforts to increase the visibility of women and minority scholars in academe have also generated discussion of how to attract, prepare, and promote women and minority faculty (Bernard, 1964; Gainen and Boice, 1993; Kulis and Miller-Loessi, 1992; Reskin and Roos, 1990; Roos and Reskin, 1992). Bowen and Schuster's (1986) book, *American Professors: A National Resource Imperiled*, calls attention to the importance of faculty as a resource in higher education and to a number of current problems, including inattention to the special needs of new and junior faculty. Boice (1992) suggests that because universities hired fewer new faculty during the 1980s, diminished emphasis was given to new faculty socialization. Studies highlighting the stresses faced by faculty newcomers, however, underscore the urgency of a closer examination of their needs (e.g., Boice, 1992; Dinham, 1992; Olsen and Sorcinelli, 1992; Seldin, 1987; Sorcinelli, 1992; Whitt, 1991).

*Authors are listed in alphabetical order.

For higher education administrators and policy makers, faculty recruitment, retention, and productivity are likely to be major issues in the next decade. Lack of attention to faculty newcomers can be costly for the individual and for the employing institution (Daly and Townsend, 1992; Trautvetter, 1992), particularly since the early experiences of new faculty are known to be critical to their success and satisfaction with an academic career (Boice, 1992; 1993; Whitt, 1991). Moreover, there are growing public demands for greater accountability in higher education, especially for teaching (Blum, 1990; Kimball, 1990; Mayhew, Ford and Hubbard, 1990). The quality of education that undergraduate students obtain owes much to the enthusiasm and effectiveness of faculty in the teaching role. New faculty, attempting to balance the demands of a complex professional role and to develop an academic career, have a vested interest in understanding how new faculty socialization occurs in the academic workplace. How well prepared are new faculty? What difficulties do they typically encounter? What resources presently are available to support their transition and assist in career development? What more can or should be done? The concept of *socialization*—generally, the process by which individuals acquire the attitudes, beliefs, values and skills needed to participate effectively in organized social life—provides a starting point for examining such questions.

Theory and research relevant to new faculty socialization appear in a number of different fields. Professional and workplace socialization and the effects of formal organizations on individual experience, and vice versa, are studied within the fields of sociology, social psychology, psychology, business management, communication, and higher education. This paper will draw primarily on the sociology of work, the social psychology of self and identity, and the study of higher education to better understand new faculty socialization. The term junior faculty is used to refer primarily to non-tenured full-time faculty below the rank of associate professor, although part-time faculty will also be considered. New faculty may include individuals at the associate rank or higher who are hired into a new college or university, but our main focus will be on newly hired faculty in their first full-time appointment.

We begin by providing an overview of graduate training and the transition to early on-the-job experiences as preparation for an academic career. Attention is then focused on the contributions of the sociology of work and the social psychology of self-concept for understanding new faculty socialization. Next, we discuss variations in workplace socialization strategies and evaluate their consequences for the new faculty member and the employing institution. We then examine diversity—among faculty (e.g., gender, race/ethnicity) and by type of academic institution (e.g., teaching versus research emphasis, standards for tenure and promotion). Programs designed to assist new faculty development are described in the next section. The final section offers concluding comments and discusses directions for future research.

STUDIES OF HIGHER EDUCATION: ANTICIPATORY AND ON-THE-JOB SOCIALIZATION OF NEW FACULTY

The first intensive phase of new faculty socialization occurs in graduate or professional schools. Graduate programs are expected to transmit the attitudes, beliefs and values of both the profession and the academic discipline, as well as to instill technical knowledge and skill. This ''anticipatory socialization''—preparation for an expected future role—may be found wanting in various respects. Graduate schools do a reasonably good job of conveying disciplinary knowledge, but do not adequately prepare students for undertaking academic careers (Bess, 1978; Fink, 1992; Rouse, 1984; Trautvetter, 1992). In a national study of 100 beginning college teachers, for example, Fink (1984b) found that although most had been teaching assistants, only one-half had been given full responsibility for courses and they had not received in-depth preparation or close supervision; rather, most were placed in a ''sink or swim'' situation to work out for themselves strategies for surviving in the classroom. Thompson and Ellis (1984) argue that little effort has been made to assess the value and effectiveness of graduate teaching assistantships for preparing college teachers.

Graduate education has been criticized also for its failure to adequately prepare new faculty to conduct and publish research. Creswell (1985) argues that new faculty have difficulty publishing their research because they lack a ''template'' for writing a research article. Graduate schools vary in opportunities provided to students to collaborate with faculty in research and publication; students may lack knowledge, or confidence, about publishing their work. The effectiveness of research assistantships as preparation for independent scholarship and publication is unclear.

While identification with an academic discipline's perspective often begins at the undergraduate level as students anticipate acceptance in graduate programs (Merton, Reader, and Kendall, 1957), this anticipatory socialization involves a rather naive and idealistic orientation toward the future work role. The effectiveness of graduate school training for fostering the development of a more realistic view of the new faculty role has been debated. Some researchers argue that informal socialization in graduate schools gradually replaces idealism with a realistic, and sometimes cynical, view (Becker and Geer, 1958; Haas and Shaffir, 1984; Lortie, 1959; Morris and Sherlock, 1972; Ritzer and Walczak, 1986). Others suggest that graduate school does not completely eradicate idealistic expectations among new faculty. Studies of new faculty that report disillusionment with the new faculty role support the latter view. For example, several researchers found that new faculty had high expectations for collegial relations, but were disappointed by a perceived lack of shared values and collaborative research (Baldwin and Blackburn, 1981; Boice, 1992; Boice and Thomas, 1989; Reynolds, 1992). In a sample of 106 male faculty members in the first three years of full-time employment, Baldwin and Blackburn (1981) found that idealistic and unrealistic career expectations were still common.

While Merton, Reader, and Kendall (1957) suggest that graduate students move incrementally from apprenticeship to fully socialized membership in the profession, other researchers argue that students are in some respects insulated from the responsibilities of the actual work role and therefore retarded in their professional socialization (Becker, 1960; Hall, 1968). Rouse (1984) notes discontinuities in the transition from graduate student to new faculty member that arise because socialization for the faculty role is necessarily incomplete. New faculty leave the relatively structured context of graduate school for the more autonomous (and isolated) setting of their first appointment with its many pressing responsibilities: new classes to teach, students to advise, a new home to establish, and though frequently displaced by the necessity of more immediate tasks, scholarship (Boice, 1992; Jarvis, 1992). Moreover, new faculty members learn early in their careers through informal socialization that becoming a part of the faculty requires more than just teaching classes, going to committee meetings, and conducting research. Significant others expect new faculty to become certain kinds of scholars and teachers—to identify with particular ideologies and areas of scholarship (Kleinman, 1983). Juggling the many demands of the first faculty appointment often proves stressful for new faculty (Boice, 1992; Whitt, 1991). Whitt (1991) observes that new faculty are expected to ''hit the ground running'' at the time of their first appointment. This expectation is based on a prevalent assumption that prior socialization has sufficiently prepared new faculty for the job. Sands, Parson, and Duane (1991) also note that the decline in mentoring experienced in the transition from graduate school to first faculty appointment reflects the notion that the Ph.D. is a terminal degree, certifying readiness to assume the role of a university professor. That so many new faculty report their early years on the job as a time of ''avoidance, distress, and unproductive beginnings'' (Boice 1992, p. 3) suggests instead that graduate school socialization, in itself, is insufficient preparation for new faculty.

Stresses and Sources of Social Support

Studies of higher education have identified a variety of strains experienced by new faculty: worry about succeeding and, especially, obtaining tenure; coping with ambiguities and inconsistencies in what is expected of them; social isolation and lack of support from other faculty and administrators; insufficient time to meet the many competing demands confronting them; financial, health, and marital problems (e.g., Baldwin, 1979; Dinham, 1992; Mager and Myers, 1982; Reynolds, 1988; Sorcinelli, 1988; Whitt, 1991). Whitt's (1991) qualitative study based on 21 interviews with six new faculty, six department chairs, and four administrators on the dean's staff in the School of Education at a large research university, emphasized ''how little assistance [faculty] were given in adjusting to their new setting'' (p. 191). New faculty in their first faculty position sometimes struggle additionally with their new identity as a professor. One faculty informant in Reynolds' (1992) study, for example, described his initial sense of being an ''imposter.'' The New Faculty Project survey of faculty at four types of institutions (research, comprehensive, liberal arts, and two-year) found that ''time pressures, lack of personal time and teaching load led the field in sources of stress'' (Dinham, 1992, p. 2). Stress factors reported by Menges and Trautvetter (1993) included personal stress, meetings and committees, teaching and time constraints, research, and the review/promotion process. Nevertheless, new faculty report being pleased with attainment of a faculty appointment and generally like the nature of academic work (Sorcinelli, 1988). New faculty seem to be enthusiastic and satisfied for the most part upon arriving at their particular institution (Trautvetter, 1992).

Parson, Sands, and Duane (1992) investigated sources of career support, which may help offset the strains experienced by new and junior faculty. In an analysis of survey responses from 347 faculty at a research-oriented public university they found that the highest ranked source of support for both male and female faculty, at all faculty ranks, was a spouse or significant other. Near and Sorcinelli's (1986) and Sorcinelli and Near's (1989) reports on relations between the work and personal lives of faculty confirm that the open-ended demands of the faculty role, as in other high status occupations, intrude heavily on personal life. With respect to the impact of family on faculty socialization, Corcoran and Clark (1984) found that about one quarter of the highly productive faculty members in their sample of 63 grew up in families in which the mother or father was also a faculty member. In these cases, parents provided anticipatory socialization and a more realistic view of the work role.

Parson, Sands, and Duane's (1992) factor analysis of types of support sources for faculty identified four major sources of career support; spouse or significant other appeared as part of the first factor, off-campus personal supports. Colleagues within the academic unit provided a second factor. The third factor was described as professional supports outside the unit (including administrators and colleagues on campus as well as colleagues off campus). Finally, for minorities, who made up 11 percent of their sample respondents, a fourth factor consisted of minority networks—minority faculty in the unit or elsewhere on campus and ethnic or cultural groups off campus. The specific kinds of support given included ''encouragement, friendship, information and advice about the profession, visibility within the profession, improved resources for research and teaching, and intellectual guidance'' (Parson, Sands, and Duane, 1992, p. 161). In Olsen and Sorcinelli's (1992) study, faculty on average rated colleagues outside their departments as the most helpful and supportive, with untenured faculty and chairs, in turn, next most supportive; deans and tenured faculty least so. ''Over one-third indicated that none of the senior faculty had ever been particularly interested in or helpful to them in their careers'' (Olsen and Sorcinelli, 1992, p. 21).

Another important source of support, or strain, for new faculty is the chair. While chairs and higher administrators were viewed by Whitt's (1991) respondents as playing a key role in the adjustment of new faculty, she noted a "striking discrepancy" between the department chairs' impressions and those of new faculty. Department chairs viewed the new faculty experience as a largely positive one and felt support from chairs was readily available. By contrast, new faculty members characterized their experience as largely negative and their chairs as not particularly helpful. Parson, Sands, and Duane (1992) suggest that the department chair is important in the career development of junior faculty since the chair evaluates performance, conveys information about tenure and promotion, provides (or withholds) resources, handles conflicts, and, ideally, maintains morale (see Bennett, 1983; Tucker, 1981). Daly and Townsend (1992) found that junior (tenure-track) faculty perceived the facilitative activities of the chair as more important than did tenured faculty. Their analysis of questionnaire responses from a sample of 485 faculty employed at doctorate-granting universities in the United States confirmed that the key activities of chairs as perceived by new faculty were conducting annual reviews, informing junior faculty about their progress toward tenure, supporting proposals for institutional funding, providing financial support for participation in national and regional meetings, and "fostering development of faculty's special talents and interests" (Daly and Townsend, 1992, p. 10).

These studies are limited to faculty in research-oriented institutions, but a more extensive literature exists on the chair's role that corroborates the chair's importance in faculty socialization and development across different types of institutions. Lucas (1990), Roach (1976), and Wylie (1985), for example, address the role of the department chair vis à vis faculty in various higher education settings. Daly and Townsend (1992) cite a dozen other references related to the chair's role in assisting new faculty. Daly and Townsend also remind readers of an important caveat—that research on the role of the chair must account for possible differences by discipline. (Biglan's [1973] model of disciplinary differences was employed by Daly and Townsend in their own analysis.) Clark's (1989) description of the American professoriate as strongly differentiated by discipline and Biglan's (1973) work on the distinctive properties of particular disciplines also suggest the importance of the chair for new faculty: the chair is the administrative officer representing the requirements of the institution who is also aware of the unique nature of a particular academic discipline. Becher's (1989) notion of variations within each discipline, reflecting specialties and subspecialties, however, speaks to the need for junior faculty to maintain professional contacts with other faculty in their specialty areas for intellectual and career support.

The increasing number of studies of new and junior faculty by higher education researchers (see also Eimers, 1990; Stanley and Chism, 1991; Turner and Boice, 1987; Van der Bogert, 1991) includes several that are noteworthy for their longitudinal designs. Olsen and Sorcinelli (1992) report findings from a five-year longitudinal study of new faculty (n = 54) at a large public research university. Changes were noted in the experiences of new faculty over the course of their pre-tenure years. "Tasks that have become routine by year five of an appointment, for example, may consume substantial time and emotional energy in year one" (Olsen and Sorcinelli, 1992, p. 15). New faculty, at all types of institutions, may initially be most concerned with teaching pressures and later become more concerned about research and publication, at the research-oriented institutions, as the tenure decision approaches. Correspondingly, Fink (1984b) reported for a sample of 97 geography faculty that teaching was initially their most overwhelming responsibility. Interviews with the 45 faculty still participating in Olsen and Sorcinelli's study after five years showed that over time teaching preparation declined as faculty became more proficient teachers and had fewer new preparations, but faculty worried more about research productivity and, depending on the discipline, grant support. Faculty also felt that teaching should weigh more heavily in tenure decisions. Faculty satisfaction with the intrinsic rewards of their position—autonomy, intellectual discovery, sense of accomplishment—remained high over time, but overall job satisfaction decreased during the five-year period in conjunction with a perceived downward turn in collegiality and social support. The proportion of faculty who characterized their work as "very stressful" rose from 33 percent in 1986 to 71 percent in 1990 (Olsen and Sorcinelli, 1992).

Another longitudinal study of new faculty, presently in its second of three years, is the New Faculty Project under the direction of Robert J. Menges. This study of 177 newly hired tenure-track faculty at five different institutions (two liberal arts colleges, one community college district, a comprehensive university, and a research university) includes faculty in humanities, social sciences, natural sciences, and applied/professional disciplines. The sample of 142 non-tenured faculty below the associate rank also includes 56.3 percent women and 18.3 percent faculty of color (Trautvetter, 1992). These data, complementing cross-sectional surveys and smaller qualitative studies, should permit a better understanding of new faculty socialization across disciplines, types of institutions, and by gender and race/ethnicity. Descriptions of new faculty socialization also need to consider individual differences. Menges' (1992) conceptual model of academic life notes that new faculty bring to the hiring institution individual psychological and social characteristics; e.g., personality traits and beliefs about themselves, about teaching, and about the hiring institution that "influence participation in the domains of professional work."

Individual characteristics are assumed to interact with organizational efforts to socialize new faculty; thus an effort to understand new faculty socialization leads us to consider further both the nature of the organizational socialization efforts in the academic work setting and the ways in which individual faculty members respond to their new work role. The following section examines socialization for the new faculty role in organizational context.

THE SOCIOLOGY OF WORK AND NEW FACULTY SOCIALIZATION

Workplace or occupational socialization refers to the social and psychological adjustment of individuals to their work roles. Organizational socialization is a related process, but refers more specifically to how the organizational context influences the nature of socialization as well as eventual outcomes (Van Maanen, 1976). Both processes involve the acquisition of values, norms, and behaviors necessary for effective participation in the workplace. During the 1950s, scholarly interest in workplace socialization intensified as Scientific Management principles for organizing work began to lose favor (Rothman, 1987). The emerging Human Relations school shifted management's emphasis from reward and punishment to subjective states of workers as the primary shapers of workplace behavior (Tausky, 1978). Contemporary work organizations continue to endorse a more humanistic approach which deemphasizes direct supervision and the application of reward and punishment, but instead emphasizes indirect control of workers through training or socialization (Van Maanen, 1983). A substantial theoretical and research-based literature has developed in response to this shift in emphasis. While much of this literature addresses the topic broadly, some addresses socialization into particular work roles or within specific work settings. Scholars have noted the lack of attention to the study of educational institutions as work organizations (Bidwell, 1965; Boice, 1992; Gross, 1956; Lortie, 1969; Pellegrin, 1976); only a few scholars who examine workplace socialization address the professoriate directly (see, for example, Bucher, Stelling, and Dommermuth, 1969; Lortie, 1968). However, much of the more general literature on workplace socialization is relevant to an understanding of the socialization of faculty members. The general themes and issues in this broader literature will be summarized and applied to the professoriate in this and subsequent sections of this paper.

Within the discipline of sociology, much of the early work on the study of occupations was devoted to study of the professions (Ritzer and Walczak, 1986), and some of that inquiry focused specifically on socialization to the professions. College professor is considered a "classic profession" (Rothman, 1987), thus much of the literature on the professions is relevant to the socialization of new faculty members. The professions—high-status, self-regulated occupations requiring specialized knowledge, skills, and experiences—present unique features of socialization (Freidson, 1970; Hodson and Sullivan, 1990). Because professionals are often employed in organizations where member compliance is achieved primarily through the internalization of norms and values and through changes in self-concept, the organization attempts to socialize individuals so their norms, values, and attitudes are congruent with those of the organization. Etzioni (1961) describes organizations of this type as normative organizations and argues that they generally lack the ability to achieve compliance of members through the control of overt behavior via punishment. The relative isolation of college professors in classrooms makes it difficult, if not impossible, to apply behavioral controls and constraints (Pellegrin, 1976), thus lengthy prior socialization methods are intense and time consuming (e.g., graduate and professional school training).

Though workplace socialization begins prior to the first day of work and continues throughout one's career, it is intensified in times of promotion or job change (Van Maanen, 1983). Socialization that occurs in the workplace may be highly structured (formal) or minimally structured (informal). Work organizations are motivated to invest resources in socialization programs because they foster predictable, efficient, and productive employee behavior (see, for example, Boice, 1992; Jarvis, 1992; Lewis and Povlacs, 1988). Individuals typically are receptive to these socialization programs because such programs reduce worker uncertainty and anxiety as they facilitate learning the work role (Van Maanen, 1976). Lortie (1968) suggests that new faculty socialization often involves experiencing a "shared ordeal." Shared ordeals, imposed on newcomers by full-fledged members of the organization, are psychologically trying, but serve to dramatize the worth of the position. When successfully completed, acceptance by colleagues is the valued reward. The rather lengthy tenure earning process which commences on entry to the university or college provides an example of a shared ordeal. The success of this socializing technique depends on the recruit's motivation to join the organization. Initial motivation must be high in order for the newcomer to tolerate the uncomfortable "shared ordeal" (Schein, 1983). Prior investment by new faculty members in lengthy professional/graduate school training indicates that motivation to become a full-fledged member of the organization is high.

Faculty Work Identification: Discipline, Profession, and/or Institution?

Work identification is conceptualized as both a product and a process. As a product, identification refers to a sense of membership, close association, belonging; a sense of common interest, similarity, oneness. As a process, identification refers to the experiences through which the individual comes to develop this sense of connection.

Much has been written about where the loyalties of professionally trained newcomers to organizations ultimately lie (Wanous, 1980). Becker and Carper (1956) argue that professional socialization results in identification with work that may be task specific or discipline (field) specific; individuals may identify with specific work tasks associated with formal job titles (e.g., professor or teacher), or they may identify more so with the larger field or discipline (e.g., electrical engineer, chemist, sociologist). New faculty are socialized also to identify with their employing institution. Organizational socialization involves communicating the institutional mission and objectives, policies, and procedures. When individuals identify with an organization's goals and decision making premises they are more likely to behave in ways that are "best for the organization" (Bullis and Bach, 1991, p. 181). One difficulty in academe is deciphering "mixed messages" about organizational goals. Also, adopting the organization's frame of reference may cause individuals to narrow their perception of alternatives, a dysfunction of organizational identification noted by Tompkins and Cheney (1985). For academics, strong organizational affiliation may attenuate or complement disciplinary identification. Faculty may identify in varying degrees with their employing institution as a whole, individual departments and/or with their disciplines. Some targets [of identification] may complement one another while others may compete. "Individuals adopt the frames of reference of those targets with which they most identify" (Bullis and Bach, 1991, p. 182).

Two targets of identification that have received considerable attention are faculty members' identification with their discipline/profession and with their employing institution (Clark, 1983). The distinction between disciplinary/professional identification and organizational identification is illustrated in Gouldner's (1957; 1958) classic work on cosmopolitans and locals. Locals view their professional futures as linked to their employing organization (college or university) and are more likely to participate in the administrative, social, and political affairs of the organization (Becker and Geer, 1958; Clark, 1987; Gouldner, 1957; 1958; Lammers, 1974). By contrast, cosmopolitans identify more with their discipline/profession, and this identification links them to national and international groups of scholars. Because the cosmopolitan's reference group transcends the organization, socializing the cosmopolitan faculty member to organization specific norms and values may be difficult. In comparison, locals tend to be far more susceptible to organizational socialization efforts (Van Maanen, 1976). Miller and Wagner (1971) argue that the basic cosmopolitan versus local orientation is established prior to organizational entry during graduate school training. The type of employing institution is also related to one's orientation. For example, at community colleges where classroom hours are high and student loads per class are heavy, the emphasis is on generalist rather than specialist approaches to disciplinary knowledge (Clark, 1987). Therefore, a local orientation is more compatible with the community college mandate. Clark (1983) expands on the local versus cosmopolitan distinction among academicians by noting that both orientations can entail either an applied or pure emphasis. According to Clark, cosmopolitans can be of two types, researchers (pure) or consultants (applied). He also envisions two types of locals, the disinterested teacher-scholars (pure) and the practical professionals (applied).

Organizational identification, a more local orientation, may be accomplished by investing resources (e.g., time, effort, money) in the newcomer in order to create feelings of indebtedness. In such cases, it is made clear to the newcomer, usually by the department chair, that rewards are differentially made available to those who meet department standards. Such debts can only be repaid by loyalty, commitment, and hard work directed toward furthering the organization's goals (Schein, 1983). Colleges and universities often offer new faculty reduced course loads, summer teaching, and other perquisites, not only to facilitate the newcomer's entry into the organization, but also to create feelings of indebtedness. However, these same resources may encourage the newcomer to be more cosmopolitan by enabling the development of a reference group that is national or international in scope. O'Briant (1991) argues that it is increasingly difficult to foster institutional loyalty among contemporary faculty because locals seldom receive a proportionate share of professional recognition and reward.

Disciplinary identification may begin with the selection of an academic major at the undergraduate level and is reinforced through both formal and informal socialization during graduate school. After the completion of the terminal degree, the activities of professional associations enhance identification with academic disciplines (Clark, 1987; Taylor, 1976). Clark (1983, p. 80) states that professional associations

> generate a steady flow of symbolic materials about themselves. The materials include: admission and membership requirements that help distinguish between insiders and outsiders; reaffirmations of the special virtues of the field; reports on how the field as a whole is doing, particularly if it is engaged in delicate relations, or even border warfare, with other fields; prizes and tributes for outstanding performers and "tribal elders"; sometimes a code of ethics; and always an obituary column.

Much has also been written about component roles within the professorship which offer dimensions along which new and junior faculty identification can be examined. Bornheimer, Burns, and Dumke (1973) discussed five functions of the faculty in higher education: teaching, research, service, advisement, and committee assignments. Similarly, Clark (1987) describes the most common dimensions as: teacher, researcher, student advisor, administrator, and consultant. The research and teaching components of the faculty role are primary targets of identification for most new faculty in universities; teaching and advising are more prominent roles in liberal arts and community colleges. One challenge in adjusting to the faculty work role is the balancing of various role components into an organizationally successful performance and personally satisfying career. For most faculty there is a blending of activities, for example, in "informal conversations with colleagues in the hallway, lonely hours of thought while grading, and one-to-one mentoring when advising students on courses and careers" (Clark, 1987, p. 71).

As the process of work identification unfolds, the newcomer may internalize his or her faculty role such that the role and the person seem to merge (Bush and Simmons, 1981; Lortie, 1959; Turner, 1978). Acquisition of the faculty role may also involve some degree of redefinition; the new faculty member may re-make the role to fit personal role expectations (Bush and Simmons, 1981; Thornton and Nardi, 1975; Turner, 1973). Schein (1968) suggests that "creative individualists" are socialized to accept only the most basic values and norms of the organization and profession but reject the less pivotal norms and values that are not absolutely necessary as the price of organizational membership. For example, creative individualists know they must be effective teachers (basic value), but may reject the university's policy of requiring student attendance (less pivotal norm). Thus, conceptualization of new faculty socialization requires recognition of different types and degrees of work identification. Organizational efforts to socialize new faculty interact with individual faculty characteristics to determine outcomes that, additionally, change over time.

Faculty Socialization, Organizational Identification, and Turning Points

Organizational identification theory addresses "the development of a relationship between individuals and organizations" (Bullis and Bach, 1991, p. 191). A member's relationship to an organization is mediated by interactions with other members; thus the finding, in studies of higher education, that new faculty place importance on collegiality is not surprising. Bullis and Bach asked a sample of "organizational newcomers" (26 entering graduate students in three communication departments) to describe their interactions with other department members. Following Tompkins and Cheney (1983), the department rather than the entire organization was studied as the target of organizational identification. Bullis and Bach (1991) found that multiplexity (variety in types of content communicated among members) was a significant predictor of organizational identification. "As diverse interactions occur, relationships develop, identities are shaped, and influence is exerted"(p. 192). Multiplexity is one of the characteristics of communication networks, hypothesized to foster assimilation, that has been studied in an educational setting using turning points analysis (Bullis and Bach, 1987).

Turning points analysis was offered as an alternative to stage and phase models of socialization, to provide a more detailed, inductive account of socialization experiences over time (Bach and Bullis, 1987). Baxter and Bullis (1986, p. 470) define a turning point as "any event or occurrence which is associated with change in a relationship." The structured "retrospective interview technique" (Bach and Bullis, 1987, p. 11) provides respondents with graphs indicating monthly intervals against which they plot level of organizational identification at points of change, followed by questioning about "how the events came about and how the events brought about change in identification.'' Respondents describe, in their own words, memorable events in their organizational experience.

Without dismissing the heuristic value of stage models (e.g., Buchanan, 1974; Feldman, 1976a; 1976b; Louis, 1980; Wanous, 1980), turning point analysis provides a more phenomenologically anchored account of organizational identification, compatible with qualitative higher education studies of new faculty socialization. Verrier's (1992) study of faculty, for example, ''presumed that we make sense by identifying and reflecting upon episodes or 'experiences' of our past'' (p. 3). The narrative segments he reports, in which four professors ''explore, recreate, and reflect upon'' their pre-tenure experiences, include accounts of critical events: a phone call from a professor providing needed encouragement to return to school for an advanced degree; a denigrating offhand remark by a senior faculty member; a decision whether to submit an article to a journal of women's studies or the dean's preferred journal; a favorable student evaluation of teaching. While further research is needed to determine the descriptive, predictive, and applied utility of turning point analysis relative to stage models, this appears to be a promising line of investigation for understanding new and junior faculty socialization.

With an explicit interest in recruitment of new faculty, Kirk and Todd-Mancillas (1991) collected data at one state university from 29 beginning graduate-student teachers in nine departments to identify critical turning points in identification with the department (as an indicator of potential commitment to an academic career). From these data, Kirk and Todd-Mancillas developed three categories of turning point experiences: intellectual identity, socio-emotional identity, and occupational identity. Turning points in intellectual identity included two subsets; those related to sense of competence and those related to compatibility with the department. Socio-emotional identity turning points signified acceptance, belonging, and support between and among peers and superordinates. Occupational identity turning points included two subcategories; status classification (awareness of ''place'') and structural support (e.g., access to an office mailbox or copy machine). The flexibility of this approach was also demonstrated by its application to relational change in student faculty interactions using the retrospective interview technique with a sample of 52 senior university students reviewing their student careers (O'Neill and Todd-Mancillas, 1992).

Theories of unobtrusive control through identification and studies examining the antecedents and consequences of organizational identification (see Bullis and Bach, 1987; Tompkins and Cheney, 1985) seem particularly appropriate for understanding faculty as professionals employed in normative organizations. However, much organizational identification literature focuses on how socialization can be managed in such a way that members identify with the organization and more readily accept its values as their own. Less attention is given to role-making, emergent norms, and the contributions of newcomers to organizational change. ''Fit'' between the individual and the organization may in fact occur as a result of selective recruiting, changing the individual to fit the organization, changing the organization to fit the individual, or terminating the relationship. Sometimes newcomers stay but never become strongly identified with the organization. Identification also can be withdrawn and/or redirected. This can occur as newcomers come to better understand organizational values and goals, if they then perceive salient differences between themselves and others. Bullis and Bach (1989) note that disappointment may be a result of participants' originally inflated and unrealistic expectations.

Bullis and Bach's (1989, p. 287) sample of graduate student newcomers in three communication departments ''were more likely to experience a decrease than an increase in identification over time,'' a finding that parallels Olsen and Sorcinelli's (1992) on new faculty satisfaction. ''Newcomers who reported at least one [turning point] instance of disappointment reported lower levels of identification after eight months than those who did not'' (Bullis and Bach, 1989, p. 287). Though Bullis and Bach's (1989) conclusion was that ''disappointment appears to create a decrease in identification from which the relationship does not recover'' (p. 289), their one-year research time frame was not long enough to determine eventual outcomes. Their conceptual model actually suggests a nonlinear course of identification. Rather than employing an incremental socialization model, organizational identification may be better understood as proceeding in fits and starts, showing unexpected reverses associated with critical events, and reflecting inherent continuing strains between individual and organizational needs.

New members do not enter organizations as a *tabula rasa.* Many of the turning points identified by Bullis and Bach (1989) demonstrate that ''newcomers are actively involved in perceiving, evaluating, and managing their relationship with their respective organizations; . . . newcomers create and define their roles within the organization'' (p. 287). Individuals strive both to maintain independence and to identify with the group; they embrace ''getting away'' as well as ''jumping hurdles.'' Bullis and Bach therefore recommend a more dialectical perspective on individual-organizational relationships.

SOCIALIZATION AND SELF-CONCEPT

With respect to learning the work role effectively, the demands that an individual makes of himself or herself are at least as salient as disciplinary expectations or organizational expectations. These self-imposed demands involve both adaptation and conformity to the role expectations and norms of the academy and the individual's discipline, and incorporate the transmission of the campus faculty culture from one generation to the next. According to self-theorists, socialization is more than just the process of learning rules, norms or behavior patterns; socialization occurs only to the extent that these rules, norms, and behaviors become part of the individual's self-concept (Gecas, 1982; Gecas and Seff, 1989; 1990). The self-concept can be defined as "the totality of an individual's thoughts and feelings having reference to himself (herself) as an object" (Rosenberg, 1979, p. 7).

Within sociology and social psychology, processes of socialization and the development of the self-concept have been studied since the writings of G. H. Mead (1934) and C. H. Cooley (1902). In these early writings, the self and processes of socialization are viewed as social in nature, anchored in language, communication, and face-to-face interaction (Gecas and Burke, forthcoming). In more recent years, a focus on adult socialization and the social context of the self has expanded to include social structural influences. Consequently, there is interest in the effect of context on the learning of work orientations and behaviors. Our emphasis in this section will be on developments within the study of self and identity, particularly as they intersect with the professorial identity. We begin with some definitional and conceptual clarifications; after which we generally proceed from discussions of various self-components and self-processes (e.g., self-motives) to definitions of the situation.

Definitions and Distinctions

To facilitate the discussion that follows, we offer several definitions and distinctions between key concepts: self, self-concept, and self-identity. The concept of self refers to the process of reflexivity or self-awareness—the ability of humans to be both subject and object to themselves. Reflexivity is a special form of consciousness which is considered the quintessential feature of the human condition (Mead, 1934; Gecas and Burke, forthcoming).

While the core of the self is the process of reflexivity, the concept of self is used generically to encompass all of the products or consequences of this reflexive activity (Gecas and Burke, forthcoming). This is referred to as the self-concept (Gecas, 1982) and is composed of various identities, attitudes, beliefs, values, motives, and experiences, along with their evaluative and affective components (e.g., self-efficacy, self-esteem).

The self-concept is a source of motivation. At least three motives emanate from the self-concept: self-esteem, self-efficacy, and authenticity. The self-esteem motive refers to the desire to view oneself in a positive light. This occurs through such cognitive activities as self-reflective perception, self-presentation strategies, and redefining the meaning of various situations (Gecas and Seff, 1989; 1990). For example, Boice (1992) found that new faculty reacting to student ratings tended to attribute disappointing ratings to the inability of students to handle challenging material. Faculty thereby avoided self-blame and maintained self-esteem by redefining the situation.

Self-efficacy refers to the motivation to perceive oneself as a competent individual in control of his/her environment. Individuals who have persistent self-doubts about their capabilities undermine their sense of self-efficacy and further expose themselves to experiences of vulnerability and stress (Bandura, 1990). A faculty member's sense of efficacy is crucial for career success (Menges, 1991). Feelings of efficacy can be encouraged or discouraged by colleagues and department chairs. For example, subtle discouragement of minority and female faculty members' research interests affect their sense of efficacy (Boice and Kelly, 1987; Boice, Shaughnessy, and Pecker, 1985).

Authenticity refers to an assessment of the meaning and significance of what one is and does. As Clark (1987, p. 106) states: ''To believe in what one does is something quite different from simply doing it.'' Although most new faculty members will acknowledge that there are many problems with their academic positions including low pay and poorly prepared students, most who stay in the academy believe in what they do, are committed, and are interested in their work. In other words, their work affects their sense of authenticity. By attributing motivational properties to the self-concept we give substance to the idea that the self is an agent in its own creation (Gecas, 1986). Brim (1968) states that small incremental shifts will take place in what an individual asks of himself or herself, which over the years makes the person much different from what he or she was when younger. Consequently, the individual changes, but without knowing how the change occurred. Self-motives, then, are important to an understanding of new faculty socialization because they provide a conception of how individuals are motivated to change.

Situational Identities

Also relevant to the self-concept is the construction of an identity as a new faculty member, and its maintenance in communication and social interaction. The approach examined here focuses on face-to-face situations which emphasize the emergence and maintenance of the new faculty role. How do individuals go about ''defining the situation'' and thereby constructing the realities within which they live? A critical aspect of these situational definitions is the construction of an identity as a faculty member. The development of identities, including the identity of faculty member, is viewed as a social construction that involves considerable negotiation, bargaining, role-taking, and impression management (Blumstein, 1973; Goffman, 1959; Strauss, 1978; Turner, 1962). Goffman (1959; 1963; 1967) describes in considerable detail the ''staging operations'' involved in an individual's presentation of his or her identity in everyday life.

''Staging operations'' apply to all academic departments. To function smoothly in an academic department composed of other faculty members, students, and staff, the newcomer needs considerable knowledge to ''properly'' stage his or her identity. Most of that knowledge is acquired slowly and informally by interacting with others and without anyone ever making a deliberate effort to teach the newcomer the rules of the game (Becher, 1989). The rules are quite different at a four-year research university than they are at a two-year college, especially with respect to the emphasis on research. For example, Clark (1987, p. 129) states:

> Only those enclosed in strong institutional cultures of major universities are positioned to go all out in deifying the outstanding researcher or scholar. In the more inchoate cultures of the middle-hierarchy institutions, that idealization diffuses into a melange of features of teaching as well as of research, practical as well as purely academic capacities, and student as well as peer-orientation. In the two-year college, where the open-door ideology reigns supreme, the idealization of scholarship is diluted even further, largely replaced by a full-throated appreciation of the capacity to stimulate beginning students.

Failure to understand and comply with these implicit rules will affect the newcomer's status within the group. Learning the rules occurs through interaction with significant others, especially colleagues and the department chair, who hold normative beliefs about the work role, and who have the power to sanction the newcomer for correct or incorrect behavior (Brim, 1966).

Much of the critical information about how to succeed professionally is tacit knowledge—information that is not taught but is critical to learn (Boice, 1992; Sternberg, Okagaki, and Jackson, 1990). There is also a distinction between two types of tacit knowledge (Gerholm, 1985). One category is the academic knowledge of a particular discipline including the kind of discourse expected. The other category of tacit knowledge is generated by the newcomers themselves as they try to make sense out of their experiences (e.g., knowing that the chairperson's secretary runs the department). Similar to academic knowledge, it is necessary for successful professional behavior. For an understanding of socialization into academic life they are both important (Becher, 1989; Gerholm, 1985).

Newcomers must be able to recognize significant scholarly contributions to their discipline, as well as how to compose a good critique of particular contributions (Rorty, 1979). They are expected to value knowledge and intellectual curiosity. Relatedly, it is expected that norms of academic honesty—the honest handling of knowledge—will be observed. All disciplines regard plagiarism, falsification of data, and the unfair treatment of students as against the rules.

Within the lexicon of a discipline Gerholm (1985), like Goffman (1959), highlights subtle nuances: the official, "front stage" style of scholarly research papers and other kinds of formal written and verbal communication; the more casual communication style that is acceptable in internal settings, such as department seminars; and the type of "back stage" discourse in which scholars engage among themselves including flip, "off the record" remarks. Being socialized to identify with an academic discipline in its fullest sense involves the ability to distinguish between "front stage" and "back stage" and to use the discourse required by the situation.

Complementing this external, socially defined component of tacit knowledge, the newcomer also has to acquire his or her own sense of the discipline's values. It is not enough to recognize and subscribe to the official norms, which were enumerated by Merton (1973) in relation to academic scientists: (1) universalism—an impersonal, objective pursuit of knowledge; (2) communalism—an open, competitive cooperation in which knowledge becomes common property; (3) disinterestedness—in which peer review gives scholarship a public and testable character; and (4) organized skepticism—a detached examination of beliefs using empirical and logical criteria. Merton (1973) acknowledges that for every norm one can find at least one counternorm prescribing a diametrically opposed line of action. The new faculty member must therefore decide the context and conditions under which one norm will be prescribed to as opposed to an alternative norm.

Additionally, because of "academic drift"—the unguided imitative convergence of universities and colleges upon the most prestigious forms—a new faculty member must familiarize himself or herself with not only the norms of his/her campus, but the norms of the more prestigious universities (Clark, 1983). Clark (1983, p. 143) states, "Imitation means adopting their meanings as our meanings, their practices as our practices, thereby diffusing values from a core toward various peripheries." Lastly, new faculty must be aware of the more Machiavellian rules of conduct that exist de facto within any academic community (Becher, 1989). This can be thought of as the "underside" of academic life. Much as the new faculty member must learn which discourse is appropriate in various "front stage" and "back stage" situations, he or she also has to acquire social skills which include knowing how to handle norms and counternorms and Machiavellian conduct rules (Becher, 1989; Blumstein, 1973; Clark, 1983; Merton, 1973; Rorty 1979).

VARIATIONS IN WORKPLACE SOCIALIZATION STRATEGIES

Socialization programs vary with respect to the devices and strategies used to accomplish the goal of integrating newcomers into work roles. Van Maanen (1983) refers to these differences as variations in people processing strategies: formal/informal, individual/collective, sequential/nonsequential, fixed/variable, tournament/contest, serial/disjunctive, and investiture/ divestiture. The implications of these different approaches for new faculty socialization programs and their consequences for faculty members' self-concepts will be discussed below.

Formal socialization programs are those in which training is segregated from the ongoing work process. The newcomer role is also emphasized in formal programs. Informal socialization programs, by contrast, resemble on-the-job, trial-and-error learning processes (Van Maanen, 1983). Socialization to the professoriate consists of both a formal and an informal component (Ritzer and Walczak, 1986; Schein, 1983).

The first formal phase of socialization for the professoriate, graduate or professional training, is a lengthy stage. The National Research Council (1981) reports that the median range of time for doctoral training is six to eight years, and the total elapsed period from baccalaureate to doctorate ranges from seven to thirteen years. Because this schooling is removed from the actual work experience, as noted earlier, it is focused more on communicating knowledge than on the practical aspects of the future work role (Lortie, 1959). Although socialization in professional/graduate schools also emphasizes the values and norms of the profession (Schein, 1983), Van Maanen (1983) argues that "trainees" are not able to generalize from what is learned in formal training to actual work situations. Consequently, formal socialization processes are often only the first round of socialization.

In formal graduate school socialization, a closer approximation of the future work role exists for those students who hold teaching and research assistantships. Hauptman (1986) reports that of all 1983 doctoral recipients, almost 90 percent held assistantships at some point during their graduate studies. Assistantships involved the student in work tasks that are similar to those that will be carried out in the college and university setting, thus skills acquired from serving as teaching and research assistants are potentially more transferable to the actual work setting.

The second phase of socialization begins when new faculty accept employment in colleges and universities. This stage is informal in that few colleges and universities have developed special training programs to facilitate the entry of newcomers (Boice, 1992; Whitt, 1991). More often, when there is an orientation session conducted by the institution, it focuses on pragmatic issues such as applying for health insurance, filling out W-2 tax forms, and reviewing university policies regarding student grades. Acknowledging the lack of structured socialization for new faculty members, Whitt (1991) says that these newcomers must be highly self-motivated. Boice (1992) argues that those who are not self-motivated will very likely not receive tenure. Lack of assistance helps to explain why many studies of new faculty members find high levels of stress and low levels of job satisfaction (e.g., Baldwin and Blackburn, 1981; Mager and Myers, 1982; Reynolds, 1988).

Learning the teaching component of the work role is the result of a kind of self-socialization wherein the new faculty member refines teaching skills through trial and error learning in the classroom (Howsam, 1967; Lortie, 1969). Studies in both teaching and research institutions indicate that the majority of new faculty members' time is spent preparing for class (Boice, 1992). Informal interaction with "old timers" in the organization may also facilitate learning the teacher role. Van Maanen (1983) notes that laissez-faire, informal socialization increases the influence of the immediate work group on the new employee. In some cases the direction provided by the work group may be at odds with the expectations of those in positions of authority. For example, colleagues are likely to inform the new faculty member about what rules can be bent or broken (e.g., how many classes a semester can be cancelled without attracting attention).

The research role associated with many faculty positions also is learned primarily through informal processes. In a national survey of college professors, Boyer (1987) found that 75 percent work in organization settings which require a commitment to publishing. Senior faculty may serve as informal mentors to new faculty through collaborative research endeavors. Trial and error learning is accomplished as new faculty submit their work for peer review, collect criticism, and embark on what may seem like endless revisions. Van Maanen (1983) argues that trial and error learning of this type induces anxiety in newcomers to organizations. Socialization to the profession which occurred in phase one of formal education may also provide guidance to new faculty navigating the channels of the publishing process. Reskin (1979) found that graduate school sponsors were a particularly important influence on the postdoctoral research productivity of new faculty. Others suggest that this kind of mentoring is less likely to occur for women and minorities, a point we will come to later in the paper.

The degree to which newcomers are socialized individually or collectively is an important structural characteristic of socialization programs (Van Maanen, 1983). Research suggests that peer group interaction in collective socialization programs eases the newcomer's passage into the organization (Becker, 1960; Bruckel, 1955; Evan, 1963). Van Maanen (1983) also notes that collective processes provide a potential base for recruit resistance to organizational demands. Recruit groups are more likely than individuals to rebel against organizational socialization because the responsibility for this risky action must be distributed across a group of individuals. Becker and Carper (1956) document a form of student collective resistance in their study of medical school socialization. They found that in the context of the student group greater cynicism about the profession and professional training was expressed while a more idealistic orientation was expressed when students met individually with the interviewers.

Socialization for academe is collective during the formal schooling phase, and primarily individual when new faculty members begin to perform their work role. The peer group is a strong source of support for graduate students. Student peer groups also assist in socializing their members through group study efforts. Ties developed in graduate school often are retained when new faculty members accept employment, and can be professional resources. Faculty-student mentoring arrangements and relationships between doctoral sponsors and their students provide an exception to the pattern of collective socialization for professional/graduate students. These relationships resemble apprenticeships in that mentors work individually with students on thesis topics and related work. LeCluyse,

Tollefsen, and Borgers (1985) examined the extent of mentoring among graduate students and found that 76 percent of the students reported having a mentor. In a study of academic career achievement of chemists, Reskin (1977; 1979) found that individuals' graduate sponsors had important and lasting consequences for career success. Van Maanen (1983) suggests that the success of individual socialization strategies is influenced by whether the trainer and trainee like one another. Thus, the matching of academic sponsors and students is a critical variable influencing successful socialization.

The recruitment of new faculty members for academic departments is an individual as opposed to collective process. Rarely do individual departments have multiple positions to fill at one point in time. The fact that the professoriate is composed of hundreds of different disciplines with varied standards for effective work performance (Bowen and Schuster, 1986) impedes the development of an "in the same boat" feeling among new faculty who are batch hired across a number of different disciplines. Within departments, tenure-track junior faculty hired at different points in time may develop a sense of camaraderie during the shared ordeal experience described earlier. Bowen and Schuster (1986, p. 147) argue that pressures on junior faculty to publish often serve to isolate them as they "burrow toward tenure." This shared experience may create feelings of peer group identification for junior faculty members.

Socialization programs also vary with respect to whether or not they contain a series of discrete stages. Sequential socialization programs are marked by a series of discrete stages, nonsequential programs are accomplished in only one transitional stage (Van Maanen, 1983). In graduate and professional schools the training of aspiring professors is largely sequential (e.g., prerequisites exist for courses, course work must be completed prior to writing the thesis, only more advanced students receive teaching or research assistantships). Each of these discrete stages provides an opportunity for mastery or failure; consequently, feelings of efficacy and worth are affected. Once hired, new faculty experience nonsequential socialization as they are immersed simultaneously in all aspects of the work role.

Whether recruits are provided with precise knowledge of the time required for completion of the socialization program is another important variable. Fixed socialization strategies provide a precise time frame for completion; variable programs do not (Van Maanen, 1983). Graduate school training contains both fixed and variable elements. Course work is scheduled and completed on a semester basis (fixed), but the time required for completion of the thesis varies greatly across students (variable) (Bowen and Schuster, 1986). Organizational socialization for new faculty operates according to a fixed time frame. The length of the tenure-track/probationary period is specified generally as part of the employment contract. While knowledge of the time frame may create feelings of pressure (Bowen and Schuster, 1986), Van Maanen (1983) suggests that the lack of a specified time frame causes anxiety because recruits want to know the length of time it will take to become a full member of the organization.

Socialization programs may be designed according to tournament or contest principles. Tournament programs involve separating recruits into tracks on the basis of presumed differences in ability. These programs are competitive in that failure to master the training material at any point results in elimination from the tournament. Contest programs avoid separating recruits into tracks, and allow newcomers to repeat phases of training as necessary (Van Maanen, 1983). Socialization of new faculty in graduate/professional schools and in their employing organizations contains elements of the tournament approach. Failure to pass courses or comprehensive examinations results in elimination from the program of study. Unacceptable annual performance reviews for junior faculty can result in non-renewal of contracts, and the tenure decision itself is permanent. Failure to receive tenure means loss of employment.

Van Maanen (1983) suggests that recruits passing through tournament socialization programs tend to adopt the safest strategy of passage due to the permanent consequence of failure. Safe strategies of passage involve avoiding risk and potentially innovative approaches. This can be thought of as an attempt to maintain self-esteem. Individuals with low self-esteem will not want to risk failure (Gecas, 1982). On the other hand, individuals with high self-esteem might view this as an opportunity to increase self esteem. However, Van Maanen (1983) suggests that the longer individuals compete in tournament activities, the more insecure they will feel. Parallels might be drawn between this consequence of the tournament socialization strategy and pressure on new faculty members in research institutions to choose safe research topics—topics most likely to result in publication.

Socialization of new faculty in graduate schools often conforms to the serial approach, while on-the-job socialization is more disjunctive. Serial socialization occurs when experienced members groom newcomers to fill similar roles. If a recruit does not have predecessors available to perform this mentoring role, socialization is disjunctive (Van Maanen, 1983). Graduate school sponsors typically train their students to follow in their footsteps by encouraging them to pursue similar research interests (Reskin, 1979). This aspect of professional socialization resembles the serial approach. Actual organizational socialization typically is disjunctive as few academic departments have the luxury of more than one faculty member in a given area of expertise. Even in instances where disciplinary specialties are duplicated with the hiring of new faculty, changing standards regarding research and publication may serve to separate junior and senior faculty (Boyer, 1987; Bowen and Schuster, 1986). On such campuses, new faculty may find that experiences passed on by senior faculty are quite removed from their own circumstances.

The final socialization strategy involves the degree to which a training program attempts to change or alter certain entering characteristics of the recruit. Investiture processes are designed to confirm the identity of the newcomer—the message is we hired you because you are a "good fit." Divestiture programs, by contrast, are designed to dismantle the identity of the newcomer, to resocialize him/her. Some degree of divestiture occurs in graduate school training as students are encouraged to shed former values and endorse those of the professional model (Schein, 1983). Schein (1983) argues that assigning work overloads to students in graduate schools is one way of sending the message that students are not sufficiently capable and must undergo basic changes in order to succeed. By the time new faculty members are hired in colleges and universities, it is assumed that prior socialization has instilled proper values and work behaviors, and further resocialization is not required. The academic search process, wherein candidates undergo lengthy interviews and make detailed presentations, is an attempt to screen potential new faculty to ensure a good fit with the organization.

Some organizations consciously design and implement socialization programs, deliberating among the various strategies presented above. Other organizations may simply drift into certain patterns of socializing new employees without ever giving the matter much thought (Ott, 1989). Graduate schools follow the former pattern when socializing their students, and colleges and universities as employers of new faculty tend to follow the latter. Curricula, examination processes, and even aspects of student life are carefully planned. When students processed through these highly structured programs become new faculty it is assumed that the bulk of the "socializing work" has been accomplished; thus, less conscious thought is given to the design of socialization programs by these employing organizations.

DIVERSITY AND NEW FACULTY SOCIALIZATION

The American professoriate is a heterogeneous professional group composed of many diverse cultures with contrasting values and traditions (Boyer, 1987; Bowen and Schuster, 1986; Clark, 1983). There are hundreds of different academic disciplines and subspecialties, and the faculty in the various disciplines exhibit significantly different backgrounds, personality characteristics, and attitudes (Becher, 1989; Bowen and Schuster, 1986; Clark, 1983). After extensive study of disciplinary differences among faculty, Ladd and Lipset (1975) concluded that there are greater differences of opinion among faculty in the various academic disciplines than among such diverse groups as the rich and poor, young and old, and white and black. Further variation among faculty exists with respect to type of employing institution—research university, liberal arts college, or community college (Boyer, 1987). At major research universities the emphasis is on quality research and student quality; community colleges emphasize equity values (i.e., open door policies); four-year colleges are a mixture of both orientations (Clark, 1987).

In addition, faculty have become more heterogeneous in terms of race and gender. The changing nature of higher education has further fragmented the faculty into diverse groups. For example, budget constraints have compelled many institutions to employ significant numbers of part-time faculty. These faculty members' work experiences and interests are often different from those of the regular faculty. Changing standards with respect to requirements for tenure and promotion also have served to divide senior and junior faculty. The following discussion will address some of the many divisions in higher education and their implications for new faculty socialization.

Disciplinary and Institutional Differences

Differences by discipline as well as by type of institution may be relevant to junior faculty research activities (Bieber, 1992) and to the relative importance attached to teaching (Creswell and Roskens, 1981). Moreover, "to the degree that procedures, practices, and criteria in tenure review vary across departments, it can be theorized that the junior faculty experience of the process and the meaning they make of it vary as well" (Verrier, 1992, p. 6).

Bieber (1992) conducted 17 interviews with full-time junior (tenure-track) faculty at research and comprehensive institutions in the fields of biology, psychology, English, and sociology to describe their sense of themselves in the researcher role. In comprehensive universities where teaching is the primary consideration for tenuring, research was more personally motivated and less tied to obtaining grants and publications. In research-oriented universities, research activities were more closely tied to professional self-concept. Disciplinary affiliation was also perceived by faculty as strongly influencing the nature of research activities, e.g., whether one's research agenda is more cumulative or eclectic.

In a study of norms governing teaching performance in higher education, Braxton, Bayer, and Finkelstein (1992) looked at institutional and disciplinary variations. Their analysis of responses from 302 faculty in departments of biology, history, mathematics, and psychology at research universities and comprehensive colleges/universities, showed some institutional differences but found "nonsubstantial variations of teaching performance norms across the four fields, suggesting that norms for the college teaching profession may be relatively monolithic" (p. 553). In their study of new faculty socialization, a corresponding interest has been expressed by Menges and Quinn (1992) in the extent to which new faculty perceive and follow teaching norms, and how they are acquired. Institutional differences in teaching norms may reflect variation in educational mission and can be expected to influence new faculty experiences.

Trautvetter (1992) reported that new faculty in two-year institutions were generally more satisfied with their institution, salary, and support at work than four-year institution faculty members, and experienced significantly less stress. New faculty at the comprehensive and two-year institutions were also older and had more career experience. "Community college faculty members perceived their environment to be more trusting between faculty and administrators, more supportive in regards to teaching and more collegial in nature" than new faculty at research universities (Trautvetter, 1992, pp. i-iii).

Teaching and/or Research Emphasis

Academic institutions differ in the extent to which they require faculty to engage in research and publishing. Community colleges emphasize teaching and may have little to no scholarly productivity requirement (Bowen and Schuster, 1986). Community colleges enroll students with poor academic backgrounds, serve students interested in vocational programs and offer more adult education and remedial classes (Clark, 1987). These teaching activities are very labor-intensive; thus, they constitute a full workload. In contrast, four-year colleges and universities increasingly require research and publication in order for new faculty to achieve tenured status (Clark, 1983). In a survey of 5,000 faculty members, Boyer (1987) found that 62 percent of the faculty at liberal arts colleges and 89 percent of the faculty at research universities are engaged in scholarly research and have published in a professional journal. He argues that "emerging" institutions, in an attempt to emulate top research universities, now emphasize scholarly productivity as the critical criterion for promotion.

Many universities and colleges use new faculty members to increase the emphasis on research (Smith, 1990). While senior faculty may remain committed to teaching, the expectation under which they were hired, new faculty are hired and rewarded under new expectations that emphasize both teaching and research. For many junior faculty, this new emphasis creates a tension between teaching and research and results in pressure to succeed at both endeavors. Such pressures may explain why the majority of advanced assistant professors find the first few years of the work role very demanding (Baldwin and Blackburn, 1981). In a sample of 186 male faculty members at 12 liberal arts colleges, Baldwin and Blackburn (1981) found that 72 percent felt stressed by pressures to achieve. Campbell (1985) and Locke et al. (1984) suggest that academic departments should choose between the teaching and research role when hiring and evaluating new faculty in order to reduce job pressures, dissatisfaction, and burnout. However, many studies show that success at teaching and scholarly productivity correlate positively (Boice, 1992).

Doctoral granting institutions typically socialize their students to conduct research (Gottlieb, 1961; Malaney, 1988), and transmit the expectation that most four-year colleges and universities will require that new faculty do research. While new faculty value good teaching, they are most likely to be rewarded financially for their scholarly reputations. Differential reward can be a powerful socialization message to new faculty in that it may encourage them to focus on research, perhaps even at the expense of teaching (Boyer, 1987). Fulton and Trow (1974) surveyed a national sample of college professors in order to assess the relationship between stage of career and self-identification as researchers or teachers. They found that with increased age faculty preferences gradually evolved such that many professors' interests and values moved away from research toward teaching. This may be due to the fact that few professors seem to enjoy writing (Boice and Jones, 1984), although they recognize that it is a necessary requirement for receiving tenure (Hartley and Branthwaite, 1989).

Reskin (1979) argues that doctoral sponsors are important in influencing their students' later research productivity. In a study of doctoral chemists, she finds that the quality of the sponsor's scientific performance is an important predictor of the number of articles published by students on completion of the Ph.D. Reskin suggests that while much of this effect is due to sponsors transmitting scientific knowledge, skills, and professional values to their students, a portion of the effect is due to ascriptive aspects of sponsorship. Sponsors ascribe to their students an origin status in the scientific stratification system. The professional stature of the sponsor can provide advantages such as introductions, nominations, and recommendations (Allison and Long, 1987; 1990; Reskin, 1979).

Changing Standards For Tenure And Promotion

At institutions where scholarly productivity in the past was rare and teaching excellence was the primary criterion for promotion, the new emphasis on publishing serves to separate junior and senior faculty (Boice and Thomas, 1989; Bowen and Schuster, 1986; Mooney, 1990; Seldin, 1987; Wright, 1992). The change in standards isolates junior faculty who may be overwhelmed with heavy workloads, and creates resentment among many senior faculty who are affected adversely by the shifting reward structure. As mentioned earlier, this fragmentation of faculty creates a situation where it is not possible for the old guard to effectively mentor new faculty. Members of the old guard may be suspicious of the upstart junior faculty (Bowen and Schuster, 1986), and junior faculty may discount the advice of their senior colleagues who do not engage in scholarly research on the grounds that the advice is outdated. In a study of career attitudes in three generations of college and university faculty, Corcoran and Clark (1984) found that more recent cohorts have internalized higher expectations of research and scholarly productivity. Whitt (1991) argues that this cohort difference creates different faculty subcultures and is a major barrier to collegiality.

Many junior faculty joined the professiorate expecting to follow in the footsteps of their mentors, to move from campus to campus as they climb the professional ladder (Boyer, 1987). These socialized achievement expectations are problematic for junior faculty members because prospects for mobility and advancement are restricted far more today than in the past. Moreover, the declining status of the academic profession exacerbates the schism between the old and the new guard. Metzger (1987, p. 125) states:

> Veteran faculty members who keep track of the purchasing power of their paychecks, of the waiting time between promotions, of the quality of work amenities and supporting services, of their chances of getting a research project funded, can attest that the previous period of rapid expansion was attended by the furnishing of concrete benefits that the next period largely snatched away.

These changes in the nature of the academic labor market cause the work experiences and career patterns of junior and senior faculty to be quite different (Rosenblum and Rosenblum, 1990), and also impede the development of senior-junior faculty mentoring relationships (Boice and Thomas, 1989; Mooney, 1990; Seldin, 1987). This results in a more disjunctive pattern of socialization for new faculty today, and greater reliance on peer group socialization.

The issues just examined are summarized by Boice (1992, p. 24) who reports the following common reasons for cultural conflicts between junior and senior faculty:

> (1) that senior faculty routinely excluded new faculty from departmental decisions, (2) that senior faculty openly grumbled about new faculty interest in gaining more national visibility than local visibility as professionals, (3) that seniors showed undisguised disdain for new faculty talk about research projects, (4) that seniors complained about new faculty's narrow preferences for teaching specialty courses, and (5) that senior faculty aggressively distinguished teaching and research as mutually interfering activities.

Socialization Opportunities for Women and Minorities in Academe

Women, racial and ethnic minorities have long been underrepresented in the professoriate (Bernard, 1964; Chamberlain, 1988; Simeone, 1987). Women represent about 27 percent of full-time faculty and racial and ethnic minorities only 11 percent (AAUP, 1990; NEA, 1993). This underrepresentation suggests that minority and women faculty are often tokens in academic institutions. Kanter (1977) argues that token status serves to marginalize individuals in organizations and provides a number of obstacles to successful careers. For this reason, the stresses associated with entering a new work role may be exacerbated for minority and women faculty.

Women are not only underrepresented in academe, they are also underrepresented in component roles of thc profession. Specifically, women are employed less often than men in research institutions (Aisenberg and Harrington, 1988; Astin and Bayer, 1973; 1979; Bernard, 1964; Fox, 1985; Simeone, 1987), they are concentrated in lower ranked positions (Baldridge et al., 1978; Cole, 1979; Finkelstein, 1984a; 1984b; Kulis and Miller-Loessi, 1992; Menges and Exum,

1983; Reskin and Roos, 1990; Rossi, 1970; Roos and Reskin, 1992; Sandler, 1979), and they do a disproportionate share of service and committee work (Reskin and Roos, 1990; Roos and Reskin, 1992). Reskin and Roos (1990) refer to this type of gender segregation as ghettoization. There are at least two explanations for the concentration of women in lower status areas of academe. First, women may self-select into these areas as a result of differential gender role socialization (Clark and Corcoran, 1986); the nurturing qualities that are a part of traditional female gender role socialization are valued in teaching and university service work. Kanter (1977) refers to this phenomenon, in the business world, as the office mother and office wife roles. Second, the discriminatory preferences and assumptions of academic institutions limit women's access to the higher status areas of academe. For example, academic administrators (mostly male) may assume that women are less career oriented because they have children; the same assumptions may not hold for men.

While ghettoization limits women's employment in research-oriented colleges and universities, those women who do hold positions in such institutions typically benefit from the existence of an environment supportive of research (e.g., lighter teaching loads, more graduate assistants, more productive colleagues, better laboratory, library, and computer resources). The lack of such resources is a major obstacle to women's productivity at teaching-oriented institutions and may explain why women publish less than men (Fox, 1983) and receive outside funding less often (Rong, Grant, and Ward, 1988). Cole and Zuckerman (1987) suggest that this research productivity gap is narrowing among recent Ph.D. cohorts, a change which may reflect movement away from traditional patterns of gender socialization for women academicians. Although many of the studies just reviewed focus on the marginalization of women in academe, scholars also note that racial and ethnic minority faculty feel pressure to emphasize university service (advising and committees) over research productivity (Boice and Kelly, 1987; Boice, Shaughnessy, and Pecker, 1985; Heard and Bing, 1993).

The important mentor/protege relationship, perhaps the only form of directed on-the-job socialization for new faculty, is important particularly for minority and women faculty whose sense of belonging within the profession may be shakier than that of their majority group counterparts (Berg and Bing, 1990; Sands, Parson, and Duane, 1991; Simeone, 1987). Unfortunately, the underrepresentation of women and minorities in the professoriate, particularly at the higher levels (Andersen, 1992), often results in a shortage of available mentors for new women and minority faculty members (Berg and Bing, 1990; Blackwell, 1989). This shortage of mentors also exists for women and minority graduate students (Adler, 1976). While majority-group senior faculty can mentor women and minorities, it is more difficult for these mentors to be role models. Sex, racial, and ethnic similarity of mentors and proteges can be beneficial in that such mentors serve as examples of success ''despite the odds.'' Furthermore, mentors who have navigated non-traditional paths can provide specific information on how they overcame the obstacles associated with token status (Simeone, 1987). Berg and Ferber (1983) found that both students and faculty are more comfortable with same-sex mentors. Goldstein (1979) found that Ph.Ds with same-sex sponsors had more publications four years after graduation than those in cross-sex mentoring situations, suggesting the importance of support from same-sex mentors/role models.

The importance of mentor/protege relationships for women and minority faculty has been acknowledged on a few campuses which have begun to actively promote the formation of these relationships (e.g., Massachusetts Institute of Technology and City University of New York) (Simeone, 1987). Minority and women's groups on campuses are also often active in their support and encouragement of mentoring relationships for students and junior faculty (Chamberlain, 1988; Simeone, 1987).

Socialization and Part-Time Faculty

Although the number of faculty positions increased throughout the 1970s, much of this increase was confined to part-time and temporary work, what Clark (1983) refers to as proletarian positions. Budget constraints and the need to maintain flexibility in staffing has led to an increase in the ranks of part-time faculty in colleges and universities (Bowen and Schuster, 1986). This pervasive hiring trend disproportionately affects younger cohorts of would-be faculty members. Metzger (1987, p. 125) points out that many new faculty members can define with first-hand knowledge the following terms that have crept into the academic lexicon: ''the 'folding chair' (the unrenewable appointment that lasts for a year and then expires); the 'nontenure track' (the renewable appointment that precludes a status promotion); the academic 'gypsy' (the jobseeker in a casual labor market who travels everywhere but in the end gets nowhere).'' Approximately 38 percent of all faculty members are employed part-time, and on some campuses the percentage is even higher (AAUP, 1992; Gappa, 1984; NEA, 1993). The largest percentage of part-time faculty are at teaching and community colleges: the American Association of University Professors (1992) found that 52 percent of all faculty in community colleges are part-time with some colleges and departments using up to 80 percent part-time faculty members. Moreover, part-time faculty members compose nearly 17 percent of all faculty at research universities, almost 30 percent at comprehensive institutions, and almost 33 percent at liberal arts colleges.

Part-time instructors exhibit a wide range of backgrounds, professional traits, and motivations (Rosenblum and Rosenblum, 1990). In a national survey of 128 educational institutions Tuckerman (1978) found that part-time faculty included students, semiretired individuals, those desiring full-time employment, those employed elsewhere, and those with responsibilities at home. Part-time faculty enjoy few work benefits, experience unsatisfactory working conditions, little job security and stability, and little or no chance for professional advancement, and rarely receive critical feedback (Clark, 1987). Part-time faculty receive much less income than tenure track faculty for comparable teaching. The American Association of University Professors (1992) reports that the mean salary for part-time faculty is $6,302 per year, with salary ranging from $900 to $3,000 per course at most institutions.

Because part-time faculty typically work under less favorable conditions (e.g., short-term contracts, fragmented schedules, fewer teaching resources), they often develop only minimal commitment to their employing institutions (Boyer, 1987; Bowen and Schuster, 1986). Moreover, most part-time faculty are not ''temporary'' employees in that they work an average of 6.5 years at a single college (AAUP, 1992). Yet minimal commitment, on the part of the institution as well as on the part of the faculty member, results in part timers being less responsive to organizational socialization. Academic institutions and their senior faculty may also be less willing to invest in the mentoring of part-timers because they are viewed as relatively expendable. Part-time faculty may lack a supportive peer group due to high rates of turnover and minimal time spent on campus. In addition, data show that over 40 percent of women faculty members are employed on a part-time basis, compared with 30 percent of men. This gender gap has widened as the number of part-time faculty members has increased: the number of part-time male faculty rose by 10.3 percent between 1975 and 1987, while the number of women rose by 54.1 percent during the same period (AAUP, 1992). These factors combine to suggest that directed on-the-job socialization experiences for part-time faculty are virtually non-existent. Informal trial-and-error learning is likely to be the norm for these relatively isolated faculty members.

PROGRAMS FOR NEW FACULTY DEVELOPMENT

With their first appointment, new faculty are expected to assume full responsibility for their primary tasks, particularly teaching. ''Yet, it seems unrealistic to expect that new faculty members will know everything necessary to fulfill their responsibilities effectively'' (Fink, 1992, p. 39). Orientation programs, not prohibitively expensive nor unreasonably time consuming for administrators to provide, offer major benefits for new faculty and for their employing institutions. Institutions that fail to provide systematic orientation and continued opportunities for faculty development add to the stresses of an academic career and increase the likelihood of high turnover among junior faculty as well as lower productivity among tenured faculty.

Boice (1990b) has demonstrated the effectiveness of writing workshops for faculty in improving their productivity and publication records. The workshops

Boice developed begin by exploring participants' reasons for not writing—reasons reflecting precisely the types of stresses so often experienced by new and junior faculty: time constraints, competing demands and distractions, unrealistically high standards and fear of failure. Lucas and Harrington (1990) found that faculty exposed to writing workshops also increased their rate of completing proposals for fellowships, external grants, and internal seed money. Based on observation of 74 faculty workshop participants at California Polytechnic State University, Lucas and Harrington reported that "almost twice as many of those who completed these [writing] workshops wrote proposals as did faculty members who completed another set of workshops designed specifically for instruction in grant writing" (p. 140). Compensating for the time required to participate in such seminars, enhanced productivity can help alleviate "the stress that accompanies the start of academic careers" (Lucas and Harrington, 1990, p. 144). To the typical grant writing workshop topics suggested by Drew and Hughes (1983)—grant-worthy activities, sponsors, contacts with program officers, organization of proposals, and budgeting—Lucas and Harrington recommend the addition of Boice's (1984; 1990a; 1990b; 1992) ideas on overcoming writing blocks.

Fink (1992) provides an overview of types of orientation programs with respect to the following dimensions: timing (several intensive days before the semester begins or shorter sessions throughout); content covered (e.g., teaching, research, institutional procedures); voluntary or mandatory; target audience (new full-time faculty or broader); and centralization (e.g., university wide, by college or by department). Five ongoing programs are outlined by Fink to illustrate successful combinations of the above elements in different institutional settings. With such programs, individual faculty members can approach their responsibilities better informed and better organized. They become more familiar with institutional supports for research and grant writing. The programs that address teaching appear to succeed in encouraging greater confidence and experimentation with more diversified teaching methods than lecture alone. Contacts with faculty and administrators help ease the sense of being an outsider, and newcomers gain added insight into the mission and priorities of a particular institution. For the institution, orientation programs convey to faculty an interest in their professional development that promotes effective functioning, job satisfaction and commitment. Program directors also believe orientation programs increase institutional identification, counterbalancing the tendency of new faculty to identify exclusively with their discipline and individual department (Fink, 1992).

Mentoring has also been examined as a program for socializing new and junior faculty. Boice (1992) provides an overview and evaluation of recent research on mentoring, noting, first, its relative novelty as a focus for systematic investigation within the academic workplace though it has been studied in other settings

(Lavery, Boice, Thompson, and Turner, 1989; Sands, Parson, and Duane, 1991). In a study of mentoring at one large comprehensive university, Boice (1990a) found that only a handful of the 40–60 new faculty hired each year on tenure-track positions had received spontaneous mentoring, but those faculty had benefited from their mentoring relationships. Boice (1992) describes a program of structured mentoring and techniques for enhancing mentoring, such as cataloguing each semester's agenda. Boice (1992) also advocates mentor-newcomer relationships that cross disciplinary lines. While more research is needed to document the effectiveness of and most favorable circumstances for mentoring, this appears to be a promising avenue for investigation. Mentoring serves to convey tacit knowledge and alleviates the sense of isolation and absence of collegiality of which new and junior faculty complain frequently.

Jarvis (1992) discusses a variety of institutional variables that influence junior faculty scholarship: administrative support for the principle of faculty development; good management (e.g., timely feedback); collegiality (fostering personal contact with other scholars on and off campus); mentoring (informal and formal); research centers and informal colloquia (for sharing ideas, keeping up with the literature, encouraging future work); institutional supports (summer funding, manuscript typing, small grants, travel money); facilities and maintenance (e.g., offices, labs, computers). Austin (1992, p. 83) recommends teaching fellow programs, which "reinforce institutional commitment to teaching excellence" and can help junior faculty to be "more competent in their teaching, more responsive to student needs, more professionally self-confident, and more connected to colleagues." Given the importance of the chair's role, institutional training programs for chairs to increase their sensitivity to gender and minority issues and to the needs of new and junior faculty in general are also suggested (Daly and Townsend, 1992).

CONCLUSION

Fink (1992, p. 39) notes that "each year American institutions of higher education appoint thirty thousand to forty thousand new full-time faculty." If these faculty members do not succeed, there are both individual and institutional costs (Daly and Townsend, 1992). For the individual denied tenure, there is often a sense of wasted time and effort; a feeling of failure. Remaining colleagues, too, may experience psychological costs; a sense of loss and disappointment, uncertainty about the future, lowered morale, and concerns about inadequate guidance provided by senior faculty (Daly and Townsend, 1992). Programs and courses developed around the special skills and interests of departing faculty must be revised. The institution has lost its initial investment in recruiting the individual and is faced with another expenditure of time and funds to replace him or her, now in a time of greater budgetary constraints. Even excellent faculty development programs cannot alleviate all the stresses inherent in the professorial role (Austin, 1992), stresses that may culminate in failure to obtain tenure, but reexamination of the ''sink or swim'' attitude toward assistant professors in their first faculty appointment is certainly warranted.

Clark and Corcoran (1986, p. 22) remarked that ''few studies of faculty role socialization have been done.'' Since that time a substantial literature on the new faculty role has accumulated in the field of higher education. Widely read works on the changing nature of higher education, such as Bowen and Schuster (1986), Boyer (1987), and Boice (1992), highlighted the need for more research on how to prepare new faculty effectively for their work role. While much of the recent higher education literature on new faculty socialization offers insight into how socialization is accomplished in graduate school and on the job (particularly, highlighting problems and deficiencies in the process), this work is still primarily exploratory.

Many of the studies conducted over the past decade are based on small samples of graduate students or university faculty. Generalization from small and/or unrepresentative samples to the larger population of graduate students and new faculty members is inappropriate. The full range of diversity of new faculty and their employing institutions remains to be studied. In many respects, it is misleading to speak of the new faculty role in the academic workplace because many such environments exist, each with different requirements, opportunities, and pressures. As Bayer (1989, p. 224) points out in his review of Becher's cross-national, ethnographic study of faculty across twelve disciplines, ''Too often in the higher education literature there is unhesitating generalization from the study of actors (students, faculty) in one or a few academic fields to all of academia.'' Studies based on small samples have enriched our understanding of commonalities and variations in new faculty experiences and suggest directions for future research based on larger, more diverse, and representative samples. This paper has highlighted some of the many types of diversity that should be incorporated into future research. Most scholars would agree that academic activities can be grouped by discipline and by type of institution, but these forms of structural variation also intersect with ascribed characteristics (e.g., race/ethnicity, gender), personality traits and situational factors. To fully understand new faculty socialization, consideration should be given to the interplay of many such variables.

An additional shortcoming of the existing body of literature on new faculty socialization is that the majority of studies are cross-sectional; information is collected at only one point in time. Yet, socialization is an ongoing process that should be studied processually, over time. Collecting data from new faculty at one point in time may distort understanding of socialization; for example, new faculty may feel isolated, anxious and pressured during their first semester, but begin to adjust (or not adjust) to the new work role in the second semester. Correspondingly, many scholars have conceptualized the new faculty socialization process as consisting of stages or of turning points. Research designed to test the predictive power of these conceptual models is conducted most appropriately with the same sample of individuals followed over time, as in the panel designs employed by Boice (1992), Menges (1991) and Olsen and Sorcinelli (1992).

Attention to the changing nature of academic work environments is another important consideration for future research on new faculty socialization. Calls for reform in higher education, combined with budgetary pressures, necessitate constant adaptation on the part of both faculty and their employing institutions. For example, faculty in colleges and universities are required increasingly not only to teach and conduct research, but also to generate external funding. Some disciplines are more vulnerable than others to these pressures. Clark (1983, p. 80) states, "Disunited within their own fields on grounds of basic approach, theory, and methods, social scientists and humanists are thereby rendered more vulnerable to specific political views or world views brought into one's work from outside sources." Research is needed to examine how, over time, different types of faculty adapt to new political climates in varied institutional settings.

Additionally, there is much scholarship outside the higher education literature that is relevant to the topic of new faculty socialization. In particular, in this paper we drew from the sociological literature on workplace socialization and the social psychology of self-concept. Workplace socialization studies show, for example, how the structural design of socialization programs predisposes certain outcomes. Self-concept theory emphasizes how socialization affects self definitions and feelings, which, in turn, influence organizational behavior.

Future research directed at better understanding socialization for the faculty role is particularly important in what many scholars find to be an era of declining work satisfaction among college and university faculty (Austin and Gamson, 1983; Finkelstein, 1984a; Locke et al., 1984). While declining work satisfaction for faculty may be attributed to the depressed academic job market and increased demands on faculty, knowledge of how to better prepare new faculty for their work may serve to mitigate the negative effects of such conditions and increase levels of faculty satisfaction.

Acknowledgments

We would like to thank Roberta Shuffitt for assistance with manuscript preparation.

REFERENCES

Adler, N. E. (1976). Women students. In J. Katz and R. T. Hartnett (eds.), *Scholars in the Making: The Development of Graduate and Professional Students*. Cambridge, MA: Ballinger.

Aisenberg, N., and Harrington, M. (1988). *Women of Academe: Outsiders in the Sacred Grove*. Amherst: University of Massachusetts Press.

Allison, P. D., and Long, J. S. (1987). Interuniversity mobility of academic scientists. *American Sociological Review* 2 (October): 643–652.

Allison P. D., and Long, J. S. (1990). Departmental effects on scientific productivity. *American Sociological Review* 55 (August): 469–478.

American Association of University Professors (AAUP). (1990). Some dynamic aspects of academic careers: The urgent need to match aspirations with compensation. *Academe* (March-April): 29.

American Association of University Professors (AAUP). (1992). Report on the status of non-tenure-track faculty. *Academe* (November-December): 39–48.

Andersen, M. L. (1992). *Thinking About Women: Sociological Perspectives on Sex and Gender*. New York: Macmillan.

Astin, H. S., and Bayer, A. E. (1973). Sex discrimination in academe. In A. Rossi and A. Colderwood (eds.), *Academic Women on the Move*. New York: Russell Sage.

Astin, H. S., and Bayer, A. E. (1979). Pervasive sex differences in the academic reward system: Scholarship, marriage, and what else? In D. R. Lewis and W. E. Becker (eds.), *Academic Rewards in Higher Education*. New York: Ballinger.

Austin, A. E. (1992). Supporting junior faculty through a teaching fellows program. In *Developing New and Junior Faculty* 50 (Summer). San Francisco: Jossey-Bass.

Austin, A. E., and Gamson, Z. F. (1983). *Academic Workplaces: New Demands, Heightened Tensions*. Washington, DC: George Washington School of Education and Human Development.

Bach, B. W., and Bullis, C. (1987). A critique of state and phase models of socialization using turning point analysis. Paper presented at the annual meeting of the Speech Communication Association, Boston.

Baldridge, J. V., Curtis, D. V., Ecker, G., and Riley, G. L. (1978). *Policy Making and Effective Leadership*. San Francisco: Jossey-Bass.

Baldwin, R. G. (1979). Adult and career development: What are the implications for faculty? *Current Issues in Higher Education*. Washington, D.C.: American Association for Higher Education.

Baldwin, R. G., and Blackburn, R. T. (1981). The academic career as a developmental process: Implications for higher education. *Journal of Higher Education* 52: 598–613.

Bandura, A. (1990). Conclusion: Reflections on nonability determinants of competence. In R. J. Sternberg and J. Kolligan (eds.), *Competence Considered*. New Haven, CT: Yale University Press.

Baxter, L., and Bullis, C. (1986). Turning points in developing romantic relationships. *Human Communication Research* 12: 469–494.

Bayer, A. E. (1989). Book review of *Academic Tribes and Territories: Intellectual Enquiry and the Cultures of Disciplines*, by T. Becher. *Journal of Higher Education* 62(2): 223–225.

Becher, T. (1989). *Academic Tribes and Territories: Intellectual Enquiry and the Cultures of Disciplines*. Great Britain: Open University Press.

Becker, H. S. (1960). Notes on the concept of commitment. *American Journal of Sociology* 65: 32–40.

Becker, H. S., and Carper, J. W. (1956). The elements of identification with an occupation. *American Sociological Review* 21: 341–348.

Becker, H. S., and Geer, B. (1958). The fate of idealism in medical school. *American Sociological Review* 23: 50–56.

Bennett, J. B. (1983). *Managing the Academic Department: Cases and Notes*. New York: American Council on Education and Macmillan Publishing.

Berg, B. L., and Bing, R. L. (1990). Mentoring members of minorities: Sponsorship and the gift. *Journal of Criminal Justice Education* 1: 153–165.
Berg, H. M., and Ferber, M. A. (1983). Men and women graduate students: Who succeeds and why? *Journal of Higher Education* 54: 629–648.
Bernard, J. (1964). *Academic Women*. University Park, PA: The Pennsylvania State University Press.
Bess, J. L. (1978). Anticipatory socialization of graduate students. *Research in Higher Education* 8: 289–317.
Bidwell, C. E. (1965). The school as a formal organization. In J. G. March (ed.), *Handbook of Organizations*. Chicago: Rand McNally.
Bieber, J. P. (1992). Research autonomy among untenured faculty. Paper presented at the Annual Meeting of the Association for the Study of Higher Education, Minneapolis.
Biglan, A. (1973). The characteristics of subject matter in different academic areas. *Journal of Applied Psychology* 57: 195–203.
Blackwell, J. E. (1989). Mentoring: An action strategy for increasing minority faculty. *Academe* 75: 8–14.
Blum, D. E. (1990). Younger scientists feel big pressure in battle for grants. *Chronicle of Higher Education* 26 (September): A1, A16.
Blumstein, P. W. (1973). Audience, Machiavellianism, and tactics of identity bargaining. *Sociometry* 36(3): 346–365.
Boice, R. (1984). Reexamination of traditional emphases in faculty development. *Research in Higher Education* 21: 195–209.
Boice, R. (1990a). Mentoring new faculty: A program for implementation. *Journal of Staff, Program and Organizational Development* 8(3): 143–160.
Boice, R. (1990b). *Professor as Writers*. Stillwater, OK: New Forums Press.
Boice, R. (1992). *The New Faculty Member: Supporting and Fostering Professional Development*. San Francisco: Jossey-Bass.
Boice, R. (1993). New faculty involvement for women and minorities. *Research in Higher Education* 34(3): 291–341.
Boice, R., and Jones, F. (1984). Why academicians don't write. *Journal of Higher Education* 55: 567–582.
Boice R., and Kelly, K. A. (1987). Writing viewed by disenfranchised groups. *Written Communication* 4: 299–309.
Boice R., Shaughnessy, P., and Pecker, G. (1985). Women and publishing in psychology. *American Psychologist* 40: 577–578.
Boice, R., and Thomas, C. T. (1989). Diagnosing academic cultures. *Journal of Staff, Program and Organizational Development* 7: 165–171.
Bornheimer, D. G., Burns, G. P., and Dumke, G. S. (1973). *The Faculty in Higher Education*. Danville, IL: Interstate Printers and Publisher.
Bowen H. R., and Schuster, J. H. (1986). *American Professors: A National Resource Imperiled*. New York: Oxford.
Boyer, E. L. (1987). *College: The Undergraduate Experience in America*. New York: Harper and Row.
Braxton, J. M., Bayer, A., and Finkelstein, M. J. (1992). Teaching performance norms in academia. *Research in Higher Education* 33(5): 533–569.
Brim, O. G., Jr. (1966). Socialization through the lifecycle. In O. G. Brim, Jr., and S. Wheeler (eds.), *Socialization After Childhood: Two Essays*. New York: Wiley.
Brim, O. G., Jr. (1968). Adult socialization. In J. A. Clausen (ed.), *Socialization and Society*. Boston: Little, Brown and Co.

Bruckel, J. E. (1955). Effects on morale of infantry team replacement systems. *Sociometry* 18: 129–142.
Buchanan, B. (1974). Building organizational commitment: The socialization of managers in work organizations. *Administrative Science Quarterly* 19: 533–546.
Bucher, R., Stelling, J., and Dommermuth, P. (1969). Differential prior socialization: A comparison of four professional training programs. *Social Forces* 48: 213–223.
Bullis, C., and Bach, B. W. (1987). Organizational identification in an educational setting: A comparative study. Paper presented at the Annual Meeting of the Speech Communication Association, Boston.
Bullis, C., and Bach, B. W. (1989). Socialization turning points: An examination of change in organizational identification. *Western Journal of Speech Communication* 53 (Summer): 273–293.
Bullis, C., and Bach, B. W. (1991). An explication and test of communication network content and multiplexity and predictors of organizational identification. *Western Journal of Speech Communication* 55 (Spring): 180–197.
Bush, D. M., and Simmons, R. D. (1981). Socialization processes over the life course. In M. Rosenberg and R. H. Turner (eds.), *Social Psychology: Sociological Perspectives*. New York: Basic Books.
Campbell, F. L. (1985). Turning toward teaching. In F. L. Campbell, H. M. Blalock, Jr., and R. McGee (eds.), *Teaching Sociology: The Quest for Excellence*. Chicago: Nelson-Hall.
Chamberlain, M. K. (1988). *Women in Academe: Progress and Prospects*. New York: Russell Sage.
Clark, B. R. (1983). *The Higher Education System*. Berkeley: University of California Press.
Clark, B. R. (1987). *The Academic Life*. New Jersey: The Carnegie Foundation for the Advancement of Teaching.
Clark, B. R. (1989). The academic life: Small worlds, different worlds. *Educational Researcher* 18(5): 4–8.
Clark, S. M., and Corcoran, M. (1986). Perspectives on the professional socialization of women faculty: A case of cumulative disadvantage? *Journal of Higher Education* 57: 20–43.
Cole, J. R. (1979). *Fair Science: Women in the Scientific Community*. New York: The Free Press.
Cole, J. R., and Zuckerman, H. (1987). Marriage, motherhood and research performance in science. *Scientific American* 225: 119–125.
Cooley, C. H. (1902). *Human Nature and the Social Order*. New York: Scribners.
Corcoran, M., and Clark, S. M. (1984). Professional socialization and contemporary career attitudes of three faculty generations. *Research in Higher Education* 20: 131–153.
Creswell, J. W. (1985). *Faculty Research Performance* (ASHE-ERIC Higher Education Report No. 4). Washington, DC: Association for the Study of Higher Education.
Creswell, J. W., and Roskens, R. (1981). The Biglan studies of differences among academic areas. *Review of Higher Education* 4: 1–16.
Daly, F., and Townsend, B. K. (1992). Faculty perceptions of the department chair's role in facilitating tenure acquisition. Paper presented at the Annual Meeting for the Study of Higher Education, Minneapolis.
Dinham, S. (1992). New faculty describe a life of stress. Paper presented at the Annual Meeting for the Study of Higher Education, Minneapolis.
Drew, J. S., and Hughes, A. O. (1983). Firing up for funding: A model faculty proseminar in grants and contracts. *Grants Magazine*: 101–107.

Eimers, M. (1990). Background and experiences of new faculty. *Instructional Developments* 1(3): 12–15.
Etzioni, A. (1961). *A Comparative Analysis of Complex Organizations*. New York: Free Press.
Evan, W. (1963). Peer groups interaction and organizational socialization: A study of employee turnover. *American Sociological Review* 28: 436–440.
Feldman, D. C. (1976a). A contingency theory of socialization. *Administration Science Quarterly* 21: 433–452.
Feldman, D. C. (1976b). A practical program for employee socialization. *Organizational Dynamics* (Autumn): 64–66.
Fink, L. D. (ed.). (1984a). *The First Year of College Teaching, New Directions for Teaching and Learning* 17. San Francisco: Jossey-Bass.
Fink, L. D. (1984b). How the new teachers performed. In Fink (ed.), *The First Year of College Teaching, New Directions for Teaching and Learning* 17. San Francisco: Jossey-Bass.
Fink, L. D. (1992). Orientation Programs for new faculty. In M.D. Sorcinelli and A.E. Austin (eds.), *Developing New and Junior Faculty, New Directions in Teaching and Learning* 50 (Summer). San Francisco: Jossey-Bass.
Finkelstein, M. J. (1984a). *The American Academic Profession: A Synthesis of Social Scientific Inquiry Since World War II*. Columbus, OH: Ohio State University Press.
Finkelstein, M. J. (1984b). The status of academic women: An assessment of five competing explanations. *The Review of Higher Education* 7: 223.
Finkelstein, M. J., and LaCelle-Peterson, M. W. (1992). New and junior faculty: A review of the literature. In M.D. Sorcinelli and A.E. Austin (eds.), *Developing New and Junior Faculty, New Directions for Teaching and Learning* 50 (Summer). San Francisco: Jossey-Bass.
Fox, M. F. (1983). Publication productivity among scientists: A critical review. *Social Studies of Science* 13: 285–305.
Fox, M. F. (1985). Location, sex-typing, and salary among academics. *Work and Occupations* 12: 186–205.
Freidson, E. (1970). *The Profession of Medicine*. New York: Dodd and Mead.
Fulton, O., and Trow, M. (1974). Research activity in American higher education. *Sociology of Education* 47: 29–73.
Gainen, J., and Boice, R. (eds.). (1993). *Building A Diverse Faculty, New Directions for Teaching and Learning* 53. San Francisco: Jossey-Bass.
Gappa, J. M. (1984). *Part-time Faculty: Higher Education at a Crossroads*. Washington, D.C.: Association for the Study of Higher Education.
Gecas, V. (1982). The self-concept. In R. H. Turner and J. F. Short (eds.), *Annual Review of Sociology* 8: 1–33. Palo Alto, CA: Annual Reviews.
Gecas, V. (1986). The motivational significance of self-concept for socialization theory. In E. J. Lawler (ed.), *Advances in Group Process*. Greenwich, CT: JAI Press.
Gecas, V., and Burke, P. (forthcoming). Self and identity. In K. Cook, G. A. Fine and J. House (eds.), *Sociological Perspectives on Social Psychology*. New York: Basic Books.
Gecas, V., and Seff, M. A. (1989). Social class, occupational conditions and self-esteem. *Sociological Perspectives* 32: 353–364.
Gecas, V., and Seff, M. A. (1990). Social class and self-esteem: Psychological centrality, compensation, and the relative effects of work and home. *Social Psychology Quarterly* 53: 165–173.
Gerholm, T. (1985). On tacit knowledge in academia. In L. Gustavson (ed.), *On Com-*

munication: No. 3. Linkoping, Sweden: University of Linkoping Department of Communication Studies.
Goffman, E. (1959). *The Presentation of Self in Everyday Life*. New York: Doubleday.
Goffman, E. (1963). *Stigma*. Englewood Cliffs, NJ: Prentice-Hall.
Goffman, E. (1967). *Interaction Ritual*. New York: Doubleday.
Goldstein, E. (1979). Effects of same-sex and cross-sex role models on the subsequent academic productivity of scholars. *American Psychologist* (May): 407–409.
Gottlieb, D. (1961). Processes of socialization in American graduate schools. *Social Forces* 40: 121–131.
Gouldner, A. W. (1957). Cosmopolitans and locals: Toward an analysis of latent social roles-1. *Administrative Science Quarterly* 2: 281–306.
Gouldner, A. W. (1958). Cosmopolitans and locals: Toward an analysis of latent social roles-2. *Administrative Science Quarterly* 2: 444–480.
Gross, N. (1956). Sociology of education, 1945–1955. In H. L. Zetterberg (ed.), *Sociology in the U.S.A.: A Trend Report*. Paris: Unesco.
Haas, J., and Shaffir, W. (1984). The fate of idealism revisited. *Urban Life* 13: 63–81.
Hall, D. T. (1968). Identity changes during the transition from student to professor. *School Review* 76: 445–469.
Hartley, J., and Branthwaite, A. (1989). The psychologist as wordsmith: A questionnaire study of productive British psychologists. *Higher Education* 18: 423–452.
Hauptman, A. M. (1986). *Students in Graduate and Professional Education: What We Know and Need to Know*. Washington, D.C.: Association of American Universities.
Heard, C. H., and Bing, R. L., III. (1993). African American faculty and students on predominantly white university campuses. *Journal of Criminal Justice Education* 4(1): 101–113.
Hodson, R., and Sullivan, T. A. (1990). *The Social Organization of Work*. Belmont, CA: Wadsworth.
Howsam, B. (1967). Effecting needed changes. In E. L. Morphet and C. O. Ryan (eds.), *Planning and Effecting Needed Changes in Education*. Denver: Designing Education for the Future.
Jarvis, D. K. (1992). Improving junior faculty scholarship. In *Developing New and Junior Faculty, New Directions in Teaching and Learning* 50 (Summer). San Francisco: Jossey-Bass.
Kanter, R. M. (1977). *Men and Women of the Corporation*. New York: Basic Books.
Kimball, R. (1990). *Tenured Radicals: How Politics Has Corrupted Our Higher Education*. New York: Harper.
Kirk, D., and Todd-Mancillas, W. R. (1991). Turning points in graduate student socialization: Implications for recruiting future faculty. *The Review of Higher Education* 14(3): 407–421.
Kleinman, S. (1983). Collective matters as individual concerns. *Urban Life* 12(2): 203–225.
Kulis, S., and Miller-Loessi, K. (1992). Organizations, labor markets, and gender integration in academic sociology. *Sociological Perspectives* 1: 93–118.
Ladd, E. C., and Lipset, S. M. (1975). *The Divided Academy*. New York: McGraw-Hill.
Lammers, C. J. (1974). Localism, cosmopolitanism, and faculty response. *Sociology of Education* 47: 129–158.
Lavery, P. T., Boice, R., Thompson, R. W., and Turner, J. L. (1989). An annotated bibliography of mentoring for new faculty. *Journal of Staff, Program and Organizational Development* 7: 39–46.

LeCluyse, E. E., Tollefson, N., and Borgers S. B. (1985). Differences in female graduate students in relation to mentoring. *College Student Journal* 10(4): 411–415.

Lewis, K. G., and Povlacs, J. T. (1988). *Face to Face: A Handbook of Individual Consultation Techniques for Faculty / Instructional Developers.* Stillwater, OK: New Forums Press.

Locke, E. A., Fitzpatrick, W., and White F. M. (1984). Job satisfaction and role clarity among university and college faculty. In J. L. Bess (ed.), *College and University Organization: Insights from the Behavioral Sciences.* New York: New York University Press.

Lortie, D. C. (1959). Laymen to lawmen: Law school, careers, and professional socialization. *Harvard Educational Review* 29: 352–369.

Lortie, D. C. (1968). Shared ordeal and induction to work. In H. S. Becker, B. Greer, D. Reisman and R. S. Weiss (eds.), *Institutions and the Person.* Chicago: Aldine.

Lortie, D. C. (1969). The balance of control and autonomy in elementary school teaching. In A. Etzioni (ed.), *The Semi-Professions and their Organization.* New York: Free Press.

Louis, M. R. (1980). Surprise and sense making: What newcomers experience in entering unfamiliar organizational settings. *Administrative Science Quarterly* 25: 226–251.

Lucas, A. F. (1990). The department chair as change agent. In P. Seldin (ed.), *How Administrators Can Improve Teaching: Moving From Talk to Action in Higher Education.* San Francisco: Jossey-Bass.

Lucas, R. A., and Harrington, M. K. (1990). Workshops on writing blocks increase proposal activity. *To Improve The Academy: Resources for Student, Faculty, and Institutional Development* 9: 139–146.

Mager, G., and Myers, B. (1982). If first impressions count: New professors insights and problems. *Peabody Journal of Education* 50: 100–106.

Malaney, G. D. (1988). Graduate education as an area of research in the field of higher education. In J. C. Smart (ed.), *Higher Education: Handbook of Theory and Research,* (Vol. 4). New York: Agathon Press.

Mayhew, L. B., Ford, P., and Hubbard, D. L. (1990). *The Quest For Quality: The Challenge for Undergraduate Education in the 1990s.* San Francisco: Jossey-Bass.

Mead, G. H. (1934). *Mind, Self, and Society.* Chicago: University of Chicago Press.

Menges, R. J. (1992). The new faculty project of the national center of postsecondary teaching, learning and assessment. Paper presented at the Annual Meeting of the Association for the Study of Higher Education, Boston.

Menges, R. J., and Exum, W. H. (1983). Barriers to the progress of women and minority faculty. *Journal of Higher Education* 54: 123–144.

Menges, R. J., and Quinn, J. (1992). Discerning norms about teaching. Presentation at the Annual Meeting of the Association for the Study of Higher Education, Minneapolis.

Menges, R. J., and Trautvetter, L. C. (1993). Socialization of newly hired female faculty across types of institutions and disciplines. Paper presented at the Annual Meeting of the American Educational Research Association, Atlanta.

Merton, R. K. (1973). *The Sociology of Science.* Chicago: University of Chicago Press.

Merton, R., Reader, G. G., and Kendall, P. L. (1957). *The Student Physician.* Cambridge: Harvard University Press.

Metzger, W. P. (1987). The academic profession in the United States. In B.R. Clark (ed.), *The Academic Profession.* Berkeley: University of California Press.

Miller, G. A., and Wagner, L. E. (1971). Adult socialization, organizational structure and role orientations. *Administrative Science Quarterly* 16: 151–163.

Mooney, C. J. (1990). Faculty generation gap brings campus tensions, debates over hiring rating of professors. *Chronicle of Higher Education* 36(41): A18-A19.
Morris, R. M., and Sherlock, B. (1972). *Becoming a Dentist*. Springfield, IL: Charles C. Thomas.
National Education Association (1993). *The NEA 1993 Almanac of Higher Education*. Washington, D.C.: NEA Publishing.
National Research Council. (1990). *Employment of Minority Ph.Ds.: Changes Over Time*. Washington, D.C.: National Academy Press.
National Research Council Office of Scientific and Engineering Personnel. (1981). *Summary Report: 1980 Doctorate Recipients from U.S. Universities*. Washington, DC: National Academy Press.
Near, J. P., and Sorcinelli, M. D. (1986). Work and life away from work: Predictors of faculty satisfaction. *Research in Higher Education* 25(4): 377–394.
O'Briant, W. H. (1991). Professional loyalty and the scholarly community: Reflections toward a philosophy for fostering faculty. *The Review of Higher Education* 14(2): 251–272.
Olsen, D., and Sorcinelli, M. D. (1992). The pretenure years: A longitudinal perspective. In M.D. Sorcinelli and A.E. Austin (eds.), *Developing New and Junior Faculty, New Directions for Teaching and Learning* 50 (Summer). San Francisco: Jossey-Bass.
O'Neill, K. L., and Todd-Mancillas, W. (1992). An investigation into the types of turning point events affecting relational change in student–faculty interactions. *Innovative Higher Education* 16(4): 277–290.
Ott, J. S. (1989). *The Organizational Culture Perspective*. Chicago: Dorsey Press.
Parson, L. A., Sands, R. G., and Duane, J. (1992). Sources of career support for university faculty. *Research in Higher Education* 33(2): 161–176.
Pellegrin, R. T. (1976). Schools as work settings. In R. Dubin (ed.), *Handbook of Work, Organization and Society*. Chicago: Rand McNally.
Reskin, B. F. (1979). Academic sponsorship and scientists' careers. *Sociology of Education* 52: 129–146.
Reskin, B. F., and Roos, P. A. (1990). *Job Queues, Gender Queues*. Philadelphia: Temple University Press.
Reynolds, A. (1988). Making and giving the grade: Experiences of beginning professors at a research university. Paper presented at the Annual Meeting of the American Educational Research Association, New Orleans.
Reynolds, A. (1992). Charting the changes in junior faculty: Relationships among socialization, acculturation and gender. *Journal of Higher Education* 63(6): 637–652.
Ritzer, G., and Walczak, D. (1986). *Working: Conflict and Change*. Englewood Cliffs, NJ: Prentice Hall.
Roach, J. H. L. (1976). The academic department chairperson: Functions and responsibilities. *Educational Record* (Winter): 13–23.
Rong, X. L., Grant, L., and Ward, K. B. (1988). Funding and sociological publication: Effects of method, gender and topic. Paper presented at the Annual Meeting of the American Sociological Association, Atlanta.
Roos, P. A., and Reskin, B. F. (1992). Occupational desegregation in the 1970s: Integration and economic equity? *Sociological Perspectives* 35: 69–91.
Rorty, R. (1979). *Philosophy and the Mirror of Nature*. Princeton: Princeton University Press.
Rosenberg, M. (1979). *Conceiving the Self*. New York: Basic Books.
Rosenblum, G., and Rosenblum, B. (1990). Segmented labor markets. *Sociology of Education* 63: 151–164.

Rossi, A. (1970). Status of women in graduate departments of sociology. *The American Sociologist* 5: 1–12.

Rothman, R. A. (1987). *Working: Sociological Perspectives.* Englewood Cliffs, NJ: Prentice Hall.

Rouse, L. P. (1984). Breaking into academe. *Academe* (May-June): 39.

Sandler, B. R. (1979). You've come a long way, maybe—or why it still hurts to be a woman in labor. *Current Issues in Higher Education* 11–14.

Sands, R., Parson, L. A., and Duane, J. (1991). Faculty mentoring faculty in a public university. *Journal of Higher Education* 62 (2): 174–193.

Schein, E. H. (1968). Organizational socialization and the profession of management. *Sloan Management Review* 9(2): 1–16.

Schein, E. H. (1983). The role of the founder in creating an organizational culture. *Organizational Dynamics* (Summer): 13–28.

Schuster, J. H. (1990). Strengthening career preparation for prospective professors. In J. H. Schuster, D. W. Wheeler and Associates (eds.), *Enhancing Faculty Careers: Strategies for Development and Renewal.* San Francisco: Jossey-Bass.

Seldin, P. (ed.). (1987). Coping with faculty stress. *New Directions for Teaching and Learning* 29. San Francisco: Jossey-Bass.

Simeone, A. (1987). *Academic Women: Working Towards Equality.* Boston: Bergin and Garvey.

Smelser, N. J., and Content, S. G. (1980). *The Changing Academic Market.* Berkeley: University of California Press.

Smith, P. (1990). *Killing the Spirit.* New York: Viking Press.

Sorcinelli, M. D. (1988). Satisfactions and concerns of new university teachers. *To Improve the Academy* 7: 121–133.

Sorcinelli, M. D. (1992). New and junior faculty stress: Research and responses. In M.D. Sorcinelli and A.E. Austin (eds.), *Developing New and Junior Faculty, New Directions for Teaching and Learning* 50 (Summer). San Francisco: Jossey-Bass.

Sorcinelli, M. D., and Austin, A. E. (1992). *Developing New and Junior Faculty, New Directions for Teaching and Learning* 50 (Summer). San Francisco: Jossey-Bass.

Sorcinelli, M. D., and Near, J. P. (1989). Relations between work and life away from work among university faculty. *Journal of Higher Education* 60(1): 59–81.

Stanley, C. A., and Chism, N. V. (1991). Selected characteristics of new faculty: Implications for faculty development. *To Improve the Academy: Resources for Student, Faculty and Institutional Development* 10: 55–61.

Sternberg, R. J., Okagaki, L., and Jackson, A. S. (1990). Practical intelligence for success in school. *Educational Leadership* (September): 35–39.

Strauss, A. L. (1978). *Negotiations: Varieties, Contexts, Processes, and Social Order.* San Francisco: Jossey-Bass.

Tausky, C. (1978). *Work Organizations: Major Theoretical Perspectives.* Itasca. IL: F.E. Peacock Publishers.

Taylor, P. J. (1976). An interpretation of the quantification debate in British geography. *Transactions of the Institute of British Geographers* 1: 2.

Thompson, M. L., and Ellis, J. R. (1984). A study of graduate assistantships in American schools of education. *College Students Journal* 18(1): 78–86.

Thornton, R., and Nardi, P. M. (1975). The dynamics of role acquisition. *American Journal of Sociology* 80: 870–885.

Tompkins, P. K., and Cheney, G. (1983). Account analysis in organizations: Decision making and identification. In L. L. Putnam and M. E. Pacanowsky (eds.), *Communication and Organizations: An Interpretive Approach.* Beverly Hills: Sage.

Tompkins, P. K., and Cheney, G. (1985). Communication and unobtrusive control in contemporary organizations. In R. McPhee and P. Tompkins (eds.), *Organizational Communication: Traditional Themes and New Directions*. Beverly Hills: Sage.
Trautvetter, L. C. (1992). A portrait of newly hired faculty at different institutions and in four disciplinary fields. Paper presented at the Annual Meeting of the Association for the Study of Higher Education, Minneapolis.
Tucker, A. (1981). *Chairing the Academic Department: Leadership Among Peers*. Washington, D.C.: American Council on Education.
Tuckerman, H. P. (1978). Who is part-time in academe? *AAUP Bulletin* 64: 305–325.
Turner, J. L., and Boice, R. (1987). Starting at the beginning: The concerns and needs of new faculty. *To Improve the Academy: Resources for Student, Faculty and Institutional Development* 6: 41–55.
Turner, R. H. (1962). Role-taking: Process vs. conformity. In A. M. Rose (ed.), *Human Behavior and Social Processes*. Boston: Houghton Mifflin.
Turner, R. H. (1973). Determinants of social movement strategies. In T. Shibutani (ed.), *Human Nature and Collective Behavior: Papers in Honor of Herbert Blumer*. New Brunswick, NJ: Transaction Books.
Turner, R. H. (1978). The role and the person. *American Journal of Sociology* 84: 1–23.
Van der Bogert, V. (1991). Starting out: Experiences of new faculty at a teaching university. *To Improve the Academy: Resources for Student, Faculty and Institutional Development* 10: 63–81.
Van Maanen, J. (1976). Breaking in: Socialization to work. In R. Dubin (ed.), *Handbook of Work, Organization and Society*. Chicago: Rand McNally.
Van Maanen J. (1983). People processing: Strategies of organizational socialization. In R. Allen and L. W. Porter (eds.), *Organizational Influence Processes*. Glenview, IL: Scott, Foresman and Company.
Verrier, D. A. (1992). On becoming tenured: Acquiring tenure at a research university. Paper presented at the Annual Meeting of the Association for the Study of Higher Education, Minneapolis.
Wanous, J. P. (1980). *Organizational Entry: Recruitment, Selection, and Socialization of Newcomers*. Reading, MA: Addison-Wesley.
Whitt, E. J. (1991). Hit the ground running: Experiences of new faculty in a school of education. *The Review of Higher Education* 14(2): 177–197.
Wright, R. A. (1992). The integration of teaching, research and service: A study in the "trickling" down of an academic role. *Free Inquiry in Creative Sociology* 20(2): 131–135.
Wylie, N. R. (1985). Helping new faculty adjust to careers at liberal arts colleges (project summary). Ann Arbor, MI: Great Lakes Colleges Association.

Author Index

Subject Index

G

H

N

O

P

R

W

Y

Contents of Previous Volumes

VOLUME I

VOLUME II

VOLUME III

VOLUME IV

VOLUME V

VOLUME VI

VOLUME VII

VOLUME VIII

Remediation in American Higher Education Darrel A. Clowes, *Virginia Polytechnic Institute and State University*
Author Index and Subject Indexes
Contents of Previous Volumes
1992: ISBN 0-87586-099-0

VOLUME IX

An Analysis of the Paradigmatic Evolution of U.S. Higher Education and Implications for the Year 2000 Hasan Simsek and Richard B. Heydinger, *University of Minnesota*
A Motivational Analysis of Academic Life in College Martin V. Covington, *University of California, Berkeley*
The Paradox of Growth in Federal Aid for College Students, 1965–1990 James C. Hearn, *University of Georgia*
Scientist and Engineer Supply and Demand Larry R. Leslie and Ronald L. Oaxaca, *University of Arizona*
Two-Year Colleges and Minority Students' Aspirations: Help or Hindrance? Amaury Nora, *University of Illinois at Chicago*
The Influence of College Residence Halls on Students Gregory S. Blimling, *Appalachian State University*
Postmodernism and Critical Theory in Higher Education: Implications for Research and Practice William G. Tierney and Robert A. Rhoads, *The Pennsylvania State University*
Qualitative and Quantitative Approaches to Academic Culture: Do They Tell Us the Same Thing? Marvin W. Peterson and Melinda G. Spencer, *University of Michigan*
Higher Education in China: Challenges of Making Foreign Knowledge Serve China Wenhui Zhong and Ruth Hayhoe, *Ontario Institute for Studies in Education*
College and University Budgeting: What Do We Know? What Do We Need to Know? William F. Lasher and Deborah L. Greene, *University of Texas at Austin*
Author and Subject Indexes
Contents of Previous Volumes
1993: 508 Pages ISBN 0–87586–109–1